Shimon Shetreet / Walter Homolka

Jewish and Israeli Law – An Introduction

Shimon Shetreet / Walter Homolka

Jewish and Israeli Law – An Introduction

—

DE GRUYTER

Prof. *Shimon Shetreet*, Hebrew University of Jerusalem
Prof. *Walter Homolka*, Abraham Geiger Kolleg, University of Potsdam

ISBN 978-3-89949-793-9
e-ISBN (PDF) 978-3-89949-794-6
e-ISBN (EPUB) 978-3-11-038702-5

Library of Congress Cataloging-in-Publication Data
A CIP catalog record for this book has been applied for at the Library of Congress.

Bibliographic information published by the Deutsche Nationalbibliothek
The Deutsche Nationalbibliothek lists this publication in the Deutsche Nationalbibliografie;
detailed bibliographic data are available on the Internet at http://dnb.dnb.de.

© 2017 Walter de Gruyter GmbH, Berlin/Boston
Printing and binding: CPI books GmbH, Leck
♾ Printed on acid-free paper
Printed in Germany

www.degruyter.com

Abridged contents

Part IV: Executive Powers and National Security Powers

Part V: Israel as a Jewish and Democratic State

Part VI: Law and Religion: International Perspectives

Part VII: Equality in Israeli Law

Detailed Contents

Part III: **Fundamental Legal Doctrines of Israeli Law**

Part V: Israel as a Jewish and Democratic State

Part VI: Law and Religion: International Perspectives

Part IX: Israeli Private and Commercial Law

Preface

This book was initiated during the 32nd National Convention of the German Society for Comparative Law in Cologne in September 2009. After Rabbi Professor Walter Homolka, rector of the Abraham Geiger College at the University of Potsdam (Germany) had given a lecture on Jewish law and its interrelations with national laws, great interest was raised among the assembled experts to learn more about the origins and development of the law in the State of Israel, about the whole variety of influences on Israeli Law, and about its current state of affairs.

At the time, an idea was suggested for a small introductory book to answer the questions of many colleagues present and to raise an awareness of the interesting case of Israel when it comes to comparative law in many respects. The work on this project began with Professor Dr. Christian Kirchner of Humboldt University Berlin, member of the board of the German Society for Comparative Law, a well-known and widely respected scholar. Unfortunately, he fell ill and passed away. In recognition of Dr. Kirchner for this endeavor, it is with appreciation that we dedicate the completed project to his blessed memory.

Fortunately, in this situation, Professor Dr. Shimon Shetreet of the Hebrew University of Jerusalem was so kind as to assume this exciting project when he spent time at the Abraham Geiger College of the University of Potsdam (Germany) as a visiting professor. With his background as a former cabinet minister of the State of Israel and an international expert in comparative law, the right person had been identified to extend the project into a thorough roadmap and an exciting guidebook.

It was then that we decided to switch from German to English to give the book a wider audience. This also gave the book another direction. There is no detailed introduction to Jewish Law in German at the moment. In English, however, we find a huge amount of literature on this subject, namely Menachem Elon's four-volume set "Jewish Law." At the same time, we found that an elaborate and contemporary analysis of Israeli Law in the English language is missing globally. Thanks to Shimon Shetreet's enormous efforts, we can now present a very detailed introduction to Israeli Law—then and now.

Over many centuries, the Jewish people developed its legal tradition and remained loyal to it in the diaspora. Walter Homolka, therefore, gives a concise overview in Part I of the book on Jewish Religious Law, its major sources, and its practice in the various religious denominations. This shall provide the necessary foundation for the question of how Jewish law is practiced in the State of Israel.

While Jewish Law is certainly one of the sources and inspirations for Israeli law, there are many more influences. Shimon Shetreet offers a multifaceted picture of the Law of Israel in the other parts of the book.

The book analyzes the Israeli legal system, its legal culture, and its categorization as a mixed jurisdiction, influenced by civil and common law traditions. In Part 2, the book examines the system of government in Israel and the basic values underlying its democratic system including: representativeness, stability, governance, efficiency, accountability, and public confidence in the government. Part 3 of the book reviews the basic principles of the legal system: the obligation of public officers to serve as trustees of the people, the duty to respect human rights, the rule of law principle, and the doctrine of the separation of powers. Part 4 analyzes the origins and operation of judicial review of legislative and administrative actions; it discusses the transition of Israeli legal culture to the constitutional era with the passing of the basic laws in 1992 and the landmark *Bank Mizrachi* decision on judicial review of laws of parliament, the Knesset. Part 5 of the book discusses the executive powers and national security powers.

Parts 6 – 8 of the book deal with central issues of law and religion, equality, and Israel as a Jewish and democratic state. In Part 9 of the book, special attention is given to holocaust dilemmas in Israel over the years including the reparation agreement with Germany, the establishment of the Yad Vashem Memorial Institute, the Eichmann, Kastner, and Demjanjuk trials, the impact of the holocaust on Israeli jurisprudence and the unfulfilled challenge of meeting the needs of holocaust survivors in Israel. The book also devotes detailed attention to private, commercial, and business law in Part 10, including environmental law and alternative dispute resolutions.

The book examines public law issues such as institutions of the state, the government, parliament, and the judiciary, but also devotes detailed attention to private, commercial, and business law.

With this analysis of Israeli law in its various facets and the presentation of exemplary legal cases by Shimon Shetreet, it is hoped that this volume will contribute to better understanding of Israeli law, and will serve as a useful and widely sought source for the study and analysis of Israeli law.

We trust that this work which is a result of eight years of preparation, four years of which were spent on concentrated writing, will make an interesting read not only for experts in law, religion, and politics, but just as well for interested general readers and students.

This project was supported by a number of organizations and foundations. We are grateful to the Abraham Geiger College at the University of Potsdam. We are also grateful to the Faculty of Law at the Hebrew University of Jerusalem for their support.

Shimon Shetreet   Walter Homolka

Table of Cases

Israeli Cases

Foreign Cases

Canada

Table of Legislation

Israeli Legislation

Foreign Legislation

Germany

Canada

Poland

Switzerland

United Kingdom

United States

International Agreements, Treaties & Standards

Glossary

C.F (Jer.) – Civil File Jerusalem
C.F.H – Criminal Further Hearing
C.A – Civil Appeal
C.C – Civil case
CL.A – Civil Leave to Appeal
Cr.A – Criminal Appeal
E.A – Election Appeal
GSS – General Security Service
H.C.J – High Court of Justice
IDF – Israeli Defense forces (the Israeli Army)
L.S.I. – Laws of the State of Israel
LB – Laws Book (Hebrew Israel Statures)
MK – Member of Knesset
P.D. "Piske'i Din" – Judgments of the Supreme Court of Israel
S.H. – "Sefer Hukim" (Hebrew Israel Statures)
Tak-El – "Takdin-Elion"

About the Authors

Shimon Shetreet, LLB, LLM (Hebrew University), MCL, DCL (University of Chicago) is the Greenblatt Professor of Public and International Law at the Hebrew University of Jerusalem, Israel. He is the President of the International Association of Judicial Independence and World Peace and heads the International Project of Judicial Independence. In 2008, the Mt. Scopus Standards of Judicial Independence were issued under his leadership. Between 1988 and 1996, Professor Shetreet served as a member of the Israeli Parliament, and was a cabinet minister under Yitzhak Rabin and Shimon Peres. He was senior deputy mayor of Jerusalem between 1999 and 2003. He was a Judge of the Standard Contract Court and served as a member of the Chief Justice Landau Commission on the Israeli Court System. The author and editor of many books on the judiciary, Professor Shetreet is a member of the Royal Academy of Arts and Science Belgium.

Rabbi **Walter Homolka** PhD (King's College London, 1992), PhD (University of Wales Trinity St. David, 2015), DHL (Hebrew Union College, New York, 2009), is a full professor of Modern Jewish Thought and the executive director of the School of Jewish Theology at the University of Potsdam (Germany). The rector of the Abraham Geiger College (since 2003) is chairman of the Leo Baeck Foundation and of the Ernst Ludwig Ehrlich Scholarship Foundation in Potsdam. In addition, he has served as the executive director of the Masorti Zacharias Frankel College since 2013. The author of "Jüdisches Eherecht" and other publications on Jewish Law holds several distinctions, among them: the Knight Commander's Cross of the Austrian Merit Order and the 1st Class Federal Merit Order of Germany. In 2004, President Jacques Chirac admitted Rabbi Homolka to the French Legion of Honor.

Part I: **Jewish Law**

Chapter 1:
The Emergence and Development of Jewish Law

Jewish law[1] is the law not of a state, but of a people: the people of Israel. In its more than 3,000-year history, this people has rarely had its own state with political sovereignty. The majority of Jewish history has been characterized by life under alien rule, particularly in the Diaspora.[2] Jews have lived and continue to live in many different countries and cultures and under quite varied systems of government and law. These have consistently had an influence on the development of Jewish law, yet the people was nevertheless able to preserve its autonomy throughout the centuries. A crucial factor was the relatively broad autonomy often enjoyed by Jewish communities in legal matters, although the degree of autonomy varied depending on time and place. This legal autonomy, and the practical use of law that it required, ensured its continuous development.

Another reason that Jewish law has preserved its autonomy and uniqueness to this day is even more significant and fundamental. The basis of Jewish law is not the authority of a worldly legislature, but ultimately the covenant between the people of Israel and God. Its original source and its actual core is thus divine revelation, as expressed in the Torah[3] and other books of the Hebrew Bible.

The Biblical phrases for law are *mishpat* and *din*. However, it is not really possible to clearly separate the meanings of the two expressions. The word *mishpat* means, among other things, "law" as a system of precepts and regulations that comprise civil, criminal, and religious law equally. It regulates people's relationships among themselves and their relationship with God.[4] The word *din*, on the other hand, refers in Deut. 17:8 to the context of interpersonal law. The word is also used in this sense later in the Talmud, although there a distinction is made between property law (*dine mamonot*), family law (*dine mishpacha*),

---

1 Revised version from *Walter Homolka, Das Jüdische Eherecht*, Berlin 2009, S. 1–12; Menachem Elon, *Jewish Law—History, Sources, Principles*, Bd. 1, Philadelphia 1994, Passim, provides a detailed account of the history of Jewish law.
2 Diaspora (Greek for "dispersion") refers to the dispersion of the Jews outside of Eretz Israel; historical terms for Diaspora include *galut* (banishment) and *tefutza* (dispersion).
3 Torah ("instruction") is the term for the five books, ascribed to Moses, of Genesis (Bereshit), Exodus (Shemot), Leviticus (Vaiyikra), Numbers (Bemidbar), and Deuteronomy (Devarim). Other common terms are the Five Books of Moses, Pentateuch, and Chumash.
4 Elon, Menachem, *Jewish Law*, pp. 105 f.; See EJ, 1971, Vol. 12, pp. 110–151 (Art. Mishpat Ivri); JL, Vol. 4, pp. 1262–1275 (Art. Jüdisches Recht).

DOI 10.1515/9783899497946-001

criminal law (*dine nefashot*), and law of the state (*dine ha-malchut*). *Dine mama-not* includes all property law issues. These include the law of civil procedure and the property law aspects of marriage and inheritance law, as well as rules regarding fines (*kenass*). *Dine mishpacha* includes all laws on issues of marriage and family, as well as personal status. *Dine nefashot* are laws dealing with the punishment of individuals (except for fines) and criminal procedure. The *dine ha-malchut* deal with issues involving the state, war and peace, appointment of kings and judges, private property and land rights, as well as rights concerning the sanctuary and the community. But the word *din* certainly also includes the rules regulating the relationship between humans and God—for overall, a division between religious and profane law (corresponding to the Roman distinction between *fas* and *ius*) is foreign to Jewish law.

After the epoch of its Biblical establishment, the period between the destruction of the Second Temple (70 CE) and the beginning of the third century was particularly important for the development of Jewish law. In this period, traditional law was reordered and systematized in a new way; thus, a novel Jewish law evolved that would, from then on, be known as *halacha*. The word *halacha* is a derivation of the Hebrew word *halach* (go). The fact that it came to denote the entirety of Jewish law is based on a metaphorical interpretation of Ex. 18:20: "... And thou shalt teach them ordinances and laws, and shalt shew them the way wherein they must walk, and the work that they must do." *Halacha* is thus "the way wherein they must walk." Depending on context, therefore, the word *halacha* (pl. *halachot*) can denote both all of Jewish law or a specific rule, a law relating to a specific matter.[5]

As the entire system of Jewish norms, *halacha* includes legal matters regarding life in all its manifestations. Two factors play a particularly important role in the practical application of Jewish law: first, different interpretations among the various currents of Judaism on the guiding principles governing the implementation of the law; second, its relationship to the "law of the state," that is, to the existing laws of the country in which it is practiced.

---

5 *Segal, Peretz*, "Jewish Law During the Tannaitic Period," *An Introduction to the History and Sources of Jewish Law*, N.S. Hecht; B.S. Jackson; S.M. Passamaneck (eds.), Oxford 1996, pp. 101–140.

1. The Classic Sources of Jewish Law

The character of Jewish law described above reveals that it is based, as a whole, on a Biblical foundation. The first and most important written source of Jewish law is thus the Hebrew Bible, and especially the Torah. The traditional Jewish interpretation counts a total of 613 legal precepts in the five books of the Torah, the so-called *mitzvot*[6]; they form the basis of all later Jewish legal codifications and of the Jewish legal system as a whole. The first texts in which the Torah of Moses is mentioned (2 Kings 14:6, 2 Chron. 25:4) refer to a King Amaziah who lived in the early eighth century. However, it is unclear whether the legal code that guided the behavior of this King of Judah, according to the Biblical narrative (written down a bit later), was really identical to the Torah in its later canonical form. In the initial years following the Babylonian exile, at the latest—that is, at the time of Ezra (fifth century CE), who is described in the Torah of Moses as a priest and scribe—the Torah emerges clearly as a written legal code, interpreted and applied by priests: "So they read in the book in the law of God distinctly, and gave the sense, and caused them to understand the reading" (Neh. 8:8). It is assumed that the books that were called "the Torah of Moses" or the "Torah of God" are more or less the same as the Pentateuch in its current form.

The Torah contains not only specific commandments, but also various collections of rules. Examples are the so-called Book of the Covenant (Ex. 20:23–23:19), the so-called Holiness Code (Lev. 17–26), and the Ten Commandments. The Book of the Covenant contains ritual, ethical, and legal rules; in Ex. 21:1–22:16 (as in, for example, Deut. 15:12–18, 19:11–13, 21:1–25:13), the focus is on rules that regulate relationships between individuals. The laws collected in Lev. 17–26 can be classified largely, though not exclusively, as religious law. The Ten Commandments, which appear in two accounts (Ex. 20:1–17 and Deut. 5:6–21), are moral demands on individuals and cannot be called "laws" in the actual sense because they do not provide for sanctions in the event of non-compliance.

The next authoritative literary sources of Jewish law are the prophets (*nevi'im*) and hagiographies (*ketuvim*), although in comparison with the Torah they contain few legally relevant passages. They can deal with matters as varied as rights of acquisition (Ruth 4; Jer. 32), royalty (1 Sam. 8; 1 Kings 21), questions of

---

6 Plural of mitzvah ("commandment"). Of the total of 613 precepts, 248 are commandments in the narrower sense ("thou shalt," called *mitzvot asseh*) and 365 contained prohibitions ("thou shalt not," *mitzvot lo taaseh*). Determining and enumerating these commandments forms its own genre of literature, the *Sefer ha-Mitzvot* ("Book of Commandments").

sureties (Prov 6:1–5), and individual or collective liability for breaking the law (2 Kings 14:6).

In the post-Biblical era, the epoch between the destruction of the Second Temple (70 CE) and the completion of the Talmud (circa 600 CE) is particularly important to the development of Jewish law. This was the period in which the classical sources of Jewish law were created: the Mishnah, the Tosefta, and the two Talmuds—the Palestinian (or Jerusalem) and the Babylonian Talmud— as well as the halachic *midrashim*. To this day, these form the starting point for the study of the sources and all legal development.

The word *midrash* is derived from the Hebrew verb *darash*, meaning "seek" and "question." This word is used to describe, for example, Ezra's behavior (Ezra 7:10): "For Ezra had prepared his heart to seek the law of the Lord, and to do it, and to teach in Israel statutes and judgments." Thus the Bible already makes a connection between interpretation of the Biblical word and findings of law. Midrash (pl. midrashim) thus means primarily "research, study," but also "interpretation" and "doctrine." The term refers, in its narrower sense, to the interpretation of books of the Hebrew Bible in general, and also to the various collections of these interpretations, which emerged largely between 70 and 300 CE in Palestine. A subgroup of the midrashim are called "halachic midrashim"; these refer to texts in the Torah, particularly the books of Exodus, Leviticus, Numbers, and Deuteronomy.

The Mishnah is a collection of laws, or a legal code, in the Hebrew language that was compiled around 200 CE. The word *mishnah* comes from the Hebrew word *shanah*, which means "repeat, learn" (*matnita* in Aramaic). The various *halachot* were for a long time passed on orally; later they were collected in academies and written down. It is assumed that the classification of the *halachot* and their ordering by subject were largely completed before the destruction of the Second Temple. The final form of the Mishnah is traditionally ascribed to Yehuda ha-Nasi[7] (circa 135–220 CE). After its completion, the Mishnah became the central reference point for the practice of Jewish legal practice. It would no longer be possible to apply a law without looking to the Mishnah for advice.

The Mishnah consists of six orders (*sedarim*), each of which represents an area of the law. The orders are "Seeds" (*zera'im*—agricultural law, which relates only to crops in Israel); "Celebration" (*mo'ed*—religious holidays); "Women" (*nashim*—family law in the broad sense); "Damages" (*nezikin*—civil law, criminal law); "Holy Things" (*kodashim*—laws regarding rites and temple taxes); and "Pu-

---

[7] Yehuda ha-Nasi was an important scholar and leader of Palestinian Jewry in the second century.

rities" (*toharot*—laws relating to the ritual purity of persons, objects, and places). The orders are subdivided in turn into tractates (*masechtot*), the tractates into chapters (*perakim*), the chapters into *mishnayot* (pl., from *mishnah*)—the smallest unit in the Mishnah. The word "Mishnah" can therefore refer to the entire code or to an individual paragraph. This structure of the Mishnah determined the systemization of Jewish law in the following centuries.

The next important work of Jewish law is the Tosefta, which was created around the same time as the Mishnah[8] and whose final editing probably took place in the late third and early fourth centuries.[9] The word *tosefta* is derived from the verb *yasaf*, meaning "collection, addition." The Tosefta is also a collection of laws. In its overall structure, it is similar to the Mishnah, and the text deviates very little from that of the Mishnah. However, the laws are organized differently in each chapter. In addition, there are legal provisions and subjects that are not found, or are found in a different version, in the Mishnah. The Tosefta sometimes names authorities as the sources of laws that are anonymous in the Mishnah, or ascribes laws to different rabbis[10] than those named in the Mishnah, and it contradicts the Mishnah regarding which halacha is valid and should be used. In addition, it contains narrative (haggadic) and interpretive (midrashic) textual materials.

The principle relationship between Mishnah and Tosefta will be discussed later in this chapter. It has not quite been resolved whether these are collections of laws by two different, rival schools of law, or whether the Tosefta is a contemporary supplement and completion of the Mishnah, which was completed a short time earlier, but had already attained authoritative status.

In the three centuries following the editing of the Mishnah, two additional central works of Jewish law emerged that would become the cornerstone of all later halachic literature. These are the Palestinian or Jerusalem Talmud, created in the land of Israel and completed in the fifth century, and the Babylonian Talmud, completed by Babylon's rabbis in the sixth century. The word Talmud means "teaching, instruction, study." The aim of both Talmuds is to interpret

---

8 The epoch up to around 200 CE is traditionally called the period of the Tannaites ("Repeaters of Law"). For an overview of the epoch, see Konner, Melvin, *Unsettled—An Anthropology of the Jews*, New York 2003.

9 Strack, Hermann Leberecht & Stemberger, Günter (translated by Markus Bockmuehl), *Introduction to the Talmud and Midrash*, T& T Clark, 1991, pp. 149–163; Zinvirt, Yaacov, *Tor zum Talmud*, Münster et. al. 2009.

10 Plural of *rabbi*, the title of ordained Tannaites and Amoraim (transmitters of traditions) in Palestine; a scholarly title since the generation after Hillel (Mt 23:7). The rabbis interpreted the Torah through halacha and aggada and taught at the academies.

the Mishnah, and they emerged through a long process of learning and teaching of the earlier halachic writings, especially the Mishnah. While the Mishnah is a thematically organized collection of briefly formulated rules, the Talmud contains discursive commentaries and analyses of them, called Gemara (from the Aramaic *gemar*—"to learn"; "to complete").

The Mishnah is the common foundation of both Talmuds. However, the Palestinian and the Babylonian Talmuds clearly differ in language and literary character, as well as in regard to the source materials they include, the Mishnah tractates they comment on, and the extent of these commentaries.

Determining the form of the Mishnah upon which the Palestinian Talmud is based is difficult; the original version contained no Mishnah texts, but only quotes and allusions within the Gemara itself. Only in later manuscripts was the previously continuous text broken up according to the Mishnah's textual units and the Mishnah texts placed before those of the Gemara chapter by chapter.[11] Thus, the Mishnah text of the Palestinian Talmud, as it has been passed down in manuscripts and print, is not the text that the rabbis discussed in the period in which the Palestinian text was being created.

The Palestinian Talmud includes the first four orders of the Mishnah: "Seeds" (*zera'im*), "Celebration" (*mo'ed*), "Women" (*nashim*), and "Damages (*nezikin*), and parts of the tractate "Impurity" (*nidda*) from the order "Purities" (*toharot*). It thus annotates 39 of the 63 tractates of the Mishnah. The theory that Gemara originally existed for all six orders has been refuted by fragments of the Palestinian Talmud found in the Cairo Geniza. The orders "Holy Things" (*kodashim*) and "Purities" (*toharot*) were probably never included in the Palestinian Talmud, although they were studied, as shown by passages in the Palestinian Talmud and quotes by Palestinian scholars in the Babylonian Talmud. Conversely, the lack of some tractates from the existing orders has been ascribed to later text losses.

Yochanan bar Nappacha[12] (d. 279 CE), a student of Rabbi Yehuda ha-Nasi, was traditionally considered the author of the Palestinian Talmud. But scholars in the late Middle Ages had already noted the difficulties facing this dating. In the Palestinian Talmud, rabbis from the fourth century and events from the same epoch are mentioned. Today, it is assumed that the final editing of the Palestinian Talmud took place in the first half of the fifth century, and that it was done in Tiberias in Galilee. The editing involved a systematic revision of the

---

11 *Strack & Stemberger:* Introduction, p. 175.
12 Yochanan bar Nappacha lived in Palestine and was one of the most important of the ancient Jewish scholars.

text which, however, did not proceed uniformly and centrally. How the details of this editing process should be understood has not yet been fully clarified.[13]

The Babylonian Talmud is also based on the Mishnah, and annotates 36 tractates, 1/2 of the Mishnah's 63. In the orders "Seeds" (*zera'im*) and "Purities" (*toharot*), Gemara are found only for the tractates "Benedictions" (*berachot*) and "Impurity" (*nidda*); in the other orders, they are omitted only for certain tractates. The traditional explanation for the general lack of Gemara for these two orders is that their laws, with the exception of the two tractates that do have commentaries, were no longer significant in practice: the agricultural laws were connected mainly with the land of Israel, and the purity rules could no longer be implemented because of the absence of a temple cult.

Although the Babylonian Talmud deals with fewer tractates of the Mishnah than the Palestinian, it is considerably more comprehensive than the latter. It integrates far more material than the Palestinian Talmud and contains, in addition to many Midrashim—which form their own literary genre in Palestine—numerous narrative texts (the Aramaic umbrella term is *aggada*), as well as myths and legends, tales of rabbis, and historical recollections. The Babylonian Talmud also contains material from various branches of science. One can, therefore, say that it is "less a thematically closed book than a national library of Babylonian Judaism whose structure emulates Mishnah."[14]

The traditional view ascribes the Babylonian Talmud primarily to Rav Ashi[15] (335–427), who wrote it down and then revised it himself. In this narrative, the text was finally completed several centuries later, so that the Babylonian Talmud was "sealed" after 500 CE. In fact, however, it must be assumed that the emergence of this corpus extended over a longer time period; that is, it began significantly earlier. The Babylonian Talmud draws from a large number of sources, which were already available in various earlier forms. Developed in this way, the text was probably considerably revised and expanded in the sixth and seventh centuries: While the participation of the rabbis of this epoch (the so-called Savora'im) was at first thought to be limited to "fine-tuning the literary final edit," it is now believed that they had a substantial role in its revision.[16] The editorial history of the Babylonian Talmud is thus considered to have been finally concluded in the early eighth century; not, however, the history of its text. Although the Babylonian Talmud, rather than the Palestinian Talmud, became

---

13 See also Lifshitz, Berachyahu "The Age of the Talmud," *An Introduction to the History and Sources of Jewish Law*, Oxford 1996, 169–195.
14 Strack & Stemberger, *Introduction*, p. 192.
15 Rav Ashi was one of the greatest of the Amoraim from Babylonia.
16 Strack & Stemberger, *Introduction*, pp. 204–206; Lifshitz, *Age*, p. 178.

over time the more important of the two Talmuds, it was long considered an "open" book whose text could be corrected, explained, and furnished with additions.[17]

The leaders of the academies in Babylonia (the so-called Geonim) established that legal cases were to be decided in accordance with the Babylonian Talmud. Moses Maimonides[18] (1135–1204) emphasized this principle when he explained that it was the duty of every Jew to follow the Babylonian Talmud, as all of Israel had submitted to it.[19] Since that time, the attempt has been made to orient justifications for legal rules around the Babylonian Talmud. The Babylonian Talmud thus developed into the legal reference work of Jewish law that is most intensively studied by scholars, while the Palestinian Talmud—less detailed and more difficult to understand in comparison—did not attain the same importance.

2. The Relationship between Biblical and Rabbinical Law

In Jewish law, a distinction is made between oral law (*tora she-be-al pe*) and written law (*tora*). The phrase *tora she-be-al pe* refers to law laid down outside the Hebrew Bible and includes not only the Mishnah, the halachic Midrashim, and both Talmuds, but also the entire halacha in all its historical manifestations.[20] From Lev. 26:46 ("These are the statutes and judgments and laws [torot, pl. of tora], which the Lord made between him and the children of Israel on mount Sinai by the hand of Moses"), the rabbis inferred that God had given Israel two Torahs: one written and one oral. This revelation contains the subtleties of Biblical exegesis: the interpretation by experts of the scripture and the hermeneutical process based on this interpretation from generation to generation.[21] Thus the halacha is a manifestation of the law revealed at Sinai, and the task of the rabbis is to constantly illuminate and supplement it and transform it into practical law.[22]

Another distinction between two types of halacha is that between *halacha de-oraita* and *halacha de-rabbanan*. The Aramaic term *de-oraita* refers generally

---

17 Lifshitz, *Age*, p. 178; Strack & Stemberger, *Introduction*, p. 201–204.
18 The philosopher, legal scholar, and doctor Moses Maimonides was among the greatest Jewish figures of the Middle Ages and lived in Spain, Fez, and Cairo.
19 Lifshitz, *Age*, p. 179.
20 Elon, *Jewish Law*, p. 191.
21 bT Meg 19b. This refers to Deut. 9:10.
22 Elon, *Jewish Law*, pp. 192–193.

to laws stemming from the Torah; *de-rabbanan* means rules ascribed to rabbinical scholars. But drawing the line between the two terms is difficult, because the criteria determining which laws can be attributed to the Torah and which to the rabbis are complex in nature. Thus *de-oraita* includes, to a limited extent, not only the laws found in the Torah, but those that have been derived from the Torah with the help of Midrash. Similarly, laws based on a sentence in the Torah are considered *halacha de-oraita*. These include some halachot known as *halacha le-Moshe mi-Sinai* (halacha to Moses on Sinai).[23] This category includes laws whose interpretation is based on a tradition that can be traced back to Moses receiving the law on Sinai and that is expressly viewed by the rabbis as Biblical in origin.[24] The group *de-rabbanan* includes laws that were created or revised by scholars through decrees or in other ways. And even if they are sometimes based on sentences in the Torah, they are still not necessarily classified as *de-oraita*.

The discussion of which rules should be viewed as *de-oraita* and which as *de-rabbanan* is not merely a thing of the past. It continues to be conducted today, since classification in one of the two categories is quite important for practical jurisprudence. When in doubt, for example, one would follow the strict interpretation of a law if it were classified as Biblical, while conversely, the rabbinic origins of a rule would allow more lenient interpretation in doubtful cases. Admittedly, the rabbis themselves generally viewed their laws as just as legally binding and effective as Biblical law.[25]

3. Post-Talmudic Developments

The post-Talmudic phase of Jewish law can be divided into three historical periods:[26]

- The Talmud commentaries and the responses of the Geonim (700 – ca. 1050 CE)
- The codification of the Rishonim (ca. 1050 – ca. 1600 CE)

---

23 Goldfine, Yitzhak: *Einführung in das Jüdische Recht. Eine historische und analytische Untersuchung des Jüdischen Rechts und seiner Institutionen*, Hamburg 1973, p. 45.
24 Elon, *Jewish Law*, pp. 204–207, 209.
25 Elon, *Jewish Law*, p. 215.
26 See Elon, *Jewish Law*, pp. 1101–1102.

- The commentaries and responses of the Acharonim[27] (ca. 1600 CE until today)

The period between the completion of the Talmud and the emergence of the Rishonim, the "early" or "first" scholars in the eleventh century, is known as the Geonic period. The name is derived from the title Gaon (pl. Geonim, literally "Excellency"), reserved for the authorities who were leaders of the academies of Sura and Pumbedita in Babylonia. It is generally agreed that the Geonic period ended in 1038 with the death of Rav Hai, the Gaon of Pumbedita.

The legal literature produced by the Geonim was very distinctive in regard to its literary character, the wealth of subjects it dealt with, and its innovative approach. It can be subdivided into four genres that have shaped post-Talmudic legal literature to this day, from the Geonim to the Rishonim to the Acharonim, the later scholars: commentaries on the Talmud, codified works, responses, and halachic treatises.

A. Commentaries

From the period of the Geonim, the works *She'iltot*, by Achai of Shabcha, and the law collection *Halachot Gedolot*, Simeon Kayyara, should be noted. One of the last of the Geonim, Rav Hai, wrote particular works on specific legal matters (purchase and sale and oaths). Traditionally, Rabbi Shlomo ben Yitzhak[28] (1040–1105), known by the acronym "Rashi," is also considered to belong to the French and German Geonic periods, though this conflicts somewhat with the temporal classification mentioned above. His commentary became a classic and an "indispensable part of the Talmud."[29] Rashi's goal was to clarify the correct way to read the texts of the Mishnah and Gemara. His Talmudic commentary gained the status of actual law.

The commentary series "Tosafot" (not to be confused with the tosefta) was begun during the time of Rashi's followers and carried on for a full two hundred years, into the thirteenth century. In editions of the Talmud published

---

27 The scholars known as Geonim (also called Kadmonim, the earliest), Rishonim (the first ones, until the sixteenth century), and Acharonim (the last ones, from the sixteenth century) were collected under the name Posekim, as "decisors" of the law that was binding for religious practice.

28 Shlomo ben Yitzhak was one of the most important commentators and teachers of the High Middle Ages at the yeshivas in Troyes, Mainz, and Worms.

29 See Elon, *Jewish Law*, pp. 1116–1117.

today, however, one finds additional commentaries alongside those of Rashi and the Tosafot. One is by Eliahu ben Shlomo Zalman[30] (1720–1797), who became known as the "Gaon of Vilna." Aside from Rashi, he is among the Talmudic scholars of highest reputation.

B. Codifications

Whenever codifications were undertaken, the legal literature immediately underwent lively development. Thus, in the eleventh century, the *Sefer Halachot* by Rabbi Yitzhak Alfasi (acronym Rif) eliminated the haggadic portion of the Talmud and the aspects that were no longer relevant since the destruction of the Jerusalem Temple. In the process, he followed the structure of the Talmud tractates and also retained the Aramaic. Rif's work inspired further developments, such as the Mishneh Torah of Moses Maimonides (1135–1204; acronym Rambam). The Mishneh Tora ("Repetition of the Torah"[31]) (also *Yad ha – Hazaka* ["Strong Hand"], taken from Deut. 4:34) is the first major Jewish legal code since the Mishnah and the two Talmuds and was produced in ten years, roughly between 1170 and 1180.[32] It consists of 14 books—14 being the numerical value of the Hebrew letters forming the word yad (hand)—of which the fourth (*Sefer Nashim*) deals in particular with the laws of marriage. Although contemporaries of Maimonides already recognized the great significance of the Mishneh Torah for the systematization of Jewish law, they—like later scholars—criticized Maimonides' methodology: They accused him of presenting the laws apodictically—without naming sources or explaining the views of earlier authorities[33]—despite the fact that transparency and reasoning are of central importance to practical jurisprudence. The Mishneh Torah, written in Hebrew, which also included all the legal matters that had been rendered obsolete (for example, by the destruction of the Temple), developed into the most authoritative source of Jewish law, in turn initiating numerous commentaries, many of which dealt with the Talmudic sources used by Maimonides.

---

30 Eliahu ben Shlomo Zalman lived in Vilna and was among the most important Jewish scholars of the eighteenth century. He vehemently opposed the emerging Chasidic movement.
31 The term "Mishneh Torah" corresponds to the Greek "deuteronomion." Just as Moses repeated the Torah in Deuteronomy, Maimonides repeated the halacha in his own time. Elon, *Jewish Law*, p. 1197.
32 See Elon, *Jewish Law*, p. 1188.
33 Goldfine, *Einführung*, p. 82.

A further classical work of Jewish law was written in Spain by the important scholar Rabbi Asher ben Yehiel[34] (ca. 1250 – ca. 1327; acronym Rosh): the *Piskei ha-Rosh* ("Decisions of the Rosh"). This book presented the important view that the decisions of earlier legal scholars did not *per se* possess higher authority than the interpretations of each era. Every scholar had the right to disagree with the opinions of past authorities.

The third son of the Rosh, Rabbi Jacob ben Asher [35] (Ha-Tur, 1270 – 1343), created his own approach to codification in *Sefer ha-Turim* ("Book of Rows"). The author collected the halachot in effect in his time into a concise summary, without mentioning the authorities or Talmudic sources. His presentation was not limited to Talmudic material alone, but also included later legal texts. However, he included an explanation of the differences of opinion on the respective subject areas and named the opposing sides. Of the four *turim*, *tur Even ha-Ezer* is the only one relevant to marriage law.

The works of Rosh, Rambam, and Ha-Tur form the basis for the last great code of Jewish law, the *Shulchan Aruch*[36] ("Set Table") by Joseph Karo[37] (1488 – 1575), first published in Venice in 1565. The *Shulchan Aruch* consists of four parts, of which the third is titled *Even ha-Ezer* ("Stone of Help") and is devoted to marriage laws. Facing divergent opinions from the three scholars, Karo decided which ones he held to be in force and thus condensed the multiplicity of positions. In time, this began to be viewed as the conclusive codification of Jewish law. Not until the annotations by Moses Isserles[38] (Rama, ca. 1525 – 1572), which made Karo's work acceptable for Ashkenazi Jews as well, did the Shulchan Aruch become a general guideline within Judaism.[39]

4. Developing Law through Responsa, Takkana, and Minhag

With the publication of the *Shulchan Aruch* in the sixteenth century, the creativity and variety of the continuing process of renewal of Jewish law diminished. As

---

34 The renowned Talmudist Asher ben Yechiel lived and worked in Germany, France, and Spain.
35 Jacob ben Asher was born in Germany and is considered the halachic authority of the late Middle Ages.
36 See Elon, *Jewish Law*, pp. 1309 – 1422.
37 The important legal scholar and kabbalist Joseph Karo lived in Safed, Palestine.
38 Moses Isserles lived in Krakow. His Haggahot ha-Rav ("Commentary on the Master") is also known as ha-Mappa ("Tablecloth").
39 On Isserles, see Elon, *Jewish Law*, pp. 1359 – 1365.

a result of the development of book printing, this code was soon widely distributed and relatively easy to access. From then on, agreement with the *Shulchan Aruch* became a criterion for what was to be considered Jewish law. As a result, a rift gradually emerged between Jewish law and daily life; it became increasingly wide due in part to the simultaneous onset of the Enlightenment.

The changes in Jewish law were essentially limited by the following factors:

1. The belief that it was based on divine revelation, which meant its principles could not change
2. The fact that, since the destruction of the Temple, and the lack of a Jewish sovereign state, Jewish law could only develop in the form of case law, that is, decisions of individual judges or courts on the basis of their interpretations of relevant authoritative sources and examples.
3. The more conservative view that predominated among representatives of rabbinic law, especially in more recent centuries, based on the principle that "a later court cannot nullify the decisions of an earlier court unless it is superior in wisdom and numbers."[40]

The above limitations did not, however, limit the development of halacha. Although the success of the *Shulchan Aruch* meant the end of the classical period of Jewish legal codification, Jewish legal discourse continued in the various branches of modern Judaism.

It was indispensable for the practical applicability of Jewish law that a decision be made between contradictory doctrines. Local authorities were often not in a position to deal with complex legal matters. Communities, rabbis, and even individuals, therefore, addressed their questions to the leading scholars of their times. The questions were collected in booklets or small books and sent on, and then answered in the same form. Thus, through the centuries a rich and comprehensive literature came into being in which answers ("Responsa") to the legal and intellectual questions of each epoch can be found.[41] In addition, legal authorities could issue takkanot in their jurisdictions—orders to establish legal regulations. This could also occur locally through *minhag*.[42]

---

40 M Ed 1:5.
41 On the development of response literature, see Elon, *Jewish Law*, p. 1472.
42 Minhag ("Custom") refers to the customary law and liturgical practice of the Jewish community of a town or region, and supplements halacha.

Chapter 2:
Jewish Law as a Pluralist Phenomenon

The Enlightenment and the legal emancipation it engendered, accomplished from the end of the eighteenth century onwards in the countries of Europe,[1] allowed Jews to participate and share in modern European culture. Contemporary questions and challenges led to heated disputes among the Jews of Europe, and also North America, that lasted throughout the nineteenth century. Three basic branches of Judaism ultimately formed, each of which applied and developed Jewish law differently. One of these branches, neo-Orthodox Judaism, considered the decrease in Jewish observance since the beginning of the Enlightenment to be a reason to follow the laws and doctrines of rabbinic Judaism as strictly and closely as possible. The movement that began to rethink the doctrines of rabbinic Judaism and revise them in practice was termed the Jewish Reform movement, or liberal or progressive Judaism. It had its roots in early-nineteenth century Germany and spread in the 1840s to North America and Great Britain. Today, liberal, reform, progressive and reconstructionist congregations are found on every continent. Since 1926 they are united in the World Union of Progressive Judaism, serving 1.200 congregations with 1.8 million members in more than 50 countries. Also in Germany, a Conservative branch of Judaism that nevertheless strove for renewal formed soon after in the form of so-called positive-historical Judaism. These conservative communities are linked worldwide today in the "Masorti" movement (*masorti* is the Hebrew word for "traditional").[2]

1. Orthodox Judaism

The Torah and its significance for Jewish life are the focus of Orthodox Judaism. According to the Orthodox view, the Torah is the Word revealed by God, spoken over three thousand years ago at Mount Sinai. The Torah is the *tora min ha-shamayim* (m. Sanh. 10:1), "the Torah from Heaven." It contains God's word as dictated to Moses and, therefore, may not be changed.

---

1 During the French Revolution, the National Assembly proclaimed the Emancipation of the Jews (1790). In Prussia, the Emancipation Edict of March 11, 1812, which recognized Jewish citizenship, was later restricted both legally and in practice. Emancipation was finally achieved in the North German Federation in 1869 and in the German Empire in 1871.
2 Rosenthal, Gilbert; Homolka, Walter, *Das Judentum hat viele Gesichter.* Eine Einführung in die religiösen Strömungen der Gegenwart, Berlin 2014, passim.

DOI 10.1515/9783899497946-002

Such was the case for post-Enlightenment Orthodox rabbis. In their search for religious guidance in Jewish legal texts, innovation was not generally desired and, even when permitted, was rarely admitted. The extreme form of this trend was expressed in the well-known aphorism by the Hatam Sofer (the Hungarian Rabbi Moses Sofer, né Moses Schreiber, 1762–1839): "This is the general rule: the new is forbidden from the Torah in any place and in any time."[3]

Orthodox Judaism also applies the principle of inviolability to oral laws, which are identified with the "oral Torah" that was also revealed to Moses on Mount Sinai. As such, it holds the key to fully understanding the "written Torah." This dual Torah thus contains the oral and written law directly revealed by God. The quintessence of this view therefore consists in the idea that, first of all, the laws are interpreted and classified as immutable and, second, decisions related to new situations in other epochs must nevertheless conform to these laws. Orthodox Judaism rejects the view that it is possible for oral law to interpret and develop the words of the Torah in a process of dynamic historical change.

Orthodox Jews are thus literally faithful to the Torah and insist that every word, every law, and every commandment in the Bible is binding. The same is true for the precepts of the oral Torah—that is, the interpretation of the Biblical text in the Jewish tradition, which is ascribed the same significance as divine revelation, and thus the same immutability as the written Torah. All 613 commandments and prohibitions in the Torah have the same status, and no one has the right to place one commandment above another. Thus, ritual laws (such as the dietary laws) and rules of morality (such as the commandment to love thy neighbor) are equally important; an Orthodox Jew takes the two equally seriously and heeds them equally. The same is true for the rabbinical interpretation of these commandments. The laws and commandments of the Torah are binding—exactly as the rabbis interpreted and explained them.

Rabbi Joseph B. Soloveitchik[4] (1903–1993) called on every Jew to become an *ish halacha*, a "man of the law."[5] He believed that the meaning of halacha need not be proven or explained because it is God's law. Because it holds our feelings and instincts in check, halacha brings us closer to God; it establishes the rules that we cannot revoke by our own will, urge, or desire. However, even in Orthodox Judaism, there are attempts to link literal interpretation with a modern worldview.

---

3 Panken, Aaron D., *The Rhetoric of Innovation: Self-Conscious Legal Change in Rabbinic Literature*, Lanham, MD 2005, p. xv.
4 Joseph B. Soloveitchik was born in Belarus and was one of the leading Orthodox rabbis of the twentieth century.
5 Soloveitchik, Joseph B., *Halakhic Man*, Philadelphia, PA 1983, passim.

For example, Soloveitchik found it important to note that halacha deals with discoveries and knowledge about human beings and the world, even with earth and space exploration by modern science. The purpose of halacha, he said, was to unite our creative actions in the universe with God's creative force. In addition, attempts have been made to link the literal interpretation of *mitzvot* with moral idealism.[6] The president of the Orthodox Yeshiva University in New York, Rabbi Samuel Belkin (1911–1976),[7] taught that all *mitzvot* serve a higher moral purpose, even if human beings cannot always recognize it. The prohibition on shellfish in Jewish cooking sounds simple, but could be connected to a higher moral purpose that we do not see. For some Orthodox rabbis, however, these explanations of the meaning of halachic provisions go too far. In their view, it is enough to know that the laws reflect the will of God. That is reason enough to honor and follow religious law, and there is no reason to change those laws. In the Orthodox view, the decrease of Jewish observance in modern times does not indicate a need to bring Judaism up to modern standards, but rather the need to bring Jews back to their duties. It is not the system but the people who are in error. Occasional reinterpretations, in this view, are permitted only by the *gedolei ha-dor*, a generation's great wise men and scholars. Thus Orthodox Judaism, under its own precepts, can do little to reduce the difficulties that, for example, some of the rules of rabbinical marriage law pose to modern Jews. Yet some Orthodox Jews hope that, someday, the Sanhedrin[8] (High Council) will be reappointed, making more substantial changes possible than is currently the case.

2. Reform Judaism

Many Jews believe not only in the value of tradition, but also in the necessity of change in order to bring traditional practice into conformity with current circumstances. For this reason, liberal or Reform Judaism emerged in the nineteenth century, when the Jews could for the first time practice their religion without restrictions by government authorities. Reform Judaism sees itself as the heir to the nearly 4,000-year-old religious experience of toledot—history as a chain of traditions that begins with the revelation on Sinai. It strives to maintain and de-

---

6 Soloveitchik, *Halakhic Man.*

7 Samuel Belkin, born in the Tsarist Reich, studied Hellenic literature in addition to Jewish law.

8 Sanhedrin (from the Greek *synedrion*, "meeting, council, court"), the term for the Jewish Council of Elders in Jerusalem in the Greco-Roman period. Its authority included the general and religious courts. The Sanhedrin was dissolved when Jerusalem was conquered by the Romans.

velop this tradition, that is, to link knowledge from the past with the reality of our present. After all, Judaism not only has a rich history; it is also a challenge for today's Jews to place these traditions in a modern context. Other expressions of Judaism are equally valid, for they pursue the same goal, if in different ways.

The most important characteristic of Reform Judaism is its attitude towards the revelation on Mount Sinai. A central belief is the historicity of divine revelation and Jewish tradition, which marks every halachic decision, even in Reform Judaism. That is, the Torah contains the word of God, but is written in human words. Its holiness is contained in what it testifies to, not in the way in which it portrays it. It testifies to the religious message that was and is heard by contemporary and succeeding generations, and must constantly be reinterpreted. Therefore, the book is a constantly renewed source of inspirational texts and practical instructions. It must be engaged closely, and every possible aspect of it examined. But the Torah remains a book written by human beings, containing errors and mistakes in copying that must be questioned and revised; its statements are in some respects completely outdated. It is, therefore, absolutely necessary to examine it critically. Only in this way can we determine which passages have a divine character and continue to speak to us today. Some parts yield less than others, and an assumption of immutability is an unjustifiable limitation on rabbinical authority. From a liberal Jewish perspective, the Torah is an authoritative text deserving of attention and appreciation, but it does not possess final authority. Solomon Freehof phrased it as follows:

> "To us the law is human, but nobly human, developed by devoted minds who dedicated their best efforts to answering the question 'What doth the Lord require of thee?' Therefore, we respect it and seek its guidance. Some of its provisions have faded from our lives. We do not regret that fact. But as to the laws that we do follow, we wish them to be in harmony of tradition."[9]

In Reform Judaism, the process of revelation is a progressive one, in which human beings strive to understand God's will. No generation has the sole claim to correct understanding of God's will; each has its insights, which succeeding generations can deepen and broaden. The Hebrew Bible, too, is the product of a long process of religious development, to which both divine revelation and human thinking have contributed essential pieces. The human element reflects the intellectual horizons and social conditions of each period. Thus, Reform Judaism opposes the traditional view that every word of the Torah—be it written or oral—must be considered, in its wording, to possess divine authority

---

9 Freehof, Solomon B., *Reform Responsa*, Cincinnati, OH 1960, p. 21.

unrelated to time. For Reform Judaism, as noted, the Bible and Talmud may be authoritative sources of Judaism, but not every single word in them. It is guided by these texts, but also takes into account modern thinking and current circumstances. It feels itself free (and, in fact, obligated) to change old commandments if they no longer fulfill their original purpose or conflict with modern knowledge or present-day ethical ideas. This does not mean, however, that such changes should be viewed as a renunciation of tradition. Mark Washofsky of Hebrew Union College in Cincinnati describes it as follows:

> "In the formative period of Reform Judaism, in both Europe and America, Reform scholars and thinkers sought to explain and justify in halakhic terms the innovations they introduced into Jewish religious observance. They did this out of their conviction that this 'new' Judaism was a direct continuation of the rabbinic religion that was the common heritage of all Jews. Thus they wrote Responsa which attempted to demonstrate that their innovations in Jewish ritual, such as prayer in the vernacular, the use of instrumental music at services, and the placing of the bimah at the front rather than in the center of the sanctuary, were entirely consistent with Jewish law."[10]

In addition to a belief in the historical, progressive character of revelation, the liberal Jewish attitude towards halacha is determined by a comparative, interdisciplinary approach. The bases of Reform Judaism cover all areas of Jewish life and take account of the development of halacha, but they do not necessarily lead to traditional conclusions. Solomon B. Freehof gets to the heart of it:

> "We make our contact with the great rabbinic intellectual tradition, see wherein it can help us. If we find cases in which the rabbinic tradition does not fit with life, then those cases will have to take their chances with life as everything else does. I follow the tentative formula that the halakha is our guidance and not our governance."[11]

Thus Reform Judaism always takes halacha into account and considers it an important starting point for decision making. But in Reform Judaism, halacha is not absolutely binding. In the search for a modern Jewish answer, other epistemological criteria are also consulted: conscience, reason, philosophical and ethical considerations, the current state of knowledge in natural and social scien-

---

10 Washofsky, Mark, *Jewish Living: A Guide to Contemporary Reform Practice*, New York, NY 2001, p. xix. See Homolka, Walter; Romain, A., *Progressives Judentum*, Leben und Lehre, München 1999.
11 Freehof, Solomon B., "Reform Judaism and the Legal Tradition: The Tintner Memorial Lecture," (Association of Reform Judaism), New York, NY 1961, p. 10; see also Freehof, *Reform Responsa*, pp. 22, 75, 218.

ces, and the like.[12] Whether or not Reform Judaism takes traditional religious law as its legal guideline depends in part on all these components. John D. Rayner, therefore, emphasizes the interdisciplinarity of Jewish law from a liberal perspective:

"[It] will therefore require the co-operation, not only of Halakhists, but of historians and theologians, and of experts in relevant secular disciplines such as medicine, psychology, sociology, jurisprudence, etc. It will lay special emphasis on moral law, which is the most enduringly valid and the most universally relevant. But it will also concern itself with civil law, which may guide us as we seek to make a Jewish contribution to the amelioration of society. And it will attend to ritual matters in so far as they call for legislation."[13]

Thus, the opinions of the rabbis are included in the current thinking of liberal rabbis, but are not binding in and of themselves.

The methodology of the liberal approach to halacha differs from the hermeneutical rules of Orthodoxy, but is also related to them, and their functions are similar as well. It is based on the principle that one first considers the traditional view—even if one ultimately cannot agree with it because it does not correspond to the current situation. Decisions by today's rabbis must take individual situations into account and avoid harmful effects that might result from observance of a law. This is achieved through the principle of prioritization. Important principles are placed above less important ones. For example, the use of the telephone to keep in contact with one's family might override the traditional prohibition on using electricity on Shabbat.[14]

Even if a commandment is observed in Reform Judaism as it is in Orthodoxy, the justification is often different. Some rules are not applied if, in the liberal view, a different prioritization would be more suitable. Consider that in an era when it is normal for women to be heads of state, Orthodox halacha provides in Mishnah Shebu 4:1that women are unsuited to be jurors. Another example is the prohibition on opening an umbrella if it rains on Shabbat. In the Orthodox understanding, this corresponds to the prohibition on putting up a tent on Shabbat. It is equally problematic to place a disabled person in a wheelchair on Shabbat, as the tracks its wheels make on the ground are similar to writing (m. Shab. 7:2 49a)—so riding in a wheelchair on Shabbat is a forbidden activity.

---

12 Rayner, John D., *Jewish Religious Law: A Progressive Perspective*, New York, NY; Oxford 1998, p. 42.

13 Cohen, Jonathan, "On the Standard of Holiness in Jewish Law," in Jacob, Walter: *Beyond the Letter of the Law: Essays on Diversity in the Halakhah*, Pittsburgh, PA 2004, pp. 142–155.

14 Shabbat ("rest") is the seventh day of the week, a day of rest and sanctification to remember God's creation of the world (Exod. 20:11) and Israel's liberation from slavery (Deut. 5:15).

This example illustrates why so many Jews have striven, since the age of 19th century of Emancipation, to develop an up-to-date halacha, in line with the traditional dynamic of Jewish teachings, and in this way to follow the Jewish mission of developing the Torah anew in every generation.

Thus Reform Judaism has revised the outdated definition of work on Shabbat, liberated women from limitations, and eliminated the prayers to restore sacrifices, to name only a few examples. However, this is not simply an effort to replace one body of rules with another. Despite the general assumption that these reforms only serve to modernize Judaism, there is a deeper meaning to them: restoring the original situation in which Jewish law served the Jewish people, met its needs, and provided guidance for everyday life. In this way, the solutions of the past are linked to the requirements of the present. For example, when it was recognized in the 1980s that burying a stillborn child without any mourning ritual for the parents could be very painful, a funeral ritual was introduced for these cases. An essential characteristic of Reform Judaism is thus its flexibility in regard to human needs and emotions, but also a refusal to take advantage of constructions that would help to preserve the illusion of Orthodoxy. For example, strictly Orthodox Jews can erect an *eruv*, an enclosed public space in which the prohibition of carrying on Shabbat is lifted.

Despite its desire for consensus, Reform Judaism strives to recognize and promote each person's individuality. Therefore, efforts are generally made to achieve unity on issues of community interest—such as status questions and forms of worship—at the national level or within a cultural framework. This permits broad agreement on customs in all of a country's liberal congregations. On the other hand, however, Reform Judaism permits exceptions and alterations, which are especially important in personal matters. Thus, the rabbis provide guidance regarding individual observance of kashrut[15] or Shabbat, but the actual decision lies with the individual's conscience—not primarily because it would be impossible in any case to enforce observance of the laws, but because ultimately each person bears responsibility for his or her own religious observance. It is the duty of each person to live his or her life with knowledge of Jewish tradition, personal integrity, and affiliation with the community. This can lead to differences in individual religious behavior. In the liberal view, there is no reason that a religious orientation of one's life within this framework must be identical for everyone, as long as religious life is lived within a recognized Jewish structure. In the process, the relationship between personal freedom and community identity must be constantly balanced. Every Jew has the right to express religiosity in

---

15 Kashrut ("fitness"), dietary laws regarding prohibited and permitted foods.

his or her own way, but also has the duty to adhere to the set of rules that makes up the People of Israel in the traditional sense.

Since its inception, Reform Judaism has been aware of the difficulty of comprehending God's will in everyday occurrences; therefore, it considers human striving to be a holy task that one must carry out to the best of one's abilities. This task is reflected in Leo Baeck's[16] observation that "being liberal is so much more difficult"[17]—more difficult because, unlike in Orthodoxy, there are no definitive answers, so that one must make individual decisions of conscience in regard to living a religious life. Engagement with such questions forces the individual to set priorities; every day it brings the challenge of reflecting on how one should behave. Reform Judaism is thus far from being "comfortable," as critics have often claimed. Rather, it embodies the literal meaning of the word Israel—"strives with God" (according to Gen. 32:29)—and is a constant attempt to link the highest ideals with the realities of daily life and to live consciously as a Jew in the midst of modern society. Thus the prominent liberal halakhist Moshe Zemer (1932–2011) concluded, in his work "A Progressive Approach to Traditional Jewish Law" (1999):

> "Finally we have seen that not only is it permitted to enact new regulations and innovate in order to repair the wounded souls of our brethren, it is also the imperative of the hour. Decisors and rabbis must cope with the situation of our generation, just as was stated by Rabbi Joseph Albo more than five hundred years ago: 'Certain general principles were only briefly alluded to in the Torah, so that the Sages of every generation may work out the newly emerging particulars.'"[18]

The principles and decisions of Reform Judaism today are not so much the result of a systematic reordering of Jewish faith and life, but rather emerged, in general, as answers to concrete questions. Their common basis, however, is a general theological principle, in light of which Reform Judaism approaches tradition: the right to change tradition according to progressive revelation. In 1983, the great contemporary halachist of Reform Judaism, Walter Jacob, described the

---

16 Leo Baeck (1873–1956), author of *Das Wesen des Judentums* (1905), is one of the best-known representatives of liberal Judaism in the twentieth century. Until his deportation to the Theresienstadt concentration camp in 1943, he was rabbi in Berlin. After World War II, he emigrated to the United States. From 1938 to 1956, he was president of the World Union of Progressive Judaism (WUPJ).

17 Quote from a speech by Leo Baeck, First Conference of the World Union of Progressive Judaism at Berlin, Saturday, August 18th – Sunday, August 20th, 1928.

18 Zemer, Moshe, *Evolving Halakhah A Progressive Approach to traditional Jewish Law*, Jewish Lights Publishing Woodstock, VT 1999, p. 653.

task and role of engagement with halacha by the Central Conference of American Rabbis and their Religious Law Commission as follows:

> "We have looked at Halacha in a different and, we believe, more creative way than other Jewish groups. We have not looked to the Orthodox for approval; rather, our response and the guides which we have written have linked the past to the present and sought to make Halacha meaningful to new generations …. The roots of Reform Halacha lie partially in our nineteenth-century past, for we have been provided with firm halachic foundations through the efforts of Geiger, Frankel, Loew, and others. They are, however, more deeply rooted in the distant rabbinic past. On occasion we may be as radical as those Tana'im and Amora'im who created Rabbinic Judaism, and thereby created [Judaism] anew. Frequently, we will find appropriate solutions within the tradition, broadly perceived. The authority of the Central Conference of American Rabbis and its Responsa Committee lies in its ability to persuade and reach a consensus. Halachic discussions will bring us closer to consensus and agreement on basic principles. As often in the past, we will proceed inductively, and specific statements will evolve into general principles."[19]

3. Conservative Judaism

Conservative Judaism seeks a middle way between the Orthodox position of *tora min ha-shamayim* and Reform Judaism.[20] It also originated in 19th-century Germany, where it was heavily influenced by the Prague-born chief rabbi of Dresden, Zacharias Frankel (1801–1875). With a group of moderate rabbis, he founded the Jewish Theological Seminary of Breslau in 1854 and became its first dean. The non-Orthodox variant of traditional Judaism taught there soon became known as "positive-historical." It was "positive" because, in contrast to the classical Jewish reform movement in Germany at the time, it sought to preserve halacha and mitzvot traditionally and to retain Hebrew as the liturgical language of prayer in the synagogues. It was "historical" because it recognized that Judaism, with its laws and institutions, had developed and changed over the centuries. Therefore, for a true understanding of Judaism, it was crucial to study its historical development. As much as Frankel did not rule out the possibility of change and development in Judaism, he also emphatically rejected fundamental inter-

---

19 Jacob, Walter (ed.), *American Reform Responsa: Collected Responsa of the Central Conference of American Rabbis, 1889–1983*, New York, NY 1983, pp. xvi, xviii.
20 Dorff, Elliot N., "Jewish Law in the Conservative/Masorti Movement," in *Periodica de Re Canonica* 96/3–4 (2007), pp. 639–652 [Prima Consultazione Romana sul Diritto Ebraico e Canonico —Erste römische Konsultation zum jüdischen und kanonischen Recht, 9–11.10.2006, Pontificia Università Gregoriana]. Elazar, Daniel J., Geffen, Rela Mintz, *The Conservative Movement in Judaism: Dilemmas and Opportunities*, Albany, NY 2000.

ference with tradition.[21] At the Breslau Jewish Theological Seminary, which existed until 1938, the critical historical method was applied in dealing with Talmud, but not with the Five Books of Moses themselves.

Despite the historical-positive approach, with few exceptions almost all conservative thinkers accept the idea that the People of Israel received the Torah directly from God. Some believe that this revelation was a one-time historical act, while others see revelation as an ongoing process in which each generation discovers more and more of the Word of God. However, most conservative Jews oppose the Orthodox view that every single word in the Torah is immutable. At the same time, both the oral and the written Torah are at heart inspired by God. For conservative Jews, faith has no basis without this notion.

In contrast to Orthodox positions, however, conservative thinkers believe that revelation is a reciprocal process, a dialogue between God and humankind. The core of divine truth may not be denied. But the way in which we think about this truth in the Torah and Talmud is deeply human, contains errors, and holds thoughts and ideas that are linked with their times. At this level, therefore, change is most definitely possible. In the conservative view, the Bible and Jewish religious laws are our answer to God's desire to make Himself known to us. The mitzvah is a human interpretation and application of God's principles in each era. Conservative Jews readily follow basic and essential principles such as the observance of Shabbat and the holidays, the Kashrut rules, Jewish marriage and divorce, the necessity of a solid Jewish education, and the study of the Hebrew language and ethical doctrines. They are, however, simultaneously aware of the necessity of adapting some Jewish rules to our daily lives. They advocate attending synagogue and, therefore, those attending services may drive there if they live too far from a synagogue to walk. Further, conservative rabbis have achieved some important changes in marriage and divorce laws. For example, they have found a solution to the problem of wives whose husbands will not or cannot grant a divorce. In such cases, a Jewish court (*bet din*) can dissolve the marriage, regardless of the existence of the traditionally-necessary divorce letter (*get*).

The question of who has the right to change laws and on what basis is difficult for conservative Judaism to answer. Rabbi Salomon Schechter[22] (1847–

---

21 See Meyer, Michael A., *Antwort auf die Moderne*, Vienna 2000, pp. 131–138. With the creation of the Jewish Theological Seminary of America (JTSA) in 1887 in New York, the conservative movement in North America created its spiritual home.

22 This scholar, born in Romania, was along with Frankel one of the pioneers of the modern conservative movement. He came to New York via Vienna, Berlin, and Cambridge and taught at the Jewish Theological Seminary.

1915) believed that religious law was so important to Judaism because no movement can survive based exclusively on noble thoughts. But he believed that the living community of all Jews—including the prophets, psalmists, sages, and rabbis—had to have the last word, across the generations, on which parts of Jewish law may be changed and which may not be; the people as a whole and its ways of life determine the interpretation of the Torah. Schechter also dealt with the Zeitgeist and with secular science, in accordance with a sentence from Mishnah tractate Abot 2:19: "Be diligent in the study of Torah. Know what to answer a heretic."

The great Talmud scholar Louis Ginzberg (1873–1955), the founder of the American Academy of Jewish Research, also emphasized that Jewish law has never been dead matter or a fixed, constant entity. It has developed and changed, keeping pace with new social and scientific situations. According to Robert Gordis (1908–1992), a student of Ginzberg's, "Growth is th law of life, and the law is the life of Judaism."[23] Gordis sees revelation as a process, for which he offers an image: Today's Torah goes back to Moses in the same the way as an oak comes from an acorn. In this way, the rules that emerged before our time make it possible for us to establish rules for our own time. Gordis believes in the necessity of halacha for four reasons:
- It links human beings with the universe in which they live.
- It teaches them ethical and social values.
- It makes life better and richer.
- It links every Jew with the Jewish people and community.

In general, the inviolability of halacha and mitzvot is central to the conservative movement. Opinions diverge on how to approach changes and the extent of such change. Some advocate more determined action, while others criticize the procedure within the conservative movement for being too insensitive. But all conservative interpreters of the law share the view that Jewish law can be molded. In the conservative movement, it is the task of the Committee on Jewish Law and Standards (CJLS) and the Rabbinical Assembly to undertake these changes.

---

23 Gordis, Robert, *The Dynamics of Judaism: A Study in Jewish Law*, Bloomington, IN 1990, p. 211.

4. Halacha as a Dialectical Process

When we consider all three branches, it is clear that the view of what halacha is has changed and developed in every era. This is not surprising if we consider that this reflects a principle that has marked the history of the Jewish people from the beginning: the community harmonized the faith of the Jewish patriarchs and matriarchs with the teachings of Sinai, the idealism of the prophets, and the pragmatic individual decisions of the rabbis. It took into account the social conditions of various epochs and responded to contemporary lifestyles and attitudes, even if it did not necessarily adapt to them. This is shown especially in the Talmudic period, when halachic principles were the subject of lively debate and critical examination. Customs that were no longer practicable were successfully eliminated through a process of interpretation that lent different meaning to the words of Torah texts. Thus the death penalty, which was provided for in Biblical literature for numerous offenses, ultimately had so many conditions attached to it that it became impossible to implement. Similarly, the sentence "eye for an eye, tooth for a tooth" (Exod. 21:24) was separated from any physical retribution and instead came to refer to purely financial settlements. Later, rabbinical decisions were applied to annul laws that had negative consequences for the community. For example, Hillel's prosbul[24] made it possible to require loans to be paid back even after the Shabbat year—the period in which fields lay fallow, which the Biblical text required every seventh year— and would not be forfeited, as the Bible required. As further evidence of how much traditional Judaism approved of changes, we may note that in the second century CE, the Shabbat service lasted only an hour, Torah portions were translated into local languages, prayers varied from community to community, and men wore no head covering, were allowed to have more than one wife,[25] and apparently did not sit separately from their wives during services.

Through the centuries there was also an intermittent, extensive debate about observing religious law, which continued after the Enlightenment in the three main strands of Judaism. Many decision makers expressly took account of actual realities in their legal decision making. For some situations, no logically based derivation was possible using halachic methods (that is, by falling back on traditional laws). In such cases, radically new approaches were introduced into Jewish law. For example, Yehuda ha-Nasi (around 165–217) felt called upon to

---

24 Prosbul is the term for the writ deposited with the court in order to cancel the remission of debts during sabbatical years.
25 According to tradition, monogomy, which was already common in Central Europe, was not established until 1040 by Rabbi Gershom ben Yehuda.

change the entire halachic basis of the laws on the Shabbat year in order to protect the population from starvation. Moshe Zemer points out that, from the Middle Ages until today, great legal scholars such as Moses Isserles (1525–1572) and David Zvi Hoffmann[26] (1843–1921) have modified laws that seemed too strict to them out of a sense of halachic responsibility. The literal implementation of the law was for them a profanation of God's name.[27] Initially, geographical differences in observance developed between the Ashkenazim and the Sephardim; only later did the aforementioned differences between liberal, conservative, and Orthodox Jews emerge.[28]

There most certainly is Jewish law, that is, halacha, that applies to all Jews equally. But there is no single way to interpret it. Judaism lives through the diversity of views represented in it. There are many correct interpretations and many ways to understand halacha. In the process, geographical differences developed between the observance by Ashkenazim and Sephardim, and only later the above-mentioned differences between liberal, conservative, and Orthodox Jews.[29]

5. The "Law of the Land" and Jewish Law

In the third century CE, the Babylonian scholar Samuel formulated the principle of *dina de-malchuta dina*—Aramaic for "The law of the land is the law." This was a result of the historical circumstances of the Babylonian exile and has four classical references in the Talmud (b. Ned. 281, bT Git. 10b, BG 113a, BB 54b-55a). Neh. 9:37 is retroactively invoked as Biblical evidence that the Jews are expected to observe the laws of their non-Jewish rulers (see also Jer. 29:4).[30] The concept of *dina de-malchuta dina* developed in the rabbinical literature and is essential for understanding Jewish marriage laws; it means that Jews are subject in civil matters (*dinim*), though not in ritual prohibitions (*issurim*), to the laws of the countries in which they live, as long as these laws do not contradict the religious and ethical rules of Judaism. This acknowledgment of the respective state laws at first

---

26 David Zvi Hoffmann was a representative of neo-Orthodoxy and served as dean of the Rabbinical Seminary for Orthodox Judaism in Berlin starting in 1899.
27 Zemer, *Evolving Halakhah, p.235.*
28 Rosenthal, Homolka, *Das Judentum hat viele Gesichter,* passim.
29 For details, see Sylvia Barack Fishman, *The Way into the Varieties of Jewishness,* Jewish Lights Publishing, Woodstock, VT 2007.
30 Encyclopaedia Judaica [EJ] Jerusalem 1971, vol. 6, 515–5 (Art. Dina de-malkhuta dina).

applied primarily to property laws, especially tax laws. Later, the meaning of the principle of *dina de-machuta dina* extended to include large areas of daily life.

The following are some remarks on the historical development of this principle. Jews always possessed quite varied amounts of legal autonomy, depending on place and time. The spectrum of Jewish law ranges from state sovereignty in Biblical times, to relative legal autonomy as a Greek or Roman province in antiquity, to only partial legal autonomy in the Diaspora. The state that enjoys an institutional monopoly regarding legislation and administration of justice is a relatively recent phenomenon; in antiquity and in Muslim and Christian polities of the Middle Ages, a large number of areas of law were left to various religious, ethnic, social, and economic communities. This changed with the development of the modern state, especially with the French Revolution. As a result, even outside of France—though generally after a long process—the modern bourgeois state replaced the medieval European societies of estates.

One consequence of this development was that Jewish communities, like other legal entities, lost the measure of legal autonomy they had heretofore enjoyed. Areas of law that had previously been dealt with by Jewish law became subject to the jurisdiction of the state. Because the modern state was able to firmly establish its claim to sole legislative authority in the nineteenth century and, through the introduction of general civil law that applied to everyone, took it upon itself to shape marriage and family to a greater degree than in the past, Jewish law (like the canonical law of the Catholic Church) was greatly reduced.

Jewish law has nevertheless been applied within the community up to the present day. In the General Regulations for the Jews of Prussia, issued by Frederick the Great in 1750, it was still expressly provided that the provisions of Mosaic Law would decide certain internal Jewish matters. Austria's *Allgemeines Bürgerliches Gesetzbuch* (Civil Code, ABGB) and the earlier Russian code also provided for the use of Jewish law, for example in marital law. Then, as now, however, members of the Jewish community could not give their blessings to marriages that conflicted with national laws.[31] In divorce, too, Jewish courts

---

31 Since Bismarck, chuch or other religious marriages were permitted only after prior civil marriage. Violations were sanctioned as misdemeanors under §§ 67, 67a of the Personal Status Law. The Personal Status Reform Law of 2007 repealed both paragraphs as of January 1, 2009. This meant that religious marriage of a couple not married civilly was no longer an offense. The end of the civil marriage obligation meant that church or other religious marriages could in the future be carried out even if the couple was not married under civil law. However, religious marriages have no civil legal consequences. Only a civil marriage is a legally recognized marriage under § 1350 of the Civil Code. A religious marriage does not support a claim for alimony,

can only reach decisions if the marriage in question has already been dissolved under civil law. In other words, Jewish marriage laws can only be applied within the bounds set by national law. And even within these bounds, it cannot necessarily be enforced. Jewish authorities cannot force any Jew to enter into a Jewish marriage or accept a Jewish divorce. They cannot prevent anyone from marrying or divorcing under civil law. Jewish marriage law is only enforceable *ex negativo*, in that the Jewish authorities can refuse to perform Jewish marriages or divorces in specific cases. In this sense, Jewish courts can refuse what national law permits; but they cannot permit something that national law prohibits. As a result of the social upheavals and political developments since the Enlightenment, and especially in the course of the nineteenth century, rabbinical (marriage) law thus lost a significant portion of its practical effectiveness—in part because its scope of authority was reduced, in part because alternative recourse to state law became an option even for members of the Jewish community.

A. Jewish Law in the State of Israel

The situation in the areas of today's State of Israel, from the Ottoman period to the present, can be examined separately.[32] While state law is applicable to foreign nationals, in family law matters, Israeli citizens are subject to the laws of their respective religious communities. This legal situation was carried over from the period of Ottoman rule in the territory of today's Israel (1517–1917).[33] The situation did not change when Palestine became a British mandatory territory. The Palestine Order-in-Council of 1922, which was essentially the constitu-

---

disadvantages fathers on childcare issues, and has no effect on child support, taxes, or inheritance. In particular, it supports no claim for a widow's pension.

32 Encyclopaedia Judaica [EJ] Jerusalem 1971, Vol. 12, 145–151 (Art. Mishpat Ivri); Shetreet, Shimon, "Between Three Branches of Government: The Balance of Rights in Matters of Religion in Israel," Jerusalem 2001, p. 9 ff.; Shimon Shetreet, "The Relationship Between Religion and State from a Jewish Viewpoint in Comparative Perspectives: Selected Issues," in *Periodica de Re Canonica* 96/3–4 (2007), pp. 589–617 [Prima Consultatione Romana sul Diritto Ebraico e Canonico – First Roman Consultation on Jewish and Canon Law, October 9–11, 2006, Pontificia Università Gregoriana]. Gotham, Meike, "Die Rechtsnation und ihr Staat, Die Geltung des Jüdischen Ehe – und Scheidungsrechts, in Israel," Hamburg 2004, p. 51 ff.; Mazie, Steven V., "Israel's Higher Law: Religion and Liberal Democracy in the Jewish State," Lanham, MD 2006, p. 165 ff. See also chapters 10 and 11 of this book.

33 Goldfine, Yitzhak, "Herkunft und Quellen des gegenwärtigen israelischen Rechts," Eine Rechtshistorische und rechtsvergleichende Studie auf dem Gebiete der Rechtsrezeption, Frankfurt/Main 1967, p. 11 ff.

tion of Palestine during the Mandatory period, subordinated personal status matters to the personal laws of the parties. The founding of the State of Israel in 1948 did not fundamentally change this law from the Mandatory period. Thus, in the State of Israel today, the family law of the parties' respective religious communities applies.[34] In particular, the Rabbinical Courts Jurisdiction (Marriage and Divorce) Law of 1953 established that Jewish law was to be applied as personal law in all matters of marriage and divorce to Jews with residence in Israel—by civil as well as rabbinical courts. Nevertheless, English law has an influence on the treatment of personal status matters, for example, in complaints regarding compensation for breach of engagement.

B. Jewish Law as the Embodiment of Jewish Ethics and the Quest for Justice

This historical overview should not create the impression that the relationship between Jewish law and state law in modern times has been merely defensive and marked by constant retreat. Rather, the unique character of Jewish law described at the outset means that—according to a formulation we owe to Leo Baeck—it can, and under some circumstances must, oppose state law purely out of ethical obligation. Jewish law must, by virtue of its own foundations, be able to withstand and oppose possible abuses or perversions of state law, such as those that occurred under the Nazi regime.

For example, in *Fragen des jüdischen Ehegesetzes* (*Questions of Jewish Marriage Law*) (1929), Baeck made it clear that Jewish marriage is first and foremost a divine institution.[35] As with Jewish law in general, its validity is religiously based. Faith, not state compulsion, is decisive when the issue is ensuring enforcement of the law. It demands absolute respect and finds support in God himself as the lawgiver. Its binding nature is only reinforced by the fact that the obligation based in it continues to have effect even if the secular power lacks the means to enforce it. Accordingly, even if punishment "is not permitted [before] a human court" (*patur be-Dinei Adam*), punishment will be had before the "heavenly court" (*be'Dinei shamayim*).

The law's reference to God in this way also has substantive consequences, in the sense of harmonious linkage of strictness and leniency. Jewish law seeks a middle ground between strict demands and merciful concession—a mid-

---

34 Goldfine, Yitzhak, "Einführung in das jüdische und israelische Eherecht," Hamburg 1975, p. 1ff.
35 Baeck, Leo, *Fragen des jüdischen Ehegesetzes*, (1929) in *Leo Baeck Werke*, ed. by Albert H. Friedlander et al., Vol. 6, Gütersloh 2005, pp. 504–507.

dle ground that formal state law, divorced, as it were, from ethics, does not necessarily attempt to find in the same way. This also means that the attitude toward law expressed in the Latin sentence *fiat iustitia, pereat mundus* ("Let justice be done, though the world perish") is alien to Jewish law. Rather, it applies the principle that law exists for the sake of human beings, not the human being for the sake of law. A legal scholar tied the Biblical injunction "Ye shall therefore keep my statutes, and my judgments: which if a man do, he shall live in them" (Lev. 18:5) to the observation that the use of law should lead to life, not to its loss (b. San. 74a). Thus the provisions on workers and work contracts, as well as those on loans, liens, and the jubilee year (*shemitta*), all contain a wealth of social considerations that indicate a tendency to ensure settlements in favor of the economically weaker party when interests collide.

This sense of social justice, demonstrated from the earliest historical period, was revived by the prophets. Later, the Talmud expanded the law in this spirit in many ways, adapting it to the requirements of a new era. The fact that knowledge of law was not limited to a small group of experts, but was part of the intellectual property of broad classes of people, additionally promoted the elaboration of this social law. (Incidentally, the particular value placed on the law by Judaism arises, among other things, from the fact that study of the Torah is generally considered a religious duty for Jews). The fact is that once given to the people, law—even God's law—was withdrawn from divinity, as it were; it would now be handed down to future generations: "And thou shalt teach them diligently unto thy children, and shalt talk of them when thou sittest in thine house, and when thou walkest by the way, and when thou liest down, and when thou risest up." (Deut. 6:7; 11:19). In Judaism, there is no divine intervention regarding the use of law; it is to be implemented by human beings alone.[36] Jewish procedural law recognizes no supernatural evidence. (Thus a legal scholar who wished to invoke a supernatural voice in a legal dispute was told, "The law is not in heaven" (bT B.M. 59b). In other words, the reality of Jewish law is divine, but it is not *tora min ha-shamayim*, not a Torah from heaven. All people are equally subject to religious law, which prevents any state or non-state violence or despotism.

The meticulous precision in observing rituals as well as the precise regulation of the cult shaped legal procedures, and lent strong impulses to the structure of the legal system. The influence of ethical perspectives on Jewish law is shown in the fact that insistence on claims according to the strict law of the

---

36 Homolka, Walter: *Judaism's Universal Gift – An Ethic for Humankind*, in Küng, Hans; Homolka, Walter, *How to Do Good & Avoid Evil – A Global Ethic from the Sources of Judaism*, Woodstock VT, pp. 21–41.

Torah (*din tora*) is not considered an ideal to be striven for; forbearance is an even higher ideal. In the Talmud (bT B.M. 30b), it is claimed that the destruction of Jerusalem resulted from the fact that Torah law was applied strictly rather than with leniency. In addition to the law (*shurat ha-din*), therefore, there is a sphere of equity lying "beyond the letter of the law" (see bT B.M. 30b). "Let the law pierce through the mountain" (bT Yev. 92a), but should always be applied while observing the limitations dictated by good faith. Thus, a fundamental principle is always at the heart of Jewish faith: the ethical obligation of Jews to face God's challenges in a constant process of purification and to make his kingdom a reality on earth. For the connection between human beings and God is justified and solidified by adherence to the instructions, the mitzvot, that God set out in his Torah. Justice is, accordingly, a gift of God with which he orders the world according to his will. The process of continuous interpretation of this divine will and the current application of the legal norms arising from it are traditionally the most prestigious task of the rabbis as Jewish legal scholars. The rabbis acted in the awareness that even divinely inspired law need not be immutable; revelation can continue to unfold in a process of discussion regarding these norms and their legal force. The Spanish philosopher of religion Josef Albo (around 1380–around 1445) formulated it thusly: because God's Torah cannot possibly be so complete that it is sufficient for all time, and because there are so many details that change in the lives of human beings and in the laws, and because too many forces are at work to fit in one book—therefore, the oral traditions received by Moses on Mount Sinai are only vaguely indicated in the written teachings, so that the halachic authorities of each generation can reach new interpretations corresponding to their respective situations.[37]

The basis of Jewish ethics is the command of emulation, the *imitatio dei* (Deut. 28:9). Because human beings are created in the image of God, they have the responsibility as well as the possibility of emulating him. We should not imagine that we are God and can, in a sort of illusion of omnipotence, raise our will to the status of law—although in practice we do this often enough. But we have the task of bringing God's justice, mercy, and love into the world through our actions. These concepts should not be seen as opposites; indeed, they are almost synonyms: in the Jewish view, justice is mercy and love.

"O how love I thy law! it is my meditation all the day. / Through thy precepts I get understanding: therefore I hate every false way. / Thy word is a lamp unto my feet, and a light unto my path. / I have sworn, and I will perform it, that I will keep thy righteous judgments. / I am afflicted very much; quicken me, O Lord, according unto Thy word. / Accept,

---

37 Albo, Josef, Sefer ha-ikkarim, 3:23.

I beseech Thee, the freewill offerings of my mouth, O Lord, and teach me Thy judgments."
(Psalms 119:97, 104–108).

It is thus crucial that halacha and ethics should not be pulled apart, but be kept
together in a fruitful mutual relationship. The ethical imperative of *imitatio dei*
forms the actual basis of halacha and the main point of contact between the divine and human spheres. This correlation between ethics and halacha, which is
essential to Judaism, makes it necessary to put tradition constantly to the test
and to find solutions to ethical problems arising from the use of religious law.
Some problems remain controversial between the various branches of Judaism.
A classic example is the problem of aguna, the "chained woman," which could
be solved through the ability of rabbinical courts to annul marriages. So far,
however, no generally accepted rule has been established on this matter.

Two points should be noted: There is certainly such a thing as Jewish law,
meaning halacha, which is equally applicable to all Jews But there is no one
way to interpret it. Judaism lives through the diversity of views represented within it. There are many correct interpretations and many ways to understand halacha. It is not least due to the various interpretations of Jewish law that Judaism
has branched out in various directions, with their respective interpretations of
halacha.

In contrast to "positive" (that is, positivist) law, Jewish law is not a firm set of
rules in which issues of justice represent a problematic area, lying, strictly speaking, beyond the sphere of "positive" law. Rather, in Jewish law, the question of
justice is found at the origin of all questions of law. It fundamentally accompanies law: *Zedek u'mishpat*, law and justice (Prov. 2:9), have always been seen as a
unit in Judaism and have been jointly promoted. The binding aspect of the Jewish legal tradition from Abraham through the prophets to the rabbis and today's
scholars of Jewish law is precisely this unending quest for justice. Every rabbi is
expected to seek to the best of his or her ability to interpret God's will in such a
way that the words of the psalm take visible shape: "The statutes of the Lord are
right / rejoicing the heart; / the commandment of the Lord is pure, enlightening
the eyes. / The fear of the Lord is clean, enduring for ever: the judgments of the
Lord are true and righteous altogether." (Psalms 19:8–9).

Part II: Legal Culture and System of Government in the State of Israel

Chapter 3:
General Introduction

1. Country Basic Data

The State of Israel is situated in the Middle East along the shore of the Mediterranean Sea, bound between Egypt to the southwest, the Gaza Strip to the west, Jordan to the east, Lebanon to the north, and Syria to the northeast.[1] Israel has a total area of 22,145 km² and includes East Jerusalem and the Golan Heights.[2] The State of Israel is divided into six administrative districts which are distributed into 15 regions. The districts include: Jerusalem, the Northern District, the Haifa District, the Central District, the Tel-Aviv District, and the Southern District. Additionally, Israel holds territory in the West Bank, which is known as Judea and Samaria.[3]

The country's population is 8,345,000 as of April 2015.[4] Most of the country (75%) is of Jewish ethnicity, while 20.7% are Muslim, and 4.4% are Christian, Druze, and of other faiths.[5]

The State of Israel was established in May 1948. Before that time, the Turks under the Ottoman Empire controlled the Israeli territory until 1917, when it was conquered by the British. The British ruled the territory until 1922, when, under the League of Nations, it was granted to England as a Mandated territory and was meant to be established as "a national home for Jewish people."[6]

2. Legal Culture

The Israeli legal system is influenced by a number of different legal sources. Historically, Ottoman legal codes were a major part of the overall legal system. Through the progress of time, most of the Ottoman legislation was voided or replaced; however, there are remnants in Israeli law. Today, Israeli law is influ-

---

1 *Land Boundaries*, CIA World Factbook: Israel, https://www.cia.gov/library/publications/the-world-factbook/geos/is.html (accessed February 9, 2017).
2 See Israel Statistical Yearbook, No. 55, the Central Bureau of Statistics (2004).
3 See *Land Boundaries*, *supra* note 1.
4 CIA World Factbook: Israel, Population
5 As of 2012 CIA World Factbook: Israel, Religion.
6 Assaf Likhovski, *Law and Identity in Mandate Palastine* (University of North Carolina Press, 2006).

DOI 10.1515/9783899497946-003

enced by both civil and common law traditions, and Israel is classified as a mixed jurisdiction.

Common law influences manifest themselves most prevalently in the court systems. Judicial decisions are considered a source of law and form Israeli common law. Therefore, precedent, judicial procedure, and decision making are very important to Israeli courts. The Supreme Court gives great importance to its previous decisions, but is not bound by its own precedent. The Supreme Court decisions are legally binding on lower courts. American common law traditions and the wisdom of American judges have heavily influenced the emerging Israeli Constitution.[7]

The civil law tradition manifests itself in the codification of mainly private laws and some public laws. Civil law manifests itself through the major role that academics play in shaping the law and through private law principles such as good faith.[8]

In addition to the common law and civil law traditions, Israel has had over seven decades to develop its own additions to the inherited legal system. All of these influences have created a mixed jurisdiction system which strongly resembles common law, but with obvious civil law influences.[9]

The Israeli legal system was influenced by three main legal traditions. The first tradition was the Ottoman rule that influences the Israeli legal system. Later on, the British rule (1917–1948), during the British mandate over Palestine influenced the Israeli legal system, and then came the Israeli independence (1948) that brought the Israeli legal system. Both old Ottoman laws and British legal traditions can be found in the Israeli legal system.[10]

The Ottoman legal system was the most predominant of the legal influences at the beginning of modern history. Up until 1948 and for some time after, Ottoman law had a significant presence in the Israeli legal system. However, the Ottoman legal regime has almost completely disappeared from Israeli law due to more recent laws that have repealed or replaced the old Ottoman laws. Ottoman legal influence, while now mostly insignificant, can still be felt in the legal autonomy that religious communities have in most family matters.[11]

---

7 See Gad Tedeschi, *The Issue of Deficiencies in the Law, Studies in Our Legal System* (2nd ed., 1959); Aharon Barak, *The Israeli Legal System – Its Tradition and Culture*, 40 Hapraklit 197 (1992).
8 *Id.*
9 *Id.*
10 *Id.*
11 Friedman Daniel, "*The Effect of Foreign Law on the Law of Israel: Remnants of the Ottoman Period*," 10 Isr. L. Rev. 192, 201–206 (1975).

British legal influence has been much deeper and long lasting in the Israeli legal system. In many ways, Israel owes its very legal structure and principles of constitutional law to British legal heritage. British rule began in 1917 after the Turks lost control of the territory. In 1922, the League of Nations officially granted the territory of Israel to Britain as a Mandated Territory. The Mandated period lasted thirty years and was meant to exist until such time as the territory was able to stand on its own.[12] This period ended upon the approval of the United Nations' decision to partition Palestine into a Jewish state and an Arab state.[13]

British laws played an important role in the country long after independence. Until 1980, Israeli courts were bound to follow common law. However, Article 46 of the Palestine Order in Council, which was the basis for following common English law, was repealed in 1980. The long adherence to common law has created an Israeli legal system that shares many similarities with common law countries like Great Britain and the United States.[14] British parliamentary system has heavily influenced the current form of Israeli government and, like the British government, the Israeli government has a parliament (called the Knesset).[15]

On November 29, 1947, the United Nations General Assembly adopted a resolution to partition Palestine into a Jewish state and an Arab state. The decision was adamantly opposed by Arab states, but was accepted by the Jewish population in Palestine.[16] The new Jewish nation produced a Declaration of Independence on May 14, 1948.[17] After the Independence, the country operated under a parliamentary democracy with the election of a Constituent Assembly, which later became the first Knesset (or Parliament). This system remained in place until 1992 when developments in the constitutional process altered the governmental system to a constitutional democracy with the passing of two laws: *Basic Law: Human Dignity and Liberty* and *Basic Law: Freedom of Occupation.*[18]

Since 1948, the Israeli legal evolution has had several areas of emphasis. First, there has been a focus on filling in the gaps left by the legal systems of

---

12 The British conquered the territory in 1917, the Mandate from the League of Nations took effect in 1922, and the UN General Assembly adopted its decision to partition Palestine into Jewish and Arab states on November 29, 1947.

13 Friedmann Daniel, *"Infusion of the Common Law into the Legal System of Israel,"* 10 Isr. L. Rev. 324–327 (1975).

14 Barak, *supra* note 7, at 203.

15 Shimon Shetreet, The Executive: Basic Law: The Government (forthcoming 2017, Yitzhak Zamir, ed.).

16 UN General Assembly Resolution 181 (Partition Plan) (29.11.1947)

17 Ruth Lapidoth and Moshe Hirsch, eds., *The Arab-Israel Conflict and its Resolutions – Selected Documents* (Dordrecht, Martinus Nijhoff Publishers, 1992), 33.

18 Suzie Navot, The Constitution of Israel, Chap. 1 (Hart, 2014).

previous ruling regimes like the Ottomans and the British. Israeli legal evolution also focused on developing new systems of law, "for private relations between individuals and the other for the rights of individuals in a democratic system". this evolution has manifested itself in the continual efforts to codify the private system and reform the public law.[19]

The Knesset is the Israeli parliament. The head of the executive government is the Prime Minister. The President of Israel chooses a member of parliament and charges that person with the task of forming a government. Normally it is the leader of the biggest faction in the parliament who has the best chance of forming a coalition and command the confidence of parliament after forming a government. The President is primarily a representative figure whereas the Prime Minister, who is the head of the executive branch, is the main executive officer of the government. The Israeli parliament consists of multiple parties which receive seats proportional to the percentage of votes that the parties carry in the elections. Under the Israeli democratic parliamentary system, voters vote for a list of candidates and not for a particular person on the list. In order for a party to have a percentage of seats in the Knesset, the party must carry a minimum of 3.25 percent of the votes from the electorate.[20]

For the period between 1992 and 2001, the Prime Minister was subject to direct elections. The purpose of the change was to provide the government with greater stability and governability and to create closer ties between the electorate and their representatives. However, the new electoral system suffered from instability; it did not help to resolve the difficulties of governance that had motivated the creation of the direct electoral system. After 2001, the process for electing the prime minister returned to its original form with a few minor alterations.[21]

3. Constitutional Infrastructure

The State of Israel does not have a complete constitution. However, Israel is considered a constitutional state. The country is a parliamentary democracy. Israel's constitutional law is based on several sources including: the Declaration of Independence, the Basic Laws passed by the Knesset (Parliament), treaties and customs, and judicial jurisprudence.

---

19 *Id.*
20 Election to the Knesset Law (amendment no. 62) 5774–2014, amending Section 81a of the Election to the Knesset Law (Consolidated Version) 5769–1969, p. 34.
21 Basic Law: The Government (passed in 2001).

The Declaration of Independence is a central constitutional document of the State of Israel. The Declaration proclaimed the new Jewish state on May 14, 1948, and constituted a provisional governmental system that was supposed to be replaced by other more permanent governmental institutions. This replacement was planned to be accomplished by the Constituent Assembly which was charged with enacting a Constitution for the state of Israel.[22] At that time, the assembly could not come to an agreement on a working constitutional draft to present for approval. The Constituent Assembly passed a resolution called the Harari Resolution[23] stating that the Israeli Constitution would be written chapter by chapter by the Knesset in the form of Basic Laws. These chapters would be approved individually and, when completed, would form the full constitution of the State. Currently, there are eleven Basic Laws. In order to complete the document, the Israeli constitution needs more Basic Laws dealing with legislative procedures and human rights. The current Basic Laws (all of which are entitled "Basic Law: ...") consist of: The Knesset; The Israel Lands; The President of the State; The Government; The State Economy; The Army; Jerusalem the Capital City; The Judiciary; The State Comptroller; Freedom of Occupation; and Human Dignity and Liberty.[24]

Before the 1947 UN Resolution that established the State of Israel, the founding fathers of the State of Israel developed an agreement which is frequently referred to as the Status Quo Letter. A detailed report on this Founding Fathers Agreement is provided in Chapter 11 of this book.

For a long period in the modern history of the State of Israel, it was uncertain whether the Basic Laws operated with constitutional supremacy over ordinary legislation from the moment they were passed or if they were only ordinary legislation until the entire constitution was complete.[25] This question was settled in 1995, when the Israeli Supreme Court ruled in the *Mizrahi Bank* judgment that the limitation clauses are meant to limit Knesset's legislative authority in relation to the Basic Law.[26] Some argue that, from that time, Israel has been considered a

---

22 Elyakim Rubinstein, "The Declaration of Independence as a Basic Document of the State of Israel" (1998) 3(1) *Israeli Studies 195*.

23 Harrari resolution 1950.

24 Basic Law: The Knesset (1958); Basic Law: Israel Lands (1960); Basic Law: The President of the State (1964); Basic Law: The Government (1968); Basic Law: The State Economy (1975); Basic Law: The Army (1976); Basic Law: Jerusalem Capital of Israel (1980); Basic Law: The Judiciary (1984); Basic Law: The State Comptroller (1988); Basic Law: Freedom of Occupation (1992); Basic Law: Human Dignity and Liberty (1992).

25 See C.A 6821/93 *United Mizrahi Bank Ltd. v. Migdal Coorperative Village*, 49(4) P.D. 221 (1995).

26 *Id.*, And see H.C.J 231/73 *Bergman v. Minister of Finance*, P.D. 23(1) 693 (1969) which is the first time the Supreme Court ruled that the Knesset may not legislate an act in violation of a Basic

constitutional democracy. But judicial review of Knesset laws was exercised much earlier in the late 1960s; the Supreme Court relied on Basic Laws to review Knesset laws, when the Basic Law required a special majority in order to be amended (an entrenchment clause). This was the case in the Bergman ruling and other rulings dealing with election laws and election financing. The Supreme Court's decision in the *Mizrahi Bank* case was possible because the Court held that the Basic Laws allow it to perform judicial review over the Knesset; thus the decision provided the Supreme Court with the limited ability to create common law.

4. Sources of Law

The domestic sources of law in the Israeli legal system are: basic laws, constitutional laws embodied in basic laws, legislation (primary and secondary), court jurisprudence, codification of private law, and custom and administrative regulations.

Legislation generally falls into two categories: primary and secondary legislation. Primary legislation takes various forms. The most common is legislation in the form of statutes passed by the Knesset. There is other legislation that exists in Israel, including constitutional laws which come from the Knesset but are different in form than regular statutes. Israeli legislation also includes Ordinances, which are based in pre-independence legislation. Secondary legislation is promulgated by the government. There are also regulations under emergency powers.

During the first period following the declaration of independence of the State of Israel, legislative authority was held by a Provisional Council of the State. The Council published a Proclamation which laid out the temporary arrangements for the State's activities. The Proclamation stated that all laws that were in force at the time of independence would remain in force, subject to laws that were inconsistent with the newly established independent State of Israel.[27]

The Council passed the Law and Administration Ordinance, which gave more detailed arrangements for governance. (In the first years of the State of Israel, the Knesset's pieces of primary legislation were called Ordinances, as they

---

Law (without the amendment of an entrenched provision [i.e., requiring a special majority]) as it was passed in violation of the required special majority.

27 See generally Shetreet, *supra* note 15.

were called during the mandate period. Later, they were called Acts.) An Ordinance was meant to be only temporary, but because a full constitution was not drafted, most of the Ordinances remained in force for a long time until the enactment of new Israeli legislation, such as the Basic Law: The Government. The Proclamation published by the Provisional Council kept most existing laws in force. The Ordinances followed the same model and adopted the Mandate laws that were passed at the time of British Rule of Palestine. This model allowed the newly established state to avoid a legal vacuum. Remnants of the Mandate legislation are called ordinances. Laws that were enacted by the Provisional Council of State are also called Ordinances. However, Ordinances do not refer to legislation passed by the Knesset.[28]

Ordinances fall into three categories: Ordinances enacted by the Provisional Council of State between independence and the first Knesset; Ordinances enacted by the British High Commissioner in Council for Palestine that subsequent Knessets have reformulated; and Ordinances of the High Commissioner that remain in their original form.[29] All of these ordinances remain in force in Israel unless repealed or modified by the Knesset or if they, by implication, are in conflict or are in non-conformity with "the nature or character of the State or its governmental structure."[30] Many of these Ordinances have been transformed from their original language, English, to the Hebrew, one of the official languages of Israel.[31] The new version of the Ordinances (in the new language) is the binding version. This differs from most laws in Israel wherein the original Hebrew language of the law is the binding text despite the existence of other translations. Some of the ordinances were consolidated after significant amendments over the years.

The bulk of legislation in Israel is passed by the Knesset.[32] In addition to its ordinary legislative function, the Knesset is also the constituent authority due to the Harari Resolution, which declared that the Israeli constitution would be created chapter by chapter by the Knesset.[33] This means that the Knesset has a dual capacity: one Legislative and a parallel one (the constitutional or constituent function) to pass the Basic Laws. These chapters, known as Basic Laws, differ in structure and impact from regular legislation. Primary legislation is passed

---

28 Shetreet, *supra* note 15.
29 Navot, *supra* note 18.
30 See Law and Administration Ordinance, Section 11.
31 This process is possible through Section 16 of the original Law and Administration Ordinance which authorized the Minister of Justice to produce new versions of laws that existed in Palestine.
32 Basic Law: The Knesset (1958).
33 Harari Resolution 1950.

by the Knesset in the form of contemporary laws. Laws are only in effect if published in the Official Gazette. The effective date of any law is the date of publication; it is presumed that the law applies to pending proceedings as well as those beginning after the adoption of the law. Amending or repealing legislation must be done by a procedure identical to which the original law was enacted. A law is usually amended or repealed by the introduction of a new law that amends or supersedes the old. If there is no amendment or repeal, laws will remain in effect. Similiar rules apply to secondary legislation or regulations.[34]

Secondary legislation is another form of legislation common in the State of Israel. Secondary legislation refers to the power of the government (i. e., the cabinet or the minister) to promulgate regulations. The government and individual ministers derive this authority from express provisions found in primary legislation created by the Knesset and from legislative power given to the government by virtue of emergency powers.[35] Secondary legislation is broadly constructed so that the government can function. The powers are confined within the boundaries of the primary legislation. If the government's actions exceed the boundaries set forth in the primary legislation, then the judiciary may declare the secondary legislation void. Emergency legislative powers, provided by Basic Law: The Government, grant the government exceptional jurisdiction to change and suspend laws as well as alter taxes and other compulsory payments.[36] This only can occur if the Knesset declares a state of emergency.[37]

Israel does not yet have a complete Constitution. Instead, Israel has Basic Laws which function as supreme norms that prevail over ordinary legislation.[38] In fact, the Israeli governmental-judicial structure has acted in a similar manner to a constitutional democracy. The Basic Laws are expressed through the constituent authority of the Knesset which is derived from the Harari Resolution shortly after the state was formed. The Basic Laws are written as chapters of the future complete Israeli Constitution. Still lacking are Basic Laws dealing with legislation and with certain categories of basic human rights.[39]

The Constituent Assembly became the first Knesset; due to political gridlock, however, it was unable to produce a working draft of the constitution. The grid-

---

34 Interpretation Law, Section 19 (1981).
35 See Chapter 12 for further discussion.
36 See originally the Law and Administration Ordinance, Section 9 (1948), and see now Basic Law: The Government Section 50.
37 *Id.*
38 Navot, *supra* note 18.
39 See Aharon Barak, *Proportionality: Constitutional Rights and Their Limitations* (Cambridge, Cambridge University Press, 2012).

lock was partially resolved by the Harari Resolution, which provided that the Constitution, Law, and Justice Committee of the Knesset would prepare a draft of the Constitution through separate chapters. Each chapter would each constitute a Basic Law which would thereafter be consolidated into a complete Constitution for the State. The Knesset passed the Transition Law which vested its powers in the second Knesset and future Knessets. Generally, it is presumed that the succeeding Knessets have both constituent and legislative authority and that enacting Basic Laws is not the same as passing ordinary legislation.

Some Basic Laws were enacted with "entrenchment" clauses, which means that the law may be changed only by a special majority. Without the entrenchment clauses, a Basic Law would be subject to amendments or repeal by a simple majority as all other legislation. Some legislation, like Basic Law: The Knesset, did have entrenchment provisions; however, the provisions did not apply to the entire law, only to certain designated sections. There have been a number of legal challenges directed at certain laws that seemed to contradict the entrenchment provisions and some decisions invalidating the conflicting laws. Even before 1995, the Supreme Court recognized the Basic Laws as supreme norms when they provided for special majority for amendment.[40] The earlier court decisions ruled that the entrenched provisions take precedence over conflicting ordinary law.[41] The Supreme Court had not recognized the normative supremacy of the Basic Laws, but only of entrenched laws.[42]

A change in this situation came about due to a plan for creating a Basic Law for human rights in parts (instead of as a completed Basic Law) just as the Harari Resolution had allowed the constitution to be created in chapters.[43] According to the compromise, the Basic Laws were to be formed in sections. In 1992, the Basic Law: Freedom of Occupation included a section that entrenched the entire law; it required a special majority of 61 Knesset members to amend the law.[44] The law also included a limitation clause which allowed regular legislation to violate the Basic Law only if certain criteria were met.[45] Developing an entrenchment provision for the entire law and also a limitation clause shifted the way in which the Knesset was able to operate in relation to this Basic Law. Any attempt of the

---

40 See H.C.J 107/73 *Negev Automobile Service Station Ltd. v. State of Israel,* 28(1) P.D. 640 (1974).
41 See H.C.J 142/89 *Laor Movement v. The Speaker of the Knesset,* 44(3) P.D. 529, at 539 (1990).
42 See A. Rubinstein & B. Medina, The Constitutional Law of the State of Israel (6th ed., 2005). See also H.C.J 148/73 *Kaniel v. Minister of Justice,* 27(1) P.D. 794 (1973) and H.C.J 60/77 *Ressler v. Chairman of the Central Committee for Elections to the Knesset,* 31(2) P.D. 556, 560.
43 *Id.,* at para. 43.
44 *Id.,* at para. 44.
45 See Basic Law: Human Dignity and Liberty Section 8.

Knesset to enact a law that would infringe on the rights in the Basic Law, if it did not follow the limitation clause, would be invalid despite being passed by a majority. This substantive limitation on the Knesset was a shift in the structure of Israeli Constitutional law. It is considered the beginning of the constitutional era in the Israeli legal system; some called it "The Constitutional Revolution".[46]

The *Mizrahi Bank* judgment was a critical decision in the new constitutional era or "Constitutional Revolution". The *Mizrahi Bank* case considered whether a law passed after the adoption of the Basic Laws of 1992 violated the right of property guaranteed in the Basic Law: Human Dignity and Liberty, and whether the law met the terms of the limitation clause.[47] The Supreme Court judgment focused on the status of the Basic Laws. The President of the Supreme Court, Justice Barak, stated "In March 1992 the Basic Law: Freedom of Occupation and Basic Law: Human Dignity and Liberty were adopted. Their adoption heralded a fundamental change in the status of human rights in Israel. They became constitutional rights. The constitutional revolution took place in the Knesset in March 1992. The Knesset granted the State of Israel a constitutional Bill of Rights."[48] The decision also stated that the Basic Laws have constitutional status[49] based on the Knesset's constituent power and that the Knesset should have such power.[50]

Inherent in the *Mizrahi Bank* judgment was the Supreme Court's jurisdiction of judicial review of laws, as is common in the majority of constitutional democratic states. The Supreme Court's willingness to invalidate laws has been historically cautious; it is measured by enforcing the precedent that invalidation is restricted to instances in which legislation infringes on the basic rights (which stem from the basic laws). Nevertheless, judicial interpretation has changed as a result of the *Mizrahi Bank* case. During the years 1992–2016, the court identified fifteen instances in which legislation unconstitutionally infringed on basic rights, and invalidated said legislation or parts of it.[51] In two other occasions, re-

---

46 Navot, *supra* note 18, at 25; This author does not accept the terminology of "revolution" because conceptually the term implies a revolt by the people against competent authorities, which certainly did not occur in 1992.

47 See C.A 6821/93 *United Mizrahi Bank Ltd. v. Migdal Cooperative Village*, 49(4) P.D. 221 (1995).

48 *Id.*, opinion of Justice Barak, 352.

49 *Id.*

50 *Id.*, see Justice Shamgar's opinion at 49. 221.

51 H.C.J 6055\95 *Tzemach v. Minister of Defense*, 53(5) P.D. 241 (1999); H.C.J 1715\97 *Investment House Chamber v. Minister of Finance*, 51(4) P.D. 367 (1997); H.C.J 1030\99 *Oron v. Speaker of the Knesset*, 56(3) P.D. 640 (2002); H.C.J 1061\05 Hof-Aza *Regional Council v. The Knesset*, 59(2) P.D. 481 (2005); H.C.J 8276\05 *Adala v. Minister of Defense* (published on Nevo, 12.12.2006); H.C.J 2805\05 *Academic Center v. Minister of Finance* (published on Nevo, 19.11.2009); miscellenious

lating to income support to *yeshiva* students and the *Tal Committee* (which dealt with the exemption of mandatory military service in the IDF given to ultra-Ortho-dox Jews), the Supreme Court found the legislation to be unconstitutional, and thus cannot be temporally extended or incorporated into future legislation.[52]

Judicial interpretation has changed as a result of the *Mizrahi Bank* case. The Basic Law: Human Dignity and Freedom includes a section that limits judicial review of laws enacted prior to the passing of the Basic Law enactment.[53] The Supreme Court's judicial review is limited in the sense that the prior laws cannot be invalidated based on any subsequent Basic Laws. However, the Supreme Court interprets any legislation prior to the Basic Law: Human Dignity and Liberty in the light of the Basic Law and under its influence.

As a result of the *Mizrahi Bank* decision, the Knesset's legislative and constituent power was confirmed; whenever the Knesset establishes norms as constituent power (Basic Laws); they have a constitutional status. Therefore, any laws passed based on only legislative authority are subordinate to those with constitutional status.

The Knesset's practices have accepted the *Mizrahi Bank* judgment. Accordingly, the Knesset has had to amend Basic Laws by an absolute majority (i.e. 61 members of Knesset) in order[54] to allow for legislation that prima facie did not meet the requirements of the limitation clause. The Constitutional Revolution changed public perception of the importance of the Basic Laws. It is now a cornerstone of the legislative process to examine legislation in terms of compliance with the Basic Laws. There is also more adherence to stability and a reluctance

---

application criminal 8823\07 *Ploni v. State of Israel* (published on Nevo, 11.02.2010); H.C.J 10662 \04 *Hassan v. National Insurance Insitutie* (published on Nevo, 28.02.2012); H.C.J 8300\02 *Nasr v. Government of Israel* (published on Nevo, 22.05.2012); H.C.J 7146\12 *Adam v. Knesset* (published on Nevo, 16.09.2013); H.C.J 7385\13 *Eitan v. Government of Israel* (published on Nevo, 22.09. 2014); H.C.J 8300/02 *Nasser v. Government of Israel* (published on Nevo, 22.05.2012); H.C.J 7146/ 12 *Adam v. The Knesset* (published on Nevo, 16.09.2013); H.C.J 7385/13 *Eitan Israeli Immigration Policy v. Government of Israel* (published on Nevo, 22.09.2014); H.C.J 5239/11 *Avneri v. The Knesset* (published on Nevo, 15.04.2015); H.C.J 8665/14 *Dasta v. The Knesset* (published on Nevo, 11.08. 2015).

52 H.C.J 4124\00 *Yekutieli v. Minister of Religious Affairs* (allowances to ultra-orthodox yeshiva students) (published on Nevo, 14.06.2010); H.C.J 6298\07 *Ressler v. The Knesset* (published on Nevo, 21.02.2012) (excemption from military service).

53 See Basic Law: Human Dignity and Liberty.

54 When the Knesset amended the Basic Law it was through another Basic Law that included an override clause. The override clause stated that a law that violated the freedom of occupation would be in effect if 61 members of the Knesset approved the law, expressly state that it shall be of effect notwithstanding the Basic Law and that the law would expire four years after the date of commencement.

to amend Basic Laws. There have also been some Supreme Court justices who have suggested that Basic Laws before 1992, which do not include limitation clauses, should also be given the effects of the limitation clause. This has not been the majority opinion of the court but it may be the direction that the Supreme Court will take in future cases.[55]

The *Mizrahi Bank* decision has arguably resulted in a formal constitution for the State of Israel, albeit incomplete. Some challenges still remain because not all Basic Laws are entrenched and, therefore, subject to easier amendment. Other Basic Laws must still be enacted. Because the Constitutional change has created tremendous tension among the Judiciary, the Executive, and the Legislative Branches, it may have slowed the process toward completing the constitution. The creation of future Basic Laws will carry greater weight than before.

Private law has also undergone a fundamental change with the codification of private law, both replacing remaining Ottoman law and modernizing the legal system. A codex may be recognized based on: wholeness, methodic nature, simplicity, scope of application, and novelty.[56]

There is a duty to publish statutes, regulations, and orders. This duty is based on the rational that there is no law in force unless it has been brought to the knowledge of the public.[57] The law outlines the extent of the duty to publish. The official platform of publication is the Reshumot. The duty of publication can be met by publication in other forums on occasion.[58] Regulations are also required to be published.[59] Government guidelines, which are not regulations and do not carry legislative weight, are not always required to be published, but recently the trend has been to require publication of general guidelines. Publication should give reasonable publicity in a way which will insure they will reach the citizens concerned[60] and the government has been required to provide access to the public of written administrative guidelines.[61]

Basic Laws are normally identified by the addition of "Basic Law" to the title and by the absence of a date of adoption.[62] Basic Laws are characterized as con-

---

55 See A. Rubinstein & B. Medina, *supra* note 42.

56 See Barak, *supra* note 7; Tedeschi, *supra* note 7.

57 See H.C.J 220/51 *Aslan v. Military Governor of the Galilee, Nazareth,* 5(2) P.D. 1480 at 1486 – 1487.

58 See The Law and Administration Ordinance, Section 10 (1948).

59 See Interpretation Ordinance, Section 17.

60 See H.C.J 3081/95 *Romeo v. Scientific Council of the Medical Federation in Israel,* 50(2) P.D. 177 at 194 – 195 See Yoav Dotan, Administrative Guidelines (1996), see also Yoav Dotan, *On the Publication of Administrative Guidelines,* 3 Mishpat umemshal 475 (1992).

61 Required under the Freedom of Information Law, 5758 -1988, LB 226 Section 6(a).

62 See Chapter 1: General Introduction.

stitutional in nature by virtue of their content containing fundamental principles, general applicability, succinct language, and majestic form. But many of
the Basic Laws take on highly detailed form and resemble ordinary legislation.
The *Mizrahi Bank* case indicated a further method of identification, material or
substantive examination.

Basic Laws can be amended only by another Basic Law.[63] This means that
the Knesset must use its constituent authority in order to change a Basic Law.
Laws that have entrenched provisions can only be amended by a special majority. Theoretically, for those Basic Laws without an entrenchment provision, a
simple majority would be sufficient to amend the Basic Law.

The Israeli court system is a three-tier system. These courts are: Trial
Courts, which establish facts, relevant law, and legal conclusions; Appellate
Courts, which review the trial courts' decisions for errors; and a Supreme
Court, whose judgments set binding precedent for lower courts and for govern-
mental and executive authorities. There is a right to appeal one tier. The second
appeal is only by leave of the appeal court.

The Israeli legal system is predominantly a common law system. As such,
courts engage in the creation and formulation of law and norms. The judiciary
creates law in three forms of law making: interpreting legal norms, developing
common law, and filling in gaps in legislation.[64] The judiciary's interpretation
of existing statutes is in fact engagement in law making because the judge
must exercise judicial discretion, selecting one of any number of interpretive
possibilities and giving it legal efficacy through judicial discretion.[65] Common
law is a major source of law in administrative law, evidence, and remedies.[66]
Common law is created not by the interpretation of an existing statute, but
where a judge creates a general norm for the entire system based on a specific
case. Filling in the gap in legislation involves judicial creativity by way of analogy to other laws and according to principles of freedom, justice, equity, and
peace of Israel's heritage.[67]

Judicial interpretation is "a process by means of which the legal significance
of the text is 'extracted' from its linguistic significance. When the judges encounter vague or ambiguous language, which raises a number of meanings, they must
decide—using their judgment—which meaning may be reconciled with the pur-

---

63 Opinion of Justice Shamgar in Mizrahi Case, *supra* note 47, at 272.
64 See The Foundations of the Law Act, Section 1 (1980).
65 See A. Rubinstein & B. Medina, *supra* note 42.
66 See Friedmann Daniel, *supra* note 13, at 327.
67 See The Foundations of the Law Act, Section 1 (1980).

pose which the language of the law seeks to achieve."[68] The judges are responsible for deciding the meaning of the text based on the intent of the legislature and according to principles of the legal system. There may be several purposes and these must be balanced between goals and aspirations; contradictory purposes must be reconciled. This leads to the judges' development of law.[69]

Under the Basic Law: The Judiciary, legal precedent or stare decisis is binding on lower courts. Any decisions from the Supreme Court are binding on lower courts. However, courts cannot bind higher courts or other courts on the same level. Although precedent is statutorily binding on lower courts, the Supreme Court is not bound by precedents of its own rulings.[70] Instead, when deciding between "truth and stability", the Supreme Court has stated that truth is preferable. That being said, the Supreme Court is cognizant of the importance of legal stability and gives considerable weight to its own precedent.[71]

Judicial discretion is based on four primary criteria; these are: fundamental value system, the aspiration to close the gaps between law and life, maintenance of the democratic nature and protection of constitutional values, and respect for the rule of law and the separation of powers.[72]

Throughout Israeli history, the development of the judicial role and judge-made law has evolved. Case law has progressed from legal formalism in the 1950s and 1960s with a focus on legal certainty to an increased reliance upon considerations of values in the 1980s. Over this period, the system adapted to shifting political and social transitions. There was greater political instability from increasing power of extremist forces, women's status, Arab minorities, and other factors. The judiciary served as an objective forum which could resolve these disputes.[73] This naturally led to the increasing prominence of fundamental values as normative considerations and a focus on the purpose, spirit, or intention of the law. The Supreme Court played its important role in formulating the

---

68 Navot, *supra* note 18, at page 79.
69 See A. Rubinstein & B. Medina, *supra* note 42. See also Aharon Barak, *Judicial Discretion* (1989); Shimon Shetreet, *The Discretionary Power of the Judge* (M. Storme and B. Hess eds.); Shimon Shetreet *Discretionary Power of the Judge: Limits and Control*, 73–116 (Procedure Ghent 2000; Kluwer 2003) (On the occasion of the 500th Anniversary of the University of Ghent and 50th Anniversary of the International Association of Procedural Law).
70 See Basic Law: The Judiciary.
71 Gavison, Kremintzer, Dotan, *Judicial Activism: For and Against* 6 (Jerusalem, Yediot Haharonot and Magnes, Jerusalem, 2000) (Hebrew).
72 See A. Barak, Forward: "A Judge on Judging: The Role of the Supreme Court in a Democracy", 116 Harvard L. Rev. 16 (2002); see also generally Barak, *The Judge in a Democratic Society* (2008).
73 *Id.*

Israeli Constitution and with it has had broader opportunities for creative interpretation, especially when dealing with rights.[74]

The patterns of court decisions for broader interpretations have led to a reputation of judicial activism. The activist approach led the courts to review the internal proceedings of the Knesset, to enforce ethical norms on public and military officials to supervise religious institutions, and to engage in judicial review of security issues. The expanded role of the judiciary has been criticized as exceeding the legitimate and proper boundaries of judicial function and trespassing legislative territories and executive powers in violation of the doctrine of separation of powers. Against this criticism, some scholars suggest that the court's decisions reflect a policy of caution and self-restraint.[75]

Another source of law in the Israeli legal system is custom. In many statutes, custom is recognized as a binding source of law; in some cases, custom can replace legislation. In most cases, custom serves to complete or supplement gaps in legislative regulation or in common law. Although custom is commonly referenced in Israeli law, it is rarely resorted. This is due to the difficulty of proving custom and to the low level of awareness of lawyers and judges to the importance of custom.[76]

Customs may gain the force of law though due to the fact that they have been respected for a long period of time and viewed as binding by the parties concerned. Often long standing customs are embodied into legislation. Legislation may adopt a custom in whole or in part. Additionally, judges often rely on interpretive customs when hearing cases. When using custom, judges attempt to interpret statutes in a manner consistent with the potentially conflicting custom. If a judge decides that there is no way to reconcile the custom and statute, then the statute prevails over the custom.[77]

Treaty making customs are an example of the interaction between custom and legislation. There is no direct legislation on how international treaties are adopted and ratified or how they are transformed into domestic law. The Supreme Court held that the government was the best branch for ratification and adoption.[78] The practice indicated that it was customary for the government to

---

74 Assaf Meydani, *The Israeli Supreme Court and the Human Rights Revolation: Courts as Agenda Setters* (Cambridge University Press, 2011).

75 See Navot, *supra* note *18*, at pg. 64–68.

76 See Shimon Shetreet, *"The Custom in Public Law"*, Klinghoffer Volume on Public Law (In Hebrew, ed. Y. Zamir, 1993) 375, 375, 380.

77 See H.C.J 547/84 *Of-Haemek v. Ramat Yishai Local Authority*, 40(1) P.D. 113, see pg. 145–147.

78 See Y. Zilbershatz, *"The Adoption of International Law into Israeli Law—The Real Is Ideal"* 25 Israel Yearbook on Human Rights, 243–249.

handle treaties.[79] The Supreme Court gave its approval to the custom despite multiple interpretations that would have indicated that the power over treaties belonged in either the Knesset or with the President. Later, the government decided to table treaties in the Knesset for ratification. However, the original custom was reinforced again in practice since the government only tables the most important of treaties in the Knesset (treaties involving territorial concessions, security issues, and human rights).[80]

Administrative authorities act within the limits of their statutorily conferred powers by Knesset legislation. Unless there is authorization, an administrative act is invalid. Executive authority is not permitted to delegate its authority unless permitted by law. Knesset legislation identifies the powers and identities administrative bodies as well as the criteria governing the manner of exercising those powers.[81] In recent years, the Israeli Supreme Court established an interpretive presumption that the legislature is presumed not to have enabled executive authority to establish primary orders. Therefore, the Knesset is required to give greater specificity in legislation in order to establish executive authority.[82]

Regulations may also be used to grant powers to another authority; the regulation is the principal source of power.[83] In order to be a valid grant of power, the regulation must establish the granting of power.[84] Under Human Rights laws, a new law cannot grant authority to violate rights unless it is in compliance with the limitation clause in the Basic Law: Human Dignity and Liberty.

It is also possible to grant power by Administrative Directive, which is a decision by a Minister to empower a local authority. Directives do not carry the weight of legislative authority nor do they establish a legal norm.[85]

General residual powers are inherent executive powers that are not expressly granted by an empowering statute; instead, they are powers granted to the government by virtue of section 32 of Basic Law: The Government.[86] These powers are residual powers, subject to law and to the boundaries of reasonableness.

Every administrative authority has general auxiliary powers which are intended to supplement primary powers of the administrative authority. Auxiliary powers have two limitations. First, they are usually applied to preliminary activ-

---

79 Cr.A 131/67 *Kamiar v. The State of Israel*, 22(2) P.D. 89 (1968).
80 *Id.*
81 See Navot, *supra* note *18*, at Chapter 5.
82 See H.C.J 3627/97 *Rubinstein v. Minister of Defense*, 52(5) P.D. 481.
83 See Section 70.
84 *Id.*
85 See A. Rubinstein & B. Medina, *supra* note *42*.
86 See Basic Law: The Government, Section 32.

ities such as visits, tours, publication, consultations, etc. Second, the powers can only be used as reasonably necessary to enable exercising the primary power.[87]

Orders are given under authority of administrations to impose prohibitions and duties. Orders can be general or personal. General orders are like a regulation or a "secondary legislation". They allow the administration to fill in gaps in the legislation where the Knesset did not have the time or expertise necessary for the legislation.

The main sources of international law in Israel are treaties, custom and jurisprudence, and general principals of law.

The Government is usually the branch that deals with treaties. This is not the case, however, when it comes to issues of major state importance such as territorial concessions, security issues, and the like. In those instances, the Knesset and President will most likely be involved.[88]

Treaty law and customary international law differ in the way that they are incorporated into Israeli domestic law. Customary international law is automatically incorporated into Israeli law unless there is a conflict, wherein Israeli domestic law will prevail.[89] Treaty law enters domestic law based on what type of treaty is involved. In the case of purely declaratory treaties, they are automatically incorporated into domestic law but do not have priority over domestic laws.[90] Constitutive treaties are incorporated through a legislative act. The government is empowered to sign and ratify treaties without Knesset approval, but the Israeli courts have declared that constitutive treaties cannot be relied upon in an Israeli court as an independent, self-executing source of law.[91] Treaties dealing with territorial concessions or significant matters must be brought before the Knesset for approval. However, Israeli courts work under the presumption that the purpose of the law is to realize the provisions of international law and not to be in conflict with them. Current Israeli-Arab conflicts, globalization, and the rising focus on human rights has lead the court more and more to attempt to harmonize the execution of domestic law with principles of international law.

---

87 See Interpretation Ordinance, Section 26 (1954) and Interpretation Law, Section 17 (1981).
88 Yafa Zilbershatz "The Adoption of International Law into Israeli Law: 'The Real Is Ideal'" (1996) 25 Israel Yearbook on Human Rights 243.
89 See Cr.A 336/61 *Eichmann v. Attorney General*, 16(3) P.D. 2033 (1962).
90 See Navot, *supra* note 18, at pp. 64–68.
91 See C.F.H 7048/97 *Anonymous v. Minister of Defense*, 54(1) P.D. 721, 743; and H.C.J. 279/51 *Amsterdam v. Minister of Finance*, 6 P.D. 945, 966.

5. The Role of Custom in Israeli Public Law[92]

Custom plays an important role in public law.[93] It is difficult to envisage the functioning of many governmental and public institutions and arrangements without the unwritten stratum of customary rules of behavior which determine modes of action. In some fields, systems of norms and institutions have developed parallel to those laid out in written laws.

An example of this is the censorship of the press. Such cases, however, are exceptional. In most instances, custom fills lacunae (or gaps) in legal arrangements deriving from both written and judge-made law. Indeed, custom serves this purpose in every realm of public law, such as: the enforcement of laws, the formulation of rules of behavior for holders of governmental office and appointments to governmental office; including the relations between governmental authorities: the government and the Knesset, the President and the Knesset, and central and local government.

Custom gradually develops from practice or repeated action (resulting from convenience or habit) into usage, i.e., the assumption that a given act will be executed in a certain way. After the elements of custom are fulfilled (sense of obligation, dimension of time, continuance), the mode of behavior becomes custom —an independent, obligatory legal norm. English law incorporates the unique institution of "constitutional conventions". Similar, although decidedly distinct, are Israel's constitutional practices, which constitute a stage in the formulation of obligatory constitutional custom.

Over the past few years, a number of articles have been published on the role of custom as a source of law,[94] making it possible to briefly discuss the role of custom as a source of public law. In addition, two relevant laws have been passed: the Foundations of Law Act (1980) and the Repeal of the Mejelle Law (1984). With regard to the Foundations of Law Act, the repeal of Article 46 of the Palestine Order-in-Council, 1922, by Section 2 of this Law, should not be viewed as prejudicial to the status of custom as a source of law.

Likewise, the absence of custom from the list of sources enumerated in the Law as guiding the judge when passing judgment (in the event of a lacuna in the law) should not be considered a tacit slight to its status as a legal source. Custom is recognized in case law; hence, it will continue to constitute a legal source even

---

92 Shimon Shetreet, *The Role of Custom in Public Law*, 21 Isr. L. Rev. 450 (1986).
93 Robbie Sabel, *International Law*, 51–57 (2nd ed., 2010, Hebrew).
94 See G. Tedeschi, *"Custom in Israel Law: Present and Future 5 Mishpatim 9"* (1973); see also D. Even, *"Custom in Public Law – Following the Agranat Report"*, (1976) 7 Mishpatim 201.

though not expressly referred to in the Foundation of Law Act.[95] This is equally valid regarding the impact of the Repeal of the Mejelle Law. Despite the cancellation of the Mejelle, custom exists as a source of Israeli law by virtue of Israeli legislation and Israeli common law.[96] Preferably, express legislation should determine custom as an independent source of law and, when appropriate opportunities arise, court rulings should eliminate any remaining doubts. Prior to the repeal of the Mejelle, custom existed as a legal source in all areas of the law, including public law, by virtue of the Mejelle, and was not restricted solely to private law.[97] At the same time, the status of custom as a legal source was further ensured by Israeli common law and legislation.

Numerous laws have recognized custom as a "legal source." The legislature was aware of the need to recognize custom and usage as part of the system of rules intended to govern various legal relations. In this context, custom and usage were even accorded legislative recognition in public law. For example, Section 17 of the State Service (Discipline) Law, 1963, determines that: *A State employee who, in Israel or abroad, does any of the following, shall be guilty of a disciplinary offence: ... (2) Does not carry out or is remiss in carrying out any duty imposed on him as a State employee by custom, law or regulation ...*.

An additional example may be seen in the Local Councils [Regional Councils] Law, 1958, which deals with the dismissal and suspension of employees. According to Section 61: *The Chairman or anyone who has been authorised by him may dismiss an employee if there is no provision derogating from any right or commitment under a contract or usage of work.* A similar provision appears in Section 133 of the Military Justice Law, 1955, as amended in 1979, whereby failure to carry out orders according to "army usage" is an offence punishable by a year's imprisonment. A prime example of legislation referring to usage in public law is Section 19 of the Basic Law: The Knesset, which determines that if the working procedures of the Knesset are not regulated by laws or regulations, "the Knesset shall follow its accepted practice and routine."

In addition to the references to usage and custom in Israeli legislation, there is a firm basis for custom as a source of law in Israeli common law, as created in the case law. Justice Landau, in his article "Rule and Discretion in the Administration of Justice," writes: "In any case, the ship of Israeli judicial interpretation has cast off the English anchor, and must sail to sea on its own. There is no com-

---

95 G. Procaccia, *"Foundations of Law, 1980"* (1984), 10 Iyunei Mishpat 147 (1984)
96 R. Gavison, *"Abolition of the Mejelle: Custom as a Source of Law"*, 14 Mishpatim 325 (1984).
97 See Tedeschi, *supra* note 94, at 52; Even, *supra* note 94, at 205–207; compare with Gavison, *supra* note 96, at 349.

pass other than written law, and, should this prove insufficient, the discretion of the courts which must create the new Israeli common law. We cannot always be guided by the wards of English justices in the eighteenth and nineteenth centuries. We must participate in the formulation of law in accordance with the needs of the twentieth century, in the State of Israel."[98] The implementation of this approach led to judicial recognition of rights by virtue of usage. Justice Witkon, in a Supreme Court case dealing with the right of a successful litigant to reimbursement of his legal expenses,[99] ruled that this "right is a substantive and not a procedural right. Even if it lacks a statutory basis I am inclined to say that the right exists, and has been upheld daily in our courts for over twenty-five years. It is too late to challenge its existence, even if we have the power to create our own common law."

The power of usage to confer rights upon citizens was recognized in the 1962 case of *Kohen v. Minister of Defense.*[100] The plaintiff served as a military correspondent for *Haolam Hazeh,* and was accredited by the Israel Defense Forces (IDF) from 1956 onward. Along with his colleagues, he was invited to participate in educational tours, visits, meetings with IDF officers, etc. After five years, his accreditation was discontinued by the head of the IDF press liaison office. The respondents claimed that the right to serve as a military correspondent accredited by the IDF was not provided for by law; hence, its denial did not constitute grounds for complaint. In the words of Justice Witkon:

"A strict approach should not be taken regarding any right the denial or prejudice of which can be brought before the High Court of Justice .... I do not maintain that the right must be a statutory one written in a law. This Court has often recognized rights not stipulated in any legal provision; upon receipt of judicial recognition they assumed forms recognized by the law. Matters of usage and concepts of natural justice that until recently were featureless and undefined ascend in this manner to the mainstream and attain the rank of right. This judicial development takes place alongside legislation and does not infringe upon it, and I would not like to limit its progress."[101]

It should be stressed that when interpreting a statute in the event of doubt, or when deciding on a legal question which legislation does not govern, there is a difference between judicial creativity and the closure of gaps via custom and usage. Justice Witkon's ruling in the *Kohen* case may very well constitute a crea-

---

98 M. Landau, *"Rule and Discretion in the Administration of Justice"*, 1 Mishpatim 292 (1969)
99 C.A 180/71 *Lavi v. Officer in Charge of Recompensation,* 26(2) P.D. 509 (1972).
100 H.C.J 29/62 *Cohen v. Minister of Defense,* 16 P.D. 1023 (1962).
101 The appellant was not successful in the *Kohen* case. But see H.C.J 509/80 *Yunes v. Director-General of the Prime Minister's Office,* 35(3) P.D. 589 (1981).

tive judicial solution to the legal question of the plaintiff's right to receive the aid of the High Court. Nonetheless, it must be acknowledged that the ruling grants status to custom and usage as a source of law. Moreover, proponents of the broad approach of "gaps" in the law, which allows for extensive reliance upon custom,[102] cite Justice Witkon's ruling as recognition of custom as a source of legal norms.

A. The Elements of Custom in Public Law

Together with legislation and case law, custom is an independent and direct source of legal norms. When the State law, through the courts, recognizes custom, it constitutes a norm which is as binding as any other legal norm. Custom is distinguished from other sources of law by the mode of its formation; rather than by legislation or the courts, it is created by a continuous pattern of behavior, accepted by the parties concerned as binding,[103] and recognized by the court.[104] Under established case law, in order to claim the existence of custom one must prove three elements: the sense of obligation, the dimension of time, and continuance. The sense of obligation, or the "awareness of obligation," as Prof. Tedeschi puts it, is the element which distinguishes custom from other behavioral patterns deriving from habit, coincidence, convenience, or free choice for any other reason. The existence of custom is proven when the parties abide by it due to the belief that they are bound to do so and thus are not at liberty to choose another pattern of behavior. The fundamental question of awareness of the obligation in custom is a central one, inasmuch as it is indicative of the binding character of the norm. It should be noted that traditional sanctions are not requisite in order to prove the existence of a legal norm.[105] The second element

---

102 For a discussion on judicial creativity and gaps, see Gavison, *supra* note 96, at 337.

103 See C.A 25/50 *Wolfsohn v. Sphinis Co. Lid*, 5 P.D. 265 (1951), in which Justice Silberg defines custom as certain behavior which the public has accepted as an obligatory legal norm as if it were the product of legislation. The pattern of behavior which constitutes custom does not have to be shared by the general public, but may relate to holders of certain office.

104 In the process of judicial recognition of custom, there is a process of filtering according to certain criteria, such as public policy or reasonableness. See Gavison, *supra* note 96, at 338–339.

105 See the discussion on the essence of international law. The test based upon the requirement of sanctions, as espoused by Austin, does not see international law as law. J. Austin, *Lectures on Jurisprudence* (Campbell, 4th ed., 1873) 231–232; J. Austin, *Lectures on Jurisprudence* (Campbell, 5th ed., 1911) 77–103. Some scholars, such as Kelsen, see the possibilities of war and retaliation as fulfilling the requirement of sanctions. See alsoY. Dinstein, *International Law and the State*, Vol. 1 (Tel Aviv, 197 1, in Hebrew) 22. Yet, not all scholars view the obligatory foundation in the

of custom relates to the dimension of time.[106] Custom, by its very nature, is a pattern of behavior formed gradually.[107] Contrary to English law, the requirement of the dimension of time—in the sense of the length of time the custom has existed—is not strict. In Israeli law, it is not necessary to prove that a custom commenced at a certain time in order to verify its existence. The duration of time required as evidence of custom is contingent upon the nature of the custom, and may be brief.

The third element of proof of custom is the requirement of continuance. Custom must be shown to be constant, i.e., the behavior purported to be custom must be repetitive throughout a certain period of time. This does not imply a minimal quantitative demand but, again, depends on the matter at hand. When dealing with a custom which refers to a mode of behavior in the context of an event that occurs every few years, such as the procedure of appointing a person to office, the numerical requirement will be small. In the case of frequent and widespread acts, such as action in accordance with internal administrative guidelines, the requirement will be greater. Therefore, in order to fulfill the criterion of continuance, the test will focus not only upon the question of how many times a pattern of behavior was repeated, but also on the number of repetitions in relation to the total number of opportunities to do so. The requirements of continuance and dimension of time are intertwined. In cases in which the rate of recurrence is high, it is not necessary to assess the period of time, although a certain duration must be shown in order to prove the existence of custom. In public law, the proof of custom is based upon two aspects: (a) positive evidence that the authorities acted according to the norm claimed to be custom; and (b) negative evidence that no mode of behavior besides that norm was ever adopted when acting on the same issue. If a different mode of action arouses criticism and censure due to the existence of binding custom, such criticism indicates support of the custom. If the deviation failed to draw criticism, this may be viewed as prejudicial to the claim of custom.

---

definition of law as requiring the existence of sanctions. Pollock, for example, maintains that the perception of an obligation to honor a norm is sufficient to term it law and that there is no need for sanctions: J. Pollock, *First Book of Jurisprudence* (London, 1896) 1–15.

106 *Salmond On Jurisprudence* 201–203 (London, 12th ed. by P.J. Fitzgerald, 1966).

107 See Silberg J.'s ruling in the *Wolfsohn* case, *supra* note 103.

B. Custom Contrary to Law

In the classification of custom, one must distinguish between custom which negates the law *(contra legem)* and that which concords with it *(praeter legem)*.[108] The latter category of custom includes rules of behavior which govern behavior in matters ignored or not comprehensively dealt with by legislation.[109] Custom negates existing law when a pattern of behavior considered to be custom contradicts a legal norm fixed by law. In this context, it is possible to speak of custom as changing, qualifying, or repealing law. Like Anglo-American law, Israeli law accords legislation status superior to that of custom. When a custom negates a law, it is rejected in favor of that law, even if the law has remained inactive and precedes later custom. The reasoning behind this is that legal norms of the sovereign are deemed to have priority over any other legal source. The implementation of this approach may be seen in all areas of the law. Its application is somewhat limited by legal acknowledgement of social reality, in spite of the declared position that law is superior to custom.

The courts extend indirect recognition to custom which negates law, even while remaining declaratively faithful to the view that law has priority over custom. This is achieved by judicial interpretation. For example, when a particular law may be interpreted in a number of ways, the court will prefer the interpretation consistent with custom, although other interpretations may be more compatible with the letter of the law. When the statute in question is one that it is possible to lawfully contract out of, the attitude towards custom contradictory to law is more flexible. Another way of mitigating the declared approach regarding custom which negates law is by interpreting the law in a manner that is compatible with custom.[110] Customs of non-enforcement of statutes, or guidelines of the

---

108 Gavison, *supra* note 96, at 340–344.

109 In this sense, custom fills lacunae in the system of written law. See Gavison, *supra* note 96, at 336–337.

110 A fascinating example of this judicial technique may be found in the issue of key-money in protected tenancy. In Israel, a custom developed whereby an incoming tenant would pay the outgoing tenant key-money, part of which would be transferred to the owner of the dwelling. This key-money embodied the difference between the real worth of the rental and the rent actually paid by a tenant protected under Tenants' Protection (Tenancy Involving Key-Money) Law, 1962 (16 L.S.I. 119). The payment was contrary to the declared intention of the legislator to protect weak socio-economic sectors, and its receipt was therefore forbidden in Article 7 of The Rent Restriction (Dwelling-Houses) Ordinances, No. 44, 1940 (Palestine Gazette, 1940, Supp. I, p. 289). Despite the prohibition, social reality prevailed over legislative imperatives, and the custom of key-money remained in effect. According to the approach of Israeli law, not only was the existence of contrary custom incapable of repealing the law, but the Court

enforcement authorities limiting the enforcement of laws in accordance with changes in social norms, are yet another technique therein, especially in situations where constraints are exercised against a legislative change in the statutory law. In light of the constitutional custom regarding the government's authority to conclude international treaties, to a certain extent even Section 11(a)(5) of the Basic Law: The President of the State, constitutes an example of interpretation of a law in order to conciliate it with contradictory custom. The wording of the section implies that the Knesset plays a general role in the conclusion and ratification of treaties. Hence, it provides that treaties approved or ratified by the Knesset will be signed by the President. This rational interpretation was rejected by the Court in the *Kamiar* case[111] in favor of the view that there is no general duty that the Knesset take part in the conclusion of treaties.

Custom provided the basis for the law regarding the imposition of concurrent prison sentences for offenses adjudicated at a single procedure.[112] In *Honigman v. Attorney-General,* Justice Halevi recognized the existence of the usage, but added that "there is no strict rule or usage against accumulative punishments." This implies that, when offenses are committed in different places and circumstances and over long periods of time, it is permissible to ignore the usage of imposing sentences. This usage was given expression in section I 1(a) of the Penal Law (Modes of Punishment) (Consolidated Version), 1970,[113] whereby a person sentenced in one case to a number of prison terms will serve them concurrently unless the Court orders otherwise. The claim "no case to answer" also originates in usage. In the words of Justice Cheshin in *Blecher v. Shamir,*[114] "it has been determined in accordance with the rule of usage in criminal cases that the courts in Israel will hear at an interim stage a claim of no case to answer." In *Attorney-General v. Hussein Hamdan,*[115] he added that "this usage is law and may not be changed." Also worthy of mention is the Court's obligation to allow the appellant to respond to the claims of the respondent in a criminal trial, the foundation of which is "in custom ... that is established and it is known that no one ignores

---

had view it as illegal and, consequently, declare it invalid. Actually, limited interpretation of the article by the courts facilitated the emergence of a number of methods of paying key-money without violating the law. The result was that the custom of key-money was no longer contrary to the law, but existed alongside of it.

111 Cr.A 131/67 *Kamiar v. The State of Israel*, 22(2) P.D. 89 (1968).
112 Cr.A 63/52 *Kapon v. Attorney-General*, 1 P.D. 793 (1948).
113 24 L.S.I. 112. The issue is currently governed by Sec. 45 of the Penal Law, 1977 (L.S.I. Special Volume).
114 H.C.J 6/53 *Blecher v. Shamir*, 7 P.D. 1105, at 1109 (1953).
115 Cr.A 26/49 *Attorney-General v. Hussein Hamdan*, 2 P.D. 837 (1949).

or violates it." Usage determines the procedure of dismissing or cancelling a criminal appeal when the appellant fails to appear in Court.

On the basis of usage as established in the courts, a criminal appeal is cancelled if the appellant does not appear for the proceedings, despite the fact that the provisions of the Criminal Procedure Law[116] do not refer to cancellation, but to the Court's right to hear the case in the absence of the appellant.[117] In procedural law, custom has played a role in determining both the relations between the Court and the litigants and the proper form of commencing the procedure,[118] i.e., "by motion or by regular action."[119] In the laws of execution, usage has developed which later received judicial recognition. In criminal law, "usage can usually serve as defense ... when it is shown that for reasons identical or similar to those proven in the trial, people act the way the accused did."[120] Custom and usage among certain groups of the population have played a role in the determination of punishment[121] and the evaluation of evidence.[122] By virtue of usage, legal arrangements have been made in constitutional and administrative law regarding relations between state authorities, stipulating powers and obligations not expressly mentioned by law.

The working procedures of the Knesset are based largely upon usage and custom; these either deal with realms not governed by the Knesset Rules of Procedure or complement provisions encompassed therein.[123] Cabinet committees (until the adoption of Section 27 of the Basic Law: The Government)[124] and the Cabinet Rules of Procedure, which are now laid down by the virtue of Section 17 of that Basic Law,[125] were previously established by usage. Constitutional custom provides the basis for the recognition of the Government's authority to conclude

---

116 Formerly, Sec. 189 of the Criminal Procedure Law, 1965 (19 L.S.I. 158), and currently Sec. 208 of the Criminal Procedure Law [Consolidated Version], 1982.

117 Cr.A 542/77 *Brand v. State of Israel*, 32(1) P.D. 277 (1978); Cr.A 7/59 *Proshinski v. Tik*, 13 P.D. 832 (1959).

118 H.C.J 64/74 *Zmiro Mahmoud Said v. District Court*, 28(2) P.D. 37, at 42–43 (1974) (correction of an error in the ruling pursuant to the appeal of the litigant's representative).

119 *Zucker v. Tax Assessment Officer*, 35 P.D. 102 (1958); C.A 355/58 *Kugot and Geller v. Official Receiver*, 13 P.D. 95 (1959).

120 D.C.A (TLV) 383/52 *Kramer v. Zingler*, 9 P.D. 36 (1953); C.A 113/71 *Stauber v. Muha*, 26(2) P.D. 416, at 419 (1972); H.C.J 50/55 *Yehezkel v. Head of the Execution Office*, 9 P.D. 1617 (1955).

121 Cr.A 773/77 *Cohen v. State of Israel*, 32(1) P.D. 575 (1978).

122 C.A 588/76 *Bukbeza v. Bukbeza*, 21(2) P.D. 3 (1967).

123 104 See A. Zidon, *The Knesset – Israel's Parliament* (Jerusalem, 5th ed., 1969, in Hebrew) 101–114.

124 22 L.S.I. 257.

125 Approved in its meeting of June 8, 1968. The Government has since then revised the text of its Rules of Procedure several times.

and ratify international treaties and the participation of the Minister of Justice in the process of pardoning offenders by the President. Until an amendment to legislation was introduced, the High Court of Justice had refused to refer petitioners against rulings regarding execution of judgments to an alternative remedy in the ordinary courts, since a petition to the High Court of Justice against a ruling of the chairman of the execution office would be "usage which has become rooted in the execution laws ... over the past decades."[126] The courts further acknowledged the capacity of custom to create preliminary conditions for the exercise of power by as a public authority, as long as these do not contradict or change the law, as distinguished from filling in the details of the framework laid down by law.[127]

The courts have used custom in the formulation of the rules of disqualification of judges. The case concerned the claim that a Druse judge was disqualified from sitting in a case in which a woman who stayed in his home was a party. The Supreme Court stated that whether or not the judge is disqualified "will largely depend on the custom of the community." When a custom creates a power, it may be that the custom grants a permit to act, or it may impose a duty. When the custom permits an act, there will be no flaw in the act if the officer permitted to act decides not to act. This is the case, for example, with regard to the pardon process, where by virtue of custom the Minister of Justice takes part in the process. If the Minister fails to play that role, the process will not be adversely affected.

Usage has played a part in the area of the relations between the citizen and the government. The usage of the fiscal authorities to regard an assessee's income tax return as an initial offer for purposes of negotiation with the Assessing Officer led to conviction on a charge less severe than that demanded by the state attorney (Section 217 of the Income Tax Ordinance (New Version) instead of Section 220).[128] Regarding taxation, it should be mentioned that the usage as to the methods of estimating inventory[129] and computing the price of imported products[130] served as a guideline for court rulings.

It has been noted that case law alternately employs the terms "custom" and "usage"; the aforementioned rulings do not unequivocally clarify which concept is being referred to in terms of the precise definition proposed herein. It may be

---

126 H.C.J 87/52 *Etzion v. Head of the Execution Office*, 6 P.D. 484 (1952).
127 H.C.J 483/77 *Barzilai v. Prime Minister*, 31(3) P.D. 671 (1977).
128 L.S.I [N.V.] 145. *Ezra Eliyahu v. State of Israel*, 32(1) P.D. 536–537 (1978); *Malka v. State of Israel*, 32(1) P.D. 250 (1978).
129 D.C (TLV) 309/59 *Publishers, Ltd. v. Tax Assessment Officer*, 27 P.D. 111 (1961).
130 C.A 245/77 *State of Israel v. Paldom Steel, Ltd*, 32(1) P.D. 16, at 18 (1978).

generally said that the establishment of a governmental power,[131] the approval of one state agency's participation in a governmental procedure assigned by law to another state agency,[132] and the establishment of conditions for the exercise of power all fall within the realm of custom, although judgments frequently refer to usage.

This is also the case regarding arrangements granting civil rights or determining legal procedures. In contrast, arrangements which create assumptions presumed by law in a given direction are usually classified as usage.[133] But beyond the ambiguity in the employment of "custom" and "usage," the preceding survey clearly indicates the extensive application of custom and usage in public law.

C. Unique Aspects of the Enforcement of Custom in Public Law

Obviously, custom in public law differs from custom in private law inasmuch as each governs issues in distinct branches of law. Custom in public law, however, is unique in the degree of its enforcement by the courts. The limitations upon the enforcement of custom in public law derive from the fact that many of the subjects governed by custom in public law, especially those dealing with interrelations among governmental authorities, may fall within the test of injusticiability according to established judicial perceptions. These limitations also originate in the rules on *locus standi* in the High Court of Justice and in judge-made rules denying the hearing of petitions to the High Court or the granting of judicial relief for reasons of justice and equity.

There are two alternate attitudes toward the question of limitations upon the judicial enforcement of custom in public law. The first of these maintains that, lacking a possibility of enforcement, no custom exists. According to this approach, custom, like all law, creates rights, authority, and power. One of the characteristics of law is the possibility of its enforcement in legal proceedings. Therefore, the absence of means of legal enforcement of custom, whether due to limitations of injusticiability, right of standing, or considerations of justice in the High Court of Justice, excludes the possibility of defining the norm as obligatory custom.[134]

---

131 See, for example, *Kamiar, supra* note 111.
132 See *Barzilai, supra* note 127.
133 Shetreet, *"Custom in Public Law,"* 21 *Isr. L. Rev.* 450, 488–89 (1986).
134 Z. Terlo, *Governmental Powers,* (Jerusalem, 1975, in Hebrew) 1–24.

The second approach contends that the limitations of legal enforcement do not deprive the norm of its status as custom in public law. While the legal norm created by custom suffers from limitations of enforcement, this situation resembles a right in private law. Although in certain circumstances the latter cannot be enforced, there is no argument as to its existence. This study supports the second approach. It is known that not every right is enforceable, and not all legal norms are accompanied by sanctions guaranteeing enforcement. For example, in a situation of prescription under the law of Israel, the owner of the right cannot enforce it upon the expiration of the stipulated period, yet the right itself remains valid. If the defendant refrains from a plea of prescription, the plaintiff can enforce the right.[135] This is also the case regarding the inability of enforcing custom in public law owing to the application of the rules of injusticiability and *locus standi*, provisions of procedural immunity of public officers, refusal to hear a case for reasons of equity (such as the principles that those who seek justice in the High Court of Justice must come with clean hands and must not delay their petitions), or refusal to grant relief out of considerations of justice. The absence of enforcement does not negate the existence of custom.

It has been held that the dismissal of a petition to the High Court due to delay does not preclude the enforcement of the plaintiff's rights in an alternate court procedure, should one exist. In the *Bank Igud v. State of Israel judgment*,[136] Justice Cohn ruled: "The fact that the plaintiff delayed suit until the High Court of Justice no longer saw a need to grant him relief for the sake of justice does not mean that there is prescription on this matter in a court which grants relief in accordance with the law. A petition that was dismissed because of delay can still be filed as a lawsuit in another court with jurisdiction, so long as the period of limitation of action has not lapsed. When the High Court of Justice dismisses a case out of hand, this dismissal does not constitute an act of court which can prevent a lawsuit on the same matter in another court."

6. The Impact of International Law on Domestic Law and Human Rights

International law has played a normalizing effect on Israel's domestic laws and judicial independence. The Israel Foreign Ministry, according to its Deputy Direc-

---

135 This approach was adopted in the Prescription Law, 1958 (12 L.S.I. 129), Sec. 2: "... prescription shall not *per se* void the right itself."
136 C.A 292/71 *Bank Igud v. State of Israel*, 27(1) P.D. 245.

tor General Robbie Sabel, tends to have an "ambivalent attitude to the world of international human rights. On the one hand we see Israel as a society that respects human rights and, by and large, complies with the most stringent of international norms. On the other hand, we are imbued with a deeply felt skepticism as to the impartiality and evenhandedness of international human rights bodies when they deal with Israel."[137]

Two decisions highlight the ambivalence. The first was the decision to withdraw Israel's acceptance of compulsory jurisdiction of the International Court of Justice at The Hague (ICJ). The second was to recommend that Israel should accede to all the major international human rights treaties.

Israel has had an unhappy experience with the ICJ. The ICJ's composition is determined by the UN General Assembly, whose representation is based on international regional grouping.[138] It is, therefore, assumed that Israel would not receive a fair hearing on any issue of political relevance. [139]

Due to the nature of Israel as a Jewish state founded after the end of World War II and the Holocaust, the Jewish people and the State of Israel felt that it was fitting for Israel to be a party to human rights treaties.[140] Furthermore, acceding to human rights treaties allows Israel to become a full member of the "club"of nations.[141] As a full member of the "club" of nations, Israel can overcome Arab states' efforts to exclude Israel from international and regional organizations.[142] Additionally, Israel has felt relatively proud of its human rights record.[143]

Another reason for acceding to the human rights treaties was to firmly ground the principles of human rights into Israeli domestic law so that they would be an inflexible, rigid standard.[144] By accepting the treaties, it would prevent legislative or executive actions from altering or compromising those standards of human rights.[145] Customary international law automatically becomes part of Israeli domestic law[146] while other treaties do not become law without an explicit legislative act in Israel. Regardless of whether international law has been

---

137 Robbie Sabel, *Israel and the Enforcement of the Norms of International Human Rights*, in Sabel, *supra* note 93, International Law.
138 *Id.*
139 *Id.*
140 *Id.*
141 *Id.*, at 2.
142 *Id.*
143 *Id.*
144 *Id.*
145 *Id.*
146 *Id.*, at 3.

brought into the domestic system, the outward expression of acceptance to these standards can have an impact on Israeli, domestic law, and judicial rulings.[147] It would seem to be a reasonable assertion that, in Israel, acceding to an international human rights treaty elevates the provisions of such treaty to that of a judicial standard, even where the treaty is not incorporated into local law.

Robbie Sabel commented that "The practical importance of human rights treaties is however a reflection of the independence of the Israel judicial system, for it is the Israel judicial system, with government acquiescence, that applies such norms. It is not a reflection of international organisational norms, for when we turn to the international scene we, in Israel, tend to find an inbuilt political bias that negates rather than fosters international human rights."

Israel's skepticism to international enforcement of human rights stems from the international enforcement machinery.[148] The veto power of each of the five permanent members of the UN Security Council is out of place in regards to enforcement of universal human rights.[149] Additionally, ad hoc international criminal courts and the newly established International Criminal Court create a gloomy political reality for Israel.[150] It is most likely that the elected judges will exclude Israel and there is concern that the way in which the list of war crimes has been drafted that Arab states will be able to pursue their feud over the status of Israel settlements.[151] It is, therefore, unlikely that the court will be able to maintain impartiality when it pertains to Israel.[152]

United Nations politicization has resulted in Israel being the only state in the world "for whom the UN has appointed a special rapporteur for human rights with an open-ended mandate" in regards to human rights international reporting systems.[153] This extra focus has caused Israel to be the only country in the Middle East to have to submit an urgent report to the Committee on the Elimina-

---

147 Israeli laws reflect the language of the treaties. Example: The Israel Penal Enactment reflects the wording against racism found in the UN Convention Against Racial Discrimination. Israel's High Court often refers to provisions of human rights treaties as a standard even when they have not been incorporated into domestic law. See H.C.J 13/86 *Shahin v. Commander of Israel Defense Forces in Judea and Samaria*, 41(1) P.D. 197.

148 Sabel, *supra* note 93 at 3.

149 *Id.*

150 *Id.*

151 See Alan Baker, *The International Criminal Court: Israel's Unique Dilemma* 18 JUSTICE, 119 (1998).

152 *Id.*

153 See reporting committees such as: the Committee on the Elimination of Racial Discrimination (CERD), the Committee Against Torture (CAT), the Committee for the Elimination of Discrimination Against Women (CEDAW), and the Committee on the Rights of the Child (CRC).

tion of Racial Discrimination (CERD) and to be challenged on their status as a non-racial state because of their use of religious symbols in government.[154]

Despite the disadvantages, international supervision is a positive element of human rights law. However, the supervision must come from a body that is impartial and elected from like-minded states. One alternative to the UN may be Israel's ascension to the Council of Europe which would provide Israel with international supervision over their human rights.[155] Robbie Sabel states, "I would welcome having Israel's actions supervised by representatives of liberal, democratic societies. I have no doubt they would find some fault with us, as they have with the UK and Italy and other European States; however, such criticism would be from judges who themselves live in democratic societies with independent judiciaries. If, however, such supervision, as in UN bodies, continues to be exercised with political bias by representatives of hostile, totalitarian States, we in Israel will continue to be deeply skeptical of international enforcement of human rights."[156]

---

154 *Id.*
155 *Id.*
156 *Id.*, at 5.

Chapter 4:
System of Government

Israel maintains a parliamentary system of government which owes much of its structure to the British parliamentary system. The Israeli parliament is known as the Knesset. The Knesset is led by the Prime Minister, who is usually the leader of the party with the highest number of seats in the Knesset. The President of Israel chooses the Prime Minister, who is then charged with organizing a government. This government is based on a coalition and consists of representatives from multiple parties. Elections for the Knesset occur once every four years, but by legislation, the Knesset can call for earlier elections. Each party which has a minimum of 3.25% of the electoral votes is represented accordingly in the Knesset. Knesset members are elected as a list and not individually.[1]

For a time, the parliamentary system was altered to provide direct elections for the Prime Minister. In this system, the Prime Minister was elected directly and had authority to create the government. The Prime Minister could resign, which would trigger elections for the Prime Ministerial position. If the Prime Minister sent his resignation to the President or had a vote of no confidence, then the Knesset would be dissolved and there would be new elections. This scenario was mostly an effort to better control the unruly governing system and to more directly connect the electorate with their representatives. Unfortunately, the change resulted in even more confusion and the Prime Minister called for three elections in a period of only five years. Ultimately the system failed to accomplish its goals and the system returned to its original configuration. The reform lasted only nine years, from 1992 to 2001. The underlying difficulty that resulted from the direct election reforms was that it was based on other electoral systems, but these models were not sufficiently researched to understand the true effects on the Israeli system.[2]

1. The Basic Values of the Democratic System of Government

US President Abraham Lincoln defined democracy as "government of the people, by the people, for the people."[3] The basic values of every democratic system

---

1 See A. Rubinstein & B. Medina, *The Constitutional Law of the State of Israel* (6th ed. 2005).
2 *Id.*
3 Abraham Lincoln, "The Gettysburg Address", http://www.abrahamlincolnonline.org/lincoln/speeches/gettysburg.htm (accessed February 9, 2017).

DOI 10.1515/9783899497946-004

of government teach us about the social and humane values which lie at the foundation of this system.

A few key fundamental values are usually mentioned when discussing the democratic system: representation—an elected government which reflects adequately of the various population groups and their preferences; stability—a continuous rule that is not constantly fearful of its term ending prematurely; governability—an effective ability of the government to achieve its declared objectives; efficiency—achieving maximize results and accomplishments with minimal resources; accountability—accountability of the government to the parliament and the public.

Among these values exist different tensions, and sometimes they even contradict each other. Therefore, although every democratic country strives to promote all of these values, in practice each country chose a slightly different system of government which gives an advantage to certain values over others.

A. Representativeness

a. General

Pure democracy is, in theory, direct democracy with no mediators.[4] Famous philosophers of democracy hold the opinion that civilian participation in the navigation and management of the political life is an integral part of the expression and exhaustion of one's liberty and personality.[5] As the renowned Jean-Jaques Rousseau stated:[6] "sovereignty cannot be represented" and "the English people believes itself to be free; it is gravely mistaken; it is free only during the election of members of parliament; as soon as the members are elected, the people is enslaved; it is nothing."

Nevertheless, it is common view that self-government by way of direct democracy is impractical in countries where the population amounts to millions or even hundreds of millions of people.[7]

Accordingly, with the formation of large sovereign units, philosophers of democracy began siding with democratic regimes governed by representatives. The United States of America was formed in the late 18th century. By the mid-

---

4 Yaron Ezrachi & Mordechai Kremnitzer, *Israel: Toward a Constitutive Democracy* 57 (Israel Democracy Institute Press, 2001)

5 *Id.*

6 Jean-Jacques Rousseau, Of the Social Contract 142 (translator Y.Or)

7 Ezrachi & Kremnitzer, *supra* note 4, at 57.

19th century, the perception that views direct democracy as a plausible option had vanished, leaving only the representative democracy as a feasible option.[8] There is still much support to the claim that, other than the practical difficulties in managing direct democracies, there are substantial limitations of such democracies, further favoring representative democracy. Main arguments supporting this claim are the fear of tyranny of the majority, denying political compromises, and the public's inability to make complex and meaningful decisions.[9] Other than these arguments, John Stuart Mill held the opinion that a representative government is preferable in order to facilitate parliament debate and create a market of ideas which will lead to the discovery of the truth. Lastly, the concern was raised about direct democracy making both the civilians and society too political and compromising the private aspect of civilian's lives.[10]

On the other hand, one might think that in the modern age, with progressed technological abilities allowing civilians to take active part in political decisions, democracy that is closer to a direct one is plausible and even desired. A good example is the common use of referendums as part of the decision-making process in democratic countries.[11]

Nonetheless, there are claims that the use of referendum might bring to tyranny of the majority, with the majority fulfilling its desires without the need to compromise politically with minority groups, thereby impairing the latter's rights.[12] Another concern is that of a manipulative use of the referendum's results as justification for government actions.

Switzerland is known for its wide use of referendums, where even its current constitution was approved by one. The Swiss constitution enumerates several areas of government that decisions relating to them must be approved by referendum. Some are: amending the constitution or denying the amendment and

---

8 Robert A. Dahl, *On Democracy*, 92 (Shahar Elizer Peled, translator, Israeli Democracy Institute, 2002).

9 See Dana Blander & Gideon Rahat, *Referendum: Myth and Reality*, 44–50 (Israel Democracy Institute, 2000).

10 Norberto Bobbio, *The Future of Democracy: A Defense of the Rules of the Game*, 26–27 (Hebrew) (Translated from Italian by Dalia Amit, 2002)

11 Bobbio, *Id.*, at 37; Bobbio views the referendum as an exclusive institution of direct democracy. See Also, H.C.J 1661/05 *Regional Council Hof Azza v. Prime Minister of Israel*, paragraph 91 (2005): The Supreme Court ruled that there was no duty to hold a referendum on the issue of disengagement from Gaza, and the process of decision by ordinary legislator is constituent with the democratic values of Israel.

12 Dan Lahav, *A Referendum—Background: Considerations and Aspects in Shaping Legislation for a Referendum*, 45 (Jerusalem: The Knesset's Research and Information Center, 2004).

joining an international organization for security cooperation.[13] The Swiss constitution further enumerates actions that, per the request of 50,000 nationals or eight cantons, must be approved by referendum. Among these are federal actions including joining specific international conventions.[14] Moreover, actions considered as federal emergency steps can be approved by referendum or even must be approved in such a way under certain circumstances, given the timeline of the actions.[15]

In the past few decades, the referendum had become an acceptable decision-making mechanism in democratic countries.[16] Nevertheless, Israel had not used the mechanism yet.[17]

Recent legislative measures indicate a change in the Israeli system of government as the representative democracy and pure parliamentary system tend toward utilizing the referendum mechanism. First, there is Amendment Number 1 to Procedures of Government and Justice (Annulment of the Applicability of Law, Jurisdiction, and Administration), 5759 – 1999, enacted in 2010. It directs that any agreement according to which the law, jurisdiction, and administration of the State of Israel shall no longer apply to territory in which they currently apply —including an agreement that involves a future undertaking, and a conditioned undertaking—after the agreement has been approved by the Knesset by an absolute majority, shall require approval in a referendum, unless it has been approved by a majority of 80 members of the Knesset. Moreover, this arrangement was enacted into Basic Law: Referendum, thereby requiring another basic law in order to amend it. These station the referendum as an almost necessary process in the making of any meaningful political arrangement, considering the Israeli political reality.

Representativeness or self-governance through representatives was meant to ease the limitations of direct democracy in large countries.[18] Representativeness allows citizens to impact governmental actions through its representatives. The purpose of representativeness is to ensure that the elected representatives will operate to fulfill the wishes of those who elected them, or at the very least put them on the governmental agenda.

The two main bodies entrusted to realize Israeli representativeness are the parliament and the government. The government represents the public in its en-

---

13 Section 140 to the Swiss Constitution.
14 Section 141 to the Swiss Constitution
15 Section 140b and 141 to the Swiss Constitution.
16 Shmuel Saadia and Liav Orgad, Referendum, 42 (2000).
17 See historical analysis of proposals for referendum in Israel, Saadia, *supra*.
18 Ezrachi & Kremnitzer, *supra* note 4, p. 51.

tirety in the areas of political, economic, and social work.[19] The parliament, however, expresses the principle of political representativeness in a stricter sense as it includes representatives from all parties that had passed the election threshold, whereas the government includes only the coalition of parties.[20]

Naturally, each representative stands for a group of citizens. The division of all nationals into these groups can be made in different ways, for example, geographical representativeness, in which every election zone has representatives in parliament who are expected to work in the best interest of that election zone. Representativeness can also be fulfilled by ideological representation, which means that the ideological sections comprising civilian society are represented in a manner that is proportionate to their share of the population. Representativeness can also reflect different public opinions on a specific political issue, which are not part of a comprehensive political agenda. It is also common to address representativeness in its theoretical meaning as Descriptive Representation. Accordingly, the parliament is expected to reflect the nation as a whole, a body that must think, feel, and act in a manner that reflects the people's will.[21]

A voting system that wishes to fully protect the principle of representativeness must base itself on two ambitions. The first is forming a voting process that will enable voters to fully express their wishes and preferences on a voting ballot; the second is creating a political map that correctly mirrors the preferences expressed on the voting ballot.[22]

The principle of representativeness is also expressed through participatory democracy that enables citizens to express their opinion and impact public progression. For example, during the legislative process the bill is published publicly and the media accompanies the entire process. This way each citizen has the power to impact the legislative process; in certain cases, even public authorities are given the chance to express their opinion on the bill.[23]

The principle of representativeness is not absolute. At times, the principle contradicts other principles of the democratic system.[24] A classic example is the contradiction between the principles of representativeness and governance and efficiency values: in high levels of representativeness, the government's ability to act efficiently and to apply its policy is sometimes restricted. It is also evi-

---

19 *Id.*, 62.
20 *Id.*
21 Vernon Bagdanor, *What Is Proportional Representation?* (1984).
22 See Also: John Stuart Mill, *Representative Government* (1861); Hanna Pitkin, *The Concept of Representation* (1967).
23 Yitzhak Zamir, *Administrative Legislation: The Price of Efficiency*, 4 Mishpatim 63, 66 (1973).
24 *Id.*, 64.

dent in democratic countries with a heterogeneous society that has many different interests and groups. In such countries, precise representation of all groups might disable the formation of a majority group that can facilitate governmental policy and government actions.[25]

The principle of representativeness similarly contradicts the principle of efficiency. For instance, when there is a multiplicity of parties, the government is often required to allocate funds for sectoral goals in order to preserve the coalition. Doing so, the government acts out of political pressures and not out of efficient economic considerations. Likewise, multiple parties might also cause "political paralysis" where the government is not capable of functioning properly and executing its policy.

Lastly, the principle of representativeness might also contradict the principle of stability as the representation of all groups compromising society prevents each body from accumulating enough power to allow it to act within its term of governance without fearing removal from power. In that context, there is a popular opinion that says that while parliamentary system have a high level of representativeness and low stability level, presidential systems enjoy high stability but low representativeness. In parliamentary systems, the parliament that represents the different groups of people enjoys superiority over the government, fulfilling the principle of representativeness. In presidential systems, the president and different secretaries that represent a single party are not inferior to parliament. Some argue that the presidential system is nonetheless preferable considering the principle of stability, as the president holds great power and can only be ousted through rare procedure.[26] Linz holds the opposite opinion, according to which presidential systems are less stable than parliamentary ones when it comes to the stability of the democracy, unlike the governance stability.[27]

b. Proportional Representation versus Plurality Voting Systems

There are two ways of guaranteeing representation of the electorate in government and parliament: one is the proportional representation system and the other is the plurality voting system.[28] In a proportional representation system,

---

25 *Id.*
26 Gidon Doron and Maoz Rozental, *President Commission to Review the Structure of Government in Israel*, Subcommittee Report: Representativeness in Presidential and Semi-Presidential Systems of Government 114–123.
27 *The Breakdown of Democratic Regimes* (Juan J. Linz and Alfred Stefan eds., 1978).
28 See, Shimon Shetreet, *The Executive: Basic Law: The Government* (forthcoming 2017, editor Yitzhak Zamir).

the electorate usually votes for a party and not an individual. The seats of parliament are divided among the different parties so that each party gets a number of seats that is proportionate to its number of votes. In such systems, every vote receives expression as each vote effects the way parliament seats are divided. Plurality voting systems are based on a "winner takes it all" mechanism. In systems of this kind, voters usually vote for candidates running for a specific seat in parliament. The candidate with the most votes gets the seat, and all votes for non-elected candidates are not expressed in any way. Consequently, the level of representativeness is lower than in a proportional representation system.[29]

On the other hand, certain aspects of the proportional representation system also compromise the principle of representativeness. In countries with proportional representation, it is common that a coalition is needed in order to form a government, as no single party wins the majority of votes. Some say that the coalition forming process removes the government-electing procedure from the public to the politicians, the latter forming coalitions that do not necessarily reflect the public's choice. Moreover, these coalitions are at times a complete falsification of the voters' wills. They are formed with great consideration of undesired factors such as the influence extremist parties have on the moderate majority during the formation of the coalition, when they are much needed.[30]

The voting system in Israel is one of proportional representation, which brings a high level of representativeness, as discussed above. Nevertheless, there are arguments saying that, since Israel is not divided into electoral districts, the level of geographical representativeness is compromised as there is less representation for the periphery. Those supporting these arguments suggest changing the system to a proportional representational system with electoral districts.[31] There are, however, important issues to consider in changing the country's division to electoral districts. For instance, separating a homogeneous voting bloc between adjacent electoral districts would prevent it from gaining the

---

29 According to one of the political known rules called "Deburjeh rule", the majoritarian system is inclined to reduce substantially the number of parties represented in parliament, so representativeness is reduced. See Itay Send, *The Powers of the Prime Minster in the Parliamentary Israeli System* in The State of Israel: New Ideas 55, 72 (Uriel Raichman and David Nachmias, editors, 2006).

30 Dani Koren and Boaz Shapira, Coalitions 16 (1997).

31 Naomi Chazan and Nir Atmor, *The President Commission to Review the Government Structure in Israel*, Subcommittee Repot: Review of the parliament system 179 (2005)

electoral expression it would have received had the entire bloc voted in one district.[32]

There have been attempts, though not successful, to change the proportional representation system. In the early 1950s, Prime Minister David Ben-Gurion described the political parties' rationale as an "ailment we inherited from our diaspora past." Ben-Gurion formulated the idea of adopting the British regional election system, and guarantee the rule of Mapai, the dominant political party of the time. At the time, Mapai had more voters than any other party; changing the system would have ensured an almost complete rule of Mapai in the Knesset. Ben-Gurion did not get his wish and the topic was removed from the agenda. In fact, there was no real justification for the change since Israel has a small territory and there are no geographic or ethnic differences between its different areas. The change would have also greatly distorted the diversity of public opinions and its translation to mandates in Mapai's favor.[33]

In the late 1980s, the political ties and plurality of small parties that affected the political stability brought the change of election system back onto the agenda. At that time, many propositions were made to turn the system into a mixed system where the majority of the members of the Knesset (MKs) would be elected on a regional-proportional basis and the rest from countrywide lists. These suggested reforms tried to mitigate the tension between the value of stability that requires a small number of parties and the value of representativeness that requires the representation of small interest groups as well. In fact, these reforms fell through due to pressures from the central parties.[34] It should be noted that such mixed systems are very successful, like the one enacted in Italy.[35] The Presidential Commission for the Examination of the Structure of Government in Israel recommended, in its report from 2007, that 60 MKs be elected in proportional national elections and 60 MKs be elected in regional elections.[36]

---

32 Boaz Shapira, *Electoral Reforms in Israel 1949–1966* in The Electoral Revolution 16, 21 (Gideon Doron editor, 1996)

33 *Id.*, at 18

34 *Id.*

35 Send, *supra* note 29 at page 73.

36 See the recommendation of the Megidor Commission to review the structure of government and the subcommittee on the system of elections presided over by Prof. Shimon Shetreet; the commission recommended introducing a mixed system of election according to which 60 members of Knesset would be elected in proportional elections, and 60 in regional majoritarian elections. https://lib.mishpat.ac.il/multimedia/%D7%93%D7%95%D7%97%20%D7%95%D7%A2%D7%93%D7%AA%20%D7%A0%D7%A9%D7%99%D7%90%20%D7%94%D7%9E%D7%93D7%99%D7%A0%D7%94%20%D7%9C%D7%91%D7%97%D7%99%D7%A0%D7%AA%20%

The election threshold also bears great significance to the number of parties and, as a consequence, on the level of representativeness. The lower the electoral threshold, the more parties can enter the Knesset, including parties that represent only small segments of the population. The 1992 elections are a great example for this. Until then, the election threshold was 1%. Starting that year, the election threshold was raised to 1.5%. Had it not been changed, Tehiya would have won one mandate at the expense of the Arab Democratic Party. That would have caused a draw between the leftist wing bloc and the rightist and ultra-orthodox bloc, a draw that would have paralyzed the political system.[37] In 2014, the election threshold was raised once again to 3.25%, which led to the Arab parties unifying to maintain their representation, while preventing the Yachad party of Eli Yishai from gaining representation in the Knesset.

c. "Personality" and Ideology: Personalization of Politics

After distinguishing the two systems for representativeness, we will now analyze the values of "personality" and ideology, which are common criteria in the assessment of different election systems. The principle of "personality" holds within it everything relating to the character and qualities of the candidates. In the "first-past-the-post" voting system, the public votes for individuals running for office. The charismatic skills are crucial for the voter's decision. Although the ideology of the party represented by the candidate is important to every voter, it is the candidate as an individual who is elected. Therefore, one holding the same opinions as party A might vote for party B if the latter's candidate has a more appealing personality.[38]

In the proportional representation systems, there are two approaches for the elections: the "closed list" and "open list" systems. In "closed list" elections, the party presents a list of candidates in the order in which they will win seats in the parliament. If the party wins ten seats, then the first ten candidates on its list will assume those seats. As a result, the personality of the candidates bears less importance and the voters are motivated more by ideological reasons. Needless to say, the parties still aspire to put their most attractive candidates at the top of the list because their personality still affects the voters. On the other hand, in

---

D7%9E%D7%91%D7%A0%D7%94%20%D7%94%D7%9E%D7%9E%D7%A9%D7%9C%20% D7%91%D7%99%D7%A9%D7%A8%D7%90%D7%9C%2012633.pdf (accessed February 9, 2017).
37 Koren and Shapira, *supra* note 30, at 30.
38 Lasse Lausten, *Choosing the Right Candidate: How Context and Polticial Ideology Affect Candidate Personality Preference*; http://dpsa.dk/papers/Laustsen%20-%20choosing%20the%20 right%20candidate.pdf (accessed February 9, 2017).

"open list" elections, the voters are given the tools to express their preferences as to specific candidates by influencing the order in which a party's candidates are elected. Hence, if a party wins ten seats of parliament, these seats will be assumed by the ten candidates with the highest voting scores from the voters. In this way, the voters are granted better control of the process of forming the list of candidates for parliament. This system also combines between the preferences of personalities of the candidates and the voters' ideological preferences.[39]

B. Stability

a. General

The principle of stability is considered an important criterion in assessing the function and efficiency of acting governments. Stability is important to the government's operation in several aspects. First, a government lacking stability will need many efforts to pass each resolution; thus, instability might paralyze the government in a way. Second, government acting with uncertainty as to its days in position will prefer to promote short-term interests, even when undermining long-term factors. Lastly, instability takes away time from effective governmental operation to political debates and controversies.

Some hold the opinion that the principle of stability in the acting government has two facets. One is winning a coalition majority stable and liable enough to support the acting government; second is an active opposition capable of being an appropriate alternative to the government in power. A unified opposition must effectively criticize the government and guarantee that the acting government will both act responsibly and consider the interest of the population in its entirety.[40] Others define governmental stability through two parameters: the government's ability to finish its term and a low rate of ministers changing roles.[41]

The election system is not the only reason for governmental stability and effectiveness. It is also the outcome of how much the voters see the elections as a tool in fulfilling their political aspirations as well as the level of trust and contentment they feel toward the acting government. The stability and effectiveness

---

39 *Id.*
40 Gideon Doron and Maoz Rozental, *President Commission to Review the Structure of Government in Israel*, Subcommittee Report: Representativeness in Presidential and Semi-Presidential Systems of Government, 114–123.
41 Amnon Rubinstein and Adam Wolfson, *Absence of Government: How to Mend Israel's Broken System*, 96 (Kineret Zmora Bittan, 2012)

of an acting government also depends on the government's ability to enact legislation that best suits the voters' interests while at the same time not discriminating against parties or interest groups that are not part of the coalition's majority. These factors have direct impact on the level of support the government enjoys and its ability to hold its position.

The level of acceptable political rivalry in the governmental system of a country also bears influence on the government's stability. The higher that the political rivalry is, the less stable the government will be.[42] The next elections also influence the government's stability. When the elections are close, the ministers of the coalition must continue with the government's regular actions while preparing for the coming elections. The preparation includes, among others, the need to appropriate successful governmental policies and hold other coalition members responsible for less successful policies. This dynamic certainly does not make the government more stable.[43]

It is commonly accepted that a "first past the post" system is preferable in maintaining stability of governance. In such systems, there is a higher probability of forming a government of one political party, or a coalition comprised of very few parties. The instability that is common in governments of many parties also leads to inefficiency; the Prime Minister is often required to make superfluous political appointments due to the large number of parties in the coalition.[44] Nevertheless, it is possible, given the suitable social structure and political culture, that certain models of the proportional representation election system will also allow a strong coalition based on one governing party with the ability to ensure stability and efficiency no less than in a "first past the post" system.[45] Some even say that history shows that a single governing party does not have a better stability record than a coalition government. Coalition governments are forced to lean toward the center of the political spectrum, thus making their policy closer to the opinions of the average citizen.[46]

The level of stability is further influenced by how easy it is to oust the acting government.[47] As stated above, presidential government enjoys better stability

---

42 Doron and Rozental, *supra* note 40, 129.

43 Dan Koren, *Time in Grey*, 20 (1994).

44 Doron and Rosenthal, *supra* note 40 at 107; for example, in the 32nd government, 34 ministers served, 6 of them without portfolio. Since then a law was passed to limit the number of ministers to 19, see Section 5 of the Basic Law: The Government.

45 David Butler, *Democracy and Elections* (1983).

46 Koren and Shapira, *supra* note 30, at 19.

47 Chazan and Atmor, *supra* note 31, at page 178, who suggest that the instability of government is due to the excessive easiness to result the vote of the no-confidence procedure.

than parliamentary government systems since the government does not depend on the parliament's support. Many reforms in Basic Law: The Government have been made in order to improve governmental stability in Israel, according to which the dismissal of a serving PM will only be allowed under specific circumstances, such as a vote of no-confidence by 80 MKs.[48] According to the March 2014 reform, a vote of no-confidence in government can be made only by a vote of confidence in an alternative government and in support of the majority of MKs.[49]

As discussed earlier, the popular opinion is that presidential government is preferable for governmental stability over the parliamentary government systems. Nonetheless, there are still opinions heard that an empirical study of governmental stability in countries around the world show that the presidential government's stability argument is only valid in regards to the United States and that, as a general rule, parliamentary governments enjoy higher levels of stability.[50]

When assessing the level of governmental stability in the state of Israel since its establishment in 1948, two periods must be differentiated. The first period stretches between 1948 and 1977. Mapai was the party dominant in power and created politics of consensus. The second period begins in 1977 and is characterized by political polarization and political rivalry.[51] During the first period, the dominant party was able to maintain governmental stability. In the second period, however, the dominant party, even when holding the center of power, was not in the heart of the consensus, making the government, since the "1977 *Mahapach*" (change of ruling party), politically unstable.[52]

As to the Israeli government structure, a comparison must be made between the double election or two notes election system of 1992–2001 and the single note system, enacted in all other elections. As the last chapter shows, the main rationale behind the 1992 reform was that direct election of the PM would impair the power of small parties and their ability to pressure the PM, thus resolving the political draw in Israel. The supporters of the reform say that this was also meant to improve governmental stability. However the reform did the exact opposite—the double election compromised stability as it enhanced the Knesset fragmentation.

---

48 Uriel Reichmann, *Introduction: The Challenges of Leadership and Crisis of Government*, in The State of Israel – New Ideas (2006).
49 Section 28 of Basic Law: The Government.
50 Chazan and Atmore, *supra* note 31, at 183–185.
51 Koren and Shapira, *supra* note 30, at 45.
52 *Id.*

Voters in a double-election system believe that once their favorite party is in power, through the direct election of PM, they can give their second vote to a sectoral party that best represents their interests. This pattern empowers small parties and consequently impairs the governmental stability. The most severe impairment of governmental stability in a double voting system occurs when the elected PM represents one political bloc while the majority of MKs represent a rival bloc. In this case, with the PM acting in contrary to the Knesset, it is nearly impossible to maintain a stable government.[53]

Some say that the main factor in determining governmental stability is the coalition members' desire to maintain it. This is the reason for small coalitions often being more stable than broad coalitions. In small coalitions, each member party gets more benefits from being part of a larger government, so their interest in dismantling the government is decreased. Similarly, the governments of Menachem Begin, which were highly dependent on all coalition members, were especially stable as every substantial crisis would have led the government falling while all members of the coalition preferred the moderate situation. Moreover, some even claim that material benefits such as jobs, budgets, and other favors are more beneficial to governmental stability than making political achievements. The arguments continue about the grand coalitions being exceptionally stable because all members of coalition understand that their ideological ambitions will not be fulfilled, in addition to a balanced distribution of government positions and the continued fear from the loss to the other rival party.[54]

b. Comparative View of Stability Mechanisms

For a parliamentary system to function properly, it must have stability mechanisms. The need for these mechanisms is vital in countries with more than two parties, since the more parties there are, the greater the chance of lack of consent in parliament, which could lead to the dismantling of the government.[55] The stability mechanisms allow the government to act regularly and efficiently. They include: (a) substantial limitations on political parties; (b) Threshold limitations; (c) parliamentary votes of no-confidence; (d) the PM's authority to dissolve the parliament.

---

53 *Id.*, at 28.
54 *Id.*, 124–128.
55 See for example Kaarlo Touri, *The Eurozone Crisis as a Constitutional Crisis*, in Polity and Crisis: Reflections on the European Odyssey (editors Massimo Fichera and Sakari Hänninen, 2014); Bruce Ackerman, *The New Separation of Powers*, 113 HARV. L. REV. 633, 650 (2000).

(1) Substantive limitations on political parties

Following World War II and the enactment of the German constitution (Grundgesetz),[56] the German constitutional court outlawed the Nazi and communist parties and determined their activity as contradictory to the constitution. These parties were found to be anti-democratic and thus in breach of the constitutional principles.[57] As a consequence of this ruling, the number of German parties gradually dropped until it reached only three parties in the 1950s. While communist parties are not forbidden in Israel, the law stipulates that a party can run only after being registered by the Parties Registrar.[58] This limitation is anchored in the Parties Law, 5752–1992. Another limitation on party registration is that the Parties Registrar will not register a party whose objectives or actions reject Israel's existence as a Jewish or democratic state, incite racism, or serve as a camouflage for any illegal activity.[59]

(2) Threshold limitations

The greatest danger of the proportional representation system is the plurality of small-scale parties. These parties are capable of significantly impairing the efficiency of legislative processes and the possibility of forming a stable and efficient government. In an effort to limit the number of small parties, many countries with proportional representation election systems adopt threshold limitations. These limitations stipulate that in order to have representatives in parliament, a party must get a minimal and known percentage of the votes. This minimal threshold is called the "election threshold". In Germany, the election threshold is 5%. This means that each party must get at least 5% of the votes in the parties election in order to have representatives in the Bundestag. Even if a party does not win 5% of the votes in the parties' election, it might still win seats of parliament if it gets more than three seats in the personal elections.[60]

In Israel, from 2004 to 2014, the electoral threshold was 2%. Thus, a party that received more than 2% of the votes could have at least two representatives

---

56 The adoption of the constitution was done in the course of May 1949.
57 Paul Franz, *Unconstitutional and Outlawed Political Parties: A German-American Comparison,* 5 B.C. Int'l & Comp. L. Rev. 51, 56 (1982).
58 For the current system of election to the Knesset see: http://main.knesset.gov.il/About/Lex icon/Pages/heb_mimshal_beh.aspx (accessed February 9, 2017).
59 Section 5 of the Parties Act 5052–1992, S.H. 190.
60 Election of Members and the Allocation of Seats in the German Parliament, https://www.bundestag.de/en/parliament/elections/arithmetic (accessed February 9, 2017).

in the Knesset. Despite this threshold limitation, Israel still has a plurality of parties. In the nineteenth Knesset, there were thirteen parties, and ten parties in the twentieth Knesset.[61]

In March 2014, the electoral threshold was raised to 3.25% of the votes[62] as part of a larger reform meant to strengthen the governance and improve governmental efficiency. It should be noted that the issue of raising the electoral threshold was under a heated debate as it has many political implications.

The supporters argued, as stated above, that limiting the number of small scale parties will strengthen the governance and the governmental stability. This strengthening will prevent small scale parties from gaining political power that is disproportional to their electoral power, thus forming large blocs.[63]

On the other hand, others argued that raising the electoral threshold compromises the principle of representation and constitutional rights of different minorities such as the Arab and ultra-orthodox populations. They hold the opinion that every change in the electoral threshold must be constitutionally reviewed and a concrete public interest in raising it must be demonstrated.[64] Moreover, raising the electoral threshold will mainly harm the small parties, whereas the problem of governance and "political blackmailing" mostly comes from medium-scale parties.[65]

(3) Parliamentary vote of no-confidence

It seems that the most efficient tool the parliament has against the government is the vote of no-confidence. The parliament uses it to pressure PMs to change their ways. With this vote, the parliament substantially elects whether to continue or halt the PM's tenure. This tool grants the parliament with much power as it can oust the presiding government and change it for one that relates more with the parliament's objectives. On the other hand, excessive use of votes of no-confidence can also bring a lack of efficiency and stability, paralyzing the executive.

---

61 The political parties in the Knesset: http://main.knesset.gov.il/mk/Faction/Pages/default. aspx (accessed February 9, 2017).

62 Amendment number 62 to the Election to the Knesset Act.

63 See the speech of M.K. Ronen Hoffman in the debate in the Knesset Committee of Law and Justice, protocol number 119, pp.s 8 – 9 (21.1.2014).

64 See comment of Prof. Barak Medina in the debate in the Knesset committee on Law and Justice, protocol number 134\10, pp. 3 – 4 (10.02.2014)

65 See comment of M.K. Dov Hanin in the Knesset committee on Law and Justice, protocol number 128, p. 7 (03.02.2014)

The German Basic Law sets a mechanism for votes of no-confidence that limits the Bundestag's power, thus empowering the Chancellor.[66] A constructive vote of no-confidence is meant to form a new government. When the Bundestag wishes to terminate the Chancellor's tenure, it is required to elect a new chancellor at the same time. If the Bundestag cannot get a majority vote for replacing the chancellor, the government will remain the same. This mechanism is a significant restraint on the vote of no-confidence: while parties are likely to agree on ousting the chancellor, it is harder to reach consent as to a replacement.[67] This technique was only used once in the German federation. It was in 1982 when the Bundestag elected Helmut Kohl to replace the presiding chancellor Helmut Schmidt through a vote of no-confidence. Other than this case, there was merely one attempt to utilize this technique, in 1972 when the Bundestag unsuccessfully tried to oust Willy Brandt from his position as chancellor.

The constructive vote of no-confidence was adopted in Israel as well. And yet, the Israeli vote of no-confidence mechanism creates more difficulties for the parliament than the German counterpart. Article 28 of Basic Law: The Government stipulates that a vote of no-confidence can be made only when confidence is given in an alternative government that has announced its policy's guidelines, its composition, and its ministers. The proper way to utilize in a practical way the vote of no-confidence mechanism, according to the 2014 amendment to Article 28, still remains unclear.

The previous version of Basic Law: The Government allowed for an easier mechanism of a vote of no-confidence. The Law specified that a vote of no-confidence in the government could be made by a Knesset resolution approved by a majority of MKs,[68] and that the President could be asked to entrust an MK with forming the new government, if the latter gave written consent to it.[69] In such situations, the government was considered to have resigned from office and the president was required to appoint the MK specified in the Knesset resolution.[70] If that MK did not succeed in forming a government, the Knesset resolution would "be deemed to be a Knesset decision to disperse prior to the completion of its period of service" and new elections would be held.[71]

---

66 Grund Gesetz (GG, basic law) Article 67.
67 Ackerman, *supra* note 55, pages 654–655.
68 In the past, there has not been a requirement for a special majority, and a no-confidence vote was based on a simple majority procedure.
69 Basic Law: The Government, Section 28(b) in version at that time.
70 *Id.*, Section 28(c).
71 *Id.*, Section 28(e).

Indeed, in light of the relative ease in which the Knesset could have brought the government's tenure to an end,[72] the Israeli vote of no-confidence was a substantial mean giving the Knesset much power. If the Knesset was not pleased with the governmental policy and actions, it could pressure the government to change its ways by motions of no-confidence.

There was only one case of a vote of no-confidence terminating the government's term: in 1990, during the twelfth Knesset's tenure, the 23rd government with Yitzhak Shamir as PM fell, following a vote of no-confidence in the Knesset.[73]

(4) The PM's authority to dissolve the parliament

As mentioned above, the vote of no-confidence mechanism was made to grant the parliament authority against the PM. There is also a tool meant to balance the powers and give the PM a certain advantage—the PM's authority to disperse the parliament. This authority originated so that the British royalty that could disperse the parliament. In Germany, the system allows the chancellor to initiate a vote of confidence in the government by the Bundestag; this vote differs from the Bundestag-initiated votes of no-confidence. A chancellor who loses the vote of confidence can dissolve the Bundestag and have early elections.[74] The Bundestag can only prevent the elections if it elects a new chancellor within 21 days. Using this mechanism, chancellors can win, by the new elections, more seats in the Bundestag for their party members and by that means get the vote of confidence. This technique has successfully been utilized twice thus far: first by Willy Brandt in 1972, after nearly being outsted by a constructive vote of no-confidence, and second by Helmut Kohl in 1983.[75]

Israel has a half-way mechanism. According to this mechanism, the PM has the sole authority to dissolve the Knesset. This authority is, however, restrained by the condition that there exists a majority against the Government that prevents it from orderly activities. Another restraint on this authority is that the dis-

---

72 The Plenum – Motions of No-Confidence, http://www.knesset.gov.il/description/eng/eng_work_mel5.htm (accessed February 9, 2017); e. g., during the 11th Knesset ,165 no-confidence motions were recorded.

73 Nissan Nave, *The Knesset as a Supervisory Institution on the Government*, accessible in the virtual library of MATAH: lib.cet.ac.il/Pages/item.asp?item=8303&kwd=6200 (accessed February 9, 2017).

74 GG Art. 68.

75 Donald P. Kommers, *The Basic Law: A Fifty Year Assessment*, 53 S.M.U L. REV. 477, fn. 17. (2000).

solution of the Knesset can be made only with an approval by the President of the State.[76] The aim of this requirement is to insure stability. Another qualification is that the Knesset can intervene in 21 days to form a new Government and frustrate a new election.[77]

C. Governance

a. General

The principle of governance reflects the government's ability to fulfill its economic, defense, social, and political goals.[78] As a general rule, the public policy in democratic countries tends to be divided in different directions and be blurry. This phenomenon is a consequence of different decision makers attempting to promote different objectives. There is also the inherent discrepancy between an optimal long-term policy and an optimal short-term policy.[79]

The level of governance displayed by the government is very much a direct outcome of governmental stability. Lack of stability leads to a situation in which the government's hands are tied or, alternatively, full by dealing with political disputes,[80] thereby impairing the government's ability to fulfill its objectives.

There are, however, other factors that bear influence on the level of governance. The governance is very much dependent on the political culture in a given society. The political culture is shaped by the national experience, the public view of the government, the level of tolerance in the interaction between individuals, majority-minority relations, and the relationships among different minorities.[81]

The level of governance is also dependent on the coalition: governments built from a single party acting unanimously have a better ability to meet their goals. On the other hand, when the coalition is comprised of several parties, they have to compromise their objectives in order to maintain the coalition.

---

76 Basic Law: The Government, Section 29(a).

77 *Id.*, Section 29(b).

78 Craig Calhoun, ed. "Governability", *Dictionary of the Social Sciences* (Oxford University Press, 2002).

79 See Asher Arian et. al., *Governance and the Executive Branch in Israel*, 26 (2002).

80 See the analysis of Prof. Amnon Rubinsthien and the Secretary of the Cabinet Israel Maimon for the Prime Minister Yitzhak Shamir and Ariel Sharon in the debate of the committee of Law and Justice, protocol number 213 (05.07.2007).

81 See Gabriel Sheffer and Eyal Tzur, *President Commission to Review the Structure of Government in Israel*, The Subcommittee Report of the Megidor Commission, Democracies in Existential Shadow, 212–216 (2005).

Some say that the "political choke ring" is a substantial cause for the lack of governance in Israel. Israeli PMs must form a coalition, and compromise the public policy they wish to lead and to share their authority with many ministers. Consequently, the government lacks a clear policy and it is difficult to establish cooperation by the many ministers representing rival parties. This problem is even more serious due to the trend of fragmentation among parties that has existed in Israeli politics for a long time.[82] Furthermore, PMs are not able, practically, to fire ministers from other parties who do not obey them without coordinating the dismissal with those parties' chairmen. This is why, for example, PM Peres could not get Minister Moda'i fired in 1986 despite ongoing disputes between the two. Peres had to agree to compromise on moving Minister Moda'I from his job as minister of finance to be the minister of justice.[83]

Another cause for the lack of governance is the extensive bureaucracy. This complex system often creates difficulties for ministers to manage their offices and be able to fulfill the policies they wish to lead. The office employees reflect archeological layers of ideologies held by different ministers who lead the office, making it harder for acting ministers to fulfill their goals.[84] In this context, the situation of 1977 should be mentioned. The Likud made political *Mahapach*, or change of ruling party; in turn, the Likud ministers, new to the bureaucratic system, had to deal with senior clerks of the opposite party, and complained of difficulties in controlling their offices.[85]

The different institutions of public service limit the latitude of the government. These institutions are very powerful and professional, thus enjoying much power and prestige, making it very hard for the government to act against their opinion.[86] A good example is the Bank of Israel and the heads of the Finance Ministry's objection to the 1983 "dollarization plan" that led PM Yitzhak Shamir to waive the services of Minister of Finance Aridor.[87]

b. Governance in Israel

Much criticism was heard in the professional literature on political science about the lack of governance in the Israeli political system. For example, Prof. Yehezkel

---

82 Compare to Uriel Raichmann, *supra* note 48, page 12 and to Arian, *supra* note 79, page 113 – 117.
83 Koren and Shapira, *supra* note 30, page 57.
84 Uriel Raichmann, *supra* note 48, page 12.
85 Koren and Shapira, *supra* note 30, page 49.
86 Arian, *supra* note 79, pages 74, 89 – 94.
87 Koren and Shapira, *supra* note 30, page 110.

Dror believes that, since its founding, the Israeli government's level of governance had consistently deteriorated.[88] He believes that the government fears making decisions and, therefore, holds prior positions, without a clear policy based on a thorough and dynamic examination of Israeli reality. One expression of this state is the heavy need of legal advice, tribunals, and semi-judicial procedures in matters that are substantially subject to political governmental decisions. This phenomenon is characteristic of the government's avoidance of decision making and an attempt to hide behind the professional bureaucracy.[89] As an example of this process, Dror mentions the extensive need of backward-looking commissions of inquiry instead of utilizing forward-looking policy committees. Similarly, some state the increasing involvement of legal advisors in governmental activities and its different offices. Unlike ordinary judicial decisions, the advisor's decisions are made prior to action, and have the ability to bring governmental actions to a halt. One must keep in mind that those advisors often hold only legal knowledge and lack the professional tools to evaluate the importance of the matter brought before them.[90]

In order to avoid governmental decisions, says Dror, the government also turns to political compromises. Compromise is not necessarily better than any of its opposite choices, and the dire need of political compromises indicates a difficulty in decision making.[91] Likewise, avoiding making decisions often leads to the point where the government has only one option, so that no decision is required of the government. Consistently relying on the last resort option is very dangerous in his opinion.[92] Prof. Amnon Rubinstein and Adam Wolfson also hold the same opinion on the Israeli governance crises. In their book, *Absence of Government: How to Mend Israel's Broken System*,[93] they claim that Israel suffers—since 1977, but particularly in the last years—from a severe lack of governance; this problem is evident in the large number of governmental decisions not implemented and the government budget not being spent according to the original plan.[94]

As this author does not share the same negative estimate of the Israeli government's level of governance. Without referring to any specific subject, Israel

---

88 Yehezkel Dror, *Memo to the Prime Minister: To Build a State*, 52 (1990)

89 *Id.*, 54.

90 Reichmann, *supra* note 48, page 13; For an expansion on the rule of the attorney general about the expense of elected officials, see Arian, *supra* note 79, pages 76–89.

91 Dror, *supra* note 88, page 56.

92 *Id.*, at 60.

93 Rubinstein and Wolfson, *supra* note 41, at 85.

94 *Id.*, 70–80.

has significant achievements in many fields, indicating that the severe criticism on the lack of governance is unjustified, at least in part.

Prof. Dror holds the opinion that managing the country by improvising and avoiding a commitment to a general strategy was more suitable for the country's first years, when there was a constant uncertainty and the governmental system was still young and not institutionalized. With time, as a consequence of the government institutions taking shape and the administrative system developing established routines, the ability to improvise decreased.[95]

Prof. Dror criticizes the lack of effort by the government to introduce and implement reforms, and suggests a few explanations to this phenomenon. We will mention the main ones: first, as noted above, the tradition of the state from its early days is a tradition of improvisation, which has been highly successful but is difficult to break free from. Add to this the fact that not many Jews in the diaspora worked in government, so that experience and knowledge in the subject was not imported from the diaspora as opposed to other subjects. Second, Israel moves like a pendulum between periods of contentment, where the need for a reform is not felt, to periods of crisis, where it seems there should be plans for improving the immediate situation rather than planing for the long term. Third, the political system benefits from the current situation; the politicians enjoy great freedom of action without administrative work and discussion of real alternatives. Finally, adherence to magic solutions such as changing the election system or establishing a constitution, as well as a lack of discussion in the media of real problems, divert the spotlight from less popular but more important subjects that would improve the government.[96]

Some believe that the best way to improve governability is through reform of the Basic Law: The Government, which will give the prime minister authorities similar to those of a president in a presidential system of government. Among other things, they recommend that the prime minister should be given a veto over legislation that the Knesset will be able to overcome only by a majority vote of its members. Furthermore, the Ministry of Finance, the Civil Service Commission, and a national planning advisory system should be added to the prime minister's office. These measures will increase the prime minister's ability to implement policies without interference. To make these improvements, the stability of the reign of the prime minister should also be improved, and the ways to achieve this goal were discussed above.[97]

---

95 *Id.*, 58–59
96 *Id.*, 64–66.
97 Raichman, *supra* note 48, at 14.

D. Efficiency

As with any activity performed by any person or body, it is clear that governmental activity should be performed efficiently, especially given the huge extent of its budget. The main significance of the efficiency principle is achieving the government's objectives by utilizing the available resources in the best way.

The efficiency of the government can be improved in different ways, such as reducing unrequired personnel, unifying government offices with limited scope to one bigger office, and more.[98] Efficiency suggestions for public service and the government authorities have been the subject of discussion in several commissions in Israel. The commission that prepared the most comprehensive report regarding deficiencies in public administration and efficiency suggestions was the Kovarsky Commission.[99] The commission published a final report in 1989 where it recommended optimizing the public service by privatizing micro-level actions to outside companies and organizations, allowing government officials to focus on formulating policies and monitoring events at the macro level. Another commission that dealt with this subject was the Sanbar Commission,[100] which sought to make the relationship between the central and local governments more efficient. In the report, published in 1981, the commission recommended decentralizing the provision of citizen services to the local authorities and intensifying their independence. Doing so would free the central government from handling these services, and allow it instead to focus on national issues and challenges. It is interesting to note that the two commissions saw both the transfer of responsibility for carrying out operations to external groups and the reduction of the number of officials who are responsible for these operations as a way to increase the efficiency of the government. The privatization policy raises questions of values and principles.[101]

The principle of efficiency is the focus of tension between the desire to maintain the status of the Knesset as a legislative authority, and the growing need for secondary legislation. As we will see in the next chapter, over the years, most of the legislative actions transferred from the legislature to the executive, which acts by the way of secondary legislation. The process of passing legislation in the Knesset has many obstacles compared to the relative effectiveness

---

98 Chazan and Atmor, *supra* note 31, at 155.
99 The Public-Professional Committee for a Comprehensive Examination of the Civil Service and Institutions Receiving State *Report* (1989)
100 The State Committee for Local Government Report (1981).
101 *Globalization, Privatization and Free Market Economy* (C.P. Rao ed., 1998).

of the executive and the public administration.[102] On the other hand, the proliferation of secondary legislation violates the separation of powers, which is one of the fundamental principles of the Israeli system of government.

In the context of secondary legislation, the principle of efficiency also stands in contrast to the principle of representativeness. As we have seen above, the cumbersome legislative process in the Knesset, which requires the bill stage and the many discussions about it, helps the realization of the representativeness principle; the length of the process and its publicity allow the citizens to take part in the legislative process and express their views on the subject through their representatives. In contrast, the simpler and quicker administrative legislative process realizes the principle of efficiency, but also harms the principle of representativeness. Some believe that it is appropriate to find the middle way between these two principles, allowing citizens to be involved, albeit less, in the administrative legislative process.[103]

E. Accountability

A basic principle in shaping the systems of government is that officials, led by ministers and executive heads, are responsible for the public and for the relevant institutions. The government and the prime minister's responsibility is for the Knesset. The ministers' responsibility is for the prime minister, and they are also responsible for the areas and activities of their offices according to the different fundamental concepts of responsibility. The responsibility of the government, the prime minister, and the ministers has many shades and dimensions. This responsibility is expressed in a series of basic concepts and mechanisms that maintain the responsibility of the government, the prime minister, and the ministers in a parliamentary system.[104] The concepts of ministerial responsibility, shared responsibility, and legal responsibility—which is divided into civil responsibility, administrative responsibility, and criminal responsibility—should also be mentioned. There are also the concepts of direct and indirect responsibilities, as well as the responsibility of the ministers to the parliament (responsible government), and the concepts of public and ethical responsibilities.

The various types of responsibility the government and its members have, can be sorted into a number of conceptual divisions. Maintaining the distinction

---

102 Zamir, *supra* note 23.
103 *Id.*
104 The government owes a duty of trust to the people, see 6163/92 H.C.J *Eisenberg v. Minister of Housing*, 47(2) P.D. 229 at 260 (1993).

between the various types of responsibilities is important, but many times they overlap in the public discourse.[105]

The public responsibility reflects the government's responsibility towards the general public, which stems from the fiduciary duty of the government to the state and the public; it embodies the government's duty to act in their favor only. This responsibility is enforced by the media, pressure groups, and the Knesset, with the latter making an important contribution to maintaining the government's fiduciary duties by encouraging public scrutiny.[106]

The political responsibility refers to the obligation to keep the political "rules of the game" fair towards the party members, the members of other parties with which an agreement was made, and the general public. In Israel, this responsibility is usually interpreted as restrictively, but sanctions in the parties' regulations may apply in cases of violation of an official's duty.[107]

The legal responsibility is to the law institutions and it is enforced by the courts. The members of the government have several types of legal responsibilities, including civil and criminal responsibilities as does any person, and administrative responsibilities in their capacity as civil servants.[108]

The moral responsibility seeks to realize the principles of morality, justice, and professionalism.[109] In Israel, efforts are being made to develop an ethical code for the ministers, but there are no formal mechanisms to enforce this responsibility.

In addition, Section 4 of the Basic Law: The Government provides for two fundamental principles of the governmental action: the principle of shared responsibility and the principle of ministerial responsibility.

The principle of shared responsibility states that the government bears collective responsibility towards the Knesset and, as a result, each of its members

---

105 see Ronald Pennock, *The Problem of Responsibility*, in Carl Friedrich ed., *Responsibility*, 3 (1960); John Lucas *Responsibility* (1993).

106 Raphael Cohen-Almagor "On Public Responsibility"; Raphael Cohen-Almagor, Ori Arbel-Ganz, Asa Kasher (editors) *Public Responsibility in Israel* 19 (2012); Itzhak Zamir "Introduction: Public Responsibility"; Raphael Cohen-Almagor, Ori Arbel-Ganz, Asa Kasher (editors) *Public Responsibility in Israel* 8 (2012); Arye Naor "On the Responsibility of the Prime Minister"; Raphael Cohen-Almagor, Ori Arbel-Ganz, Asa Kasher (editors) *Public Responsibility in Israel* 161 (2012); Ori Arbel Ganz and David Nachmias, *Public Responsibility of Elected Officials in Israel: Crossing the Bounds of Reasonableness*, Israel Affairs 602 (2008).

107 Frank Knight, *Political Responsibility in a Democracy*, in Carl Friedrich ed., *Responsibility*, 171 (1960); H.L.A Hart, *Punishment and Responsibility: Essays in Philosophy of Law*, 211 (1968).

108 The government members do not have criminal and civil responsibility like any other person as they enjoy immunity.

109 Harry Frankfurt, *Alternate Possibilities and Moral Responsibility*, 66 J. Phil 829, 860 (1969).

is fully responsible for its actions and omissions. By virtue of this principle, the government members are obliged to present "a united front" and to refrain from expressing stances opposite to that of the government, except in cases where prior authorization was given, for example, in a coalition agreement. This principle may be enforced through the transfer of disputed powers or by dismissal of the aberrant minister.[110]

The principle of ministerial responsibility states that ministers have responsibility towards the Knesset regarding the activities of their office, on subjects they have authority to intervene in and guide. This principle is derived from the fact that, while the government is the head of the public administration, the ministers are the ones who run most of the administrative offices. As part of the English model implemented in Israel, there are many expressions of ministerial responsibility, such as responsibility to report and update the Knesset, correcting omissions and deficiencies that were found in the functioning of the office, and in exceptional cases taking personal responsibility for deficiencies in the minister's area of responsibility.[111]

F. Public Confidence in Government

A fundamental principle of the government is keeping and fulfilling the public confidence in the government and in the public officials who operate its various branches. The government cannot function efficiently unless it enjoys the public confidence. The requirement of maintaining the public confidence in the government is important for all the systems of the government: the judiciary branch, the executive branch, and the legislative branch. In the case of the executive branch, public confidence is required in the government as a body, in the prime minister as the head of the executive branch, and in each of the ministers separately. Rules and norms on both the legal sphere and the public sphere are derived from the public confidence principle. In the public sphere, public officers who do not have the public confidence cannot continue to hold their office. This principle is true for every position in every state authority. On the legal front, many rules were derived from the fundamental principle of the public confidence in the government.

This principle is reflected in a long line of decisions covering different subjects and angles of the government and its ministers' functions. In the Deri de-

---

110 *Id.*
111 *Id.*

cision, the court ruled that following the serious charges brought against Minister Deri, if the prime minister did not exercise his power to dismiss Deri according to Article 21a of the Basic Law: The Government (today Article 22(b) of the Basic Law), it would be unreasonable under the circumstances, notwithstanding the fact that the government enjoys the Knesset confidence and there is no explicit provision in this case.[112] Following this matter, it was decided in the case of Deputy Minister Pinhasi that, when exercising his discretion, the prime minister has to consider the effect on the public confidence of leaving the deputy minister in his role, which leads inevitably to the conclusion that he has to be dismissed.[113] It is important to note that the courts have created a connection between the fundamental principle of the public confidence in the government and the principle that the minister is devoted to the public. By virtue of this relationship, laws regarding the rules of conduct that apply to ministers were established.

In the case of *Tzaban*, the court ruled that because they are part of the judiciary branch, rabbinic judges cannot engage in political activity, even if it is permitted by the rabbinate, because this kind of behavior undermines the public confidence, the judiciary branch, and the principle of separation of powers.[114] In the case of *Eisenberg*, the court disqualified the appointment of Yossi Ginosar as the director general of the Ministry of Construction and Housing because the appointment was extremely unreasonable, given his involvement in the Bus 300 affair and the Izzat Nafso affair during his tenure as head of a department in the Shin Bet.[115] Similarly, regarding Sarid, the appointment of Ehud Yatom as the head of Counter-Terrorism was disqualified because of his involvement in the Bus 300 affair.[116] In the case of *Ometz*, the court ruled unlawful the decision of the city council to refrain from discussion of removing from their positions the mayor of Nazareth Illit, Shimon Gapso, and the mayor of Ramat Hasharon, Itzhak Rochberger, despite the fact that indictments were handed down against the two.[117] In this affair, it was decided that even if the public would have chosen

---

112 H.C.J 93/3094 *The Movement for Quality Government in Israel v. The Government of Israel,* 47(5) P.D. 404, 419 – 423 (1993).
113 H.C.J 4267/93 *Amitai—Citizens for Good Governance and Integrity v. The Prime Minister of Israel,* 47 P.D. 441, 466 – 467, 474 (1993).
114 H.C.J 84/732 *MK Yair Tzaban v. The Ministry of Religious Services and Rabbinic Judge Rabbi Ovadia Yosef,* 40(4) P.D. 141.
115 H.C.J 92/6163 *Eisenberg v. The Ministry of Construction and Housing,* 47(2) P.D. 229 (1993).
116 H.C.J 01/4668 *Sarid v. The Prime Minister of Israel,* 56(2) P.D. 265 (2003).
117 Decision without explanations: H.C.J 4921/13 *Ometz Citizens for Good Governance and Integrity v. Mayor of Ramat Hasharon Itzhak Rochberger* (published on Nevo,, 17.09.2013); the reasoned decision from 14.10.2013.

these mayors again in the upcoming elections the court would have needed to intervene to maintain the public confidence and good governance.[118] A similar statement was made in the case of the *Mayor of Bat Yam*, Shlomo Lahiani, after the city council decided not to remove him from office.[119]

G. The Reforms Regarding the Government and the Knesset in 2014

a. General

On March 11th, 2014, the Knesset passed a series of amendments to various laws relating to the functioning of the government in Israel.[120] One group covered amendments to Basic Law: The Government, Basic Law: The Knesset, and Basic Law: The Economy of the State. A series of amendments to the Elections Law to the Knesset, the Party Financing Law, and the Knesset Law were also added. Before the series of amendments was accepted, the bill for the first group of laws was called "The Basic Law Bill: The Government (Amendment) (Increasing the Governance)." The second group of amendments was called "Knesset Elections Bill (Amendment 61) (Raising the Electoral Threshold and Increasing Governance)." According to the proponents of the bills,[121] the proposed law changes are intended to enhance the governance of the Israeli government and increase its stability.[122] In general, we can say that the guiding line of these legislative reforms was emphasizing stability and governance considerations at the expense of the representativeness principle. Hereinafter, we will discuss and give a bit of detail about the major changes that were made.

b. Restrictions on the Government Composition and Size

A series of provisions which were accepted in a legislative reform reflect a tendency to reduce the number of members of the cabinet. These provisions were put in the amendments of Clauses 5 and 25 of Basic Law: The Government.

---

118 *Id.*, at 53–54.
119 H.C.J 6549/13 *Ometz Citizens for Good Governance and Integrity v. Bat Yam Mayor* (published on Nevo, 20.10.2013)
120 This legislation has been named in the media discourse as "The Governance Laws".
121 MKs David Rotem, Robert Ilatov, Hamad Amar, and Ronen Hoffman.
122 Explanatory Notes to the Bill: Knesset Bills, 512 – 15 Av 5773, 22.7.2013, p. 46–47. It should be noted that, naturally, changes have occurred between the bills versions and the corrections that have been actually received, though the principles are similar.

In Clause 5 of this Basic Law, a limit was imposed on the number of ministers in general. A small provision was added in Clause 5(f) saying that the number of ministers, including the prime minister, will not exceed 19, unless the Knesset authorized a bigger government from the beginning or, alternatively, if additional ministers were added later by a majority of seventy MKs. This clause is not applicable to the 20th Knesset.

2. The Institutions of the State

A. The President

When Israel was established, "the Provisional Council of State enacted the Law and Administration Ordinance, which laid the foundations of government and its powers."[123] While the Ordinance made no mention of a presidency, the chairman of the Council, David Ben-Gurion, suggested that the body elect Dr. Haim Weizman as the president of the Council. The suggestion was accepted; however, it was clear that the position was symbolic and did not have any legal powers. The president acts as a non-partisan, representative head of state, whose actions must be approved by the prime minister or another government minister that is authorized to act for that purpose.[124]

All the functions of the president are defined by Basic Law: The President of the State. Outside of the ceremonial functions,[125] the president has three primary powers: pardons and sentence reductions, appointing Knesset members to the Government, and consent to Knesset dispersal at the request of the prime minister.[126] The Knesset elects the president to a seven-year term. Any Israeli citizen may be a candidate and the presidency is limited to a single term.[127]

The Israeli president has both substantive and procedural immunity. Substantive immunity shields the president from legal action relating to presidential functions and exercise of powers. Procedural immunity shields the president from any criminal charges being brought against him while in office.[128] Substan-

---

123 *Id.*, at 67.
124 *Id*; see also H. Klinghoffer, *Die Stellung des Staatsprasidenten im Israelischen Verfassungsrecht"*. Die Moderne Demokratie und ihr Recht, II, 743, Tubingen, J.C.B. Mohr (1966).
125 These functions include signing laws enacted by the Knesset, signing conventions with foreign states that have been ratified by the Knesset, and confirming the appointment of judges.
126 Basic Law: The President of the State, 1964, S.H. § 11.
127 *Id.*, Article 6.
128 Basic Law: The President of the State, §§ 13–14.

tive immunity does not apply to prohibited functions that are not connected to the functions of the president. For example, if the president has accepted a bribe, he will have procedural immunity only, and only for the period of his presidency.[129] Additionally, there is no judicial review of presidential decisions.[130]

While most of the president's powers are ceremonial, the greatest power is that to grant pardons. The power to pardon leaves much discretion to the president, who may set the conditions for the pardon and decide how a particular prisoner will be pardoned (annulment of a conviction, rehabilitation, etc.).[131] The grounds for granting pardon are varied, and include absence of guilt, state reasons, considerations of justice, and more.[132]

B. The Knesset

The Knesset is Israel's unicameral legislature. It has 120 members who are elected to four-year terms. Because there is no formal written constitution in Israel, there are no prima facie restrictions on the Knesset. However, there are two types of limitations. The first limitation was imposed by Israel's Supreme Court. The Court recognizes Basic Laws to have supreme constitutional status, meaning that no legislation can violate any of the Basic Laws. The second limitation is more theoretical. While the Supreme Court has not repealed a statute for violating a democratic value, the Justices have stated many times that they can and will.[133] Despite these limitations, the Knesset can enact, amend, or repeal Basic Laws by a simple majority,[134] except for Basic Law: Freedom of Occupation and Basic Law: The Government, which requires 61 members to amend or repeal.

Members of the Knesset are not representative and free; they must act according to the will of the people of the State. The platform of the parties is pre-

---

129 *Id*; see also Knesset Member Immunity, Rights and Duties Law, 5711–1951 about Knesset Member and Prime Minister immunity.

130 *Id.*, at p. 69. Basic Law: The President, Article 13–14.

131 Article 18 Criminal Register and Rehabilitation Law, 5741–1981

132 See for example A.D. H.C.J 219/09 *Minister of Justice v. Nir Zohar*, p.10 (29.11.2009) available at (Hebrew): http://elyon1.court.gov.il/files/09/190/002/N09/09002190.N09.htm

133 See for example the opinon of Justice Barak in H.C.J 910/86 *Ressler v. Minister of Defense*, 42(2) P.D. 441; see also Aharon Barak, *Foreword: A Judge on Judging: The Role of a Supreme Court in a Democracy*, 116 Harvard Law Review 19, 103 (2002) available at http://digitalcommons.law.yale.edu/fss_papers/3692 (accessed February 9, 2017).

134 See for example H. Klinghoffer, *Legislative Reactions to Judicial Decisions in Public Law"*, 18 *Isr. L. Rev. 30 (1954)*.

sented to the public; however, they can change their platform if needed. Members of the Knesset can change their minds regarding issues without sanction.[135]

Members of the Knesset enjoy many privileges and immunities. They are immune for acts performed within the scope of their duties,[136] as well as being immune from criminal prosecution during the time they are in office. The details of Knesset member immunity are laid out in the Immunity of Knesset Members, their Privileges and Obligations Law, 1951.[137]

Immunity for acts performed within the scope of duties cannot be removed and protects a member for life. In order to be protected, the member's action must be legal and official. Any normal or reasonable action that has a close relation to the member's official functions will be assumed to have immunity.[138]

Criminal immunity for Knesset members protects procedurally against actions that do not rise out of Knesset duties and functions. This immunity can be removed and does not apply after a member's term has concluded. Until 2005, when a Knesset member had committed a criminal offense, the Attorney General had to ask the Knesset to remove that member's immunity. In 2005, the Knesset amended the Immunity Law to revoke immunity for members if an indictment has been filed against them; if such situation occurred, then that Knesset member must request for the immunity to apply.[139]

In addition to immunities, Knesset Members enjoy the privileges of freedom from arrest, exemption from compulsory military service, and complete freedom of movement.[140]

Generally, a Knesset member's term of office terminates with the Knesset's term, and removing a member prior to that is quite difficult. If members are unable to perform their functions, they keep his seat unless they resign. Members can be removed early only if they have been "convicted of an offence which is

---

135 Knesset Member Immunity, Rights and Duties Law, 5711–1951; see also Gregory Mahler, *The Knesset: Parliament in the Israeli Political System, 88 (Associated Press, 1981)*.

136 Including votes, written or spoken expression of viewpoints, or acts performed within the framework of his function; see also *The Rules of Ethics For Members of the Knesset*, available at http://www.knesset.gov.il/rules/eng/Ethics_Rules.pdf (accessed February 9, 2017).

137 *Id.*

138 *Id.*, see also "The Rights and Duties of Members of Knesset" at the Knesset website, available online: https://www.knesset.gov.il/description/eng/eng_work_chak1.htm (accessed February 9, 2017).

139 Knesset Member Immunity, Rights and Duties Law (Amendment no. 33), 5765–2015 available at (Hebrew): https://www.knesset.gov.il/Laws/Data/law/2015/2015.pdf (accessed February 9, 2017).

140 *Id.*

tainted by moral turpitude."[141] The Attorney General determines if the offense bears moral turpitude, and then the member's removal is automatic.

The primary function of the Knesset is to pass legislation. It has exclusive authority to enact law. Laws can pertain to any subject so long as they do not contradict the Basic Laws. The Knesset also has a representative function, being that they are elected proportionally through the people of Israel. Additionally, the Knesset supervises the executive branch—the Government must resign if the Knesset offers a vote of no confidence.[142] A vote of no confidence must be joined by sixty-one members of the Knesset. Another supervisory fuction is the Knesset's ability to enact legislation regarding sources of financing and use of the state budget.[143]

One of the most unique functions of the Knesset is its constitutional power. It has the ability to enact "constitutional" provisions by adding to and amending the Basic Law. This power is not unlimited, and the Knesset is limited to enactments that express the fundamental values of society.[144]

During the legislative process, bills are read and debated three times. This process allows members to reconsider their positions, brings the bills to the public's attention, allows the public to express an opinion, and assures that there will be enough time for an examination of the bill. Bills can be introduced by the Government, Knesset committees, and Knesset members. Knesset committees can summon experts and interested parties in order for them to express their viewpoint regarding bills being discussed. If the Government does not support a bill, it requires the support of at least fifty members during each reading of the bill. If an individual member proposes a bill, it must pass two preliminary stages before it can be read. First, the Speaker and his or her deputies must confirm that the bill can be tabled and, second, a vote is held in the chamber to approve the submission of the bill to a committee in preparation for the first reading.[145]

The first reading of a bill is a general debate. If the bill achieves a majority vote, it will be transferred to the most suitable committee, where it will further

---

141 *Id.*
142 See for example the Knesset press release regarding the 2014 revision to the vote of no-confidence available at: https://www.knesset.gov.il/spokesman/eng/PR_eng.asp?PRID=11200 (accessed February 9, 2017).
143 Foundations of Budget Law, 5745 – 1985; see also Menachem Mautner, *Law & the Culture of Israel*, 148 (2011) discussing budgetary allocations to religious institutions by the Sass party.
144 Daphne Barak-Erez, *Broadening the Scope of Judicial Review in Israel: Between Activism and Restraint*, 118 – 119 Indian J. ConLaw 8 (2009).
145 Mahler, *supra* note 135, at 90 – 95.

be debated. This is when the expert opinions are heard. After these debates, the bill is tabled for its second reading to the chamber. In this reading, each clause of the bill is considered separately. If there are reservations, the bill must be sent back to the committee to reflect the reservations. The third reading usually takes place immediately after the second reading, with no further debate. If there were reservations, the third reading will take place one week after the second reading. If a bill has been approved in the third reading, the legislative process is complete. In order to become law, the president must sign it and then it must be published in *Reshumot*.[146]

The Knesset has the power to determine its own rules and procedures by a majority vote, subject to judicial review by the Supreme Court.[147] However, the court has rarely exercised this power, saving it for "extreme circumstances, when a substantive defect which affects the basic principles of our constitutional regime and our democratic concepts is discovered in a provision of the rules adopted by the Knesset plenum, will judicial review be exercised over a provision of the rules."[148]

The Knesset can debate and decide issues with any number of members present; decisions are made by a majority vote of those participating. The Knesset is headed by the Speaker of the Knesset, who is elected from the Knesset. The Speaker conducts the sessions and debates, determines voting order for motions, and decides the results of the votes. He or she grants the right to speak to other members, comments while they speak, calls the members to order, and can even remove members from the chamber. The Speaker is also in charge of preparing the Knesset's annual budget. Additionally, when the president is abroad, the Speaker stands in.[149]

Most of the Knesset's work is done through committees. Composition of the committees is determined proportionally in accordance to party representation. The Organizing Committee contains all factions according to size, and this committee proposes the composition of the standing committees. Committee proceedings occur regardless of the number of members present. Additionally, the sessions are made public only if the committee allows it.[150]

---

146 *Id.*, at 95–97.
147 H.C.J 389/80 *Dapei Zahav Ltd. v. The Broadcasting Authority*, 35(1) P.D. 421 (1980).
148 H.C.J 669/85 *Kahane v. Speaker of the Knesset*, 40(4) P.D. 393, 399.
149 Article 16 of Basic Law: The Government.
150 Id., Article 31.

C. The Executive

The executive branch is in charge of implementing laws adopted by the Knesset. The executive has broad discretion concerning how government powers will be exercised. "The Government is the executive authority of the State."[151] The government consists of the prime pinister and the other ministers. The prime minister must be a Knesset member, but the other ministers do not have this requirement. However, most of the ministers are Knesset members.[152]

The prime minister must form the Government, subject to Knesset approval. Subject to government approval, the prime minister may appoint a deputy minister. Deputy ministers must be Knesset members.[153]

In order to be a minister, a person must be a citizen and a resident of Israel. People who have dual citizenship with another country must renounce that citizenship in order to serve.[154] A person cannot be a minister if they are serving as president, chief rabbi, state comptroller, or in judicial and other positions. Also, once appointed, a minister cannot serve as a head to a local authority, chairman of a governmental authority or institution, or in a public body.[155] Additionally, a person who has been convicted of an offense and sentenced to prison, and seven years have not passed since the punishment was concluded, is not eligible to be a minister unless the chairman of the Central Election Committee states that the offense did not carry moral turpitude.[156] Further, if ministers are convicted of an offense carrying moral turpitude, their tenure will be terminated.[157]

The prime minister may, at will, remove ministers from their position.[158] However, the Supreme Court has ruled that there are circumstances in which this removal is mandatory. For example, ministers must be removed if they have been indicted for acts carrying moral turpitude, even if there is no conviction. Criminal investigation does not warrant removal.[159]

The president chooses a Knesset member to form the Government. The member has twenty-eight days; however, the period can be extended for no more than

---

151 *Id.*, Article 1.
152 *Id.*, Article 5.
153 *Id.*, Article 3.
154 *Id.*, Article 6.
155 *Id.*
156 *Id.*
157 *Id.*, Article 23.
158 *Id.*, Article 22.
159 H.C.J 3094/93 *Movement for the Quality of Government v. Government of Israel*, 47(5) P.D. 404, 419, 428 (1993).

fourteen additional days. If that member is unable to form the Government, the president may select another member, who has twenty-eight days with no possibility of extension.[160] If a Government cannot be formed, the Knesset will be dismissed and there will be new elections.[161]

Once the member has formed the Government, he or she must notify the president and the Speaker of the Knesset. Within seven days, the Knesset must vote on the new Government. The Government convenes as soon as the Knesset gives a vote of confidence.[162]

A new Government must be formed when a new Knesset is elected, when the prime minister has resigned, when the prime minister dies or is unable to fulfill duties for more than 100 consecutive days, when the prime minister has been convicted of an offense that carries moral turpitude, when a prime minister is no longer a Knesset member, or if the Knesset has expressed no-confidence in the prime minister.[163]

Members of the Government have the same immunities as Knesset members. They also have the same prohibitions pertaining to additional occupations as Knesset members.[164] However, there are additional prohibitions that apply only to members of the Government. Members of the Government cannot be on the board of directors of a company or other association for three years after termination from office if that company received a concession from the State during their tenure. This applies to prime ministers and deputy ministers, if the concession was received from the office in which they served.[165] Additionally, ministers cannot handle matters in which they have a personal interest.[166]

"The Government is collectively responsible to the Knesset."[167] This makes all members of the Government responsible for its decisions, regardless of whether they supported or proposed the decision. It also "restricts activities of members of the Government with respect to their criticism of the Government, the initiation of legislation [,] and voting in the Knesset against the Government's position on a particular issue."[168] Additionally, a prime minister can re-

---

160 Article 8 Basic Law: The Government.
161 *Id.*, at 9.
162 *Id.*, at 13.
163 *Id.*, at 20 – 21.
164 *Id.*, at 17 and 23.
165 Section 14 of the Immunity Law.
166 Government Resolution No.2801 (440/61) (28.11.02).
167 Article 4 of Basic Law: The Government.
168 Suzie Navot, *Constitutional Law of Israel*, 106 (2007).

move ministers if they undermine the Government's position on a particular issue.[169]

The ministers have many governmental powers. Each minister has powers conferred to them by specific laws that pertain to the activities of their ministry. Ministers can delegate their powers to civil servants in other bodies. However, the power of enacting regulations cannot be delegated.[170]

Ministers must report to the Knesset, the public, and all the bodies related to their ministry "regarding all acts, omissions, and failures of the ministry in his charge."[171] Ministers bear responsibility for all acts and omissions of their ministry. The ministers determine the general policy of their ministry.[172] They can also intervene and exercise governmental powers that belong to other bodies.[173]

Members of the Government are responsible for developing the policy of the executive branch. This function is distinctly political. Because of this, their actions are not bound by administrative laws that bind other bodies, such as the requirements to base decisions in a factual basis, to listen to all bodies that may be harmed by a decision, to give reasoned decisions, or to publish decisions.[174]

The Government has wide discretion to determine its working procedures. Section 31(f) of Basic Law: The Government states that "The Government will set work and debate procedures, and decision-making processes in the Government, whether permanent or for a specific matter."[175] The section does not contain any provisions relating to the number of members required to form a quorum at government meetings.[176] With the approval of the Knesset, the Government may change the division of the roles of the ministers, combine or divide ministries, abolish or create new ministries, or transfer areas of duties from one to another.[177]

Government and ministerial committee debates and decisions that relate to state security and foreign relations are to remain confidential. Disclosure or publication of them is prohibited. Additionally, if the Government declares that the secrecy of matters are essential to the State, they cannot be disclosed or publish-

---

169 Article 26 of Basic Law: The Government.
170 *Id.*, at 33.
171 Navot, *supra* note 168, at 109.
172 *Id.*
173 Article 34 of Basic Law: The Government.
174 See Articles 1, 4, 32. 37 of Basic Law: The Government.
175 *Id.*, Article 31.
176 *Id.*
177 *Id.*

ed.[178] To prevent leaks, the Government will convene a regular meeting, and then declare it a Ministerial Committee for Matters of National Security. However, government leaks remain a permanent fixture of Israeli politics.[179]

D. The Judiciary

Israel enjoys an independent judiciary with great public confidence in the courts. The judiciary is divided into three categories: criminal, civil, and public. Criminal and civil matters are adjudicated by the general courts: Magistrates, Districts, and the Supreme Court. The Supreme Court hears appeals from the lower courts. Public matters, disputes between the citizen and the sovereign authorities, are adjudicated differently. These matters are submitted directly to the Supreme Court.[180]

Along with the general courts, there are specialty courts. These courts include religious, labor, military, and administrative courts. The general courts have general jurisdiction over criminal, civil, and administrative matters. Religious courts have jurisdiction over matters of personal status, such as marriage and divorce. Labor courts have jurisdiction over matters of labor relations. Military courts have jurisdiction over individuals in the military. In recent years, other specialty courts have been established. The Court of Administrative Affairs was established to alleviate the docket of the Supreme Court. Additionally, family courts have been established in order to keep all family matters in the same court, in front of judges that specialize in family law.[181]

Civil and criminal trials are adversarial. Advocates present the positions of the parties, and the judge seeks to find the truth in each case. The parties or their attorneys submit the evidence and ask the questions. The judge plays an active role, asking clarifying questions. The judge also acts as the gatekeeper, deciding of the admissibility of the evidence and the questions. In certain cases, a judge may request specific evidence or ask questions that the parties have deliberately left out. This helps the judge find the factual truth.[182]

---

178 *Id.*, Article 35.
179 Mohammed El-Nawawy, *The Israeli-Egyptian Peace Process in the Reporting of Western Journalists*, 167 (2002).
180 Basic Law: The Judiciary.
181 Articles 32–59 Courts Law [Combined Versioned], 5744–1984 and Family Courts Law, 5755–1955.
182 Issachar Rosen-Zvi, *The Civil Process* 31 (Sacher Institute, Hebrew University Press, 2015) (Hebrew).

Judges in Israel are appointed by the president once they have been elected by the Judges Election Committee. The committee has nine members: the Minister of Justice, one other minister, two Knesset members, three Supreme Court justices, and two representatives from the Israel Bar Association. These appointments are free from political consideration. Judicial appointments are for life, but in practice, judges typically retire at age seventy. To be a magistrate judge, an individual must be a lawyer, member of the Israel Bar Association, and have practices or taught law for five or more years, two of which must be in Israel. To be a district court judge, an individual must have been a magistrate judge for at least four years, and practiced law, held a judicial position, or taught law for six or more continuous years. To be a Supreme Court Justice, an individual must have been a district court judge for five years, or have been an attorney, held a judicial position, or have taught law for ten or more years. If someone does not meet these criteria, one can still become a Supreme Court Justice if they are regarded as an "eminent jurist." The Supreme Court has traditionally consisted of females, religious judges, and in 2003, an Arab judge.[183]

The judiciary must be completely independent. To ensure this, judges are guaranteed substantive, personal, and institutional independence. Substantive independence means that a judge is not subject to any authority other than the law itself. Essentially, there is no person of authority above a judge. Judges cannot be held criminally liable for their decisions, even if they exceed the boundaries of their powers. Personal independence means that judges are not supervised by the executive branch. Judges can be removed only in extraordinary circumstances, and the decision is made by the Judges Selection Committee, requiring a majority vote of seven of the nine members.[184] Institutional independence means that the Minister of Justice is in charge of the administrative affairs of the judicial branch. At first glance, it appears that the judicial branch is dependent on the executive branch; however in practice, there are mechanisms to ensure judicial independence. For example, the law imposes restrictions on expressing opinions in response to judicial decisions, or regarding pending decisions. These laws are intended to prevent any sort of influence on the decision-making process.[185]

Each city in Israel has a magistrate court. Concerning criminal matters, magistrate courts have jurisdiction over offenses that are punishable by fines and offenses that carry a statutory prison sentence of less than seven years. In regards

---

183 For the legislative provisions, see Article 4 of Basic Law: The Judiciary; Article 6 Courts Law.
184 *Id.*, at 14.
185 *Id.*, Article 71.

to civil matters, magistrate courts have jurisdiction over all claims except those relating to immovable property where the value is more than ILS 2,500,000.[186] The courts sit as a one-judge panel; however, the president of the court may decide that a particular matter be heard by a three-judge panel. Magistrate court decisions are appealed to the district courts.[187]

Israel is divided into six districts in which the district courts sit. These districts are Jerusalem, Tel-Aviv, Haifa, Be'er Sheva, Centre, and Nazareth. The district courts serve as a trial court for matters not under the jurisdiction of the magistrate courts, as well as an appellate court for magistrate court decisions. As a trial court, the district courts hear civil claims with a value in dispute more than ILS 2,500,000, and criminal offenses with a punishment of more than seven years of imprisonment. Generally, the courts sit as a one-judge panel, but specific matters statutorily require a three-judge panel. These matters include offenses carrying a potential punishment of ten or more years of imprisonment, appeals, and any other matter that the president of the district court orders.[188]

The Supreme Court serves as a court of last resort for appeals of district court decisions, as well as the High Court of Justice. The Supreme Court is composed of fifteen justices. It sits in three-judge panels, but the President of the Supreme Court can request for a case to be heard by a larger panel. For example, cases that present constitutional questions are often heard by panels of nine or eleven justices.[189]

While all trial court judgments may be appealed, there is no automatic right of appeal for appellate court decisions. A second appeal can only be heard if it was granted by the original trial court, or the appellate court itself. Supreme Court decisions cannot be appealed, even when acting as a trial court. If the Court sits as a three-judge panel, it can decide to conduct a further hearing in front of a five- or more-judge panel. Further hearings can be held when a Supreme Court ruling contradicts an earlier ruling, or if a case is important, difficult, or novel so as to warrant a further hearing. This ensures the stability of the judicial system.[190]

Claims that an individual has been aggrieved by the State can be submitted directly to the Supreme Court. Through this jurisdiction, the Court develops the constitutional law of the State. While the Court can invalidate lower court decisions, it can also invalidate military decisions on the ground that they are unrea-

---

186 At the time this text was written, this sum was approximately € 531,712.
187 *Id.*, Article 52 of the Courts Law.
188 *Id.*, Article 40.
189 *Id.*, Article 26.
190 *Id.*, Article 30.

sonable or exceed powers. The Court has also extended its review powers to internal procedures of the Knesset, and broadened the scope of the rules of public law (for example, the principle of equality) to apply to government companies and certain private bodies.[191]

The Supreme Court has wide discretion in determining whether or not to hear a case. Petitioners must show that they have standing, meaning that they have been personally, significantly, and directly harmed by the matter addressed in their petition. There must be a true dispute to be decided, not merely a public grievance. However, in high profile cases, the Court has intervened even if the petitioner had no personal interest in the matter. A petitioner's claim must also be justiciable. Some petitions are inappropriate for the Court because they present a political question that must be resolved by other branches of the government. This allows the Court to avoid sensitive public issues. Political questions include matters of political parties, foreign relations, and review of military authorities. More recently, the Court has relaxed its barriers concerning standing and justiciability and have heard cases that do not completely meet these standards.[192]

The Administrative Affairs Courts were established in 2000. District courts may sit as an Administrative Affairs Court and decided matters relating to "municipal taxes, education, religious councils, tenders, non-profit organizations, licensing of businesses, tourism, planning and construction, weapons, population administration, public housing, transport, renovation and maintenance of houses, parties, credit supply services, registration of currency supply services, [and] animals."[193] Formerly, these matters were under the jurisdiction of the Supreme Court, but in 2000 the law sought to reduce the burden of the High Court, granting the jurisdiction to the district courts. If a case before the district court raises an issue of great importance, sensitivity, or urgency, it may be transferred to the Supreme Court. Cases before the Administrative Affairs Court are heard by a single judge. To sit as an Administrative Affairs judge, a district court judge must be specially trained in administrative law. These judges sit for four-year terms.[194]

In 1995, the family courts were established in order to hear cases involving family affairs. These courts hear cases involving "maintenance, guardianship, maternity and paternity, return of abducted minors, and actions based on specific legislation, such as marriage age, legal competency and guardianship, determination of age, property relations between spouses, adoption of children, and

---

191 See for instance Itzhak Zamir, *Courts and Politics in Israel*, 523 Public Law (1991).
192 Navot, *supra* note 168, 127.
193 Article 1 of Administrative Courts Law, 5760–2000
194 *Id.*

prevention of domestic violence."[195] Marriages and divorces are the exclusive jurisdiction of the religious courts. In family court, each family has its own judge that will adjudicate any matters relating to that same family. The rationale is that the judge will have a familiarity with the family and will have a better understanding of their dispute. Family courts seek to preserve the family unit and will exhaust all avenues of dispute resolution, namely mediation. The family courts involve social workers and psychologists in their decision-making.[196]

The religious courts have been around long before the establishment of the State. These courts apply religious law of each community. Because there are multiple religious communities, the religious court system consists of *Shara'ite* courts (Muslim), Druze Courts, and Rabbinical courts (Jewish), which apply the religious laws of each community. The jurisdiction of the Rabbinical courts is limited to marriage and divorce of Jews who are citizens and residents of Israel, whereas the *Shara'ite* courts have general jurisdiction over all matters of personal status of Muslims.[197]

The labor courts provide a specialized forum for labor disputes in order to balance the interests of workers and employers. There are regional courts which serve as courts of first instances, with the National Labor Court serving as the appellate court. These courts have jurisdiction over worker-employer relations and disputes, as well as some criminal matters "such as the Minimum Wage Law, the Equal Opportunities for Labor Law, the Prevention of Sexual Harassment Law and others."[198] Along with the judges, cases are decided along with public representatives, including a representative for the worker and a representative for the employer.[199]

In addition to formal courts, Israel also has administrative tribunals. There are about one hundred of these judicial and quasi-judicial tribunals. These tribunals resolve disputes between citizens and authorities, saving time and money.[200]

The status of the judiciary and the definition and authority of the court structure are spelled out in the Judges Law of 1953, the Courts Laws of 1957, the Rab-

---

195 Family Court Law, *supra* note 181. See also Shaul Shochat, *Family Courts – A Court Indeed?*, 2 Mishpaha Bamishpat 2009.

196 Family Court Law, *supra* note 181, Article 5.

197 Yüksel Sezgin, The Israeli Millet System: Examining Legal Pluralism Through Lenses of Nation-Building and Human Rights, 43 Israel Law Review 631 (2010).

198 Labour Courts Law, 5726 – 1969.

199 *Id.*, Article *18.*

200 Itzhak Galnoor, *Public Management in Israel: Development, Structure, Function and Reforms*, 39 (2011).

binical Courts Jurisdiction (Marriage and Divorce) Law of 1953, the Dayanim Law of 1955 (s., *dayan*, rabbinical court judge), the Qadis Law of 1961 (sing., *qadi*, Muslim religious judge), the Druze Religious Courts Law of 1962 (*qadi madhab*, Druze religious judge), the Jurisdiction in Matters of Dissolution of Marriages (Special Cases) Law of 1969, and the Judiciary Law of 1984.

The Israeli general court system is divided into three categories: magistrates' courts, district courts, and the Supreme Court. The Supreme Court is the highest court in the land. The general court system also includes some special courts such as: labor courts, military courts, and religious courts. These special courts are restricted in jurisdiction. The Supreme Court has limited review jurisdiction to the appellate level of the special courts.

The Supreme Court, which is located in Jerusalem, is composed of fifteen justices and generally sits as a bench with three judges. The President or the Deputy President may direct larger benches; if the Supreme Court has already heard the matter and requires further hearings, then a larger bench is also used. The Supreme Court has jurisdiction throughout the country.

The Supreme Court has jurisdiction to hear criminal and civil appeals from judgments of the district courts, which have appeal as a matter of right. Other matters must receive permission from the Supreme Court in order to appeal. The Supreme Court also has special jurisdiction for appeals regarding administrative detentions, disciplinary rulings of the Israel Bar Association, rulings of the Civil Service Commission, and appeals regarding Knesset elections. The first appointments to the Supreme Court were made through the workings of a number of bodies. There was an advisory body composed of the Presidium of the Bar Association.

From the outset, the Supreme Court and, in fact, the entire judicial system demonstrated complete independence in their rulings. It must be remembered that the State was threatened with destruction from external powers and faced major security problems from the time of its inception; any analysis of the court system of this time and perception of its role in the new society must take this fact into consideration. The state had to survive the War of Independence upon its establishment in 1948, with heavy casualties amounting to one percent of the total population at the time. This situation emphasizes the success that was affected by the creation of an independent judiciary.

Magistrates' courts hold original jurisdiction on criminal matters that have a maximum punishment of up to seven years and on certain civil matters, mostly dependent upon the monetary value of the claim. Magistrates' courts may also act as specialized courts such as juvenile court, family court, or small claims courts. Magistrates' courts are generally presided by one-judge benches. However, the president of the magistrates' court or the judge hearing the case may call for a bench of three judges. There are twenty-nine Magistrates' Courts in Israel, based upon geographic areas.

District courts have jurisdiction over all criminal and civil matters that do not fall within the jurisdiction of the magistrates' courts, and general residual jurisdiction to hear any matter that is not under the exclusive jurisdiction of any other court or tribunal. District courts are generally presided by one-judge benches, but in criminal matters of great severity, they may be presided by three-judge benches. District court can be seen as the middle level of courts in the general court system. District courts are broken down into geographic districts: Petah-Tikva, Nazareth, Beer-Sheva, Haifa, Tel-Aviv, and Jerusalem. Magistrates' courts and district courts have jurisdiction only in their respective geographic area (with the exclusion of Jerusalem, which covers the Jerusalem geographic area and any areas that are not covered by the other five geographic areas).

The unique characteristic of Jewish law is its dual nature, it being both religious and national law.[201] 1948 saw the establishment of the State of Israel, and the eventual rejection of Jewish law as the national law directly applicable in the new State; Jewish law remains a source from which the law of the land draws traditions and values.

In December 1947, a "Legal Council" of 31 members was created. This body was to be the nucleus of the new Justice Ministry, and one of its aims was to "examine the functioning and administration of the courts" in the post-Mandate period.[202]

On the establishment of Israeli in 1948, a major debate took place in the country concerning the proper place and role of Jewish law within the new state.[203] Eventually, it was decided to maintain the existing status quo, incorporating Jewish law only in matters of personal status.[204] Jewish law, therefore, has no official place within the Israeli legal system, except in matters relating to personal status.[205] Nevertheless, it should be noted that some principles of Jewish law have been incorporated into the Israeli legal system through legislation

---

201 See further, M. Elon, "The Sources and Nature of Jewish Law and its Application in the State of Israel," 2 Is. L. Rev. (1967) 515, at 517.
202 I. Shabo, "The Legal Council," 32 *HaPraklit* 127 (Hebrew).
203 M. Elon, *Supra* note 201 Part III, 3 Is. L. Rev. 1968, 416, at 441–446.
204 Sec. 11, Law and Administration Ordinance 1948, 1 L.S.I. 7 provided that the law in force in Palestine on May 14, 1948, should continue in force, subject to necessary changes deriving from the establishment of the State and its authorities.
205 See Secs. 1 and 2, Rabbinical Courts Jurisdiction (Marriage and Divorce) Law 1953, 7 L.S.I. 139.

and have thus become a part of the modern Israeli criminal and civil law. Jewish law is also frequently resorted to and applied by some judges in the regular courts.[206]

In 1980, the Foundations of Law Act was enacted. It determined that instead of deciding cases where there is a lacuna in the law in light of British common law, cases should be decided "in the light of the principles of freedom, justice, equity and peace of the Israeli heritage."[207] Currently there is no decisive view as to the impact of the Foundation of Law Act and the role of Jewish law in the Israeli legal system.

The judicial role has emerged as the result of gradual development and the cumulative effect of a number of factors. These factors include the individual judges themselves and their conception of the nature and scope of the judicial role; previous judicial decisions; the obligation to write reasoned decisions; the principle of precedent; and social and professional controls operating within the courts. System factors also have an effect on the nature and scope of the judicial function and help define the role of the judiciary. These system factors include the existence of judicial review of statutes,[208] the extent of legislative activity in adopting law to change conditions, and the public acceptability of judicial decisions.[209]

Although Israel does not have a written constitution, there are a number of special laws termed "Basic Laws" which regulate the main institutions of Israeli government.[210] The Basic Law: Adjudication[211] declares the independence

---

206 For further reading on the subject of Jewish Law and the State of Israel, see Z. Warhaftig, *Constitution for Israel, Religion and State*, (Jerusalem, 1988); I. England, *Religious Law and the Law of the State* (Jerusalem, 1975) 67; M. Chigier, *The Rabbinical Court in the State of Israel*, 2 I.L.R. (1967) 147.

207 Foundations of Law Act 34 L.S.I. 81, Sec. 1.

208 In Israel, the courts do not have an express power of judicial review of statutes. In the past, it was proposed to establish a constitutional court, that is, the Supreme Court, sitting as a constitutional court to review the constitutionality of statutes. Thus, what was under discussion was a regular court that would also sit as a constitutional court, and not a separate constitutional instance, as is customary on the Continent. This proposal is still pending. See Chapter 1 Shimon Shetreet, Justice in Israel: A Study of the Israeli Judiciary, 497–522 (Martinus Nijhoff: London, 1994).

209 S. Shetreet, "Judicial Independence and Accountability in Israel," 33 L.Q.R. (1984) 979, at 980.

210 Basic Law: The Knesset (1958); Basic Law: Israel Lands (1960); Basic Law: President of the State (1964); Basic Law: the Government (1968); Basic Law: State Economy (1975); Basic Law: the Army (1976); Basic Law: Jerusalem the Capital of Israel (1980); Basic Law: Adjudication (1984); Basic Law: State Comptroller (1988).

of the judiciary; it regulates a number of aspects regarding the position of judges, including their appointment, tenure, and remuneration.[212] However, this Law is not entrenched against amendment by subsequent Knesset legislation, only against amendment by emergency regulations.

The rule against ad hoc or special tribunals is protected by Section 1(c) of the Basic Law: Adjudication, which expressly prohibits their establishment. A Draft Constitution for Israel, formulated by scholars from Tel-Aviv University, also proposes a similar rule.[213]

Numerous post factum validation laws have been enacted in the state of Israel.[214] Due to the fact that there is no constitution in Israel, the Knesset is free to enact whatever legislation it desires, including amendments concerning courts and judges.[215] The only limitation on this power are the various provisions in the Basic Laws, for example, those in Basic Law: Adjudication forbidding the amendment or alteration of this latter law by emergency regulations.[216]

Basic Law: Adjudication provides[217] that the reduction of judicial salaries may be made only if the reduction does not apply solely to judicial salaries. This provision in effect enables judicial salaries to be reduced by a decision of the Knesset, so long as an additional group of persons is also covered by the salary reduction.

In Israel, the task of assigning cases is vested in each of the presidents of the various courts. The advantage of such a system of case assignment is twofold: problematical and charged cases are placed in the hands of more experienced judges, as a matter of course; and the possibility of assigning cases according to the expertise of the judges thus reinforces the efficiency of the judicial process. The disadvantage of this method is in the influence on the final outcome of each case, which it places in the hands of the president of the court. The *St. John's Hospice* case demonstrates that, in Israel, courts are determined to prevent "judge shopping" and are willing to set aside rulings obtained by the improper practice of judge shopping.

---

211 Basic Law: Freedom and Integrity of Man, 1992; Basic Law: Freedom of Occupation (1992). See further, R. Gavison, "The Controversy over Israel's Bill of Rights," 15 Is. Yearbook on Human Rights (1984) 113. S.H. 1984, at 78.
212 Secs. 4, 7, 10 respectively.
213 Sec. 140, Draft Constitution for Israel (Tel-Aviv University).
214 See Chapter 21, *Justice in Israel*, supra note 208.
215 See A. Rubinstein, *Israel Constitutional Law* (3rd ed., 1980, Hebrew) 214–15.
216 Sec. 22, Basic Law: Judicature. There are a number of entrenched provisions in Basic Laws such as Basic Law: The Knesset, Section 4, which can be amended only by a special majority.
217 Sec. 10(b) Basic Law: Adjudication.

The scope of legal aid in Israel is quite narrow.[218] This is a breach of the value of accessibility. A drastic change is called for in this area if Israel wishes to adequately respect the value of accessibility. Recommendations of a committee chaired by Justice Bechor to introduce a major reform in the eligibility for legal aid, particularly in criminal proceedings, have not as yet been implemented.

The "open court" principle is one of the fundamental principles in the legal system, and it has also found a basis in statutory law. Section 3 of Basic Law: Adjudication[219] states that "[a] court shall sit in public unless otherwise provided by Law or unless the court otherwise decides under Law." This principle has also attained a wide recognition in decisions of the Supreme Court. This Court has designated the open court principles as "one of the pillars of criminal and civil procedure, and are of the most important means of ensuring a fair and impartial trial."[220]

The Basic Law does not state the open court principles as an absolute, but rather allows for the reservation, if provided for by law, or when directed by the court under law. Restrictions on the principle have, indeed, been enacted in law – in Sections 68–69 of the Courts Law [Consolidated Version], 1984.[221] These reservations allow for the hearing of a matter *in camera*, or for the removal of a person from the court, both at the discretion of the court and on grounds which are enumerated in the statute. These grounds include: the safeguarding of state security and its foreign relations, the protection of morality, the security of witnesses, the protection of the interests of the parties involved in a sex offence, the privacy of the parties involved in a personal status case, and the protection of minors. An additional reservation on the open court principles is the *sub judice* rule, found in Section 70 of the Courts Law, which emphasize a wide ranging prohibition on the publication of court-related matters except with the permission of the court.

The outcome of this legal situation is that, indeed, the substantive principle of open proceedings is laid down in Basic Law: Adjudication. However, when it conflicts with other important principles, it is within the court's discretion to strike a balance between them and, if necessary, to retreat from the open court principles. Even though the open court principle is one of the most signif-

---

218 For the legal aid generally, see M. Cappelletti and B. Garth, *Access to Justice* (1978); for Israel see *Id..*, Vol. II, 627, 634 (1978); see also Lieberman, "Israel's Legal Aid Law: Remedy for Injustice?" 9 Is. L. R. 413 (1974). For the Israeli statute: Legal Aid Law 1972, S.H. 654, at 95.
219 S.H. p. 78; 38 L.S.I. 101.
220 Cr.A 334/81 *Haginzer v. State of Israel*, 36(1) P.D. 827.
221 Courts Law (Consolidated Version) 1984, S.H., p. 198; 38 L.S.I. 271.

icant principles in the legal system, even if it is not absolute; when it is in conflict with another fundamental principle, it is only correct that the open court principles should give way.

In Israel, the duty to state reasons for a decision is based on the Civil Procedure Regulations, 1984,[222] and on the Criminal Procedure Law [Consolidated Version], 1982.[223] Even the procedural rules of the rabbinical courts provide for a duty to state reasons, although they also allow for an exception from this duty. The foundation of the duty to state reasons, in the Israeli legal system, is inadequate as regards to the High Court of Justice. There are no legal provisions which directly impose such a duty upon the High Court. Section 20(b) of the Rules of Procedure Regulations in the High Court of Justice, 1984, grants the High Court the discretion to adopt the provisions of civil and criminal procedures, and in this way it may impose upon itself the duty to state reasons; however, this is within its discretion. Another way to impose this obligation upon the High Court of Justice is through application of the duty which is found in the Administrative Procedure Amendment (Statement of Reasons) Law, 1958.[224] This law applies, among others, to public officers and contains a very broad definition of this term, which includes "any authority vested with any power under any Law."[225]

The importance of public confidence in the courts is also reflected in the rather strict tests applied for self-disqualification of judges for bias.[226] The test does not require proof that bias has actually influenced the judge, but rather that there is a real likelihood that it will influence the judge.[227] The traditions of the bench go even further than the strict requirement of the law of bias.[228]

There are two main legal restrictions on public comment on courts, judges, and judicial proceedings. These are the rule prohibiting comments which may influence matters pending before the court, otherwise known as the *sub judice* rule,[229] and the prohibition of scurrilous attack on judges.[230] Both restrictions

---

222 Sec. 192 and Sec. 460 Civil Procedure Regulations, 1984.
223 Sec. 182 and Sec. 218 Criminal Procedure Law [Consolidated Version], 1982.
224 Sec.7 and Sec. 13 Administrative Procedure Amendment (Statement of Reasons) Law, 1958.
225 *Id.*, Sec. 1.
226 See Shetreet, "The Administration of Justice: Practical Problems, Value Conflicts and Changing Concepts," 13 U.B.C.L. Rev. 52 (1979).
227 For English examples, see S. Shetreet, *Judges on Trial, A Study of the Appointment and Accountability of the English Judiciary* (1976) at 204. Also see sec. 77(a) of the Courts Law [consolidated Version] 1984.
228 *Id.*, at 304–314.
229 Sec. 71 Courts Law (Consolidated Version) 1984.
230 Sec. 255 Penal Law 1977.

are sanctioned by penal statutory provisions; in English common law, these restrictions are known under the term of "contempt of court."[231] The *sub judice*
rule in Israel is enshrined today in Section 71 of the Court Law [Consolidated Ver-
sion], 1984,[232] and forbids publication in a matter pending before the court to
the extent that it may affect the conduct of the trial and its result. There is an
exception to this rule in Section 71(c) of the Law, which provides a defense for
publication in good faith of anything said or any event occurring at a public
hearing of the court. This arrangement enables the flowing of information in
one direction, from the court to the public, through the media, so far as it refers
to things which were stated or occurred in the court. It also provides an absolute
prohibition on the transfer of information in the opposite direction—from the
public and the media to the judge. Thus, public criticism, and the opinions of
the public and its assessments, cannot reach judges so as to affect their views.

The statutory prohibition against scurrilous attacks on judges has been interpreted broadly, and the avowed policy of the prosecution is to press criminal
charges for what is viewed as a scurrilous attack on a judge.[233] Section 255 of
the Penal Law does expressly exclude from the offense frank criticism in good
faith on the nature of a judicial decision on a matter of public interest. Statisti-
cally the recorded cases of prosecutions for scurrilous attacks on judges are very
few.

It is to be noted that petitioners to the High Court of Justice who seek redress
against the administration are expected to refrain from interviews and comments
to the press after they have submitted the case to the High Court. If they violate
this restriction, they may lose the case on this ground alone. The rationale behind this restriction is that once the matter has been put before the court for resolution, the party to the case should refrain from a public campaign.[234] Appeal to
public opinion after the case has been submitted to court might be taken as an
expression of lack of confidence in the court, or as an attempt to influence the
judges by public pressure.

The law in Israel provides for security of tenure of judges until the statutory
retirement age of 70. A judge may be removed from office prior to retirement age
only on the basis of a medical certificate, subject to carefully defined grounds;

---

231 For details on the relations between English common law and Israeli law on this issue, see
E. Harnon, *Contempt of Court by Disobedience*, (Jerusalem, 1965) at 6–15, 34–37, 43–47.
232 See Sec. 71 of the Courts Law (Consolidated Version), 1984 S.H. 198; Sec. 255 of the Penal
Law, 1977.
233 Cr.A 364/73 *Seidman v. State of Israel*, 28(2) P.D. 620; Cr.A 49/58 *Herouti v. A.G.*, 12 P.D. 1541;
Cr.A 53/49 *Weil v. A.G.*, 3 P.D. 93; Cr.A 37/50 *Sternhal v. A.G.* 6 P.D. 119 (1950).
234 H.C.J 114/78 *Bourkan v. Minister of Finance*, 32(2) P.D. 800, at 803–804.

where the judge has been found guilty of a disciplinary offence under the Courts Laws,[235] or where the Judicial Selection Committee so decides on a majority vote of at least seven of its nine members.[236]

A judge in Israel may be transferred to a court in another locality if the consent of the presidents of the courts concerned is obtained.[237] Where the transfer is a permanent one, Basic Law: Adjudication requires either that the consent of the President of the Supreme Court be obtained, or that a decision to this effect be reached by the Disciplinary Tribunal.[238]

In Israel, lower ocurts are bound by the principle of precedent, but only those precedents set by the Supreme Court. Only the Supreme Court is not bound by its own previous rulings, although in practice the judges of the Supreme Court do tend to follow them.

Presidents of the Supreme Court have wider and different powers than the Presidents of the other courts in the Israeli system. They are elected by the Judicial Appointments Committee,[239] unlike the presidents of the district and magistrates courts, who are appointed by the Minister of Justice with the consent of the President of the Supreme Court.[240] It is to be noted that there is a practice to appoint the President of the Supreme Court and the deputy strictly according to seniority. The powers of the President of the Supreme Court touch both the administration of the judiciary in general, and the appointment and discipline of judges in particular. The President of the Supreme Court is a permanent member of the Judicial Appointments Committee,[241] and is the only one who may propose candidates for judicial appointment.[242] With the approval of the Minister of Justice, the President has authority to appoint registrars.[243] The Minister of Justice requires the President's approval to appoint judges to temporary positions;[244] consent is also needed from the President for the appointment of the Presidents and Deputy Presidents of the District and Magistrates' Courts.[245]

---

235 Courts Laws [Consolidated Version], 1984, S.H. 1198.
236 See Sec. 7(4) Basic Law: Adjudication, S.H. (1984) at 78.
237 Secs. 36 and 46 of Courts Law [Consolidated Version], 1984, S.H. 1198.
238 Sec. 9 and See Sec. 7(4) Basic Law: Adjudication, S.H. (1984) at 78.
239 Sec. 8, Courts Law [Consolidated Version] 1984, 38 L.S.I. 271 and Sec. 4(a) Basic Law: Adjudication, 38 L.S.I. 101.
240 Sec. 9, Courts Law 1984.
241 Sec. 4(b) Basic Law: Adjudication.
242 Courts Law 1984, sec. 7(2).
243 *Id.*, Sec. 84.
244 *Id.*, Sec. 10(a).
245 *Id.*, 23c. 9.

The President of the Supreme Court has authority to suspend a judge against whom a disciplinary complaint has been filed or a criminal investigation is being held.[246] Upon the recommendation of the judges of the Supreme Court, the President appoints all members of the judicial disciplinary tribunal and determines its size and composition.[247]

Regarding general administrative powers, any permanent transfer by the Minister of Justice of a judge from one court to another of the same instance, must be approved by the President of the Supreme Court;[248] similarly, the President must approve any extra-judicial activity or other public function carried out by a judge.[249] The Minister of Justice consults the President of the Supreme Court when altering the financial jurisdiction of the magistrates' court.[250] When exercising the power to punish a person disturbing court proceedings, a judge has an obligation to notify the President of the Supreme Court.[251]

The President of the Supreme Court has informal powers to deal with breaches of judicial standards of behavior. This power is vested in the President, by virtue of being head of the judiciary, by means of the above mentioned legal powers relating to the judiciary, and because of the fact that the Supreme Court determines the composition of the judicial disciplinary tribunal. The President of the Supreme Court is considered the moral leader of the judiciary. Since the early days of the State of Israel, the President of the Supreme Court has been seen as having general responsibility over the judiciary. From this position of general responsibility, the President of the Supreme Court is seen as bound to protect the independence and status of the judiciary before the executive and the legislature.

The presidents of the district and magistrates courts are generally responsible for the smooth operation of the courts within their areas of jurisdiction. They have the legal responsibility to determine which judges are to sit on what case,[252] and for setting dates for hearing cases, as well as responsibility for ensuring that judgments are given within a reasonable time after the hearing and the submission of summations.[253] Under the Rules of Procedure, judge are under a duty to report to the President of their court cases where the judgment was not handed

---

246 Sec. 14 Basic Law: Adjudication.
247 Sec. 17(a) Courts Law 1984.
248 Sec. 9(a) Basic Law: Adjudication.
249 *Id.*, Sec. 11.
250 Sec. 51 Courts Law 1984.
251 *Id.*, Sec. 72.
252 Sec. 38(a), 48(a) Courts Law 1984.
253 Secs. 38(b), 48(b) *Id.*

down within thirty days after the hearing of evidence and concluding arguments had been completed. With regard to matters concerning the administration of the courts, the presidents of the district and magistrates courts have the power to ensure the smooth and efficient running of court proceedings, by acting reasonably and efficiently.

Apart from matters concerning the administration of the courts, the presidents of the lower courts have moral authority to act on behalf of the court, both internally and externally. They may respond to actions and statements of other bodies in matters regarding the courts in which they sit. However, in general, only the Supreme Court President or the Director of Courts have reacted publicly to statements made in the press about a specific court, a judge within that court, or the judiciary as a whole.[254]

Jewish law recognizes the importance of junior judges not being open to influence. Judges have an obligation to consult with each other.[255] During deliberations, junior judges commence with their opinions followed by the more senior judges. This avoids the influence of senior judges on their opinion, and may be seen as a clear example of an emphasis on the protection of internal judicial independence.

In Israel, the law leaves a possibility for minority decision. Apart from that, there are no special procedures in the Supreme Court regarding decision making. The procedure generally depends on the number of judges sitting and the complexity of the case. Single judges often pronounce their decision at the end of the hearing. Where there is a panel of judges, they may give a unanimous decision at the end of the hearing, following a short consultation in the courtroom or during a break. Alternatively, a decision may be handed down after the judges have studied the whole case, or after submissions of written summations. This allows time for consultation among the judges, and the opportunity for majority and minority views.

The Courts Law of 1984 lays down the qualifications for persons to be appointed as judges of the various courts. Those eligible to be appointed to the Supreme Court must have either served for five years as a district court judge; or have either practiced law, acted in an adjudicatory function, or taught law for a period of at least ten years, and be inscribed on the Roll of Members of the Chamber of Advocates during that period.[256] District court judges are selected

---

254 Landau commission Report on Judicial Ethics, *Judges Bulletin*, No. 6 of September 1985, at 7.
255 Mishna, Sanhedrin, 4, 1: 5, 8.
256 Sec. 2, Courts Law 1984. An eminent jurist is also qualified by a decision of a special majory. This has been used only once in the history of the country.

from amongst magistrates court judges who have served at least four years or from amongst persons who have practiced law, served in an adjudicatory function, or taught law for a period of at least six years.[257] Magistrates court judges are selected from amongst those who are registered or entitled to be registered in the Israeli Chamber of Advocates and have continuously or alternatively practiced law, served in an adjudicatory function, or taught law for at least five years (at least two of them in Israel).[258]

One cannot be appointed to the office of District Court judge or Magistrate Court judge, unless one is inscribed on the Roll of Members of the Chamber of Advocates, or at least entitled to be inscribed on it. However, the office of a Supreme Court judge may be occupied by a candidate who is not inscribed or eligible to be inscribed on the Roll of Advocates. This is so because of the special provision allowing "an eminent jurist" to be appointed to the Supreme Court, but not to other courts. All judges in Israel must have Israeli nationality to be appointed; a judge who has dual nationality must take all the necessary actions to renounce the second nationality.[259]

In Israel, appellate controls are exercised by the Supreme Court and the district courts. The Supreme Court, which is the highest court in the land, hears appeals from the district courts, which are the courts of general jurisdiction. The district court itself hears appeals from the magistrates' courts. The Supreme Court does not confine itself to passing criticism on an improper judicial act or omission. The Court also reacts to judicial irregularities in operative orders by reversing judgments in civil cases[260] and setting aside convictions in criminal cases.[261] Sometimes judicial misconduct is in itself a ground for reversing a judgment or conviction; in other cases, judicial misconduct together with other grounds of appeal results in the reversal. In criminal cases, improper judicial conduct may serve as a reason to reduce the sentence passed.[262]

Appellate courts not only ensure judicial conduct, and in appropriate cases amend or reverse judgments, they also guide lower courts as to the proper way of

---

257 *Id.*, Sec. 1.
258 *Id.*, Sec. 4.
259 *Id.*, Sec. 5.; see also Sec. 5, Basic Law: Adjudication.
260 For reversal of civil judgments, see C.A 322/74 *Jabur v. Saad*, 29(a) P.D. 233, where judgment was rendered 27 months after the end of the hearing; C.A 803/75 *Monrof v. Kleinmiz*, 30(3) P.D. 179, where judgment was rendered after more than 22 months, the Supreme Court reversing the findings of fact at first instance, and ruling in favor of the appellant.
261 For criminal cases, see Cr.A 152/51 *Trifous v. Attorney General*, 6(1) P.D 17 at 17 (the judge had met in his house with a close friend of the defendant in the trial).
262 See Cr.A 125/74 *Merom v. State of Israel*, 30(1) P.D. 57, at 77; Cr.A 1/52 *Deutsch v. A.G.*, 8(1) P.D. 456; Cr.A 568/72 *Ezra v. State of Israel*, 27(1) P.D. 806, at 810.

conducting cases. They suggest the proper way in which the particular circumstances should be subsequently handled in order to avoid possible deviations from high standards of behavior and to eliminate possible damage to public confidence in the courts.

The role of the appellate courts in assuring high standards of conduct is not limited, however, to post factum correctional action and to establishing standards of judicial conduct. They also have a restraining and preventive effect on lower court judges. Most judges hope for promotion; frequent reversal or reprimand may adversely affect their chances of judicial promotion. There may be some doubt as to whether reversals due to error of judgment in substantive law alone have a negative effect on the chances of a judge being promoted.

The interrelations between the judiciary and the Legal Advisor to the Government—as the Attorney General is called in Israel—are of a unique nature. Legal Advisors are public servants who are part of the executive, but are independent officers in the exercise of their duties relative to administration of criminal justice and the giving of legal opinions. Their appointment and dismissal are carried out by the government upon a recommendation of the Minister of Justice.[263] Nevertheless, the law entrusts them with wide powers for substantial intervention in the judicial process. Section 62 of the Criminal Procedure Law (Combined Version) 1982 grants the Legal Advisor (and the Advisor's representatives) discretionary powers to decide whether or not a person should be indicted. Section 231 of the aforementioned Law empowers the Legal Advisor to stay criminal proceedings at any time within the time interval between the submission of the indictment and the adjudication of the case.

The Legal Advisor's intervention is anchored in the Law. This distinguishes it from intervention lacking any legal basis. In addition, the Legal Advisor's intervention is not objectionable from the substantive aspect. This is due to the special nature of this institution. Despite being subordinate to the executive regarding both personal appointment and dismissal, the Legal Advisor is in fact a totally independent body with regard to substantive decisions.

Although the Supreme Court has always maintained its right to interfere with the Legal Advisor's decisions,[264] in the past the rule has been that the scope of its intervention would be extremely limited.[265]

---

263 Section 5 of the State Service (Appointments) Law, 1959, S.H. 84; 13 L.S.I. 87.
264 H.C.J 156/56 *Schor v. The Legal Advisor to the Government*, 11 P.D. 285; 2 S.J. 283 (1958–1960)
265 *Id.*

Judicial appointments in Israel are made for life until retirement at the age of 70 for judges at all levels of the judicial hierarchy.[266] There is a special procedure for compulsory retirement for health reasons if the Judicial Selection Committee so decides, based upon a medical certificate.[267] Judges may retire earlier if they have served at least 20 years and have reached the age of 60, or have served at least 15 years and have reached the age of 65.[268] In addition, magistrates' court judges may retire after having served 20 years on the bench if they have reached the age of 50, or after having served 15 years, if they have reached the age of 55, so long as they notify the Minister of Justice a year prior to retirement.[269]

A judge may be removed from office under Section 7(4) of Basic Law: Adjudication, where the Judicial Selection Committee so decides by a majority of at least seven of its nine members.[270] A judge may not be removed for incompetence. A judge may also be removed from office or disciplined by a Disciplinary Tribunal,[271] only on one of the four grounds specified in the Courts Law [Consolidated Version].[272] The President of the Supreme Court has authority to suspend judges for a fixed period where a disciplinary complaint or criminal charges[273] have been filed against them.[274]

It should be noted that the outcome of a civil litigation does not have to be adjudicative. The Knesset has passed a legislative amendment that encourages out-of-court compromises to lighten the burden of an overloaded court system. The result is that many cases are settled by means of compromise or are transferred to arbitration or mediation.[275]

The right to appeal is provided for in Section 17 of Basic Law: Adjudication. In general, a judgment from a court of first instance is appealable as a right.[276]

---

266 Sec. 7 Basic Law: Adjuciation, S.H. 1984, at 78; Sec. 13(a)(1), Courts Law [Consolidated Version] 1984, S.H. 198.

267 Sec. 13(a)(2), Courts Law [Consolidated Version].

268 Sec. 13(b)(1) and (2), *Id.*

269 Sec. 13(c), *Id.*

270 Under Amendment 15 of the Courts Act, the Committee must provide fair hearing to a judge who is proposed to be removed under Section 7(4) of the Basic Law: Adjudication. Likewise, the Committee may determine the date for the judge's retirement and pension. See Sec. 14 of the Courts Law, and see Sec. 6 of the Courts Law (Amendment 15) 1992, S.H., 68.

271 Disciplinary Tribunal is composed of three or five members as the Supreme Court President decides. Sec. 13 Basic Law: Adjudication.

272 Sec. 18, *Id.*; See further, Chapter 15 of *Justice in israel*, supra note 208.

273 Criminal charge against a judge may be pressed only by the Attorney General.

274 Sec. 14, Basic Law: Adjudication.

275 Courts Law (Amendment No. 15), 1992, Sec. 10.

276 Excluding, of course, cases in which the Supreme Court is the court of first instance, sitting as the High Court of Justice. See Sec. 15 of the Basic Law: Adjudication.

Judgments from courts of second instance as well as interlocutory (or interim) decisions in civil matters may be appealed only by leave of a judge of the court to which application for appeal is made.[277] Israeli law does not normally allow for appeal of interim decisions in criminal matters.[278]

3. The Political System

Israel is a parliamentary system. The people elect parliament, called the Knesset, and the Knesset elects the Prime Minister. The President consults with the heads of parties after each election in order to form the Government. Generally, this will be the leader of the party that has the most representation in the Knesset.[279]

The government of Israel has three main branches: the unicameral legislature (the Knesset), the executive (the Government, headed by the Prime Minister), and the independent judiciary. The Knesset's primary function is to enact laws and to oversee the Government. They also elect a President every seven years. The President is a figurehead with practically no legal power.[280]

Israel's political system was largely influenced by the British due to the admiration held for it by first Prime Minister of Israel, David Ben-Gurion. While there are many similarities, there also exist significant distinctions between the Israeli and British parliaments. Two parties dominate the makeup of the British parliament, whereas the Israeli parliament consists of multiple parties. Also, England is divided into constituencies where individual voters elect a representative. Israel uses a "nation-wide proportional representation." This means that voters vote for a party rather than for individual candidates. The Knesset has 120 seats and a proportional number of members from each party are selected. The parties themselves select the individual representatives, either by internal elections or selection by the party leader. Elections are held every four years, but the Knesset or Prime Minister can call for elections at earlier intervals. Additionall, a Knesset may be in session for more than four years in special circumstances.[281]

---

277 See Sections 41, 52 of the Courts Law [Consolidated Version], 1984.
278 Generally on this point see H.C.J 541/81 *Fogel v. Religious Council Ashkelon*, 35(iv) P.D. 813 (1984). The basic exception to this general rule relates to a judge's decision following a disqualification request by one of the parties.
279 Sec.7 Basic Law: The Government
280 Navot, *supra* note 168, 61–63.
281 *Id.*

It should be noted that between 1996 and 2001, Israel's political system was a presidential parliamentary system. In the elections of 1996, 1999, and 2001, voters selected only a Prime Minister. During this period of revolution, there was a rise in formation of political coalitions and conduction of political bargaining. The change was due to public dissatisfaction with political stalemate in the Knesset.[282]

The original system was eventually restored after it became clear that the presidential parliamentary system was instable and inefficient. For example, the Prime Minister was still dependent on the Knesset, the Prime Minister's only sanction for the Knesset was to dismiss them, and there remained a social imbalance in Israel. Repeal of the direct democracy system in Israel has allowed the opportunity for the political parties and the parliament to be renewed; however, it is too soon to indicate whether the system has been completely stabilized.[283]

In Israel, a political party is a unit with constitutional status. Only a party may submit a list of candidates for election to the Knesset. Additionally, the parties of Israel determine the character of the government, both personally and ideologically. Parties enter into political agreements, form coalitions, and plan government policy.[284]

Party status and primary party functions are regulated by The Parties Law, although internal affairs are largely left up to the parties themselves.[285] It states that a "party" is a "group of persons who have associated in order to legally promote political or social goals and bring about their representation in the Knesset by delegates."[286] It goes on to state that a party is formed by registering one hundred or more adult citizens and residents of Israel with the Party Register. The Parties Law continues:

"A party will not be registered if in one of its objectives or actions, explicitly or suggested, is one of the following:

(1) The rejection of Israel's right to exist as a Jewish and democratic state.
(2) Incitement of racism.
(3) Support of the armed struggle of enemy states or terrorist organizations against the state of Israel.

---

282 Id.
283 Id.
284 Article 5a, Basic Law: The Knesset.
285 Parties Law, 5752–1992.
286 Id., Article 1.

(4) A reasonable basis to conclude that the party will be used for illegal activities."[287]

Parties must be formed for the purpose of achieving representation in the Knesset; their political and social purposes must be specified. A party must also have a central institution, an auditing institution, and a body responsible for managing party affairs.[288]

The Registrar of Parties may refuse party formation by refusing to register it, and all adult citizens may oppose the registration of a new party. Because refusing to register a party interferes with the right to be elected, the Registrar must carry out this power cautiously.[289]

While internal affairs of a party are largely unrestricted, the Supreme Court of Israel has suggested that affairs should conform to democratic principles. For example, the Court has held that "proper procedures and an orderly and fair system of decision-making" are very important for parties. However, the Court has not mandated parties to act democratically. Further, attempts to amend the Parties Law to require parties to have democratic procedures have failed. Examples of parties that do not operate democratically include the religious and Orthodox parties. These parties have only male members and a religious authority selects the candidates.[290]

Lobby and interest groups in Israel, unlike the United States, are not institutionalized.[291] In the Knesset, there are two types of lobby groups: lobbies of interest groups and Knesset members' lobbies. The former consist of public relations professionals who represent interest groups; the latter consist of Knesset members who unite for a particular issue. While Knesset member lobbies are free to form, there are many rules regarding interest group lobbies. The Knesset Speaker must approve their presence and they are not allowed to coerce votes or mislead Knesset members about the facts relating to legislation.[292]

Israel's chief lobby group for women's rights, the Israel Women's Network (IWN) has had great success. The group, which was founded in 1984 by a

---

287 *Id.*, Article 5.
288 *Id.*, Article 18.
289 Ariel Bendor, *The Right of Candidacy in the Knesset Elections*, 18 Mishpatim 269 (1988).
290 C.A 197/89 *Agudath Yisrael v. Shwartz*, 45(3) P.D. 320 at 326.
291 See Knesset articles on Lobbyists and Lobbies available at (respectively): https://www.knesset.gov.il/lexicon/eng/lobbyist_eng.htm and https://www.knesset.gov.il/lexicon/eng/lobby_eng.htm (both accessed February 9, 2017)
292 For a full list of Lobbies in the Twentieth Knesset see: https://www.knesset.gov.il/lobby/eng/lobbylist_eng.asp (accessed February 9, 2017).

group of women professionals, seeks to improve the status of women in Israel. IWN "provides free legal advice against discrimination and sexual harassment in the workplace [and] runs campaigns to raise public awareness about the fundamental need for equal rights for women."[293] IWN is active in the Knesset and provides legal representation. IWN brings many cases to the courts. For example, IWN "represented Alice Miller in a landmark decision granting women the right to volunteer for pilot-training courses in the Israeli Air Force."[294]

4. Reforms and Government System

On March 11th, 2014, the Knesset adopted a series of amendments to laws forming how Israel's system of government operates. One group of amendments addressed Basic Law: The Government, Basic Law: The Knesset, and Basic Law: State Economy.[295]

In addition to these amendments, the Knesset adopted amendments affecting elections to the Knesset, political party finance, and the Knesset law. Before the adoption of these amendments, the draft of several laws was called the "The Draft Law: Basic Law: The Government" (amending the reinforcement of governance). The second group of amendments was called Draft Law: Election to the Knesset Amendment Number 61; it increased the threshold of percentage and the reinforcement of governance.

The MK who presented the original bill stated that the amendments were aimed at increasing the ability of the executive branch to govern and to promote the stability[296] of government in Israel. The main changes[297] that were adopted were the following:
A. Restrict the number of ministers to 19 and deputy minister to 4.
B. Abolish the institution of the minister without portfolio.
C. Change the no-confidence vote, providing a requirement of electing an alternative government to the present one.
D. Extend the time for passing the budget of the state to 100 days.
E. Increase the threshold percentage of entry to the Knesset from 2% to 3.25%.

---

293 See IWN's website: http://www.iwn.org.il/pages/about-the-israel-women-s-network- (accessed February 9, 2017).
294 H.C.J 4541/94 *Miller v. Minister of Defense*, 49(4) P.D. 94 (1995).
295 Members of Knesset David Rotem, Robert Elitov, Hammad Amar, and Ronen Hoffman.
296 Explanatory notes for draft laws, H.H. 512, page 46–47, 5773–2013.
297 There were a number of changes in the original text proposed, but the principles were maintained.

F.   Abolish the possibility of splitting from a faction in the Knesset unless the split is by one-third of the faction.

G.   Impose further conditions on getting political parties financed by members of Knesset who resign from their factions.

Of specific interest is the increase of the threshold percentage; this increase is likely to decrease the number of small political parties[298] and, by that, to ease the composition of the operating coalition. Similarly, the restriction on splitting from factions will support a better operation of the coalition, as does the extension of time for adopting a budget, which will make it easier to obtain approval. The change in the confidence vote system will reduce the risk of ending the government's term of office[299] and also promote stability. In addition, the restrictions on the government's size by restricing the number of ministers and deputy ministers should improve governance and efficiency. The amendments were met with criticism[300] by the opposition. Members of the opposition withdrew from voting on these proposals, in fact, from passing the governance amendments as well as the equality law on military service and the referendum act.[301]

---

298 Explanatory notes on the draft law, HH 515, p. 54, 5773–2013.

299 *Id.*

300 See for example, Moran Azulai, "The Opposition Will Boycott Knesset Debates: The Government is Planning Exceptional and Extreme Measures", YNET available at www.ynet.co.il/ar ticles/0,7340,L-4496861,00.html (accessed February 9, 2017). (See the comments of the leader of the opposition, Yitzhak Hertzog.)

301 Moran Azulai, "Split Knesset: 'Rock Bottom' v. 'Tramping the Democracy'", YNET available at http://www.ynet.co.il/articles/0,7340,L-4497140,00.html (accessed February 9, 2017).

Part III: **Fundamental Legal Doctrines of Israeli Law**

Chapter 5:
Basic Principles of the Israeli Legal System

1. Introduction

The Israeli legal system is not based on any single, central document. Rather, it is based on a series of basic laws and the Supreme Court's jurisprudence. Justice Barak has stated that the system's basic principles include principles of equality, justice, and morality.[1] Also included are principles of separation of powers, the rule of law, freedom of expression, freedom of procession, worship, occupation, human dignity, purity of adjudication, public peace and security, the democratic values of the state, and its existence as such. This list of principles is not a closed list. Usually there are no conflicts between these values and principles, but in the event that there are, the values must be taken into account and weighed in the circumstances.

The Israeli Declaration of Independence asserts that the State of Israel will be based on the precepts of liberty, justice, and peace as envisaged by the prophets of Israel.[2] Additionally, the Declaration of Independence upholds the full social and political equality of all its citizens and guarantees full freedom of conscience, worship, education, and culture. The Declaration of Independence may serve as a normative force from which legal rights can be derived or a charter of the nation's values according to the Supreme Court.

The State of Israel holds several fundamental principles as part of its legal system. These include: Israel as a democratic state, the separation of powers, judicial independence, the rule of law, and Israel as a Jewish state. These points will be discussed below.

Israel as a Democratic state is based on the principles of equality espoused in the Declaration of Independence. President Barak wrote that: "It appears to me that just as the existence of the state is a fundamental tenant in our legal system, so is its existence as a democratic state."[3]

Being a democratic state, Israel holds the separation of powers between the legislative, executive, and judicial branches as one of the most prominent characteristics. Separation of powers is characterized by two fundamental features: first, the division of powers between various authorities; second, the recip-

---

1 See Cr.A 677/83 *Borochov v. Yefet*, 39(1) P.D. 205.
2 Declaration of Establishment of State of Israel (14.05.1948).
3 E.A 2/84 *Naiman v. Chairman Central Elections Committee*, 39(2) P.D. 255, 314.

DOI 10.1515/9783899497946-005

rocal supervision between authorities and mechanisms for balancing between authorities. First, each authority has established powers to perform the functions that pertain to the branch. The legislative branch has authority to give legal expression to decisions regarding central issues regarding the relationships between society, individuals, and administration.[4] The executive branch has authority to implement the decisions established by the legislative branch. The judicial branch has the power to resolve individual disputes concerning matters in which the other branches have exercised their respective authorities.[5] Second, the supervision among these authorities is reciprocal in nature and there are mechanisms established to balance the supervisory authorities. Examples of these mechanisms include judicial review and the Knesset supervision of the executive branch. These mechanisms create balancing and supervisory bridges between the branches of government.[6]

The judicial branch enforces restrictions imposed on the other sovereign authorities. This only can occur if the judiciary is independent from the political system. Indeed, an independent judiciary is one of the basic values of the state.[7]

The Rule of Law requires that all persons and bodies of the State act in accordance with the law and that any act which is not according to law must be sanctioned by organized society. This is a hallmark of all democratic legal systems. Sovereign powers are subject to provisions of law; power is held as part of a comprehensive network of norms that bind all, including those who are in positions of authority. The law is both the source and limitation of power. Therefore, the legislature's authority is circumscribed by the constitution and the administration may only act in accordance with the authority conferred by law. The rule of law also means the substantive rule of law. This means that all sovereign decisions must comply with certain basic requirements like prohibition of imposing sanctions absent legal authorization.[8]

Israel is a Jewish State and constitutes a basic principle of Israeli law. In the Basic Law: Freedom of Occupation and in Basic Law: Human Dignity and Liberty, it states that the Basic Law's purpose is to establish the values of the State of Israel as a Jewish and democratic state.[9] The purpose of establishing the State of

---

4 Suzie Navot, *The Constitution of Israel*, 83 (Hart, 2014).
5 *Id.*
6 C.A 6821/93 *United Mizrahi Bank Ltd. v. Migdal Cooperative Village*, 49(4) P.D. 221 (1995).
7 See H.C.J 14/86 *Laor v. Film and Plays Censorship Council*, 41(1) P.D. 421, 433.
8 See Navot, *supra* note 4.
9 See Section IA of Basic Law: Human Dignity and Liberty; Section 2 of Basic Law: Freedom of Occupation.

Israel was to realize the yearnings of the Jewish people to renew their national life and fulfill the Zionist vision.[10]

As a result of being a Jewish State, many aspects of the country demonstrate the Jewish tradition including: the right of Jews to emigrate to Israel, the Hebrew language[11], holidays, and days of rest. The State of Israel as a Jewish state establishes the basic values of Judaism and not the religion as a whole. The goal is to "anchor the laws of the state of Israel in its values as a Jewish and democratic state. The natural way of achieving this synthesis is to find the common ground between the Jewish and democratic systems, the principles that they share or at least those that can be used to integrate the two systems."[12]

Further expression of Israel as a Jewish state can be found in the Foundations of the Law Act of 1980. The Act authorizes the court to look to the principles of freedom, justice equity, and peace that are part of the Israel heritage when faced with a legal question that cannot be answered by reference to legislation or case law.[13]

2. Constitutional Protection of Human Rights

Human rights are based on democratic and judicial tradition. These rights have been consolidated by judicial rulings in many different fields; for example, the recognition of freedom of speech was recognized in the *Kol Ha'am* and *Bezerano* rulings. Furthermore, in 1992, the Basic Laws were instituted, providing these rights a constitutional recognition.

Israel's Declaration of Independence set forth the credo upon which the State was to be founded. The third section of the Declaration has fulfilled an important role in reinforcing the protection of civil rights by the courts; it has served the courts as a means of creating basic assumptions as to the democratic and the Jewish character of the State.[14] The following passage is of particular importance:

"The State of Israel will be open for Jewish immigration and for the Ingathering of the Exiles; it will foster the development of the country for the benefit of

---

10 See E.A 2/84 *Naiman v. Chairman Central Elections Committee*, 39(2) P.D. 255, 314.

11 The official languages of the state are Hebrew and Arabic.

12 See C.A 506/88 *Yael Shefer, Minor Represented by Her Mother v. State of Israel*, 48(1) P.D. 87, 96–97.

13 See Section 1 of the Foundations of the Law Act, 1980.

14 Shimon Shetreet, *Developments in Constitutional Law: Selected Topics*, 24 Isr. L. Rev. 368–460 (1990) (Hereinafter: *Developments in Constitutional Law*).

all its inhabitants; it will be based on freedom, justice and peace as envisaged by the prophets of Israel; it will ensure complete equality of social and political rights to all its inhabitants irrespective of religion, race or sex; it will guarantee freedom of religion, conscience, language, education and culture; it will safeguard the Holy Places of all religions; and it will be faithful to the principles of the Charter of the United Nations."[15]

The Declaration goes on to express Israel's readiness to cooperate with the UN, the Arab inhabitants of Israel, neighboring states, and the Jewish people. The UN is asked to receive Israel into the family of nations and to assist in the building up of the State; the Arab inhabitants are urged to preserve peace and to participate in building the State "on the basis of full and equal citizenship," and are ensured political and social equality as inhabitants; neighboring states and their inhabitants are asked for cooperation and peace; and the Jewish people are called to rally round the State, to immigrate, and to join in its formation.[16]

The Declaration does not directly confer any right to any citizen, nor does it impose any duty on the government. However, it does have some legal significance. It works as a tool of legal interpretation. When faced with multiple interpretations of a statute, the court will prefer the interpretation that is consistent with the Declaration, conferring a broader protection of civil rights, specifically freedom of expression, freedom of movement, and the right to equality.[17]

The Supreme Court first employed the Declaration of Independence in the 1953 decision of the *Kol Ha'am* case. The issue presented in that case was in regards to the Minister of the Interior's closing of a newspaper due to the publication of an article about the Korean War. Ministers can exercise this power if a newspaper publishes something that, in their opinion, endangers public peace. The Court held that in order to close a newspaper, the Minister must show a real likelihood of danger to the public peace. A tendency towards such danger would not suffice.[18]

Whenever individuals have a dispute with the government, they seek a remedy from the courts.[19] The Supreme Court of Israel has expanded its role of judicial review in regards to questions of civil and human rights since its inception. This concept can be illustrated in the case of *Bergmann v. Minister of Finance*. In that case, the Supreme Court resolved the issue of the word "equal" as it applies

---

15 *Id.*
16 *Id.*, at 412.
17 *Id.*
18 H.C.J 87/53 *Kol Ha'am* v. *Minister of Interior*, 7(1) P.D. 871 (1953).
19 Shimon Shetreet, "Reflections on the Protection of the Rights of the Individual: Form and Substance," 12 Isr. L. Rev. 32, 34 (1977).

to the Knesset being elected by equal elections and employed judicial review of a statute in context of the Basic Laws. To define this concept, the Court looked outside of the provisions in Basic Law: The Knesset and held that the fundamental principle of equality before the law "can exist also on its own, without reliance upon a provision in a written constitution which expressly sets forth the principle of equality of everyone before the law. We do not have such a provision, neither in a written constitution nor in an 'entrenched' provision of a Basic Law. Nevertheless, this unwritten concept is a vital and indispensable element of our entire constitutional system."[20]

The expansion of judicial review can be attributed to two main factors: first, the failure of political branches of government to solve problems; second, deliberate evasion of decision making on the part of those political branches in respect of certain problems.[21]

In regards to the first factor, the public is aware that the political branches and administrative authorities (the Knesset, the Government, and the Government departments) have not always been able to solve the problems facing them. In light of this realization, the public has resorted to the courts for settlement of those problems that have remained unsolved by the political authorities. As a result, the Court is now a forum for resolving human rights violations. With regard to the second factor, the executive will often intentionally divert decision making to the judiciary, forcing the judiciary to resolve political and economic issues.[22]

Because the courts have a prominent role in society, citizens are increasingly aware of their rights of recourse for enforcement of their constitutional and human rights. The Supreme Court has demonstrated willingness to extend judicial review to the substantive decisions of the government.[23]

Since Israel's founding, security considerations in Supreme Court decisions have diminished while considerations of civil rights have increased. In the early years of the State, the Court annulled security decisions if it was proven that the public officeholders exceeded their authority or did not fulfill the procedural requirements laid down by law. Until the end of the 1970s, the Court refused to intervene where the plea was an attack against the security decision itself, rather than challenging excess of jurisdiction or procedural defect.[24] In 1979, the Court decided the *Elon-Moreh* case and changed the way that the Court reviewed secur-

---

20 H.C.J 98/69 *Bergmann v. Minister of Finance*, 23(1) P.D. 693, 697 (1969).
21 *Developments in Constitutional Law, supra* note 14, at 405.
22 *Id.,* at 406.
23 *Id.,* at 407.
24 *Id.,* at 416.

ity decisions. In that case, private land was seized in order to establish a Jewish settlement on the West Bank. The Court undertook an examination of the considerations that motivated the authorities that made the decision. It ultimately decided that the motivations were safety and political, not militant, in violation of international law.[25] Since this case was decided, security considerations are now examined on their merits.

Examples of security decisions that the Court has annulled include: refusal of family reunification;[26] the seizure of property of the East Jerusalem Election Company in Judea and Samaria;[27] and the banning of publication of an article about Israel's intelligence agency in a Tel Aviv newspaper.[28] The Court has also held that individuals are afforded the right to a hearing before a demolition order from Defense (Emergency) Regulations can be executed;[29] the holding of detainees form the occupied territories in Israel is legal; however, the conditions must meet certain minimum standards.[30] Additionally, when a Court denies a petition, it recommends that the government act in accordance with the petitioner's request. In most cases, the executive will bow to the authority of the High Court and carry out the recommendations.[31]

In light of this new standard of review, many challenges of security decisions are settled before the petitioners reach the High Court. Often times, a petition is filed, but the matter is resolved in favor of the petitioner before the matter can be adjudicated. This clearly demonstrates the impact that the Court's jurisprudence has had on the government.

Sometimes when resolving an issue of individual civil rights, the courts will look to the norms and values held by the majority of society. This often occurs when the question is more social, or political, rather than legal. This increases the public opinion and confidence of the courts, making it more likely that the public will approve of the decisions. If a judicial decision is too far removed from the norms and values of society, the legislature can act as a counterbalance, effectively reversing the decision.[32]

---

25 H.C.J 390/79 *Dweikat v. The Government of Israel*, 34(1) P.D. 1 (1979)
26 H.C.J 802/79 *Samara v. Commander of Judea and Samaria*, 34(4) P.D. 1 (1980).
27 H.C.J 7957/04 *East Jerusalem Electric Company v. Minister of Energy and the Commander of Judea and Samaria*, 35(2) P.D. 673 (1981).
28 H.C.J 680/88 *Schnitzer v. Chief Military Censor*, 42(4) P.D. 617 (1988).
29 *Association for Civil Rights in Israel v. Commander of the Central Region*, 43(2) P.D. 529 (1989).
30 H.C.J 253/88 *Sejdiah v. Minister of Defense*, 42(3) P.D. 801 (1988).
31 *Developments in Constitutional Law, supra* note 14, at 420.
32 Shetreet, *Reflections, supra* note 19, at 40 – 42.

For example, the *Shalit* case presented the question of "who is a Jew" in Israel. In that case, a Jewish father and an agnostic mother of non-Jewish parentage requested that their minor children be registered in Israel's population register as of Jewish ethnicity, but "without religion." The registration officer refused to register the children as Jews because, according to the halachic rules, a child born to a non-Jewish mother cannot be registered as a Jew. The father petitioned the High Court of Justice, which sat in full bench to hear the case. The majority opinion was that the registration officer was bound to effect registration in accordance with the parent's request unless he had reasonable grounds to believe that the declaration was not correct. The majority further held that for the purposes of registration of nationality the religious test was not determinative. Accordingly, the Court ordered the registration officer to register Shalit's children as Jews as requested.[33]

In the 1953 *Kol Ha'am* case, the Minister of the Interior closed down Kol Ha'am, Israel's communist newspaper, for ten days, in light of the high tensions between Israel and Russia. The Supreme Court ruled that this was within the Minister's statutory authority in light of the potential danger to the public's peace. However, nine months later, after tensions between the two countries had eased slightly, the Minister ordered the paper to close again. In light of this second closing, the Supreme Court held that the Minister must show that a publication will "probably" endanger the public peace before a newspaper can be closed down.[34]

While the Court normally upholds individual rights, it has sometimes restricted them in light of public necessity. For example, in *Yeridor v. Chairman of the Central Elections Committee*, the Court sustained a decision of the Election Committee to refuse to approve a list of candidates submitted by the "Al Ard" group for the Knesset elections in 1965. The Committee disqualified the list on the ground that it was an illegal association because its sponsors repudiated the integrity of the State and its very existence. Because the object of the group was to annihilate the State, the Committee could lawfully disqualify it.[35]

In *Kremer v. Jerusalem Municipality et al.*, the Court allowed the educational board to refuse applications of parents to transfer their children from a public school to an officially recognized private school on the grounds that this policy was to ensure the success of the Ministry of Education's program to reform elementary and secondary education. The purpose of the program was to raise the

---

33 H.C.J 56/68 *Shalit v. Minister of Interior*, 23(2) P.D. 477, 505 (1970) (Hebrew); S.J. at 35.

34 H.C.J 73/53 *Kol Ha'am v. Minister of Interior*, 7(2) P.D. 165, 871 (1953).

35 Election Appeal 1/65 *Yeridor v. Chairman of the Central Elections Committee*, 19(3) P.D. 365, 369 (1953).

standard of education of the school children who came from underprivileged neighborhoods, and to provide equality in educational opportunities among all social strata.[36] In this case, the Court denied that parents a basic right of freedom to choose non-public education of their children in favor of supporting equality in education.[37]

3. The Fundamental Principles of the Legal System

The executive branch in Israel, i. e., the government, is subjected to a number of fundamental principles that stem from the prevailing governmental system and stand at the basis of our existence as a society. The Israeli ruling acknowledged the fundamental principles as principles from which, according to them, the public law should be developed[38] and legislation should be repealed.[39] In addition, rules that contradict the fundamental principles should be disqualify.[40] Some of these principles are anchored in basic legislation such as the principle of respecting human rights, which is partially anchored in Basic Law: Human Dignity and Liberty and in Basic Law: Freedom of Occupation. On the other hand, there are many principles that are not explicitly anchored in primary or secondary legislation; they are learned from different sources, such as the Israeli Declaration of Independence,[41] Israel's heritage,[42] and liberal literature.[43]

Many references to the "basic principles of the system" can be found in the Israeli ruling. However, it seems that in every decision that dealt with the "basic principles of the system," certain basic principles were specifically recognized in accordance with the circumstances of the case in question. For example, in the

---

36 H.C.J 152/71 *Kremer v. Jerusalem Municipality et al.*, 25(1) P.D. 767, 771 (1971).

37 Shetreet, *Reflections, supra* note 19, at 58.

38 See for example 273–293/1127 *The State of Israel v. Klein*, 48(3) P.D. 485, 39 according to Justice Cheshin (1994).

39 See for example H.C.J 1/49 *Bejarno v. The Minister of Police*, 2(1) P.D 80; H.C.J 9098/01 *Genis v. The Ministry of Construction and Housing* (published on Nevo, 22.11.2004).

40 See for example H.C.J 142/89 *Laor Movement v. The Speaker of the Knesset*, 44(3) P.D. 529 (1990) (Hereinafter: Laor Affair).

41 See for example H.C.J 73/53 *Kol Ha'am v. Minister of Interior*, 7(2) P.D. 165, 871 (1953).

42 See for example: H.C.J 1635/90 *Jerzhevski v. The Prime Minister of Israel*, 45(1) P.D. 749 (1991).

43 See for example: H.C.J 2605/05 *The College of Law and Business v. The Finance Minister*, paragraph 23 to President Beinisch's judgement (published on Nevo, 2009), the majority opinion rejected the privatization of prisons, in part relying on the words of the philosopher John Locke, who is considered one of the fathers of liberalism. See, in contrast, what Justice E. E. Levy said in the minority opinion, paragraph 13 to his judgement.

Yardor decision,[44] the majority opinion recognized the state's right to act against bodies seeking to deny its existence as a Jewish and democratic state as a fundamental principle and allowed that a party could be disqualified on the basis of its platform, without an explicit law that authorizes it. In light of this, a defined and closed list of the basic principles that were recognized as such by the ruling cannot be described.

However, with regard to the government's activities, an overview of the literature and the ruling shows[45] that it is possible to point to five fundamental principles to which the government is subjected in every step of the way: the government as the public trustee; respecting human rights; the principle of legality and the rule of the law; Israel as a Jewish and democratic state; and the principle of the separation of powers. We will discuss these principles in detail in the following pages.

A. The Government and Ministers as Trustees of the People

A fundamental principle of government activities is the principle that the government is the trustee of the public. The rationale for this principle stems from the idea that the public administration and the government were formed by the public and for the public; therefore, their entire purpose is to act only in favor of the public, while maintaining its trust.[46] The principle of the government and the administration's trust towards the public is reflected in the Supreme Court's ruling from the first days of the state. In a number of decisions, the Supreme Court ruled that the State Authority is a public trustee and that this characteristic has to serve as a guideline in its customs and procedures.[47]

Justice Haim Cohn described it thus in The Shapira affair:

> "It is not the private property but the public property, which gives what it wants and denies what it wants, whereas it was created entirely to serve the public, and it has nothing of its own: as long as it is entrusted a trustee, and for itself has no other rights or duties, or dif-

---

44 E.A 1/65 *Yardor v. Central Elections Committee*, 19(3) P.D. 365 (1965).

45 H.C.J 8600/04 *Hof Aza Regional Council Head v. The Prime Minister*, 59(5) P.D. 673, paragraph 13 to President Barak's judgement (2005).

46 Itzhak Zamir, *The Administrative Power*, Vol A 36 – 37 (Second Edition, 2010); Yoseph M. Edrey Basic Law: The Economy of the State 170 (2004).

47 H.C.J 262/62 *Israel Peretz v. Kfar Shmaryahu*, 16(3) P.D. 2101, at 2115 (1962); H.C.J 5364/94 *Welner v. "Alignment" The Labor Party*, 49(1) P.D. 785 – 786 (1995).

ferent and separate from those, which stem from this trust or which were given or imposed on it by virtue of statutory provisions."[48]

From this trust duty of the law, the general law is derived, which is applicable to any governmental authority, including the government, the prime minister, and the ministers, because the discretion that is granted to a public authority must be operated fairly, honestly, from practical considerations alone, and with reason.

Vice-President Justice Elon noted:

> "A public authority, which appoints a civil servant, functions as a public trustee. It is a big rule in our hands, that this trust must be operated fairly, honestly, without extraneous considerations, and in the public interest, which by its power and for it the authority can make appointments."[49]

Justice Barak also ruled thus:

> "The state, by means of the acting in its name, is a public trustee, and have been entrusted with the public interest and properties to use them for the common good[...] This special status is imposing on the state the duty to act with reason, honesty, purity of heart and good intentions. The state may not discriminate, act arbitrarily, in lack of good faith or in a conflict of interest. It must maintain the principles of the natural justice. In short, it must act with fairness."[50]

The question of the government's incidence of the duty of loyalty arose during the Ginosar Affair, where the appointment of Yossi Ginosar as Director of the Ministry of Construction and Housing during the second Rabin government was discussed. The problem lay in the fact that Ginosar was involved in the Bus 300 Affair and the Nafso Affair while he worked at the Shin Bet. Ginosar was not put on trial in these affairs because of a presidential pardon in the Bus 300 Affair and because of the decision of the Landau Commission in the Nafso Affair.

The Supreme Court judges noted that the duty of loyalty to the general public in Israel is imposed on the government as well, being "the executive authority of the state" according to Section 1 to Basic Law: The Government.[51] Therefore,

---

48 H.C.J 142/70 *Shapira v. The District Committee of the Bar Association, Jerusalem*, 25(1) P.D. 331, 325 (1971).
49 H.C.J 90/4566 *Dekel v. The Finance Minister*, decision, 45(1) P.D. 28, 33 (1990).
50 H.C.J 840/79 *The Contractors and Builders in Israel Center v. The Government of Israel*, 35(3) P.D. 729, 745–746.
51 H.C.J 6163/92 *Eisenberg v. The Ministry of Construction and Housing*, 47(2) P.D. 229, 260 (1993).

it was determined that when considering the question of the appointment of a person with a criminal record to a senior position, the government must consider the damage to the public confidence in the government authorities that this kind of appointment might lead to.[52]

It was also noted regarding the exercising of discretion by the government on the subject that: "we must distinguish between questions of capacity (or power) and questions of judgment. The absence of an express statutory provision regarding the disqualification of a person with a criminal record, meets the qualifications of the candidate, but it does not rule out the possibility of considering his past in using the administrative discretion given to the appointing authority ... the duty of the public authority to take into account the criminal record of a candidate when it appoints a person to a public office is derived from the status of the public authority. The public authority is the public's trustee."[53]

B. The Duty to Respect Human Rights

The State of Israel has not gone the way of other new democratic countries, and did not enact a constitution in which the human rights that the state has to respect are listed.[54] Although in some laws, indirect protection was given to some rights,[55] it can be said with certainty that the human rights in Israel were a creation of a court ruling, which drew inspiration from the Declaration of Independence and the democratic nature and character of the State of Israel.

Although the basic rights are not anchored in legislation, the ruling has always viewed human rights as legal rights "that are not written in a book."[56] Over the years, the ruling that protects human rights consolidated in several ways. Already in the 1950s, in the *Kol Ha'Am* case,[57] which is considered one of the

---

52 Id., p. 259. See also: H.C.J 3094/93 *The Movement for Quality Government v. The Government of Israel,* 47(5) P.D. 404, 419, 428 (1993); H.C.J 4267/93 *Amitai—Citizens for Good Governance and Integrity v. The Prime Minister of Israel,* 47 P.D. 441, 462 (1993).

53 *Eisenberg, supra* note 51, at 256 – 257.

54 The Administrative Power, *supra* note 46, at 163 – 165.

55 See for example: Women's Equal Rights Law, 5711 – 1951, 68 190; Defamation Law, 5725 – 1965, 68 240; and Privacy Protection Law, 5741 – 1981, 68 128. Itzhak Zamir, The Administrative Power, *supra* note 46, 165 – 166.

56 Justice Landau in H.C.J 243/62 *Israel Film Studios LTD. v. Levi,* 16(1) P.D. 2407, at 2415 (1962).

57 *The Kol Ha'Am Case, supra* note 41; it should be noted that earlier the decision in the Bejarno case was given, which cancelled an administrative decision because of a violation of the freedom of occupation. See: H.C.J 1/49 *Bejarno v. Minister of Police,* 2 P.D. 80 (1949). The decision in the Kol Ha'Am case is considered more of a milestone because of the fact that it abolishes the Min-

most important decisions of the Supreme Court, Justice Agranat set the near certainty of a severe danger test. According to this test, the right to freedom of expression, which is considered a basic right, will not be violated unless there is a near certainty of a severe danger to another important public interest. In addition, the court interpreted laws and regulations that violate basic rights narrowly. This requires that an agreement in the law to make regulations that violate human rights should be explicit and clear.[58] Moreover, it was ruled that if an administrative action might violate a basic right, there is a duty to consider this violation in the balance of the considerations guiding the discretion of the administrative authority when it comes to taking that action. Thus, a duty is imposed on every administrative authority to balance between human rights and the public's interest when exercising administrative discretion.[59]

Despite this, until the Basic Laws were legislated, a law had the power to violate human rights, provided that the violation was made explicitly.[60] Over the years, attempts have been made to subordinate the human rights legislation in a judicial ruling and to ensure a stronger protection of them. Yet the court did not have an opportunity to cancel a law because it violates human rights.[61] To these attempts Justice Barak referred in the *Laor* case, which dealt with the violation of the right to equality:

> "According to the social and legal concept accepted here, the court does not take on itself the authority to announce the abolition of a law which contradicts the basic principles of our system [...] this is how we have acted for more than forty years. reflects the social consensus in Israel, and it enjoys the agreement of the enlightened public [...] It would not be appropriate if we deviate from our accepted approach, which reflects our legal-political tradition, and it would not be appropriate if we adopted a new approach that recognizes the power of the Supreme Court to announce an abolition of a law—which does not contradict

---

ister of Interior's decision due to his harsh statements and remarks, as well as because of the reversal of the decision in spite of it concerning, apparently, a political issue in the consensus. See: Pnina Lahav "The Hand of the Embroider: Individual Freedoms Sheet According to Justice Agranat" *TAU Law Review* 97 475, 505–503 (1992); and on the other hand see: Orit Rozen "Kol Ha'Am the Portrait of a Struggle" *Quite, We Are Speaking!—The Legal Culture of the Freedom of Expression in Israel* 71 (2006). Rozen believes that, in the decision, Justice Agranat articulated the public opinion versus the government opinion.

58 For a detailed discussion on the issue of defense of human rights through the principle of administrative legality, and the development of Jewish law which, according to a violation of a basic right, requires an explicit agreement in legislation, see Daphne Barak-Erez, *Administrative Law* vol. A 100–106, 121–125 (2010).

59 Itzhak Zamir, The Administrative Power, *supra* note 46, p. 104, 166–171.

60 H.C.J 337/81 *Mitrani v. Minister of Transport*, 37(3) P.D. 337 (1983).

61 Itzhak Zamir, The Administrative Power, *supra* note 46, p. 171.

an instruction reinforced in a Basic Law—and which contradicts the basic principles of the system."[62]

In 1992, several human rights were expressly anchored in the Israeli law book in two basic laws: Basic Law: Human Dignity and Liberty and Basic Law: Freedom of Occupation. As a result, these human rights received a super-legal status and their normative supremacy was established.[63] The test prescribed in the Basic Laws, under which the legality of a violation of human rights will be examined, is compliance with the terms of the limitations clause. According to this test, a violation of Basic Rights will be allowed when it is done "by a law which is befitting the values of the State of Israel, enacted for a proper purpose, and to an extent no greater than is required, or by such a law as before-mentioned from the power of express authorization."[64]

The limitations clause in Basic Law: Human Dignity and Liberty affects only laws subsequent to it, as written in Section 10 of the law.[65] Nevertheless, in the *Ganimat* case, the court took another important step and ruled that laws prior to the Basic Law will also be interpreted in light of the Basic Law.[66] Thus, violations of basic rights which rose from laws prior to the Basic Law were reduced.

The Basic Laws that anchor the human rights led to the enactment of more detailed laws, which are designed to protect human rights. For example, Section 1 of the Equal Rights for People with Disabilities Law, 5758 – 1998, notes:[67]

"Rights of people with disabilities and the obligation of Israeli society toward these rights are founded upon recognition of the principle of equality, man's worth—created in God's image—and on the principle of respect for all human beings."

The rights to equality and freedom of expression are not among the human rights which are explicitly detailed in the Basic Laws. However, the popular opin-

---

62 The Laor Case, *supra* note 40, 554. See also: Adi Parush "Judicial Activism, Legal Positivism and Natural Law—Justice Barak and the Doctrine of the Omnipotent Knesset" *TAU Law Review* 17 717 (1993); Yizhar Tal "The Omnipotent Legislature—Is That So?" *TAU Law Review* J 361 (1984).
63 Itzhak Zamir, *The Administrative Power, supra* note 46, p. 171–175; for the review of the impact of the Basic Laws on the administrative law, see Barak-Erez, above 21, p. 72–76.
64 Section 4 to Basic Law: Freedom of Occupation. For the analysis of the limitations clause, see: H.C.J 1715/97 *The Israeli Investment Managers Association v. Minister of Finance*, 51(4) P.D. 367 (1997); according to 4424/98 *Silgado v. the State of Israel*, 56(5) P.D. 529, 546–551 (2002); Itzhak Zamir, *The Administrative Power, supra* note 46, at 182–189.
65 *Id.*, p. 175–176.
66 M.C.A 537/95 *Ganimat v. State of Israel*, 49(3) P.D. 355, 410 (1995); Itzhak Zamir, *The Administrative Power, supra* note 9, 176.
67 SB 152.

ion is that these rights are implicitly included in the basic rights.[68] On the other hand, the Supreme Court ruled that overexpansion of human rights should be avoided, and that human dignity does not include all civil, political, and social rights.[69]

An important subject which the law regulated is the balance among different rights and between rights and public interests.[70] Regarding the second type of decisions, the court decided that the necessary balance is a vertical balance in light of either the limitations clause or according to the balancing formula that was decided upon in the *Kol Ha'Am* case ("the probability of the public peace being endangered"). For example, in the *Horeb* case,[71] the court dealt with the closing of Bar-Ilan Street on Saturday and with the question of what is the proper balance between respecting the freedom of movement of those who seek to use the road on Saturday and respecting the religious public sensibilities. The court ruled that the damage to the public sensibilities justifies the dismissal of individual rights only where there is a likelihood of the probability of the public peace being endangered ("beyond the level of intolerable degree").[72] In this case, that also meant a compliance with the principle of proportionality is demanded, i.e., that the violation of the basic right will not be excessive.[73]

Unlike the balance between human rights and a public interest, when the court has to balance between different rights, the balance is horizontal. In the *Dayan* case[74], the court dealt with the demands of protesters to hold pickets outside Rabbi Ovadia Yosef's private house and in the need to balance between the freedom to protest and the right to privacy. The meaning of the horizontal balance is the creation of a compromise between rights so that no right will be denied completely. In this case, the horizontal balance was reflected by the decision to delineate the pickets in a time and a place, and thus, on the one

---

68 On discrimination, see: H.C.J 5394/92 *Huppert v. "Yad Vashem", The World Holocaust Remembrance Center*, 48(3) P.D. 353, 360 (1994). For Justice Dorner's dissenting opinion, see: H.C.J 4541/94 *Miller v. Minister of Defense*, 49(4) P.D. 94, 113 (1995). On the subject of freedom of expression, see: P.C.A 294/91 *Chevra Kadisha Burial Society "Jerusalem Congregation" v. Kestenbaum*, 46(2) P.D. 464, 520 (1992) (Hereinafter: *The Kestenbaum Case*). See also Itzhak Zamir, The Administrative Power, *supra* note 46, p. 177–182.

69 H.C.J 4128/02 *Adam Teva V'Din Israel Union for Environmental Defense v. Prime Minister of Israel*, 58(3) P.D. 518 (2004).

70 Itzhak Zamir, The Administrative Power, *supra* note 46, at 182–183.

71 H.C.J 5016/96 *Horev v. Minister of Transport*, 51(4) P.D. 1 (1997).

72 *Id.*, p. 41.

73 *Id.*, p. 55.

74 H.C.J 2481/93 *Dayan v. Jerusalem District Police Commander*, 48(2) P.D. 456 (1994).

hand, limit the extent of violation of the Rabbi, and, on the other hand, not deny completely the right to protest.

Another issue which occupied the Supreme Court was applying human rights in the framework of the private law. In principle, the Basic Laws apply only to the state authorities.[75] In a few specific legislations, the legislature implemented the obligation to protect human rights on the individual as well. Example include Section 2 of the Employment (Equal Opportunities) Law, which prohibits discrimination in hiring; the Prohibition of Discrimination in Products, Services, and Entry to Entertainment Venues and Public Places Law, 5761–2000, which anchors the obligation of equality in these contexts; and the Protection of Privacy Law, which anchors the right to privacy.

With regard to areas where there is no specific legislation, both public bodies and bodies that fulfill functions of a public nature, though working in private law, are obliged to respect human rights by virtue of the doctrine of the bi-material bodies. According to this doctrine, their public nature obligates them to comply with certain public norms.[76] However, not all of the public law principles should be applied to these bodies, because this goes against the purpose of transferring the activity to the private law area—facilitating its function and giving it more freedom of action, similar to companies in the private sector. The Supreme Court ruled that between the private and the public law there is "a twilight zone, where the private and the public law are tangled."[77] The question about which principles should apply to hybrid bodies remains vague, and was not cleared enough in the ruling.

In the case of *Mifal HaPayis v. Gadot*,[78] Mifal HaPayis (Israel National Lottery) appealed to the Labor Court of Israel, claiming that the pension benefits that some of the former senior personnel received do not meet the requirements of fairness and reasonableness which hybrid bodies are committed to, according to principles of the public law. Mifal Hapayis also claimed the pension benefits drastically deviated from the accepted pension conditions for senior executives in government-owned companies. The court discussed the nature of Mifal HaPayis and determined that it is indeed a hybrid body due to its characteristics and background. According to the court, one of the factors that justified inter-

---

75 Section 11 of Basic Law: Human Dignity and Liberty.
76 The criteria that define a hybrid body were also not clarified enough in the ruling, and their characteristics were described only in general. See P.C.A 3414/93 *On v. Israel Diamond Exchange Industry, Ltd.*, 49(3) P.D. 196, 205 (1965).
77 *Id.*, p. 214.
78 Labor Appeal 300851/98 *Mifal HaPayis v. Gadot* (published on Nevo, 23.10.2003).

vention in the terms of contract was that Mifal HaPayis was a hybrid body.[79] The court balanced between the need to fulfill the contractual obligation and the public interest by using the money going to Mifal HaPayis for the public benefit, while using the grounds of probability, which is known from the public law; consequently, the court ruled that the defendants' pension terms should be compared to those of government-owned companies CEOs. If significant differences were found, the pension terms of the defendants should be reduced and refunds should be demanded.[80]

In another case, the court ruled that the Jewish National Fund has to act equitably because it is a hybrid body. Accordingly, the court rejected the claims against the appointment of an Israeli-Arab to the board of directors in Kakal. The petitioners argued that the appointment is a crucial one as it changes the fundamental business basis of the organization, which is to advance the Jewish settlement in Israel.[81]

In addition to the dual or hybrid bodies doctrine, the court applied the obligation to respect human rights on distinctly private bodies as well, using public law norms. For example, in the *Kestenbaum* case,[82] Justice Barak ruled that the obligation to respect human dignity should be applied in certain cases to private bodies through the public policy doctrine.[83] According to him, the statement that a contract violating a public policy doctrine is void allows the basic principles of the law to flow into private law, including the obligation to protect human rights.[84] For example, a contract which limits the freedom of occupation might be disqualified by virtue of being contrary to the public law.[85] This model has been called "the indirect applicability model," and it seems that it has yet to fully take root in the ruling.[86]

---

79 *Id.*, paras 26–30.
80 *Id.*, para 69.
81 Motion 5299/06 *Bank v. the Jewish National Fund*, p. 3, 27–30 (27.6.07).
82 *The Kestenbaum* Case, *supra* note 68, which dealt with restrictions on a burial company.
83 Section 30 of the Contracts (General Part) Law 5733–1973, 68 118.
84 *The Kestenbaum* Case, *supra* note 68, p. 531.
85 P.C.A 6601/96 *AES System Inc v. Saar*, 54(3) P.D. 860 (2000).
86 Hillel Sommer "From Childhood to Adulthood: Open Issues in the Implementation of the Constitutional Revolution," *Law and Business* A 59, 74 (5764).

C. The Rule of Law Principle

One of the basic principles which governs the administrative work in the democratic system of government is the rule of law ("Administrative Legality"). This principle is also accepted in the system of government in Israel. The rule of law determines that the administrative authority is not allowed to do anything without authorization by the law. This is a basic rule which is used to check the legality of any administrative decision, without exception.[87]

The rule of law arises from the perception of the public administration in a democracy. According to this perception, the power of the public administration is derived from the public and is for the public. It is clear, therefore, that all the authorities of the public administration are derived from the authorization of the public, which is reflected in the laws that are the creation of the public's representatives—the Knesset— and it is not allowed to act of its own accord without permission. In other words, an administrative authority is committed to act only by virtue of law, while any action which is not subject to or under the law shall be considered invalid.

At the basis of the rule of law are several rationales. First, by virtue of the separation of powers principle, the legitimacy of the executive branch's actions is derived from the laws that are enacted by the legislative branch by virtue of its role as the elected legislator that represents the people. Furthermore, this principle allows the judiciary and the legislature branches to criticize and better monitor the actions of the government. Second, the rule of law was designed to reduce the fear of abuse of power that might occur if there is not a framework of rules defined for action. Third, this principle is intended to ensure that the administrative authority will be a public trustee.

Nonetheless, due to the expansion of modern state functions, and due to the fast pace of modern life, operating the administration's rule of law precisely might make the government activity very problematic, and might prevent the administration from the flexibility it needs. The solution lies in the residual power of the government, stipulated in Section 32 of Basic Law: The Government which states that "[t]he Government is authorized to perform in the name of the State, subject to all laws, any act, which is not assigned by law to another authority."

Because of the need to balance the residual power with the administration's rule of law,[88] the residual power is limited by a number of ways: a) The residual

---

87 Zamir, *supra* note 46, at 49, 73–76; Barak-Erez, *Administrative Law, supra* note 58, at 97–100, 106–109.
88 Barak-Erez, *supra* note 58, at 139–143.

power cannot violate constitutional human rights; b) The residual power will exist only if the authority of a certain action is not in the jurisdiction of another authority; c) Its operation is subjected to the law.[89] For more information on Section 32 of the law, see Chapter 8 hereinafter.

Alongside the obligation to act only under explicit authorization of the law, the government is also obligated to honor the rule of law as the public's trustee. This is achieved, either through obeying and honoring the existing legislation (which is made with, among other things, the assistance of the Attorney General) or through making sure that the law is being enforced on the citizens and bodies operating in it, this while operating the different responsible authorities.

D. Israel as a Jewish and Democratic State

In every system there are principles that reflect the basic values of law and society. In Israel, these values are derived, among others things, from Israel's essence as "a Jewish and Democratic State." The Supreme Court's judges described it thus in the *Kaadan* case,[90] which dealt with the right of an Israeli Arab to build his house on state land allocated to the Jewish Agency:

> "Alongside the specific purposes underlying the authority and discretion of the administration, there are also general purposes which are spread out as a normative umbrella over all the legislations. These general purposes reflect the basic values of the Israeli law and society. They show that every legislation has an integral part in the comprehensive legal system. The basic principles of the system 'seep' into every legislation, and constitute as its general purpose [[....]] These basic principles also reflect the essence of Israel as a Jewish and democratic state."

Israel's essence as a Jewish and democratic state can also be found explicitly and implicitly in the Israeli Declaration of Independence:

> "Accordingly we, members of the people's council, representatives of the Jewish community of Eretz-Israel and of the Zionist movement, are here assembled on the day of the termination of the British mandate over Eretz-Israel and, by virtue of our natural and historic right and on the strength of the resolution of the United Nations general assembly, hereby declare the establishment of a Jewish state in Eretz-Israel, to be known as the State of Israel."

---

89 *Id.*, at 145.
90 H.C.J 6698/95 *Kaadan v. Katzir*, 54(1) P.D. 258, paragraph 20 according to Justice Barak (2000) (Hereinafter: *The Kaadan case*).

In addition, Israel's essence as a democratic state is reflected in the Declaration of Independence implicitly:

> "The State of Israel will be open for Jewish immigration and for the Ingathering of the Exiles; it will foster the development of the country for the benefit of all its inhabitants; it will be based on freedom, justice and peace as envisaged by the prophets of Israel; it will ensure complete equality of social and political rights to all its inhabitants irrespective of religion, race or sex; it will guarantee freedom of religion, conscience, language, education and culture; it will safeguard the Holy Places of all religions; and it will be faithful to the principles of the Charter of the United Nations."

Israel's Jewish character finds expression in the day-to-day life of the state and in its laws, such as: the ban on pig breeding; setting Jewish holidays as days of rest, marriage, and divorce under the Jewish laws; and the Law of Return, 5710 – 1950.[91] Israel's democratic character also has a wide expression in legislation. The court was not satisfied with a narrow meaning of democracy as the majority rule, but also interpreted the democracy in Israel as a system that includes essential principles, such as protection of human rights and other liberal values.[92]

The phrase "a Jewish and democratic state" was first introduced into Israeli legislation in the amendment to Basic Law: The Knesset, which stated that:

> 7 A. A candidates' list shall not participate in elections to the Knesset, and a person shall not be a candidate for election to the Knesset, if the objects or actions of the list or the actions of the person, expressly or by implication, include one of the following:
>   (1) Negation of the existence of the State of Israel as a Jewish and democratic state [...].

Later, the term "Jewish and democratic state" was also anchored in the aim section of Basic Law: Human Dignity and Liberty:

> "The purpose of this Basic Law is to protect human dignity and liberty, in order to establish in a Basic Law the values of the State of Israel as a Jewish and democratic state."

A similar section was also inserted into Basic Law: Freedom of Occupation in 1994.

---

91 Daphne Barak Erez "The Evolution of a Pig: A National Symbol of Religious Interest?" *Law* 33 403 (2003); Zamir, *supra* note 46, at 40, 60 – 62. And see about distinguishing between religious and national norms, Shimon Shetreet, *Freedom of Conscience and Religion: No Imposition of Religious Norms and No Limitations on Religious Grounds*, 3 Mishpatim 467–493, (1974) (Hebrew).
92 *Id.*, at 46, 67–70.

The interpretive question raised by the phrase "Jewish and democratic" is twofold. First, it requires clarification of the meaning of each of these terms alone. For example, there are several different interpretations to the term "Jewish," such as "a Jewish-religious character" compared to "a national or culture Jewish character."[93] In the same way, the term "democracy" can be interpreted as "liberal democracy," which includes in it, among other things, perceptions about human rights, the rule of law, etc., or it can be interpreted in a narrower sense as purely procedural democracy. Second, clarification is needed about the meaning of the term "Jewish and democratic" as a whole, and about the relationship between its two components. For example, some claim that these are two completely contradictory terms, which cannot exist together,[94] whereas some claim that they fall into line with each other.[95]

Others will claim that a certain tension exists between the terms, but that tension can be resolved by balancing between them and giving preference to one of them. Thus, for example, Justice Elon claims that the fact that the term "Jewish" appears before the term "democratic" in the Basic Laws means that the principles should be balanced with a priority given to the state's Jewish character.[96]

However, there is an approach which claims it is possible to reconcile the tension between the terms using the appropriate interpretation of them. Thus, Prof. Gavison interprets the term "Jewish state" in its content-culture sense— that is, a nation state which draws inspiration from unique religious frameworks. She adopts a basic definition of democracy in the sense of a humanist legal system, one that attributes a principle to the human right to participate equitably in determining the future of the society in which he or she lives. Thus, Prof. Gavison seeks to reconcile the terms.[97]

---

93 *Id.*, at 62.
94 Avigdor Levontin "Jewish and Democratic—Personal Reflections", A Jewish and Democratic State 57, 74 (5756): "Saying Jewish and Democratic is almost like saying "hot and cold." "Hot and cold" is not impossible, but it is lukewarm; and "lukewarm" is usually used to describe not-hot-and-not-cold, and in any case, what point does it have?" See also: Oren Yiftachel and As'ad Ghanem "Understanding Ethnocratic Regimes: The Politics of Seizing Contested Territories", State & Society 4, 761 (2005).
95 Alexander Yakobson and Amnon Rubinstein *Israel and the Family of Nations* 8–18 (2003).
96 See Menachem Elon "Through Constitutional Law: The Values of a Jewish and Democratic State in Light of Basic Law: Human Dignity and Liberty" TAU Law Review 17 p. 659, 666–670, 678 (5753).
97 Ruth Gavison "A Jewish and Democratic State: Challenges and Risks," A Jewish and Democratic State, p. 169, 224–225 (5756).

Another possibility is the interpretation of the term "Jewish" as "Traditional-Jewish." Under this model, the democratic character of the state is maintained, alongside the recognition of the Jewish religion and tradition as a rich heritage, which will influence the character of the state, its values and its culture. A similar definition was only recently adopted by the European Union (EU) in the Treaty of Lisbon, under which the EU sought to declare its ethical and cultural vision. The treaty states that the EU will draw inspiration from the cultural, religious, and humanist heritage of Europe. Alongside these characteristics, the EU provided in the preamble of the treaty the universal concepts of human rights, freedom, democracy, equality, and the rule of law—which developed in the light of the unique European heritage.[98]

In fact, although the characterization itself was accepted by a large part of the nation, the question of the proper interpretation of "Jewish and democratic state" has become the focus of another political debate between those who are religious and those who are secular, and between Zionist and other parties. Every side prefers to interpret the term in a way it finds convenient.

The Supreme Court preferred to interpret the terms in a way that reduces the tension inherent in the phrase. Thus, in the *Ben-Shalom* case, the Supreme Court interpreted that "a Jewish and democratic state" means: "The state is a Jewish state; its regime is an enlightened democracy, which provides rights to all citizens, Jewish and not Jewish."[99] A full expression of this concept was given in the *Kaadan* case, where it was determined that the allocation of land for the settlement of Jews only is unconstitutional based both on democratic and Jewish values:[100]

"Indeed, the return of the Jewish people to their homeland is derived from the values of the State of Israel as a Jewish and democratic state …. From these values of the State of Israel— from each of them individually and their integration—there are a few conclusions: thus, for example…Jews and non-Jews are citizens with equal rights and obligations in the State of

---

98 For an emphasis and discussion of the role the Jewish tradition played in shaping the character of the State of Israel and its legal arrangements, and for a discussion of the desired combination between the democratic character of the State of Israel and the Jewish tradition, see Shimon Shetreet, *The Good Land: Between Power and Religion*, p. 168–179, 493–508 (1998); Treaty of Lisbon amending the Treaty on European Union and the Treaty establishing the European Community, signed in Lisbon, 13 December 2007, 2007/C 306/01, available at: http://eurlex.europa.eu/JOHtml.do?uri=OJ:C:2007:306:SOM:EN:HTML (accessed February 9, 2017).

See also Shimon Shetreet *On Citizenship and National Identity in Europe and Israel* The Israel Journal of Foreign Affairs, pp. 115–124 (2011).

99 E.A 2/88 *Ben-Shalom v. The Central Elections Committee for the Twelfth Knesset*, 43(4) P.D. 221, 231 (1989).

100 *The Kaadan Case, supra* note 90, paragraph 31 to President Barak's judgement (2000).

Israel …. Moreover: not only do the values of the State of Israel as a Jewish state does not require discrimination on the basis of religion or nationality, but also that these values forbid discrimination and require equality between religions and nationalities …. True, a special key to enter the house was given to the Jewish people, but when a person is a lawful citizen in the house, he or she enjoy equal rights like all other household members …. There is, therefore, no contradiction between the values of the State of Israel as a Jewish and democratic state and the absolute equality of all its citizens. Quite the opposite: equal rights for all people in Israel, whatever may be their religion and nationality, is derived from the values of the State of Israel as a Jewish and democratic state."

E. The Separation of Powers

a. General

Alongside the other basic principles, the separation of powers doctrine is one of the bases of a democracy. Its aim is to ensure the freedom of the citizens of the state by preventing the concentration of too much power in the hands of the government.

At the basis of this principle stands the concept that the greatest danger for a person's freedom is from the government, especially in the modern state, which holds the monopoly on the power. Splitting the governmental power by dividing it between the different authorities is meant to be a key tool in preventing a dangerous tyranny that can be caused by concentration of power in the hands of one person or one body:[101]

The accumulation of all powers, legislative, executive, and judiciary, in the same hands, whether of one, a few, or many, and whether hereditary, self-appointed, or elective, may justly be pronounced the very definition of tyranny.[102]

And in the words of Lord Acton: "Power tends to corrupt, and absolute power corrupts absolutely."

This pronunciation of the principle of separation of powers is usually attributed to the 18th-century French scholar Montesquieu, who described the model that prevailed at that time in England, which he considered to be the appropriate model. In fact, the birth of the idea was in the writings of the 17th-century philosopher John Locke, who explained that the principle that stood at the basis of

---

101 Zamir, *supra* note 46, p. 66, 91; Amnon Rubinstein and Barak Medina, *The Constitutional Law of the State of Israel* Volume 2, p. 333 (2005); Ze'ev Segal, Constitutional Principles in the State of Israel 50 (1988).
102 *The Federalist No. 47*, The Particular Structure of the New Government and the Distribution of Power Among Its Different Parts, *New York Packet* Wednesday, January 30, 1788 [James Madison].

the glorious revolution in England in 1688 was the principle of separation of powers.[103]

The roles of government are usually divided into three branches: legislative, executive, and judicial. In general, legislative action includes the creation and acceptance of new laws, which tend to be of a general nature. The Executive's branch action includes the administering and implementing of laws and making decisions related to specific cases within the authority prescribed by law. Judicial action is the implementation of the law in order to settle disputes in court. However, it should be kept in mind that it is difficult to find an exact definition of the three roles, and that the boundaries among them may be quite murky.[104]

The classic concept of separation of powers maintained a complete separation among the three branches, each dealing only with its unique characteristics: the legislative branch only legislates; the executive branch only executes; and the judiciary branch only judges. This concept has never been fully implemented due to its lack of practicality.[105] Indeed, every branch has its own distinct characteristics that constitute its raison d'etre; however, every branch also carries out acts that are distinctly included within the bounds of the other branches. In Israel, for example, the executive branch enacts secondary legislation and runs administrative courts; the legislative branch enacts a quasi-judicial proceeding while examining the question of removing the immunity of a MK; and the judiciary branch has administrative functions in different matters, such as in a writ of execution.[106]

The dominant view in the world today is that, in order to protect freedom, the actions of the three branches should be bound together, allowing, alongside free action, a close mutual supervision. This approach is supposed to ensure that the principle underlying Montesquieu's idea will be fulfilled—preventing the concentration of too much power in the hands of one branch. According to this doctrine, the doctrine of checks and balances, whose clearest expression is found in the US government, the separation of powers is based on a balance of

---

103 Segal, *supra* note 101, p. 51.
104 Barak-Erez, *supra* note 58, at 86 – 95.
105 Even England of the 18th century, which Montesquieu described as having a complete separation of powers, did not have a complete separation of powers. For example, Lord Chancellor was the Speaker of the House of Lords and a member of the legislative branch, a judge, and a member of Government. For more examples, see Segal, *supra* note 101, at 51.
106 For a description of the wide range of powers which is in the hands of the executive branch, including legislative and quasi-judicial powers, as well as a description of the difficulty in distinguishing between the natures of the various powers, see Barak-Erez, *supra* note 58, p. 83 – 95.

powers between the branches, which creates non-dependence between them and a capability for mutual supervision.[107]

Such a mechanism ensures that the authorities will be interwoven, and conduct a dialogue and interact and review each other constantly. As noted by the Supreme Court:

> "An enlightened democratic system of government is a system of separation of powers. This separation does not mean that every branch is for itself, without any consideration of the other branches. Such a view will deeply hurt the foundations of democracy itself, as the meaning of this is that every branch will be a dictatorship in its on framework. On the contrary, separation of powers means mutual checks and balances between the various branches. Not walls between the branches but balancing and supervising bridges."[108]

In another case, the Supreme Court expressed a similar idea by President Shamgar:

> "Separation of powers does not mean the creation of a buffer which decisively prevents any contact between the branches, but its expression is mainly in the balance between the branches, in theory and in practice, which allows independence and defined mutual supervision."[109]

It should be noted that the principle of separation of powers is not implemented the same in every democratic country. For example, in a parliamentary government like Canada's, there is no clear constitutional separation between the legislative and the executive branches.[110] The cabinet, which is the heart of the government, is granted executive powers and legislative powers. The cabinet ministers are also members of the legislative branch. The prime minister, who heads the executive branch, is also a member of the cabinet and the legislative branch.[111] The cabinet gets its members and governing power from the legislative

---

107 Zamir, *supra* note 46 at 92–93; Segal, *supra* note 101, at 51–52.

108 The words of Justice (his title at the time) Barak in H.C.J 73/85 *The "Kach" Faction v. The Speaker of the Knesset*, 39(3) P.D. 141, 158 (1985).

109 President Shamgar in H.C.J 306/81 *Platto-Sharon v. The Knesset Committee*, 35(4) P.D. 118, 141 (1981).

110 Francois Venter, *Constitutional Comparison: Japan, Germany, Canada, & South Africa as Constitutional States*, 219 (1st ed., 2000).

111 Patrick Malcolmson and Richard Myers, *The Canadian Regime* (2nd ed., Broadview Press, 2002) at 120. The centralization of the cabinet was probably less pronounced in the days when the queen had more power.

branch, while also controlling the parliament.[112] The absence of a clear separation is not considered a shortcoming of the Canadian system. To the contrary, the merging of roles is seen in Canada in a positive light, and is an important component of responsible parliamentary government which exists in the country.

b. The Separation of Powers in Israel

The State of Israel accepted, in principle, the doctrine of the separation of powers, in the sense of the division of powers between the various branches: the Knesset is mainly engaged in legislation, the government is mainly engaged in execution of laws, and the judiciary is mainly engaged in adjudication.[113] It would be a mistake to see only the government as the executive branch according to Montesquieu's model—notwithstanding Paragraph 1 of Basic Law: The Government, which states that "The Government is the executive authority of the State of Israel"—rather that the government's agencies, including the public administration, are the executive authority.[114]

Apparently, as part of the balance of power among the three branches, the legislative branch receives the precedence, being the elected body representing the people.

In particular, it can be argued that the Knesset is superior to the government in two major respects: first, the Knesset establishes the government and can disperse it; and second, the Knesset can determine and limit the powers of the government by legislation. (It should be noted that this does not mean that the government operates directly as an organ of the Knesset, because it has its own operation power.)[115] For these reasons, the academic discourse in Israel focuses mainly on the tension between the legislative branch and the judicial branch, mainly because of the fundamental review that the Supreme Court began to give on the constitutionality of laws in the 1990s, after the enactment of Basic Law: Human Dignity and Liberty and Basic Law: Freedom of Occupation.

The problem is that this analysis about the superiority of the Knesset does not reflect the true situation, due to the enormous weight of the executive branch in the everyday life of the individual and the state. Focusing on the tension be-

---

112 Indeed the ministers of the cabinet are the political leaders of the factions of the parliamentary. *Hogg*, 9.5(e).

113 Zamir, *supra* note 46, at 36, 68, 412–413. However, as mentioned, there is a mixture of powers between the various branches. Thus, the executive branch also deals with legislative and quasi-judicial duties, and the other branches also deal with executive duties.

114 Id., p. 328.

115 Segal, *supra* note 101, at 54.

tween the judiciary branch and the legislative branch blurs the fact that, among the three branches, the executive branch is the most dominant. In fact, it can be determined that the principle of separation of powers eroded significantly, mainly with regard to the executive branch.[116] If in the 19th century the permissive liberal approach (laissez faire) was common, according to which the state's role is limited to maintaining the public order and not intervening in other areas, in the early 20th century, and especially after WWII, the welfare state approach began to develop quickly. The rise of the welfare state comes in light of the significant harm caused by the permissive approach to the weaker sectors, as well as the recognition that there is a need for governmental regulation of the free market and the supply of services by the state agencies.[117]

The governmental authorities now deal with detailed planning of the national economy, including everything that is connected to the areas of finance, industry, agriculture, and other industries. The population is entitled to services of housing, welfare, education, health, etc., which the state regulates and determines the way of acceptance and scope. The state also works on protecting fair trade, improving safety at work and on the roads, ensuring social working conditions, and more. Even in the current era, where there is a tendency to privatize services that once were public, there is governmental control over the provision of those services; service providers must meet terms that were defined in advance by the public administration. The welfare state has developed so much that today almost every action a person performs, whether simple or complex, depends to some extent on an administrative decision, or is affected by an activity regulated or supervised by an administrative body.[118]

The intensive involvement of the executive branch in the life of the population naturally led to the expansion of its areas of activity.[119] Moreover, due to the special circumstances in Israel, its executive branch is stronger and less restrained than in other countries. For example, the security problems with which Israel has had to deal since its establishment, and the need to absorb enormous amounts of immigration movements which arose in different periods, forced the delegation of more powers than normal to the executive branch.[120]

---

116 Basic Law: The Government.

117 Zamir, *supra* note 46, at 31–34, 68–69, 95; Barak-Erez, *supra* note 58, at 23–28, 48–49.

118 Zamir, *supra* note 46, at 34–35; see also Asher Arian, David Nachmias, and Ruth Amir *Executive Governance in Israel* p. 33–35 (2002).

119 Baruch Bracha *Administrative Law*, Vol. A 53–55 (1986). (Hebrew); Arian, Nachmias and Amir, above 87, p. 28, 32–33.

120 Zamir, *supra* note 46, at 95–96, 444 (2nd ed., 2010). Zamir counts additional factors for the growth of the executive branch's authorities in the Israel. Among other things, he refers to the

It should be noted that the emergence of parties led by one leader, such as Yesh Atid in the 19th and 20th Knessets, as well as Kulanu in the 20th Knesset, weakens the Knesset; "individual" parties controlled by the leader violate the freedom of opinion and judgment of the Knesset members of those parties.

4. The Relationship between the Executive and Legislative

In Israel, there are very close relationships between the government, which is the executive branch, and the legislature, which is the Knesset. In the process of building the government, the member of Knesset (MK) who has been selected by the president of the state as the candidate having the greatest likelihood of composing the government. That candidate has to compose a coalition of the majority of parliament (the Knesset) who would support a cabinet presided by the MK composing the cabinet. In fact, it is not possible to separate the process of composing the coalition from the process of selecting the ministers who will serve in the government. The ministers are chosen from the members of the Knesset who represent the coalition parties.[121] The positions that each party receives in the cabinet is one of the fundamental terms of the coalition negotiations.[122] Whereas other presidential systems maintain a clear separation between the legislature and the cabinet, in parliamentary systems like Israel's, the separation is amorphous. As long as the government holds a stable coalition, it can maintain discipline with all of the MKs belonging to the coalition. In this way, the government can control the Knesset, and the MKs of the coalition compose the majority of the Knesset.

The inherent dependency of the Knesset on the government comes from the characteristics of the system—a process of expanding the secondary legislation in Israel which contributes to the empowerment of the executive against the legislator. This process has been partially suppressed by the Supreme Court of Israel, which has enforced the notion that the legislature is the branch that legislates the rules shaping the main principles which guide the different bodies.

---

lack of a complete and reinforced constitution, which can outline the relationship between the various branches while protecting each branch from being harmed by another branch, and, more generally, which can maintain the checks and balances of the government as a whole (for example, keeping the balance between the central government and the local authorities). See also Arian, Nachmias, and Amir, *supra* note 118, at 43.

121 Apart from such instances when a Minister is not an MK.

122 See generally Dani Koren and Boaz Shapira, Coalitions (1997).

One cannot ignore the fact that the Knesset holds many supervising mechanisms designed to supervise, control, and manage other operations of the governments, thus, ensuring that the obligation of the government towards the Knesset is maintained. These mechanisms include the motion of no-confidence and budget supervision.

A. The Interaction between the Executive Branch and the Judicial Branch

a. General

The Israeli branch which is the closest to Montesquieu's theory of separation of powers is the judiciary. In order to realize the principles of the rule of law and of equality before the law, the judicial branch must have full independence with regard to other branches, or as close as possible to it.

Currently in Israel, although the court has the authority to rule, decide in disputes, and issue orders that bind the executive branch, in practice the final word rests with the executive branch, which holds the power of enforcement of those judgments. Execution depends on the executive branch's discretion and respect for the court.

b. The Involvement of the Executive Branch in the Powers of the Judiciary Branch

The principle of separation of powers requires, as stated, a separation between the executive branch and the judiciary branch. However, the executive branch has a legitimate role in the eyes of the judiciary branch, which is manifested in the executive branch's responsibility for the Directorate of Courts. In addition, the executive branch takes on itself—and, in our opinion, wrongly—additional powers from the judiciary branch powers.

The proper approach regarding the responsibility of the executive branch over the judicial system is that, other than responsibility for the Directorate of Courts, there should be no intervention of any kind by the executive branch in the judicial branch's field of activity. Although intervention is not the norm, it is done in many cases, sometimes even with the consent (or on the basis of the advice) of the judiciary branch itself. Hereinafter, we will discuss the various ways through which the executive branch gains influence and control over the field of the judiciary branch.

The control of the executive branch over the Directorate of Courts is influenced by the tension between two principles. On the one hand, the independence of the judiciary branch requires its control over its regular management.

On the other hand, the government's responsibility for the functioning of all branches under the principle of democratic responsibility requires that it will have responsibility for the activity of the Directorate of Courts. In practice, the Israeli model gives the Minister of Justice wide powers. However, in many cases, the minister is under a duty of consultation with the President of the Supreme Court or the duty to obtain the President's consent. Sometimes it is only a force of custom and does not have a legal status.[123]

The powers of the Minister of Justice include establishing courts and determining their places,[124] appointing court presidents (with the consent of the President of the Supreme Court),[125] and filing complaints against judges. The appointment of judges is entrusted on a commission that includes ministers, judges, MKs, and attorneys,[126] but, in this context as well, the Minister of Justice enjoys significant power, because he or she is responsible for summoning the commission (with the agreement of the President of the Supreme Court).[127] The administrative authority of the Minister of Justice finds clear expression in the fact that he or she appoints the Director of Courts, and is responsible for the orderly management of the courts.[128]

In our opinion, the current situation in which great power is given to the Minister of Justice is inappropriate. Preserving the power of the judiciary branch requires the transfer of administrative powers regarding adjudication from the Minister of Justice to the Supreme Court. Here are some guidelines to the required changes: a) Do not give the executive branch control over judicial matters or matters relating to judges; b) The authority of the central administration of the courts should be in the hands of the Minister of Justice, but should be transferred to the judiciary branch on a local level; and c) The power to enact procedural regulations should be in the hands of the minister and the head of the judiciary branch, especially regarding civil procedure.[129]

The appropriate model in our opinion is as follows: The responsibility for the Director of Courts will be given to the Minister of Justice and to the President of

---

123 For more details, see Shimon Shetreet *On Adjudication*, 234–235 (2004) (Hebrew).
124 Section 33 and Section 43 of The Court Law [Consolidated Version], 5744–1984, The Law Book 198.
125 Section 10 of The Court Law.
126 Section 4 of Basic Law: The Judiciary.
127 Section 7(a) of The Court Law.
128 *Id.*, Section 82(a). The appointment of the Director of Courts is made with the consent of the President of the Supreme Court.
129 Shetreet, *On Adjudication, supra* note 123, at 239–241, 356–357 (Hebrew); Shimon Shetreet "The Culture of Judicial Independence in Israel" *Law & Business* 10 525, 534–537 (5769) (Hebrew).

the Supreme Court jointly. The appointment of the Director of Courts will be made with the consent of the President of the Supreme Court. The budget will be prepared by the two, as part of the budget of the Ministry of Justice. The court staff will be disconnected from the Civil Service Commission and will be subjected to the Director of Courts. The authority to make regulations will be given to the Minister of Justice and to the President of the Supreme Court; that authority will be made according to the recommendations of a commission that will be established by law. A Council of Court Presidents will be set up, empowered to determine the procedures. In this way, a proper balance between the principle of the judiciary branch's independence and the principle of parliamentary responsibility and democratic accountability can be achieved.[130]

As for the appointment of judges, it seems that our existing arrangement is appropriate. Although the Minister of Justice has a priority in driving the wheels of the Judicial Selection Commission, priority is also given to the President of the Supreme Court. This is because, in order to present a candidate who is not supported by neither the President of the Supreme Court or by the Minister of Justice, the votes of at least three committee members are required, i.e., more than the number of seats allocated to each of the bodies represented in the committee, except for the Supreme Court.[131] The committee represents all state authorities, and the executive branch has only two votes out of nine.[132]

The arrangement in Israel regarding disciplinary proceedings against judges is also appropriate. The Minister of Justice has the authority to initiate disciplinary proceedings, while the disciplinary hearing itself is conducted by an independent tribunal whose composition is determined by law.[133]

---

130 Shetreet, "The Culture of Judicial Independence in Israel," *supra* note 129, p. 561 (Hebrew); Shimon Shetreet, *On Adjudication, supra* note 123, p. 235–238, 357–358 (Hebrew).
131 Section 7(a) of The Courts Law.
132 Section 4(b) Basic Law: The Judiciary; Shimon Shetreet, On Adjudication, *supra* note 129, at 266–295 (Hebrew); Shetreet *"The Culture of Judicial Independence in Israel," supra* note 135, at 560–561 (Hebrew); for a comparative review of the procedure for the appointment of judges, see: Assaf Shapira "Judges Appointment Procedures—A Comparative Perspective," *Parliament* issue 72 on the Israel Democracy Institute website (Hebrew).
133 Sections 17–21 of the Courts Law; on this regard in a comparative perspective see *Trial: A Study of the Appointment and Accountability of English Judiciary* (1976); Shimon Shetreet, J. Déschenes, *Judicial Independence: The Contemporary Debate* (1985); Shimon Shetreet, Christopher Forsyth, Eds., *The Culture of Judicial Independence: Conceptual Foundations a Practical Challenges* (2011); Shimon Shetreet, Ed., *The Culture of Judicial Independence: Rule of Law and World Peace* (2014); Shimon Shetreet and Sophie Turenne, *Judges on Trial: Independence and Accountability of the English Judiciary*, 2nd ed. (2013).

The executive branch can exercise its powers in a way that interferes in the judicial process, and by personal intervention and influence over the judicial process. An example of the second type of intervention can be seen in the *Shalit* case, where the court dealt with the question who is a Jew. Justice Zussman testified[134] directly that there was an attempt by people from the executive branch to take advantage of their status and respect in order to tip the court's ruling. In the Jewish Underground case, there was also an intervention of public personalities (mostly Knesset members); they demanded a stay of proceedings, the replacement of the judge, etc.[135]

The executive branch may intervene in the activity of the judiciary branch through secondary legislation on a matter pending before a court. If the legislative branch enacts secondary legislation corresponding to the position of a petitioner on a matter pending before a court, there is no problem because the legal conflict is basically resolved and the legal expenses are saved. However, the question arises whether it is appropriate for the executive branch to rule in secondary legislation on a matter pending before a court. The independence of the judiciary requires avoiding secondary legislation on a matter pending before a court (against the position of the petitioner) and, even more so, when it comes to giving an individual court order.[136]

Organizationally, the Attorney General belongs to the executive branch. However, the law gives the Attorney General the power to intervene in a significant way in the judicial process. For example, the Attorney General can make the decision whether or not to prosecute a person for a criminal law[137] or make the decision to delay legal proceedings at any stage between the filing of the indictment and the giving of the court's decision.[138] However, the Attorney General is not subjected to the government when making substantive decisions in matters of prosecution and when providing legal opinions,[139] but only formally in matters of his or her appointment and dismissal; therefore, this involvement does not strengthen the executive branch at the expense of the judiciary branch.[140]

---

134 H.C.J 56/68 *Shalit v. Minister of Interior*, 23(2) P.D. 477, 505 (1970) (Hebrew).
135 Shimon Shetreet, *On Adjudication*, *supra* note 123, at 358–361; Shimon Shetreet "The Culture of Judicial Independence in Israel", *supra* note 129, p. 551, 553–554 (Hebrew).
136 *Id.*, p. 554; Shimon Shetreet, *On Adjudication*, *supra* note 123, at 361–362 (Hebrew).
137 Section 62 of the Criminal Procedure [Consolidated Version] 5742–1982, LB 43.
138 *Id*, Section 231.
139 The "Commission of Jurists on the Powers of the Attorney General of the Government" Report, p. C (Jerusalem, 1962).
140 Shimon Shetreet, *On Adjudication*, *supra* note 129, at 380–385 (Hebrew).

The court is limited to adjudicating only petitions that were brought before it; it cannot initiate a judicial review on the government's activity. This limitation can be exploited by the government through a quick action of establishing facts before the court has the opportunity to review the government's activity. In this way, the executive branch may change the situation in practice, essentially thwarting judicial decisions in advance, without the court having a viable option of preventing it. Such actions are not common, but have happened a few times, such as in the case of the expulsion of Hamas activists to Lebanon in late 1992.[141]

5. Judicial Review of Legislative Actions

As discussed above, despite the principle of separation of powers, the three branches of government interact through a system of "checks and balances." An important component of this system, which is central to the judiciary branch's independence from the executive branch, is the judiciary branch's ability to monitor the actions of the executive branch and intervene. In recent years, an important development in this issue occurred in Israel.[142]

The authority of the court to review the actions of the executive branch have been anchored for many years in Section 15 of Basic Law: The Judiciary. The Supreme Court made it clear that this power is not limited to low-level governmental authorities, but also applies to decisions about the government itself.[143] Initially, the court reviewed administrative decisions on two levels: a formal examination of the legality of the administrative action and an examination of the reasonableness of an action, which was added later.[144] As part of the judicial review, the court granted protection to basic rights, even in the absence of a constitutional grounding or a formal law, through creative interpretation and judicial activism.[145]

The nature of the judicial review in the first years of the state was, as mentioned, quite formal. In those years, the court refrained from interfering in political matters. For example, the court refrained from intervening in the issue of the

---

141 *Id.*, p. 362–366.
142 For further details, see Shimon Shetreet, *On Adjudication, supra* note 123, at 394–399 (Hebrew).
143 *Eisenberg v. The Ministry of Construction and Housing*, judgement, *supra* note 51, at 275 (Hebrew).
144 Menachem Hofnung "Authority, Power and Separation of Powers—Judicial Criticism in Israel in a Comparative Perspective" *Mishpatim* 28 211, 221–222 (5757) (Hebrew).
145 Shimon Shetreet, *On Adjudication, supra* note 123, at 399. (Hebrew).

entry of the first German ambassador to Israel who served in the Wehrmacht in his past, claiming that it is a political matter that cannot be examined in legal standards.[146] The court also dismissed many petitions on the grounds that the petitioner has no "locus standi" on the issue. For example, the petition of a single petitioner regarding the recruitment of yeshiva students was denied on the grounds that the petitioner does not have more interest in the topic than the rest of the public, who think that the exemption of yeshiva students from military service is wrong.[147]

In recent years, there has been a development in the scope of judicial review of administrative actions.[148] The court relaxed its threshold tests a lot, with the justiciability and locus standi tests serving as important examples for this trend.

With regard to justiciability, the court suspended the normative justiciability doctrine based on the concept that, in principle the legal standards can be applied to any action of the branch and review them.[149]

With regard to locus standi, the court expanded significantly. It determined that in balancing between the importance of locus standi on the one hand, and the fear of imposing an overload on the courts on the other hand, locus standi should be favored when it comes to a petitioner who can point to an issue of public interest, an issue involving a substantial public defect, or an act or dispute which touches an issue with a special constitutional significance.[150] Moreover, in the past, the dominant perception was that the individual had to point out a self-interest that was hurt in order to get the locus standi. In the 1980s, however, this perception was replaced by the perception that the role of the court is broader than giving personal support. Instead, its role is to maintain the rule of law; that is why there is a justification for expanding locus standi to cases in which the individual petitioner was not directly hurt by an illegal act.[151] As a rule, the court's tendency today is not to reject petitions that deal with substantive matters without discussing the case in question. The result of this tendency is a significant expansion of the criticism's scope.

---

146 H.C.J 186/65 *Reiner v. Prime Minister*, 19(2) P.D. 485, 487 (1965) (Hebrew).

147 H.C.J 40/70 Becker *v. Minister of Defense*, 24(1) P.D. 238, 247 24(1) 238, 247 (1970) (Hebrew).

148 See, for example, Suzie Navot, *The Constitutional Law of Israel*, 37–40 (2007).

149 Zamir, *supra* note 46, at 122–130.

150 H.C.J 651/03 *Association for Civil Rights in Israel v. Chairman of the Central Elections Committee of the 16th Knesset*, 57(2) P.D. 62, 68 (2003) (Hebrew). For an analysis of the change in the status of locus standi, see Shlomo Levin "Is There a Right of Standing to the Right of Standing?", *HaPraklit* 39 4531 (5751); David Kretzmer "On the Occasion of the Fortieth Anniversary of the Public Law", *Mishpatim* 19 551 (5750). (Hebrew); Ze'ev Segal *Locus Standi in the High Court of Justice*, 253–251 (2nd Ed., 1994) (Hebrew).

151 Zamir, *supra* note 46, at 117–122.

The expansion tendency is also reflected in the nature of the criticism. In the past, criticism of the administration's work was made in relation to a limited number of principles, while focusing mainly on whether the action that was made was authorized. The judicial perception was that only cases where the operation of administrative discretion was made in an unreasonable way would be disqualified by the court on grounds of unreasonableness. This approach was taken because of the assumption that an extremely unreasonable action exceeds the powers conferred on the administrative authority. However, today, every action of the administration must meet the test of reasonableness to the extent that even unreasonableness which is not extreme may lead to disqualification.[152]

Subsequently, in addition to the reasonableness test, the proportionality test was introduced, in which the administration action had to go through more stringent tests. The proportionality test involves the question of whether the balance made by the administrative authority between various considerations that guided it is suitable, and not only whether it significantly exceeded its bounds of discretion.[153] As part of this tendency of expanding the judicial criticism, the traditional tests of power and good faith were assimilated into the reasonableness and proportionality tests. Most of the judicial criticism today focuses on the general principles of reasonableness and proportionality.[154]

Expanding the criticism is also expressed in the fact that today the court does not restrict itself from discussing certain issues as it did in the past. Today the criticism encompasses all the government and public administration actions, including political-diplomatic issues and issues in which the executive branch has special expertise, such as military and security decisions.[155] Howev-

---

152 H.C.J 840/79 *Contractors and Builders Union in Israel v. Government of Israel*, 34(3) P.D. 729; for a different opinion, see the words of Zamir, who believes that in the area of judgment the court did not expand its stronghold, but continued the ancient legal tradition: Zamir, *supra* note 46, at p. 136–139.

153 See for example, H.C.J 3477/95 *Ben-Atiya v. Minister of Education, Culture and Sport*, 49(5) P.D. 1 (1995) (Hebrew); H.C.J 3648/97 *Stamka v. Minister of Interior*, 53(2) P.D. 728, 776–777 (1999) (Hebrew); H.C.J 2056/04 *Bet Surik v. The IDF Commander in Gaza*, 58(5) P.D. 807. 836, 839. 841 (2004) (Hebrew).

154 See for example, H.C.J 680/88 *Schnitzer v. Israeli Military Censor*, 42(4) P.D. 617 (1988) (Hebrew); Aharon Barak *Proportionality—Constitutional Rights and Their Limitations* 2010 (Hebrew); Aharon Barak "Human Dignity as a Constitutional Right", *Hapraklit* 41, 271 (1994) (Hebrew); Aharon Barak, Human Dignity: The Constitutional Value and the Constitutional Right (Cambridge University, 2015).

155 *Beit Surik Case*, above 147, 842–846. The court emphasizes that the assessment of proportionality is in its field of expertise, as opposed to various factual and empirical assessments which are not in its field of expertise. However, as was in the Beit Surik case, sometimes disa-

er, it should be noted that the court sometimes still hesitates to intervene in decisions that have a clear political nature.[156]

Several factors account for the expansion of the court's criticism on the executive branch actions: the failure of the political bodies to solve problems on their own, deliberate avoidance of those bodies to make decisions on controversial issues, and an increasing public awareness of civil rights and the importance of the court as a defender of those rights.[157]

An important factor in the expansion of judicial criticism was the legislation of the Basic Laws, which anchored some of the basic human rights. This legislation opened a new era in the relations between the executive branch and the judiciary branch. Following adoption of the Basic Laws, the court gained the ability to criticize administrative decisions and actions based directly on grounds anchored in these laws. The court is not afraid to use the tools that the Basic Laws give it; in many cases, the court applies the Basic Laws to impose duties or to cancel a public administration action.[158]

The power of judicial review that the court has also works indirectly. Since the government knows there is a reasonable chance that its actions will undergo judicial review, it plans its actions in anticipation of review from the court, and refrains from acting in a way that will arouse petitions to the court. This means that the law casts its shadow beyond actions taken by the administration, and indirectly prevents actions which are not appropriate.

The expansion of the judicial review under the power of the Basic Laws supposedly points to a growth in the judiciary branch's power relative to that of the executive branch. However, some argue that it is precisely the increase of the scope of judicial review into the limelight which increased the public criticism of the involvement of the Supreme Court in the executive branch. As a result, various political branches work to restrict the scope of authority of the judicial branch.[159]

---

greements break out between the experts themselves about factual matters related to the petition.

156 See for example, H.C.J 4169/10 *Cohen v. Minister of Defense*, Section 7 of Justice Beinisch's judgement (published on Nevo, 2.6.2010) (Hebrew); H.C.J 7523/11 *Almagor Terror Victims Association v. Prime Minister*, Section 3, 10 of Justice Beinisch's judgement (published on Nevo, 17.10.11) (Hebrew).

157 Shimon Shetreet, *On Adjudication, supra* note 123, p. 398–399. (Hebrew).

158 For example: H.C.J 3872/93 *Mitral Ltd v. Prime Minister and Minister of Religious Services*, 47 (5) P.D. 485 (1993); H.C.J 4541/94 *Miller v. Minister of Defense*, 49(4) P.D. 94. (Hebrew); Shimon Shetreet, *On Adjudication, supra* note 123, p. 399–402 (Hebrew)

159 Menachem Hoffnung, *Power, Jurisdiction and Seperation of Powers—Judicial Review in Israel in Comparative Perspectives*, 28 Mishpatim 211, at 237–238 (1997).

The built-in downside to judicial review of the executive branch is the phenomenon known as the "politicization of the courts." The tendency to refer issues of a political nature to the courts[160] is done out of the assessment of its independence and neutrality, but in this way the court becomes involved in controversial issues.[161] For example, the court has ruled in issues at the heart of a public controversy, such as imposing a total ban on torturing detainees in General Security Services interrogations;[162] an order to release Lebanese detainees held in administrative detention for many years as a bargaining chip in the release of Israeli prisoners;[163] and, in a slightly different context, the prohibition to discriminate Arabs on the question of admission to a residential community village.[164] In Aharon Barak's opinion, because the court only examines the legality of the government's actions but not the merits of those actions, it does not intervene in political activity.[165] However, he agrees that since the public is not always able to recognize this distinction, there is a place for the doctrine of injusticiability in rare cases where the fear that the public confidence in the judges will be harmed is greater than the fear that the public confidence in the court will be harmed.[166]

---

160 See e.g.: H.C.J 217/80 *Segal v. Minister of Interior*, 34(4) P.D. 249 (Hebrew); H.C.J 448/81 *Ressler v. Minister of Defense*, 36(1) P.D. 81 (1981) (Hereinafter: *The Ressler Case*) (Hebrew); H.C.J 246/81 *Derech Eretz Association v. Israel Broadcasting Authority*, 35(4) P.D. 1 (1981) (Hebrew); H.C.J 141/82 *Rubinstein v. Speaker of the Knesset*, 37(3) P.D. 141 (1983) (Hebrew).

161 Shimon Shetreet, *On Adjudication, supra* note 123, p. 464 (Hebrew). In several cases, the court recognized expressly this issue. See H.C.J 2031/13 *Regavim v. Benjamin Netanyahu*, Prime Minister of Israel (published on Nevo, 22.6.15), in paragraph 10 of Justice Rubinstein judgement:

"This petition, like other petitions from another side of the Israeli public-political map, is among other things part of a political struggle in a legal cloak. In H.C.J 5377/09 *Regavim v. Minister of Defense* (published on Nevo,) (2011), I happened to say (Paragraph 13):

"Within our own people we are sitting, and we are aware that this petition, which comes from the right side of the Israeli political map, is based on a struggle against organizations from the left side of the political map, and in counterweighting their work, and also to the authorities' actions regarding illegal Jewish construction against illegal Palestinian construction; unwillingly, the court was dragged in some way or other into these struggles, which in themselves are not in its field. We have, therefore, to remind ourselves, as well as to various petitioners, what is supposed to be obvious, that the law and its interpretation should be before our eyes, and that we do not want to be drawn into the political polarization districts.

162 H.C.J 5100/94, *The Public Committee Against Torture in Israel v. Government of Israel*, 53(4) P.D. 817 (1999) (Hebrew).

163 A.D.C 7048/97 *Anonymous Persons v Minister of Defense*, 54(1) P.D. 721 (2000).

164 *The Kaadan Case, supra* note 90.

165 *Ressler v. Minister of Defense, supra* note 160, p. 492.

166 *Id.*, at 496.

The criticism directed at the court about dealing with and deciding on matters that are ideological in nature is based on two foundations.[167] First, in a democracy, the role of legislation, which reflects decision making in ideological issues, is given to the elected body, which reflects the majority opinion. Therefore, decision making by judges who are not elected by the people violates this principle.[168] Second, in such decisions, there is a greater concern than usual that the personal views and inclinations of the judges will affect their decision. Such issues usually have a great legal ambiguity; they tend to be quite sensitive to the worldview of the person dealing with them.

The Supreme Court's judicial review of the executive branch's activity also applies to secondary legislation that is legislated by the executive branch. The principle of legality promises that acts will be issued in the field of authority which was granted to the minister. Therefore, if ministers exceed the authority granted to them by law, or issue a regulation that contradicts a piece of legislation, the court will revoke the regulation.[169] There is an explicit provision in Section 16(4) of the Interpretation Ordinance [New Version], which states that: "No regulation shall contradict the provisions of any law." Overstepping an authority happen in one of two ways: one is violating the procedural requirements established in a law. Another is a substantial deviation from the authority that was granted to the minister who issued the regulation.[170]

Beyond the basic review of the principle of legality, the Supreme Court had already ruled in its first years that, as with every administrative action, the authority to issue a regulation is subjected to the principle of reasonableness and to judicial review of its reasonableness.[171] However, only in cases of extreme unreasonableness will the court invalidate a regulation on the grounds of unreasonableness.[172] The fact that in extreme cases a regulation will lead to injustice is not a justified ground for revoking the regulation, as long as its results are not extremely unreasonable according to the majority.[173] The review of the reasona-

---

167 Shimon Shetreet, *On Adjudication, supra* note 123, p. 467 (Hebrew).
168 Asher Maoz "The Boundaries of Justiciability: Parliament, Government and Courts" *Plilim*, Vol. 8, 412 (5760) (Hebrew).
169 C.A 521/61 *State of Israel v. Haz*, 50 P.D. 2193 (1961).
170 H.C.J 156/75 *Daka v. Minister of Transport*, 30(2) P.D. 94, 101 (1976) (Hebrew).
171 For further information, see Nathan Mayer "On the Status of Secondary Legislation," *TAU Law Review* 1 374 (5731) (Hebrew); see also P.C.A 311/57 *Attorney General v. M. Dizengoff and Co. (Sailing) Ltd.*, 13 P.D. 1026, 1037 (Hebrew).
172 *Id.*, p. 1039.
173 H.C.J 4769/90 *Zidane v Minister of Social Affairs and Social Services*, 47(2) P.D. 147, 165 (1993). (Hebrew). See also Barak-Erez, *supre note* 58, at p. 765 – 766 (Hebrew).

bleness of the regulation will be made according to the existing conditions at the time. Therefore, if a regulation which was reasonable at the time it was issued has become unreasonable, the court is authorized to order the minister to revoke or change it.[174] Even when the regulation does not contradict legislation, if the court finds that the regulation was not issued in order to achieve the purpose that was granted to the minister by law, it can invalidate the regulation.[175]

Expanding the judicial review over secondary legislation stemmed from two main considerations. First, the parliamentary supervision over secondary legislation is not effective and comprehensive; therefore, the Supreme Court is required to carry out the inspection in full. Second, the trust that existed during the establishment of the state between the courts and the administration was weakened as a result of the vast growth of secondary legislation, and the secondary legislature's attempts to extend its powers.[176]

In Britain, judicial review of primary legislation is exercised under the UK Human Rights Act. Judicial review of secondary legislation is common. If secondary legislators have exceeded the authority granted to them by the primary legislation, the secondary legislation will be found unconstitutional.[177] In doing so, the court is seen as helping to fulfill the will of the parliament.[178]

6. The Interaction between the Judicial Branch and the Legislative Branch

The main point of conflict between the court and the Knesset relates to the power of the Supreme Court to invalidate Knesset legislation. In recent decades, significant development has occurred in this subject.[179]

---

174 H.C.J 4157/98 *Tzevet—IDF Veterans Association v. Minister of Finance*, 58(2) P.D. 769, 805 (2004) (Hebrew).

175 H.C.J 98/54 *Lazarovitch v. Maintenance Supervisor*, 10 P.D. 40, 47 (1956) (Hebrew).

176 Aharon Barak "Court Supervision on Secondary Legislation" *HaPraklit* 21 463, 476 (5725). (Hebrew).

177 David Yardley, *Introduction to Constitutional and Administrative Law*, 134 (8th ed., Butterworths, 1995).

178 Colin Turpin & Adam Tomkins, British Government and the Constitution 654–656 (6th ed. 2009).

179 What follows below are primarily the essence of a broad article of the author on the subject. See: Shimon Shetreet "The Supreme Court at a Crossroads: The Appropriate Model for Judicial Review of Laws in Israel," *Mozney Mishpat* 5 23 (5766) (Hebrew). For further details, see Shimon Shetreet, *On Adjudication*, *supra* note 123, p. 407–460 (Hebrew).

Until 1992, the Supreme Court used its authority of judicial review in certain cases where primary legislation of the Knesset was announced as invalid because of a conflict with provisions of a Basic Law. However, the constitutional judicial review of the Knesset legislation was limited only in cases where the legislation stood against entrenched provisions.[180]

The High Court of Justice's willingness to invalidate the law was restrained. The reason is that the law was valid in the 1990s, according to which such disqualification is limited only to circumstances where an entrenched section in a Basic Law is violated, i.e. in contrary to the conditions set out in that section. The court firmly refused to disqualify laws or to stop the legislation process for reasons related to the content of those laws, even if its mind is not at ease at the content of those laws.[181] For example, Deputy President Justice Miriam Ben-Porat replied to the claim in *H.C.J. Cohen v. Minister of Social Affairs and Social Services* that a certain law discriminates against the petitioner: "However, as negative as the opinion of the judiciary branch will be on this agreement, without a constitution, the Knesset has the authority and the power to legislate a law that suffers from discrimination, and after doing so, there is no escape from complying with it."[182]

After the decision in the *Bank Mizrahi* case,[183] according to which the court has a constitutional authority to revoke Knesset laws, the Supreme Court found fifteen cases between 1992 and 2015 where a law unconstitutionally restricted human rights and therefore it, or part of it, was subsequently revoked.[184] In

---

180 See H.C.J 98/69 *Bergman v. Minister of Finance*, 23(1) P.D. 693 (1969) (Hebrew); H.C.J 246/81 *Derech Eretz Association v. Israel Broadcasting Authority*, 35(4) P.D. 1 (1981) (Hebrew); H.C.J 141/82 *Rubinstein v. Speaker of the Knesset*, 37(3) P.D. 141 (1983) (Hebrew).
181 See H.C.J 889/86 *Cohen v. Minister of Social Affairs and Social Services*, 41(2) P.D. 540 (1987) (Hebrew); 345/88 *Vinitzky v. Speaker of the Knesset* (published on Nevo, 7.6.1988) (Hebrew).
182 *The Cohen Case*, supra note 181, p. 546 (Hebrew).
183 C.A 6821/93 *United Bank Mizrahi Ltd. v. Migdal Cooperative Village*, 49(4) P.D. 221 (1995).
184 H.C.J 6055/95 *Zemach v. Minister of Defense*, 53(5) P.D. 241 (1999) (Hebrew); H.C.J 1715/97 *Israel Investment Managers Association v. Minister of Finance*, 51(4) P.D. 367 (1997) (Hebrew); H.C.J 1030/99 *Oron v. Speaker of the Knesset*, 56(3) P.D. 640 (2002) (Hebrew); H.C.J 1661/05 *Hof Aza Regional Council v. Knesset of Israel*, 59(2) P.D. 481 (2005) (Hebrew); H.C.J 8276/05 *Adalah v. Minister of Defense* (12.12.2006) (Hebrew); H.C.J 2605/05 College of Law and Business, Human Rights Department v. Minister of Finance (published on Nevo, 19.11.2009) (Hebrew); Criminal Motions 8823/07 *John Doe v. Slate of Israel* (published on Nevo, 11.2.2010) (Hebrew); H.C.J 10662/04 *Hassan v. National Insurance Institute* (published on Nevo, 28.2.2012). (Hebrew); H.C.J 8300/02 *Nasser v. Government of Israel* (published on Nevo, 22.5.2012); H.C.J 7146/12 *Adam v. Knesset* (published on Nevo, 16.9.2013) (Hebrew); H.C.J 7385/13 *Eitan Israeli Immigration Policy v. Government of Israel* (published on Nevo, 22.9.2014) (Hebrew); H.C.J 5239/11 *Avneri v. The Knesset* (published on Nevo, 15.04.15); H.C.J 8665/14 *Dasta v. The Knesset* (published on Nevo, 11.08.2015).

two other cases, concerning the Tal Law and the payment of unemployment benefit income to yeshiva students, the Supreme Court ruled that because the legal arrangement is unconstitutional, the Knesset cannot extend the validity of the law, or to include it in the new law about to be legislated.[185] In another case, the Tel Aviv Magistrate's Court dismissed a section in the Income Tax Ordinance which contradicted Basic Law: Freedom of Occupation.[186] The number of laws which were revoked since the *Bank Mizrahi* case is, therefore, fairly limited.

However, recently there has been a significant development in the context of the relationship between the judicial and the legislative branch, and especially in the extent of judicial review of Knesset legislation. At the beginning of 2012, the Knesset passed a series of amendments[187] to the Prevention of Infiltration (Offences and Jurisdiction) Law, 5714–1954. The purpose of the amendments was an attempt to deal with the rising phenomenon of infiltration into Israel from the Egyptian border. According to the law, Section 30a(c)(3) sought to apply a temporary provision, which meant, in practice, that infiltrators against whom a deportation order was issued could be held in custody for three years without a trial. In the *Adam* HCJ,[188] the petitioners argued that the amendment was unconstitutional. The court, with a panel of nine judges, accepted the petitioners' position; it ruled that the temporary provision, which allows holding infiltrators in custodial facilities for three years, violates the right to liberty and the right to dignity of people in custody in a way which does not comply with Basic Law: Human Dignity and Liberty. The majority opinion was that the law did not meet the terms of proportionality in Section 8 of Basic Law: Human Dignity and Liberty.[189] According to the opinion of all the members of the panel, it was determined that the violation of the freedom and dignity of the people in custody did not meet the terms of proportionality according to the narrow test—that is, the extent of the violation of their freedom (placing them in custody for three years and almost without an individual examination of the identity and the circumstances of the person in custody) compared to the social benefit gained from dealing with the phenomenon of infiltration.[190] Consequently, the court ruled

---

185 H.C.J 6298/07 *Ressler v. Knesset of Israel* (published in Nevo, 21.02.2012) (Hebrew); H.C.J 4124/00 *Yekutieli v. Minister of Religious Services* (published on Nevo, 14.06.2010) (Hebrew).
186 C.R 4696/01 *State of Israel v. Handelman* (published on Nevo, 14.04.2003) (Hebrew).
187 The Prevention of Infiltration (Offences and Jurisdiction) Law (Amendment No. 3 and Temporary Order), 5772–2012.
188 H.C.J 7146/12 *Adam v. Knesset* (published on Nevo, 16.09.2013) (Hebrew).
189 *Id.*, paragraphs 96–104, 108 of Justice Edna Arbel's judgement (Hebrew). To be precise, it was decided that the law does not meet all three tests of proportionality.
190 *Id.*, paragraphs 109–115 of Justice Edna Arbel's judgment (Hebrew).

that Section 30a of the Law was unconstitutional and null.[191] President Grunis finished his opinion in the decision by saying that revoking the section did not dismiss the Knesset's ability to re-legislate it if the circumstances changed, for example, if the phenomenon of infiltration exacerbated. Alternatively, the Knesset could re-legislate the in a way that would permit holding infiltrators in custody for a significantly shorter period of time.[192]

The invalidation of the section by the court in September 2013 made waves in the Knesset and outside it. Already in December of that year, as a response to the revocation of this section, the Knesset passed a new amendment to the law,[193] according to which an infiltrator could be held in custody for a period of only one year. In addition, the legislature added a new chapter to the law[194] that sought to create a parallel "detention center" (the one known by the name "Holot Detention Facility"), to which infiltrators for whom there is a difficulty in their deportation will be moved. Soon a petition was filed against the constitutionality of this settlement, which was discussed in the *Eitan* HCJ.[195] The High Court ruled by a majority that, despite the changes made by the Knesset[196]—reducing the time in custody for a year and determining that the application of the law is prospective, i. e., applies only to infiltrators who entered Israel hereafter—the law severely violates the right to dignity and the right to liberty of the people in custody. The High Court of Justice ruled that the injury is not proportional and, therefore, the section should be cancelled.[197] Furthermore, the majority opinion ruled that the additional arrangement in the amendment —a detention center in which the infiltrators who are not in custody will be as-

---

191 *Id.*, paragraph 122 of the decision of Justice Edna Arbel's judgement (Hebrew). It should be noted that Justice Hendel, as opposed to the other eight members of the panel, thought that the provision about regarding imprisonment of only three years should be revoked and that the section should be left as it is. See: *Id.*, paragraph 1 of Justice Hendel's judgement.

192 *Id.*, paragraph 5, of Justice Grunis's judgement.

193 The Prevention of Infiltration (Offences and Jurisdiction) Law (Amendment No. 4 and Temporary Order), 5774–2013.

194 Chapter 4, "Detention Facility for Infiltrators—Temporary Order," Sections 32a–32k of the law (Hebrew).

195 H.C.J 8425/13 *Eitan Israeli Immigration Policy v. Government of Israel* (published on Nevo, 22.9.2014). Attached to the petition was H.C.J 7385/13, in which the petitioners argued that the state is not doing enough to alleviate the suffering of the residents of south Tel Aviv in light of the infiltration phenomenon. This petition was rejected, see p. 139, paragraph 106 of the judgement of Justice Vogelman (Hebrew).

196 *Id*; Details of the changes between the previous amendment and this amendment are in pp. 39–40, Section 44 of the judgement of Justice Vogelman. (Hebrew).

197 *Id.*, pp. 52–61, Sections 67–71, 78–79, 80–83 of the judgement of Justice Vogelman (Hebrew).

sembled—also violates the rights to liberty and dignity of the people held in it in a way which is not proportionate, and therefore is also null.[198] This is mainly due to the fact that the agreement required that the infiltrators staying at the center must report for registration three times a day; therefore, they will not be able to work. In addition, the majority judges ruled that the fact a person staying at the facility is subjected to the authority of the Israel Prison Service employees also violate their right to dignity. According to the majority opinion, the authority to apply sanctions against the people in the facility if they violate the terms of stay constitutes a disproportionate violation of the right to due process.[199]

In the decision, Justice Vogelman referred to the fact that this was a second disqualification of the Knesset legislation on the subject:

"There is no dispute that special care is required when the subject of conversation is a law which was legislated shortly after its previous version was revoked by this court (in the *Adam* decision). However, this caution does not mean that this court is exempt from fulfilling its role in our constitutional regime."

President Grunis and Justices Amit and Hendel[200] were in the minority—they believed that shortening the maximum time in custody to one year and determining that the application of the law is prospective are sufficient to put the new legal arrangement into the perimeter of proportionality and prevent the revocation of this section of the law. President Grunis warned in his opinion that revoking a law which was passed by the Knesset, while not giving room to maneuver and discretion to the legislature, may look as if the court was treading on the legislature's territory.[201]

This was the first case of its kind in the Israeli constitutional law in which the court revoked a main law; after the Knesset responded by creating a new legislative arrangement, the High Court disqualified that law as well. Needless to say, the *Eitan* decision aroused a lively debate among the political and legal communities regarding the court's role and the limitation of its intervention in legislative acts. This debate remains the focus of a strong tension between the Knes-

---

198 *Id.*, pp. 61–62, Sections 85–87 of the judgement of Justice Vogelman (Hebrew).
199 See p. 113, Section 65 of the judgement of Justice Vogelman (Hebrew).
200 Justice Amit joined the majority opinion in regarding the disqualification of the sections of Chapter 4 of the law, i.e., detention facility agreement. President Grunis and Justice Hendel believed that only Section 32 h(a), according to which those staying at the facility must report for registration three times a day, should be revoked, whereas the rest of the agreement details should be left unchanged.
201 Paragraph 20 of President Grunis's judgement.

set, the government and the court, while there are people who wish to limit the authority of the High Court in disqualifying laws.[202]

Afterwards, the Knesset changed the custody agreement in response to the disqualification of the final agreement.[203] The new agreement limited the time an infiltrator can be held in custody to three months at most.[204] Simultaneously, the law ruled that those staying at the detention center will only have to report for registration once a day.[205] Furthermore, staying at the center will be limited to 20 months top.[206]

Another source of considerable tension between the court and the Knesset is the issue of legislative interpretation. The institutional role of the court, according to the principle of separation of powers, is to interpret laws legislated by the parliament. For this reason, when interpreting a law, it is natural and appropriate that the court will mainly consider the intention of the legislators when they legislated the law. However, the customary approach of the Supreme Court is largely not this approach, but rather the purposive approach, whose main representative is President Barak.[207] According to this approach, the legislation's interpretation is determined by its purpose.

A third point of conflict between the Knesset and the Supreme Court is connected to the judicial review by the court on the activity of the Knesset. The court's authority to intervene in the parliamentary activities of the Knesset was already established in the early 1980s, in the *Platto-Sharon* case.[208] Regarding the scope of the review, the court determined that it has to act with restraint when intervening in the Knesset's internal parliamentary proceedings.[209] According to the ruling, the court will intervene in internal Knesset procedures only when they pose a considerable violation of fundamental principles of our constitutional government.[210] The Knesset's internal procedures include the legisla-

---

202 See for example: Omri Efraim and Moran Azulay "The Initiator of the Law Against Infiltrators, Minister of Interior Gideon Sa'ar: 'Limit the High Court of Justice Authority, We Are Left Without Tools'," *Ynet* (22.9.2014) (Hebrew).

203 Amendment from 17.12.2014, 68 5775 No. 2483, p. 84.

204 Section 30a(c) of the law.

205 *Id.*, Section 32 h(b).

206 *Id.*, Section 32 u(a).

207 Aharon Barak *Legal Interpretation* Vol. 2: Legislation Interpretation 151 (5753) (Hebrew).

208 *The Platto Case, supra* note 109, p. 125, and see the dissenting opinion of Justice Landau in p. 135 (Hebrew).

209 *Id.*, p. 142.

210 H.C.J 652/81 *Sarid v. Speaker of the Knesset*, 36(2) P.D. 197, 204 (1982) (Hereinafter: *H.C.J Sarid*) (Hebrew). For further details, refer to Suzie Navot "Twenty Years to the 'Sarid' Test: "Re-

tive process in its various stages until its completion,[211] the discussions in the Knesset committees, determining how to vote, and the methods of the discussion in the plenum. They also include making proposals to the agenda, presenting parliamentary questions, raising no-confidence motions in the government, debating bills on behalf of the government, debating private member's bills on behalf of the MKs, and other such matters that are under the title "The Knesset's Work" and are mainly regulated in the Knesset Rules of Procedure.[212] However, the court added that the scope of the review will vary according to the type of activity.[213] For example, regarding the decision of the House Committee about the MKs' positions, which was made with an inherent conflict of interest, the court ruled that the decision is exposed to "a dense and thorough review,"[214] Unlike a review of internal parliamentary procedures, where the Knesset is under quasi-judicial authority (such as the removal of immunity), review of the conduct of the Knesset will be done the same way that the court reviews ordinary administrative activity.[215]

7. The Legal Norms

A. Basic Laws

Basic Law: The Government is the Basic Law which went through the most changes among the Basic Laws. Scholars argued that this fact points to a lack of understanding of the importance of Basic Law: The Government as a constitutional foundation that should enjoy stability and that does not change frequently. Another expression of this is in making the decision that Basic Law: The Government should be separated from Government Law, which was made in the last meeting of the Constitution, Law, and Justice Committee (which lasted 15 minutes), while accepting the Attorney General's position indisputably.

---

consideration of Judicial Supervision over Parliamentary Proceedings," *Law Studies* 19 720 (2003) (Hebrew).

211 The court already mentioned its authority to review the legislation process in H.C.J 761/86 *Miari v. Speaker of the Knesset*, 42(4) P.D. 868, 873 (1989) (Hebrew); The court's authority to revoke a law where a fault was found in its legislation process was decided in H.C.J *Nimrody Land Development v. Speaker of the Knesset*, 45(3) P.D. 154, 157.

212 H.C.J 971/99 *Movement for Quality Government in Israel v. The Knesset Committee*, 56(6) P.D. 117, 167 (2002) (Hereinafter: T*he Movement for Quality Government Case*) (Hebrew).

213 H.C.J *Sarid*, *supra* note 210, at 201.

214 *The Movement for Quality Government Case*, 210, p. 153.

215 H.C.J *Sarid*, *supra* note 210, at 20.

Some argue that on that occasion almost everything which was not related to the direct election did not interest the MKs. Another problematic aspect is the fact that the application of the law was applied immediately to the elections to the Knesset ("The 16th Knesset"). This was in contrast to the step taken by legislating Basic Law: The Government in 1992 (at the 12th Knesset), which was applied only as of the elections to the 14th Knesset. The problem with this step is that it constitutes an opening for frequent changes in the electoral system, in accordance with the mood of the majority of the Knesset, who see a chance to improve their chances to be reelected at the next elections as well.[216]

Basic Law: The Government serves as part of the Israeli constitution, which is anchored today in the Basic Laws. Basic Law: The Government was the third Basic Law legislated by the Knesset after Basic Law: The Knesset and Basic Law: The President of the State. Therefore, the debate on Basic Law: The Government and its sections should begin with an analysis of theoretical foundations relating to the status of the constitution and an analysis of theoretical aspects relating to the system of government in the State of Israel.

A constitution is defined as "a set of laws, customs and conventions which define the division of powers between the organs of the state, and regulate the relationship between the various organs of the state and between them and the citizens."[217] The constitution expresses a statement on a particular political settlement; it also reflects the unique culture and history of the government and its procedures. Therefore, a necessary condition for understanding the constitution properly is understanding the way it was consolidated.

Most of the democratic countries have a written constitution. For example, the United States has had a written constitution since 1787, which is the oldest constitution. Unlike many other nations, the United Kingdom has no single constitutional document. Its constitution consists of a collection of laws, customs, and documents with a superior value, along with the Human Rights Act from 1998.[218] Therefore, regarding the constitution of the UK, it is not enough to settle for an analysis of a single document in order to learn about the constitutionality of a particular topic. In the UK, a matter which is "unconstitutional" is usually a matter which contradicts the constitutional conventions. In accordance with the Human Rights Act from 1998, the courts were authorized to declare a law of the

---

216 See Arian, Nachmias, and Amir, *supra* note 118 p. 8 (2002).

217 David Yarley, *Introduction to Constitutional and Administrative Law*, p. 4 (8th ed., Butterworth, 1995); S. Shetreet, & S. Turenne, *Judges on Trial: The Independence and Accountability of the English Judiciary* (2nd ed.), Cambridge University Press (2013).

218 *Id.*, p. 3; Colin Turpin and Adam Tomkins, *British Government and the Constitution*; pp. 3–9 (6th ed. 2009).

parliament incompatible, and then the parliament is allowed to amend the law or leave it as it is.[219]

In Israel, there is a special significance to the existence of a constitution. The society in Israel is a divided society within which there is serious tension between groups on grounds of religion and nationality. Furthermore, the security risk the state has been in since its establishment reinforces the need for a constitution which will protect the minority rights on the one hand, and give the majority a sense of security on the other hand.[220]

In the Declaration of Independence, the adoption of a written constitution was explicitly mentioned: "We declare that, with effect from the moment of the termination of the Mandate[...] until the establishment of the elected, regular authorities of the State in accordance with the Constitution which shall be adopted by the Elected Constituent Assembly not later than the 1st October 1948, the People's Council shall act[...]." The first Knesset held a lengthy discussion on the subject of the constitution, and eventually decided on the Harari Decision, which states that: "The First Knesset assigns to the Constitution, Law and Justice Committee the preparation of a proposed constitution for the state. The constitution will be made in parts, each of which will constitute a separate Basic Law. The parts will be brought to the Knesset, as the Committee completes its work, and all the chapters together will constitute the constitution of the state."[221]

In practice, the Knesset did not work on the preparation of the constitution. With time, the government submitted regular bills that deal with classic constitutional issues, such as the Law of Return and the Citizenship Law. The Supreme Court ruled immediately after the establishment of the state that the Declaration of Independence is not a constitutional norm above the law.[222]

The first Basic Law that was brought to legislation was Basic Law: The Knesset. Until the Constitutional Revolution,[223] which began in 1992, additional Basic

---

219 The Constitutional Reform Act 2005, which regulated constitutional issues relating to the judicial and the executive branch, should also be mentioned.

220 For an analysis of the important constitutional development, see Ruth Gavison, *The Constitutional Revolution—Reality or Self-Fulfilling Prophecy?* 98 (1998).

221 S. Navot, *supra* note 4, at 14–16

222 H.C.J 10/48 *Ziv v. Gubernik*, 1(1) P.D. 85, 89 (1948) (Hebrew). However, the ruling of Justice Dov Levin in the Clal case, that the Basic Laws made the Declaration of Independence an independent source for human rights, should be noted. H.C.J 726/94 *Clal Insurance Enterprises Holdings Ltd v. Minister of Finance*, 48(5) P.D. 441, 461 (1994) (Hebrew). According to this viewpoint, the Declaration of Independence was given a supra-law status.

223 The expression was coined by Prof. Claude Klein in his article "The Silent Constitutional Revolution," *Maariv* 27.3.1992 (Hebrew). See more: Aharon Barak, "The Constitutional Revolution," *Selected Writings*, Vol 1 349 (Haim H. Cohn and Itzhak Zamir eds., 2000) (Hebrew); Aharon

Laws had been legislated, such as Basic Law: The President of the State; they mainly reflected the existing legal situation and did not address human rights. These issues did not raise many problems because there is a large degree of consensus in them.[224] In addition, the Supreme Court did not see these Basic Laws provisions at a constitutional level above the law.[225]

In 1992, Basic Laws dealing with human rights were legislated: Basic Law: Human Dignity and Liberty and Basic Law: Freedom of Occupation. According to the Supreme Court's interpretation, these Basic Laws anchored for the first time the human rights and gave them a preferable constitutional status. In the first years after the legislation of the Basic Laws, there was ambiguity regarding the legal status and superiority of those laws. Significant systematic treatment of the status of Basic Laws by the Supreme Court was expressed in the *Bank Mizrahi* decision.[226] The majority opinion, led by Justice Barak, was that the Knesset has authority to enact a constitution in Israel, and that the Basic Laws are chapters of the constitution. Barak states (paragraph 54): "The Knesset has constitutive authority. From this power it granted Israel a constitution. It did so in chapters according to the Harari Decision."[227]

As for the theory underlying the Knesset's authority to enact a constitution, the opinions in the Supreme Court were divided. President Shamgar's opinion is that the Knesset is omnipotent; it is in its authority to set a normative hierarchy and limit its own hands.[228] In contrast, Justice Barak's approach is the "two hats" approach, according to which by enacting Basic Laws the Knesset does not work under the "hat" of the legislative branch, but under the "hat" of the constituent authority.[229]

The minority opinion of Justice Cheshin was that the Basic Laws are not a supreme normative level similar to that of the constitution, in his opinion, the

---

Barak, "The Constitutional Revolution: Protected Human Rights," *Mishpat Umimshal* 1 9 (1992) (Hebrew).

224 Gavison, *The Constitutional Revolution, supra* note 220, p. 68. For further details, see: Shimon Shetreet and Sophie Turenne, Judges on Trial: Independence and Accountability of the English Judiciary (2nd ed., 2013).

225 Aharon Barak, "The Constitutional Revolution—Twelve Years Old," *Law and Business* 1 5, 19 (5764) (Hebrew).

226 *The Bank Mizrahi* case, *supra* note 6.

227 *Id.*, in paragraph 54.

228 *The Bank Mizrahi Case, supra* note 6, Justice Shamgar's opinion on p. 271. See also: Meir Shamgar, "The Constitutional Powers of the Knesset in the Legal Field," *Mishpatim* 26 3 (1995) (Hebrew).

229 *The Bank Mizrahi Case, supra* note 6, Justice Barak's judgement on p. 355.

power of the Knesset to create a constitution of a supreme normative status should not be recognized.[230]

A third approach is that of President Landau, who, similarly to Justice Barak, agrees that the Knesset is authorized to enact a constitution. However, on the question whether the Basic Laws collectively make up a constitution, he disagrees with Justice Barak; he thinks that the Basic Laws do not contain the identification marks that are characteristic to a constitution.[231]

In September 1997, the Supreme Court disqualified for the first time a statutory provision of the Knesset because it contradicted a Basic Law.[232] Afterwards, the Supreme Court disqualified other provisions of the Knesset.[233] Compared with other countries, the number of disqualifications of Knesset laws is not great. There are several reasons for this. First, the observance of the law sections in the Basic Laws[234] reduce in advance the constitutional review of laws which were legislated after the Basic Laws were legislated. Second, many basic rights are not anchored in the Basic Laws. Third, the number of petitions that request revoking a Knesset law is not great. Finally, in many cases, the Supreme Court faces Knesset laws which contradict Basic Laws in the way the law is interpreted

---

230 *Id.*, Justice Cheshin's opinion p. 567 (Hebrew).
231 Moshe Landau, "Thoughts on the Constitutional Revolution," *Mishpatim* 26 419 (1996) (Hebrew); Moshe Landau, "Giving a Constitution to Israel on the Way of Court Ruling," *Mishpat Umimshal* 3 697 (1996) (Hebrew); Moshe Landau in "A Symposium: The Bank Mizrahi Decision—After Three Years," *HaMishpat* 5 249, 254 (2000) (Hebrew).
232 H.C.J 1715/97 *Israel Investment Managers Association v. Minister of Finance*, 51(4) P.D. 367 (1997).
233 See: H.C.J 6055/95 *Tzemach v. Minister of Defense*, 53(5) P.D. 241 (1999) (Hebrew); H.C.J 1030/99 *Oron v. Speaker of the Knesset*, 56(5) P.D. 640 (2002) (Hebrew); H.C.J 8276/05 *Adalah—The Legal Center for Arab Minority Rights in Israel v. Minister of Defense* (published on Nevo, 12.12. 2006) (Hebrew); H.C.J 1661/05 *Hof Aza Regional Council v. Knesset of Israel*, Section 191–195 for the majority opinion (published on Nevo, 9.6.2005) (Hebrew); H.C.J 2605/05 *The College of Law and Business (RA) 58 – 026630 – 02, Human Rights Division v. Minister of Finance* (published on Nevo, 19.11.2009) (Hereinafter: *The Human Rights Division Case*) (Hebrew). In H.C.J 212/03 *Herut—The National Movement v. Central Elections Committee for the 16th Knesset*, 57(1) P.D. 750 (2003) (Hebrew), the court interpreted an express statutory provision, according to which "no court will need a request for relief," as such that does not limit the authority of the High Court to address a petition regarding the law, due to its contradiction of Basic Law: The Judiciary. The practical significance in this case, similarly to the other cases that were mentioned, is the revocation of a statutory provision that contradicts a Basic Law.
234 Section 10 of Basic Law: Human Dignity and Liberty, and Section 10 of Basic Law: Freedom of Occupation.

in accordance with the Basic Laws, which leads to the nullification of the contradiction.[235]

Despite the adoption by the Supreme Court of Justice Barak's perception that the Basic Laws constitute, at least, chapters of a constitution, it should be noted that in the academia there is disagreement on this issue. The figure most identified as an opposition to Justice Barak is Prof. Ruth Gavison. In her view, despite the increased power of the Basic Laws, the Knesset enjoys today a status of a constituent authority; therefore, the Basic Laws should not be viewed as chapters of a constitution.[236]

In recent years, there have been more changes in the constitutional process progress. The Constitution, Law and Justice Committee of the 16th Knesset decided to act for the completion of the constitution. For this purpose, it held many discussions involving representatives from a variety of sectors. In light of the conclusions from these discussions, the committee prepared a constitution proposal that it presented to the president and to the Speaker of the Knesset, in order to put it to on the Knesset's table and to get a future decision by the Knesset that will approve the proposal.[237]

On February 13, 2006, the Knesset's birthday and Tu BiShvat 5766, the 16th Knesset plenum approved a draft decision of the Constitution, Law and Justice Committee, headed by MK Eitan, that called for the 17th Knesset to engage in the process of approving a complete constitution for Israel while shifting from the previous multi-stage legislation model of the constitution to a model of a complete constitution. The draft resolution that the Constitution, Law and Justice Committee accepted refers to the Declaration of Independence, mentions the elections for the Constituent Assembly and the transitional law which transformed the Constituent Assembly into the Knesset of Israel. Thus, the draft resolution of the committee confirms its role of the Knesset as a constitution constituent authority. The decision mentions the Harari Proposal, which assigned the Constitution Committee with the task of preparing a constitution in parts. Finally, the version of the operative decision that the Knesset plenum was asked to accept mainly called the 17th Knesset to approve a constitution for Israel on the basis of the proposals brought before it.

The proposal of the Constitution, Law and Justice Committee to a "constitution in broad consensus" reflects the considerable effort invested in shaping a political culture and instilling a constitutional culture in the Israeli system of

---

235 Barak "The Constitutional Revolution—Twelve Years Old," *supra* note 225, at 28.
236 Gavison, *The Constitutional Revolution, supra* note 220, at 106.
237 Meeting protocol No. 658 of the Constitution, Law and Justice Committee, the 16th Knesset (2 February 2006) (Hebrew).

government. The "constitution in broad consensus" proposal for enacting a complete constitution in one document is part of the realization of the Zionist vision; it is the realization of the Zionist revolution. The constitution embodies the formulation for recognizing the State of Israel as a Jewish state, and as a place where Jewish people can exercise their right to self-determination. At the same time, by recognizing the rights of the Arab minority, the proposed constitution recognizes the right of all the citizens of the State of Israel to preserve their language and culture.

Some argue that it does not seem that Israel will have a complete constitution in the foreseeable future because there has been no real change in the fundamental and structural disagreements that prevented the adoption of a constitution over the years.[238] Another argument is that we do not need a complete constitution because the tactic of the decision not to enact a formal constitution actually fulfilled the goals and needs that lead nations to enact a constitution in the first place.[239] Another key argument is that, with an agreed version of a constitution, there is no real way to mediate the gaps between the conflicting views on the role of the Supreme Court.[240]

Despite this, in the last decade we have witnessed encouraging steps towards the establishment of a constitution in Israel. These steps, and mainly the "Eitan Decision," evoke a cautious optimism about the chances that Israel will have a constitution.[241] Furthermore, it does not seem that the need for a compromise is a sufficient ground for rejecting the enactment of a constitution, even in a later unforeseen date. Postponing the enactment of a constitution and leaving Israel for many more years without one—and as a country different from the democratic and non-democratic countries that have one—has a lasting damage; its image and normative disadvantages are visible to all. Not accepting a complete constitution perpetuates until an unknown date the lack of superior norms that determine the guidelines to the governing authorities.[242]

Unlike the new Basic Laws from 1992, Human Dignity and Liberty and Freedom of Occupation, Basic Law: The Government suffers from several shortcom-

---

238 Yehoshua (Shuki) Segev "Why Israel Does Not Have and Will Not Have a Constitution (At Least in the Foreseeable Future)? On the Merits of the Decision Not to Decide," *Mozney Mishpat* 5 125, 174–175 (5766).

239 *Id.*, p. 197.

240 *Id.*

241 From this writer's remarks in his speech before the Knesset guests in a festive event on 13.02.06.

242 See Israel Democracy Institute *Constitution by Consensus* 13 (The Israel Democracy Institute Constitution proposal, led by Justice Meir Shamgar, 2005) (Hebrew).

ings. This Basic Law was changed many times over the years. Its style, which deals with somewhat technical subjects, makes it hard to bequeath it to the general public.[243] In addition, the Basic Law does not tend to handle fundamental conventions which, by their nature, are suitable to appear in a Basic Law.[244] On the other hand, Basic Law: The Government regulates the most important branch of the government – The Executive Branch.

B. Legislation

Upon its establishment, the State of Israel did not have a constitution. The Constituent Assembly was unable to agree upon a completed draft to submit for approval. Instead, the Constituent Assembly passed a resolution creating the first Knesset and granted them power to draft the constitution in chapters known as Basic Laws.[245] The Knessets have adopted several Basic Laws, but attempts to pass comprehensive bill of human rights have been unsuccessful.[246] Attempts have been made to pass the bill, but ultimately it was decided that the bill of human rights should be passed chapter by chapter, just as the constitution would be passed through the Basic Laws.[247] To date, the Knesset has adopted Basic Law: Human Dignity and Basic Law: Freedom of Occupation in 1992.[248] The 1992 Basic Laws introduced the constitutional era in the history of legal culture in Israel. The courts held that, through these Basic Laws, the Knesset had created constitutional limits for the country and had limited the Knesset's ability to restrict the rights established therein.[249]

Despite not having a comprehensive bill of human rights or regular law, the Israeli Supreme Court has produced the bill of judicial rights by developing special rules of interpretation and relying on the Declaration of Independence, which is Israel's source of commitment to protecting human rights.[250] This developed slowly throughout Israel's history. At first, the Declaration of Independence

---

243 Elyakim Rubinstein "Basic Law: The Government, in its Original Form—in Practice," *Mishpat Umimshal 3* 576 (5756).
244 Barak Medina *"Regulating the Activities of the Executive Branch in the Constitution"* (A position paper to the Constitution, Law and Justice Commission).
245 The Harrari Resolution 1950.
246 *Id.*
247 Shimon Shetreet, *Developments in Constitutional Law: Selected Topics,* 24 IsLR 386 (1990).
248 *The Bank* Hamizrachi case, *supra* note 6.
249 *Id.*
250 Shetreet, *supra* note 247.

was not considered a legal document and could not be relied upon for the protection of rights.[251] This has changed and the court now relies on the Declaration of Independence as a source of human rights. As the courts have recognized new rights and established these rights, it has formed the judicial bill of rights. In this manner, the court has recognized many basic human rights.[252] The Supreme Court has shown its willingness to interpret the Basic Laws so as to incorporate rights not expressly enumerated in the Basic Laws.[253]

The first two sections of the Basic Laws are the principles clause and the purposes clause. They serve as an introduction and provide a general standard for all human rights.[254] The Basic Laws open with a section devoted to a statement of the basic principle underlying human rights, which are the value of human beings, the sanctity of their lives, and their freedom.[255] The purposes clause states that the Basic Law(s) is to protect human dignity and liberty in order to anchor the Basic Law values of the State of Israel as a Jewish and democratic state.[256] The Basic Laws include a limitation clause which allows the legislature to violate human rights in certain circumstances established in the clause.[257] The limitation clause states that there can be no violation unless by law, designed for a proper purpose and to an extent no greater than required.[258] The Supreme

---

251 See H.C.J 73/53 *Kol Ha'am v. Minister of Interior*, 7(2) P.D. 165, 871 (1953).

252 See e.g. H.C.J 355/79 *Katalan v. The Prison Services*, 34(3) P.D. 294 (1980) (right of privacy); see also Cr.A 2145/92 *The State of Israel v. Guetta*, 46(5) P.D. 704.

253 Hillel Sommer "From Childhood to Adulthood: Open Issues in the Implementation of the Constitutional Revolution," *Law and Business* A 59, (5764).

254 See sections 1 and 2 of the 1992 Basic Laws.

255 See Section 1 Basic Law: Human Dignity and Liberty: "Fundamental human rights in Israel are founded upon recognition of the value of the human being, the sanctity of human life, and the principle that all persons are free; these rights shall be upheld in the spirit of the principles set forth in the Declaration of the Establishment of the State of Israel"; see identical text in Basic Law: Freedom of Occupation.

256 See Section 1 A of Basic Law: Human Dignity and Liberty: "The purpose of this Basic Law is to protect human dignity and liberty, in order to establish in a Basic Law the values of the State of Israel as a Jewish and democratic state"; see also Section 2 of Basic Law: Freedom of Occupation: "The purpose of this Basic Law is to protect freedom of occupation, in order to establish in a Basic Law the values of the State of Israel as a Jewish and democratic state."

257 See Section 8 of Basic Law: Human Dignity and Liberty: "There shall be no violation of right under this Basic Law except by a law befitting the values of the State of Israel, enacted for a proper purpose, and to an extent no greater than is required or by regulation enacted by virtue of express authorization in such law"; see also Section 4 of Basic Law: Freedom of Occupation.

258 Barak Medina, *Human Rights Laws*, pp. 142–273 (published on Nevo and Sacher, 2016) (Hebrew).

Court examines whether the violating law is compatible with the values of the State of Israel. Next the court examines the intended purpose of the law, both subjectively and objectively. A purpose is proper if it serves an important social goal which is sensitive to human rights; the violation must be to only a minimal extent and does not exceed what is necessary.[259]

These rights are expressly listed in the Basic Laws: Freedom of Occupation; sanctity of life, body, and dignity; personal freedom; right to property; right to leave and enter Israel; and privacy. Other rights have found legal recognition in Israel in varying degrees, but are not mentioned in the Basic Laws. These include: right to equality; freedom of expression and association; right to due process; personal autonomy; and the freedom of contract, freedom of religion, and freedom of movement.[260]

Freedom of occupation entitles all persons an inherent right to engage in the work or trade that they choose and the state is to refrain from interfering in that exercise. There are some restrictions that the state can make such as licensing and regulations. The right of sanctity of life, body, and dignity entitles all persons to protection from physical force, death sentence, torture as a form of punishment, and degrading conditions of imprisonment as well as minimal living conditions.[261] Personal freedom means no deprivation or restriction on the liberty of a person by imprisonment, extradition, or any other means. A person cannot be subject to degrading or harsh conditions, or a life sentence without possibility of release. Punishment must be proportional to crime.[262] The right to property applies to real and contractual rights.[263] The right to leave and enter Israel is subject to balancing against competing interests. The court has the power to issue temporary injunctions on travel in the event of criminal prosecutions, the payment of court fees, and the like.[264] Privacy is not defined except for what acts are prohibited by the government. The right of privacy protects against entrance

---

259 *Id.*
260 Recognition of freedom of religion and conscious as a constitutional right.
   H.C.J 7622/02 *Zonshein v. Advocate General*, 57(1) P.D. 726 (2002); Aharon Barak, Proportionality in Law: The infringement of the Constitutional Rights and its Limits 726 (2002); Medina, *supra* note 258; Hillel Sommer, *supra* note 86; H.C.J 721/94 *El Al Airlines v. Danilovich and others*, 48(5) P.D. 749 (1994) (right of equality); C.A 2512/90 *Supergas Ltd. v. Saar*, 45(4) P.D. 405 (1991) (freedom of contract).
261 See Section 2 of the Basic Law: Human Dignity and Liberty.
262 *Id.*, Section 5.
263 *Id.*, Section 3.
264 See H.C.J 3914/92 *Lev v. District Rabbinical Court of Tel Aviv*, 48(2) P.D. 491 (1994); C.R.A 7208/93 *Weissgels v. Weissgels*, 48(4) P.D. 529 (1994).

to a private premise; searches of person, body, or belongings; and privacy of records.[265]

The right to equality has achieved a constitutional status despite not being explicitly expressed in the Basic Laws.[266] Freedom of expression and association finds its protection in the purpose clause of the Basic Law: Human Dignity and Liberty, although it is not expressly mentioned.[267] The right to due process is derived mostly from the rights of property and the rights belonging to the criminal process.[268] Religious freedom and freedom of conscience are constitutionally founded in the Declaration of Independence and in the Basic Laws, but there are limitations on religious freedom in Israel. In some areas of the law, all citizens are subject to religious law. Some of these areas are marriage and divorce, burials, and kosher food status. Freedom of movement allows every person lawfully present to move freely within Israel and to choose a place of residence.[269]

Israel has not expressly provided for the right of equality in Basic Law.[270] No law, as of yet, has expressly provided for constitutional entrenchment of the principle of equality. However, the right of equality has a long history in Israel; it has found expression in the Declaration of Independence.[271] In the absence of a constitutionally established right by legislation, the Supreme Court has recognized the duty to act equally toward citizens.[272] The court gives presumption to the interpretation that laws are meant to act equally on all citizens.[273] The Supreme Court agreed to recognize the right of equality as a constitutional and protected right within the general provision of the Basic Law: Human Dignity and Liberty.[274] This may lead to other rights being read into the existing Basic Laws, and the Supreme Court has adopted the implied rights approach, that is to recognize rights not explicitly enumerated in the Basic Law: Human Dignity and Liberty.

---

265 Navot, *supra* note 4, para. 584. See Section 7 of the Basic Law: Human Dignity and Liberty.
266 *Danilovich* case, *supra* note 260.
267 Sommer, *supra* note 86.
268 See Section 5 of the Basic Law: Human Dignity and Liberty.
269 *Id.*, Section 6.
270 Equality is not mentioned in neither 1992 Basic Laws. See H.C.J 6427/02 *The Movement for Quality Government v. The Knesset*, 61(1) P.D. 619 (2006).
271 Decleration of independence: "The state of Israel will ensure complete equality of social and political rights, to all its inhabitants, irrespective of religion, race or gender."
272 See H.C.J 7052/03 Adala v. Minister of Interior, 61(2) P.D. 202 (2006).
273 H.C.J 98/69 *Bergman v. Minister of Finance*, 23(1) P.D. 693; H.C.J 507/81 *Abu Hazera v. Attorney General*, 35(4) P.D. 561, 585.
274 H.C.J 6427/02 *The Movement for Quality Government v. The Knesset*, 61(1) P.D. 619 (2006).

Under the Declaration of Independence, there is a guarantee of complete civil and political equality to all inhabitants and the Supreme court judisprudence enforces the guarantee.[275] At the same time, Israel is defined as a Jewish state. The two statements, Jewish and Democratic, can be argued to pull in different directions on the equality spectrum.[276] As the Or Commision of Inquiry on the events of October 2000, reported in practice that there are challenges that Arab citizens face in a number of fields.[277]

Prima facie, the designation as a Jewish state and the preferences given to Jews, can be argued to violate equal protection.[278] The Law of Return gives a clear preference to Jews in the matter of immigration where non-Jews must comply with much stricter immigration codes. However, There are a number of principles that provide Israel with the justification to create a Jewish state as a homeland for the Jewish people. First, Israel has the right to determine the composition of its population and its character.[279] Second, the Jewish Agency Law provides legal authority to focus the country on gathering the exiles. Third, other statutes officially establish Jewish Sabbaths and holidays as well as symbols. Fourth, the Declaration of Independence defines the State of Israel as a Jewish State. Fifth, the courts have upheld decisions to ban parties from elections when those parties specifically deny Israel as a Jewish State, suggesting they were trying to undermine the state's existence.[280] The court reasoned that the existence of the state of Israel as Jewish was a basic constitutional fact. It cannot be negated; therefore, those that attempt to negate this fact cannot stand for election.[281]

Military service is required for all citizens of Israel who have reached the age of eighteen.[282] All are required to serve, but enlistment officers have discretion on who is enlisted. The policy has been to not enlist Arab citizens. This has led to some differences in benefits for which Jews are eligible for their military service and Arabs are not eligible.[283] Military personnel are compensated for

---

275 See *supra* note 271.

276 See S. Samooha "Minority Status in Ethnic Democracy: The Status of the Arab Minority in Israel," 13 Ethnic & Racial Studies (1990) 349.

277 Or Commision of Inquiry available online at: http://elyon1.court.gov.il/heb/veadot/or/in side_index.htm (accessed February 9, 2017).

278 Samooha, *supra* note 276.

279 This right is expressed in the International Covenant for the Elimination of All Forms of Racial Discrimination adopted by the UN on Dec. 21, 1965 and ratified by Israel on Jan. 3, 1979.

280 See Section 7 A of Basic Law: The Knesset.

281 See E.A 1/65 *Yardor v. Central Elections Committee*, 19(3) P.D. 365 (1965).

282 See The Defense Service (Consolidated Version) Law (1986).

283 *Id.*

the time spent in service, payment exemptions in certain circumstances, and priority in returning to a place of work. While Arabs' rights to education, housing, child benefits, and general social rights[284] are not limited by their lack of service, the special benefits given to mostly Jews who serve in the army have caused resentment among Israeli Arabs in the past.

C. Administrative Regulations and Orders

Administrative authorities act within the limits of its powers statutorily conferred by Knesset legislation.[285] Unless there is authorization, an administrative act is invalid.[286] Executive authority is not permitted to delegate its authority unless permitted by law.[287] Knesset legislation provides the powers and identities of administrative bodies as well as the criteria governing the manner of exercising those powers.[288] The Supreme Court established an interpretive presumption that legislature is presumed not to have enabled executive authority to establish primary legislation. Therefore, the Knesset is required to give greater specificity in legislation in order to establish executive authority.[289]

Authority to act can be vested in a government agency in several ways. Authority can be vested through primary legislation, as established by the Knesset. Authority can also be vested through regulations, administrative directives, and general governmental powers.

Regulations may be used to vest powers in another authority and the regulation acts as the principal source of power. In order to be a valid vesting of power, the regulation must establish the vesting of power. Under Human Rights laws, a new law cannot vest authority to violate rights unless it meets the requirement of the limitation clause in the 1992 Basic Laws.[290]

It is also possible to vest power through Administrative Directive, which is a decision by a Minister to empower a local authority. Directives can be oral or

---

284 See Absorption of Discharged Soldiers Law (1994).
285 Criminal Appeal Request 8135/07 *Goren v. State of Israel* (published on Nevo, 11.02.2009).
286 H.C.J 355/79 *Katalan v. The Prison Services*, 34(3) P.D. 294 (1980)
287 H.C.J 3267/97 *Rubinstien v. Minister of Defense*, 55(2) P.D. 255 (9.12.1998); H.C.J 2918/93 *Manucipality of Kiryat Gat v. State of Israel*, 47(5) P.D. 832 (28.11.1993).
288 *Id.*
289 Article 31 of Basic Law: The Government; H.C.J 1384/98 *Avni v. The Prime Minister*, 52(5) P.D. 206 (1998).
290 See section 8 of the Basic Law: Human Dignity and Liberty and section 4 of Basic Law: Freedom of Occupation.

written; they do not carry the weight of legislative authority nor do they establish a legal norm. Directives are an informal administrative norm with legal consequences.[291]

"General Governmental Powers" are authorities that are not regulated by an empowering statute but are powers granted to the government by Section 32 of Basic Law: The Government. These powers are residual powers and subject both to law and to a number of conditions.[292]

Every administrative authority has general auxiliary powers which are intended to supplement primary powers of the administrative authority. Auxiliary powers have two limitations. First, they are usually applied to preliminary activities such as visits, tours, publication, consultations, etc. Second, the powers can only be used as reasonably necessary to enable exercising the primary power.[293]

Orders are given under authority of administrations to impose prohibitions and duties. Orders can be general or personal. General orders are like regulations or secondary legislation. Orders allow the administration to fill in gaps in the legislation where the Knesset did not have the time or expertise necessary for the legislation.[294]

D. Local Government Bylaws

The State of Israel is geographically small and is particularly centralized. This is a result of the geography as well as the British legacy and the social and military challenges that confronted the state immediately after its establishment. Political power is concentrated in the hands of the central government.

The local government is an outgrowth of the framework under British Mandate. The framework is one of a number of local governing units that consolidated into legal structures. These structures were maintained after the State of Israel was established.[295] Regional councils are a combination of a number of rural local authorities and are at the top of local governmental hierarchy with local committees at the lowest level. There are 60 municipalities, roughly 140 local councils, and 50 regional councils. Authorities fall into two categories: municipal and village.[296] Municipal authorities can either be a city or a local council.[297]

---

291 Criminal Appeal 213/56 *The Attorney General v. Alexsandrovich* (1957).
292 See *Municipality of Kiryat Gat, supra* note 287.
293 H.C.J 402/63 *Ronen v. Minister of Education and Culture,* 18(3) P.D. 172 (1999).
294 H.C.J 653/79 *Azriel v. Licensing Division,* 35(2) P.D. 085 (1980).
295 See Municipalities Ordinance of 1934; Local Councils Ordinance of 1940.
296 The principal difference between city and local councils is the number of residents.

Municipal authorities are governed by the Mayor and the Council, where the Mayor functions as executive and the Council as legislative.

In large part, the original local governmental structure was based on the British system which was designed to give the largest amount of autonomy as possible to the settlements.[298] At the time of Independence, the local government was considered to be the executive arm of the central government.[299] Local government is confined to act only within the powers explicitly conferred upon it by law.[300] The Ministry of the Interior has absolute authority to establish or abolish local authority. The Ministry of the Interior is to act as supervisor and has the power to override any local decision—local government decisions are conditional upon approval from the central government. Despite the broad supervisory powers, the central government does not usually interfere with local authorities. Israeli courts also are reluctant to interfere because the Ministry of the Interior has exclusive authority over local authorities. The Israeli court system will get involved only in exceptional cases when Ministers exceed the scope of their powers.[301] This lack of supervision leads the local government frequently to exceed formal boundaries of power.[302] Budgetary changes since the 1980s have led to more income for local authorities, leading to further independence.

297 Navot, *supra* note 4, at para. 492.
298 See I. Rozen-Zvi, "Taking Space Seriously; Law Space and Society," Contemporary Israel, (2004) pp. 23–27.
299 See I. Rozen-Zvi, "The Place of Justice: The Law of Local Government and Social Injustice."
300 See the ultra vires doctrine H.C.J 36/51 *Chet v. Haifa Municipality*, 5 P.D. 1553; H.C.J 230/73 *S.Z.M Inc v. Jerusalem Manucipality*, 28(2) P.D. 113.
301 See H.C.J 51/68 *Azur Local Municipality, v. Minister of the Interior*, 22(2) P.D. 226; H.C.J 94/174 *Rishon Le-Tzion Municipality v. Minister of the Interior*, 28(2) P.D. 711.
302 See Rozen-Zvi, *supra* note 298.

Chapter 6:
Judicial Role in Society

1. Introduction

The Israeli judiciary has long enjoyed independence in its personal and substantive meanings, that is, the independence of the individual judge's security of office and terms of service, and independence in adjudicating cases. However, the constitutional position of the judiciary remains inadequate.[1]

Over the years, the role of the judiciary in Israel has increased significantly. Still, the constitutional position of the judiciary is lacking. A simple legislative majority could change every provision relative to the judiciary. The challenge has become much greater since 1992 when the Knesset passed two very important constitutional pieces of legislation: The Basic Law: Human Dignity and Liberty and The Basic Law: Freedom of Occupation. These two Basic Laws opened a new era in the Israeli legal system. They established constitutional standards that cannot be violated by ordinary legislation. Thus, by implication, they gave the courts the power to invalidate legislation found to be contrary to the Basic Laws.[2] In effect, they constitutionalized the Israeli legal system.[3]

Israel's judiciary is led by a Supreme Court which has a strong role in governance, yet lacks constitutional protection. This anomaly poses a critical challenge. The court has been asked to rule on numerous politically charged issues. These rulings often bring about threats to the collective independence of the judiciary that are "structural" in nature: proposals to limit the jurisdiction of the courts or to change the terms of office of judges. In the absence of adequate constitutional protection, such changes require only a simple majority vote of the Knesset. At the same time, amendments of the Basic Laws require a special majority, thus putting much greater pressure on the courts in their adjudication of constitutional cases. Legislative measures amending judicial rulings require a special majority.[4] Such majority has been mobilized in the Knesset in the Meat Import cases.[5]

---

1 S. Shetreet, *The Challenge of Judicial Independence: Constitutional Protection of the Israeli Judiciary*, in P. Russell and D. O'Brien (eds.), Judicial Independence in the Age of Democracy, 233 (2001)(hereinafter: *The Challenge of Judicial Independence*) .
2 *Id.*, at 234.
3 A. Barak, *Constitutionalisation of the Israeli Legal System*, 31 Isr. L. Rev. pp 3–23 (1994).
4 *The Challenge of Judicial Independence, supra* note 1, at 234–235.

DOI 10.1515/9783899497946-006

In recent decades, there has been a trend in expansion of the Supreme Court's role and a decline in the power of the executive. Litigators and petitioners began to bring politically charged issues before the Court. At the same time, the High Court of Justice demonstrated a willingness to adjudicate these issues on the merits and to interfere with the executive's decisions. By adopting a more liberal approach to the rules of justiciability and standing, the Court opened its doors to many issues that were not adjudicated in the past.[6]

The public resorted to the courts for settlement of problems that the political authorities failed to resolve. Thus, the courts adjudicated the validity of non-orthodox conversion conducted in Israel, the closing of streets on Sabbath, the validity of the General Security Service interrogation practices, the introduction of summer daylight savings time,[7] the exemption from drafting Yeshiva students,[8] the constitutionality of allocating broadcasting time for election propaganda,[9] the retroactive increase in allocations of funds to political parties for financing campaigns, and the immunity of Knesset members.[10] The Supreme Court adjudicated cases regarding the rights of a one-man faction in the Knesset, the validity of a pardon granted to the heads of the general Security Services in the midst of a heated public debate, the power of the Minister of Justice to refuse to surrender a criminal fugitive declared extraditable by the courts, and even the time when a Speaker of the Knesset ought to put a motion of no confidence to a vote.[11] Sometimes the executive intentionally diverted the onus of making decisions from itself to the judiciary. The Government so acts whenever it is reluctant to pay the political price involved in making the decision itself.[12]

---

5 See The *Mitrael* Cases: H.C.J 3827/93; H.C.J 5009/94; and S.Shetreet, *Between Three Branches of Government: The Balance of Human Rights in Matters of Religious Liberty*, (Floersheim Institute of Policy Studies, 1999).
6 *The Challenge of Judicial Independence, supra* note 1, at 236.
7 H.C.J 217/80 *Segal v. Minister of Interior*, 34(4) P.D. 429 (Hebrew); H.C.J 297/82 *Berger v. Minister of Interior*, 37(3) P.D. 29.
8 H.C.J 448/81 *Ressler v. Minister of Defense*, 36(1) P.D. 81 (1981); F.H 2/82 *Ressler v. Minister of Defense*, 36(1) P.D. 708; H.C.J 179/82 *Ressler v. Minister of Defense*, 36(4) P.D. 421; H.C.J 910/86 *Ressler v. Minister of Defense*, 42(2) P.D. 441. See also H.C.J 3267/97 *Rubinstein and others v. Minister of Defense* , 52(5) P.D. 481 (1998), which declared unlawful the policy to exempt Yeshiva students from army service.
9 H.C.J 246/81 *Agudat Derech Eretz v. Broadcasting Authority*, 35(4) P.D. 1.
10 H.C.J 620/85 *Miari v. Speaker of the Knesset*, 41(4) P.D. 169; H.C.J 141/82 *Rubinstein v. Speaker of the Knesset*, 37(3) P.D. 141 (1983) (Hebrew).
11 *The Challenge of Judicial Independence, supra* note 1, at 237.
12 See *supra* notes 9 – 10.

The increasing role of the courts in the system of government has been manifested by the greater willingness of the High Court of Justice to review substantive decisions of the executive as distinct from procedural defects, defects of jurisdiction, or other technical defects. This phenomenon is most strongly manifested in the Court's willingness to examine security decisions of the executive on their merits.[13]

2. System Factors Affecting Judicial Role in Society

The justice system is shaped by a network of powers and processes shared by members of the judiciary, executive, and legislative branches. All of them deserve appreciation, respect, and gratitude for establishing and maintaining an independent judicial system and democratic government based on the rule of law.

The role of the judiciary and the balance of powers between the judiciary and the executive branches on the one hand and the legislature on the other have undergone substantial change in Israel. The change was enhanced and completed with the enactment of two Basic Laws in 1992—Basic Law: Freedom of Occupation and Basic Law: Human Dignity and Liberty. These laws began the new constitutional era in the Israeli legal system, and have further reinforced the broad scope of the role of the judicial branch with the Supreme Court at its head. This change in the balance of powers between the branches of government in Israel is credited mainly to the Supreme Court, which, under the leadership of Presidents Barak and Shamgar, brought about important changes in the nature of the judicial review of executive, legislative, and administrative actions. This change in the balance of power and the increasing judicial role was effected by introducing flexibility into the law of standing and justiciability, thereby creating a judicialization of social process and governmental actions. The process has been further extended as a result of the relative weakening of the legislative branch and the executive branch in the 1980s and the 1990s. As Robert Bork wrote, the Israeli Supreme Court is making itself the "dominant institution in the nation, an authority no other court in the world has achieved."[14] This process has brought about judicial involvement in almost all fields of activity, including

---

13 See S. Shetreet, *Developments in Constitutional Law: Selected Topics*, 24 Isr. L. Rev. 368–460 (1990) (hereinafter: *Developments in Constitutional Law*).
14 Robert H. Bork, *Coercing Virtue: The Worldwide Role of Judges* (AEI Press, 2003).

legislative actions and executive actions that until the middle of the 1970s were held to be beyond the scope of judicial review by the Supreme Court. The ever-increasing role of the Supreme Court in the activities of the government added new dimensions to the interrelations between the judiciary branch and the executive and legislative branches. In addition, the 1992 enactment of the two Basic Laws—Basic Law: Freedom of Occupation and Basic Law: Human Dignity and Liberty—have proven crucial to this development because they have changed the checks and balances between the branches of government, giving more power to the courts. In the process of increasing the role of the judiciary, a tension has been created between the courts and the other branches of government—the legislative and executive. Sometimes this tension has been imperceptible and unobtrusive; at other times, it has been obvious and intrusive. This tension may cause the legislative and executive branches to take action to restrict the powers of the Supreme Court and its jurisdiction, and to intervene in its independence.

Judicial independence is vital for any justice system. An illustration of this possible trend is the proposal to establish a constitutional court, which is still on the public agenda. Although having been dismissed once already in the Knesset, the proposal still attracts the substantial support of numerous MKs. This proposal reflects the dissatisfaction and the loss of confidence on the part of a significant portion of the public vis-à-vis the judiciary of Israel. This dissatisfaction stems both from the failure of the Supreme Court's composition to fairly reflect the diversity of society and from the increase in judicial activism in sensitive and controversial matters pertaining to judicial review of Knesset statutes. The debate became very heated when Prof. Daniel Friedman took office as the Minister of Justice. After his appointment in the latter part of 2006, Prof. Friedman proposed a number of controversial changes.[15]

A majority of these reforms deal with appointment and service of judges. One of the main reforms is the 45th amendment to the Law of Courts, which limits the term of service of presidents and vice-presidents of courts. An additional reform is the method of appointing presidents of the Supreme Court and of other courts.[16] Furthermore, a global reform in the committee for the election of judges is proposed.[17] A proposed amendment to the Law of Terms limits the time of

---

15 Isabel Kershner, *"Friends' Clash Reflects Battle Over Israeli Court"*, New York Times, 22/11/2007.

16 Article 1 to the Law of Courts: Amendment—Ways of Election and Appointment of President and Vice-President and Cancellation of Temporary Appointments.

17 Proposed amendment to the Basic Law: Judiciary (the composition of committee for the election of judges).

service of presidents and vice-presidents of courts. In addition, there is a proposal to change the members of the committee for the appointment of judges and the method of appointment.[18] In addition, according to the proposed amendment to the Law of Courts, the practice of appointing judges for a temporary period will be cancelled. Currently, district court judges are assigned temporarily to the Supreme Court and later can be appointed to it permanently. Furthermore, it is proposed to change the model of judicial review of statutes. Another proposal is a division of the authority of Attorney General. According to the proposal there will be a distinction between legal counseling to the government and between the duties as Attorney General.[19]

All of these issues and others divide the Israeli public, divide scholars, and divide the judiciary on the one hand and the executive on the other.[20]

Here is a proposal to focus on a central issue going to the root of the role of the Supreme Court in Israeli society. This analysis considers the development of the constitutional discourse and public debate on constitutional adjudication and on the role of the Supreme Court in Israeli society. At the center of the debate lies the issue of judicial review of the constitutionality of Knesset laws.

The analysis begins with a judicial review of Knesset laws in the era before, and after, the enactment of the 1992 Basic Laws—Basic Law: Human Dignity and Liberty and Basic Law: Freedom of Occupation. Special attention will be paid to the discussion in legal writings, court decisions and public discourse of the controversy regarding the desired model of the judicial review of statutes. In the ensuing discussion, this chapter will examine the process of constitutional adjudication with reference to the models of the judicial review of Knesset laws.

The models of judicial review may be placed in a number of categories as follows: the adjudicative model, the declaratory model, the pre-legislation model, the centralized and decentralized model, and the adjudicative model coupled with the legislative power to amend after judicial ruling (the override procedure). These models will be briefly analyzed.

After the analysis of the models of judicial review and the model proposed by the Israeli Justice and Constitution Committee of the Knesset (the centralized adjudicative model coupled with the Knesset override procedure), the chapter

---

18 The Law of Courts: Amendment—Members of Committee for Judges' Election, Memorandum of the Law of Courts.

19 Dan Izenberg, *Friedmann Moves to Split Functions of Attorney-General*, Jerusalem Post, 24/07/2008.

20 Dan Izenberg, *Mazuz: Friedmann's Bill to Split Duties of A-G a "Catastrophe,"* Jerusalem Post, 13/08/2008.

will outline the model that is recommended for adoption in Israel—the centralized declaratory model.

The author's proposal is that the court's role be limited to the declaration of a statute's compatibility or incompatibility with existing law, while the act of striking down, or amending, such a statute is to be carried out only by parliament. This would not constitute a dramatic change in current constitutional practice, as it is consistent with the de facto practice of the Supreme Court of suspending the invalidation of a statute in those cases where it has ruled that the statute contradicts the Basic Laws, and allows the Knesset to respond to the court's ruling. The proposal set forth is similar to the declaratory model of judicial review introduced by the United Kingdom's Human Rights Act of 1998.

The chapter's main thesis is that in order to resolve the issue of the crisis of confidence in the Israeli Supreme Court, there is a need for reform. The author's proposal is to provide a new method of deciding constitutional questions in order to reinstate the confidence of substantial parts of the Israeli public in the Supreme Court. According to the proposal, the Supreme Court would have the authority only to declare that a law contradicts a Basic Law, and the Knesset would then amend or nullify that law. According to the new proposal, the Supreme Court would rule on constitutional issues in a special panel. The new proposal also provides that the appointment of the members of this special panel be based on the principle of a fair reflection of society: the adjudication on the validity of the laws will be before a panel of at least nine judges, including at least three women, a traditional-religious person, and judges from different social backgrounds. In order to minimize the friction between the Supreme Court, the Knesset, and the executive branch, the court should grant standing only to petitioners who have been personally harmed by the actions of the authorities. In light of the fierce and ongoing debate about the role of the courts in society, this reform should be carried out by the legislature.

3. The Rules of Justiciability and Standing

In a democratic society, greater recourse to the courts to solve political questions can be paradoxical. People turn to the judiciary because it is independent of politics and, in so doing, inevitably immerse it in politics. The cases with political-ideological ramifications which have been brought before the court by the public force it, in effect, to pass judgment. The court has reacted by developing procedural barriers to filter out petitions, thus restraining this phenomenon to a certain degree. The clearest example of such an instrument is the development of the doctrine of justiciability.[21]

Literally speaking, a dispute is justiciable in its normative meaning, if there exists a threshold for its resolution.[22] This formulation emphasizes the objective element of the concept, but conceals more than it reveals. It focuses on the courts' ability to adjudicate a conflict rather than on the desirability of a judicial decision. The Court no longer accepts the view that certain activities of public authorities are not subject to adjudication by legal standards. On the contrary, the Court has held that the law governs every action (i. e., normative justiciability), but non-interference may result from exercise of the court's discretion (i. e., institutional justiciability).[23] The court maintains that in some cases, even though legal standards can be applied, the courts may choose not to exercise their power.[24]

Another important test, which determines whether or not the court will take up the case, is the test of *locus standi*, or "standing." With this test, the Supreme Court abandoned altogether the traditional approach, according to which a public petitioner lacking a direct interest in the petition would be deemed to lack standing. The Court formulated a more liberal approach, based on a pragmatic balancing between two competing considerations: the importance of recognizing public petitions as safeguards for the rule of law, and the fear of overburdening the Court with petitions. The Court held that a proper balance between these two considerations would be struck by granting standing to a petitioner who was able to point to an issue of special public importance, to a seemingly serious fault in the action of the authorities, or to the fact that the act in dispute is of special constitutional importance. The Court stressed that these categories did not constitute a closed list, but were markers for sorting out the competing interests.[25]

Moreover, in the *Becker* case, the Court pointed out the functional link between standing and justiciability: "The stronger the right of standing which the petitioner can show …. The greater will be the Court's willingness to over-

---

21 *The Challenge of Judicial Independence, supra* note 1, at 238.
22 S.Shetreet, "Standing and Justiciability," in I. Zamir and A. Zysblat, eds., *Public Law in Israel*, 265–274 (Oxford: Oxford Univ. Press (1997).
23 *See* A. Ben-Dor, *Justiciability in the High Court of Justice*, Mishpatim 17 (1987): 592–636, and H.C.J 732/84 *Tzaban v. Minister of Religious Affairs*, 40(4) P.D. 141 (1986).
24 *The Challenge of Judicial Independence, supra* note 1, at 239.
25 *Id,.* at 239–240.

come its reluctance to interfere in political matters, and vice versa: a weak right of standing strengthens this reluctance."[26]

4. The Development of the Judicial Review of Laws in Israel

A. Judicial Review Prior to 1992

Until 1992, the power of judicial review of laws was exercised by the Supreme Court in several cases in which the Knesset's primary legislation was declared unconstitutional. The Supreme Court intervened when the legislation violated the requirements of Section 4 of the Basic Law: The Knesset, regarding equality of Knesset elections. However, the constitutional review of the Knesset legislation was limited only to matters that were provided for in an explicit, entrenched provision in Knesset legislation, requiring a special parliamentary majority to amend the statutory provision. Such was the issue in the *Bergman* Case,[27] in which the court nullified a law that contradicted Basic Law: The Knesset, by violating the equality principle mentioned in Section 4 without sustaining the required majority mandated in that same section. The court left it to the Knesset to decide whether to pass the law by a majority of MKs (61 votes), as Sections 4 and 46 of Basic Law: The Knesset demands, or to amend the law in order to remove the inequality. It is noteworthy that the Knesset embraced both recommendations. From this point going forth, a series of petitions claiming the invalidity of laws were filed; the court discussed all of the cases by and in themselves, without addressing the question of jurisdiction or justiciability of the problem. For instance, the Supreme Court ruled in the *Kaniel* Case that should a law be passed under the terms set in Section 46 mentioned above, it would be valid even if the change in Section 4 was implicit and has not been carried out explicitly or by a basic law.[28]

The second time the High Court of Justice nullified a Knesset law was in 1981, following a petition filed by the "Derekh Eretz Association,"[29] again on grounds of a violation of the elections law (means of propaganda; Amendment No. 6, 1981), and the equality principle mentioned in Section 4 of the Basic Law: The Knesset. Furthermore, the High Court ruled that the law had not been passed by the necessary majority. This issue was raised again in the petition filed by MK

---

26 H.C.J 40/70 *Becker v. Minister of Defense & Others*, 24(1) P.D. 238.
27 H.C.J 98/69 *Bergmann v. Minister of Finance*, 23(1) P.D. 693, 697 (1969).
28 H.C.J 148/73 *Kaniel v. Minister of Justice*, 27(1) P.D. 794 (1973).
29 H.C.J 246/81 *Agudat Derech Eretz v. Broadcasting Authority*, 35(4) P.D. 1.

Professor Amnon Rubinstein. This time the law in question was the amendment to the Party Financing Law, passed in the Knesset following the elections and designed to retroactively increase each party's financing unit in order to cover the negative balance in some parties' accounts incurred by the election campaign. As before, this petition was prompted by the violation of the equality principle in the famous Section 4. The court upheld the petition, as well as the equality violation claim, and declared the law invalid. Surprisingly, the Knesset refrained from reacting this time by amending the law or upholding it by the necessary majority and embraced the Supreme Court ruling as written. The High Court of Justice's willingness to invalidate a law was limited, due to the judicial rule that existed until the 1990s whereby such an annulment was restricted to situations in which the statute contradicts specific terms in an entrenched clause, i.e., the amendment thereof requires a special majority.

The court refused to nullify laws or impede the legislative process based solely on the content of those laws, even when it considered the content objectionable. For instance, the vice-president, Justice Miriam Ben-Porat, responded in the following manner to the claim made in the *Cohen*[30] case that a certain law discriminated against the petitioner: "Be the judicial branch's opinion of this arrangement as negative as it may. In the absence of a constitution, the Knesset has the authority and the power to legislate a discriminatory law and once it has done so, there is no option but to act in accordance with it." Another instance of the unwillingness of the court to intervene was in the *Vinitzky*[31] case, where a petition regarding the validity of a law was instantaneously overruled. The court cited the fact that it does not become involved in legislative proceedings within the Knesset's jurisdiction, as the law in question was. The same attitude was adopted by the court regarding the reinstitution of the validity of the Emergency Regulations.

B. The Constitutional Discourse on the Appropriate Model of Judicial Review after 1992

Until 1992, the Basic Laws were institutional laws dealing with the state agencies and the branches of government—the executive, the legislator, and the judiciary. In 1992, two Basic Laws dealing with human rights were passed: Human Dignity

---

30 H.C.J 889/86 *Cohen v. Minister of Social Affairs and Social Services*, 41(2) P.D. 540 (1987) (Hebrew).
31 345/88 *Vinitzky v. Speaker of the Knesset* (published on Nevo, 7.6.1988) (Hebrew).

and Liberty, and Freedom of Occupation. A heated constitutional controversy began following the Supreme Court's interpretation of these two Basic Laws in the *Bank HaMizrahi*[32] case, which granted the court the power to annul laws contrary to these Basic Laws. With this ruling the constitutional era in Israel began, with a focus on substantive rights, not just institutional issues that may have touched only tangentially on principles of equality, as had been the case in the past. Following the *Bank HaMizrahi* case, numerous drafts of Basic Laws were submitted, but never came into law.

In the case of *Herut*,[33] the court ruled that an ordinary law cannot contradict the provisions of the Basic Law unless it meets the conditions set forth in the limitation clause. Therefore, a provision proposing to exclude the High Court of Justice's jurisdiction could not prevent the High Court from reviewing the decision of the Central Election Committee. Some writers interpret this case as holding that if an ordinary law meets the conditions of the limitation clause, it can change a provision of the Basic Law. Others hold the view that the *Herut* case affirms the ruling that an ordinary law may not change a provision of the Basic Law unless the Basic Law contains an explicit provision allowing such a change.

There was a very limited number of cases involving the invalidation of statutes for violating the 1992 Basic Laws and the suspension of invalidation. Between 1992 and 2002, the Supreme Court annulled only three laws that violated the Basic Laws. These were a section of the Investment Managers' Law, the instruction regarding soldier detainment, and the instruction legalizing pirate radio stations.

In the *Sagi Tzemach* case,[34] the instruction of the Military Justice Law–1955, whereby a soldier may be detained for 96 hours before being brought before a judge, was discussed. The Supreme Court, in a majority ruling of 10 out of the 11 judges, invalidated this section of the law because it contradicts the Basic Law: Human Dignity and Liberty, by violating personal liberty and does not comply with the "limitation clause" because the harm done exceeds requirement. This ruling was extremely far-reaching. The law's strict instructions, legislated prior to the Basic Law, were immune to constitutional review, whereas the provision enacted after the Basic Law and invalidated in the case actually improved detainee conditions remarkably in comparison to the previous situation. The

---

32 C.A 6821/93 *United Mizrahi Bank Ltd. v. Migdal Cooperative Village*, 49(4) P.D. 221 (1995).

33 H.C.J 212/03 *Herut—The National Movement v. Central Elections Committee for the 16th Knesset*, 57(1) P.D. 750 (2003) (Hebrew).

34 H.C.J 6055\95 *Tzemach v. Minister of Defense*, 53(5) P.D 241 (1999).

court noted that declaring a law, or a provision of the law, as contradictory to a Basic Law does not constitute its immediate invalidation; adequate time must be provided for the purpose of dealing with the outcome of the court ruling. Therefore, the court's ruling to invalidate this section of the Military Justice Law took effect six months after the ruling was handed down. In the *Office of the Investment Managers* case,[35] a petition was submitted claiming that the Regulation of Investment Advice, Investment Marketing and Investment Portfolio Management Law,[36] which was intended to regulate the profession of investment managers and consultants, contradicted Basic Law: Freedom of Occupation because it placed heavy restrictions on the occupation of investment management. The court, sitting in a special panel consisting of 11 judges, ruled unanimously that one of the statutory provisions excessively harmed the freedom of occupation. Therefore, it did not meet the conditions specified in the limitation clause of the Basic Law, which provides that the freedom of profession cannot be constricted unless done by a statute consistent with the values of the State of Israel, aimed at a proper purpose, which is proportional and is expressly authorized by the statute.

In the *Eitan Cabel*[37] case rendered in March 2002, a petition was submitted against an amendment to the Bezeq Law—1982, which granted licenses to radio stations that had been operating for five continuous years. This amendment was enacted in order to legalize the right-wing religious radio station, Channel 7. Channel 7 had transmitted for many years as a pirate radio station, operating without a license. The Supreme Court ruled that this amendment, which granted licenses to specific parties without tenders and equal criteria, damaged freedom of competition of those who wanted to use the public resource of radio frequencies; thus it violated the Basic Law: Freedom of Occupation. This violation was not proportional to any positive results of the law because the legislation did not promote the intended purpose of the law, which was to increase pluralism in radio broadcasts. The law de facto completely blocked new competitors from entering the field, and was at odds with the rule of law by rewarding unlawful actions. Therefore, the bench of nine judges ruled unanimously that the amendment did not meet the conditions of the override section in the Basic Law: Freedom of Occupation. Consequently, the amendment was invalid.

---

35 H.C.J 1715\97 *Office of the Investment Managers v. Minister of Finance*, 51(4) P.D 367 (1997).
36 Regulation of Investment Advice, Investment Marketing and Investment Portfolio Management Law, 5755–1995.
37 H.C.J 1030/99 *Oron v. Speaker of the Knesset*, 56(5) P.D. 640 (2002) (Hebrew).

In 2005, in the *Hof Aza*[38] case, the Supreme Court invalidated a provision in the law implementing the Gaza Disengagement Plan that limited damages to people ordered to evacuate. One can also count the *Pesaro*[39] case as well. In the first decade after the Basic Laws of 1992, the court has declared statutory provisions unconstitutional in four cases (or five cases if we count Pesaro). As of the end of 2016 the Supreme Court invalidated a total of fifteen laws.[40] The court refused to invalidate the provisions of the Citizenship and Entry to Israel Law, which limited the entry of persons from Palestinian territories in violent conflict with the State of Israel who married Israeli citizens.). The court refused to invalidate the provisions of the Citizenship and Entry to Israel Law, which limited the

---

38 H.C.J 1661/05 *Hof Aza Regional Council v. Knesset of Israel*, 59(2) P.D. 481 (2005) (Hebrew).

39 H.C.J 1031/93 *Pesaro v The Minister of Interior*, 49(4) P.D. 661 (1993).

40 Based on Bank *Hamizrahi* ruling C.A 6821/93 *United Bank Mizrahi Ltd. v. Migdal Cooperative Village*, 49(4) P.D. 221 (1995). The Supreme Court invalidated fifteen provisions as unconstitutional. Three were invalidated in the decade after the 1992 Basic Laws. They are H.C.J 6055/95 *Zemach v. Minister of Defense*, 53(5) P.D. 241 (1999) (Hebrew) detention of a soldier without a warrant; H.C.J 1715/97 *Israel Investment Managers Association v. Minister of Finance*, 51(4) P.D. 367 (1997), provision regarding a requirement for investment managers; and H.C.J 1030/99 *Oron v. Speaker of the Knesset*, 56(3) P.D. 640 (2002) (Hebrew) law validating pirate radio; In the following decade 2003–2012 the Supreme Court ruled unconstitutional seven statutory provisions: H.C.J 1661/05 *Hof Aza Regional Council v. Knesset of Israel*, 59(2) P.D. 481 (2005) (Hebrew) provision for compensation of settlers evacuated from Gaza in the disengagement plan, H.C.J 8276/05 *Adalah v. Minister of Defense* (12.12.2006) (Hebrew), provision exempting the state from tort liability for injuries caused by security officers in conflict zones; H.C.J 2605/05 *College of Law and Business, Human Rights Department v. Minister of Finance* (published on Nevo, 19.11.2009) (Hebrew) legislation establishing a privatized prison; Criminal Motions 8823/07 *John Doe v. State of Israel* (published on Nevo, 11.02.2010) (Hebrew) provision allowing for court hearing on arrest extension without the presence of the suspect; H.C.J 10662/04 *Hassan v. National Insurance Institute* (published on Nevo, 28.02.2012) (Hebrew) provision depriving eligibility for income allowance when recipient uses a car; H.C.J 8300/02 *Nasser v. Government of Israel* (published on Nevo, 22.05.2012 income tax benefits provisions); H.C.J 6298/07 *Ressler v. Knesset of Israel* (published in Nevo, 21.02.2012) (Hebrew) law granting exemption from military service to yeshiva students; If we also count Yekutieli case it will amount to eight. see H.C.J 4124/00 *Yekutieli v. Minister of Religious Services* (published on Nevo, 14.06.2010) (Hebrew). provision in the Budget Law for a minimum wage allowance to yeshiva students in the years 2013–2016 the court struck down four statutory provisions, three of them dealing with provisions of the same law dealing with detaining persons illegally entering the country; H.C.J 7146/12 *Adam v. Knesset* (published on Nevo, 16.09.2013) (Hebrew) provisions for detaining persons illegally entering the country; H.C.J 7385/13 *Eitan Israeli Immigration Policy v. Government of Israel* (published on Nevo, 22.09.2014) (Hebrew) provisions for detaining persons illegally entering the country; H.C.J 5239/11 *Avneri v. The Knesset* (published on Nevo, 15.04.2015) restrictions on boycott; H.C.J 8665/14 *Dasta v. The Knesset* (published on Nevo, 11.08.15) provisions for detaining persons illegally entering the country.

entry of persons from Palestinian territories in violent conflict with the State of Israel who married Israeli citizens. The court struck down a provision which imposed limitations on the ability of Palestinians to sue the State of Israel for damages suffered from the activities of the army.

Considering the relatively small number of cases in which the court exercised its power of judicial review to invalidate Knesset laws, it seems doubtful whether Israeli society should pay the social price of maintaining the present adjudicative model. The social price is paid in a loss of public confidence in the Supreme Court.

5. Judges in Democracy

The judicial role in any society is determined and influenced in part by individual judges and their perceptions regarding the scope and essence of their role. Indeed, the judges' characters and the manner in which they perceive the social role played by the judicial branch are key in establishing the courts' role in society. A certain tension is evident in Israeli legislation. This tension emanates from two separate approaches. On the one hand, judicial restraint or formalist law is based upon the view that the law is a closed logical system divorced from social, cultural, and historical circumstances; the law is composed of a system of rules created to establish facts. By implementing relevant legal rules in concrete cases, the court will make a logical decision that is not based on the judges' social and subjective preferences. On the other hand, judicial activism, of which one of the greatest supporters was Judge Holmes, is based upon the perception that judicial life is reality rather than logic. The law is dynamic and forms part of a process of development, uniting within it a synthesis of opposing perceptions and approaches. An active judicial branch reaches decisions within a certain social context; the law's goal is to detail the policy by which social conflicts are resolved. Perceiving the court as an entity that resolves disagreements on the basis of socio-political norms also characterizes the school of legal thought known as Critical Legal Studies (CLS). Israeli judges have been forced to adopt a view midway between these two competing approaches.

All agree that the current approach common in the Supreme Court, as reflected in its rulings, is the activist approach. Indeed, the *Mizrahi Bank* ruling is a striking example of the judicial branch's desire to have legislation judicially reviewed, a possibility that, until recently, would not have crossed anyone's mind. The activist approach adopted by the court is especially apparent in matters of state and religion, as well as in security related issues.

In the Courts' adjudication in matters of state and religion ever since Israel was established a controversy has raged regarding the character of the state. One approach has emphasized the role of civil rights, while the other has stressed the role that religion should play in the administration of public life in the country. The court walks a fine line in matters of state and religion, striving to refrain from tipping the scales in socially and politically charged cases. The key to a solution whereby the continuity of Jewish democratic life in Israel is ensured lies in the formation of a constitutional formula that breathes traditional democratic life into the notion of a "Jewish democratic state." The need for this formula is underlined by the realization that ideological disagreements cannot be resolved in a manner all agree upon; the common ground that is agreed upon by the majority should be the basis for this formula. Design of this formula should be inspired by traditional Jewish precepts, respect for religion, and tradition. However, the formula must be committed to democracy and oppose religious coercion. Tradition is maintained by respecting our ancestors' legacy and heritage, not by establishing the state constitution on religious foundations. Therefore, the appropriate interpretation is the middle path acceptable to the majority of the public in Israel: an interpretation that is not too strict in terms of adherence to religious commandments, but rather symbolizes an identification with Jewish tradition in a manner that will become the accepted norm in society and will not contradict freedom of religion and conscience. The difference of opinion surrounding the character of the State of Israel was also manifested in the actions taken by various government authorities, each one contributing, positively or negatively, to the shaping of the democratic traditional Jewish identity and to protecting civil rights or violating them.

A. The Judicial Review of Security Decisions

In Israel's early days, judicial monitoring played an important role in reviewing the decisions of the executive branch which were based on security factors and violated basic civil rights. However, this review focused on procedural violations and excess of jurisdiction rather than the review of the administrative authorities' decision based on its merits.

Therefore, in Israel's early days, the Supreme Court annulled security decisions when it was proven that civil servants or executives had exceeded their jurisdiction or failed to follow the statutory-procedural requirements. For example, the court refused to approve the issue of an administrative arrest warrant because the counselling committee had not been established as required in accordance with the relevant statutory instruction; annulled a closing warrant because it had not been published; and annulled an administrative arrest warrant that did not specify the place of arrest. On the other hand, until the late 1970s, the court refused to intervene when the petition was not based on a deviation from authority or procedural flaw, but rather on a claim that challenged the decision itself. When the claim was that security factors justified the decision, the court dismissed the petitions, as long as the ministers or military commander stated that their actions were within their jurisdiction and performed honestly. However, there are cases in which the court has intervened in substantive aspects of administrative decisions based on improper considerations by interpreting the law in such a manner as to render administrative actions motivated by security factors impossible. In later years, the courts expressed growing willingness to subject the executive branch's substantive decisions to judicial review. Such was the situation in the *Elon Moreh*[41] case where the court stated that security considerations were subject to essential review, even when the authorities acted within their jurisdiction. Immediately following this case, the court overturned the decision handed down in the *Samara*[42] case that had denied families the right to reunite. The original decision barring the meetings was based a priori on security factors.

In the matter of the *East Jerusalem Electric Company*,[43] the court annulled the confiscation of the company's property. In the *Schnitzer* case,[44] in which the court annulled the military censor's decision to prohibit the partial publication of an article that discussed the Mossad in a Tel Aviv newspaper, Justice Barak explicitly addressed the ever-increasing tendency to expand the extent of the judicial monitoring of security factors. Over the years, judicial review of security authorities taken sensibly has become more and more similar to the review applied to any other governmental activity. One might argue that the importance of security factors is diminishing, while the factors pertaining to the rule of the law are ever increasing. Even if the formal judicial framework were but slightly altered, the use of legal authorities has changed as Israel's security has strengthened. Moreover, the public attitude, as well as that of the judges, towards security considerations has changed, particularly in light of events such as the failure in the Yom Kippur (1973) and the Lebanon (1982) wars, errors that undermined the status of the security establishment in that it shook the confidence that the public once had in the security forces.

---

41 H.C.J 390/79 *Dweikat v. The Government of Israel*, 34(1) P.D. 1 (1979).
42 H.C.J 802/79 *Samara v. Commander of Judea and Samaria*, 34(4) P.D. 1 (1980).
43 H.C.J 351/80 *Electric Company of East Jerusalem v. Minister of Energy*, 35(2) P.D. 373.
44 H.C.J 680/88 *Schnitzer v. Chief Military Censor*, 42(4) P.D. 617 (1988).

The Supreme Court's contribution to the protection of civil rights against abuse by security forces was manifested in two recent judgements. In the *Surik* case,[45] the court ruled that several segments of the security fence failed to meet the proportionality standard because they separated local inhabitants from their agricultural lands, thus violating their rights according to international humanitarian law.

In another case, the court prohibited the use of an early warning procedure by the security forces. This procedure allowed IDF troops to be assisted by a local Palestinian inhabitant when attempting to arrest a Palestinian accused of engaging in terrorism, in order to give him an early warning and prevent any possible harm from coming to him or whoever was with him at the time of the arrest. The court ruled that this procedure contradicted international law, and therefore prohibited it.[46] Thus, the Supreme Court has expanded the extent of its judicial review on security matters by including not only aspects of authority and procedure, but also a review of the content of the decisions made.

B. Judges as Chairmen of Commissions of Inquiry

The important role judges play in Israeli public life is by no means confined to adjudication on the bench. Judges are frequently appointed to lead inquiries into major public controversies and matters of the highest national importance. These commissions are instituted by law and their terms of reference defined by the government. The President of the Supreme Court determines the composition of the commission.[47] In addition, judges have been asked to chair non-statutory governmental committees for the investigation of various matters, some of which were very sensitive, such as the task of reviewing the structure and function of the Israeli secret services, or the remuneration of teachers.[48]

Perhaps the most significant inquiries conducted by judges have been those related to war. Justice Shimon Agranat, former President of the Supreme Court, chaired a Commission on the Yom Kippur War of 1973. Following the Commission's report, Prime Minister Golda Meir, and Minister of Defense, Moshe Dayan, were forced to resign under popular pressure, even though the report had placed the responsibility for the neglect and misjudgment of the projected

---

45 H.C.J 2056/04 *Bet Surik v. The IDF Commander in Gaza*, 58(5) P.D. 807 (2004) (Hebrew).
46 H.C.J 3799/02, *Adala v. Central Command*, 60(3) P.D 67 (2005).
47 *See* Sections 1–4, *Commissions of Inquiry Law*, 23 L.S.I. 32, 1968. For an analysis of the Law, *see* P. Elman, *The Commissions of Inquiry Law*, 6 Isr. L. Rev. 398 (1971).
48 *The Challenge of Judicial Independence, supra* note 1, at 243–244.

plan of the enemy on the military, rather than the political level. Justice Itzhak Kahan, another former Supreme Court President, chaired a commission of inquiry into the massacres in the Sabra and Shatila refugee camps during the 1982 Lebanon War. The commission concluded that there were no grounds whatsoever for a finding of direct responsibility for the massacres on the part of any Israeli. However, after establishing very exacting moral standards, the Commission found that there was indirect responsibility on the part of both the military command and the political leadership. It therefore recommended that Defense Minister Ariel Sharon, as well as several senior army officers, be removed from office. Although the Commission's recommendations were not legally binding, their moral authority and the strong public confidence which judges enjoy in Israeli society compelled the government to implement them.[49] There is a division of opinion on the legitimacy of appointing judges to chair commissions.[50] But it would appear that in times when there is a loss of public confidence in the political branches, it is generally accepted as justified.[51]

C. The Judicial Resolution of Sensitive Cases

The High Court of Justice made a unique contribution to political affairs during the Israeli political system's crisis in the middle of 1990, when the two main parties were negotiating deals with isolated MKs to form a coalition. The success of each one of the main parties depended upon one or two MKs. The Supreme Court was the governmental institution that had to find the solution to this crisis, as well as to other political crises.

The Supreme Court's willingness to hear cases brought by groups and organizations representing a public that had lost its faith in the political system allowed the court to provide an institutional answer to what society perceived to be a time of political crisis and governmental vacuum. The court's institutional role was made possible by important legal developments. The Supreme Court nearly revolutionized the laws pertaining to the right of standing; it expanded judicial doctrine, as well as the extent of the judicial review, by including the probability component in it. All of these changes enabled the court to intervene

---

49 *Id.*, at 244–245.
50 *The Commission of Inquiry into the Events at the Refugee Camps in Beirut* (1983). For further discussion, *see* Y. Zamir, *A Commission of Inquiry from the Legal Aspect*, 35 HaPraklit 323–329 (1984).
51 For further discussion, *see* S. Shetreet, *The Yom Kippur War Commission of Inquiry: The Overall Judgment—Favourable*, 8 Mishpatim 74–90 (1977).

in issues of policy and in political matters, leading to an extremely positive influence on the way the government functions. The Supreme Court intervened in countless cases related to significant political issues, including political agreements, setting the summertime clock, exempting yeshiva students from military service, allocating broadcasting slots for election propaganda, removing parliamentary immunity, decisions made by the Knesset and its chairman, presidential clemency, and the refusal to hand over a fleeing criminal designated for extradition.

In the past, this author supported a broader right of standing, and a flexible doctrine of justiciability. I represented the petitioners in the well-known cases of *Shiran*,[52] where the owners of televisions were given the right to petition against the Broadcasting Authority, and in the case of *Aloni*,[53] where citizens were given the right to petition against the refusal to extradite a criminal. During this time, I promoted a wide-ranging concept of judicial review of the decisions of the administrative authorities and a review based on reasonableness, a flexible concept of standing to petition the High Court of Justice, and a broad doctrine of justiciability. I believed that after a lengthy period of time of broadening judicial review and the judicial role, extending the concept of standing to petition the High Court of Justice, and broadening the doctrine of justiciability, there would come a period of fine-tuning that would reduce the friction between the judicial branch and political branches. The judicial wisdom of approaching the interrelationships between the judicial branch and the other branches would reduce conflicts between the Supreme Court and the Knesset, thus preventing the Supreme Court and influential sectors within Israeli society from continuing their heated debates and confrontations in the public arena, including in the Knesset.

My approach was that the fine-tuning of the judicial role in society and the adjustment of the boundary lines between the judicial branches and the other branches had to be done by the courts themselves. This fine-tuning would have been accomplished just as the judges themselves had broadened judicial review, through the use of the test of the extent of essential harm to the rule of law, or the test of substantive harm to the fabric of the parliamentary system of government. Fine-tuning has not taken place, and the conflict between the executive and the judiciary has only intensified. The Supreme Court is deterred from intervening in political authorities' decisions, even when the court rules in religious matters of similar content against the authorities.

---

52 H.C.J 1/81 *Viki Shiran v. Broadcasting Authority,* 35(3) P.D. 365 (1981).
53 H.C.J 852/86 *Shulamit Aloni v. The Minister of Justice,* 41(2) P.D 1 (1987).

Today my opinion regarding the interrelationship between the judiciary and the other branches of government has changed. I now believe that there is a need for renewed consideration of the basic issues concerning the judiciary's role in society. This change came about because of the intense conflict within Israeli society concerning the role of the Supreme Court and its authority to annul the laws of the Knesset through judicial review of the laws' validity in light of the Basic Laws and the intense opposition faced by the Supreme Court because of its judicial activism. After a rapid expansion of the judicial role, a more flexible concept of standing to petition the High Court of Justice, and a broad doctrine of justiciability, we have arrived at the point where the Supreme Court has reached the outer borders of the territory that divides the judicial branch from the legislative and the executive branches. At this stage, it is necessary to engage in the fine-tuning of the boundaries between the various branches. This fine-tuning and clear delimitation are essential because of the critical voices that are gathering strength with respect to the scope of the judicial role in Israeli society.

Many have claimed that the boundary lines that have been drawn lie outside the jurisdiction of the judicial authority. This claim reflects broad public opinion; the court must heed and address this strong public sentiment. It cannot disregard public opinion and social reality. The court must have the support of the public in order to fulfill its task. One of the most controversial matters regarding the role of the judiciary in society is the judicial review of parliamentary legislation. This topic was widely discussed in the Knesset Justice Committee during the debates on the new Israeli constitution draft.

6. Drawing the Proper Boundaries of Judicial Function

A. Procedural Tools and Substantive Tests for Fine Tuning of Judicial Roles in Society: The Israeli Experience

In the early years of the State of Israel, judicial supervision played an important role in reviewing executive decisions which were based on security considerations and which interfered with civil rights. However, this review was based on procedural or jurisdictional defects and did not involve an examination of the substantive decision of the administrative authorities.[54]

---

54 S. Shetreet, *Creating a Culture of Judicial Independence: The Practical Challenge and the Conceptual and Constitutional Infrastructure*, in S. Shetreet and C. Forsyth (eds.), The Culture of Judicial Independence: Conceptual Foundations and Practical Challenges 12, at 41 (Martinus Nijhoff- Brill Publishers, 2012)(hereinafter: *Creating a Culture of Judicial Independence*)..

In more recent years, the courts have shown a greater willingness to review substantive decisions of the executive, as distinct from reviewing decisions on the grounds of procedural or jurisdictional deficiencies. Many thought that, because judges are not members of the security establishment, they should refrain from interfering in security considerations. Over the years, it has been held that security considerations are not unique insofar as judicial review is concerned. Judges are not administrators, yet the principle of separation of powers requires that they review the lawfulness of administrative decisions. In this regard, security considerations do not enjoy a different status.[55]

Several of the Israeli Supreme Court's decisions reveal a tendency to limit governmental authorities in other areas related to the employment of security considerations.[56] Supreme Court jurisprudence—ruling that the scope of judicial review in security matters is basically similar to that in other matters—has had a very important impact on the practice of the security authorities, and on the handling of challenges directed at the validity of security measures and actions.[57] Sometimes the court's influence is visible in cases settled out of court, or when the requested remedy is given by a governmental authority before or during judicial proceedings,[58] when the very possibility of lodging a petition brings about a change in the authorities' attitude.[59]

The judiciary has not limited itself to the review of specific administrative actions. More than once, the Israeli Supreme Court has expressed a deep concern regarding the exercise of emergency powers used to regulate general economic matters unrelated to dangers emanating from a state of emergency, and which should instead be regulated by ordinary parliamentary legislation.[60] Judicial review of discretionary powers in matters of security in Israel has essentially become similar to the review of any other governmental activity. Israeli democracy is very hesitant to rid itself of legal emergency mechanisms instituted to protect

---

55 H.C.J 680/88 *Schnitzer v. Chief Military Censor,* 42(4) P.D. 617 (1988).

56 For example, the Court has ruled that if an authority is allowed by law not to reason its decision, yet chooses nevertheless to do so, then those stated reasons are subject to High Court review. H.C.J 2/79 *Al-Asad v. Minister of Interior,* 34(1) P.D. 505; H.C.J 541/83 *Asli v. Jerusalem District Commissioner,* 37(4) P.D. 837.

57 Briksman, "High Court of Justice Petitions on Occupied Territory Matters – Practitional Aspects" (1990) 2 Israel Association of Public Law Journal 13.

58 *Id.*

59 *Id.*

60 Accordingly, the Court has decided that economic matters, such as the regulation of slaughterhouses or transport of bread to shops, should be regulated by normal legislation, and not by emergency powers granted to Ministers under the Supervision of Commodities Law. Commodities and Services (Control) Law, 1957, S.H 24; 12 L.S.I 24.

state security. However, it can be said that the significance of security considerations is gradually diminishing, whereas considerations relating to the rule of law are being reinforced.[61]

Since 1994, the controversy regarding the scope of judicial review of the decisions of the political branches of government and the controversy regarding the role of the Supreme Court and its power to invalidate Knesset legislation just became more intense.[62] The controversy regarding the scope of judicial review has an impact on public confidence in the justice system in Israel. The court cannot exercise its power in total detachment from the social and public discourse. In order to continue to faithfully execute its role in society, the court must demarcate in a very finely tuned manner the boundaries between the Supreme Court and the other branches. The test and the basis for the boundary lines between the judiciary and the other branches of government should be based on the following idea: when judicial intervention in a certain area will bring about a substantial disruption or imbalance between the judicial branch and another branch of government, the court should redefine the lines between the judiciary and the other branches and should refrain from intervening in this area. It is appropriate that the court and the Legislature will develop, parallel to this test, tools that will prevent substantial disruption or imbalance in the relationship between the branches of government. In the context of this fine-tuning, the court should refrain from interfering with a case which is predominantly political and which lacks significant legal issues.[63]

The task of demarcating carefully the boundaries between the judiciary and the political branches is not less challenging than the task of expanding the scope of judicial review. The challenge is to refrain from unnecessary withdrawal of the judiciary from vital areas that must remain under a judicial supervision. At the same time, the challenge is to refrain from continued judicial intervention in areas where such intervention substantially disrupts the proper relationship between the courts and the political branches. Effective tools that may be used for promoting public purposes while preserving the lines of demarcation are the public debate and public discourse.[64]

---

61 Shimon Shetreet, *Law and Social Pluralism* (LexisNexis 2002) at 265–271.
62 See the proposed draft law to amend Basic Law: The Judiciary (Amendment Justiciability) 5768/208; See: Sela, "Fridman: 'The Supreme Court is an Institution without Control'" 14.11. 2007, available at: http://www.ynet.co.il/articles/0,7340,L-3471170,00.html (Hebrew; accessed February 9, 2017).
63 Shetreet, *Culture of Judicial Independence in Israel: Substantive and Institutional Aspects of the Judiciary in Historical Perspectives* (2009) 10 Law and Business 525 at pp.576 (Hebrew).
64 *Creating a Culture of Judicial Independence*, supra note 54, at 42–43.

The press and pressure groups such as human rights organizations and social organizations exercise supervision of the activities of the administrative and governmental agencies. The proper supervision, and control of the governmental activities by these organizations should be by public criticism and not by judicial review. This criticism can have an impact on public opinion and have a positive impact on desirable social change. The pressure groups, the non-governmental organizations, the social organizations, and the human rights organizations can help introduce changes outside the courts, without disrupting the careful and sensitive balance that should exist between the branches of government, and avoiding the excessive recourse to the courts as an instrument of social change.[65]

The controversy over the judicial role in society is commonplace in many jurisdictions. The ensuing discussion of the Israeli scene can serve as a basis for possible solutions in order to moderate the controversies in other jurisdictions as well. Over the years, Israel has seen an expansion in the right of standing of petitioners before the High Court of Justice. In the wake of this expansion, there exists a need to fine-tune the boundaries between the judiciary and other branches of government. This should be done by the courts themselves taking into consideration these tests: 1) substantial interruption of the relations, as a qualification for judicial intervention and, 2) the test of substantial violation of the rule of law, and the test of the adverse impact on the parliamentary system of government, as a basis for judicial intervention.[66]

The Supreme Court needs to redefine its role in the coming years. This is because of the heated controversy which is raging in the Israeli society regarding the position of the Supreme Court and its power to set aside Knesset legislation by judicial review based on Basic Laws. The need to redefine the role of the Supreme Court is also required due to the strong opposition to the Supreme Court as a result of the constitutional and public law activism that it exercises as well as the unfortunate trend of the continued loss of public support of the Supreme Court in Israeli society.[67]

So long as the court had an ample institutional capital of public confidence, and the public controversies regarding its intervention in matters that were brought to its adjudication based on public petitions, it was justified to use the judicial institutional capital for the purpose of insuring good government, ethics, and rule of law and wider values of society by judicial decisions. After

---

65 *Id.*, at 43; Justice in Israel: A Study of the Israeli Judiciary (Martinus Nijhoff: London, 1994) (hereinafter: *Justice in Israel*) at pp. 519 – 21.

66 *Id.*

67 *Creating a Culture of Judicial Independence, supra* note 54, at 43.

a long period of extending the role of the judiciary in society by the court, the judicial capital was drained in the eyes of the public. It is now time, therefore, to consider limiting the right of standing by legislation only to those who have been affected personally (rather than allowing standing for petitioners who have general grievances). Limiting the right of standing is required in the Israeli context, in order to stop the phenomenon of solicited petitions. Because of the Israeli courts' deep involvement in the political governance of Israel, solicited petitions are generated from all sectors of the political spectrum, sometimes even from within the executive and public administration; thus, involving the courts in controversies which are beyond their power to resolve.[68]

Additional justification for limiting the right of standing to persons who were affected personally can be found in the fact that non-governmental organizations and civil society organizations in Israel are now very strong. They are able to attain legislative amendments, changes in executive policy, and other remedies by lobbying, public and parliamentary campaigns, and the use of investigative press. Therefore, deficiencies and problems that in the past could be remedied only by the courts, through public petitions to the Supreme Court, can now be remedied by alternative means without draining the judicial institutional capital. This capital is essential and vital for the Supreme Court in order to adjudicate the classical judicial controversies of petitioners and other litigants who have personally been affected and for the performance of the classical judicial role in society of dispute resolution in the ordinary cases.[69]

B. Classification of Models of Constitutional Adjudication

Models of constitutional adjudication may be classified based on a number of parameters. One parameter of classification is the nature of the court's decision when asked to exercise its power to pass judgement on the constitutionality of a statute. In this regard, one can distinguish between two main models: the adjudicative model and the declaratory model. The adjudicative model of judicial review authorizes the court to rule on the constitutionality of the statute and, in appropriate cases, to set aside the statute as invalid. The other model, the declaratory model, only empowers the court to declare that the challenged statute is incompatible with the constitutional provisions. It remains up to parliament to decide whether or not to amend or abolish the statute in question.

---

68 *Id.* at 43–44.
69 *Id.* at 44.

Another parameter is the timing of the judicial review. In the prelegislation model of judicial review of statutes that exists in France, examination of the constitutionality of the statute takes place before the law is passed by parliament. In the other, more widespread model, judicial review is exercised after legislation is passed.

A third parameter of classification is the judicial forum exercising judicial review. One can distinguish between the centralized model of judicial review where only one court, usually the highest court of the land, may exercise judicial review of statutes, and the decentralized model of judicial review in which every court may engage in constitutional adjudication, with the court of last resort having the final judgement.

The adjudicative model is one of the most significant traditions of judicial review. It originated in the United States and is practiced there as well as in Canada. An approach consisting of the judicial review of laws and a comprehensive review of the executive branch is practiced in Israel as well. Article III of the US Constitution states that "the judicial Power of the United States shall be vested in one supreme Court, and in such inferior Courts as the Congress may from time to time ordain and establish." The Supreme Court's authority in the United States begins with declaring the annulment of laws and ends with the essential examination of the executive and legislative branches' decisions. The authority to declare laws unconstitutional and to invalidate them is granted to any court. One of the roles played by the Supreme Court is the interpretation of the US Constitution.

The court may find itself annulling state laws as well as Congressional laws, should they violate the constitution. Such is the famous case in *Marbury v. Madison*, where the Supreme Court ruled that Congress, by sustaining the 1789 judicial law empowering the court to issue writs of mandamus, had granted the central government more authority than the constitution intended. This judgement implies that judges have the authority to decide whether a law or governmental act contradicts the constitution. In the United States and Canada, the judicial review model is identical.

Judicial review of laws exists, as well as comprehensive review of the actions taken by the executive branch. However, contrary to the United States, in Canada the court's judicial review leads to parliament's amendment of the law. In this case, judicial review is fundamentally different from the American model. The Canadian Supreme Court functions as a judicial review apparatus and is the ultimate court of appeal. The Canadian Supreme Court is the court of last resort in Canada, as well as the final court of constitutional adjudication, by virtue of the Charter of Rights of 1982. The judicial review of constitutionality is not exclusive to this court and is granted to all federal instances. Article 33 of the Canadian

Charter of Rights in the Canadian Constitution grants the legislator or parliament override power (the ability to legislate a law that overrides certain sections of the Canadian Charter of Rights). The legislator must explicitly state in the law that the new law is valid despite what the Charter says. The existing power granted to the judicial court in Canada is in fact to suspend a certain legislative act rather than to annul it. Nevertheless, there is concern with this model in that the override clause may prompt the legislative branch to legislate laws that are immune from essential judicial review, as long as the law explicitly states ("notwithstanding") that it is contradictory to the constitution. The overriding tool's effectiveness lies in the legislative branch's self-restraint in using it. Excessive use of the override may result in the undermining of laws protecting human rights. An example of the severe problem this apparatus may cause is the *Mitrael* case.

Israel has looked at incorporating aspects of the Canadian provisions into its own laws. In the new constitution draft, which was tabled to the Knesset plenum in 2006, the Knesset Justice Committee proposed the adoption of the adjudicative centralized model of judicial review of statutes coupled with legislative amending power modelled after the Canadian override parliamentary procedure. Such a provision would allow the Knesset to amend the legislation after it has been held unconstitutional by the court. The amending statute has to be legislated by a special majority, and after it has passed, cannot be challenged again in court. In addition to the proposed model, the Committee also presented alternative models, including the declaratory model and a separate constitutional court. The Knesset plenum resolved to call upon the next Knesset to complete the project of adopting a new constitution for Israel.

Since 1998, the United Kingdom has adopted the declaratory model for the judicial review of statutes. The UK Human Rights Act provides that, to whatever extent possible, in primary and secondary legislation both before and after the Act, contested laws will be interpreted and enforced in a manner that is consistent with the rights protected by the European Convention of Human Rights. The courts have the power to declare a parliamentary provision incompatible with the provisions of the European Convention of Human Rights.

A number of countries follow pre-legislation constitutional review. In Italy, for example, this model exists regarding certain bills. In Norway, the parliament may ask for an opinion prior to legislation. In France, this model has been adopted as a significant part of the legislative process. The main goal of the model is to ensure that the bill is compatible with the constitution before it is enacted.

If Israel were to adopt the pre-legislative model, there would be a council designated to review bills in the legislation stage. The council would be diverse and composed of representatives from all three branches of government, as well as members who do not belong to any of the three branches and academic scholars. This council would review the laws being proposed in the Knesset, then advise the Knesset and the government to amend constitutional flaws in the bills before they are passed. This suggestion, made by Kremnitzer and Carmon, is based on the prelegislative constitutional review idea that exists in France and restricts their constitutional council to pre-legislative judicial review only.

The model is innovative in several regards. First, it pertains to the legislative branch separately from the judicial branch. The model attempts to deal with a situation in which the legislative branch's status needs strengthening, as well as the situation whereby constant friction exists between the legislative and executive branch. This model's advantage is that it may prevent the legislation of laws that do not comply with the Basic Laws from the outset. This model also maintains the status of the Knesset by reducing the chances that the court will declare a law annulled and by preventing the possibility of rash legislation that is not thoroughly thought through. However, this model may complicate the process of legislation and create unwanted tensions with the Supreme Court.

The dissatisfaction of various factions in Israeli society and some academic members with the Supreme Court gave rise to the proposal for the establishment of a constitutional court along the lines of a centralized constitutional court model. The proposal, presented by Knesset members Eliezer Cohen (National Unity-Yisrael Beiteinu Party) and Yigal Bibi, provided for a constitutional court that would exercise judicial review based upon the Basic Laws and the principles and values of the State of Israel as a Jewish and democratic state. No other court would rule on the issues under the authority of the constitutional court. The proposal provided that the constitutional court would be composed of three judges from the Supreme Court, two judges from the Rabbinical Court, one judge from the Muslim Court, four members of the academy, and a new immigrant. Its decisions would bind all other courts, and it would have the power to void any laws legislated by the Knesset. Supreme Court president Barak and others opposed the bill to establish a constitutional court, noting that it presented a threat to the Supreme Court. Other justices also expressed the opinion that establishing a constitutional court would harm Israeli democracy. The authors' view is that the Supreme Court must deal with the criticism directed against it by adopting a more vigorous approach to ensuring the fair reflection principle, thereby bolstering the faith of all sectors of Israeli society in the judicial system.

Ensuring the fair reflection principle would be an appropriate and valid response to the ideologically and socially based criticism. The authors, too, oppose the establishment of a constitutional court, in the format proposed, as it may harm the delicate balance of the Supreme Court in Israel. We believe that the constitutional council or constitutional court models practiced in France and Germany respectively are incompatible with Israeli reality and circumstances. Such a move would be erroneous and would result in a return to the current model in due course.

7. Ideas for Reform

A. Past Proposals

In the past, members of academia and the Knesset have suggested that Israel develop a constitutional court in order to legitimize and increase public confidence in judicial review of government decisions. The constitutional court would be used whenever a constitutional question arose. It would hear cases requiring a determination in the light of the basic principles concerning the values of the State of Israel as a Jewish and Democratic State; no other court would rule on these issues under the authority of the constitutional court. In addition, the proposal stated that the constitutional court would be composed of three judges from the Supreme Court, two religious judges, four academics, and a new immigrant. Its decisions would bind all other courts, and it would have the power to void any laws legislated by the Knesset.[70] However, this proposal is dangerous to a democratic system; because the judges would be chosen on a political basis, it has the potential to make the justice system political. It also has the potential to weaken the Supreme Court because there would be two separate High Courts.[71]

It has also been proposed that the Judiciary needs to draw a more precise line between the Knesset and the Government, avoiding involvement in certain areas where it would cause a lack of balance between the branches. Under this model, it is up to the courts and the Knesset, in tandem, to develop the tools to prevent major distortion of lack of balance in the internal relationship between the various branches of government, as a doctrine that is self-defining, that will bring about fine-tuning and clearer boundary lines between the judicial authority and the other branches of government. For example, in this framework of fine-tuning, it is up to the courts to avoid getting involved in a petition that deals with issues of clear political character and which lack dominant legal aspects.[72] However, this is quite a challenging task. It would be best if the Court

---

70 See G. Alon, *Majority Against the Proposal to Establish a Constitutional Court*, Ha'aretz (Tel Aviv) October 31, 2001; G. Alon, *Two Law Proposals to Establish a Constitutional Court Were Postponed*, Ha'aretz (Tel Aviv) November 6, 2001.

71 See R. Gavison, "There are More than Two Options," *Yediot Acharanot*, May 21, 2001.

72 S. Shetreet, *Standing and Justiciability*, in I. Zamir & A. Zysblat, eds., *Public Law in Israel* (Oxford: 1996) at 265, 272–273.

could use legislative intent when making decisions. However, the Knesset legislates in order to achieve its goals, and places little weight on its intentions behind the legislation.[73]

B. A Three-Step Proposal

Public confidence in the Supreme Court could be restored if 1) the Court would
introduce a new form of decision making of constitutional questions, giving the
Knesset a final say; 2) decide constitutional matters by a panel consisting of a
special composition based on the principle of reflection of the society by the judiciary, consisting of at least nine judges; and 3) restrict the right to petition only
to those whom have been personally harmed by an act of the government.[74]

The first principle of the proposal is to provide a new method of deciding
constitutional questions in order to reestablish substantial parts of the public's
faith in the courts. According to the proposal, the authority to declare a law contradictory to a Basic Law, will remain in the hands of the Supreme Court, who
will judge on this matter in a constitutional panel. The final decision of whether
to preserve the law that was declared as contradictory to the Basic Law, or
whether to annul it, will be passed on to the Knesset. This is similar to the British
model introduced by the 1998 Human Rights Act. This would not constitute real
revolution in the matter of judicial review of Knesset laws, for this is how the Supreme Court currently operates. Illustrations of this *de facto* practice are the
cases of *Pesaro* and *Rubenstein*, mentioned above.[75]

The second principle of the proposed reform is that, on constitutional
matters, an arrangement will be established by which the Court will sit on a special panel to adjudicate when the constitutionality of a statute is challenged. On
other matters, they will continue to judge according to the arrangements which
exist at present, i.e., in a panel of three, seven, or more judges according to the
decision of the Court's President. In practice, the Supreme Court has revealed
that it believes that matters of constitutional adjudication cannot be decided
by a regular panel. Proof of this is illustrated by the fact that, in constitutional
cases, the Court sits in large compositions of eleven or thirteen out of its total

---

73 Shimon Shetreet, "Models of Constitutional Adjudication", in The Legal Cultures of China
and Israel-The Proceedings of Legal Conference of Zhengfa University, Beijing, and Hebrew University (Zhengfa University, 2005) at 211–213.
74 *Id.*, at 218.
75 *Id.*, at 218–219, 222.

fourteen judges.[76] It must be established in the law that a constitutional panel should be based on the principle of fair reflection of society and social diversity. In accordance with this, the constitutional panel should include at least three women, a traditional religious observer, and judges from varying social strata. These principles will provide a suitable answer to the reservations heard in recent years concerning the Supreme Court's lack of social transparency. They promise that this transparency will exist, not only in composition of the courts but also in the constitutional panel deciding on constitutional issues.[77]

The third principle is to restrict the right to petition to only those personally harmed by government action. Where this instated, there would be a reduction in friction between the courts and the political authorities. It would appear that with the closing of the period of broadening the judicial role by the court, the time has come to reduce, via legislation, the right to petition to only those personally harmed. There is one further consideration in favour of restriction of standing. The restriction is needed in order to put an end to the phenomenon of solicited petitions. In light of the deep involvement of the court in the political realm, a situation has arisen whereby petitions are made to the Supreme Court of Justice that are "solicited" from all extremes of the political spectrum, and sometimes even from within the executive authority through quiet and indirect involvement by opponents of governmental decisions. For these reasons, it would be appropriate to restrict the right to petition only to those who have been personally harmed.[78]

C. Public Confidence in the Courts

The courts can only perform their function as an institution to resolve disputes in society if they enjoy public confidence. In order to enjoy such confidence, the judiciary must appear to be as independent and unbiased as possible, and the process of resolving disputes must be fair, efficient, expedient and accessible.[79]

---

76 See for example H.C.J 6055/95 *Tzemach v. Minister of Defense*, 53(5) P.D. 241 (1999); H.C.J 1715/97 *The Israeli Investment Managers Association v. Minister of Finance*, 51(4) P.D. 367 (1997); H.C.J 4562/92 *Zandberg v. Broadcasting Authority*, 50(2) P.D. 793.

77 *Models of Constitutional Adjudication, supra* note 73, at 222–223.

78 *Id.*, at 223–224.

79 See S. Shetreet, *The Administration of Justice: Practical Problems, Value Conflicts and Changing Concepts*, 13 Univ. of British Columbia Law Review 52 (1979) (hereinafter: *The Administration of Justice*); S. Shetreet, *Judicial Independence and Accountability: Core Values in Liberal Democ-*

The judiciary, especially the Supreme Court, enjoys public support and legitimacy.[80] The public is ready to accept the Court's judgments, even when they contradict personal opinions and expectations.[81] Although there is broad general support for the Supreme Court, support will vary significantly from one decision to another. When the judgment is a judicial review of the army authorities, support for the decision declines. This phenomenon is a result of the Israeli public's conception of security matters as "veto-areas" in which the civil authorities should not interfere. The public sees the Supreme Court as the civil authority that is supposed to supervise the other civil authorities. Thus, there is support for its activism over other political authorities and governmental institutes.[82]

In this context, the new basic laws[83] allegedly contributed to the legitimacy of the Supreme Court's review of the other authorities. However, analysis of developments since the introduction of those basic laws reveals that public criticism of the judiciary has increased. This phenomenon has found a political expression: political actions aimed at eliminating the results of court decisions and attempts to initiate reforms that would limit the power of the court.[84]

In this politically charged environment, and following well established legal traditions, the Supreme Court and the judicial system have followed a number of principles and practices aimed to assure that justice will not only be done, but also that it will be seen to be done.[85] This includes the "open court" principle, which is one of the fundamental principles of the legal system with a basis in

---

racies, in H.P. Lee (ed.), Comparative Judiciaries 3, 13 (Cambridge University Press, 2011) (hereinafter: *Judicial Independence and Accountability*).

80 See *Justice in Israel*, *supra* note 65; *Judicial Independence and Accountability*, *supra* note 79, at 14; According to a 2016 survey, the public's confidence in the Judiciary, and especially the Supreme Court, is at its highest since 2001 (Chen Maanit, "Change: A Rise of Public Confidence in the Judiciary", Globes 23.01.2017); In contrast, for discussion regarding the low levels of public confidence in the state, including the judiciary, see Yael Hadar "The Israeli Public Confidence in Government Institutions in the Last Decade" Israeli Institute for Democracy (2012) (Hebrew) https://www.idi.org.il/parliaments/3467/8205 (accessed February 9, 2017).

81 Justice Barak has held, in the *Tzaban* case that "public confidence in the judiciary is the most valuable asset that this branch possesses. This is also one of the most valuable foundations of the nation." H.C.J 732/ 84 *Tzaban v. The Minister for Religious Affairs*, 40(4) P.D. 141 (1986).

82 *Id.*, at 183;

83 Basic Law: Freedom of Occupation and Basic Law: Human Dignity and Liberty.

84 See Y. Dotan, *A Constitution for the State of Israel—The Constitutional Dialogue after the "Constitutional Revolution,"* 28 Mishpatim 149–193 (Hebrew, 1997).

85 For English examples, see S. Shetreet, *Judges on Trial: A Study of the Appointment and Accountability of the English Judiciary*, p.204 (North Holland Publishing Company, Amsterdam,1976).

statutory law,[86] and a court's duty (again grounded in statute) to state reasons for its decisions.[87] The open court principle is not absolute.[88] These restrictions allow for the hearing of a matter in camera, or for the removal of a person from the court, both at the discretion of the court and on grounds which are enumerated in the statute.[89] These grounds include: the safeguarding of state security and its foreign relations, the protection of morality, the security of witnesses, the protection of the interests of the parties involved in a sex offense, the privacy of the parties involved in a personal status case, and the protection of minors.[90]

The importance of public confidence in the courts is further reflected in the rather strict tests applied for self-disqualification of judges for bias.[91] The test does not require proof that bias has actually influenced the judge, but rather that there is a real likelihood that it will influence the judge.[92] The traditions of the bench go even further than the strict requirement of the law of bias.[93]

Concern for maintaining public confidence is also evident in guidelines issued by the President of the Supreme Court on the assignment of cases.[94] No specific guidelines govern how the President is to choose particular judges to sit on any case. The desirability of an assignment based on a judge's particular specialization in a certain area has been questioned. Such a deliberate assignment may harm judicial independence if all decisions in one area are based on the views of one judge rather than incorporating the views of the whole court. The Supreme Court Working Guidelines support rotation of judges so that judges decide all sorts of cases, thereby gaining broader experience and knowledge.[95] Nonetheless, this has not prevented some judges from gaining a strong reputation for

---

86 Section 3 of the *Basic Law: Adjudication* states that "[a] court shall sit in public unless otherwise provided by Law or unless the court otherwise decides under Law."

87 For a general discussion of the duty to provide a reasoned decision, see R. Gavison, *The Court and the Duty to Reason*, 2 Mishpatim 89 (1970); M. Gavish, *The Duty to State Reasons for Decisions*, 17 Israel Tax Quarterly 207 (1989).

88 Israel Courts Law (Consolidated version) 1984, S.H., p. 198; 38 L.S.I. 271. In ss 68–69.

89 S. Shetreet, *Judicial Independence and Accountability: Core Values in Liberal Democracies*, in H.P. Lee (ed.), Comparative Judiciaries 3, 6 (Cambridge University Press, 2011).

90 An additional reservation on the open court principle is the sub judice rule, found in s 70 of the Israeli Courts Law.

91 See *supra* note 77.

92 *See Justice in Israel, supra* note 56, at 303–305; *See also* Sec. 77(a) of *Courts Law* [Consolidated Version] 1984, S.H. 198 (hereinafter: "*Courts Law*").

93 *Justice in Israel, supra* note 65, at 305–314.

94 Sec. 27(a), *Courts Law 1984*.

95 Guideline 60. This regulation applies only to the lower courts.

their expertise in certain areas of the law. Another point to be taken into account in the assignment of cases is consideration of a fair reflection of social classes, ethnic and religious groups, and ideological inclinations. It is particularly important in sensitive cases for panels to be either altogether neutral or balanced.[96]

As Lord Hailsham said in his Lionel Cohen Lecture,[97] there is a continuous tension between judicial independence and public accountability of judges in a democracy. This tension should be reconciled by the exercise of wisdom and good judgment so that the proper balance between these very important principles is maintained.[98]

D. Attempts to Resolve the Controversy between the Judicial Role and the Other Branches

The High Court of Justice has reached its limit on the border separating it from the political branches. Many have claimed that the borderlines have been pushed into territory that lies beyond the appropriate domain of the judiciary. This claim reflects a widely held public sentiment, of which the court cannot operate in disregard.[99]

The Court has developed a number of judicial strategies for this task. One strategy is to rule on a case, but to postpone the operative order to a later date to allow the Executive and the Legislature to respond to the Court decision. This pattern was followed in the case of *Pessaro-Glodstein*[100] in which the Supreme Court declared that non-orthodox conversion in Israel was legitimate and state authorities exercising civil powers (as distinguished from religious halacha on marriage and divorce) could not refuse recognition of such conversion. The Court postponed operative application, giving the Executive and the Legislature a grace period to respond to the ruling. The Court followed the same strategy in 1999 when it declared as unlawful the administrative policy on Yeshiva students' exemption from army service.[101]

---

96 *See Justice in Israel, supra* note 65, at 251–252.
97 Lord Hailsham, "The Independence of the Judicial Process," (1978) 13 *Israel Law Review* 1, at 8–9; See also, P.A. Nejelski, "Judging in a Democracy: The Tension of Popular Participation," (1977) 61 *Jud.* 166.
98 *Judicial Independence and Accountability, supra* note 79, at 9.
99 *See Justice in Israel, supra* note 65 at 250–251.
100 H.C.J 1031/93 *Pesaro v The Minister of Interior*, 49(4) P.D. 661 (1993).
101 H.C.J 3267/97 *Rubinshtein v. Minister of Defense*, 55(2) P.D. 255 481.

To avoid clashes with certain segments of the community, sometimes the Court strikes the balance of interest in a way that gives more weight to certain social interests. This was done in the *Lior Horev* case on the closing of Bar Ilan Street in Jerusalem.[102]

E. Strengths of the Israeli Supreme Court

Despite the criticism of certain aspects or weaknesses of the Israeli judicial system, the judiciary is independent. Judges make decisions in a fairly independent fashion with the highest professional standards. The Supreme Court of Israel, as the highest legal authority, provides an important contribution to the democratic system of government, civil rights, and the fair and standard administration of the government.[103]

In 1990, two of the government's largest political parties were making deals with individual Knesset members in order to control the coalition government. As a result, these large parties were dependent on one or two Knesset members. The willingness of the Supreme Court to adjudicate on petitions presented by public petitioners, who had lost faith in the political system in this time of crisis, allowed the Supreme Court to provide an institutional solution to what society perceived as a time of political crisis and lack of governance. This role of the Supreme Court was allowed due to a complete revolution and widening of the laws concerning standing, justiciability doctrine, and judicial review to the extent that it included the ground of reasonableness in judicial review. All this allowed the Supreme Court to intervene in the area of policy and political issues, and was positively influential on the functioning of the government.[104]

During this time, the Supreme Court intervened in a large number of cases that involved political topics and agreements, such as changing to daylight savings time, granting exemption from army service to Yeshiva students, allotment of broadcasting time to election propaganda, removal of parliamentary immunity, decisions of the Knesset and its Speaker, presidential pardon, and refusal to confine an escaped felon who already denounced confinement.[105] The Supreme Court also broadened the boundaries of legal criticism on security matters so that it not only includes aspects of authority and procedure, but also criticism

---

102 H.C.J 5016/96 *Horev v. The Minister of Transport*, 54(4) P.D. 1 (1997).
103 *Models of Constitutional Adjudication, supra* note 73, at 211-213.
104 *Id.*, at 214.
105 For these cases and others, *see Justice in Israel, supra* note 65 Chapters 13 – 15. See also *Developments in Constitutional Law, supra* note 13, at 406.

on the planning of the decisions.[106] The Supreme Court criticized the opinions of the government's legal advisor for the decision not to press charges against bankers involved in the 1983 banking scandal, along with other decisions. The court decided that this decision not to press charges against the bankers was completely unreasonable.[107]

F. Executive and Legislative Intervention in the Justice System

The change in the role of the Supreme Court in the Israeli system of government can be clearly seen in the tone of its reaction to executive action aimed at frustrating the results of court decisions. The executive has on occasion used physical action to render judgments ineffective. More often, judicial rulings invalidating executive action were overcome by retroactive parliamentary legislation and at times even by resorting to administrative emergency legislation.[108]

In recent years, the Supreme Court has reacted very strongly to any attempt by the executive to avoid the result of judicial decisions by physical action. For example, the deportation of persons before they had an opportunity to file a petition in the High Court of Justice, or while a petition was pending or being filed, has been met by a strong rebuke from the Court. Indeed, the Court seriously reprimanded the Legal Advisor to the Government in 1975 when an order for deportation was carried out while the petition to the High Court was being filed.[109] The Supreme Court has also insistently required strict executive obedience to court orders and has reacted fiercely to any attempt by the executive to deviate from commitments given to the Court by state attorneys.[110] An instructive illustration of this trend is the *Elon Moreh* case,[111] where the Court ordered the evacuation of a settlement on the West Bank, which was erected on seized property and which the Court held to be motivated by considerations other than "military needs," the recognized justification under customary international law for seizure of private land by an occupying power.[112]

---

106 See *Justice in Israel, supra* note 56, Chapter 15.
107 See *Id.* Chapter 13.
108 J. Freudenheim, *The Laws of Validation and the Rule of Law*, 23 HaPraklit 381 (1967).
109 *The Challenge of Judicial Independence, supra* note 1, at 253.
110 *See* the Alnatsche Affair referred to in H.C.J 320/80 *Kawasme v. Minister of Defense*, 35(3) P.D. 113, at 119. And see H.C.J 179/79 *Abu Karen v. Lands Administration*, 34(4) P.D. 567.
111 H.C.J 390/79 *Dweikat v. The Government of Israel*, 34(1) P.D. 1 (1979).
112 *The Challenge of Judicial Independence, supra* note 1, at 254.

The status of the Israeli judiciary is not entirely unassailable. Governmental and legislative intervention often occurs in various spheres of judicial activity and takes on many forms. Different patterns of intervention have been discerned during different periods in the history of the State.[113]

The weakest form of intervention by political elements in the judicial system is that of political debates of matters concerning the courts, particulary judges, and their decisions. In general, there is nothing wrong with such intervention. The modern concept of the doctrine of separation of powers requires a system of "checks and balances." One expression of this system is the right of the executive and legislative branches of government to be at liberty to discuss the way in which the judicial branch is functioning. Respect for the judiciary would suffer if judges themselves aroused public debate on the issues dealt with in their decisions. Therefore it is the executive and the Knesset's function to bring the issues to the attention of the public. Indeed, such discussions may very well further the interests of the judiciary.[114]

A somewhat more serious pattern of intervention is that of executive supervision of the judicial system. This pattern is also generally acceptable. Intervention at the central level of the administration of the judicial system does not necessarily encroach upon the independence enjoyed by the judiciary. There are, however, reasons for restricting the scope of this type of intervention, since the executive may be tempted to use its powers as a means of influencing the judicial process itself. Such influence could be either direct, e.g., determining the constituent bodies of the various courts, or indirect, e.g., worsening the working conditions of particular judges whose decisions do not meet with executive approval.[115]

Legislative intervention in the administration of the judiciary occurs in relation to the sensitive issue of judicial salaries. In order to ensure that the Knesset does not use financial measures as a means of "punishing" judges, the law prohibits any decrease in judges' pay alone. This statutory protection is, however, insufficient because there is no legal bar to the reduction of judicial pay for reasons other than general economics.[116]

Another sensitive form of intervention is the appointment of judges. It is generally accepted that political intervention in this area is legitimate. Indeed, it is a positive phenomenon, since it is important to ensure that the judiciary reflects the whole spectrum of political opinion in the state. The existing situation,

---

113 *Judicial Independence and Accountability, supra* note 79.
114 *Id.*, at 22–23.
115 *Id.*, at 23.
116 *Id.*

whereby judges are appointed by a collegial committee consisting of three judges, two representatives of the Bar Association, two representatives of the executive, and two from the legislature, is entirely satisfactory. Although the Minister of Justice chairs the Judicial Selection Committee, the majority of its members are drawn from the ranks of the legal profession and not from those of the politicians.[117]

However, regarding appointments to the bench, it is regrettable that legislative intervention in this area has gone beyond mere representation on the committee. An example of this intervention was the passing of the "Rabbi Assaf Law." The sole purpose of this law was to grant retrospective legitimacy to the appointment of Rabbi Assaf to the Supreme Court, notwithstanding his lacking the qualifications required by law for such an appointment. Another example of this phenomenon is the "Binyamin Halevi Law."[118] This law was designed to prevent Binyamin Halevi, President of the District Court, from appointing himself to preside over the bench in the Eichmann trial. Judge Halevi had expressed strong sentiments against Eichmann in another case, and it was felt that it would be politically damaging to allow him to preside over the trial. The attempts made to change the law regarding the retirement age of judges in order to allow the President of the Supreme Court, Yizhak Olshan, to remain at his post for several more years, is yet another example of illegitimate intervention on the part of the legislature. Although there are only a few examples of this type of intervention, they are sufficient to alert us to the dangers of unfettered political intervention in the administration of the court system in Israel.[119]

A much more serious form of intervention is direct and unmediated political interference in matters pending in court. Unfortunately, there are a number of cases of intervention of this type on record in the history of Israeli law. Such cases tend to occur in relation to issues of profound public concern and controversy. Particularly serious was the pressure brought to bear upon the judges in the *Shalit* case, which involved the definition of Jewish identity under the Law of Return. Justice Sussman made explicit reference to this pressure in his written opinion.[120] Pressure was also applied on Justice Landau in the *Abuhatzera* af-

---

117 *Id.*, at 24.

118 For the Statutes, see *Confirmation of Appointment of Supreme Court Justices Law*, 1950, S.H. 157(Rabbi Asaf Law) and *Courts (Capital Offences) Law*,1961, 5721 S.H. 24 (Judge Binyamin Halevi Law) and see also *supra* Chapter 13 Section 4.B, "The Knesset's Intervention in Setting the Composition of the Court."

119 *The Challenge of Judicial Independence*, *supra* note 1, at 256–257.

120 H.C.J 58/68 *Shalit v. Minister of the Interior*, 23(2) P.D. 447, 505.

fair.[121] In another case, Yitzhak Zamir, then Attorney General, was subjected to intense pressure in an attempt to persuade him to delay the judicial proceedings against members of the Jewish Underground. Direct political interference has also taken place in relation to sub judice matters that were not the subject of intense public controversy. For example, during his tenure as Minister of Commerce and Tourism, Gideon Patt approached Justice Gross in his chambers with a request to speed up a trial, the outcome of which was significant for a group of foreign investors whom the Minister hoped would make substantial investments in Israel.[122]

Even more serious is intervention aimed at preventing justiciable matters from coming before the Court. Most of the cases in this category involved hasty government measures designed to "create facts on the ground" in such a way that either the individual has no time to petition the High Court of Justice for relief, or the issue becomes moot. An example of this form of intervention was the expulsion of Dr. Soblen in the 1960s, and of two deportees from Hebron in the 1970s immediately prior to a judicial hearing against the order. In effect, the Executive rendered the legal proceedings moot and prevented the hearing from taking place.[123] Intervention in the same form was used in the expulsion of Fahad Khawasmeh, which was implemented too quickly to allow him to petition the High Court of Justice for relief. It should be noted that a petition by Mrs. Khawasmeh eventually brought the matter before the Court, and the executive was the subject of judicial criticism.[124]

This frustrating form of intervention is invoked by both the Executive and the Knesset. For example, in the *Ata* case,[125] the petitioner had sought and obtained injunctive relief against the noise level emanating from the respondent's premises. However, immediately after the Court granted an order in support of the petitioner's claim, his land was expropriated under a government order. The most disturbing feature of the episode was undoubtedly the fact that the Court itself had recommended this step to the State at the time of handing down its order in favor of the plaintiff.[126]

The Knesset has also used legislation as a form of intervention to nullify the effects of legal decisions. The first such case involved legislation passed by the

---

121 Ha'aretz, 23.2.81, 24.2.81

122 *The Challenge of Judicial Independence, supra* note 1, at 257–256.

123 See in detail in *Justice in Israel, supra* note 65, Chap. 20; *Khawasmeh v. Minister of Defense,* 35(3) P.D. 113, 120.

124 *The Challenge of Judicial Independence, supra* note 1, at 258.

125 H.C.J 114/77 *Schwarz v. Finance Minister,* 21(2) P.D. 800.

126 C.A 44/76; M. 101/76 *Ata Textile Co. Ltd. v. Schwarz,* 34(3) P.D. 785.

Knesset in 1955 in the wake of the Court's ruling that the appointment of Rabbi Nissim as the Sephardic Chief Rabbi of Israel was invalid. The Knesset issued an act changing the qualifications for the office of the Chief Rabbi, thereby nullifying the Court's decision. Similar improper legislative interventions have occurred in more recent times. Following a Court ruling that a municipal by-law restricting the opening hours of factories and recreational facilities on the Sabbath and Religious Festivals was invalid, the Knesset passed a law permitting municipalities to make by-laws of precisely this nature. The objectionable intervention was the retrospective provision in the law stating that all by-laws relating to this issue are to be regarded as if they had been made in accordance with its provisions.[127]

The most blatant form of intervention of this sort consists simply of ignoring the courts' decisions and failing to execute judgments. The enforcement of legal decisions is always dependent upon the executive. It is also accepted, even by the courts, that, given limited resources, it is not possible to enforce every single legal decision.[128] The greatest temptation to adopt this blatant type of strategy arises in cases involving major public controversies. In such cases, there may very well be pressure on the part of the public to avoid complying with a legal decision. However, it is in these very cases where preservation of the honor and independence of the judiciary is at stake that strict enforcement of its decisions is of utmost importance. It is to the credit of Israeli governments that they have never refrained from enforcing a legal decision on the grounds of public pressure. The *Elon Moreh* case involved an order of the Supreme Court requiring the dismantling of a settlement and the restoration of land to its legal owners.[129] There was no declaration on the part of any person or body that the Court's decision ought to be ignored. In fact, the Government waited ten weeks before commencing with the evacuation of the property, thereby indicating a most execrable tendency to view legal decisions as neither final nor binding.[130]

It appears from the preceding analysis that there are many diverse forms and patterns of government and legislative intervention against the independent functioning of the judiciary.It must be emphasized that it would be incorrect to claim that such intervention is the norm in the State of Israel. The norm is that judicial independence is maintained. But the many examples cited above of such

---

127 H.C.J 291/55 *Rabbi David Dayan v. Minister of Religion and the Chief Rabbinical Council of Israel*, 9 P.D. 997; Chief Rabbinical Council Law (Various Provisions) 1955, S.H 117; Cr.F (Jerusalem) 3471/87 *State of Israel v. Kaplan*, 5748(2) P.D. 265; Municipalities Law Amendment Law (no. 40) 1990.
128 *The Challenge of Judicial Independence, supra* note 1, at 260.
129 H.C.J 390/79 *Dweikat v. The Government of Israel*, 34(1) P.D. 1 (1979).
130 *The Challenge of Judicial Independence, supra* note 1. at 260–261.

intervention indicate a real danger to the standing of the judicial system and the need for action to ensure that these exceptional cases though rare are not repeated.[131]

G. The Need for Constitutional Protection of the Judiciary

It is vital that the judiciary receive the constitutional protection necessary for maintaining its independence. At present, the status and jurisdiction of the judicial branch is anchored in the Basic Law: Adjudication. This Law, however, fails to provide sufficient protection, in terms of its specific provisions, and more generally in terms of the binding nature of the Law itself.[132] Proof of its inadequacy is afforded by the many cases over the years in which its ideal of judicial independence has been compromised.[133]

From a normative standpoint, it is desirable that the protection of judicial independence takes place at the constitutional level. However, the constitutional status of the Basic Law is no different from any other legislation, except insofar as it remains unaffected by orders made under the emergency regulations.[134] Indeed, this exception protects the judiciary against orders issued by the executive under the emergency powers. However, there is no provision which would shield the Basic Law: Adjudication from amendment by ordinary parliamentary legislation, even if such an amendment is not explicitly stated.[135]

It is fairly evident that there is still a long way to go before Israel achieves proper constitutional protection of the independence of its judicial system. One of the reasons for this lack of constitutional protection is the inability of the judges to organize themselves effectively and to defend their status. A major factor contributing to this lack of effectiveness is undoubtedly the judicial tradition of avoiding any type of conflict or protest in the political arena, especially if it takes place in public.[136]

---

131 *Id.* at 261.
132 *See* Sec. 22 of Basic Law: Adjudication, and S. Shetreet, "Judicial Independence: Conceptual Dimensions and Contemporary Challenges" in S. Shetreet, ed., *Judicial Independence— The Contemporary Debate*, 590–687 (Dordrecht: Martin Nijhoff, 1985).
133 *The Challenge of Judicial Independence, supra* note 1, at 261.
134 C. Klein, *The Founding Authority in Israel*, 2 Mishpatim 51–56 (1970).
135 *Developments in Constitutional Law, supra* note 13.
136 *The Challenge of Judicial Independence, supra* note 1, at 265.

Chapter 7:
Culture of Judicial Independence

1. Introduction

Judicial independence is a significant component of governmental culture in every country. It is shaped by the relations between the branches of government and is one of the basic values which lie at the foundation of the administration of justice. Judicial independence must be supported by the political climate and social consensus. The political leadership and the professional and legal elite must work together to develop a culture of judicial independence along several very significant guidelines and levels. They must do this in a long and gradual process.[1]

The culture of judicial independence is created by five important and essential aspects: creating institutional structures, establishing constitutional infrastructure, introducing legislative provisions and constitutional safeguards, creating adjudicative arrangements and jurisprudence, and maintaining both ethical traditions and a code of judicial conduct. The institutional structures regulate the matters relative to the status of the judges and the jurisdiction of the courts. The constitutional infrastructure embodies in the constitution the main provisions of the protection of the judiciary. The legislative provisions offer detailed regulations of the basic constitutional principles. The courts add to the constitutional infrastructure and the legislative provisions complementary interpretations and jurisprudence on different aspects of the conduct of judges and the operation of courts. The ethical traditions and code of judicial conduct cover the judge's official and non-official spheres of activities, and shield the judge's substantive independence from dependencies, associations, and even less intensive involvements which might cast doubts on judicial neutrality.[2]

International law plays a significant role in creating the culture of judicial independence in domestic law. International law influences domestic law by virtue of international human rights treaties which provide for principles of fair procedures and for the right to be tried before an impartial and independent tribunal. In addition to international treaties, there are international standards

---

1 S. Shetreet, *Creating a Culture of Judicial Independence: The Practical Challenge and the Conceptual and Constitutional Infrastructure*, in S. Shetreet and C. Forsyth (eds.), The Culture of Judicial Independence: Conceptual Foundations and Practical Challenges, 12–45, 12 (Martinus Nijhoff- Brill Publishers, 2012).
2 *Id.*

DOI 10.1515/9783899497946-007

which non-governmental and academic study groups have developed.[3] One such recent project is the Mt. Scopus International Standards of Judicial Independence ("Mt. Scopus Standards").[4]

The principle of judicial independence is one of the fundamental values of the administration of justice. These values include procedural fairness, efficiency, accessibility, and public confidence in the courts. In addition, there is a requirement that the fundamental values, including judicial independence should be protected by constitutional provisions and not only by legislative provisions.[5]

The culture of judicial independence can exist only in a system which is based on the doctrine of separation of powers. After it is established, the mainteneance of judicial independence is not a matter of course. It is constantly subject to challenges, sometimes by other branches of government, and at other times as a result of different types of internal circumstances.[6]

2. Creating a Culture of Judicial Independence in Domestic Law

The culture of judicial independence in every jurisdiction is based on a number of levels. One is the institutional level, which regulates the matters relative to status of the judges and jurisdiction of the courts. Another is the constitutional level, which embodies in a constitution the institutional aspects and ensures that the independence of the judiciary shall not be adversely affected by legislation or by executive action. An additional level is the legislative level, which regulates in detail the constitutional principles. Last, there is the adjudicative level, which is the jurisprudence of the courts; it provides for interpretation and additional elements in all the levels. From the review of court decisions on the matter of judicial independence, it is possible to observe the rules and elements that each country is forging in order to create a culture of judicial independence and maintain this culture.[7]

Those who are responsible for formulating and creating the culture of judicial independence are the political leaders and the judges. The political leaders

---

3 *Id.*, at 12–13.
4 Mt. Scopus International Standards of Judicial Independence (Mar 19, 2008) (hereinafter: "Mt. Scopus Standards"), see Appendix I of The Culture of Judicial Independence: Conceptual Foundations and Practical Challenges.
5 *Creating a Culture of Judicial Independence, supra* note 1, at 13.
6 *Id.*
7 *Id.*, at 14.

are responsible also for preserving the culture after it is shaped. The judges, whose role is expressed in adjudication in court decisions, also lay down appropriate ethical rules and play a role in the judicial selection and judicial appointments. Sometimes, judges are also involved in court administration and assist in the creation of the constitutional infrastructure and the constitutional framework for the judiciary.[8]

The culture of judicial independence in each jurisdiction must facilitate and ensure judicial independence in the substantive adjudication, both in public and constitutional law, as well as in the private law in all its aspects and branches. In addition, the culture of judicial independence must ensure institutional and administrative functioning of the judiciary as an institution as well as the substantive and administrative functioning of the individual judge.[9]

The ensuing discussion will analyze the various arrangements that jurisdictions normally provide for the purpose of creating a culture of judicial independence. These arrangements will illustrate the various models that countries have used to ensure the creation and the maintenance of the culture of judicial independence.[10]

The process of building a culture of judicial independence is long and gradual. This process may make significant changes in the judicial branch and might demand changes and cooperation of the other branches of government. The development of self-judicial governance in the United States Federal Judiciary is a good example of such a gradual process for building a culture of judicial independence.[11] It took 140 years for the United States Federal Judiciary to undergo a process of a gradual change from being under total control of the Executive branch to attaining the stage of a self-governing judicial system.[12]

In the beginning of the process, the administration of the federal judiciary and the courts was governed by the Department of Treasury.[13] Later, in 1849, governance over the judicial branch was entrusted to the Department of the Interior.[14] In the next stage, in 1870, governance was transferred to the Department of

---

8 *Id.*

9 *Id.*

10 *Id.*

11 For a detailed description of this process, see: Markus Zimmer, *Judicial Independence in Central and East Europe: The Institutional Context* (2006 – 2007) 14 Tulsa. J. Comp. & Int'l L 53 – 87, at pp. 62 – 69.

12 *Creating a Culture of Judicial Independence, supra* note 1, at 14.

13 See: Act of Mar. 3, 1849, Ch. 98, 9 Stat. 395 (1849).

14 *Id.*

Justice.[15] Seventy years later, in 1939, responsibility for the administration of courts and judges was transferred from the executive branch to the judicial branch.[16] A few years later, in 1948, the Judicial Conference of the United States was established.[17]

The process of building self-judicial governance has to be gradual, as it requires a long process of education, both on the professional level and the political level. Self-judicial governance means control of the Judiciary over the judicial system. This control includes budgeting, financial managing, managing human resources, and managing a large system. It also includes professional management, such as managing case assignment, engaging in rulemaking of the procedures of the courts, and enforcing these procedural rules. Likewise, judicial self-governance includes the development and the enforcement of judicial ethics and a code of conduct. In order for the Judiciary to engage in self-governance, it should have a wide diversity of abilities. Administrative abilities are required for managing the system of justice. Self-governance also requires the judiciary to act in coordination with the other branches of government. In addition to these abilities, self-judicial governance requires a Judiciary which has financial qualifications. Another area of responsibility in the administration of courts is security and safety.[18]

In countries where dramatic changes in the system of government or in the economic system have been introduced, it is very important to develop a culture of judicial independence to help the society and the branches of government to adopt to the new constitutional system of government or to the new economic system which is based on the free market. This was the situation in Poland, when it changed from a communist system of government to a constitutional democratic system of government.[19] The proper functioning of government branches, and the development of a culture of Rule of Law in societies which are at the transition period of post-communism, depends very much on the ability to create an independent judiciary, which is assisted by the independent legal

---

15 See: Act of June 22, 1870, Ch. 150, 16 Stat. 162 (1870).
16 See Act of Aug. 7, 1939, Ch. 501, 53 Stat. 1223 (1939).
17 See 28 U.S.C §331 (2000).
18 *Creating a Culture of Judicial Independence, supra* note 1, at 14–15.
19 For a detailed analysis of the subject of Poland, see Tomaz Wardynski & Magdalena Niziotek (eds.), *Independence of the Judiciary and Legal Profession as Foundations of the Rule of the Law: Contemporary Challenges* (LexisNexis 2009, English version begins at pp. 310) (hereinafter: "Independence of the Judiciary and Legal Profession").

profession.[20] Similarly, the courts and the legal profession play a very important role in the first formative years of independent countries in developing areas of the world.[21] A similar situation was seen in China when it started moving to a free market economy.[22]

Part of the culture of judicial independence in all countries is the maintaining of traditions and rules that ensure independence of the legal profession, and independence of the prosecutors.[23]

A. Institutional Structures

Institutional structures that ensure judicial independence must be provided in a number of aspects regarding the relations of the judiciary branch with the legislative and the executive branches. Debate in the legislature on judges and on the judiciary are legitimate; they are even required as part of the legislative function of supervising and controlling the other branches of government, including the administration of justice. Some of the debates concern the legitimate interest in the protection of judicial independence and the proper functioning of the courts. Other legislative debates on the judiciary in most jurisdictions are critical of the judiciary, and generally deal with legal matters which are at the center of public controversies. Normally, in most jurisdictions, there is no statutory provision prohibiting the debate of pending cases in courts, but there are self-rules in parliaments which restrain parliamentary debates on pending cases. The proper model

---

20 See Stawceki, "Independence of the Legal Professions and the Rule of Law in Post-Communist Society," in Wardynski & Niziotek, *Id.*

21 See Henderson, "Halfway Home and a Long Way to Go: China's Rule of Law Evolution and the Global Road to Judicial Independence, Judicial Impartiality, and Judicial Integrity," in Randall Peerenboom (ed), *Judicial Independence in China: Lessons for Global Rule of Law Promotion* (Cambridge University Press, 2010); De-Silva, "The Role of Law in Society in Developing Countries," Chapter 31 of *The Culture of Judicial Independence: Conceptual Foundations and Practical Challenges.* For an analysis of the difficulties in creating proper standards of judicial conduct and proper relationships between the judiciary and the political leadership, see: Forsyth, "The Failure of Institutions: The South African Judicial Service Commission and the Hlophe Saga," Chapter 3 of *The Culture of Judicial Independence: Conceptual Foundations and Practical Challenges.*

22 For a detailed analysis of the case of China, see *Judicial Independence in China, Id.*

23 See *Independence of the Judiciary and Legal Profession, supra* note 19; also see: S. Shetreet, "Independence and Responsibility of Judges and Lawyers," General Report to the 1991 International Congress of the World Association on Procedural Law in Role and Organization of Judges and Lawyers in Contemporary Societies, *Papers of the IXth Conference of World Association on Procedural Law,* pp. 119–186 (Coimbra-Lisboa 1991).

is to formulate a rule that will balance between the conflicting interests. One is the principle of separation of powers; the other is legislative sovereignty and the importance of public debates on matters of vital public importance. There are also parliamentary internal rules excluding the debate on a specific judge. However, these rules have not prevented parliamentary criticism of specific judges.[24] The proper view on parliamentary or legislative criticism of specific judges is that the legislature should be permitted to engage in criticism subject to proper style and good taste. Legislative criticism is desirable and is a proper exercise of the principle of democratic accountability of the judiciary. [25]

Judicial independence is maintained by proper methods of judicial selection and appointments, as well as careful regulations of the procedure and grounds for judicial discipline and removal. Likewise, a careful and secure provision for the age of retirement is a necessary constitutional requirement. According to the Mt. Scopus Standards of Judicial Independence, it is proper for the Executive and the Legislature to take part in the judicial selection process.[26] These international standards require special concern for merit considerations and respect for judicial independence. However, they do not exclude participation in this process by the legislative and executive branches. The standards regulate the conditions for discipline and removal of judges and their retirement age.[27] From time to time,

---

24 For English examples, see S. Shetreet, *Judges on Trial: A Study on the Appointment and Accountability of the English Judiciary* (North Holland 1976), pp. 162–178 (hereinafter: "*Judges on Trial*"). For Israeli example, see criticism on the Eichmann trial decisions while the case was still pending in S. Shetreet, *Culture of Judicial Independence in Israel: Substantive and Institutional Aspects of the Judiciary in Historical Perspectives* (2009) 10 Law and Business 525 (Hebrew. hereinafter: "Shetreet, Law and Business").

25 *Creating a Culture of Judicial Independence, supra* note 1, at 15–16.

26 Mt. Scopus Standards , *supra* note 4, provide that:

2.4 Judicial appointments and promotions by the Executive are not inconsistent with judicial independence as long as they are in accordance with Principles 4, and regarding the legislator role.

2.14 The principle of democratic accountability should be respected and therefore it is legitimate for the legislature to play a role in judicial appointments and central administration of justice provided that due consideration is given to the principle of judicial independence.

27 Mt. Scopus Standards, *supra* note 4, provide that:

4.3 Judicial appointments should generally be for life, subject to removal for cause and compulsory retirement at an age fixed by law at the date of appointment. And

4.3.1 Retirement age shall not be reduced for existing judges.

4.2 a) The principle of democratic accountability should be respected and therefore it is legitimate for the Executive and the Legislature to play a role in judicial appointments provided that due consideration is given to the principle of Judicial Independence.

legislatures in some jurisdictions have interfered in judicial independence by changing the tenure or retirement age of judges.[28] For example, in 1973, judicial tenure in Uruguay was abolished.[29] In Bangladesh, the retirement age was changed to bring about the end of term of service of two specific judges.[30] This is the reason why the International Standards of Judicial Independence regulate specifically the retirement age.[31]

Another example comes from Ecuador, where on April 24, 2007, all nine judges of Ecuador's Constitutional Court were removed following an unpopular ruling. The removal was executed by a congressional vote lacking any legal basis. According to Ecuadorian law, the Constitutional Court's judges are removable only by impeachment. Still, this was the third time in three years that judges were removed by Congress.[32] Another example is the case in Russia regarding the president of the Constitutional Court, which we shall refer as the Zorkin-Yeltsin affair. After the collapse of the Soviet Union, the constitutional court was led by Chief Justice Valery Zorkin in several cases involving the transition of rule from the Soviet to the post-Soviet era. These cases were controversial, and included both an invalidation of one of President Yeltsin's decrees and a finding that Yeltsin's actions were unconstitutional. In response to these and other decisions, Yeltsin shut down the constitutional court for several years. When it reopened, Valery Zorkin remained with the court.[33] However, the court's perspective was notably different after its reopening; it began to regularly agree with government actions.[34] The selection of judges must also reflect the principle of reflective judiciary.[35]

---

b) The recent trend of establishing judicial selection boards or commissions in which members or representatives of the Legislature, the Executive ,the Judiciary and the legal profession take part ,should be viewed favourably, provided that a proper balance is maintained in the composition of such boards or commissions of each of the branches of government.

28 *Creating a Culture of Judicial Independence, supra* note 1, at 16.

29 See S. Shetreet, *Judicial Independence: New Conceptual Dimensions and Contemporary Challenges*, in Shimon Shetreet and Jules Deschênes (eds.), *Judicial Independence: The Contemporary Debate* 591, at pp. 607 (Martinus Nijhoff 1985) (Hereinafter: "*Shetreet, The Contemporary Debate*").

30 *Id.*

31 § 4.3 of Mt. Scopus Standards, *supra* note 4.

32 Human Rights Watch, *Ecuador: Removal of Judges Undermines Judicial Independence* (May 10, 2007), available online at: http://www.hrw.org/en/news/2007/05/10/ecuador-removal-judges-undermines-judicial-independence (accessed February 9, 2017).

33 *Creating a Culture of Judicial Independence, supra* note 1, at 16–17.

34 Tushnet, *Leadership in Constitutional Courts*, Conference Materials, Krakow (Mar 2008).

35 See Justice Dobbs, *The Judge and the Defendant: Demographics and Diversity in the Criminal Justice System*, New Developments in Criminal Justice Lecture at King's College London (April 24,

Personal judicial independence is secured by the provision of appropriate and adequate remuneration protected from undue interference by the Executive or by the Legislature, not related to previously established standards. This does not mean that judicial salaries cannot be affected by general economic measures which are applied to the whole country in situations of austerity.[36] This issue was a center of controversy in 1931 in England when the judges argued that they should not be included in the measures requiring the reduction of the salaries of all public servants.[37] The judges were right that they were not included in the term "persons in His Majesty's service." However, in terms of general approach, judges should not be expcluded from general economic measures applied to all the sectors of the public service.[38]

One of the central issues in which conflict arises between the judicial branch and the executive branch is the responsibility for the courts' administration. In this matter, a number of central points have to be noted. An important principle is that the Executive should not have control of judicial functions or matters regarding the judicial process, such as case assignment, scheduling of trials, judges vacations, and determination of salaries of specific judges. Whereas the Executive cannot have control of matters of court level, it may have control of the central level and powers over court administration. This includes budgeting, housing of courts, and alike.[39] The Executive controls at the central level of court administration and judicial matters, must be exercised with utmost care

---

2008): "By being reflective of society, the courts are given legitimacy. Members of society are more likely to respect and trust courts whose judges include people like themselves. It increases accountability and thus public confidence."; See also the Mt. Scopus Standards, *supra* note 4:

2.15: The process and standards of judicial selection shall give due consideration to the principle of fair reflection by the judiciary of the society in all its aspects, and for a discussion on surveys of social background of judges in England see: The Judiciary: The Report of a Justice Sub-Committee on the Judiciary (1972), based on an unpublished Master's dissertation by Jenny Brock.

2.15.1: Taking into consideration the principle of fair reflection by the judiciary of the society in all its aspects, in the selection of judges, there shall be no discrimination on the grounds of race, colour, gender, language, religion, national or social origin, property, birth or status, subject however to citizenship requirements.

36 Mt. Scopus Standards, *supra* note 4, provides that:

2.22: Judicial salaries, pensions, and benefits cannot be decreased during judges' service except as a coherent part of an overall public economic measure.

37 Shetreet *Judges on Trial, supra* note 24, at 67.

38 *Creating a Culture of Judicial Independence, supra* note 1, at 17.

39 *Id.*

for judicial independence, to avoid adverse effects on matters that relate directly to judges and judicial affairs.[40]

There have been cases in a number of jurisdictions of members of the Executive interfering in judicial proceedings. This could happen in the form of public statements violently criticizing a decision of a judge. Such was the case in the Canadian 1976 judges' affair.[41] Critical statements by the Executive of judicial decisions is frequent and widespread in many jurisdictions and the proper response is a proper service of the courts that will provide a timely and detailed response by the relevant judicial officer to the criticism of the Executive or public officer.[42]

Judges must be separated from the Legislature and the Executive and cannot assume legislative or executive functions. However, from time to time, judges are asked to assist in functions that have strong association with the Executive. Such a practice is the appointment of judges to head committees for the study of the revision of legislation. More frequently, judges are required to head public inquiries into issues of vital importance. The principle of separation of powers requires the total detachment between the Judiciary and the Executive. Judges who are engaged in an executive function are subject to the Executive in performing this function. Although this situation is temporary, it is inconsistent with the judicial function, which requires total independence and impartiality of the judges in adjudicating disputes between the citizen and the Executive branch. Even though in fact the judges are qualified to distinguish between their Executive function and their judicial function, the appearance of independence and impartiality may be affected in the eyes of the public. This may adverse-

---

40 Mt. Scopus Standards, *supra* note 4, provides that:

2.12 Judicial matters are exclusively within the responsibility of the Judiciary, both in central judicial administration and in court level judicial administration.

See also Shetreet, *The Contemporary Debate, supra* note 29, at 611–612.

41 See the statement of Minister Ullet which stated that the decision of the Canadian judge was stupid, and the consequence of this statement. Willet had to quit due to public pressure. See Russel, *The Judiciary in Canada—The Third Branch of Government* (McGraw-Hill Ryerson 1987), pp. 78–81. There were a number of cases in Israel where there was an attempt to influence the judges in highly publicized cases, for reports see the cases of *Shalit* (H.C.J 58/68 *Shalit v. Minister for Interior Affairs*, 23(2) P.D. 477, 505), *Abuhazeira* (Cr.A 5/82 *Abuhazeira v. State of Israel*, 36(1) P.D. 247); *The Jewish Underground* (H.C.J 144/50 *Scheib v. Minister of Defense*, 5 P.D. 399 (1951); *The Medical Center in Hertzelia* (H.C.J 256/88 *Medinvest Medical Center-Herzliya Ltd. v. The Director-General of the Ministry of Health*, 44(1) P.D. 19). See also S. Shetreet, *Justice in Israel: A Study of the Israeli Judiciary* (Martinus Nijhoff 1994) (hereinafter: *"Justice in Israel"*), Chapters 6, 8, and 21.

42 *Creating a Culture of Judicial Independence, supra* note 1, at 18.

ly affect public confidence in the independence and impartiality of the judiciary.[43]

The judges may not serve in legislative or Executive functions. Specifically, they should not be ministers of the government, nor can they be members of the Legislature or municipal councils, and they should not hold positions in political parties.[44] The exclusion of judges from assuming executive functions or legislative functions does not apply only to official appointments as Ministers or MKs, but also to judges assuming special tasks on behalf of the state or temporary positions which are associated with the Legislative or the Executive.[45] The involvement of Justice Aharon Barak in Israel, in the peace negotiations conducted by Prime Minister Begin in Camp David in 1978, where the Israeli-Egyptian peace agreement was forged, was criticized as improper involvement of a judge in an executive function.[46] Another example from an earlier period in the United Kingdom is Lord Reading, who was Lord Chief Justice of England; during his term of office, he took part in a delegation to raise funds in the United States in 1918. Likewise, while serving as Lord Chief Justice, he served as British ambassador to the United States.[47] This would be unthinkable in modern practice. The exception is when the law expressly provides that a judge may exercise a certain extra judicial function such as serving as members or presiding over commissions of inquiry. This is a very widespread practice in many jurisdictions.[48]

The principle of separation of the judiciary from the other branches of government requires that there should be post-judicial restrictions after a judge retires or resigns from the bench. There should be a cooling-off period before the

---

43 *Id.*

44 Mt. Scopus, *supra* note 4, provides that:

    7.1 Judges may not serve in Executive or Legislative functions, including as:

    7.1.1 Ministers of the government; or as

    7.1.2 Members of the Legislature or of municipal councils.

    7.2 Judges shall not hold positions in political parties.

45 *Creating a Culture of Judicial Independence*, *supra* note 1, at 18.

46 Shetreet, "Judge on a Political Mission," Haaretz 25.10.78 (Hebrew).

47 *Judges on Trial*, *supra* note 24, at 351–352.

48 For British examples, see Lord Hutton inquiry of Dr. David Kelly's death, available at: http://www.the-hutton-inquiry.org.uk/content/rulings.htm (accessed February 9, 2017); and see also Justice Jackson Review of Civil Litigation Costs, available at https://www.judiciary.gov.uk/publications/review-of-civil-litigation-costs/ (accessed February 9, 2017). For Israeli examples, see: Justice Shamgar (1st) inquiry on the massacre in the Patriarchs Tomb; Justice Shamgar (2nd) inquiry on the assassination of Prime Minister Rabin; Justice Cohen inquiry on the kidnapping of Yemenite children; and Justice Or inquiry on the October 2000 clashes.

judge could assume legislative or executive function. Equally, it is desirable that there should be a cooling-off period between the end of service in a legislative or executive function before assuming a judicial office. This cooling-off period should not be too long, but should serve the purpose of separating the branches in the eyes of the public.[49] This rule should be a customary rule and not rigid statutory restriction. The restrictions on judges do not apply only to association of judges with the executive or legislative branches. Judges are also excluded from engaging in business or remunarative business.[50]

B. Constitutional Infrastructure

In a country where a culture of judicial independence exists, there is a formal constitutional framework and legislative framework which protects the position of the judiciary. This framework regulates central principles which relate to the operation of the courts and the conduct of judges and embodies them in a constitution. It aims to regulate the position of the judges and their independence. The scope of the details of this arrangement in each jurisdiction is different; however, there are a number of matters which are normally regulated in the constitution. These include the qualification of judges, the process of their appointment, the rules of discipline, and such additional matters which are necessary to secure their independence.[51]

In order to achieve this purpose, it is important to lay down the principles of judicial independence in the constitution. This provision ensures and enhances the independence of the judiciary.[52]

The American Founding Fathers adhered to the doctrine of separation of powers in the US Constitution. They adopted the doctrine of checks and balances, based on the concept that no function of one branch of government should

---

49 A judge, other than a temporary or part-time judge, may not practice law. See also Shetreet "Who Will Judge—Reflections on the Process and Standards of Judicial Selections," 61 Aust. L. J. (1987) 766.

50 Mt. Scopus Standards, *supra* note 4, provides that:

7.4 A judge should refrain from business activities and should avoid from engaging in other remunerative activity, that can affect the exercise of judicial functions or the image of the judge, except in respect of that judge's personal investments, ownership of property, the business activities or ownership of property of family members, or that judge's teaching at a university or a college.

51 *Creating a Culture of Judicial Independence, supra* note 1, at 19.

52 For the Israeli section, see Section 2 of Basic Law: The Judiciary, which provides that there is no authority on the judge except the authority of the law.

be exercised by another branch and that each branch should function as a check on any improper use of power by the other branches.[53]

The Founding Fathers wished to ensure judicial independence. The Declaration of Independence charged George III with making "Judges dependent on his Will alone, for the tenure of their offices, and the amount and payment of their salaries."[54] The foundations of judicial independence are laid out in Article III of the US Constitution, which states that "[t]he Judges, both of the supreme and inferior Courts, shall hold their Offices during good Behaviour, and shall, at stated Times, receive for their Services a Compensation which shall not be diminished during their Continuance in Office."[55]

This is a very classic illustration of the embodiment of the independence of judiciary in a formal constitution. This is not always the case. A number of countries provide judicial independence in the legislative level rather than the constitutional level, which is not the desirable position. By judicial interpretation, the courts accord to this legislative provisions' semi-constitutional status, as is the case in Israel.[56]

C. Legislative Provisions and Constitutional Safeguards

It must be recognized that certain matters should be regulated in the constitution whereas others may be regulated by ordinary legislation. When a matter is regulated in ordinary legislation, the legislature can introduce an amendment by simple majority. In contrast, the protection granted by the constitution is modifiable only by a constitutional amendment. An example of the importance of regulating substantive issues in the constitution occurred during the controversy over New Deal legislation when US President Franklin Roosevelt attempted to pack the court—increasing the number of judges—which he could do by ordinary legislation.[57]

---

53 *Creating a Culture of Judicial Independence, supra* note 1, at 19–20.
54 United States Declaration of Independence (1776).
55 US Const., Art. III.
56 See Shetreet, *Law and Business, supra* note 24, at 547.
57 Carson and Kleinerman, "A Switch in Time Saves Nine: Institutions, Strategic Actors, and FDR's Court-Packing Plan," (2002) 113 Pub Choice 301; Nelson, "The President and the Court: Reinterpreting the Court-Packing Episode of 1937," (1988) 103 Pol Sci Q 267; Caldeira, "Public Opinion and The US Supreme Court: FDR's Court-Packing Plan," (1987) 81 Am Pol Sci Rev 1139. For cases dealing with issues of judicial independence in the United States, see *United States v. Will*, 449 U.S. 200 (1980); *Chandler v. Judicial Council*, 398 U.S. 74 (1970).

In addition to general constitutional protections of judicial independence, a more detailed constitutional protection should include six fundamental substantive principles.[58]

In England, the very important step to provide judicial independence was made in 1701, in the Act of Settlement. For centuries, the king was an absolute monarch and thus the source of all governmental and political power. Judges were an integral part of the royal administration. There was an obscure distinction between judicial and administrative duties.[59] The king enjoyed the cooperation of the judiciary, which was widely accepted. The sovereign did not seek to use judges as instruments in political struggles.[60] In that period, it was obvious that judges were not independent.[61] The central issue in the struggle between Parliament and the Crown was security of tenure. However, it was not until the Act of Settlement in 1701 that an important measure of security was finally guaranteed.[62]

The Act of Settlement provided for judges to be appointed during good behavior (*quam diu se bene gesserint*) and for their salaries to be ascertained and established, but upon the address of both Houses of Parliament, it may be lawful to remove them. Judicial tenure was still not yet completely secured. It took the initiative of George III in 1760 to help secure the term of judicial office beyond the lifetime of the monarch so that neither the King nor Parliament would be capable of attaining their particular political objectives or ambitions by exercising control over the decisions of the judiciary. The king could no longer dismiss every judge at his pleasure, nor could Parliament attain its own ends by an equally pre-emptory and almost as effective withdrawal of livelihood.[63]

The current formula evolved from the consolidation of the Act of Settlement and the said 1760 Act. Section 12(1) of the Supreme Court of Judicature (Consolidation) Act of 1925, which is the modern formulation of the historical development, stated: "All the judges of the High Court and of the Court of Appeal, with the exception of the Lord Chancellor, shall hold their offices during good behaviour, subject to a power of removal by His Majesty on an address to His Majesty by both Houses of Parliament."[64] Yet, the situation in 1760 was in need of further

---

58 See Section IV of this article.
59 *Judges on Trial, supra* note 24, at 2.
60 *Id.*, See also Sir William Searle Holdsworth, *A History of English Law* (Sweet & Maxwell, 2d ed., 1937) at p. 347.
61 *Creating a Culture of Judicial Independence, supra* note 1, at 20.
62 Act for the Further Limitation of the Crown, 12 & 13, Will 3, Ch 2, 10 Statutes at Large at 360.
63 *Beauregard*, 130 DLR 3d 433.
64 Act of 1925, 15 & 16 Geo 5, Ch. 49 (Eng).

change because the system relied on litigants' fees for judicial remuneration, which left the system open to abuse and misconduct. The salary became substantial, and a prohibition against supplementing it was added only at a later stage. In this way, "[t]he additional sources of income were eliminated in a very long gradual evolution extending over three centuries."[65]

An important development affecting judicial independence was the fundamental reform of the Courts Act of 1971,[66] introduced on the recommendations of the Beeching Commission Report.[67] The Courts Act eliminated centuries of local control over courts, established a new class of judges (called circuit judges), set up an administrative hierarchy across the country, and made court personnel a part of the national civil service. The Act, which restructured the criminal court system in England, has been described as a "radical, even a spectacular reform."[68] However, this reform carried with it mixed blessings for the independence of the judiciary in England. While it promoted judicial independence by reducing the dependence of the criminal justice system on part-time judges, the centralization of judicial administration in England brought increased executive control and thus posed a challenge to judicial independence.[69] This was to be resolved only three decades later in the Constitutional Reform Act and the additional arrangements regarding the establishment of the Courts Service.[70]

In Israel there is a wide debate on the normative level of the provisions relative to judicial independence in Basic Law: The Judiciary and in the ordinary legislation.[71] It has been suggested that even when ordinary legislation regulates matters relative to judges and courts, they should be viewed as norms of higher level than ordinary legislation. Thus, it has been argued that judicial independence, being one of the fundamental principles of the system of government, en-

---

65 *Judges on Trial, supra* note 24, at 11.
66 Courts Act 1971, Ch. 23 (1971) (UK), available online at: http://www.opsi.gov.uk/acts/acts1971/pdf/ukpga_19710023_en.pdf (accessed February 9, 2017).
67 Lord Beeching, *Royal Commission on Assizes and Quarter Sessions, 1966–1969*, Cmnd 4153 (HMSO 1969).
68 Lord Hailsham, 312 HI Deb 1247 (Nov 19, 1970).
69 Lord Lane, *Judicial Independence and the Increasing Executive Role in Judicial Administration*, in Shetreet, The Contemporary Debate, *supra* note 29 above, at 525–28.
70 *Creating a Culture of Judicial Independence, supra* note 1, at 21.
71 See Basic Law: The Judiciary, and see Section 15(c) which regulates the jurisdiction of the high court of justice to adjudicate any matters which it sees necessary to give remedy for the sake of justice and which are not in the jurisdiction of any other court or any other tribunal. See the case of *Herut*, and the case of *The Forum Co-Existence in the Negev*, see Shetreet, Law and Business, *supra* note 24, at 25.

joys higher normative value, even if it is regulated in regular normative legisla-tion. This approach is supported by recourse to international law and jurispru-dence on the subject in various jurisdictions.[72]

D. Adjudicative Arrangements and Jurisprudence

Court decisions serve the purpose of bridging the gaps which constitutional pro-visions or legislative provisions leave unanswered. The jurisprudence of the courts contributes significantly to the creation of the culture of judicial inde-pendence. In the following analysis, we shall offer a number of examples how jurisprudence in several countries provided for interpretation of the constitution and of legislation in a way that contributed to the building of culture of judicial independence. This was done with regard to a number of aspects that are neces-sary and meaningful for building this culture of judicial independence. It is note-worthy that, in the 17th century, there was a conflict between two schools of thought in the courts in England. The Act of Settlement settled the conflicting approaches, as well as the struggle between the King and the Parliament.[73]

In *Valente v. the Queen,* one of Canada's central cases concerning judicial independence, the Supreme Court of Canada listed three major components of judicial independence: security of tenure, financial security, and institutional in-dependence. The Court clarified that judicial independence needs to be consid-ered in a dual perspective: objective and subjective. The subjective perspective looks at whether a common person would perceive in any particular situation that judicial independence exists.

One of the most significant components for the preservation of the inde-pendence of the judiciary, which the supreme court of Canada emphasized, was the terms of service of the judges. When judicial salaries are subjected to the discretion of the other branches of government, which can interfere in the terms of service and salaries, this creates perception of dependence. However, in a number of countries, there was a need to introduce changes in the condi-

---

72 See: Barak, *Interpretation in Law—Constitutional Interpretation* (published on Nevo, 1993), Vol. 3, pp. 411–435; Shetreet, Law and Business, *supra* note 24, at 547; see generally Shimon She-treet, *The Normative Cycle of Shaping Judicial Independence in Domestic* and *International Law: The Mutual Impact of National and International Jurisprudence and Contemporary Practical and Conceptual Challenges,* 10 Chicago J. of Intl. Law 275–332, (2009); See also Canadian Charter of Rights and Freedoms, Part I of the Constitution Act, 1982, Art. 11(d).
73 See generally Judges on Trial: A Study of the Appointment and Accountability of the English Judiciary, xxii + p. 432 (North Holland Publishing Co. ,1976).

tions of service of the judges. As a result, the judiciary was faced with the challenge of adjudicating and resolving this issue.[74] For example, in the Canadian case of *Beauregard v. The Queen*,[75] it was ruled that not every change in the condition of the service of the judges is unconstitutional. In certain circumstances, a change can be legitimate, for example, when a reduction or freezing of a previously approved salary increase is made as a general economic austerity measure. In 1985 this matter was debated in Israel; it was agreed that the possibility of reducing the salaries of judges in the framework of a general austerity measure is acceptable. It is so provided in Section 10 of Basic Law: The Judiciary.[76]

When the issue arose whether the judges can adjudicate the constitutionality of a decrease of judicial salary when they are affected by such a ruling, it was decided in *United States v. Will*[77] that, despite the fact that judges are adjudicating in a matter that relates to their own conditions, they should not be disqualified because of the rule of necessity. This is because there is no other forum that could adjudicate this matter.[78]

It is known that legal proceedings continue for long periods of time, due to several reasons, and so there are attempts to increase the efficiency of the system. But too much emphasis on efficiency might affect the quality of the judicial process. In the case of *Chandler*, the US courts had to resolve a conflict between efficiency and judicial independence. The matter arose when the Judicial Conference for the Ninth Circuit ordered that no cases would be assigned to Judge Chandler until he finished his backlog. The US Supreme Court rejected Chandler's case on the grounds that it was legitimate for the Judicial Conference to regulate the allocation of cases and, that for efficiency purposes, it may order, for a certain period, cases should not be assigned to the judge with a backlog. Similar controversies regarding assignment of cases arose in other jurisdictions, such as in Germany.[79;80]

The tension between efficient judicial administration and judicial independence was a matter of concern to Israeli former judge Avigdor Mishali, who said after his retirement from the District Court: "The amount of files is in-

---

74 *Creating a Culture of Judicial Independence, supra* note 1, at 22.

75 *Beauregard v. The Queen* [1986] 2 S.C.R. 5

76 See Basic Laws of Israel: The Judiciary § 10, available online at: http://www.knesset.gov.il/laws/special/eng/basic8_eng.htm (accessed February 9, 2017); See also *Justice in Israel, supra* note 41, at Chapter 4.

77 *United States v. Will*, 449 U.S. 200 (1980).

78 *Creating a Culture of Judicial Independence, supra* note 1, at 22.

79 *Id.*, at 22–23.

80 Shetreet, *The Contemporary Debate, supra* note 29.

sufferable ... Many times you can't dedicate the time that you should, and you—not willingly—do things normally you wouldn't, if you considered the case more calmly ...."[81] Isgav Nakdimon, another former Israeli judge, resigned due to the excessive amount of cases a judge has to adjudicate. This situation did not allow him give the proper consideration for each case.[82]

E. Ethical Traditions and Code of Judicial Conduct[83]

In the process of decision-making, judges should be free from irrelevant controls, both overt and covert. Two dimensions of this principle should be recognized. First, there is a significant social interest in attaining actual impartiality and neutrality of the judge. Second, but no less important, there is the appearance of the impartiality and neutrality of the judge. The necessity of maintaining not only impartiality, but also the appearance of impartiality, is mandated by the value of public confidence in the courts and the judges, and also in the judicial process.[84] From this emanates a theoretical approach, which requires the creation of a set of rules that covers the judge and protects the judge's substantive independence. This set of rules covers the judge's official and non-official spheres of activities, and shields the judge's substantive independence from dependencies, associations, and even less intensive involvements which might cast doubts on judicial neutrality.[85]

Thus, we find a series of protective rules, some of which restrict judicial conduct, and others which restrict the conduct of others when they relate to judges. For instance, there are restrictive rules of conduct excluding judges from association with the other branches of the government, limiting their business associ-

---

81 Cited in *Judges on Trial, supra* note 24, at 192.

82 Six months after being appointed, Judge Nakdimon declared, "I am not able to fulfill my duties due to the amount of cases I have to adjudicate," Haaretz 30.06.10.

83 See *The Guide to Judicial Conduct*, available at http://www.judiciary.gov.uk/publications-and-reports/guidance/guide-to-judicial-conduct (accessed February 9, 2017). See also *Revised Draft of Proposed New Canon to American Bar Association's Model Code of Judicial Conduct* (2005).

84 See *Regina v. Bow Street Metropolitan Stipendiary Magistrate and Others, Ex Parte Pinochet Ugarte (No. 2)*, [2000] 1 A.C. 119, in which a first judgment was set aside on the ground of bias.

85 For an analysis of the rules of judicial conduct in the American context, see J.P. MacKenzie, *The Appearance of Justice* (Charles Scribner's Sons 1974); and, in the English context, see *Judges on Trial, supra* note 24, at 269–377.

ations, and excluding them from matters of public controversy and matters which might put into question the dignity and the integrity of the judiciary.[86]

In this context, it is noteworthy that the standards of judicial conduct in civil law countries tend to be very permissive in terms of political activities of judges. This is in sharp contrast to the rather restrictive standards prevailing in common law countries.[87] Similar trends are also seen in relation to the nature of professional associations of judges. In civil law countries, judicial associations tend to resemble trade unions, whereas this unionization trend is absent in common law countries.[88]

International standards generally forbid all political activities for judges in office, with the exception of mere membership in a political party. A fairly large number of countries prohibit all forms of political involvement, and allow only a passive party membership. The compromise is expressed in the Mt. Scopus Standards, reflecting directives from the earlier IBA Standards, which states that judges may not hold positions in political parties, except where such practice is supported by a long and democratic tradition.[89]

The international standards provide for guidelines regarding the engagement of judges in cases where they used to be advisor, defendants' counsel, and the like.[90] In such cases, the standards provide for disqualification of the judge as well as in a case where there is personal interest of the judge.[91]

---

86 *Creating a Culture of Judicial Independence, supra* note 1, at 23.

87 Section 7 of The Mt. Scopus Standards, *supra* note 4, direct that judges may not serve in executive or legislative functions, including serving as ministers of the government, members of the legislature, or in municipal councils. Section 7 also forbids judges from holding positions in political parties, and provides that judges should refrain from remunerative activities as well as other activities that can affect the exercise of judicial functions or the judges' image.

88 Shetreet, *The Contemporary Debate, supra* note 29, at 630–632.

89 *Creating a Culture of Judicial Independence, supra* note 1, at 24.

90 Mt. Scopus Standards of Judicial Independence, *supra* note 4, provide that:

18.1 Judges shall not serve in a case in which they have previously served as agent, counsel, advisor, advocate, expert or in any other capacity for one of the parties, or as a member of a national or international court or other dispute settlement body which has considered the subject matter of the dispute or in a case where they had previously commented or expressed an opinion concerning the subject matter in a manner that is likely to affect or may reasonably appear to affect their independence or impartiality.

19.1 Judges shall not sit in any case involving a party for whom they have served as agent, counsel, advisor, advocate or expert within the previous three years or such other period as the court may establish within its rules; or with whom they have had any other significant professional or personal link within the previous three years or such other period as the court may establish within its rules.

91 Mt. Scopus Standards of Judicial Independence, *supra* note 4, provide that:

This norm is a matter of course, but it illustrates the importance of the set of the rules of conduct and ethical standards which is required for the purpose of keeping impartiality and integrity of the judiciary. This practice is required even if it is not expressed and regulated in the constitution, in legislation, or in jurisprudence of any jurisdiction. It must be enforced in any jurisdiction which aims at preserving and maintaining judicial independence and maintaining public confidence in the justice system.[92]

3. The Fundamental Values of the Administration of Justice

The proper administration of justice is dependent upon adherence to certain fundamental values that lie at the foundations of most judicial systems.[93] These values include: procedural fairness, efficiency, accessibility, public confidence in the courts, judicial independence,[94] and the value of constitutionality, in the sense of the constitutional protection of the judiciary. Each of these values allows the courts to fulfill their main function, which is the resolution of disputes. These fundamental values are interrelated. Sometimes they strengthen one another or one being the result of the other; and sometimes one is the con-

---

20.1 Judges shall not sit in any case in the outcome of which they hold any material personal, professional or financial interest.

20.2 Judges shall not sit in any case in the outcome of which other persons or entities closely related to them hold a material, personal, professional or financial interest.

20.3 Judges must not accept any undisclosed payment from a party to the proceedings or any payment whatsoever on account of a judge's participation in the proceedings. See standards: Shimon Shetreet & McCormeck, *Culture of Judicial Independents in the Globalized World*, Appendix I (Brill—Nijhoff, forthcoming 2017).

92 *Creating a Culture of Judicial Independence, supra* note 1, at 24.

93 For a detailed discussion see: Shetreet, "Judicial Independence and Accountability: Core Values in Liberal Democracies," in HP Lee, ed., *Comparative Judiciaries* (Cambridge University Press, 2010).

94 For a detailed discussion of the fundamental values of the administration of justice, see Shetreet, "Practical and Value Problems in the Administration of Justice" in Shetreet (ed.), *Recent Developments in Israeli Case Law and Legislation, Collection of Lectures Delivered at the Judges' Conference* (Jerusalem: the Harry Sacher Institute 1977), 80; Shetreet, "The Administration of Justice: Practical Problems, Value Conflicts and Changing Concepts" (1979) 13 *University of British Columbia Law Review* 52; Shetreet, "The Limits of Expeditious Justice" in Justice Howland (ed.), *Expeditious Justice* (Canadian Institute for Administration of Justice 1979) 1; Shetreet, "Time Standards of Justice" (1979) 5 *Dalhousie Law Journal* 129; Shetreet, "Adjudication: Challenges of the Presents and Blueprints for the Future," in *Festschrift in Honour of Professor Walther J. Habscheid* (W Germany, 1989)

dition to the existence or to the application of the other, while at other times there may be a tension between them. A proper legal system is one which advances each of these values on its own, and achieves a suitable balance between them whenever they conflict with one another.[95]

As to the value of constitutionality, it is expected that constitutional provisions will protect the judiciary. There are six principles which lie at the foundation of constitutional protection of judicial independence. The first principle is the separation between the Judiciary and the Executive, which means judges must not be part of the administrative arm of the executive branch of the government. The second principle is the prohibition of the diversion of cases from ordinary courts. The third principle is post-decisional independence of the judgment and its respect by the other branches of government. The fourth principle requires that cases be heard by judges according to an internally predetermined plan or schedule prior to commencement of the case. The fifth principle is excluding ac hoc or special tribunals, which is widely accepted and implemented. The sixth principle is that changes in the terms of judicial office should not be applied to presently sitting judges unless such changes serve to improve the terms of judicial service.[96]

The value of efficiency requires that the courts must be efficient in terms of time and cost. The courts are the machinery for enforcing laws and regulations. The legal system might have very good laws, but these laws are of little value if the legal system does not provide an accessible, convenient, and efficient method for enforcing laws and obtaining redress for violation of rights; hence, the demand for efficient court procedure, for a judicial process which is not unreasonably slow, and for judicial services which can be obtained at a reasonable cost.[97]

The justice system must be based on the value of procedural fairness and justice. In order to ensure procedural fairness and justice, special procedural rules have been established to govern the method and manner in which the courts will resolve disputes. An elaborate body of rules governs court procedures, which regulate the method of evaluating and weighing the facts as well as evidence submitted to the courts. The purpose of these rules and laws is to attain justice and to ensure a fair trial by subjecting the conflicting claims to a vigorous and thorough investigation in order to ascertain the truth. These rules include procedural rules and rules of evidence.[98]

---

95 *Creating a Culture of Judicial Independence, supra* note 1, at 27–28.
96 For detailed analysis, see: Shetreet's Normative Cycle, *supra* note 72, at 289–293.
97 The demand for efficiency in the administration of justice is equally strong in the criminal and civil spheres.
98 *Creating a Culture of Judicial Independence, supra* note 1, at 28.

Public confidence is another basic value of the justice system. The courts can perform their function as an institution to resolve disputes in society only if they enjoy public confidence. They have recognized the indispensability of this value to the functioning of the legal system, but they can enjoy such confidence only if they are seen as independent and unbiased, and if the process of resolving the dispute is fair, efficient, expedient, and accessible. The fundamental principles of the legal system are the "open court," and the court's duty to state reasons for the decisions at which it has arrived. This significant obligation contributes to the development of logical-analytical methods of thought which lie at the foundations of the legal process; it also allows for the review of decisions on appeal and for reliance upon them as precedents. Public confidence in the courts is enhanced by broad reflection of the judiciary of all social strata, ethnic groups, and geographical regions in a given country.[99]

Accessibility of the courts and access to justice is a fundamental value of the justice system. The significance of accessibility is to be found in the opening up of the doors of the courts to the public. The courts have emphasized the great importance of this value. Accessibility includes the provision of judicial services to the public at reasonable cost, provision of the means to go to court for those unable to pay the cost, and the increase of community awareness so that citizens within the community appreciate that they are entitled to turn to the courts in order to defend their rights.[100]

The principle of judicial independence is the last, but not least, of the basic values of the justice system. The meaning and content of this principle vary somewhat from one country to another depending upon the system of government, local traditions, and climate of political opinion; even in the same country, it may carry different meanings in different time periods.[101]

The importance of the principle of an independent judiciary has grown, particularly as a result of the expanding role of the judiciary in society.[102] This in-

---

99 *Id.*

100 Article 6(1) as interpreted by the European Court of Human Rights; it also ensures the fundamental values of access to justice.

101 *Creating a Culture of Judicial Independence, supra* note 1, at 28–29.

102 See further, Cappelletti, "Who Watches the Watchmen? A Comparative Study on Judicial Responsibility," (1983) 31 *American Journal of Comparative Law* 1, at pp. 7-9. For further discussion on the increasing judicial role in society, see E Vescovi, "La Independencia de la Magistratura en la Evolucion Actual del Derecho," in W Habscheid (ed.), *Effectiveness of Judicial Protection and Constitutional Order* (Gieseking 1983) 161, at pp. 169-172. See also Das and Chandra, *Judges and judicial Accountability* (Commonwealth Lawyers Association 2003). For an in-depth discussion of the cultural influences on judicial dispute resolution, see Chase, *Law Cuture and Ritual: Disputing Systems in Cross-Cultural Context* (New York University Press 2005).

creasing judicialization is in part a result of social developments. Wide-ranging primary and secondary legislation have been enacted and, consequently, there has been a corresponding expansion in litigation against government services, as well as the development of "social rights," a typical by-product of the welfare state. In addition, collective procedures such as the American class action have developed, which have brought about a "massification" of the law, transforming the traditional two-party litigation into a major multi-party complex litigation.[103] The increased role of the judiciary in society may be seen as natural and objective, but there are also causes for increased judicialization that may be viewed as convenience-based processes of judicialization. This refers to the judicialization of issues largely for the political convenience of the other branches of government.[104]

Judicial independence requires that judicial accountability be shaped in a very careful way. One of the important points is that incompetence will not be grounds for removal of judges. This is because it may serve as a pretext to removal of judge on undefined ground.[105]

In the transnational jurisprudence, Article 6(1) of the European Convention on Human Rights represents the formulation of the core values of the justice system. It refers both to the position of the judge and the tribunal that adjudicates. It also refers to the rights accorded to everyone who stands before the tribunal. Article 6(1) of the Convention provides that: "In the determination of his civil rights and obligations or of any criminal charge against him, everyone is entitled to a

---

103 For an examination of the massification of the judicial system in criminal cases, see DH Whitbread (ed.), *Mass Production Justice and Constitutional Idea* (Charlottesville Va: Michie Co. 1970) 1. It is worth noting that massification occurs in civil cases as well.

104 As Sir Ninian Stephen wrote, in "Judicial Independence—A Fragile Bastion," in Shetreet, The Contemporary Debate, n. 29 above, at p. 543:

"Both the legislature and the executive may find it very convenient to shift to the judiciary the task of initiative—taking in [sensitive] areas ... Elected bodies may have much to fear if they have to decide such issues for themselves; wise politicians may well prefer to avoid the issue for fear of an electoral backlash."

A similar trend may be observed in Israel, where the relative role of the executive has declined, whereas the judicial role has increased. Two major processes are taking place. First, the realization of the public that the ordinary bureaucratic and political institutions are failing to solve issues has diverted the public to seek judicial redress where these other institutions have failed. Secondly, the executive has sometimes intentionally shifted questions to the courts in order to secure a judicial resolution of disputes which are economic or political in nature, to avoid having to pay the political price of the decision.

105 See *Judges on Trial*, *supra* note 24, at 330;

fair and public hearing within a reasonable time by an independent and impartial tribunal established by law."[106]

One of the more recent statements of the requirement of judicial independence was introduced in the new legislation in the United Kingdom Section 3 of the Constitutional Reform Act 2005, which provides that: "The Lord Chancellor, other Ministers of the Crown and all with responsibility for matters relating to the judiciary or otherwise to the administration of justice must uphold the continued independence of the judiciary." It also provides that: "The Lord Chancellor and other Ministers of the Crown must not seek to influence particular judicial decisions through any special access to the judiciary." The Act also imposes a duty on the Executive government to uphold judicial independence. It provides that: "The Lord Chancellor must have regard to (a) the need to defend that independence; (b) the need for the judiciary to have the support necessary to enable them to exercise their functions; (c) the need for the public in regard to matters relating to the judiciary or otherwise to the administration of justice to be properly represented in decisions affecting those matters."[107]

4. The Conceptual Foundations of Judicial Independence

In enumerating the theoretical elements of judicial independence, a distinction must be made between two aspects of the concept of the independence of the judiciary: the independence of the individual judges, and the collective or institutional independence of the judiciary as a body. The independence of the individual judge comprises two essential elements: substantive independence and personal independence. Substantive, or decisional independence means that in making judicial decisions and exercising other official duties, individual judges are subject to no other authority but the law. Independence of the judiciary implies that judges should be removed from financial or business entangle-

---

106 *Human Rights Act 1998*, s 1(3) Sch 1 incorporates the European Convention on Human Rights into United Kingdom law; Grocz, Beatson and Duffy, *Human Rights: The 1998 Act and the European Convention* (2nd ed., London: Sweet & Maxwell Ltd 2008); Janies, Kay, Bradley, *European Human Rights Law: Text and Materials* (3rd ed., Oxford University Press 2008); Clayton and Tomlinson, *The Law of Human Rights* (2nd ed., Oxford University Press 2008). For example, see *Procola*, 326 Eur Ct HR in which the plaintiffs complained before the ECtHR of an infringement on their right to an independent and impartial tribunal, and *Starrs and Chalmers v PF Linlithgow*, [2000] JC 208 (Scotland), where the Court ruled that an appointment dependent on the discretion of the minister of executive government renders the judge not independent and violates the ECtHR.

107 *Creating a Culture of Judicial Independence, supra* note 1, at 30.

ments likely to affect or rather to seem to affect them in the exercise of their judicial functions.

Personal independence means that the judicial terms of office and tenure are adequately secured. It is secured by judicial appointment during good behavior terminated at retirement age, and by safeguarding judicial remuneration. Thus, executive control over judges' terms of service—such as extension of term of office, remuneration, pensions, or travel allowance—is inconsistent with the concept of judicial independence. Still much less acceptable is any executive control over case assignment, court scheduling, or moving judges from one court to another, or from one locality to another.[108]

A modern conception of judicial independence must include collective or institutional independence of the judiciary as a whole. The concept of collective independence of the judiciary, which has been accepted by the emerging transnational jurisprudence, has not as yet received adequate scholarly attention. One of the important contributions of the international standards of judicial independence developed by the International Bar Association and in the Montreal Conference was the recognition of this important conceptual component of the principle of judicial independence in modern society.[109]

Another aspect of judicial independence is the internal independence of the judiciary, that is, the independence of judges from their judicial superiors and colleagues. This also transcends both the substantive and personal independence of judges vis-à-vis their colleagues and superiors.[110] Whether and to what extent the judiciary in any country can be viewed as independent will not only depend on the law and constitution of that country, but also on the nature and character of the people who hold the office of judge, on the political structure and social climate, on the traditions prevailing in that country, and on the institutional and constitutional infrastructure of judicial independence.[111]

The concept of judicial independence must recognize realities as well as perceptions. As Chief Justice Howland of the Ontario Supreme Court said in the *Valente* case, where the principle of judicial independence was discussed at length, "it is most important that the judiciary be independent and be so perceived by the public. The judges must not have cause to fear that they will be prejudiced by their decisions or that the public would reasonably apprehend this to be the case."[112] The recognition of public perceptions is required by the

---

108 *Id.*
109 *Justice in Israel, supra* note 41. For the same provisions, see also Mt. Scopus Standards § 2.3.
110 *Justice in Israel, supra* note 41, at Chapter 16.
111 *Creating a Culture of Judicial Independence, supra* note 1, at 31.
112 *R. V. Valente*, 2 C.C.C. (3rd ed.) (1983) 417, at 423.

need to assure public confidence in the courts. It is submitted that the reasonable man test should only be employed in the absence of other, more defined criteria. The accepted wisdom of human experience coupled with a high commitment to the value of assuring completely neutral judicial dispute resolution can establish a more definitive test, namely, that the existence of Executive controls over judicial terms of service makes the tribunal dependent or not independent. This conclusion can be drawn without recourse to the test of the reasonable person.[113]

The existence of personal controls on judges inevitably casts a cloud of doubt on their independence. For example, court martial judges are military officers, subject to the ordinary personal controls under the military hierarchy and rules, who are personally dependent; therefore, they cannot try ordinary criminal offences, as distinguished from military offenses. According to accepted concepts, their tribunal cannot be considered an independent tribunal.[114]

The importance of substantive adjudication by judges is evident in various areas, including the resolution of civil disputes, criminal cases, administrative disputes, and constitutional controversies. In all these cases, judicial review is a significant foundation necessary for effective judicial review and proper adjudication of these cases.[115] Substantive independence encompasses administrative, procedural, and substantive aspects of adjudication.[116] It means that, in the making of judicial decisions and exercising of other official duties, individual judges are subject to no authority other than the law and the commands of that judge's conscience. This aspect of the concept of judicial independence refers to the neutrality of mind of the judge, to that judge's impartiality, and total freedom from irrelevant pressures. Adjudicative functions are those official functions for which judges are responsible in the discharge of their official duties. Adjudication is composed of three main aspects: administrative, procedural, and substantive adjudication.[117]

---

113 *Creating a Culture of Judicial Independence, supra* note 1, at 31.

114 *Id.*

115 For a detailed analysis, see: Harlow, "Judicial Review and Administrative Justice," in *Effective Judicial Review: A Cornerstone of Good Governance* (Forsyth, Elliott, Jhaveri, Scully-Hill and Ramsden eds., Oxford: 2010); See also Shetreet, *Judicial Independence and Judicial Review of Government Action: Necessary Institutional Characteristics and the Appropriate Scope of the Judicial Function, Id.*; See also: Stack, "The Statutory Fiction of Judicial Review of Administrative Action in the United States," *Id.* at 317.

116 Shetreet, "Judicial Responsibility," in Goldstein (ed.) *Israeli Reports to the XIth International Congress of Comparative Law* (1982) 88, at 88–89 (hereinafter: "Judicial Responsibility").

117 See Shetreet, *The Contemporary Debate, supra* note 29, at 590–601.

Substantive independence of the judiciary demands that a judge should be removed from financial or business entanglement likely to affect, or likely to appear to affect, the exercise of judicial functions. It also considers both case scheduling and the disposition of procedural motions as just as integral to the adjudication function as substantive decision-making; as such, they must also be protected against any external interference.[118]

The term "judiciary" does not have a set definition across all jurisdictions. Adjudication, which is the function of the judiciary, encompasses administrative and procedural aspects, as well as substantive decision making.[119] The judiciary could be defined as the organ of government not forming part of the executive or the legislature; it is not subject to personal, substantive, and collective controls, and it performs the primary function of adjudication. The latter can be exercised by direct resolution of disputes between private parties, between state organs, or between a private party and a state organ. Adjudication could also be by way of review of adjudicative decisions of tribunals outside the ordinary court system.[120] The definition should exclude military tribunals from the scope of the term "judiciary," as well as administrative law judges in the United States, or the officers of administrative tribunals in England, and their equivalents in other countries, including Israel. However, independence and impartiality must be respected and maintained by administrative judges as well and this must be a central aim for the upcoming years.[121]

5. The Principle of Democratic Accountability

One of the most important principles in the contemporary debate on the role of the judiciary in society and its relationship with the executive and the legislature is the principle of democratic accountability of the judiciary. This principle has strong relevance to the method of judicial appointment and the models of con-

---

118 *Id.*, at 598, 630; L. Atkins, *The Shifting Focus of Judicial Reform: From Independence to Capacity*, in EUMAP (Aug 2002), available online at: http://www.eumap.org/journal/features/2002/aug02/indeptocapacity (accessed February 9, 2017).

119 Judicial Responsibility, *supra* note 117. Cappelletti generally accepting this thesis, see: Cappelletti, *supra* note 102, at 570–575.

120 *Creating a Culture of Judicial Independence, supra* note 1, at 32.

121 See the concluding remarks of this chapter.

stitutional adjudication of the constitutionality of executive actions and parliamentary and legislative acts.[122]

Section 4.2 of the Mt. Scopus Standards recognizes the importance of legislative and executive participation in judicial selection. It considers such participation as legitimate.[123] This model of involving the legislature and the executive in judges' selection introduces a form of democratic accountability of the judiciary in the selection process in the beginning of their term of office. This resolves the dilemma of judges making value judgments and issuing constitutional rulings without being accountable to the general society.[124]

This brings us to the linkage between the model of constitutional adjudication and the model of judicial selection. Democratic accountability demands that a state select the model of constitutional adjudication that complements its method of judicial appointments. This is in order to ensure that the power of the judiciary to rule on the unconstitutionality of legislation corresponds with that country's form of judicial appointments. In countries where judicial selection models include the participation of legislative and executive input into the process, it is justifiable to adopt an adjudicative model that grants the courts a power to rule that statutes are unconstitutional.[125] On the other hand, where the judiciary is appointed on a professional basis only, without democratic input, then the model of giving the final word to the judiciary in deciding the constitutionality of statutes is not appropriate, and other models should be considered. The two alternative models are the declaratory model and the override model. The first, the declaratory model, as adopted by the UK Human Rights Act,

---

122 For a detailed discussion over the various procedures for appointment of judges, see Malleson and Russell (eds.), *Appointing Judges in an Age of Judicial Power: Critical Perspectives from Around the World* (Toronto University Press 2006); Melleson and Moules, *The Legal System* (3rd ed., Oxford University Press 2010); Blom-Cooper, Drewry and Dickson (eds.), *The Judicial House of Lords* (Oxford University Press 2009), Chapters 7–8.

123 Mt. Scopus Standards of Judicial Independence, *supra* note 4, provide that:

a) The principle of democratic accountability should be respected and therefore it is legitimate for the Executive and the Legislature to play a role in judicial appointments provided that due consideration is given to the principle of Judicial Independence.

b) The recent trend of establishing judicial selection boards or commissions in which members or representatives of the Legislature, the Executive, the Judiciary and the legal profession take part, should be viewed favourably, provided that a proper balance is maintained in the composition of such boards or commissions of each of the branches of government. Mt. Scopus Standards, § 4.2(a), (b).

124 *Creating a Culture of Judicial Independence*, *supra* note 1, at 32–33.

125 See Shetreet, "Models of Constitutional Adjudication A Comparative Analysis" *in* Pellegrini, Grinovner and Calmon (eds.), *Papers Presented at the XII Congress of Procedural Law* 769–98 (Forensa 2007).

is that constitutional judgments of the court will be declaratory only. In this model, the judiciary does not have the power to invalidate a statute, but only the power to declare incompatibility between the law and the constitution. The second model for resolving the lack of democratic accountability, the override model, allows the court to invalidate a statute, but provides for a parliamentary power to override this invalidation. This model exists in Canada. In both models, after the decision of the court, the legislature may either modify a statute to fit the court's constitutional interpretation, or else decline altogether to engage in statutory modification.[126]

An analysis of the models of constitutional adjudication reveals the link between the scope of judicial review and the provision for democratic accountability.[127] It is generally accepted that the principle of constitutionalism requires limiting the power of the legislative branch. This idea is widely accepted, in spite of the reservation voiced in this regard. The dilemma relates to the democratic legitimacy of constitutional adjudication, and the nature of the method of constitutional settlement of disputes in each society.[128]

The fact that the judicial branch serves for longer periods should not be viewed as a deficient element. However, the fact that the judicial branch exercises judicial review over legislative judgments while exercising constitutional adjudication, yet is not subject to any accountability, is clearly contrary to the doctrine of separation of powers and the principle of constitutionalism. The dilemma is that in constitutional adjudication the judiciary may limit the political branches, but the judiciary itself is not democratically accountable.[129]

To resolve this issue, there are a number of possibilities. One strategy is to formulate a constitution in a precise manner, using detailed and specific rules, so that the constitutional guidelines will advise the judges in the exercise of judicial review of the constitutionality of statutes.[130] A second strategy focuses on the method of the selection of judges. The American model ensures democratic

---

126 *Creating a Culture of Judicial Independence, supra* note 1, at 33.
127 See Dotan, "Judicial Review and Accountability: A Comparative Analysis" (2007) 10 Mishpat Umimshal (Hebrew).
128 See, for example: Gavison, "The Constitutional Revolution: Description of Reality or a Self-Fulfilled Prophecy" (1997) 28 Mishpatim 23, at pp. 28–32 (Hebrew); Dotan, "Constitution for Israel? The Constitutional Dialogue after the Constitutional Revolution" (1996) 27 Mishpatim 149; Ackerman, "The Storrs Lectures: Discovering the Constitution (1984) 93 Yale L. J. 1013, at pp. 1030–31, 1045–47; Sunstein "Constitutionalism and Secession" (1991) 58 U. Chi. L. Rev. 633, at pp. 638, 647.
129 *Creating a Culture of Judicial Independence, supra* note 1, at 33.
130 See Craig, *Administrative Law* (3rd ed., Sweet & Maxwell 1994) 3; Stewart, "The Reformation of American Administrative Law" (1975) 88 Harv. L. Rev. 1667, at pp. 1694–95.

input into the federal and state procedures of judicial appointments through the congressional confirmation of presidential nominations on the federal levels, and by general elections in some states and by executive and legislative participation in judicial appointments in other states.[131]

The European model, adopted by several countries, including Germany and Italy, attempts to resolve this dilemma of democratic accountability with regard to constitutional adjudication by entrusting the power of judicial review not to the ordinary court system, but rather to constitutional courts. These courts use a different process to meet requirements of democratic accountability by providing for special procedures for the selection of their members. This view recognizes that constitutional adjudication requires a wider value-oriented approach and also that the European career judiciary in the ordinary court system cannot adequately ensure democratic accountability.[132] Normally, the process of electing members of the separate constitutional court is done in the National Legislature; it is more political than the appointment in the ordinary system, which is primarily based on judicial career.[133] As mentioned above, Section 4.2 of the Mt. Scopus Standards considers as legitimate such participation of the Executive and the Legislature in the appointment on judges.[134]

The democratic accountability of the courts helps ensure the existence of the rule of law and enhances constitutionalism. The underlying principle of the rule of law is provided for in Section 1 of the Mt. Scopus Standards: "The significance of the Independence of the Judiciary [is to] ensure that all people are able to live securely under the rule of law." This brings to realization the principle of democratic accountability and emphasis that "Judges are the servants, not the masters....Servants are accountable, so are judges."[135]

There are other models as well. One is to resolve the issue of the lack of accountability and the possible conflict between the branches of government by providing that the court can only declare incompatibility between a parliamentary statute and constitutional provisions, but the parliament (possibly together

---

131 See Resnik, "Judicial Selection and Democratic Theory: Demand, Supply, and Life Tenure" (2005) 26 Cardozo L Rev 579, at pp. 593–94.

132 This is the reason for the criticism regarding the absence of term limitations for federal justices. See *Id.*, at 615–616; Stras and Scott "Retaining Life Tenure: The Case for a 'Golden Parachute'" (2006) 83 Wash. U. L. Q. 1397, at p. 1426.

133 Bell, *Judiciaries within Europe: A Comparative Review* (Cambridge 2006).

134 *Creating a Culture of Judicial Independence, supra* note 1, at 34.

135 As said by Canadian judge, Mr. Justice Riddell. See *Shetreet, The Contemporary Debate, supra* note 29, at 593 (referring to *Davis Acetylene Gas Co v Morrison*, [1915] 34 OLR 155, 23 DLR 871 (Canada)). See also Constitution Act 1982, Schedule B to the Canada Act 1982, ch 11, §33 (1982) (UK).

with the executive) must decide what to do next. This is the model adopted in the United Kingdom where the basic norm is not a constitutional one but borrowed from the European Convention of Human Rights and adopted into the law.[136]

Another model designed to respond to the lack of accountability in the judiciary is the common law model. The common law model focuses on restricting the scope of judicial review and abstention from rigid constitutions, thus resolving the issue of the lack of judicial accountability by restricting the circumstances under which the judiciary will find itself in a position where it overrides legislative decisions.[137] Rigid constitutionalism was adopted only in federal common law states such as Canada and Australia, in order to regulate the interrelationship between their federal and provincial units.[138]

6. The Preferred Relationship between the Judiciary, Executive, and Legislative Branches

A. The Principle of Mutual Respect between the Branches of Government

When we deal with building a culture of judicial independence, it is important to view that culture as part of the operating system of government. The culture of judicial independence cannot exist in every governmental climate. It must exist in a system that is based on separation of powers. In its classical form, the separation of powers was developed by Montesquieu based on the English system of government in the 18th century.[139] The doctrine of separation of pow-

---

136 *Creating a Culture of Judicial Independence, supra* note 1, at 34
137 Canada's system of constitutional override allows Parliament to declare that certain types of legislation shall operate, notwithstanding their unconstitutionality, on the condition that Parliament makes this declaration expressly, and that such declaration expires after five years. The wording is as follows:

(1) Parliament or the legislature of a province may expressly declare in an Act of Parliament or of the legislature, as the case may be, that the Act or a provision thereof shall operate notwithstanding a provision included in Section 2 or Sections 7 to 15 of this Charter.

(2) An Act or a provision of an Act in respect of which a declaration made under this section is in effect shall have such operation as it would have but for the provision of this Charter referred to in the declaration.

(3) A declaration made under subsection (1) shall cease to have effect five years after it comes into force or on such earlier date as may be specified in the declaration. Canada Const, § 33.

138 *Creating a Culture of Judicial Independence, supra* note 1, at 34
139 See Baron de Montesquieu, *The Spirit of the Laws*, (T. Nugent, trans., Hafner 1949).

ers requires a total separation between the three branches of the government: the judiciary, the legislature, and the executive. The legislature is the only branch of government which is empowered to create general norms in society and to issue primary legislation. The executive is responsible for issuing individual orders and enforcement of the statutes issued by the legislature. The judiciary is engaged and entrusted with dispute resolution. This separation is the guarantee for freedom. The total separation is a utopia that cannot really be enforced in any system of government.[140]

The organizational separation between the three branches is possible and it is implemented in most modern systems of government. However, from the functional point of view, it is not possible to implement a separation of power. There is no system which does not empower the executive branch to perform semi-adjudicative functions and issue delegated legislation. There are also administrative powers that are given to the judiciary and there are some administrative powers and some semi-adjudicative powers that are given to the legislature. This deviation from the classic doctrine of separation of powers is warranted; given the realities of operating a system of government, without such a deviation it is not possible to have an effective and efficient government.[141] Today, the classical theory of separation of powers is not adopted on its pure form. Nevertheless, it is widely accepted that government powers must not be centered in one power and should be divided and subject to control and review by other authorities. This remains a principle that is adopted and practiced. This principle has been expressed in modern times by the American concept of "checks and balances." This concept divides the power between the different branches of government; however, unlike the classical theory, these powers are subjected to checks and balances of the other branches of government.[142]

Even once achieved, the maintenance of judicial independence is not a matter of course. It is constantly subject to challenges, sometimes by other branches of government, and at others as the result of internal developments, changing political circumstances, or social and economic pressures. Violations of accepted principles of judicial independence have occurred in countries that represent all forms of government and all geographic regions in the world. Challenges to judicial independence include interference with personal independence through

---

140 *Creating a Culture of Judicial Independence*, *supra* note 1, at 35.

141 Klinghofer, *Administrative Law* (Hebrew, 2nd ed., Akademon 1974) 10. Klein, "On the Legal Definition of the Parliamentary Regime and on the Israeli Parliamentarism" (1973–1974) 5 *Mishpatim* 308, 309–311, and 324–331 (Hebrew).

142 Rubinstein, *Israel's Constitutional Law* (Hebrew, 3rd ed., Shoken 1990) at 225–226.

legislation, including legislation abolishing security of tenure, lowering the retirement age, or abolishing certain courts so as to effectively end the service of a judge.[143]

It is important to note the significant reform in the UK judicial system. Before the Constitutional Reform Act (2005), the Lord Chancellor was entrusted with three important roles: speaker of the Upper House of Parliament (the House of Lords);[144] a member of the executive branch and member of the senior cabinet; and head of the judiciary. The Constitutional Reform Act[145] established new lines of demarcation between the Lord Chancellor and the judiciary, transferring all of the Lord Chancellor's judicial functions to the judiciary, and entrusting the Lord Chancellor solely with what is considered conceptually to be administrative and executive, and not judicial, matters. Thus, the Lord Chancellor became a representative of the executive, and not of both the executive and the judiciary. The Constitutional Reform Act laid down a number of other reforms aimed at providing constitutional safeguards protecting the position of the judiciary. This law established the Supreme Court of the United Kingdom, and passed on to it the jurisdiction of the Judicial Committee of the House of Lords. The law also introduced a major reform in the method of judicial appointments; it provides in Sections 3 and 4 that ministers, and other holders of office who have responsibility in matters of the administration of justice, promote and enhance the principle of judicial independence.[146]

In 2007, the English judiciary had many concerns that arose in connection with the establishment of the Ministry of Justice. In 2008, the Lord Chief Justice and the Lord Chancellor announced a new partnership with respect to the operation of the Courts Service. On matters for which responsibilities have been moved from government ministers to the judiciary, thought has been given re-

---

143 Tushnet, n. 34 above. See also *Shetreet, The Contemporary Debate, supra* note 29, at 607–08.

144 See *The Judicial House of Lords, supra* note 122, Chapters 4 and 5.

145 *Constitutional Reform Act* 2005, for details, see Shimon Shetreet and Sophie Turenne, *Judges on Trial: The Indepenence and Accountability of the English Judiciary* (2nd ed., xxx+463 pp, Cambridge University Press, 2013).

146 Malleson, "Selecting Judges in the Era of Devolution and Human Rights" in Le Sueur (ed.), *Building the UK's New Supreme Court* (Oxford University Press 2004); Malleson, "Promoting Diversity in the Judiciary: Reforming the Judicial Appointments Process," in Thomas (ed.), *Discriminating Lawyers* (Cavendish Press 2000).

garding how to ensure a measure of accountability consistent with the principles of judicial independence.[147]

Discussing judicial independence from the British perspective, Neil Andrews notes that there has been a long-standing constitutional perception that English judges form a separate arm of the state, and that the principle of "judicial independence" is also recognized in the European Convention on Human Rights. The Constitutional Reform Act provides that the executive must uphold the continued independence of the judiciary. The new order sees the Lord Chief Justice, as the head of the judiciary, representing the judiciary and holding responsibility for disciplinary matters. In addition, the Ministry of Justice and the Secretary of State for Justice have executive responsibility for the administration of justice in civil and criminal matters, an arrangement which creates the potential for friction between the judiciary and the executive. The matter is covered by "the Concordat," a Constitutional undertaking between the government and the judiciary, which sets out the agreements between the Lord Chancellor and the Lord Chief Justice on their new roles.[148]

B. Post Decisional Independence: Legislative Reversal of Judicial Decisions and Executive Enforcement of Judgments

One of the objectionable forms of legislative intervention in judicial decisions is the retroactive reversal of judicial decisions by legislation. Retroactive legislation is a violation of a number of constitutional principles. Such legislation in fact turns the legislature into an additional appellate instance above the final court of appeal in a certain jurisdiction. Such legislation also violates the rule of law, which requires that laws shall be applicable only prospectively. This is because the public should know of legislation and should conduct their behavior based on their notice of the law. Such retroactive legislation also is a violation of the principle of judicial independence in its substantive meaning because it frustrates the enforcement of the decision of the court.[149]

---

147 Jack Beatson, "Reforming an Unwritten Constitution," Law Querterly Review 126(Jan) 48 (2010), available at: http://www.ka.edu.pl/download/gfx/ksw/pl/defaultaktualnosci/1162/14/1/krakowunwrittenconstitution.pdf (accessed February 9, 2017).
148 Andrews, *Judicial Independence: The British Experience.* (The Culture of Judicial Independence: Conceptual Foundations and Practical Challenges, Chapter 24).
149 *Creating a Culture of Judicial Independence, supra* note 1, at 36–37.

The Mt. Scopus International Standards of Judicial Independence provide that retroactive legislation is inappropriate.[150] Nevertheless, in a number of situations, legislative bodies passed retroactive legislation in order to reverse decisions of Supreme Courts.[151]

In general, retroactive legislation should be viewed negatively and it must be avoided. The very exceptional cases where retroactive legislation could be justified occur when a judgment of a court will invalidate a great number of governmental actions and those which reverse a decision according to which the government or the general public acted on for a long time. In such cases, even though the law upon which the general public relied on may have been erroneous, it is not in the public interest to invalidate a great number of government actions. Therefore, the courts should apply their decisions prospectively as they have done from time to time. Doing so in those cases will not cause a conflict between court decisions and retroactive legislation. In those cases, the legislation will only reinstate the legal situation as it had been before the judgment.[152]

Retroactive legislation may be justified when the judiciary exceeds its role, as it is accepted in a particular jurisdiction. In such a situation, the legislative branch may, or perhaps should, reinstate between the two branches of the government the balance that was in fact breached by the judiciary in that case. However, in most cases, retroactive legislation is not consistent with the accepted restrictions on the legislative branch, which exclude legislation that impacts judicial decisions.[153]

Legislative reversal of court judgments exists in established democracies such as Britain (the state immunity in times of war)[154] and Canada (injunction on nuisance case).[155] An illustration of legislative responses to judicial decisions is illustrated in the Canadian case of *K.V.P. Co. Ltd. v. McKie* (1949). In *McKie*, owners of property along the Spanish River in Ontario sued the operator of an upstream pulp and paper mill for polluting the river's waters. The court ordered

---

150 Mt. Scopus Standards of Judicial Independence, *supra* note 4, provide that:
   3.1 The Legislature shall not pass legislation which reverses specific court decisions.
151 For Israeli cases of legislative reversals of judicial decisions, see *Justice in Israel, supra* note 41.
152 *Creating a Culture of Judicial Independence, supra* note 1, at 37.
153 *Id.*
154 *Burmah Oil Co (Burma Trading) Ltd v. Lord Advocate*, [1965] AC 75, [1964] 2 All ER 348, which was reversed by War Damage Act 1965 (1965 c 18).
155 K.V.P. Co. v. McKie, [1949] S.C.J. No. 37; See also Shetreet, *The Contemporary Debate, supra* note 29, at 610 – 623.

an injunction restraining the KVP Company, the defendant, from depositing foreign substances in the Spanish River. The company appealed, the appeal was dismissed, and the case was then appealed to the Supreme Court of Canada. The Lakes and Rivers Improvement Act was amended, altering the situation of the KVP Company. However, despite the amendment, the company's appeal was dismissed, with the Supreme Court holding that the amended act would not enable the Court to give a judgment that was contrary to law at the time of the Court of Appeal decision.[156] In response, retroactive legislation was passed: the KVP Company Limited Act. Section I of the Act read: "Every injunction heretofore granted against the KVP Company Limited (...) restraining the Company from polluting the waters of the Spanish River, is dissolved."[157]

The second case, crucial for British constitutional law, is *Burmah Oil Company v. Lord Advocate.* The case arose out of the destruction of oil fields in Burma by British forces in 1942 in order to prevent the installations from falling into Japanese hands. The appellants claimed that they were entitled to payment of a sum amounting to the amount of damages sustained by them due to the destruction. Although it was admitted that the demolitions were carried out lawfully, it was argued that every act of requisition done for the good of the public should be compensated.[158] The legislature reacted and passed the retrospective War Damage Act (1965), which abolished rights to compensation with respect to destruction of property authorized by the Crown during the war. This Act had the effect of reversing the court's judgment and thus undermining judicial independence.[159]

Another phenomenon is the preemption of the enforcement of judicial decisions by actions of the executive. Judicial independence of the decision continues after the case is decided. Judicial independence requires that the executive should respect the decisions of the courts and that the executive shall not use its powers in a way that will preempt the enforcement a judgment that has been handed down by the courts. Preemptive measures that frustrate the enforcement of a judgment are a violation of the rule of law and of the doctrine of separation of powers. They are also a violation of the principle of finality of judgments. In general, most jurisdictions do not engage in preemptive actions that frustrate judicial decisions. However, there have been cases in a number of jurisdictions and those cases should be avoided.[160]

---

156 *K.V.P. Co. Ltd. v. McKie et al.,* (1949).
157 Weinrib, *Tort Law: Cases and Materials* (Edmond Montgomery Publication 2009) 40–41. For the Ontario Act, see also *K.V.P. Company Ltd. Act 1950,* S.O. c. 33.
158 *Burmah Oil Co (Burma Trading) Ltd v. Lord Advocate* [1965] AC 75.
159 War Damage Act 1965 (1965 c 18).
160 *Creating a Culture of Judicial Independence, supra* note 1, at 38.

The post-decisional independence of court judgments imposes upon the executive a duty to enforce the courts' decisions—civil or criminal—and refrain from frustrating them by legal or physical actions or omissions. This principle also requires that the legislature refrain from retroactive reversals of specific judicial decisions. The Mt. Scopus Standards of Judicial Independence imposes a duty on the State to provide adequate budgets for the proper execution of court judgments.[161]

In optimal conditions, it is to be expected that judgment should be executed expeditiously. However, in reality, this expectation is not practical. In the absence of adequate budgets and resources, there has frequently been a backlog in the execution of judgments.[162] This failure to execute judgment is not always intentional. One should recognize that there are practical limits for expeditious enforcement of judgments because of lack of resources. However, failure to enforce judgments is to be recognized as improper although it cannot be viewed as a violation of judicial independence. There are cases where there is selective enforcement when the executive decides to enforce certain categories of cases or intentionally decides not to enforce judgments. In such a situation, this executive decision of selective enforcement or failure of enforcement should be viewed as a violation of judicial independence.[163]

C. Executive Delegated Legislation and Preemptive Actions in Pending Matters before the Courts

Executive intervention in judicial proceedings is affected generally by the exercise of executive powers. This could take place by way of ministers using their position to influence judicial proceedings. Such interventions prevent the court from independent and impartial adjudication.[164]

---

161 § 15.1 of the Mt. Scopus Standards of Judicial Independence, *supra* note 4, provides that:
15.1 States, parties and international organisations shall provide adequate resources, including facilities and levels of staffing, to enable courts and the judges to perform their functions effectively.
162 See H.C.J 309/62 *Bank Hapoel Hamizrahi v. Head of the Execution Office*, 16(4) P.D. 2602, in which the Israeli Supreme Court has refused to give a decree stating the police has to arrest a person, because it was convinced that due to lack of resources, the police will not be able to follow the decree.
163 *Creating a Culture of Judicial Independence, supra* note 1, at 38.
164 *Id.*

In this context, one could envisage delegated legislation in matters pending before the court. In these cases, one should clarify the nature of the delegated legislation which is aimed at regulating the issue that lies at the center of the dispute between the citizen and the administrative authority. When the delegated legislation regulates the matter in favor of the citizen, then it is acceptable. However, if the delegated legislation is aimed at frustrating the judicial process and regulating the matter in the opposite direction, which supports the position of the executive, then it is unacceptable. Delegated legislation of the latter category, which adopts the solution that is advocated by the executive, is inappropriate and violates judicial independence. It is true that prohibiting such delegated legislation limits the legislative powers of the executive, but such a limitation is necessary for the protection of judicial independence.[165]

It should be noted that the general approach, which excludes delegated legislation in pending matters before the court, does not mean that the delegated legislation is totally excluded, but it is excluded from affecting the specific case pending before the court. Such delegated legislation can apply to other parties who are not party to the case.[166]

The rule that excludes delegated legislation on matters pending before the court should be confined to situations when the litigation was initiated by the citizen in bad faith. This is a situation where the petitioner knew that the executive was going to introduce delegated legislation and, nevertheless, this petitioner went to court. It is not proper that in such a way, by filing a petition to the court such citizen can tie the hands of the executive from regulating the matter in delegated legislation. The exception is where it can be shown that the petitioner intended to limit the freedom and the discretion of the executive. Normally, the executive should not legislate in such pending matters.[167]

Another form of executive intervention in judicial adjudication is by preemption of such a decision. The court is limited to deal only with cases that are brought before it and only when its decision is effectively enforceable. Preempting actions by the executive is possible because it can engage in an action that will frustrate the adjudication.[168]

An important element of judicial independence vis-à-vis the executive is the duty to refrain from actions which frustrate judicial remedies. In other words, the executive may not engage in preemptive frustrations of judicial remedies

---

165 *Id.*, at 38–39.
166 *Id.*, at 39.
167 *Id.*
168 *Id.*

by parties to case. Such an action is, for example, when petitioners who file a legal challenge to their deportation are deported before the case is adjudicated.[169]

---

169 Such a case took place in the Dr. Soblen affair. Dr. Soblen was expelled from Israel and, by his expulsion, the judicial review of his deportation was frustrated. For a detailed discussion, see *Justice in Israel, supra* note 41, at Chapter 12.

Part IV: **Executive Powers and
National Security Powers**

Chapter 8:
The Executive and Legislative Power

1. Treaty Making & Conducting Foreign Affairs

Israel has no statutes with regards to foreign relations. The Government is authorized to exercise foreign powers without statutory authorization. Traditionally, it is understood that these powers are conferred to the Government as a general power of governance.[1] The statutory basis for this understanding comes from Section 32 of Basic Law: The Government, which states: "The Government is authorized to perform in the name of the State and subject to any law, all actions which are not legally incumbent on another authority."[2]

Section 32 allows "the Government to recognize other states and foreign governments, to establish diplomatic relations with them, and to confer diplomatic status to their representatives."[3] The Supreme Court will rarely review Government action relating to foreign relations, exercising great restraint. The Court views management of foreign affairs as unjusticiable.[4]

In *Reiner v. Minister of Justice*, petitioners sought to prevent German ambassadors to Israel from entering Israel if they had served in the German Army during World War II. The petition was rejected.[5] Similarly, the Court "rejected petitions requesting it to order the Government to refrain from conducting negotiations with the Syrian Government, for the removal of the Golan Heights from Israeli sovereignty, and it also rejected a number of petitions filed against the release of Palestinian prisoners pursuant to agreements signed with the Palestinian Authority."[6] The Court ruled that:

> The Government's decision to release prisoners is a political decision adopted on the basis of political considerations, being within the Government's competence, and as is well known, this Court is not supposed to intervene in such matters, and nor does it make a practice of intervening in its considerations. The decision resides with the Government and is subject to the criticism of the Knesset or public opinion, and not of the Court.[7]

---

1 S. Navot, *The Constitutional Law of Israel* (Kiuwer 2007) at 248 (hereinafter: *"The Constitutional Law of Israel"*).
2 Basic Law: The Government, Section 32.
3 *The Constitutional Law of Israel, supra* note 1, at 248–249.
4 *Id.*
5 H.C.J *Reiner v. Minister of Justice*, 19(2) P.D. 485.
6 *The Constitutional Law of Israel, supra* note 1, at 249.
7 H.C.J 9290/99 *M.M.T. Movement for Victims of Terrorism v. Government of Israel*, 54(1) P.D. 472.

DOI 10.1515/9783899497946-008

In *Weiss v. Prime Minister*, the Court rejected a petition that objected to Israel's negotiations with the Palestinian Authority during the transitional government. President Barak (at the time) ruled that "intervention in such matters will be in extreme cases only," and that such a political question remains with the Knesset or national polls.[8] Justice Zamir preferred to firmly deny the justiciability of these types of issues by stating that "the Court ... lacks the requisite qualifications for assessing the reasonability of any particular negotiations, or whether it exceeds the boundaries of reasonability, and it is forbidden for the Court to assume the responsibility involved in issuing an order prohibiting political negotiations."[9]

In regards to foreign relations, there is a distinction between petitions challenging the constitutionality of government policy and petitions alleging violations of basic rights. For example, in *Oyev v. Minister of Defense*, the Court rejected claims of nonjusticiability in regards to claims that the settlements in the Occupied Territories—expropriation of Palestinian owned land—violated rights. The Court stated that in matters of foreign policy, the judicial branch does not belong, but continued that if "a person's property was damaged or illegally denied him...it is difficult to believe that the Court would avert its eyes from that person, just because that person's right is also liable to the subject of political debate."[10]

Recognition of a foreign state is an act of government; therefore, only diplomats from recognized states may have diplomatic immunity. In this context, the Court held that "the Government is entitled to determine what the factual situation is in matters pertaining to the State's foreign relations, such as whether a particular person has diplomatic immunity, which is a matter for the determination of the Foreign Ministry."[11] This ruling was in regards to actions against the Palestinian Authority for damages caused by terrorist attacks. The Court decided that it is for the Government, not the Court, to determine whether or not an Authority is a sovereign body for purposed of applying immunity.[12]

Signing an international convention is also a power of the Government. There are two steps to becoming a party to an international convention: first is signing by a representative of the government, second is ratification. A convention only becomes binding after ratification. In Israel, as in England, a convention only binds the state in regards to international law and does not become

---

8 H.C.J 5167/00 *Weiss v. Prime Minister*, 5(2) P.D. 433, p. 472.
9 *Id.*, at 479.
10 H.C.J 606/78 *Oyev v. Minister of Defense*, 33(2) P.D. 113, 123.
11 C.F (Jer.) 2538/00 *Noritz v. The Palestinian Authority* (published on Nevo, 30.03.2003).
12 *Id.*

domestic law unless passed as Knesset legislation.[13] Because establishing and maintaining international relations is a power of the executive branch, not the legislative, the act of signing an international convention is not ipso facto an act of legislation; it must have Knesset force to receive legislative status.[14] However, signing an international convention often prompts the Knesset to adjust domestic law.[15]

Ratification of an international convention is left to the executive. However, some argue that ratification should be a process for the Knesset.[16] Currently, the executive gives notice to the Knesset of conventions prior to their ratification, but there is no oversight.[17]

In recent years, there has emerged a custom of requiring Knesset ratification for especially important treaties, such as those involving transfer and possession of foreign sovereigns and territories. Additionally, since the Yom Kippur War, all treaties involving political-military agreements have had Knesset debate and approval prior to taking effect. These treaties include the Disengagement of Troops Agreement, the Peace Agreement with Egypt, the 1983 Peace Agreement with Lebanon, agreements for Palestinian Self-Rule (Oslo Accords I), and the Peace Agreement with Jordan. With all of these treaties, the executive maintained that it did not need Knesset approval to ratify the treaties, but that it preferred approval for public and political reasons.[18]

Nevertheless, there has yet to be a Court ruling regarding Knesset constitutional authorization to ratify treaties of great public importance. For example, in the *Weiss* case, the Court ruled that the executive could declare that agreements regarding the Palestinian Authority be presented before the Knesset for ratification, but made no mention of whether this is a constitutional requirement.[19]

---

13 Hodaya Kain and Dafna Ben-Porat, *The Part of the Parliament in Ratifiying International Conventions and Agreements,* (Knesset Research and Information Center, 2003); Article 14(a)(5) Basic Law: The President.

14 *Id.*

15 *Id.*

16 R. Lapidot, *The Authority to Conclude International Treaties on Behalf of Israel,* Mehkarim, Bemishpat, Beinleumi, Pumbi (In Hebrew-1962), 247; Y. Blum, "The Ratification of Treaties in Israel," 2 Israel Law Rev. (1967) pp. 120, 125.

17 *The Constitutional Law of Israel, supra* note 1, at 251.

18 *Id.*

19 *Weiss v. Prime Minister, supra* note 8.

2. Taxing and Spending Power

Israel is similar to other democracies in that it embodies the phrase "no taxation without representation." The decision to levy taxes must be adopted by the legislature. Section 1 of Basic Law: The State Economy states:

(a) Taxes, compulsory loans and other compulsory payment shall not be imposed, and their amounts shall not be varied, save by or under Law; the same shall apply with regard to fees ...

(b) Where the amounts of any taxes, compulsory loans or other compulsory payments, or fees, payable to the Treasury are not prescribed in the Law itself, the amounts prescribed therefor[e] by regulations shall require approval—in advance or within the period prescribed by the Law—by a decision of the Knesset or of a committee of the Knesset empowered by it in that behalf. [20]

The Supreme Court of Israel is mindful of the broad grant of power with respect to the allocation of the public budget. In *Adallah Legal Center for Rights of Arab Israeli Minority v. Minister for Religious Affairs*, the Court stated that, factoring in all of the considerations that go into the Budget Law, it is a role that fundamentally belongs to the legislature, restricting the possibility of Supreme Court intervention.[21]

3. The Budget Law

Government expenditures for each year are determined by a special law, known as the Budget Law. The government submits a proposal for the budgetary framework to the Knesset; it is then up to the Knesset to approve or reject the proposal. The Knesset's deliberations of the Budget Law differ from its deliberations of draft bills.[22]

Section 3 of Basic Law: The State Economy deals with Israel's budget. It states:

(a) (1) The State Budget shall be prescribed by Law.

    (2) The Budget shall be for one year and shall set out the expected and planned expenditure of the Government.

---

20 Basic Law: The State Economy, 1975, S.H. §1.
21 H.C.J 240/98 *Adallah Legal Center for Rights of Arab Israeli Minority v. Minister for Religious Affairs*, 52(5) P.D. 167, 190.
22 The Budget Foundations Law, 5745–1985.

(b) (1) The Government shall lay the Budget Bill on the table of the Knesset at
the time prescribed by the Knesset or by a committee of the Knesset empowered by it in that behalf.

(2) The Budget Bill shall be detailed.

(3) The detailed Budget Bill of the Ministry of Defense shall not be laid on
the table of the Knesset but on the table of a joint committee of the Finance Committee and the Foreign Affairs and Security Committee of the
Knesset.

(4) The Budget Bill shall be accompanied by an estimate of the sources for
financing the Budget.

(c) In case of necessity, the Government may bring in an Additional Budget Bill
during the financial year.

(d) Where it appears to the Government that the Budget Law will not be adopted
before the beginning of the financial year, it may bring in an Interim Budget
Bill.

(e) The Minister of Finance shall submit to the Knesset every year a report on
the implementation of the State Budget. Particulars shall be prescribed by
Law.[23]

The proposed budget must include an itemization of all expenses, and the Finance Minster must submit to the Knesset an annual report regarding the implementation of the budget. The budget must be very specific, with allocations to
well-defined activities.[24]

Section 3(c) of the Budgetary Principle Law states: "the Budget shall indicate
the amounts of expenditure, divided into budget items, fields of operations and
schemes." An issue in this area is the allocations of "special funds" for areas of
activity in the framework of the Government's coalition commitments. Special
funds can be allocated to various bodies in accordance with the discretion of
the minister responsible for that area of governance. This arrangement was
strongly criticized by the public, leading to the amendment of the Budgetary
Principles Law. There is now a provision that mandates the consideration of
the principle of equality when allocating the budget. However, a minister has
the authority to determine the criteria for allocation, so long as there is "equality
based" criteria.[25]

---

23 Basic Law: The State Economy, §3.
24 *Id.*, at Article 2.
25 Article 3a(d)-(8) of the The Budget Foundations Law 5745 – 1985; H.C.J 10808/04 *The Move-*
ment for Quality Government in Israel v. Minister of Education (published on Nevo, 11.07.2006).

The Supreme Court has ruled that the Budget Law cannot violate the requirement to allocate the budget in accordance with equality-based criteria. If a provision of the Budget Law does violate this requirement, the Court may force the minister involved to ignore that provision and to act on the basis of equality.[26] Annual government expenditures are thus controlled by two laws: The Budgetary Principles Law and the Annual Budget Law. The Budgetary Principles Law prescribes the method of enacting the budget laws and includes provisions that enable the enforcement of the particular Annual Budget Law, which is enacted each year and determines the specific expenditures for the upcoming year. The existence of these two laws raises questions regarding the relationship between the two. The issue was referenced in dicta by the Supreme Court in the case of *HaTenua HaMesoratit v. Minister for Religious Affairs*. The Court said that Section 3(a) of the Budgetary Principles Law, requiring the budget to be allocated in accordance with principles of equality, has a superior status to the Annual Budget Law. Therefore, the Court can annul provisions of the Annual Budget Law if they violate the Budgetary Principles Law.[27] These provisions are essentially futile if they have no binding effect on the Annual Budget Laws. Notably, Justice Cheshin stated that Section 3(a) of the Budgetary Principles Law "is normatively equivalent to the provisions of a Basic Law or Constitution."[28]

Section 3(d) of Basic Law: The State Economy refers to situations where the Budget Law has not been adopted prior to the start of the financial year.[29] It states that "Where it appears to the Government that the Budget Law will not be adopted before the beginning of the financial year, it may bring in an Interim Budget Bill."[30] With an Interim Budget Bill, the Government is entitled to spend one-twelfth of the previous annual budget each month. The funds are prioritized: first designated for the payment of the State's obligations under the law, contracts, and treaties; the remainder of the funds are to be used for providing essential services and for actions included in the previous year's annual budget.[31] If no Budget Law is passed within the first three months of the financial year, the Knesset will be dispersed and elections must be held within three months.[32]

---

26 *Id.*
27 H.C.J 1438/98 *HaTenua HaMesoratit v. Minister for Religious Affairs*, 53(5) P.D. 337.
28 *HaTenua HaMesoratit*, *supra* note 30,
29 Basic Law: The State Economy, §3(d).
30 *Id.*
31 *Id.*, at 3b(b)
32 Article 36a Basic Law: The Knesset.

Any expenditure outside of the Budget Law is subject to an inspection by the State Comptroller.[33] Additionally, the Court can enforce the requirement that every expense have budgetary authorization by ruling that any expenditure outside of authorization is invalid.[34] The Budgetary Principles Law establishes a number of measures that enable the Government to allocate resources to finance its activities when a proposed expenditure is deemed invalid. When the proposal is received, the Finance Committee of the Knesset can authorize expenditure of revenues in excess of forecasted revenues, and reduce or prevent price increases in existing plans. The Government may update the budget during the year in light of actual revenues and inflation. The Government may also submit an additional budget with specified additional expenditures during the year. Furthermore, the Finance Minister can order that expenditure sums prescribed for one area be transferred to another.[35]

The Budget Law itself does not impose a duty of action on the State. It merely permits the Government to spend money for a particular purpose. However, the Court is occasionally prepared to recognize the Budget Law as an authorization for the exercise of governmental power in a particular area. In *Gross v. Ministry of Education*, for example, the Budget Law granted financial assistance to discharged soldiers in excess of the amounts prescribed in the Discharged Soldiers (Adjustment Grant) Law of 1988. The Court determined that the Government was authorized to do this not on the basis of generalized authority, but under the authorization of the Annual Budget Law.[36]

4. Omnibus and Apropriation Acts

The State Economy Arrangements (State of Emergency) Law 5745 – 1985 ("The Arrangements Law") was enacted after economic crisis struck Israel in 1985. The goal was to establish arrangements for the state of emergency where the Government could compile multiple laws and amendments to be presented to the Knesset and approved in one unit. In 1985, this was essential to the decision making of the Economic Plan, but it has subsequently become a standard feature of Israeli economic legislation. It contains a wide range of legislative subjects. The unifying feature is the Government's perception that these subjects are impor-

---

33 Article 29a of The Budget Foundations Law, 5745 – 1985; see Basic Law: The State Comptroller
34 e.g., see H.C.J 609/85 *Tzuker v. Tel-Aviv—Jaffa Mayor*, 40(1) P.D. 775.
35 Article 3a The Budget Foundations Law, 5745 – 1985.
36 H.C.J 381/91 *Gross v. Ministry of Education*, 46(1) P.D. 53.

tant to the fulfillment of economic policy. The Arrangements Law is presented annually to the Knesset and works as a supplement to the Budget Law.[37]

In recent years, there has been a decline in the number of legislative amendments contained within the Arrangements Law. However, there have been economic reforms that resemble the Arrangements Law, but not passed as an appendix to the Budget Law.[38]

In *Poultry Growers Association et al. v. The Government of Israel*,[39] the Supreme Court dealt at length with Arrangements Law and seemed to criticize it. Justice Beinish described the development and explosion of the use of Arrangements Law in the following way:

> Over the years the use of the legislative mechanism of the Arrangement Law has developed and expanded, and a number of "Arrangements Laws" were passed not as an ancillary supplement to of the State Budget, but rather as an element of the Government's economic policy. The Arrangements Law and its cognates, such as the Economic Program law forming the subject of the petitions before us, have grown into massive legislative projects that deal with an ever larger agglomeration of subjects covering a broad range of areas, even extending to areas bearing no overt and necessary connection to the budget itself. Furthermore, over the years, the Arrangements Law has increasingly been utilized not only for necessary legislative amendments required to adjust the existing legislation to the Budget Law, but also as a "platform" for substantive and far reaching legislation. In that capacity, they operate as a tool for effecting structural changes in the economy and the society, including with respect to publicly disputed topics, which the Government would have had difficulty in passing by a regular legislative procedure.[40]

While the Court pointed out the flaws of Arrangements laws, it ruled that these flaws were not sufficient to invalidate the law.[41] The case is an example of judicial restraint with respect to intervention in the legislative process.[42] However, the case law of the Supreme Court demonstrates that restraint is not always used. The Court regularly issues innovative rulings and criteria for intervention in cases where the original petitions were rejected.[43] Essentially, the Court lays

---

37 *The Constitutional Law of Israel*, *supra* note 1, at 256–257.
38 *Id.*, at 257.
39 H.C.J 4885/03 *Poultry Growers Association et al v. The Government of Israel*, 59(2) P.D. 14 (2004).
40 *Id.*
41 *Id.*
42 *The Constitutional Law of Israel*, *supra* note 1, at 257.
43 See H.C.J *Sarid v. Knesset Speaker*, 35(2) P.D. 197.

the groundwork for future intervention without implementing it in the case at hand.[44]

The petition in the *Poultry Growers Association* case challenged the chapter relating to agriculture in the Program for Israel's Economic Recovery (Legislative Amendments for Attainment of Budgetary Objectives and Economic Policy for Fiscal years 2003 and 2004) ("Economic Program Law"). Prior to this legislation, poultry growers had dominance in regards to the activities of the agriculture councils; they were mostly independent to manage and regulate the agricultural branches. In an accelerated legislative session, the Knesset adopted the Economic Program Law, which reformed the agricultural sector and transferred power from the agricultural councils to the Minister of Agriculture. The Knesset's Finance Committee "devoted less than one meeting to the debate on the agricultural section, the second reading of the law was conducted almost immediately thereafter, and the voting on each section of the law took place from the afternoon of that same day until...early morning the next day."[45] The petitioners claimed that this accelerated process was improper, and was similar to the procedure of the Arrangements Laws, which are adopted with the Annual Budget Law.[46] The Supreme Court rejected the petition, but noted that the legislative process of Arrangements Law has problems regarding "appropriate democratic procedure."[47] The Court said that this type of procedure prevents proper legislative discussion, restrains Knesset member's abilities to take a position on bill content, and precludes objective inspection of the legislative process by the Knesset.[48]

The Court ruled that judicial intervention is warranted when a flaw in the legislative process harms a fundamental principle. The judgment provided four examples of such flaws: 1) the principle of participation; 2) the principle of majority decision; 3) the principle of publicity, and; 4) the principle of formal equality. On the merits, the Court stated that there was no flaw harming a fundamental principle which would warrant intervention, but recommended that the Knesset reevaluate its reliance on Arrangements Law.[49] The Court left it up to the Knesset to make a change and it is unclear whether the Court's remarks have influenced the Knesset yet.[50]

---

44 *The Constitutional Law of Israel, supra* note 1, at 257.
45 *Id.*
46 *Id.*, at 257–258.
47 *Poultry Growers Association, supra* note 39.
48 *Id.*
49 *Id.*
50 *The Constitutional Law of Israel, supra* note 1, at 258.

Chapter 9:
War Powers—Relations between Civil Authorities and the Military

1. Wartime and State of Emergency Powers

Israel has been in a state of war since its formation, which influences Israeli law, especially in the area of emergency powers in the executive branch. At the time of Israel's founding, a state of emergency was declared. This state of emergency continues today. The executive emergency powers, however, are limited.[1]

Israel has been involved in many wars. Declaration of war is regulated by Section 40 of Basic Law: The Government, which says:

(a) The state may only begin a war pursuant to a Government decision.
(b) Nothing in the provisions of this section will prevent the adoption of military actions necessary for the defense of the state and public security.
(c) Notification of a Government decision to begin a war under the provision of subsection (a) will be submitted to the Knesset Foreign Affairs and Security Committee as soon as possible; the Prime Minister also will give notice to the Knesset plenum as soon as possible; notification regarding military actions as stated in subsection (b) will be given to the Knesset Foreign Affairs and Security Committee as soon as possible.[2]

In sum, the power to begin a war remains with the government. The law distinguishes between declarations of "war" under Section 40, and declarations of emergency situation by force under Section 38. Section 38 says:

(a) Should the Knesset ascertain that the State is in a state of emergency, it may, of its own initiative or, pursuant to a Government proposal, declare that a state of emergency exists.
(b) The declaration will remain in force for the period prescribed therein, but may not exceed one year; the Knesset may make a renewed declaration of a state of emergency as stated.
(c) Should the Government ascertain that a state of emergency exists in the State and that its urgency necessitates the declaration of a state of emergency, even before it becomes possible to convene the Knesset, it may declare a

---

1 Michal Tzur, The Defense (Emergency) Regulations 1945, 5 (Opinion Paper, The Israeli Institute of Democracy, 1999).
2 Basic Law: The Government, 2001, S.H. Section 40.

DOI 10.1515/9783899497946-009

state of emergency. The declaration's validity shall expire upon 7 days from its proclamation, if not previously approved or revoked by the Knesset, pursuant to a decision by a majority of its members; should the Knesset fail to convene, the Government may make a renewed declaration of a state of emergency as stated in this subsection.

(d) The Knesset and Governmental declarations of a state of emergency will be published in Reshumot; should publication in Reshumot not be possible, another appropriate manner will be adopted, provided that notification thereof be published in Reshumot at the earliest possible date.

(e) The Knesset may at all times revoke the declaration of the state of emergency; notification of its revocation will be published in Reshumot.[3]

Because a state of emergency was declared at the time of Israel's formation, the executive branch is authorized to exercise an array of emergency powers. A state of emergency pursuant to Section 38 and being at war pursuant to Section 40 are not identical. During war, it may be justified to confer full authority to many of the ministers due to a full or partial disruption of governmental power. This is not the case in a state of emergency in which the institutions of government are fully functional.[4]

Israel does not recognize a special category of constitutional powers known as "wartime powers" that are distinct from state of emergency powers. Because of this, the Supreme Court of Israel will readily review military activities, even in times of military conflict. For example, in 2000, the Supreme Court adjudicated petitions concerning the conduct of military operations in Judea and Samaria during times of combat. The intifada began in October of 2000. The Supreme Court had to adjudicate appeals alleging illegitimate action by Israeli forces. Because the petitions were made during combat, decisions had to be made quickly.[5]

One of the most interesting petitions dealt with the evacuation of bodies from the Jenin Refugee Camp. In April 2002, the Israel Defense Forces (IDF) conducted "Operation Defensive Wall" against Palestinian militant infrastructure in major cities of the West Bank. During this operation, the IDF entered the Jenin Refugee Camp and heavy combat resulted. After a few days of combat, the IDF took control of the camp. Over twenty IDF soldiers had been killed. The media reported that it was a massacre and that many innocent civilians had also

---

3 Basic Law: The Government, Section 38.
4 Article 5 of The Defense (Emergency) Regulations 1945.
5 H.C.J 3239/02 *Iad Ashak Mahmud Marab v. IDF Commander in the West Bank*, 57(2) P.D. 349 (2003).

been killed. The petitioners asked the Supreme Court to order the IDF to refrain from identifying and evacuating the bodies, and from burying them in the "enemies of Israel" cemetery in the Jordan Valley. At the time the petitions were served, thirty-seven bodies had been found: eight were handed over to the Palestinian side and twenty-six had yet to be evacuated. The petitioners requested that the task of locating and collecting the bodies be assigned to the Red Cross.[6] The Supreme Court's ruling, made in accordance with international law, assigned responsibility for the identification, evacuation, and burial of the dead with the Commander of the IDF forces in the West Bank. Representatives of the Red Cross were ordered to be part of these teams. The IDF (respondents to the petitions) agreed to include local community members in the process of identification. The local community will be liable for the burial, which shall be carried out with respect for the dead and according to religious laws. The Court ruled that these activities were to be carried out as quickly as possible while maintaining the balance between respect for the dead and safeguarding the security of the forces. Both the petitioners and the respondents accepted this arrangement and the petition was formally rejected. In his judgment, President Barak mentioned the rumors of massacre and civilian casualties. He stated that "In Jenin there was a battle—a battle in which many of our soldiers fell. The army fought from house to house, not by bombing from the air, in order to prevent, to the extent possible, civilians' casualties …. A massacre is one thing. A difficult battle is something else."[7] The Court reiterated that it would not take a position with regard to the combat that was managed.[8]

This is an example of a degree of Supreme Court intervention in military activity, even in times of war. The petition itself was rejected, as were most of the others; however, it should be noted that the petition was not rejected on grounds of injusticiability. The Court actually evaluated the exercise of the emergency powers and the military decisions on their merits.[9]

---

6 H.C.J 3114/02 *Barake et al. v. The Ministry of Defense et al.* (14.04.2002) available at: http:// elyon1.court.gov.il/Files_ENG/02/140/031/A02/02031140.A02.pdf (accessed February 9, 2017).

7 *Id.*

8 *Id.*

9 *Id*; See also Aharon Barak, *The Supreme Court and the Problem of Terrorism, 8* in Judgements of the Israel Supreme Court: Fighting Terrorism within the Law (2005); See e.g. a rejected petition: H.C.J 5591/02 *Yasin v.The supervisor of Camp kziyot*, 57(1) P.D 403.

2. State of Emergency and Related Legislation

The common definition of a state of emergency is a situation in which society faces danger of its existence from an outer or inner threat. In times like this, a need for special regulations for dealing with the situation may arise. The Israeli law has numerous regulatory statutes that grant the government the power to legislate in times of need.

A. Regulatory Statutes

a. Defense (Emergency) Regulations 1945

The British authorities in mandate Palestine first promulgated the defense regulations in 1945. The regulations were a means to govern emergency matters the British mandate faced in Palestine. Later, the new Israeli government incorporated the regulations into the Israeli domestic law.

The regulations include instructions in a number of subjects. Today, the authority to exercise this regulation is within the power of Israel security authorities. These acts may cause a severe interference with human and citizen rights. The regulations are part of Israel's primary legislation. They also apply by virtue of relevant legal orders in the West Bank.

Over the years, many criticized the regulations strongly because of the possible interference with human rights by the authorities.

Today, Israel relies on the Mandatory regulations when facing terror. Many subjects, which used to be included in the regulations, are now part of the new Israeli law. Still, most of the regulations remain valid, so there are times when the new laws and the old regulations conflict.

b. Commodities and Services Supervision Act 1957

According to this law, regulatory legislation can be applied only by declaring a state of emergency. The Commodities and Services Supervision Act grants a wide legislative power in a state of emergency to the Minister in charge of the law. This Situation exceeds normal and common financial-economical supervision and the Israeli Supreme Court observed that it is against the rule of law; therefore, it will be subject to judicial review.

c. Basic Law: The Government

The Basic Law: The Government was legislated in 2001. The law qualifies the Knesset to declare a state of emergency and authorizes the government to legislate regulations accordingly.

B. Declaring a State of Emergency

a. Definition of the Term

According to Section 38(a) to Basic Law: The Government, the Knesset can declare a state of emergency for one year, and it can be renewed.[10] The government can declare it as well but only for a period of 7 days.[11] The section does not define the situations or causes that constitute as a state of emergency. Therefore, the Knesset has absolute discretion when declaring a state of emergency and no judicial review on the decision can be applied.

b. Declaration Procedures

Section 38(a) states that the power to declare a state of emergency for periods no longer than a year is in the hands of the Knesset. The state of emergency will expire within a year from the declaration, unless it has been set for a shorter period. Section 38 does not limit the Knesset in terms of maximum declarations; therefore, a state of emergency may be in use all the time. However, there is great importance in the duty to rediscuss, every year, the necessity for the declaration.

Section 38(c) gives the power of declaration to the government. The declaration holds the power to legislate regulations for a state of emergency. The regulations may revoke existing laws. When it happens, and not by the legislature, there is serious harm to the principle of the rule of law. This is the reason why the law restricts the government by limiting the possibility to declare only for times when there is urgent necessity for a state of emergency. Even then, the declaration is valid for 7 days or until it is approved or disapproved by the Knesset. At least 61 Knesset members must approve the decision. This level of approval applies only to the government's declaration; when the Knesset is making the declaration, there is no need for a special majority of 61 Knesset members.

---

10 Basic Law: The Government, Section 38(b).
11 *Id.*, Section 38(c).

Section 38(d) states that there is a duty to publicize the declaration in every way possible. However, the section does not mention if publication in every way possible is mandatory when canceling a state of emergency or if publication can be in official registries only. There is logic in this publication arrangement; once the state of emergency is canceled, everything is back in order and it is possible to publish in official ways.

Section 38(e) states that the Knesset has unlimited power when repealing a state of emergency. Therefore, the decision to cancel and the decision to declare will not be under judicial review.

c. State of Emergency in Israel

The first declaration of a state of emergency was in 1948, four days after declaring Israel's independence. The purpose was to give power to the government to deal with the difficulties facing the new country. Although the circumstances have changed, the state of emergency is still applied. The reason is that many laws that have been legislated through the years rely on the existence of a state of emergency. Canceling the state would revoke them.

In 1999, ACRI (Association for Civil Rights) argued before the Supreme Court of Israel for the declaration of the state of emergency to be cancelled. They claimed that the laws that rely on the declaration violate human rights. ACRI's petition hastened government efforts to make the necessary statutory changes. Additional appeals generated detailed review of the government work by a designated team.

a. "Special" state of emergency

The Israeli legislation contains sections in numerous laws that define special arrangements for declaring state of emergency in relation to the specific law. The government can declare state of emergency for a certain serious matter.

b. State of emergency—from here on

As a direct extension to the discussion on the controversial state of emergency, this author suggests introducing a number of changes in order to limit the resort to the emergency legislation field:

i. Limit the declaration of state of emergency to situations that involve a national security threat.

ii. Distinguish between a "special state of emergency" and a "general state of emergency." A special state of emergency will be declared only when there is military conflict or serious internal danger. Only then, civil rights limitations will apply as necessary.

iii. Total exclusion of the possibility of regulating economic issues by virtue of state of emergency legislation.

iv. Use accurate and narrow terms for the state of emergency definition, causes for implementing an emergency, and what constitutes a serious threat to the national interests.

C. The Government's Power to Legislate Emergency Regulations

Section 39(a) gives the government the power to legislate emergency regulations when a state of emergency applies. The section restricts the regulations by limiting them to "defend the country, public safety and maintaining essential supplies and services." These limitations enable very important judicial review.

Throughout the years, the Supreme Court has had a significant change in the measure of judicial review needed for Section 39(a). In the past, the Supreme Court rarely intervened in the legislative process, all in the name of the broad discretion provided by the law. The current approach, however, is the opposite one. The broad discretion now means that a more thorough judicial review is needed to prevent the government from taking advantage of the state of emergency legislation. In addition, the section states that emergency regulations will be under review by the Foreign Affairs and Defense Committee, as soon as possible. This duty assures a fast and fixed review mechanism by the Knesset of the government legislation.

In the 1980s, the courts' approach started to change. In the *Clupeper-Nave* case, a new test was set for examining the legitimacy of regulations that were legislated as part of a state of emergency.[12]

The test contains three cumulative requirements:
1. Legitimate specific purpose: from the term "necessary action" in Section 39(a).
2. Legitimate mean: authority by the law that the regulations rely on.
3. Legitimate discretion of the ratio between purpose and mean: the proportionality demand.

The courts' change in approach accelerated in the 1990s in a series of cases. The Supreme Court used the test above in a strict way for the third requirement. The proportionality was measured by a reasonability test: the damage that the government is trying to prevent is proportionate to the harm that using the regulations will cause. In another case, it was determined that regulations may be legislated only for subjects that have direct relation to the state of emergency. Another determination by the Supreme Court is that emergency legislation is

---

12 H.C.J 372/84 *Clupeper-Nave v. The Minister of Education and Culture*, 38 (3) P.D. 233.

the last resort for the government. It may be used only if the state of emergency prevents the Knesset from legislating quickly enough; then the government can use this tool.[13]

D. The Prime Minister's or Other Minister's Power to Legislate Emergency Regulations

Section 39(b) states a special arrangement that grants prime ministers, or ministers acting on their behalf, the individual power to legislate emergency regulations. The section states two cumulative conditions for this to happen:
1. Unable to convene the Knesset members.
2. A necessary and urgent need for emergency regulations.

This section indicates the most severe degree of a state of emergency—the unusual event when the function of the government is negatively affected. The section does not mention any causality between the state of emergency and the effect of the government, but it seems to be interpreted that way.

E. The Power of Emergency Regulations

Section 39(c) defines the power of emergency regulations and their status among other legislation. The section states that the regulations can change any law, temporarily revoke its validity, set terms for the law, and tax or increase taxes. The legislature restricts this supremacy unless "there is no other instruction by the law." However, most legislation is not secured against change or revocation. This means that emergency regulations are subject to Basic Law only as fundamental values of state and society.

Emergency regulations, as any secondary legislation, will be subject to judicial review.

---

13 See e.g. H.C.J 6971/98 *Fritzki v. The Government*, 53(1) P.D 763; H.C.J 2994/90 Poraz v. The State of Israel, 44(3) P.D. 317.

F. Restrictions on Emergency Regulations Power

Section 39(d) protects three basic values from being changed or revoked by emergency regulations: the right of access to courts, ex post facto law, and human dignity. The ex post facto is only for criminal punishment; other retroactive applications are possible.

G. Time Limits, Publication, and end to State of Emergency

Section 39(f) states the expiration period of emergency regulations. The regulations have a maximum period of three months expiration date from the legislation date. The Knesset has the power to prolong the expiration date and, of course, cancel the regulation.

Section 39(g) states the duty of publication in formal listings for the regulations. If publication in formal listings is unavailable, there is a duty to publicize the regulations in another adequate method, until formal publication is available again. The validity of the regulations is dependent upon publication.

Section 39(h) deals with the validity of emergency regulations after the end of the state of emergency. The sections state that the regulations will expire within 60 days from the end of the state of emergency. However, regulations that had their period extended by the legislature will still be valid and their status is equal to regular legislation. The extension demonstrates that the legislature will bring back the principle of rule of law.

H. Defense Regulations—Future Glance

In February 2012, the Ministry of Justice released a new bill. The bill suggested that regulations that are no longer needed, regulations that have replacement in Israeli legislation, and regulations that are unworthy for democratic system of government will all be repealed.

I. Section 40—Declaration of War

a. Section 40 in General
Section 40 first appeared in 1992 in the renewed Basic Law: The Government. The subject in Section 40 used to be partially regulated in different laws and practice.

In 1992, the law was amended after a few proposals, including one from this author, who chaired a public committee.[14]

b. Historical Development of the Power to Declare War

a. Before the Basic Law: The Government 1992

Until the legislation of the Basic Law: The Government, the power to declare war or start a military attack was not settled formally in Israeli constitutional law. It was considered a natural part of the government's general powers. The lack of specific legislation created a vast gray area, which led to criticism through the years about the inconsistency of authorizing actions.

b. After the Basic Law: The Government 1992

The subject of war powers was first added to the Basic Law: The Government in 1992 in Section 51, and today in Section 40. The section's goal is to prevent war being waged without cabinet approval. It states that, in order to declare war, there is need for government approval and a notice to the Knesset and the Defense and Foreign Affairs Committee. Military actions required for the defense of the state are authorized without prior approval. However, and despite its important purpose, Section 40 has a few flaws.

First, there is no clear definition of the term "war" in distinction to other armed conflicts and different military actions as specified in Section 40(b). The section's premise is that every major military action needs to be part of a government decision and under parliamentary review, but there is no definition for this situation in the section. In addition, in Section 40(b) "necessary military actions" is too ambiguous and covers a vast variety of actions. Using this section with an extensive interpretation can leave Section 40(a) as a dead letter, thus bypassing the government approval.

Another issue raised by Section 40 is that there are no instructions about actions during war or instructions for the case that the enemy is first to attack. With no limitations or other instructions, Ministers of Defense, being in charge of the army, are given a very wide discretion.

c. The Government Power for Declaring War

Section 40 provides that the state may only begin a war pursuant to a government decision. With that said, Section 40(b) states that this provision does not detract from the power to react in defensive actions in order to protect the country.

---

14 See Shimon Shetreet, New Direction Position Paper, 1980.

In addition to the government, there are a few other forums that can act in matters of state defense:

a. The Cabinet: "Ministers Committee for National Security" is a legal forum under section 6 of Basic Law: The Government 2001.

b. Sometimes the government acts only by the relevant ministers who manage defense matters. These include the prime minister, who as the head of the executive branch is in charge of the Security Service and Mossad, and the Minister of Defense as the Minister in charge of the army. Also involved in these forums are the chief of the general staff, the head of the Security Service, and the head of the Mossad.

c. In the past, there were political consultation forums that were not officially regulated by law. These forums had an important part in providing policy formulation leading into the formal government deliberation and resolution.

J. Section 41: The Inapplicability of Emergency Regulations

The legislature protected the Basic Laws from any change, condition, and revocation by emergency regulations. Section 41 is a complementary mechanism for the mechanism in Section 44, which states that at least 61 Knesset members are needed in order to change the law. Section 41 was legislated in order to prevent undermining the laws' stability by temporarily revocation or changing the Basic Laws by emergency regulation.

3. Judicial Review of Security Decisions

Since its inception, Israel has lived in a state of emergency marked by recurrent wars and periods of relative quiet. Because of the state of emergency, the Government will often make security decisions that infringe upon the individual rights of citizens. For example, the Knesset has enacted legislation granting wide powers of detention and search;[15] emergency regulations are valid for 90 days unless they get an extension;[16] and the Defense Regulations enable interference within many areas of civil rights, including censorship, restrictions on political associations, and freedom of movement. The Supreme Court, sitting as the High Court

---

15 Emergency Powers (Detention) Law, 1979, 33 *L.S.I.* 89.

16 For the earlier law see Sec. 9, Law and Administration Ordinance, 1948, and now see Section 38(c) of Basic Law: The Government.

of Justice, is charged with protecting the basic rights of the citizens of Israel. This function is difficult because there is no comprehensive Bill of Rights in Israel.[17] However, over the years the Supreme Court has greatly increased its review, and in 1992 two Basic Laws concerning human rights were passed: Basic Law: Human Dignity and Liberty and Basic Law: Freedom of Occupation.

A. The History of Judicial Review of Security Decisions

In the early years of the State, judicial review of security decisions was limited to procedural or jurisdictional defects, and did not involve an examination of the substantive reasoning behind the decision.[18] As Justice Witkon put it in *Hilu v. Government of Israel:*

> "The scope of our review of such a decision [which is based on security decisions] is limited to two [grounds]: review of the legal authority upon which the decision was based, and the review of the question whether the considerations were genuine security considerations or whether they were imaginary and designed only to disguise a refusal motivated by improper motives."[19]

The reluctance of the Court to review the substance of decisions based on security reasons was clearly illustrated in the case of *Abu Gosh v. Military Commander of the Jerusalem Corridor.*[20] In that case, the petitioners were removed from their village for periods of three to five months for security reasons, which were not disclosed because they were "privileged." However, police officers told the petitioners that they were being removed because they refused to cooperate with the police in the investigation of a hand grenade attack on a youth village near the village of Abu Gosh. After long and hard deliberation, the Court nevertheless decided to accept the version of the military commander, that genuine security considerations were the grounds for the removal orders.[21]

---

17 S. Shetreet, *The Scope of Judicial Review of National Security Considerations in Free Speech and Other Areas: Israeli Perspectives*, 18 Israel Yearbook on Human Rights 35–47, 35–36 (1988) (hereinafter: "Israel Yearbook on Human Rights").
18 Geva, *On the Question of Balance between Security Considerations and the Protection of Human Rights*, 5 Mishpatim 685 (Hebrew, 1973–74).
19 H.C.J 302/72, *Abu Hilu v. Government of Israel*, 27(2) P.D. 169.
20 H.C.J 188/53 *Mahmud Rashid Abu Gosh v. The Military Commander of the Jerusalem Corridor*, 7 P.D. 941 (1953).
21 Shetreet, Israel Yearbook on Human Rights, *supra* note 17, at 42.

Many early cases in the High Court's jurisprudence appear, at first glance, as if they are invalidating security decisions because of their substance. However, taking a closer look, it is evident that the Court found either a procedural or jurisdictional defect.[22] For example, in *Al-Kharbotly v. Minister of Defense*,[23] the Supreme Court invalidated a detention order because, at the time it was issued, an advisory committee provided for by the statute had not been constituted. Also, in *Aslan v. Military Governor of the Galilee*,[24] a closure order for an area was set aside for failure to publish the order. Additionally, in *Alkhuri v. Chief of Staff*,[25] a detention order was set aside because it did not refer to the place where the detainee should be held. Further, in *Alrahman v. Minister of the Interior*,[26] an expulsion order was invalidated because it was signed by a military commander to whom the Minister of Defense had delegated his power of expulsion. The Court ruled that the Minister himself should have signed the order, and that the delegation was not permissible under the statute in question.

At times, the Supreme Court would set aside decisions based on security decisions by holding that such considerations fell outside of the scope of the statute of which the decision was based. In *Kardosh v. Registrar of Companies*,[27] the Registrar refused to register a company on the ground that it might be used to harm national security. The Supreme Court held that the use of the powers under the Companies Ordinance for the purpose of protection of national security was not within the Registrar's statutory powers, despite the fact that the language of the statute grants the Registrar absolute discretion. Similarly in *Sheib v. Minister of Defense*,[28] the Director of the Education Department in the Education Ministry dismissed the petitioner from his post as a teacher on the grounds that the Minister of Defense objected to his employment for security reasons. The objection was due to the petitioner's past association with Lehi, an underground organization which had existed before the establishment of the State. The Court held that in the absence of Knesset legislation, the Defense Minister had no authority to disqualify former Lehi Members from serving as teachers. Likewise, an education officer may not act on the instructions of another Minister, as he did in this case.

---

22 *Id.*
23 H.C.J 7/48 *Al Karbuteli v. Minister of Defense*, 2 P.D. 5.
24 H.C.J 220/51 *Aslan v. Military Governor of the Galilee*, 5 P.D. 1480.
25 H.C.J 95/49 *Alkhuri v. Chief of Staff*, 4 P.D. 34.
26 H.C.J 240/51 *Alrahman v. Minister of the Interior*, 6 P.D. 364.
27 H.C.J 241/ 60 *Kardosh v. Registrar of Companies*, 15 P.D. 1151.
28 H.C.J 144/50 *Scheib v. Minister of Defense*, 5 P.D. 399 (1951).

B. Elon Moreh case and the Rise of Judicial Review of Security Decisions

It may be said that the attitude of the public and the attitudes of the judges towards security considerations has changed to some extent due to the erosion of the status and image of the defense establishment. These attitudes crystallized following the findings of the Agranat Inquiry Commission on the Yom Kippur War,[29] and the Kahan Commission on the events at Sabra and Shatilla,[30] which showed clearly that even the security authorities are not devoid of defects and serious mistakes. Consequently, the absolute trust that the public had placed in the executive and the security establishment diminished.[31]

The previous judicial policy of the Courts to review security decisions based on only procedural or jurisdictional grounds changed in the *Elon Moreh* case.[32] In *Elon Moreh*, the Supreme Court reviewed a challenge to the security decision of the Cabinet and the Chief of Staff, to take possession of a privately owned land in the West Bank for the construction of an Israeli settlement. The Court found, after intensive factual investigation and inquiry, that the decision was based on general security needs, rather than on "military needs," which are not sanctioned by conventional international law, which is part of Israeli domestic law. The Court also found that these rules apply to officers of the State, even when they are acting outside of the territorial boundaries of Israel.[33]

Elon Moreh established that security considerations were reviewable, even where the authorities had acted in good faith within their jurisdiction. The concepts of injusticiability and the limited scope of review of security considerations were relinquished in favor of placing security considerations on the same footing as other considerations relied upon by a government authority. With these newly recognized powers of review, the Court continued to apply them when security decisions were challenged.[34] In *Samara v. Commander of Judea and Samaria*,[35] the Court intervened to reverse the decision of the Commander, who had applied pre-established criteria on security grounds to the question of whether the petitioner, a resident of Germany, could reunite with his wife and children in Judea and Samaria. Additionally, in *Asly v. Jerusalem District Commissioner*,[36] the Court

---

29 Report of the Agranat Commssion of Inquirey into the Yom Kippur War (1975).
30 Commssion for the Inquiry of the Events in the Refugee Camps in Beirut (1984).
31 Shetreet, Israel Yearbook on Human Rights, *supra* note 17, at 38.
32 H.C.J 390/79 *Dweikat v. The Government of Israel*, 34(1) P.D. 1 (1979).
33 Israel Yearbook on Human Rights, *supra* note 17, at 44.
34 *Id.*
35 H.C.J 802/79 *Samara v. Military Commander of Judea and Samaria*, 34(4) P.D. 1 (1980).
36 H.C.J 541/83 *Asli v. Jerusalem District Commissioner*, 37(4) P.D. 837.

held that a decision for the withdrawal of a newspaper license due to security considerations must be backed by sufficient evidence and should prove to be a reasonable conclusion from such evidence.

Judicial review of government decisions in security matters depends largely on the extent to which the authorities are prepared to disclose the reasons for the exercise of their powers. Under Israeli law, where the authority exercising a statutory power is granted absolute discretion, the authority may refuse to disclose the grounds for its decision. However, if the authority decides to disclose the grounds, even though it is not legally bound to do so, the Court will review the reasons and will, in addition, require the authority to reveal evidence to support its conclusion.[37] Likewise, when the authority produces a certificate showing that the reasons are privileged, the court that has jurisdiction to review such a certificate in fact reviews whether the evidence indeed supports the decision based on security grounds.[38]

After the Court established that security considerations are reviewable, it had to develop tests for the adjudication challenges directed at the substance of security considerations. In the area of free speech, the Court used the "near certainty" or "imminent danger" test, as laid down in *Kol Ha'am*.[39] But in other areas, the Court employed the "reasonable and honest suspicion" test for reviewing security considerations.[40]

C. An Example: Protections of Freedom of Speech

Free speech is a vital and indispensable foundation of a democratic government.[41] However, because of Israel's constant state of emergency, there exists a tension between free speech and State security. In the landmark decision of *Kol Ha'am v. Minister of the Interior*,[42] the Supreme Court laid solid grounds for the protection of free speech. In that case, the Court set aside the Minister's decision to suspend the publication of a newspaper for having published an article dealing with the Korean War. The Court held that because the state is a democracy, its executive agencies, political institutions, and judicial tribunals must pay due respect to civil liberties, including free speech, stating:

---

37 See H.C.J 2/79 *Al-Asad v. Minister of the Interior*, 34(1) P.D. 505.

38 See H.C.J 322/81 *Mahul v. Jerusalem District Commissioner*, 37(1) P.D. 789.

39 H.C.J 73/53 *Kol Ha'am v. Minister of Interior*, 7(2) P.D. 165, 871 (1953).

40 Shetreet, Israel Yearbook on Human Rights, *supra* note 17, at 45.

41 *Id.*, at 35.

42 H.C.J 73/53 *Kol Ha'am v. Minister of Interior*, 7(2) P.D. 165, 871 (1953).

The system of laws under which the political institutions in Israel have been established and function is witness to the fact that this is indeed a State founded on democracy. Moreover, the matters set forth in the Declaration of Independence, especially as regards the basing of the State "on the foundations of freedom" and the securing of freedom of conscience, mean that Israel is a freedom-loving State. It is true that the Declaration "does not consist of any constitutional law laying down in fact any rule regarding the maintenance or repeal of any ordinances of laws" ... but in so far as it "expresses the vision of the people and its faith" ... we are bound to pay attention to the matters set forth in it when we come to interpret and give meaning to the laws of the State, including the provisions of law made in the time of the Mandate ... for it is a well-known axiom that the law of a people must be studied in the light of its national way of life.[43]

Based on the democratic nature of the State, the Court ruled that only when there was a near certainty that the speech would endanger public peace could the government suspend publication.[44]

In the area of free speech, it is interesting to mention the case of *Zichroni v. Board of Directors of the Israel Broadcasting Authority*,[45] which invalidated a general unrestricted policy of forbidding interviews with people who identified with the PLO. The Court held that free speech prevailed over the general interest of preventing a PLO sympathizer from using the IBA to disseminate its views.

In later cases, the Supreme Court has strengthened the fundamental right to free speech in Israeli society. In one of the leading cases dealing with censorship of news movies, *Israel Film Studios v. Levi Geri and the Film Theater Censorship Board*,[46] the Court stressed that in a democratic society, the public's "right to know" is very central. Justice Landau stated that "a government which assumes the power to determine what is good or bad for a citizen to know, eventually is the one which determines what is good for a citizen to think, and there is no greater contradiction than this."[47]

Although the Court takes a strong approach toward protecting free speech rights, Israel still maintains relatively harsh censorship laws. There is an important customary arrangement, which substantially moderates the harsh effect of the censorship laws. According to the Defense (Emergency) Regulations of 1945,[48] censors are entitled to declare unfit for publication anything which

---

43 *Id.*, at 884.
44 Israel Yearbook on Human Rights, *supra* note 17 at 36.
45 H.C.J 243/82 *Zichroni v. Board of Directors of the Israel Broadcasting Authority*, 37(1) P.D. 757 (1982).
46 H.C.J 243/62 *Israel Film Studios LTD. v. Levi*, 16(1) P.D. 2407, 2415 (1962).
47 *Id.*, at 2416.
48 [1945] *Palestine Gazette* (No. 1442) (Supp. 2) 1055.

they deem detrimental to State security.[49] This is an extremely broad grant of power, giving censors absolute discretion. Despite this provision and the importance of censorship in the eyes of the security agencies of the State of Israel, an arrangement has developed whereby censorship of the daily newspapers that are members of the Editors' Committee is based upon a customary and voluntary agreement.[50]

The main provisions of the agreement stipulate that: (1) the defense regulations are valid, but will not be applied against those newspapers which are members of the Editors' Committee; (2) no censorship will be exercised regarding political affairs, opinions, commentary, or any other publication unless the article discloses military information; (3) certain issues will be submitted for prior censorship; and (4) a special committee will be established, to include an officer appointed by the Chief of Staff, an editor who is a member of the Editors' Committee, and a public official elected by the two former members, who will serve as the committee chairman. This committee is authorized to decide on complaints of the censor and the newspapers regarding violations of the agreement. The decisions of the committee are subject to the veto of the Chief of Staff (unless unanimous). However, if exercising the right to overrule a decisions against the censor, the Chief of Staff must personally hear the arguments of the editor involved prior to overruling the decision. The arrangement is perceived by all parties as obligatory and, except for very few violations, has been respected since its inception.[51]

This arrangement prevents many censorship issues from going before the courts. Before making a decision, censors must turn to the censorship tribunal (unless they are willing to violate the arrangement), which is composed of the censorship committee of the Editors' Committee. The tribunal has a civilian majority: it is composed of two representatives of the press and the public. The procedures of the hearing, the nature of the jurisdiction, and any ensuing sanctions are all based upon usage, and are generally to the benefit of the press. The custom has a positive effect on free speech, but this is of no comfort. The regulations should be reformed, the earlier the better.[52]

It should be noted that the spirit of the agreement applies to all the newspapers, even those that are not members of the Editors' Committee, i.e., the foreign press, radio, and television. The difference lies in the sanction. The press organ-

---

49 See The Defense (Emergency) Regulations, Secs. 86–101.
50 Israel Yearbook on Human Rights, *supra* note 17, at 45–46.
51 *Id.*, at 46.
52 *Id.*, at 46–47.

ized by the Editors' Committee turns into a special committee. The rest of the media do not, due to the Editors' Committee objection to receiving newspapers which are not dailies; the parties have no choice, therefore, but to refer to the courts. Special guidelines apply to radio and television, directed by the Israel Broadcasting Authority, which is a statutory body.[53]

---

53 See S. Shetreet, "Custom in Public Law," 21 *Isr. L. Rev.* 450, 488–489 (1986).

Part V: **Israel as a Jewish and Democratic State**

Chapter 10:
Law and Religion in Israel

The question as to whether freedom of religion in all its aspects is adequately protected in any society can be answered by a careful examination of the relevant doctrines and practices of its legal system. There are significant sources for the protection of religious liberty in Israeli law. There have also been various efforts to incorporate religious norms or restrictions that reflect religious sources into the law of the land; an evaluation of these is part of any investigation of Israel's adherence to principles of freedom of conscience and religion. This chapter will discuss the scope of protection of religious liberty through constitutional and legal norms; the relationship between religion and state; and recent developments in religious liberty such as marriage, day of rest, conversion, and religious courts. Finally, the chapter considers the contribution of the Supreme Court and state funding for religious institutions.

1. Sources of Protection of Freedom of Religion in Israel

A. The Palestine Mandate

The Palestine Mandate includes a number of provisions ensuring freedom of religion and conscience, and protection of the Holy Places, as well as prohibiting discrimination on religious grounds.[1] But the Israeli significance of the Mandate in domestic law is a matter still in dispute. The decisions of the Israeli Supreme Court show an inclination to diverge from the approach taken in Mandatory times, when no legally binding force was attached to the Mandate unless its provisions were embodied in the Palestine Orders in Council.[2] Instead, legal signifi-

---

1 See Articles 2, 13 – 18 of the Mandate for Palestine, and Articles 83 and 17(1)(a) of the Palestine Order in Council of 1922.
2 For the legal effect of the Mandate before 1948 as apprehended by the courts, see P.C. 98/25, *Jerusalem District Officer v. Murra and others*, Palestine Law Report 11 (ordinances made under Article 17 of the Palestine Order in Council may be examined in the light of the Mandate and be invalidated if repugnant thereto); Misdemeanour A. 18/28, *Attorney General v. Altshuler*, 1 Palestine Law Report 283 (an ordinance and the regulations made thereunder, which are discriminatory on religious grounds, are invalid) ; H.C.J. 19/41, *Rosenblatt v. Haifa Lands Registrar*, 14 Palestine L.R. 286 (the restrictions in Article 17 do not apply to Orders in Council or the regulations made thereunder, even if repugnant to the Mandate; Misdemeanour A. g/36, *Shanti v. Attorney*

DOI 10.1515/9783899497946-011

cance now tends to be attributed to the Mandate so as to require the abrogation of any Mandatory law inconsistent with its provisions. But this tendency is not consistent and cases are to be found which follow the Mandatory approach.[3]

Article 83 of the Palestine Order in Council of 1922 provides that "all persons ... shall enjoy full liberty of conscience and the free exercise of their forms of worship, subject only to the maintenance of public order and morals," Article 17(1)(a) lays down that "no ordinance shall be promulgated which shall restrict complete freedom of conscience and the free exercise of all forms of worship." The importance of these articles lies in the fact that any Mandatory Ordinances and Regulations which are inconsistent with their provisions are void and, therefore, have not been received into Israel law under Section 11 of the Law and Administration Ordinance, 1948. They are also instructive of the policy of the Israeli legal system in safeguarding freedom of conscience and religion.[4]

B. The Declaration of Independence and Israeli Statutory Law

The Declaration of Independence guarantees freedom of religion and conscience, and equality of social and political rights irrespective of religion. "Even if the Declaration itself has not conferred rights upon the citizen enforceable by way of legal action, it provides a pattern of life for citizens of the State and requires every State authority to be guided by its principles."[5] The courts resort to the Declaration of Independence only when there is doubt as to the intent of the legislature, in which case the court will prefer the construction which extends greater protection to individual freedom. However, when the legislative intention is clear, it will be upheld, even if it infringes upon individual freedom, contrary to the Declaration of Independence.[6]

To support the fundamental existence of the right to freedom of conscience and religion, the courts have relied on the fact that Israel is a democratic and enlightened State. In dealing with questions of religious freedom, as well as other human rights, the courts have also resorted to the Universal Declaration of Human Rights and the International Covenants on Political and Civil Rights

---

General, (1937) *Annotated Judgments S.Ct.* (Palestine) 31 (Ottoman laws may be inconsistent with the Mandate).

3 Shimon Shetreet, *Some Reflections on Freedom of Conscience and Religion in Israel*, 4 Israel Yearbook on Human Rights 194 (1974) (hereinafter: Shetreet, Reflections).

4 *Id.*, at 195.

5 H.C.J 262/62 *Israel Peretz v. Kfar Shmaryahu*, 16 P.D. 2101, 2116 (per Justice Summon).

6 Shetreet, *Reflections, supra* note 3, at 195–196.

that reflect "the basic principles of equality, freedom and justice which are the heritage of all modern enlightened States."[7] In doing so, the courts have required that two conditions be met: that the principle in question is common to all enlightened countries and that no domestic law exists contrary to it.[8]

Many provisions of Israeli statutory law are devoted to the protection of Holy Places and sites which serve for prayers and other religious purposes.[9] For example, Penal Law lends its protection to freedom of conscience and religion. Section 146 of the Criminal Code Ordinance, 1936, makes it an offense to cause damage to any place of worship or to any object sacred to any religion, with the intention of affronting the religion of any class of persons. Section 148 imposes penal sanctions for trespass on places of worship and burial, for indignity to corpses, and for disturbances at funeral ceremonies.[10]

After the enactment of the 1992 Basic Laws, The Declaration of Independence is now a part of the Israeli constitutional norms under section 1 of both 1992 Basic Laws. Which provide that the fundamental rights of a person in Israel "will be respected in the spirit of the principles in the Declaration on Independence of the State of Israel." Freedom of religion has been held to be included in the non-enumerated basic rights protected under Basic Law: Human Dignity and Liberty.[11]

2. The Scope of Protection of Religious Liberty

These protections include founding documents of the State of Israel, international law, Israeli court decisions, and Israel's establishment as a democratic state. One of the first fundamental sources of the protection of religious liberty comes from the 1922 Palestine Mandate where a number of provisions protect freedom of religion, conscience, and holy places, and prohibits discrimination on reli-

---

7 H.C.J 301/63 *Streit* v. *Chief Rabbi*, 18(1) P.D. 598, 612.

8 Shetreet, Reflections, *supra* note 3, at 196.

9 E.g., Section 3 of the Local Authorities (Vesting of Public Property) Law, 1958, excludes property used for religious purposes and services from that which a local authority is empowered to acquire compulsorily for public purposes.

10 4 Israel Yearbook on Human Rights, at 197.

11 Hillel Sommer "From Childhood to Adulthood: Open Issues in the Implementation of the Constitutional Revolution," *Law and Business* A 59 (5764); H.C.J 7622/02 *Zonshein v. Advocate General*, 57(1) P.D. 726 (2002); Aharon Barak, Proportionality in Law: The infringement of the Constitutional Rights and its Limits 726 (2002); Medina, *supra* note 258; Hillel Sommer, *supra* note 86; H.C.J 721/94 *El Al Airlines v. Danilovich and others*, 48(5) P.D. 749 (1994) (right of equality); C.A 2512/90 *Supergas Ltd. v. Saar*, 45(4) P.D. 405 (1991) (freedom of contract);

gious grounds.[12] The Palestine Order in Council provided that "all persons... shall enjoy full liberty of conscience and the free exercise of their forms of worship, subject only to the maintenance of public order and morals."[13]

Additionally, the Israeli Declaration of Independence guarantees freedom of religion and conscience as well as equality of social and political rights, irrespective of religion.[14] The Declaration of Independence does not have binding legal authority, but it does provide a pattern of life for the citizens.[15] The Israeli court system has relied on the fact that Israel is a democratic and enlightened state wherein religious freedom is ensured in every enlightened democratic regime.[16]

The courts have also relied on pervasive international treaties and standards such as the Universal Declaration of Human Rights. Israel has therefore established a standard for finding that a right exists. First, the principle in question must be common to all enlightened countries and no contrary domestic law exists.[17] Justice Landau stated that, while freedom of conscience was partly based on founding documents of the state, they are also partly based "directly from the nature of our state as a peace-loving, democratic state."[18]

The law and practice in Israel regarding religious freedom may best be understood as a hybrid between non-intervention in religious affairs, on the one hand, and the inter-involvement of religion and government in several forms on the other. The most notable forms are legislation establishing the jurisdiction of religious courts of the different faiths in specified matters of "personal status" by government funding of authorities which provide religious services to several of the religious communities; and a series of legal institutions and practices which apply Jewish religious norms to the Jewish population.[19] Although Israel does establish religious precepts through the State, such as the prohibition of work on religious days of rest, Israel does not compel Jews or non-Jews to violate the precepts of their chosen faith. At the same time, freedom of religion is not an absolute right, but rather is subject to limitations and derogation. Thus, freedom

---

12 Shimon Shetreet, *Freedom of Religion in Israel: A Report Submitted to the International Convention against Racism*, 1. See Articles 2, 13–18 of the Mandate for Palestine.
13 See Articles 83 and 17(1)(a) of the Palestine Order in Council of 1922.
14 Shetreet, *supra* note 12, at 2.
15 See H.C.J 262/62 *Israel Peretz v. Kfar Shmaryahu*, 16 P.D. 2101, 2116.
16 See Cr.A 112/50 *Yosifof v. Attorney General*, 2 P.D 486, 598, 612.
17 See H.C.J 103/67, *American Orphan Beth El Mission v. Minister of Social Welfare*, 21(2) P.D 325.
18 See H.C.J 501–96 *Horev v. Minister of Transportation* (97 Takdin 421, (1997)), H.C.J 5394/92 Huppert v."Yad Vashem", The World Holocaust Remembrance Center, 48(3) P.D. 353, 360 (1994).
19 Shetreet, *supra* note 12, at 3.

of religion must be balanced with other rights and interests, and may be restricted for reasons of public order and security. In practice, however, Israeli authorities have exercised their power with great caution.[20]

Religious institutions in Israel enjoy financial support through direct funding and tax exemptions. The level to which a religious organization is financially or officially supported varies depending on the community. However, religious communities still have the ability to practice their religion freely or to maintain communal institutions.

A. Religion-State Relationship and Freedom of Religion

There are several ways in which to view freedom of religion and the relationship between the State and religions. The prevailing view is that the establishment of religion and its recognition by the state, or the separation of religion from the state, do not, as such, violate religious freedom or constitute unlawful discrimination for religious reasons or religious intolerance. The nature of the regulation matters and the measure of statutory protection of religious freedom does not vary with states where separation exists or where there is a state-recognized religion.[21] In fact, the relationship between church and state has no significant effect on the free exercise of religion.[22] What is important is whether preferential treatment is given to some religions over other religions, involving an infringement of the principle of religious freedom.[23]

B. Conceptual and Comparative Analysis

There are five models which reflect the relationship between a state and a religion. These are: the theocratic model, the absolute-secular model, the separation of state and religion model, the established church model, and the acknowledged religions model.[24] Of these models, two are not democratic in nature: the theocratic and the absolute secular model.

The separation of church and state is most clearly exemplified by the United States, which forbids establishing an official religion and guarantees the free ex-

---

20 *Id.*
21 *Id.* at 4.
22 See International Draft Convention on the Elimination of All Forms of Religious Intolerance.
23 Shetreet, *supra* note 12, at 4.
24 *Id.* at 5.

ercise of religion.[25] The purpose of this model is to ensure that the pluralism of religions and views are respected and preserved.[26]

The established church model is when the state recognizes a certain religion and a certain church as the state's national church. This recognition does not mean that other religions are prohibited.[27] England is a good example of this model.[28] In England, there is a preferred religion in the state wherein certain governmental requirements carry a religious nature. For example, the King or Queen must be a member of the Anglican Church and is the head of the church. In addition, Parliament is often involved in approving aspects of the religious structure, such as confirming the measures of the Anglican Church.[29]

3. State and Religion and Freedom of Religion

The state of Israel was established as the state of the Jewish people; it allows for the Jewish people to realize their rights to self-determination. Prior to the establishment of Israel as an independent national state, Israel was internationally recognized as a political entity that would maintain a certain level of religiosity—specifically Judaism. Israel is characterized by the dual identity of being an independent nation-state of the Jewish people and a state of the people believing in the Jewish faith; there is no definitive separation of state and religion. This lack of division has historically and currently presented challenges that affect practical issues on the national agenda and legal concerns.

As David Ben-Gurion put it, "The convenient solution of separation of church and state, adopted in America not for reasons which are anti-religious but on the contrary because of deep attachment to religion and the desire to assure every citizen full religious freedom, this solution, even if it were adopted in Israel, would not answer the problem."[30]

The fact that Israel is a Jewish state does not mean that fundamental Jewish values and traditions, while influential, necessarily dictate the values and laws of Israel. It does not mean that Jewish citizens are automatically granted additional rights. It also does not mean that the Jewish religious laws are established as the law of Israel. Nevertheless, fundamental Jewish values may be seen in the

---

25 *Id.*
26 *Id.* at 6.
27 *Id.* at 5.
28 *Id.* at 6.
29 *Id.* at 5.
30 See David Ben-Gurion, Nezah Yisrael, 154–155.

Declaration of Independence of the State and in the 1992 Basic Laws regarding human rights.

Israel is justified as a place of the Jewish people for three primary reasons: (1) the 1947 Partition Plan which allowed for the establishment of the State of Israel as a Jewish State; (2) the internationally recognized right to self-determination; and (3) international mores which indicate that a democratic system does not necessarily mean state neutrality in a national perspective.

Specifically, the majority view in Israel is that in order to have self-determination, Israel must maintain a decisive Jewish majority. This is viewed as necessary because, without the Jewish majority in a Jewish state, the Jewish people would be unable to preserve self-determination. It is also viewed as necessary based upon the various disputes in which the Jewish people, and Israel as a nation state, find themselves—specifically, the continuing Jewish-Palestinian dispute. While maintaining self-determination for the Jewish citizens is an important function of the State of Israel, this is not the only function; Israel is vested in its entire citizenry.

The interests of the Jewish people as a national-cultural group are realized through a variety of benefits: the Law of Return (allowing for preference for Jews in entry to Israel), special measures to continue the Jewish values and traditions in public life, state provisions for religious services, and maintenance of close ties with the Jews of the Diaspora.

The role that Jewish law plays in the Israeli legal system is unique; state mechanisms are not used to enforce individual performance of religious precepts. Besides the law of personal status, religious law lacks the same status as legally enforceable Israeli state law. The state enforces norms that come from religious commandments. This is such that Israeli public life will maintain the Jewish fundamental values and traditions, to promote societal goals, and to avoid offending religious sensibilities. One way in which the State of Israel enforces these norms is by its involvement with religious rituals and services, for example, by it maintaining religious holy sites and ritual bath sites.

The Israeli legal system has allowed the State to regulate activities as they relate to religious rituals. For example, women may be exempt from the obligatory military service because of religious conviction, men with beards (for religious reasons) may be provided with special gas masks, and even when "summer time" is established may be affected by certain religious needs. The Israeli Supreme Court ruled that, "considerations pertaining to the observance of commandments, as such, cannot be countenanced in the actions of the administration, except to the extent permitted by law; however considerations of the person as such, and when appropriately balanced, are certainly acceptable ... the underlying foundation of the balance lies in the rule that it is possible, and even obligatory to take account of the person, or the interests of a certain section of the population, provided that it does not lead to the coercion of commandments on another person."[31]

Various statutory bodies have been established in Israel that provide religious services to the Jews in Israel: the Council of the Chief Rabbinate of Israel and the Chief Rabbis, town rabbis, and religious counsels under the Jewish Religious Services Law. These bodies are vested with sovereign power in providing these services.

The Council of Chief Rabbinate has two Chief Rabbis, four town rabbis, and ten rabbis who are elected by the Electoral Assembly (eighty rabbis and seventy public representatives—including heads of councils, members of Knesset, and government appointees). The Electoral Assembly also appoints the two Chief Rabbis who act as President of the Council and as President of the Rabbinical Court of Appeals for five years in each position. The Council provides religious services to the religious public. The legal power granted to the Council authorizes them to give answers and expert opinions in halakhic matters, to give *kashrut* certificates, and to determine competency for the position of town rabbi. Finally, the Council also acts as advisors to the government on halakhic questions and this advice is subject to judicial review.

The role of the Council of Chief Rabbinate was at issue in the *Shakdiel*[32] case when the Supreme Court overturned the Council's decision about the halakhic position on the competence of women to serve in the religious councils. The Court found that Council's role is limited to the provision of services only and does not require any religious halakhic decision regarding the services themselves. The Court continued by finding that, under both state and religious law, there is nothing preventing the appointment of a woman as a member of the Council of Chief Rabbinate. Specifically, the Court disagreed with the Council's position that women cannot be appointed to public positions; the Court held this an inaccurate and incomplete representation of the halakhic position, which was further established by a number of halakhic experts (rabbis) who disagreed with the Council's position. Also at issue in *Shakdiel* was whether a nonorthodox individual could be appointed as a member of the religious council. When local authorities are going to appoint an individual to a religious council, they must consider two factors: (1) the composition of the religious council in comparison to the composition of the local authority and (2) a test of personal

---

31 H.C.J 217/80 *Segal v. The Minister of Interior*, 34(4) P.D. 429 (Hebrew), para 108 to Justice Barak's judgement.

32 H.C.J 153/87 *Shakdiel v. Minister of Religious Affairs*, 42(2) P.D. 221 (1988).

suitability—meaning that a person must take a positive attitude to religious matters. The Court held that "the disqualification of a candidate for reasons relating to his worldview, such as his affiliation with a non-orthodox stream, constitutes illegal discrimination and will be rejected." Notwithstanding the rulings in *Shakdiel*, the Council of Chief Rabbinate does not always accept the decisions of the Court.

Another system of religious courts are the Rabbinical Courts which gain their authority under the Rabbinical Court Jurisdiction Law. This law provides the Rabbinical Courts with exclusive jurisdiction over all matters related to marriage and divorce of Jewish people in Israel. It also provides the Rabbinical Courts with concurrent jurisdiction for any case that is related to divorce, such as maintenance (e. g., alimony). Finally, the law provides the Rabbinical Courts with concurrent jurisdiction for any other matter agreed upon by the parities that relate to personal status and inheritance.

The Rabbinical Courts follow Din Torah (Jewish religious law), but the Israeli general court system occasionally reviews Rabbinical Court decisions. This happens when the general court system finds that there is a substantive issue raised in the matter such as equality of women, best interest of children, or violations of natural justice.[33] The Rabbinical Courts, when at odds with the general court system, regularly will not recognize the general court system's authority or decisions.

Due to the special position of religion in Israel, there have been a number of substantive legal rights afforded so as to preserve the Jewish culture and character of public life. Some of these legal rights infringe upon individual rights of freedom of religion, freedom from religion, freedom of occupation, and freedom of movement.

It is a balancing act between legal rights of the individual and the position of religion; this is often referred to as the status quo. So as to preserve the status quo, authorities are given the power to operate in accordance with religious considerations. The status quo is—and was—created as a political compromise before the establishment of the state by leaders of all sectors of Jewish political groups. This status quo is involved in areas such as educational autonomy, marriage and divorce, *kashrut* in governmental offices and institutions (including the army), and observance of the Sabbath and days of rest. Over time, the influence of the status quo has declined due to political developments. Specifically, attempts to formalize the status quo in the legislature or the framework of the

---

33 See e. g. H.C.J 10736/07 *Ploni v. The Rabbinic Court of Appeals* (published on Nevo, 21.01. 2008).

Basic Law have failed. The status quo was based on Founding Fathers Agreement. [34]

Individual freedom may be restricted by a government authority in order to nurture the Jewish character of public life; such laws are allowed to take "considerations of religious traditions." Under this guise, regulations have occurred related to the Matzot Law, 1986, which disallows the public display of any leavened product for sale or consumption during Passover; the Pig-Raising Prohibition Law, which disallows the raising or keeping of pigs and the selling of pork or pork products for consumption; and the prohibition of businesses being opened on the Sabbath.

These regulations are subject to judicial review under the Basic Law: Freedom of Occupation and Basic Law: Human Dignity and Liberty. The general court system has narrowly interpreted these provisions, but has not invalidated any of the regulations. As an example, when interpreting the opening of business on the Sabbath, the Court found it a "coercively formulated statutory provision, which ... to protect the interests of the religious public, to prevent damage to the character and spirit of the day of rest ... when any statute is intended to restrict or impair an individual rights, its interpretation must be appropriately narrow."

In the case of the *Solodkin*[35] judgment, the general court system judicially reviewed provisions restricting human rights on the basis of religious considerations. There the Court held that there needed to be a balance between offending religious conscience and protecting freedom of conscience and freedom of occupation. The issue at hand was the powers of the local authorities to prohibit the sale of pork in their geographic boundaries. The Court held that the local authorities must consider two factors: (1) the appropriate protection of the feelings of the offended residents and their percentage of the population and (2) whether there was a relatively close and accessible location where pork and pork products could be purchased. The Court stated, "In a mixed settlement, in which there is even a minority whose freedom would be abridged if the sale of pork and its products is prohibited, it is imperative to ensure that the violation of their freedom is proportional. This condition is satisfied if there are arrangements to ensure that there is a place in the settlement (even in its outskirts)— or nearby, in which one can purchase and sell pork and its products ... It must ensure that the selling point is accessible and that it is actually possible to maintain a location for the sale and purchase of pork products in that place." Basically the Court found that the local authority had discretion to pro-

---

34 See Chapter 11 for a detailed analysis of the Founding Fathers Agreement.
35 H.C.J 953/01 *Solodkin v. Municipality of Beit Shemesh*, 58(5) P.D. 595.

hibit the sale of pork, but that this is not an unlimited discretion; social factors of the local area populace must be taken into consideration.

An additional area requiring State involvement regarding religious services is the behavior in Holy Places. This is because of the large number of holy places for different groups all within the State of Israel. The regulating provision is the Protection of Holy Places Law, 1967, which reads in part that holy places are "protected from desecration and any other violation and from anything likely to violate the freedom of access of members of different religions to the places sacred to them or their feelings with regard to those places." Therefore, each Holy Place must be treated in a manner acceptable to each group that desires to use the Holy Place; if necessary, arrangements must be made to show consideration of the feelings of all peoples visiting the Holy Place.

A question that has been raised necessarily regarding Holy Places is the regulation of permitted forms of prayer in Holy Places. This issue was discussed in the *Hofman* case,[36] in which the issue was the right of a woman's prayer group praying at the Western Wall. The women did not ask that the separation between men and women be removed. However, they did want to carry Torah scrolls, wear *tallitot*, and read out loud from the Torah while there. Many of the individuals praying at the Western Wall found this unacceptable, at least partially due to the fact that these were customs normally exclusive to men. Great disturbance resulted—including physical disturbance. At the crux of the issue was how much consideration must be allowed for the intolerant attitude of a group in society and whether local custom should equal status quo.

The *Hofman* case lasted more than ten years and resulted in multiple judgments. The petitioners were not asking for the State to merely allow them to pray as they desired, but rather were asking for State assistance in forcing their own discriminatory practices upon others.

In the first *Hofman* judgment,[37] in a split decision, the Court found that the women had a right to pray at the Western Wall according to their own custom. It was recommended that the government determine a course of action that would establish the conditions necessary for the petitioners (the women) to pray at the Western Wall in their own customs. The suggested course of action was that the women be allowed to use a site adjacent to the Western Wall, but they rejected this, with Justice Mazza accepting their rejection, in the second *Hofman* judgment.[38] Justice Mazza stated that this recommended course of action contradict-

---

36 H.C.J 257/89 *Hofman v. The Supervisor of the Western Wall*, 48(2) P.D. 265.
37 *Id.*
38 H.C.J 3358/95 *Hofman v. Director General of the Prime Minister Office*, 54(2) P.D. 345.

ed the judgment allowing the petitioners to pray *at* (not near) the Western Wall; he said the government must make arrangements to that point. The case went to yet another hearing where Justice Mazza's finding was basically overturned.[39] The majority found that, when balancing the women's rights to pray at the wall, other people's rights to pray at the wall were in direct conflict. This conflict required a compromise that ultimately resulted in the women having to pray at a site adjacent to the Western Wall such as to not offend other worshippers. It was ruled that a proper place of prayer, adjacent to the Western Wall, must be made for the women within one year.

The *Hofman* case, and its many judgments, showcased a variety of approaches that are available with regard to Holy Places. First is the concept that this sort of case is not appropriate for judicial review. Second is the concept that this is a perfect example of why the status quo is appropriate; it reflects the feelings of the majority. Third, which ultimately was adopted in *Hofman*, was the finding that Holy Places will always require some sort of balancing act so as to best preserve the rights of all individuals who wish to worship at the site and that reasonable alternatives must be provided when appropriate, such as an adjacent prayer site for the women. However, what constitutes a "reasonable alternative" will always be subject to some controversy, depending on the individual points of view and desires.

Because one of the purposes of the State of Israel is to preserve the Jewish people's right to self-determination, Israel necessarily has a special link with the Jewish people in the Diaspora. Israel budgets money for and provides assistance to Jewish communities all over the world. It grants special standing to institutions that officially promote Jewish interests. For example, Section 5 of the World Zionist Organization—Jewish Agency Law, 1953 states "the mission of gathering in the exiles, which is the central task of the State of Israel and the Zionist movement in our days, requires constant efforts by the Jewish people in the Diaspora; the State of Israel, therefore, expects the cooperation of all Jews, as individuals and groups, in building up the State and assisting the immigration to it of the masses of the people, and regards the unity of all sections of Jewry as necessary for this purpose."

National institutions in Israel operate to promote the interests of Jews. Examples are the Jewish National Fund, which helps settle Jews in lands under its ownership, and the settlement department of the Jewish Agency, which creates settlements for the inhabiting of Jews. While these are private organizations, they help perpetuate the goal of the State to maintain Jewish character.

---

39 A.D H.C.J 4128/00, *CEO of the Prime Minister's Office v. Hofman*, 57(3) P.D. 289.

The question is to what extent the national institutions can adopt discriminatory policies based on national-ethnic considerations? This was discussed in the *Kaadan* ruling,[40] which found that the Jewish Agency cannot adopt discriminatory policies (i. e., Jewish-only settlements) when it is creating settlements on lands that were provided to it by the State. In other words, institutions that receive an allocation of state resources, and the State itself, cannot discriminate on the basis of religion and nationality.

In conclusion, Israel was formed so as to be a state for the Jewish people. However, by law, Israel is also the home of all its resident citizens, including the Arab minority. It is a Jewish and democratic state that faces ongoing challenges to balance the traditions, ideals, and values of a Jewish state and a democratic state. It also faces the challenge of ameliorating the tensions that being a Jewish state creates in granting equal civil rights to Arab and other minorities.

4. An Absence of Separation

There is no separation of religion and state in Israel. At the same time, there is no recognized religion in the accepted sense. The peculiar nature of Judaism, both in its being a way of life and not consisting merely of religious dogmas, along with its intermingling of religious and national elements, is not conducive to any separation of religion and State. As Ben-Gurion put it, "The convenient solution of separation of Church and State, ... even if it were adopted in Israel, would not answer the problem."[41]

The integration of religion and state in Israel is visible in many fields, some expressly regulated by statutory law, some relying on a legal regulation. Among them are the exclusive application of religious jurisdiction and religious law in matters of marriage and divorce, the election of the Council of the Chief Rabbinate, the application of a religious test to the Law of Return providing for Israeli citizenship to Jews wishing to permanently reside in Israel, the conduct of religious education financed out of State funds, the prohibition of the breeding of pigs, the observance of *kashrut,* the existence of special bodies for ministering to the religious needs of the population, the prescription of binding provisions on religious matters in the Army, allocations in the State Budget for religious affairs, and the establishment of a special Ministry of Religious Affairs.[42]

---

40 H.C.J 6698/95 *Kaadan v. The Land Management Organization of Israel,* 54(1) P.D 258.
41 Ben-Gurion, *supra* note 30, at 154–155.
42 Shetreet, Reflections, *supra* note 3, at 206.

The population's religious needs are supplied for by authorities established by law (through the religious councils), budgets are allocated for religious purposes, and there is a minister of the cabinet responsible for religious affairs. Religion's involvement in the state's matters is further expressed, for example, by the fact that kosher food is provided for by law in the Israeli Defense Force, the Israeli army, and government facilities, and special orders in the matters of religion were set in the Israeli Defense Force. Many laws are of a religious nature, such as the laws limiting the raising of swine, or the laws forbidding the public showing of leaven ("hamet") during Passover.[43]

In Israel, many religious institutions receive government funding. This funding has multiple sources within the government. Various ministries provide this funding, including the Ministry of Religious Affairs, the Ministry of Education, the Ministry of Internal Affairs, the Ministry of Labor and Welfare, and other ministries that allocate budgets for specific purposes, many of which are ostensibly non-religious, but which indirectly contribute to the development of those religious institutions. The main supporter, however, is still the Ministry of Religious Affairs, whose budget is mostly designated to the ultra-orthodox ("Haredi") educational and social services, religious educational institutions (the "yeshivas"), religious youth movements, religious cultural institutions (institutions that hold Torah lessons for the ultra-orthodox public), and the religious research institutions. A much smaller part of the Ministry's budget is designated for services to the whole public, such as synagogues, the Chief Rabbinate, the religious courts, and cemetery development. It should be mentioned that the religious education system is also supported by the Ministry of Education.[44]

The system of distribution of public funds has been challenged in the Supreme Court. An association named "Ma'ale" appealed to the Court after its request for allocations had been denied. This association was a nonprofit organization whose activity focused on "organizing and maintaining religious services by combining the Torah of the Israeli people, the Israeli nation, the land of Israel and the State of Israel." It requested funding by virtue of the budget section that was concerned with cultural activities for the Haredies. The Supreme Court dismissed the petition. Justice Barak reviewed the legal arrangement and decided that it was valid. The law, according to his reasoning, properly expressed the principle of equality in the distribution of allowances and in the authority's

---

43 Shimon Shetreet, *State and Religion: Funding of Religious Institutions—The Case of Israel in Comparative Perspective*, 13 Notre-Dame Journal of Law Ethics and Public Policy, 421–453, 430 (1999).
44 *Id.*, at 433.

duty to act equitably according to reasonable guidelines and clear, relevant criteria. In his opinion, Justice Barak failed to examine both the actual discrimination in the distributions of allowances and the priority that was clearly given the Haredi institutions. He also dismissed the arguments of the "Ma'ale" association, by determining that the association was not a Haredi one and, therefore, was not allowed to receive the allocations.[45]

5. The Enforcement of Religious Norms

The most difficult problem relating to religious liberty in Israel is the imposition of Jewish religious norms and restrictions of a religious nature on all Jews, whether or not they are religiously observant. To determine whether the enforcement of a norm of religious origin infringes freedom of conscience and religion, a distinction must be drawn between a norm of religious origin which is not generally recognized and adopted by the society and one which is. The enforcement of a norm of the first type—such as the application of religious law in marriage and divorce—involves a violation of religious liberty. The enforcement of a norm of the second type—such as the prescription of a day of rest—does not, for in that case, the enforced norm is treated like any norm, regardless of source, which has been accepted by society, and which the state may enforce through legislation.[46]

In *Izramax* v. *State of Israel*, Justice Silberg distinguished between the "rational" and the "creedal" commandments of Judaism.[47] While the former may, in his opinion, rightly be enforced on the public without prejudicing religious freedom, the coercion of the latter does not offend against that freedom. However, this distinction should not be maintained so strictly. The fact that a religious norm is rational does not justify its compulsion until it has won the social approval required to render it a norm binding upon society. It is possible also for such societal approval to be gained by creedal norms. Ultimately, the test for justifying coercion of norms is the measure of social consent which they have received, and not their content. Justice Agranat held alternatively, that one must find out whether the general public will exert itself to turn the religious norm in question into a norm of socially binding effect.[48] The point is that the test of whether a norm having its source in religion deserves to become a binding one in society cannot be a religious test—namely, its classification as rational or creedal within

---

45 *Id.*, at 434.
46 Shetreet, Reflections, *supra* note 3, at 207.
47 Cr.A 217/68 *Izramax* v. *State of Israel*, 22(2) P.D. 343, 354 et seq.
48 H.C.J 58/66, *Shalit v. Minister of the Interior*, 23(2) P.D. 477 (602).

the Jewish religion—but solely the test of whether it has won contemporary social consensus.[49] Ultimately, the test for justifying coercion of norms is not their content, but the measure of social consent which they have received.

A religious norm may, in its totality, be a positive social norm, but the specific acts involved may not have gained the necessary consensus that would justify coercion. Thus, no one disputes that the introduction of the Saturday day of rest, for all its religious origin, is a positive social norm. However, one should not infer that every restriction regarding the kind of things that may be done on the Sabbath is thereby justified and involves no invasion of religious freedom. Army regulations relating to the Sabbath and the festivals provide that entertainment in army units should be so arranged as to avoid "profanation" of the holiness of the day. Soldiers have thus been prohibited from listening to the radio and recordings in messes and clubrooms on those days. Manifestly, these regulations have nothing to do with the positive norm of a rest day that has social value, but are connected with the religious prescript in Jewish law against "profanation" of the Sabbath day. Nothing, then, can be deduced from the fact that observance of a weekly rest day is a positive norm as regards whether these regulations are, or are not, repugnant to religious freedom. Conversely, a prohibition imposed by a religious norm is not necessarily invalid because although the norm may not have received a majority consensus and, consequently, may not have obtained the imprimatur of a positive norm, the prohibition has itself met with societal approval.[50]

Israeli law is rich in examples of coercion of religious law which has not yet become a positive norm of society. Both the application of Jewish law to marriage and divorce and the subjection of citizens and residents to the exclusive jurisdiction of the religious courts provide examples of an improper coercive enforcement of a religious norm. They entail a serious encroachment upon freedom of religion. The very necessity to marry before a religious authority results in a number of religious restrictions of wider scope. A woman who has left the faith loses property rights. A woman and those guilty of profanation of the Sabbath are incompetent to act as witnesses. An illegitimate child *(mamzer:* a child born to a married woman from a man not her husband) cannot get married ex-

---

49 Even were the distinction adopted, it is not practical nor can it always help to justify the coercion of norms. Justice Silberg himself faced difficulties in explaining the nature of the Sabbath commandment and found in it both "rational" and "creedal" elements intermingled. He also found it difficult to justify the closing of businesses on Jewish festivals and had to appeal to the fact of those festivals being national values. See Cr.A 217/68, *Izramax v. The State of Israel,* 22(2) P.D. 343, 356–358.

50 Shetreet, Reflections, *supra* note 3, at 210.

cept to another illegitimate child. The marriage of a *Cohen* (a member of the priestly caste) and a divorcee is forbidden. In Jerusalem, at least, a bride is compelled to take a ritual bath before her wedding, the wedding must be held in a *dasher* (ritually pure) place, and the wedding may not be celebrated during the bride's menstrual period or within the seven days following it. None of these are to be found in any statute.[51]

In *Rodnitski*, Justice Landau observed that "the enforcement of religious law in marriage and divorce under Section 2 of the Rabbinical Courts Jurisdiction (Marriage and Divorce) Law, 1953 is not actually the same as the full operation of all the halachic rules affecting marriage and divorce …. Section 2 is not to be read as imposing any prohibition which is really religious in origin and substance on the Jewish population of Israel, including those for whom the observance of religious prohibition is not a matter of religious belief."[52] The section "is not intended to offend against freedom of religion guaranteed to all citizens of our State or to impose the observance of religious precepts on the non-religious public. We must adopt an interpretation of the Law of 1953 which avoids such inconsistency with the basic principles of the law of the State."[53]

Because the Army controls the lives of serving soldiers more than the State controls the lives of its citizens, religious norms are enforced on soldiers to a larger extent than they are in civilian life. Army regulations regarding the High Holy Days *(Rosh Hashana* and *Yom Kippur)* provide for obligatory participation in a Spiritual Revival Project conducted by the Army Chaplaincy. In the *Knesset,* the Minister of Defense has explained that this does not involve any assault upon the freedom of conscience and religion, for two reasons. First, the regulations do not oblige any soldier to do anything apart from listening to talks on the values of the Penitential Days and the Jewish festivals. Secondly, the talks correspond to those on other subjects given by Education Officers, where attendance is also mandatory.[54]

A similar problem arises in connection with the study of the Holy Scriptures and the like in State schools. The use of the Bible and other religious literature as "religious instruments" within the compass of prayer or religious preaching is forbidden as being repugnant to freedom of conscience and religion. However, that use is totally different from the use of this literature for teaching "Jewish cul-

---

51 *Id.*, at 211–212.
52 H.C.J 51/69, *Rodnitzki v. The Rabbinical Court of Appeals*, 24(1) P.D 704, 712. There are further grounds for this view, but they lie outside the scope of the present study.
53 *Id.*
54 Shetreet, Reflections, *supra* note 3, at 212

tural values" and inculcating Jewish moral values and their contribution to civilization.[55]

Israel excessively uses state funds from religious institutions for the formal education system, as well as in the formal education and social services. Education systems of religious movements in Israel—"El-Hamaayan" and the "Independent Haredi Education"—tend to have an advantage over the regular education system, as they provide lower or no cost education. The result is that these systems divert students and their families to a Haredi Ultra-Orthodox way of life, competing with the secular way of life. This is not merely a matter of belief, but it results in a structural social change because it causes the exclusion of the student from the work force and regular military service as well as from reserve duty.[56]

6. Analysis of Freedom of Religion in Specific Matters

A. The Right of Marriage

Under the Rabbinical Courts' Jurisdiction (Marriage and Divorce) Law of 1953, marriage and divorce of Jews in Israel will be carried out in accordance with the laws of the Torah.[57] Other religious communities have a similar legal situation.[58]

The Supreme Court has been instrumental in establishing a broader right of marriage by including recognition of registration of civil marriages performed abroad, and recognition of private marriages of individuals whom, according to Jewish law, are forbidden from marrying one another.[59] The Supreme Court has also upheld private marriages for those whose marriages are required to be religious by Jewish law: namely, Cohen with a convert, a widow, or a divor-

---

55 State Education Law, 1953, Section 2: "The object of State education is to base elementary education in the State on the values of Jewish culture and the achievements of science, on love of the homeland and loyalty to the State and the Jewish people."

56 13 Notre-Dame Journal of Law Ethics and Public Policy, at 421–422.

57 Shetreet, *supra* note 12, at 11. See also Section 2 of the Rabinnical Courts' Jurisdiction Law of 1953.

58 *Id.* at 12.

59 See H.C.J 143/62 *Funk-Schlesinger v. Minister of Interior*, 17(1) P.D. 225 (1963); C.A 566/81 *Shmuel v. Shmuel*, 39(4) P.D. 399 (1985); See also, for example, Family Court Appeal 23464–10–09 *A' S' v. D' S'* (published on Nevo, 06.10.2011), in which a "chained woman" (*aguna*) was awarded 700,000 NIS for the refusal of her husband to give her a certificate of divorce (*get*) for over 30 years.

cee.[60] Those that are forbidden to be married have seen some legal remedies in the Supreme Court. In 1975, Professor Aharon Barak, then the Attorney General, looked into the legality of lists of individuals who in the view of the Chief Rabbinate were forbidden to marry, according to Jewish law. In his legal opinion, Barak determined that the lists of persons forbidden to marry were compiled without any evidentiary foundation, and were therefore illegal. He concluded that compilation of the lists had to be regulated in such a way as to permit the right to be heard to individuals on the lists. He set up a bureaucratic mechanism by which the addition or deletion of names from the lists could be properly supervised. These rules were hardly complied with. The result was that two decades later, when this author assumed the office of Minister of Religious Affairs, he had to deal with the list of disqualified for marriage, and had to initiate a process, conducted by Chief Rabbi Bakshi Doron, to clear almost 5,000 out of 5,200 names from those lists.[61]

B. Kosher Rules

In 1992, the Basic Law: Freedom of Occupation was passed. The Knesset's enactment of this Basic Law made a positive contribution toward enhancing civil rights in matters of religion in general, and restrictions placed for *kashrut* reasons in particular. The subject came up for judicial discussion in the *Mitral* case, in which a suit was brought by a meat importer who had been issued a permit to import non-kosher frozen meat. At the time, there was no relevant Knesset legislation on the books; the issue was regulated by the Minister of Industry and Trade and the government, which used the Import-Export Ordinance to implement its decisions and policies. The High Court of Justice, responding to a petition brought by the Mitral Company, determined that the government's refusal to grant an import permit was inappropriate, since it stemmed from religious considerations that were extraneous to the Import-Export Ordinance. In passing, Jus-

---

60 See H.C.J 130/66 *Segev v. Rabbinical Court*, 21(2) P.D. 505 (1967).

61 Shimon Shetreet, The Good Land Between Power and Religion, at 265–274 (Hemed Yediot Achronot, 1998); An example of the Supreme Court provding remedy to those who are forbidden to marry under Jewish Law can be seen in C.A 10280/01 *Yarus Hakak v. Attorney General*, 59(5) P.D. 64 (2005) in which a lesbian couple was permitted to mutually adopt each other's children; See also H.C.J. 3045\05 *Ben Ari and others v. Director of Ministry of Interior Population Registry* (21.11.2006) the Supreme Court ruled in a 7 Justices decision that same sex marriage performed overseas can be registered in the population registry provided that an official certificate is presented to the registering officer.

tice Orr noted that any legislation stipulating that imported meat had to be kosher would restrict freedom of occupation, in contravention of the restriction
clause in the Basic Law: Freedom of Occupation. This meant that such legislation
could only be passed in the Knesset by a 61-member majority, as stated in Section 7 of the Basic Law.[62] The Knesset subsequently passed an amendment to the
Basic Law: Freedom of Occupation, ratified on March 9, 1994. The new Section 8
permits overriding the restriction clause of the Basic Law by law or according to
law by a 61-member vote in the Knesset, and which expressly states that it shall
be in effect, notwithstanding the provision of this Basic Law; such law expires
four years from its commencement. In line with the amendment, the Knesset
passed the Import of Frozen Meat Law, 1994.[63]

C. Civil Burial

Until the 1990s, the Minister of Religious Affairs and the Israel Lands Authority,
by invoking a laissez faire approach, avoided processing requests for burial permits and allocation of land for civil burial.[64] This changed with the *Menucha Nechona* case. The petitioners sought a secular burial. The Supreme Court agreed
and said through Justice Shamgar that the petitioner deserved to receive a burial
license posthaste from the Minister of Religious Affairs, as well as land to be allocated by the Israel Land Administration (ILA). At this point in time, Justice
Shamgar declined to intervene any further, since both the Minister of Religious
Affairs and the ILA informed the High Court of Justice that they were prepared
to satisfy the petitioner's requests on principle. The meaning of Justice Shamgar's declaration was recognition by the judiciary of the citizen's right to secular
burial.[65] This right was further promoted by the Alternative Civil Burial Act of
1996, passed during this author's term of office as Minister of Religious Affairs.
Also, lands were given to a number of civil burial societies to facilitate the opening of alternative civil cemeteries. However, the provision of civil burial sites remains generally limited.[66]

---

62 See H.C.J 3872/93 *Mitral, Ltd. v. Prime Minister and Minister of Religious Affairs*, 47(5) P.D. 485
(1993).
63 Shetreet, *supra* note 12 at 12.
64 *Id.*
65 *Id.* at 13; See H.C.J 397/88 *Menucha Nechona v. Minister of Religious Affairs* (published on
Nevo, 31.12.1988).
66 Shetreet, The Good Land, supra note 61, at 275–293.

D. Conversion

The issue of the validity of conversions was first addressed by the judicial branch in the *Miller* case,[67] in which the petitioner had completed the conversion process in the United States and received a conversion certificate from the Reform movement. The Minister of Interior decided that under the "nationality" entry on the petitioner's Israeli identity card, the word "converted" would appear alongside the word "Jew." The High Court of Justice ruled that according to the Population Registry Law, 1965,[68] data pertaining to national and religious affiliation must be recorded in accordance with the declaration made by the citizen himself, as determined by Section 19b of the law. The registry clerk had no authority to add any data that is irrelevant to the subject at hand. The result was that the court ruled that the petitioner should be listed in the population registry as a Jew, without notation of the word "converted."

Under the *Shas Movement v. Director of the Population Registry Authority*[69] case, the High Court further strengthened the legal principle that the conversion of an immigrant would be recorded in the population registry in accordance with his or her own declaration and may be accompanied by a document verifying the conversion, if necessary. Additionally, it makes no difference whether the conversion is Orthodox, Conservative, or Reform in order to be valid.[70] That being said, the court has left the ideological question of conversion to the legislature by defining only what conversion is not and not defining what conversion is in precise parameters.[71]

---

67 Shetreet, *supra* note 12 at 13; See H.C.J 230/86 *Miller v. Minister of Interior,* 40(4) P.D. 436 (1986).
68 See 19 L.S.I. 288.
69 See H.C.J. 264/87 *Association of Torah-Observant Sephardim—Shas Movement v. Kahane—Director of the Interior Ministry Population Registry,* 43(2) P.D. 723 (1989).
70 See H.C.J 1031/93 *Pesaro v The Minister of Interior,* 49(4) P.D. 661 (1993). According to Shamgar, in interpreting the Religious Community Ordinance (Conversion), one must also take into account the principles of equality and freedom of conscience and religion. Therefore, the Ordinance should be interpreted according to its narrow meaning, so that it does not rule out recognition of non-Orthodox conversion in Israel for the purpose of registration.
71 Shetreet, *supra* note 12 at 12. The result is that while the *Pissaro* case determined what the Religious Community Ordinance (Conversion) "was not"—that its jurisdiction did not extend beyond matters of personal status—it did not determine what it "was." It did not delineate the precise parameters of what constitutes conversion in Israel. The ruling made it clear that "what it was" had to be determined by the legislature.

E. Status of Religious Court Judges

A short while after Israel's establishment, the government initiated legislation with the aim of regulating the function and status of religious court judges in the legal system. As a result of this initiative, the Knesset enacted the Rabbinical Courts' Jurisdiction (Marriage and Divorce) Law, 1953.[72] However, this law has a weakness: aside from the specific jurisdiction invested in the religious court judges by the law, it leaves their status as clergymen unclear. The courts have since stated that religious court judges' role are equivalent to that of a general court judge. Therefore, religious judges are bound by the same rules as normal judges in that they hold judicial positions and the norms of the judicial system apply to them.[73]

Despite the court rulings, existing legislation in Israel does not fully regulate the status and the authorities of the religious courts. The deficiency of the existing legal arrangements is their lack of clarity regarding the status of the halachic bodies and the question of whether they are permitted and authorized to act in a capacity that extends beyond the powers determined in the framework of the legislation.[74]

F. Transportation and Commerce on the Day of Rest

Under the Traffic Regulations, 1961, based on the Traffic Ordinance, the government authorized the Central Road Sign Authority to instruct local road sign authorities regarding the determination, modification, cancellation, or maintenance of traffic arrangements. This has led to road closures on the Jewish day of rest and closing sections of roads in highly religious communities during prayers at local synagogues.[75] These regulation decisions have been upheld in a number of instances.[76]

The contention between the religious and secular publics regarding the closure of streets on the Sabbath becomes more acrimonious when the street under

---

72 *Id.* at 15. See 7 L.S.I. 139.
73 See H.C.J 732/84 *Tzaban v. Minister of Religious Affairs*, 40(4) P.D. 141 (1986).
74 Shetreet, *supra* note 12 at 15.
75 *Id.* at 16.
76 *Id.* See H.C.J 174/62 *League for Prevention of Religious Coercion v. Jerusalem City Council*, 16(4) P.D. 2665 (1962); H.C.J 531/77 *Baruch v. Traffic Commissioner of Tel Aviv and Central Districts—Central Road Sign Authority*, 32(2) P.D. 160 (1978).

discussion has a mainly ultra-Orthodox population, but serves as a main traffic artery through the city. One such example is Jerusalem's Bar-Ilan Street.[77]

In the *Bar-Ilan* case, two committees recommended closing the road while the Sabbath and holiday prayer services are in progress. The first committee was headed by Elazar Shturm. Its recommendations regarding the closure of the street during prayer hours sparked fierce opposition from secular circles, which petitioned the High Court of Justice against implementation of the recommendations.[78] The High Court of Justice avoided making any decision on the matter, and recommended the appointment of a public committee to fully investigate the matter. The High Court of Justice suggested that the makeup of the committee reflect the variety of opinions and perspectives on religious-secular relations in Jerusalem and its environs. The committee's recommendations would be taken into consideration by the government authorities in formulating an overall policy on the transportation issue, including Bar-Ilan Street. A hearing on the petition was postponed for two months in order to permit the committee to complete its work. During this period of time, the High Court of Justice issued an interim order that Bar-Ilan Street would continue to be open to traffic without limitation.

In the wake of the High Court of Justice's recommendation, the Minister of Transport appointed a second committee, headed by Tzvi Tzameret. This committee also recommended closing the road during hours of prayer, while ensuring a transit arrangement for the secular public in the framework of the existing status quo. In addition, the Tzameret committee recommended that an agreement be reached vis-à-vis the opening of other streets to traffic on the Sabbath. Based on the recommendations of the Shturm and Tzameret committees, the Minister of Transport decided to close Bar-Ilan Street during prayer hours on the Sabbath and holidays. During such times, the nearby Ramot Road, the entry road to Jerusalem, and Jaffa Road would remain open to traffic.

Based on these cases, it is clear that the issue of traffic arrangements on the Sabbath depends on the character of the community and its particular traditions.[79]

---

77 Shetreet, *supra* note 12 at 17. See Don-Yehiya, *The Politics of Accommodation: Settling Conflicts of State and Religion in Israel,* 1997, pp. 50–51.

78 H.C.J 5016/96, 5025/96, 5090/96, 5434/96, *Horev v. Minister of Transport,* 51(4), P.D. 1 (1997).

79 Shetreet, *supra* note 12 at 17. See Don-Yehiya, *The Politics of Accommodation: Settling Conflicts of State and Religion in Israel,* 1997, pp. 48.

G. Developments in the Protection of Religious Liberty: The New Era of Basic Laws

There are two Basic Laws which are of significant importance to religious liberty: Human Dignity and Liberty and Freedom of Occupation.[80] These two Basic Laws have provisions which place limits on future Knesset legislation through a restrictive clause. The clauses limit religious factions from being able to push through laws which bypass the High Court of Justice's rulings on religious freedom.[81] That being said, religious factions have been able to take advantage of amendments to the Basic Laws which allow the Knesset to pass a law that is contradictory to the guaranteed rights of the Basic Laws if passed by a 61-member majority.[82] This amendment is a step back from the passage of the Basic Laws which create constitutional rights for the State of Israel. Ultra-Orthodox circles regularly feel threatened by the guarantees in the Basic Laws; they seek many political avenues to negate and bypass the Basic Laws as they find them restricting on the existing religious arrangements in the state.[83]

H. Impact of the Jurisprudence of the Supreme Court on the Protection of the Freedom of Religion

The Judicial Branch has been the chief contributor to enhancing religious civil rights. There are numerous examples of favorable judicial rulings by the Supreme Court that have contributed toward enhancement of civil rights in matters of religious practice. For example, the court has recognized marriages of Israeli residents performed abroad as well as private ceremonies of individuals forbidden to marry;[84] the court ruled that issuance of *kashrut* certificates by the Chief Rabbinate would be carried out solely in accordance with the "hard core" of the halachic laws; and the court struck down municipal bylaws that forbade the sale of pork.[85] The Supreme Court also recognized the right to alternative burial, years

---

80 *Id.* at 19.
81 *Id.*
82 *Id.*
83 *Id.* at 20.
84 *Id.* See State Comptroller, Annual Report for 1990, No. 40.
85 See H.C.J 117/55; 72/55 *Siegfried Avraham Fraidi v. Tel Aviv-Jaffa Municipality and others, Shmuel Mendelsson v. Tel Aviv-Jaffa Municipality*, 10(2) P.D. 734 (1956).

before the Knesset set this right into law.[86] The Supreme Court also clarified that the Chief Rabbinate, religious court judges and rabbinical courts, are public bodies and are subject to the rule of law and the judicial review of the High Court of Justice.[87] In the *Kaplan* case, the Supreme Court ruled that public television could operate on the Sabbath.[88] It developed that the Supreme Court also played a primary role in defending the status of female members of public religious bodies.[89]

In spite of the generally positive trend whereby Supreme Court rulings enhanced the quality of civil rights in matters of religious practice, there are also cases in which the Supreme Court hesitated to intervene, preferring to leave the decision in the hands of other bodies. One example is the issue of conversion. When the question of recognition of Reform conversion performed in Israel was brought before the High Court of Justice, a majority of the justices preferred to defer the ideological task of determining the sum and substance of conversion in Israel.[90] Another example of the Supreme Court's hesitancy to rule on issues pertaining to rights in matters of religion is the *Bar-Ilan Street* case. As noted, the Supreme Court at first avoided ruling on the matter and, instead, recommended the establishment of a public committee to study the issue.[91] The Supreme Court also avoided handing down any clear decision on the issue of drafting yeshiva students, when the question again came up before it in 1997.[92] The Supreme Court justices determined that the present-day arrangement was unreasonable, but they avoided taking the next step of declaring the arrangement null and void.[93]

---

86 See H.C.J. 397/88 *Menucha Nechona v. Minister of Religious Affairs* (published on Nevo, 31.12. 1988).

87 Shetreet, *supra* note 1 at 20; See H.C.J 732/84 *Tzaban v. Minister of Religious Affairs*, 40(4) P.D. 141 (1986); H.C.J 3269/95 *Katz v. Jerusalem Regional Rabbinical Court* 50(4) P.D. 590 (1996). The case involved the issue of a writ of denial by the rabbinical court against an individual who refused to have his civil matter be adjudicated by the rabbinical court in accordance with the terms of a complaint filed according to the Torah code.

88 See H.C.J 708/69 *Adi Kaplan v. Prime Minister and Broadcasting Authority*, 23(2) P.D. 394 (1969).

89 Shetreet, *supra* note 12 at 21; See H.C.J 153/87 *Shakdiel v. Minister of Religious Affairs*, 42(2) P.D. 221 (1988); H.C.J 953/87 *Poraz v. Tel Aviv-Jaffa City Council*, 42(2) P.D. 309 (1988).

90 Shetreet, *supra* note 12 at. See H.C.J 1031/93 *Pesaro v The Minister of Interior*, 49(4) P.D. 661 (1993).

91 See H.C.J 5016/96, 5025/96, 5090/96, 5434/96, *Horev v. Minister of Transport*, 51(4), P.D. 1 (1997).

92 See H.C.J 3267/97 *Rubinstein and others v. Minister of Defense* 52(5) P.D. 481 (1998).

93 Shetreet, *supra* note 12 at 21.

I. State Funding of Religious Institutes

Government funding for religious institutes varies by department. The main supporter of religious institutes is the Ministry of Religious Affairs, whose budget is mostly designated for the ultra-orthodox (Haredi) educational and social services, the religious educational institutions (the yeshivas), religious youth movements, the religious culture institutions (which are institutions that hold Torah lessons for the ultra-orthodox public), and the religious research institutions.[94]

In the past, the government included in the Budget Law a list by name of the sums allocated to religious institutions. This caused a great deal of controversy and was amended in an attempt to more equally distribute an inclusive sum to support every category of public institutions. Unfortunately, the amendment still allowed for unequal distribution within categories and the discrimination persisted.[95]

J. State and Religion in Israel: Challenges and Problems

Religion is involved in state matters in many ways.[96] This situation causes a continuous debate. There are scholars who claim that the lack of separation results in the absence of "freedom from religion," which is, as described above, a fundamental value in a democratic state, and in the system of fundamental civil rights.

Thus, all citizens in Israel is subject to the authority of religious institutions in matters of marriage and divorce, even against their will.[97] There is no civil alternative for religious marriage. The situation creates difficulties, especially when religion forbids the marriage of a couple (such as in the case of a divorced

---

94 For the numerical review, see: S. Shetreet, *The Good Land between Power and Religion* (Tel-Aviv, 1998), at page 230.

95 *Id.*

96 Shetreet, *supra* note 12 at 23. Examples of religious involvement include: Kosher food in governmental organizations, laws of a religious nature involving raising of swine and the public showing of leaven in Passover. See Swine Growing Prohibition Law (1962) and the amendment to this law from 1990; Matzoth Holiday Law [Hametz Prohibition] (1986). In this subject of religious legislation, see: A. Shaki "Religious Legislation—For and Against," 7 *Tchumin* (1986) 521–525 (Hebrew).

97 The Rabbinical Courts Jurisdiction Law [Marriage and Divorce] (1953) apply to all Jewish citizens and residents by the "'Halachah of Israel Religious Law Criteria," even despite their will. About religious marriage, see: P. Shifman, "State Recognition of Religious Marriage: Symbols and Content," 21 *Isr. L. Rev.* 501 (1986).

woman and a "Cohen"), but also in the case of a secular couple that refuses to marry in a religious ceremony.[98] This legislature's choice of an exclusive form of religious marriage violates freedom of marriage, but also freedom from religion, because it obliges the couple to get the services of a religious agency in its most intimate hour.[99]

Furthermore, the deprivation of the freedom from religion, which results from the lack of separation, can be found in the subject of the "Sabbath" (Saturday), the day of rest, and especially concerning the issue of opening businesses on the Sabbath. The Government, which was supported by a coalition also composed of religious parites, advanced an amendment to the Municipalities Ordinances,[100] that in fact reversed the court's decision, and allowed the municipalities to forbid businesses from opening on the Sabbath.[101] This development in the law has shown that the lack of separation between law and religion enables the legislature, influenced by political considerations to command the support of the religious parties in the Knesset, to diminish the civil rights and freedom from religion.

---

98 In the matter of marriage and the democratic right for civil marriage and divorce, see: Y. Berlin, "The Judaism and Israel as a Democracy," *Secular Humanistic Judaism* (1988) 2, 4–7 (Hebrew).

99 See: P. Shifman, *Who is Afraid of Civil Marriage?*, (Jerusalem, 1995) (Hebrew); S. Shetreet, "Freedom of Conscience and Religion: The Freedom from Coercion of Religious Norms, The Compulsory Recourse to a Religious Authority and Imposition of Religious Restrictions," 3 *Mishpatim* 467 (Hebrew).

100 See Cr. P (Jerusalem) 3471, 3472/87 *State of Israel v. Kaplan*, 1988(2) P.D. 265. The court overruled a bylaw allowing the closing of businesses on the Sabbath. In reaction to this law, the above-mentioned amendments were passed by the Knesset.

101 The Municipalities Order Amendment Law (No. 40), 1990. However, the municipalities usually do not force the law in this field and, by this, allow the opening of cinemas and restaurants in Saturday. See: S. Shetreet, *Between the Three Branches of Government—The Balance of Rights in Matters of Religion in Israel*, (The Floersheime Institute for Policy Studies, Jerusalem, 1998) at pages 25–26 (Hebrew).

Chapter 11:
The Historical Roots of Israel as a Jewish and Democratic State: The Founding Fathers Agreement of 1947

The Jewish character of the State of Israel, being the homeland of the Jewish people, has always been the center of constitutional discourse. This element was recognized in the Balfour Declaration 1917[1] and in the text of the British Mandate in Palestine in 1922[2] given by the League of Nations to Great Britain when it was made the Mandatory Power in Palestine after the First World War. The definition of the area of the Mandate, Palestine, Eretz Yisrael, as the homeland of the Jewish people has dual meaning. On the one hand, "Jewish" means the Jewish people as an ethnic group. On the second hand, "Jewish" means Jewish religious as well. The discourse on the Jewish character of the State of Israel began long before the establishment of the state, going back to the emergence of the Zionist Movement. The matter has become a focal issue involving the international community, led by the United Nations after the end of the Second World War. Over the years, Israel developed a consensus regarding its Jewish cultural and national identity. Following the commitment made in the Declaration of Independence of Israel, 1948, and after important jurisprudence of the Israeli Su-

---

1 The words found in the Balfour Declaration, of Arthur James Balfour to Lord Rothschild, are "His Majesty's Government view with favour the establishment in Palestine of a national home for the Jewish people, and will use their best endeavors to facilitate the achievement of this object, it being clearly understood that nothing shall be done which may prejudice the civil and religious rights of existing non-Jewish communities in Palestine or the rights and political status enjoyed by Jews in any other country."

2 See full text of the British Mandate for Palestine, available at http://www.jewishvirtuallibrary. org/jsource/History/Palestine_Mandate.html (accessed February 9, 2017), and see particularly the preamble which reads in part as follows:

Whereas the Principal Allied Powers have also agreed that the Mandatory should be responsible for putting into effect the declaration originally made on November 2nd, 1917, by the Government of His Britannic Majesty, and adopted by the said Powers, in favor of the establishment in Palestine of a national home for the Jewish people, it being clearly understood that nothing should be done which might prejudice the civil and religious rights of existing non-Jewish communities in Palestine, or the rights and political status enjoyed by Jews in any other country; and Whereas recognition has thereby been given to the historical connection of the Jewish people with Palestine and to the grounds for reconstituting their national home in that country; and Whereas the Principal Allied Powers have selected His Britannic Majesty as the Mandatory for Palestine;

DOI 10.1515/9783899497946-012

preme Court, Israel defined itself in the two Basic Laws of 1992 as a "Jewish and Democratic State." In both the Basic Law: Human Dignity and Liberty and the Basic Law: Freedom of Occupation, it is stated that Israel is committed to the "values of the State of Israel as a Jewish and Democratic State."[3] The two Basic Laws also include a provision that basic human rights will be respected in the spirit of the principles in the Declaration of the Establishment of the State of Israel.[4]

The historical roots of the state of Israel as a Jewish and Democratic State were shaped in 1947. David Ben-Gurion, Itzhak Grinboim, and HaRav Fishman in fact signed a Founding Fathers Agreement—a decision to uphold the Jewish character of the state. The agreement was signed by virtue of a decision of the Executive of the Jewish Agency. This agreement was more than just a political agreement with only historical importance. It played a more important role in the analysis of the constitutional history of Israel, shaping as such the Jewish character of the state. It should play a role in legislative debates and judicial proceedings as an interpretive tool of a higher constitutional standing than any other political agreement.

This chapter suggests that the Founding Fathers Agreement should be acknowledged as the beginning of Israel's constitutional history on the issue of law and religion as well as cultural and national identity. It should be recognized as having constitutional significance when making judicial decisions or shaping legislation in these matters. Since its establishment, and even before in its lead up to become a state, the state of Israel has aimed to be a society in which its heritage plays a part in its future. This chapter aims to analyze the developments leading to the signing of the Founding Fathers Agreement, normally referred to as the "Status Quo Letter" of 1947. The chapter will detail how the decisions made by the founding fathers of Israel regarding its heritage should influence the legislative policies in Parliament and the legal decisions made in the courts today.

The opening section of this chapter examines the historical role of religion in the different political sectors of the Zionist Movement: the socialist and secular Zionists; the general Zionists; and the religious Zionists (Mizrahi). The second section analyzes the development leading to the formulation of the consensus in the leadership of the Jewish Agency and then the signing of the agreement between the three main Zionist streams, with the non-Zionist group, Agudat Israel.

---

3 Section 2, Basic Law: Freedom of Occupation; Section 10, Basic Law: Human Dignity and Liberty.
4 Section 1, Basic Law: Human Dignity and Liberty, Section 1, Basic Law; Freedom of Occupation.

This agreement is called the Status Quo Letter of 1947. We argue that the real nature of this agreement is not just a political agreement but also, in fact, it is a Founding Fathers Agreement having constitutional importance. Later, this chapter examines the social challenges of the State of Israel in its formative years regarding its efforts to carry out its task of ingathering the exiles.

The chapter then compares the definition of cultural and religious identities in other jurisdictions such as the European Union.

1. The Historical Role of Religion in the Zionist Movement

The Zionist Movement began at the end of the 19th century. The first Zionist congress was held in 1897 in Basel, Switzerland. As a result, the saying goes "In Basel I created the Jewish State."[5] At its beginning, the movement was a secular one. They wanted to create a new kind of Jew. David Green, later to be known as David Ben-Gurion and his colleagues in the Zionist leadership, thought that to establish a Jewish State, the Zionist movement had to be disassociated with anything to do with the diaspora. This included the religious lifestyle, which was a main characteristic of the shunned diaspora of the past.[6]

A considerable dispute formed in the world of Halachic Jewish Law regarding the right path to take with the growing Zionist movement. The radical circles of ultra-orthodox Judaism refused to reconcile themselves with the secular character of any potential state. They refused to accept the fact that a Jewish state could be a product of human, rather than divine, efforts. These extreme ultra-Orthodox groups think of Zionism in general, and the State of Israel in particular, as a blatant violation of the pledge of loyalty that the people of Israel took on themselves to await the end of days when the Messiah comes once again to have their own rule in the Land of Israel.[7] "Agudat Yisrael" was the political group of the ultra-orthodox sector.

Mainstream ultra-Orthodox Judaism considered the State of Israel to be a religiously neutral phenomenon that existed only within the secular realm, as a geopolitical event of the exile period. A Jewish State's establishment could be

---

5 Amnon Rubinstein, *From Hertzl to Rabin and Further*, 14 (2000).

6 *Id.*, at 20 – 21.

7 A. Ravitzky, *Messianism, Zionism and Jewish Religious Radicalism*, 1993, p. 29.For background on ultra-orthodox political parties, see Rebecca Kook, Michael Harris, and Gideon Doron: *In the name of G-D and Our Rabbi: The Politics of the Ultra-Orthodox in Israel*, Israel Affairs 5 (1998), p. 1– 18.

neither pure nor impure; it could only be a historical phenomenon with no negative or positive religious elements.

The essential part of their dispute with the State of Israel concerned the question of the secular nature of the country. The dominant approach among most ultra-Orthodox circles today is that they are willing to recognize the State of Israel in practice, but will not recognize the secularity of the Jewish state. Representatives of the ultra-Orthodox sector can cooperate with the state institutions on a qualified, pragmatic basis, but reject the national ideology and identification that goes along with it. They are willing to cooperate with the state, but only on an ad-hoc basis. If the state uses its institutions and its budgets to support yeshivas and Torah institutions, it will be judged in a positive light. But if, in turn, the state alienates itself from the world of Torah, it will be judged in a negative light.[8]

With the purpose of realizing their Zionist dream based on socialist and secular ideals, members of the Zionist Movement settled in Palestine. The legal reality, however, caused the leaders of the movement to realize the need for a change in ideology as to what needed to be represented by the movement.

The legal regulation of the Ottoman Empire, and after that of the British mandate, was based on the religious affiliation of every individual. Based on his or her religious identification, the regime would enforce personal family laws that applied to his or her community, including personal status, marital, divorce, inheritance, and guardianship laws. There were already elected institutions, recognized by the authorities, that were responsible for providing communal services to various population groups, on the basis of religious identification. "Knesset Israel" was one such institution. As a result, during the lead up to the establishment of the state, the leaders of the movement understood that they could not disassociate the movement from its Jewish heritage. This secular movement had to modify itself to involve a certain religious perspective, and they had to include their religious background to fit in with the legal reality of their new home.[9]

---

8 *Id.*, pp. 200–225, and also D. Schwartz, *The Theology of the Religious Zionist Movement*, 1996. For further reading into the tensions between the religious anti-Zionist stream and the Zionist Movement, see Chapter 10 of Hertzl, footnote 1.

9 Shimon Shetreet, *Between Three Branches of Government: The Balance of Rights in Matters of Religion in Israel*, p. 169 (The Floersheimer Institute for Policy Studies 2001 (from now on, Shetreet, Three Branches). See also Zvi Triger, "Freedom from Religion in Israel: *Civil Marriages and Cohabitation of Jews Enter the Rabbinical Courts"* (also published in 27 Israel Studies 1 (2012): http://papers.ssrn.com/sol3/papers.cfm?abstract_id=2102460 (accessed February 9, 2017); Yuksel Sezgin, "The Israeli Millet System: Examining Legal Pluralism through Lenses of Nation-

In addition to understanding the need for including a Jewish heritage in its platform, the leaders of the movement also understood that they had to adapt from a completely socialist movement to a constructive socialist movement. The labor movement, led by David Ben-Gurion, aspired to build the Jewish nation based on socialist beliefs. It was its belief that having property ownership as the rule of law tears nations apart. Only the victory of the working class could help rebuild the inner tiers of a society; Ben-Gurion believed that the only way to achieve national unity would be with the working class winning the class warfare.[10] The labor party worked hard at the beginning to achieve its socialist ideals; led by Ben-Gurion, it did not rest on empty words.

The problem came with the realization that, in the Land of Israel in the 1920s, there was no class system to fight against. There was no capitalist market, no substantial private ownership, no bourgeois, and no proletariat—just a land empty of the defining features of any capitalist or socialist society befitting a European nation. Socialist definitions and ideals from a different place could not be used to define the reality of what was happening in Israel at that time. The party leadership understood that there was a need for allowing private ownership in order to actually build up the nation and work on the state when it came to be. The need for raising funds for the settlers of the Land of Israel, building up a proper workforce, and dealing with the different financial needs of the upcoming nation was a bigger problem to be dealt with, bigger than the war fought against property ownership, because anyone who owned property was practically non-existent.

The energy of the movement turned towards more constructive horizons. The historical experiment of constructive socialism took place, an idea that a socialist state can be built from the ground up, while using the country's national funds.[11]

Building and Human Rights," 43 Israel Law Review 631 (2010); Shimon Shetreet, *Justice in Israel*, (Martinus Nejhoff, 1994) chapter 3.

10   Arieh Yaadi, *With No Alternative*, p. 578.

11   Reuven Shoshani, *Anatomy of the Socialist Criticism of Jabotinski, Part 2: Review of the Socialist Consideration in the World and in Israel*, at 87. See also Arieh Yaadi, *supra* note 10, at 579. In addition to what David Ben-Gurion thought the state of Israel should look like, before the establishment of the state, Jabotinsky also thought that the main focus of Zionism should be the establishment of a Jewish majority, and on that to make the state of Israel, thereby solving the problem for the European Jewry. One of the most efficient ways to do that was to take a bourgeois attitude, meaning to state clearly the preferred and special class of the bourgeois in the Jewish settlement, and to protect this totally and completely, as an integral part of the Zionist system. Jabotinski wanted to build the state from the top down, whereas David Ben-Gurion wanted to build the State from the ground up. These two ideas fought against each other, with the

The religious sector then joined the Zionist movement. This religious Zionist stream, Mizrahi, was led by Rabbi Fishman Maimon. It believed that Halacha does not just allow them to take part in the Zionist movement, but obligates them to participate. They built their theories on the basis of the ideas of "The Beginning of the Redemption," afterwards called "The Redemption." They became a central and inseparable force of the Zionist movement. The Zionist leadership actually hoped it would be able to use the Mizrachi movement as a means of bringing the religious public closer to the Zionist vision. Even if that at first meant the religious-Zionist vision, the assumption was that the religious would contribute to the Zionist effort, or at the very least not harm it by joining an anti-Zionist lobby that would weaken the movement's show of unity vis-à-vis the British government and the rest of the international community.[12]

The third and final stream that joined the Zionist movement was the general Zionist group, led by Itzhak Grinboim, who was acting for the Jewish Agency executive council.[13]

2. The Developments Leading to the Status Quo Letter:

In June of 1947, an investigative committee from the United Nations Special Committee on Palestine, UNSCOP, came to visit to inspect the proposed establishment of the State of Israel. Their recommendations later led to the Partition Plan to divide Palestine between Jews and Arabs. It was very important for the Zionist Movement leaders to present a united and consolidated front in the name of the entire Jewish Community (*Yishuv*) in Palestine to the committee.[14]

The big fear was that the ultra-Orthodox sector would publicly disagree with Ben-Gurion, or even defy the need for the establishment of the Jewish State. In addition to the fear that once again the fate of the Jews hung in the balance, with any wrong act on the part of the movement potentially bringing about its doom, Ben-Gurion decided that a compromise was needed in order to earn the political support of the ultra-Orthodox sector.[15]

---

idea of constructive socialism—that a socialist state can build itself up from its foundations using national funds. For further reading, See Shoshani, *Id*, at Chapter 4.

12 Shetreet, Three Branches, *supra* note 9, at 71.

13 Rubinstein, *supra* note 5, at 268.

14 Shetreet, Three Branches, *supra* note 9, at 70.

15 Shimon Shetreet, *The Good Land Between Power and Religion*, 170 (1998 Yedioth Ahronot, Hemed Books) (from now on: Shetreet, The Good Land).

The three different schools of thought towards Zionism acted together as the leadership of the Jewish Community in Palestine. They had to find a way in which they could compromise about the potential establishment of the Jewish State, as well as find a way to assuage Agudat Yisrael's doubts about the secularity of the future Jewish state. They decided among themselves what the Jewish character of the state should look like. Acting as the Executive board of the Jewish Agency and the Jewish Community in the land of Israel, they took the decision that there would be full recognition of freedom of religion and conscience for everyone, regardless of their religious affiliation. They together decided that in the future Jewish state, four central matters would be executed; they would be recognized by the state:

- The days of rest for the Jewish people would be the Jewish Sabbath and the Jewish holidays (other communities would keep their own days of rest).
- Government facilities would serve only kosher food (according to Jewish dietary laws).
- Marriage and divorce of Jews would be conducted according to Jewish religious law.
- Those who so desired would be entitled to religious education.

After the executive of the Jewish settlement in Palestine had made its decision, they worked together on the text of the letter to Agudat Yisrael, stating explicitly their decision to make the obligation for the Jewish character of the state.

The text of the letter is self-explanatory. They expressed their decision that the Jewish State would have a public Jewish lifestyle, based on traditional Jewish matters that had followed the Jews in the Diaspora for their term of exile:

"From: The Jewish Agency for Palestine, etc.

"To: The World Organization of Agudath Israel, etc., Jerusalem

"Dear Sirs,

"The Agency's Executive has learned from its chairman of your requests concerning guarantees on matters of matrimony, Shabbat, education, and *kashrut* in the Jewish state, once it is established in our days.

"As you were informed by the Chairman of the Executive, neither the Agency's Executive nor any other body in the country is authorized to determine the law of the Jewish state in advance. The establishment of the state requires the approval of the United Nations, and this is impossible unless freedom of conscience in the state is guaranteed to all its citizens, and unless it is clear that there is no intention of establishing a theocratic state. The Jewish state will also have non-Jewish citizens, Christians and Muslims, and, evidently, it will be necessary to ensure in advance full equal rights to all citizens and the absence of coercion or discrimination in matters of religion or in any other matter.

"We were satisfied to hear that you understand that there is no body authorized to determine in advance the constitution of the state, and that the state will be, in some spheres, free to determine its constitution and regime according to its citizens' wishes.

"Still, the Executive appreciates your demands, and is aware that these are matters that worry not only the members of Agudath Israel, but also many of the religious faithful in all Zionist parties or in no party, and it is sympathetic to your demands that the Agency's Executive inform you of its position regarding the issues you have brought up, and what it is willing to do, as far as its influence and directives reach, in order to fulfill your wishes regarding the said issues.

"The Agency's Executive has authorized the undersigned to formulate its position regarding the issues you have mentioned at the meeting. The position of the Agency's Executive is as follows:

"A. Shabbat. It is clear that Shabbat will be the legal day of rest in the Jewish state. Permission will naturally be given to Christians and to those practicing other religions to rest on their weekly day of rest.

"B. Kashrut. All means should be pursued to ensure that every state-run kitchen for the use of Jews serve kosher food.

"C. Marital Law. All the members of the Executive appreciate the seriousness of the problem and the grave difficulties pertaining to it, and all the bodies represented in the Agency's Executive will do whatever possible to satisfy the deep need of the religiously observant in this matter, lest the House of Israel be divided in two.

"D. Education. Full autonomy will be guaranteed to every education network (incidentally, this policy already exists in the Zionist Federation and Knesset Yisroel) and the state will not infringe on the religious philosophy or the religious conscience of any part of the Jewish people. The state will naturally determine the minimum requirement of compulsory studies in Hebrew language, history, science, and so forth, and will supervise this minimum, but will allow full independence to each network to educate according to its outlook and will avoid any injury to the religious conscience.

"Sincerely,

"On behalf of the Jewish Agency Executive, D. Ben-Gurion, Rabbi Y.L. Fishman, Y. Grinboim."

Exemptions from the army service were granted for yeshiva students in 1948, after the establishment of the State. Initially, only about 300 exemptions were granted. Throughout the years, however, the number of army exemptions given to yeshiva students has risen exponentially. This brings up modern issues for the State of Israel with the burden of army conscriptions for Israel's secular and non-Charedi (i.e. religious Zionist sector in Israel). In the defining judgement of the Israeli Supreme Court,[16] it was claimed that the law for deferment of army service for yeshiva students is unconstitutional, for violating the principle of equality. It was expressed, by non-yeshiva students, that: a) they feel like they are solely responsible for the national security of Israel; b) only they are suf-

---

16 H.C.J 6427/02 *The Movement for Quality Government v. The Knesset*, 61(1) P.D. 619 (2006).

fering the loss of life as a result of the continuous struggles that the IDF is involved in on a daily basis, in addition to forced conscription encumbering their constitutional rights to autonomy over their own lives; c) they are being treated unfairly with inequality as opposed to the Charedi people of their age, who are not forced to enlist in the IDF, in a way that is even consistent with hurting their constitutional right to human dignity.[17] This contemporary issue comes as a result of army exemptions granted at the establishment of the state. The issue came up again before the Supreme Court after what is referred to as the "Tal Law", which was aimed at introducing equality in military service.[18]

Additionally, the obligation made to provide Jewish education causes a contemporary issue concerning core studies and what the Charedi community is required to teach their students. In 2008, a law was passed that allowed Charedi communities an exemption from learning the core studies of mathematics, English, sciences, and the social sciences, while other schools were not granted this exemption.[19] This causes an even bigger rift to be formed between the Charedi community and the rest of the country, as they are held further apart by not being taught what the rest of the country defines as core studies—studies that are mandatory to be taught in order to become a part of society. This issue came up before the High Court, and the Court decided not to compel core studies on Charedi community (i.e. the ultra-Orthodox).[20]

After receiving the letter from the executive management of the Jewish settlement, Agudat Yisrael understood that the only practical way that they could strengthen their position in the future State was to cooperate with the Zionist movement on a purely pragmatic basis.[21] The spiritual leaders of the ultra-Orthodox community avoided publicly airing their own opinions regarding an halachic state, or their opinions opposing the establishment of the state, and even advised Agudat Israel to avoid any public expression of support or opposition, so that they could not be accused of sabotaging the establishment of the state, while at the same time preserving the influence they might be able to wield when the state came into being.

---

17 For further reading about the problems caused by the inequality of the burden of conscription, read H.C.J 6427/02 *The Movement for Quality Government v. The Knesset*, 61(1) P.D. 619 (2006).

18 H.C.J 6298/07 *Ressler v. Knesset of Israel* (published on Nevo, 21.02.2012) (Hebrew).

19 The High Court asked to impose core studies on Haredi Schools. http://www.haaretz.com/print-edition/news/high-court-asked-to-impose-core-studies-on-haredi-schools-1.290548 (accessed February 9, 2017).

20 H.C.J 3752/10 *Rubinstein v. The Knesset* (published on Nevo, 17.09.2014).

21 Shetreet, The Good Land, *supra* note 15, at 172.

Each representative, from the secular Zionists to the Ultra-Orthodox, had to make a compromise. As a result of the letter to Agudat Yisrael, representatives of all the population sectors signed the Declaration of Independence, forming the national consensus that is considered one of the basic principles of the state.

This letter that was written was also effective in legitimizing the religious Zionist stream into the Zionist Movement, leading to a strong alliance between the socialist Zionists and the moderate religious Zionists, who were led by HaRav Maimon.[22]

This commitment manifests itself in Israeli legislation, in governmental decisions, and in many other facets of Israeli life. Based on the obligation made by Ben-Gurion and company to uphold a public Jewish lifestyle, the Knesset, after it was first established, enacted legislation ensuring that Jewish tradition would be observed in public life. Laws that marriage, divorce, and *kashrut* in governmental institutions would be in accordance with religious law were adopted. Subsequent laws were legislated forbidding the raising of pigs, establishing the Sabbath as a day of rest for Jews, and setting guidelines for both the selection of Chief Rabbis and the establishment of religious councils to furnish religious services to the Jewish public. The system of governmental religious arrangements was based on a philosophy that the Jewish character of the state had to be maintained in the fields of marriage, divorce, days of rest, and education. Army exemptions for yeshiva students were also part of the fresh legislations.[23]

Ben-Gurion did not separate religion from state. Some commentators believe he did not do so because he wanted to control religion and use it for his own needs. He believed that by funding it and integrating it into the secular system, he would be able to weaken the forces of religion in Israel and gain control over them. Some commentators have even claimed that Ben-Gurion did not need to

---

22 For an analysis of the thesis of Prof. Friedman on the relationship between Ben-Gurion and the Agudat Israel movement, see, for example, M. Friedman, "The Status Quo History: Religion and State in Israel," in Filovski, Ed; *The Transition from Yishuv to State* (Haifa, Herzl Institute, 1991), pp. 48–79. See also on Agudat Israel and the Zionist movement: Y. Fund, *Separation or Participation: Agudat Israel, Zionism and the State of Israel* (Jerusalem, Magnes Press, 1999), N. Horowitz, "The Haredim and the Supreme Court: Breaking the Framework in Historical Perspectives," Kivunim Hadashim, Oct. 2001, pp. 22–78. This alliance between the Zionist Socialist Movement led for many years by Ben-Gurion and the Religious Zionist Movement was preserved even after the establishment of the state, and what had been the Hapoel Mizrachi Movement evolved over the years into the National Religious Party, Mafdal, which maintained a well-known alliance with Mapai until 1977.

23 Barak Erez, "Law and Religion under the Status Quo Model; between Past Compromises and Constant Change," Carduzo Law Review, Vol. 30, Issue 6, June 2009, pp. 2495–2508. (from now on Barak Erez, Law and Religion)

compromise with Agudat Yisrael, as he already had enough support without them to make a united and strong front before UNSCOP. His fears for a new subsequent loss of the Jewish people were maybe exaggerated.

Ben-Gurion himself may have realized that he should have separated religion and state. In a conversation a few months before his passing away, in his home in Sde Boker, he stated that he made a mistake in not separating religion from state; he observed he would have succeeded in doing so if he had wanted to, as he had succeeded in all the other activities he had done. But since the Jewish character of the state has been set in stone, and religion has not been separated from the state, questions of the relationship between religion and democracy have arisen in the State of Israel.[24]

3. The Historical Challenge of Ingathering the Exiles: Separate and Together

In the first decade or so, Israel absorbed hundreds of thousands of immigrants, fulfilling the Zionist dream that the State of Israel is the Jewish homeland for all the Jewish people. David Ben-Gurion believed that it was the duty of the State of Israel to bring about the "ingathering of the exiles." Accordingly, he even decided to decrease the defense budget in order to divert scarce resources to immigrant absorption.[25]

In spite of the generally positive attitude towards ingathering the exiles from all corners of the world, the actual integration of all the new immigrants posed serious challenges to Israeli society. Democratic issues arose since the beginning of the state. For example, it took many years until a non-Ashkenazi judge was appointed to the Supreme Court of Israel. Ben-Gurion was dedicated to the universal values of justice and equality, and took an active part in convincing the judiciary to make such an appointment, of a Sephardi judge.[26]

Ben-Gurion, himself a native of Russian Poland, was a firm believer in the "melting pot" theory. He sought to integrate immigrants from Diaspora Jewish communities from all over the world. Ben-Gurion did not strive to achieve a balanced blend of independent autonomous cultures of the different Diaspora com-

---

24 The Good Land, *supra* note 15, at 173.
25 Shimon Shetreet, *Reflections on Citizenship and National Identity in Europe and Israel*, Isr. J. Foreign Aff. 115, 117 (2011) (hereinafter: *Reflections*).
26 See Shimon Shetreet, *Justice in Israel: A Study of the Israeli Judiciary, supra* note 9.

munities. On the contrary, he wanted to create a modern Israeli identity that would be shared by all Israelis, irrespective of their origin.

Especially controversial were selective policies adopted by the government in relation to Sephardi immigrants, policies that sparked massive protests by the immigrants themselves. For example, in 1959, during Ben-Gurion's tenure as Prime Minister, riots erupted in Haifa, becoming the first popular social protest staged by North African Jews in Israel.[27] Social protests continued for years, with the Black Panthers[28] during Golda Meir's reign as Prime Minister, as well as social unrest igniting the Tents Movement, focusing on the housing problems.[29] Later, there was the establishment of the Tami Party, led by Aharon Abuhatzira, and subsequently the establishment of the Shas party, which is still a significant political force that currently holds no less than eleven seats in the Knesset. Shas was led first by Yitzhak Peretz, then Arieh Deri, then by Eli Yishay, and now again be Arieh Deri, all with North African roots, continuing the social protests of North African immigrants. Its spiritual guide, former Chief Rabbi Ovadia Yosef, is a native of Iraq. These social protest groups sometimes sought redress from the Supreme Court.[30]

It can be said that the long line of protest movements led by the Jewish immigrants from North Africa contributed to the democratization of Israel's social discourse and agenda. It created pressure on all political parties to respond to social issues and to appoint Jews from non-European countries to public offices and nominate them for elected positions. These social protest movements also greatly contributed to the passing of legislation and public policies that gradually built a modern welfare state with an advanced social safety net.[31]

---

27 See "The Wadi Salib Inquiry Report 1959" (Etzioni Report), in Shimon Shetreet, *Halutzim Bedim'a* [Hebrew] (Tel Aviv, 1991), pp. 225 – 239; see also Moshe Etzioni, "Retrospective Reflections on Wadi Salib Events," in Shetreet, *Halutzim Bedim'a*, op. cit., pp. 240 – 243.

28 This name was adopted from the Black Panthers in the United States, but the Israeli movement had no real connection with its American namesake.

29 Shimon Shetreet, Reflections, *supra* note 25, at 118 – 119.

30 For the case, see H.C.J 407/80 *Azar Cohen v Minister of Interior and Police Administration*, 34(4) P.D. 477. Also, see additional case of H.C.J 1/81 *Vicki Shiran v Broadcasting Authority*, 35(3) P.D. 365 (1981). In both cases this author represented the petitioners.

31 Shimon Shetreet, Reflections, *supra* note 25, at 119.

4. Implementing the Founding Fathers Agreement: The Heritage of Israel and Other Matters

The commitment to upholding the Jewish character of the state continued throughout the years after the establishment of the State of Israel. The Declaration of Independence refers to the Jewish character of the State, as well as the historical links of the State of Israel to the Jewish people, to Jewish history, and to the Jewish spiritual heritage. The framers of the Declaration of Independence worked on its wording until moments before the declaration ceremony. The wording eventually reflected the compromise formula which had begun with the letter of the Status Quo on the Founding Fathers Agreement.

The concluding sentence of the Declaration reads "Out of faith in the Rock of Israel we attach our signature on this Declaration." The use of the phrase "the Rock of Israel" was a compromise between the secular and the religious. Members of the Provisional Court of the State, just an hour before the Declaration ceremony, broke out in disagreement over the phrase "Out of faith in the Rock of Israel." Claims were made that this wording forced the signatories to proclaim against their wishes their belief in God. In defense of the phrase, David Zvi Pinkas argued that it united the majority of the people of Israel. Ben-Gurion was in favor of the "Rock of Israel" version.[32]

The final wording that was accepted was: "Out of faith in the Rock of Israel, we hereby affix our signatures as witnesses to this declaration, at the session of the temporary state council that took place in the homeland, in the city of Tel Aviv, this day, Sabbath eve, the fifth of Iyar 5708, May 14, 1948."[33]

This line of compromise continued over the years, and it is also embodied in legislation with the Foundations of Law Act, 1980.[34] This law determined that when the judiciary is unable to reach a decision through interpretation, analogy, or inference of the existing law, the court must invoke the legal "principles of freedom, justice, equity, and peace of Israel's heritage".

The wording of the phrase itself constitutes a compromise solution between those who preferred a direct reference to Jewish law and those who categorically

---

32 Although the phrase "Rock of Israel" was used as a compromise between the secular and religious parties to the decision to use it, after looking at the source of this phrase, Psalm 19:17 of the Old Testament of the Bible, in which God is referred to as the "Lord, my Rock and my Redeemer," it is clear that this phrase has more religious significance than not. In religious terms, "Rock" means God, who protects the Jewish people and is the center of their faith, which is immutable.

33 Z. Sharf, *Three Days: 12, 13, 14 of May 1948*, 1965, pp. 214–226.

34 34 L.S.I. 181.

vetoed any such reference. The phrase "heritage of Israel" refers to the sum total of Jewish cultural values, and not necessarily to their narrower meaning from Halachic, Jewish Law. Section 1 of the Foundations of Law Act, 1980, was eventually passed with the following wording: "Should the court consider a legal question that requires resolution, and the solution is not to be found in the existing legislation, judicial precedent, or by means of analogy, the court will resolve the question in the light of the principles of freedom, justice, equity, and peace of Israel's heritage."

The question was left to the judiciary. In the majority in the deciding case,[35] Justice Aharon Barak was of the opinion that it is permissible to refer to Jewish law in order to learn, as a sort of treasury of legal thought which might provide inspiration to the judiciary. The reference here is to "law" in its cultural meaning, rather than its normative meaning. In Justice Barak's view, Jewish law refers to the universal values which can be drawn from the Jewish tradition. It exists for the purpose of providing a comparative legal system from which to draw inspiration if the judge so desires, not a legal system that the judge is bound to.

Alternatively, Justice Elon, expressing the minority opinion, considered that the "law" refers to Jewish law in order to clear up any uncertainties as to its own content, not the universal values that can be derived from it. Jewish law may not constitute a binding body of laws, but it can provide guidance to the court regarding the issue that it faces.[36]

Later on, the description of Israel as a Jewish and Democratic state first appeared in Basic Law: Freedom of Occupation and Basic Law: Human Dignity and Liberty, within the attempt to extend the protection of individual rights in Israeli law.[37]

The Declaration of Independence defined the state as Jewish, but did not explicitly make the reference to the term "democratic" as well. It refers to democratic values in the third chapter of the declaration, that "complete equal social and political rights will be granted to all of its citizens without discrimination of religion, race or gender."[38] Since the above-mentioned Basic Laws, the courts have had to discuss the question of the Jewish and democratic character of Israel because decisions have to be made on questions that are directly related to the formula of how these two attributes interrelate.

---

35 C.A 546/78, *Kupat Am Bank Ltd. v. Handles*, 34(3) P.D. 57 (1980).
36 Shetreet, Three Branches, *supra* note 9, at 73.
37 *Id.*, at 66.
38 Id.

Generally speaking, the Israeli Jewish public today can be divided into four primary groups on the question of attitude toward religion. When the status quo letter was written, even the secular public was closer to a religious lifestyle, with most secularists exposed to tradition in their childhoods, while most of population, regardless of religious belief, were willing to compromise and accept the religious aspects in public lifestyle for the sake of national unity.[39] Today, approximately 43 percent of the public describe themselves as completely secular, with no religious belief, and see the religious aspects of the public lifestyle of the country as a burden and a sacrifice. Approximately 15 percent describe themselves as religious. Seven percent of the public describe themselves as ultra-Orthodox. The remaining 30 percent consider themselves traditional. The traditional Jews, like their religious observant contemporaries, respect and uphold the Jewish tradition, but are opposed to religious coercion. They observe tradition out of a sense of obligation to the customs of the forefathers and the history of the Jewish people, but there is no rigid approach to observance. The traditional Jews may be described as Jews who adopt conscious freedom of choice in the observance of Jewish law and religion, and have certain freedoms that the religious Jews do not allow themselves. They might be described as people who on Sabbath morning go to pray at the Orthodox synagogue, while in the afternoon drive by car to the soccer field. The traditional Jews keep kosher in their home, build a sukkah, and observe the customs of mourning as prescribed by Jewish custom.[40]

While the courts must discuss the question of the Jewish and Democratic characteristics of the State of Israel, and the relationship between them, there are different opinions as to what the relationship should be between the Jewish and Democratic elements of the State.[41]

In order for the courts to try to make positive contributions to civil rights in the matter of religious practice, the "Jewish" component of the Jewish and democratic state needs to be more clearly defined. In order to achieve a social cohesion that benefits the whole of society, it is necessary to find as wide a common denominator as possible between the different sectors in Jewish society.[42]

There is obviously not one formula that all parties can agree upon; in most cases, it is not possible to settle ideological arguments in a way that satisfies all

---

39 Barak Erez, Law and Religion, *supra* note 21, at 2499; See also Gutman Study on Religious Attitude and Identity, available online at: http://m.ynet.co.il/Articles/4180860 (accessed January 23, 2017).

40 Shetreet, Three Branches, *supra* note 9, at 67.

41 *Id.*, at 66.

42 *Id.*, at 67.

sides. On the social level, this objective can be achieved only through cooperation and partnership between the moderate elements of society—traditional and
religious public, which recognizes Judaism's important role in shaping the cultural face of the State of Israel—and the liberal secular public, which, while respecting Jewish tradition and maintaining a close cultural link with the Jewish
historical heritage, also values democracy and civil rights.[43]

As long as the courts must decide on legal issues according to the Jewish
and Democratic elements of the Basic Laws, they must bridge the gap between
the groups that are willing to accept compromise and reconciliation with the dif-
fering schools of thought on what is the "Jewish" component of the Jewish Democratic State.

What is needed is an approach that accepts "the heritage of Israel" and its
precepts, for example, *kashrut* in its basic meaning. It is crucial to find an interpretation that recognizes the cultural and religious importance of the Jewish
Law, without spreading beyond that limit and without affecting the religious
freedoms and, just as important, without the freedom from religion and the freedom of conscience for all sectors of society.[44]

5. Comparative Aspects: The EU Model—Humanist and Religious Inheritance

In the course of European Union (EU) efforts to adopt a constitution, a very intensive debate took place on how its religious identity should be defined. The
late Pope John Paul II suggested making "reference to the religious and, in particular, the Christian heritage of Europe."[45] Another suggestion was to "recognize
the openness and ultimate otherness associated with the name of God," and a
third was to note that the EU was "characterized by a spiritual impulse always
present in its heritage."[46]

Eventually, the draft constitution was rejected because France and the Netherlands did not approve it in their referenda. Later, in 2009, the EU adopted the
Lisbon treaty, the preamble of which clearly stated that the EU drew "inspiration
from the cultural, religious and humanist inheritance of Europe, from which

---

43 *Id.*, at 67.
44 *Id.*, at 79.
45 COMECE—Commission des Episcopats de la Communauté Européenne.
46 Draft Constitution: http://news.bbc.co.uk/2/shared/bsp/hi/pdfs/09_01_05_constitution.pdf
(accessed February 9, 2017).

have developed the universal values of inviolable and inalienable rights of the human person, freedom, democracy, equality and the rule of law.[47] Clearly, the Israeli approach is similar to that of the European Union and there are parallels between the debate in Israel on the Jewish and democratic character of the state and the need to preserve the "heritage" of Israel and the present debate in Europe on the adoption of the notion of the "cultural, religious and humanistic inheritance of Europe."[48]

Israel adopted the model of a Jewish and democratic state and the recognition of the heritage of Israel. This is a clear parallel to the formulation in the Lisbon Treaty of 2009. It is clear from all of this that there are parallels between the debate in Israel on the Jewish and democratic character of the state and the need to preserve the "heritage" of Israel and the debate in Europe on the adoption of the notion of the cultural, religious, and humanistic heritage of Europe. In the end, the EU adopted in the Lisbon treaty the formula: humanistic and religious inheritance.[49]

Canada chose to address the issue of its religious heritage in a different way. The Canadian Charter of Rights and Freedoms, adopted into the Constitution of Canada in 1982, governs the relationship between individuals and the government, ensuring that the legislative branch cannot pass laws that infringe unfairly on citizens' rights and freedoms. The Charter states outright that Canada is founded upon principles that recognize the supremacy of God and the rule of law.[50] Contrary to the system in Israel and Europe, the Canadian Charter has no qualms explicitly mentioning its connections to God and its religious connections. This manifests itself in a different way than it does in Israel. Israel's heritage, as stated before, still plays an extensive role in judicial decisions; questions involving the nature of the Status Quo agreement and the Jewish character of the State still make it difficult for the judiciary to decide between the Jewish and democratic elements of the state.

As a result of globalization, and the increase in migration of whole or partial populations of different religions and cultures becoming a widespread phenomenon, modern societies now are very rarely homogeneous. They almost always include communities of different religions and cultures. In most instances of migration to other regions, there is a dominant majority community alongside a minority community. Even societies that in the past have had a more homogeneous

---

47 Lisbon Treaty—The Preamble; available at: http://www.lisbon-treaty.org/wcm/the-lisbon-treaty/treaty-on-european-union-and-comments/preamble.html (accessed February 9, 2017).
48 *Id.*, Initial Draft Constitution.
49 Lisbon Treaty—The Preamble, *supra* note 47.
50 The Canadian Charter of Rights and Freedoms, 1982.

character have in recent decades been compelled to accept people of different cultures into their midst due to economic and social developments. This is true of former colonial powers that admitted people from their own overseas possessions, as well as of countries that needed foreign workers to supplement their work force. The massive influx into Europe of displaced persons from Syria, as a result of a civil war there, as well as the illegal immigrants from Africa via Libya, causes a major challenge for Europe.

These developments present a major challenge to modern societies, the members of which must formulate an attitude toward people of different cultures and religions within their own society. This includes the recognition of the other's religion, customs, educational needs, and language. This proves a difficult task, as communities are reluctant to abandon the religion and culture, from which they derive their own identity, and to tolerate and accept people of other cultures and religions. For their part, the immigrant populations sometimes refuse to integrate into the majority host community.[51]

In William Kymicka's book, *Multicultural Citizenship*, the right to culture is akin to the right to freedom, but a cultural right should only be granted when it contributes to autonomy of the individual. In other words, these rights should not be granted to groups which violate the autonomy given to them by host communities.[52] This is part of the negative aspects of migrating populations that refuse to integrate into the communities that host them. The majority society should be allowed to limit the requirements for minority groups to migrate to their countries if they stand to breach the liberal rights of the majority.

In recent times, these negative sides have received considerable publicity in Europe. Along the same lines as Kymicka, German Chancellor Angela Merkel stated in 2010 that multiculturalism has failed and that immigrants must make more efforts to integrate into German culture and society.[53] British Prime Minister David Cameron expressed the same sentiment. In February 2011, in a speech in Munich, he questioned the success of state multiculturalism. This new attitude toward immigrants is not without foundation and must be taken into consideration in discussions on immigration.[54]

---

51 Shimon Shetreet, "On Citizenship and National Identity in Europe and Israel," The Israel Journal of Foreign Affairs, pp 115–124 (2011).
52 Will Kymlicka, *Multicultural Citizenship: A Liberal Theory of Minority Rights*, 52 (1995).
53 Tom Heneghan, "Analysis: Germany Holds Inflamed Debate on Islam and Migration," Reuters.com, October 18, 2010, http://www.reuters.com/article/idUSTRE69H36U20101018?page Number=1 (accessed February 9, 2017); "Merkel Says German Multiculturalism Has Failed," Reuters.com, http://www.reuters.com/article/idUSTRE69F1K320101016 (accessed February 9, 2017).
54 *Id.*

In his February 2011 speech in Munich, Prime Minister Cameron openly called for a reappraisal of European policy:

> "Frankly, we need a lot less of the passive tolerance of recent years and much more active, muscular liberalism... Let's properly judge these organizations [Muslim groups]: Do they believe in universal human rights—including for women and people of other faiths? Do they believe in equality of all before the law? Do they believe in democracy and the right of people to elect their own government? Do they encourage integration or separatism? These are the sorts of questions we need to ask. Fail these tests and the presumption should be not to engage with these organizations."[55]

Modern society can increasingly be expected to apply these criteria to evaluating the role of newcomers in their midst. The issue of citizenship is especially important in the Israeli context. In Israel, national identity has to do with the definition of the character of the state of Israel as a Jewish and democratic state.

Recent events in the Arab World have only exacerbated the problem and accelerated the flow of illegal immigration to Europe. Europe as a whole is facing challenges due to the change in population. This change in population raises issues of a cultural nature, including the donning of headscarves, hijabs, and burkas; ritual slaughter of animals; building minarets of mosques; and the issue of integration in the general communities, as well as certain cultural groups advocating discrimination against women or barring women from the work force.[56]

6. The Status Quo Letter Is A Founding Fathers Agreement:

The Executive of the Jewish Agency was in fact the official leadership of the majority of the Jewish community before the establishment of the state of Israel. It is our opinion that the agreement they made should be considered as a Founding Fathers Agreement, basing strong constitutional links to what the Jewish component of the state should be. This kind of agreement is different from what is known in the United States as the Federalist Papers. There, eighty-five essays were published anonymously in New York newspapers from 1787 to 1788, in an attempt to convince its inhabitants of the advantages to be obtained by ratifying the new Constitution. The idea for these papers was the brainchild of Alexander Hamilton, with John Jay and James Madison contributing several of the essays. The essays proved to be very popular, and were turned into a book

---

55 See http://www.bbc.co.uk/news/uk-politics-12371994 (accessed February 9, 2017).
56 Shimon Shetreet, *Reflections, supra* note 25, at 7.

called *The Federalist* in the spring of 1788, still anonymous.[57] These essays were about the need for a union and a powerful national government, the inadequacy of the Confederation, and last, the rationale that the Constitution would give additional security to liberty and property.[58] The power of *The Federalist* stems not only from its effect on American society the year it was written, but from its effect on the course of events as a uniquely authoritative commentary on the new American Constitution of 1789; the essays are a great source of political theory.[59] But the Federalist Papers are a commentary on the constitution of the United States of America, indicating the original intention of the American Founding Fathers.

Although the Federalist Papers are of high importance, they are not like the Founding Fathers Agreement of Israel. The Founding Fathers agreement should be viewed much more than the Federalist Papers of the United States of America, which although taken into consideration and studied in American Universities alongside the Constitution. It is the author's view that the Founding Fathers Agreement made by David Ben Gurion, Yitzchak Grinboim, and HaRav Fishman Maimon, by virtue of a resolution taken by the leadership of the Jewish Community, i.e., the Executive of the Jewish Agency, should be held as a binding tool of interpretation, one that must be taken into account when making choices in Parliament (the Knesset) or when deciding cases involving the Jewish and democratic elements of the state.

7. Conclusion

The State of Israel continues the commitment to the Jewish heritage started with its founding fathers. Still, the definition of the Jewish state needs to be more clearly defined.

This Status Quo commitment to keep the public lifestyle of the State of Israel a traditional Jewish one, as proposed in the Founding Fathers Agreement, is the most acceptable meaning of the "Jewish State" that is provided for in the Declaration of Independence of the State of Israel. It has continued through the years in legislation, in the Foundations of Law Act, 1980, and in the Basic Laws. It sets the description of Judaism as traditionalism—it keeps and maintains the spirit of

---

57 Douglas Adair, *Fame and the Founding Fathers*, edited by Trevor Colbourn, Liberty Fund Indianapolis, 1974, page 38–39.
58 *Id.*, at 78–79.
59 *The Federalist Papers*, edited by Clinton Rossiter, New American Library, 1961, New York, page xiii.

the Jewish people's cultural heritage. This interpretation does not demand an extensively strict reading of Jewish Law, nor is it excessively lenient. The commitment to the public Jewish lifestyle in the Status Quo is not one that is forced upon anyone.[60]

In this respect, it would seem that the position expressed by Professor Aharon Barak supports our own view:

> "A Jewish state" is, then, the state of the Jewish people; 'It is the natural right of the Jewish people to be like any other people, occupying its own sovereign state, by its own authority.' A state to which every Jew has the right to immigrate, and in which the ingathering of the exiles is one of the basic values. 'A Jewish state' is a state whose own history is integrated and intertwined with the history of the Jewish people, whose language is Hebrew, where most of the holidays reflect the national renewal. 'A Jewish state' is a state in which the settlement of Jews in its fields, cities and villages and towns, is one of the primary concerns. 'A Jewish state' is a state that commemorates the memory of the Jews that were annihilated in the Holocaust, and which is meant to constitute "a solution to the problem of the Jewish people, which lacked a homeland and independence, by means of renewing the Jewish state in the Land of Israel.' 'A Jewish state' is a state that nurtures Jewish culture, Jewish education and love for the Jewish people. 'A Jewish state' is 'the realization of the generations-long yearning for the redemption of Israel.' 'A Jewish state' is a country that espouses the values of freedom, justice, equity and peace that are part of the heritage of Israel. 'A Jewish state' is a state whose values are drawn from its religious tradition, in which the Bible is the basis of its literature and the prophets of Israel are the foundations of its morality. 'A Jewish state' is a state in which Jewish law plays an important role, and in which marriage and divorce of Jews is decided in accordance with the laws of the Torah. 'A Jewish state' is a state in which the values of the Torah, the values of Jewish tradition and the values of Jewish law are among its most fundamental values."[61]

Our view is that the text of the obligation of the Founding Fathers' Agreement is not just a political agreement. It was not just a political agreement of a limited and isolated importance in Israel's history. It was vital in shaping the Jewish character of the State—not just important in forging a united front at the time when a united front was needed to represent all the sectors of the Jewish community before UNSCOP, but also an important tool in forging the modern spirit of the state itself. It should be used as an interpretive tool in judicial and political decisions, with a higher official legal standing than any political agreement. It expresses most adequately the definition of the heritage of Israel. It explains the link of the Israeli people to its history and defines the traditionalism that should guide the judiciary when making the decisions about the Jewish and

---

60 Shetreet, *Three Branches, supra* note 9, at 79.
61 A. Barak, *Interpretation in Law—Vol. 3: Constitutional Interpretation*, 1994, p. 332.

democratic elements of the state. When trying to define the "heritage of Israel" in a way that best fits the majority of Israeli society, the traditionalism expressed in the agreement should be the answer. It should be used when legislative choices are made and when judicial decisions are adjudicated on relevant matters.

The spirit of compromise that guided the Founding Fathers in the formative years should guide the contemporary debate in Israel on the national Identity Bills.[62] That spirit should also guide the development of the Basic Laws which help form the Israeli constitution, as it is written chapter by chapter. This spirit of compromise guided past leaders in forging the Founding Fathers Agreement in 1947, the Declaration of Independence in 1948, and the Foundation of Law Act in 1980. It should and must continue to guide contemporary leaders.

It must be emphasized that the Founding Fathers Agreement contains a commitment to freedom of conscience and religion of Jews and non-Jews alongside the recognition and commitment to preserve the elements of the Jewish character of the state.

---

62 See http://www.haaretz.co.il/news/politi/.premium-1.2493673 (accessed February 9, 2017).

Chapter 12:
The Jurisprudence of the Supreme Court on Non-Orthodox Communities

1. Early Case of Renting Hall for High Holiday Worship: Peretz v. Kfar Shmaryahu Municipal Council

From the early days of the State of Israel the issue of the non-Orthodox community was on the public and legal discourse. In one of the early cases dealing with the rights of members of non-orthodox Jewish community in Israel, the Supreme Court ruled that the refusal of a local municipal council cannot deny a request to rent a property to a non-orthodox congregation for the purpose of holding prayers in that property in the high Holidays. The court ruled that the local government council is managing the properties under a duty of trust and as such cannot discriminate against the non-orthodox community.[1] This was a landmark case establishing the right to freedom of religion and worship without discrimination. It relied on the Declaration of independence.

2. Legal Recognition of Non-Orthodox Jewish Conversion

The issue of the validity of conversions was first addressed by the judicial branch in the *Miller* case,[2] in which the petitioner had completed the conversion process in the United States and received a conversion certificate from the Reform movement. The Minister of Interior decided that under the "nationality" entry on the petitioner's Israeli identity card, the word "converted" would appear alongside the word "Jew."

The High Court of Justice ruled that according to the Population Registry Law, data pertaining to national and religious affiliation must be recorded in accordance with the declaration made by the citizen himself, as determined by Section 19b of the law. The registry clerk had no authority to add any data that is irrelevant to the subject at hand. The upshot is that the court ruled that the petitioner should be listed in the population registry as a Jew, without notation of the word "converted."

---

1 H.C.J 262/62 *Israel Peretz v. Kfar Shmaryahu*, 16(3) P.D. 2101, VI Selected Judgements of the Supreme Court (1961–1962).
2 H.C.J 230/86 *Miller v. Minister of Interior*, 40(4) P.D. 436 (1986).

DOI 10.1515/9783899497946-013

Additional reinforcement of the *Miller* ruling came in the form of the High Court of Justice ruling on the case of *Shas Movement v. Director of the Population Registry Authority.*[3] Then President of the Supreme Court Shamgar ruled that the conversion of an immigrant would be recorded in the population registry in accordance with his or her own declaration. If needed, this declaration would be accompanied by a document or public certificate testifying to the conversion. According to Justice Shamgar, this declaration, when accompanied by a document testifying to a conversion performed in a Jewish community abroad, was sufficient to obligate the individual's registration as a Jew. It made no difference whether the community was Orthodox, Conservative, or Reform.

In the *Miller* case and the *Movement* case, the High Court of Justice took measures to afford civilian protection for non-Orthodox conversions performed abroad. This judicial ruling may make a positive contribution to the enhancement of civil rights in matters of religious practice in the State of Israel.

Subsequently, the High Court of Justice considered the validity of non-Orthodox conversions carried out in Israel. The question arose in 1993 in the *Pissaro* case,[4] and touched on the validity of Reform conversion performed in Israel as it pertained to the Population Registry Law and the Law of Return. Then the Minister of Interior claimed that Section 2 of the Religious Community Ordinance (Conversion) did not sanction recognition of non-Orthodox conversions performed in Israel. Justice Shamgar took the opposite approach, determining that there was no need to interpret the Ordinance as possessing general civil-legal impact. Shamgar argued that one could interpret the Ordinance as possessing impact solely within the jurisdictional limits of matters of individual status. According to Justice Shamgar, in interpreting the Religious Community Ordinance (Conversion), one must also take into account the principles of equality and freedom of conscience and religion. Therefore, the Ordinance should be interpreted according to its narrow meaning, such that it does not rule out recognition of non-Orthodox conversion in Israel for the purpose of registration. Therefore, there is no stipulation that the "head of the community" must give his approval to the conversion as a prerequisite for its investment with "legal impact." In his judicial ruling, Justice Shamgar also referred to the Law of Return. He declared that the Religious Community Ordinance (Conversion) applied only to issues that fall within the jurisdiction of the rabbinical courts; it thus goes

---

3 H.C.J 264/87 *Association of Torah-Observant Sephardim—Shas Movement v. Kahane—Director of the Interior Ministry Population Registry,* 43(2) P.D. 730.
4 H.C.J 1031/93 *Pesaro v The Minister of Interior,* 49(4) P.D. 661 (1993).

without saying that the Ordinance has no bearing on the issue of the Law of Return.

Justice Barak, who concurred with Justice Shamgar's ruling, made it clear that in its decision on the *Pissaro* case, the court had simply recognized that conversions that have been performed in Israel solely to fulfill the requirements of the Law of Return or the population registry are not conditional upon the requirements of the Religious Community Ordinance (Conversion). Justice Barak emphasized that the court had not made any decision beyond that. In other words, the justices had not expressed any opinions vis-à-vis requisites of the conversion process in Israel that would qualify an individual for coverage under the Law of Return or declaration as a Jew in the population registry. Therefore, the court did not issue an order to recognize the petitioner as a Jew as called for in the Law of Return, nor was any directive given to register her as a Jew in the population registry.[5]

The result is that while the *Pissaro* case determined what the Religious Community Ordinance (Conversion) "was not"—that its jurisdiction did not extend beyond matters of personal status—it did not determine what it "was." It did not delineate the precise parameters of what constitutes conversion in Israel. The ruling made it clear that this "was" had to be determined by the legislature. Nevertheless, Justice Barak noted in his ruling that if the legislature chose not to have its own say in the matter, the court would have no choice but to make a judicial decision on the matter. By a majority opinion, then, the Supreme Court was seeking to simultaneously bolster freedom of religion and apply it to the different streams of Judaism. Nevertheless, the court preferred to leave the ideological questions to the legislature, while at the same time warning the Knesset that if it did not do so, the court would take the job upon itself.

Unmistakable signs of the *Pissaro* case could be discerned in the coalition agreement that was signed with the religious parties following the 1996 elections. The agreement included a commitment to prevent—by force of law—recog-

---

5 Justice Zvi Tal, representing the minority opinion, determined that the Religious Community Ordinance (Conversion) can also influence civil issues unrelated to issues of personal status. Therefore, in his opinion the ordinance is also relevant to the Registry Law and the Law of Return. Since "the head of the religious community" is the Chief Rabbinate, only through its agreement can the act of conversion be recognized. However, according to Justice Tal, there is a substantive difference between conversion performed abroad (to which the *Miller* ruling and the *Shas Movement* ruling refer) and conversion performed in Israel (in reference to which Registry clerks must refuse to register an individual as a Jew on the basis of a conversion certificate issued in Israel, if they have a reasonable basis for assuming that the certificate was not issued by a body authorized to do so).

nition of non-Orthodox conversions performed in Israel for the purpose of registration as a Jew.[6] In accordance with the agreement, the government initiated a conversion bill according to which only Orthodox conversions will be performed in Israel. The proposed conversion law passed the Knesset in a preliminary reading. This sparked a vigorous struggle by the Reform and Conservative movements, which enlisted highly influential leaders and institutions among diaspora Jewry, especially in the United States. These groups threatened to cut off monetary and political support for Israel and disrupt ties should the conversion law be passed. Following the debate, the Ne'eman Committee was appointed to deal with the issue.

From the discussion outlined above, one can see that while the High Court of Justice was interested in enhancing and expanding protection of freedom of religion—of all the different streams—the government and the Knesset made negative contributions on this matter. In our opinion, the Ne'eman committee,[7] which was set up by the government to recommend ways of solving the issue, drafted a good, workable formula. The committee decided in favor of setting up a conversion institute in which the non-Orthodox streams would also be represented, whereas the final conversion procedure would be performed in accordance with the practices of the Orthodox rabbinate—meaning that only one type of conversion would be performed. The Ne'eman committee's suggestions are acceptable to the non-Orthodox streams, and offer an appropriate solution to a complicated issue.

In the case of *Naamat v. the Minister* of Interior it was decided by the Supreme Court that non-orthodox conversion performed in Israel and abroad is recognized for the purpose of the Law of Return,[8] and the officer in charge of population registry must register the petitioners as Jews in the population registry upon the presentation of adequate certificate proving the conversion.[9] This ruling was based on a previous landmark Case – *Funk Schlezinger.*[10]

In the case of *Regchova v. Minister* of Interior the Supreme Court held that conversion may be performed not only in the official system created by the state but also by extra-official conversion rabbinical procedures arranged by non-government rabbis. In this case the non-governmental conversion system

---

6 E. Don-Yehiya, *The Politics of Accommodation: Settling Conflicts of State and Religion in Israel,* 1997, p. 60.

7 The Ne'eman Committee, *Report and Recommendations for Initiating Ideas and Proposals on the Issue of Religious Conversion in Israel,* 1998.

8 As distinguished from The Rabbinical Jurisdiction Act regarding marriage and divorce

9 H.C.J 5070/95 *Naamat v. Minister of interior,* 56(2) P.D. 721 (2002).

10 H.C.J 143/62 *Funk-Schlesinger v. Minister of Interior,* 17(1) P.D. 225 (1963).

that performed the conversion belonged to the ultra-orthodox group (*Charedi – Litai*).[11] Although the Regchova court decision dealt with orthodox non-governmental conversion, the ruling opens the door for recognition of performed conversion by other non-governmental procedures, including non-orthodox.

3. Status of Female Members of Public Bodies Concerned with Religious Affairs

Another example of the Supreme Court's contributions toward enhancing the quality of civil rights in matters of religious practice is the issue of the status of female members of public bodies concerned with matters of religion.

The legal arrangement as it now exists adversely affects the equal rights of women. The Equal Rights for Women Law states that "there will be one law for men and women in every judicial action." This principle is violated when religious laws of matrimony are made into state laws of matrimony, despite the lack of equality between men and women in this matter. Women serve as rabbinical pleaders (barristers), but do not serve as judges in the rabbinical courts. Until the 1990s, women were denied the right to serve on local religious councils (in charge of providing religious services such as kosher oversight or marriage registration) or in the elective body that selects the Chief Rabbis and the local rabbis.[12] The change came about as a consequence of the intervention of the High Court of Justice.

In the *Shakdiel* case,[13] in accordance with Section 5 of the Jewish Religious Services Law, 1971, an interministerial committee claimed that throughout the years of Israel's existence as a state, women had never been candidates for membership on the religious councils due to the councils' close relationship with the rabbinate, and the Halachic precepts affecting their operation. Their concern was that should the petitioner be allowed to take a seat on the religious council, this would disrupt the work of the council. Justice Elon reached the conclusion that the reason for the petitioner's disqualification was the fact that she was a woman, which contravened the principle of equality in Israel's legal system. Therefore, the decision by the ministerial committee was invalidated.

A similar question was raised by the *Poraz* case:[14] Could a local authority which is one of the three bodies that make up the assembly that selects the

---

11 H.C.J 7625/06 *Martina Regchova v. Ministry of Interior* (published on Nevo, 31.3.2016).

12 B. Neuberger, *Religion and Democracy in Israel*, 1997, p. 33.

13 H.C.J 153/87 *Shakdiel v. Minister of Religious Affairs*, 42(2) P.D. 221 (1988).

14 H.C.J 953/87 *Poraz v. Tel Aviv-Jaffa City Council*, 42(2) P.D. 309 (1988).

city's rabbi be permitted not to choose a woman as a delegate to the elective assembly simply by virtue of her being a woman? Justice Barak determined that in its decision, the city council had disregarded the principle of equality. It had not assessed the full effect of the appointment of women to the elective assembly on the work of the rabbi of the city. Consequently, the authority's decision was struck down.

The Supreme Court played an important role in enhancing women's status vis-à-vis the roles they perform on bodies that furnish religious services to the public, in the selection of officials on religious councils, and in the elective assembly for rabbis. Yet this judicial ruling of the Supreme Court carries no weight, since the religious bodies have avoided complying with it. Nor has the executive branch made any effort to enforce the court's ruling on the matter. As a result, although the court has made a positive contribution toward enhancing the status of women on bodies that engage in religious affairs, there has been no noticeable practical improvement, due to the executive branch's failure, intentional or not, to implement the judicial rulings.

From time to time the court adjudicates petitions regarding appointment of women to administrative officers in the Rabbinical Court system.[15] Similarly, private bills have been proposed to guarantee election of women to the religious services councils.[16]

4. Status of Non-Orthodox Members of Public Bodies Concerned with Religious Affairs, Religious Services Councils, and Councils to Elect Rabbis

The exclusive recognition granted to the Orthodox rabbinate in Israel on matters of religion, and the avoidance of conferring recognition on non-Orthodox rabbis, adversely affects the democratic principle of equality of all religions and of all religious streams before the law. In Israel, non-Orthodox rabbis are not permitted by law to officiate at wedding ceremonies or to carry out conversions. To date, they have also been prevented from becoming members of the religious councils, even though the court has ruled that there is no legal justification for their disqualification from membership on religious councils. Furthermore, budgetary al-

---

15 H.C.J 8213/14 *Dror Cahana v. Religious Services Minister* (published on Nevo, 07.01.2016).
16 Private bill 2118–19 proposing to remove the requirement that the rabbinical court director should be a rabbi or a rabbinical court judge (dayan), thus opening the way for women to this office.

locations made by the Ministry of Religious Affairs to Reform and Conservative Torah-culture projects is minuscule.

The issue of membership of the non-Orthodox on a religious council was taken up in the High Court of Justice's ruling on the *Hoffman* petition.[17] The petitioners claimed that the city council had to an unreasonable degree deferred the nomination of candidates for the religious council; it had avoided declaring the petitioners as its candidates to the council due to the fact that they belong to non-Orthodox streams of Judaism. Before the petition could be addressed, the council held the elections. The court registrar, A. Efal-Gabai, required the respondents to pay court costs, having determined that the council acted illegally. Nevertheless, new elections for the council were not held. This, then, constitutes an example of a negative contribution made by the executive branch to the quality of civil rights in matters of religious practice, in its disregard for the High Court of Justice ruling.

More recently, the Supreme Court has been characterized by greater determination to persuade the executive branch (primarily the Ministry of Religious Affairs) to comply with its judicial rulings, when they repeatedly engage in foot dragging and long delays in the seating of delegates from the non-Orthodox streams on religious councils. This occurred in the *Brenner* case, when the Supreme Court issued a binding injunction to seat the petitioner, Joyce Brenner, who is not Orthodox, on the Netanya religious council, as a replacement for another incumbent member of the council.[18] In response, after only one meeting in which Ms. Brenner participated, the religious council decided to set up a limited management committee. Only the latter committee holds any sessions, in effect locking out the female member of the religious council.

A petition was brought before the High Court of Justice by *the Movement for Progressive Judaism*,[19] the subject of which was an exhibition held as part of "Jewish Religious Services Week," which was organized by the Ministry of Religious Affairs and the Chief Rabbinate. The Movement for Progressive Judaism asked that it be permitted to have a booth at the exhibition. The relevant ministerial ministry turned down the application, arguing that Jewish services week was intended to display Jewish religious services as they are provided by bodies funded by the Ministry of Religious Affairs, under the supervision of the Chief

---

17 H.C.J 4560/94 *Hoffman v. Ehud Olmert and Jerusalem City Council* (published on Nevo, 15.01. 1995).

18 H.C.J 3551/97 *Joyce Gila Miller v. Ministerial Committee According to the Jewish Religious Services Law,* 51(5) P.D. 754 (1997); See also H.C.J 7237/95 *Shosh Arar v. Minister of Religious Affairs,* 51(1) P.D. 193 (1997).

19 H.C.J 650/88 *Movement for Progressive Judaism v. Religious Affairs Minister,* 42(3) P.D. 378.

Rabbinate. The Movement for Progressive Judaism does not meet these criteria. In light of this decision, the movement appealed to the High Court of Justice. Justice Shamgar ruled that freedom of conscience and religion required that governmental authorities treat all believers in the same degree, without differentiating between the different streams. Specifically regarding this case, however, the judge ruled that since the petition was brought only two days before the opening of the exhibition, there was no time for factual discovery; therefore, the petition was rejected.

This case constitutes an example of how, working alone, bureaucracy is liable to adversely affect the quality of civil rights in matters of religious practice. The denial of government aid to Reform and Conservative institutions in Israel causes harm not only to equality, but also to freedom of religion and ceremony; it is difficult to sustain these freedoms without budgets to construct houses of worship and furnish salaries for rabbis and cantors.

5. Prayer of Non-Orthodox Women in the Western Wall

The arrangement of prayer in the Western Wall area have given rise to a number of cases in the Supreme Court. The non-orthodox women group insisted on conducting a prayer according to non-orthodox mixed gender prayer in the area of the Western Wall. These issues were adjudicated by the Supreme Court in a number of cases.[20]

In all three cases the Supreme Court decided to take up the review on the merit, in spite of the Order InCouncil on the holy places (which provides that no court shall deal with dispute of holy places), the Supreme Court ordered the government to set up arrangements that will insure the right of worship of the women to pray in the area of the Western Wall. Following that, the government approved an arrangement that was proposed by the secretary of the cabinet Dr. Avichai Mandelblit, this arrangement has not yet been fully implemented due to objection of the orthodox rabbis, so this issue is still pending public discourse and further government decisions.

---

20 H.C.J 257/89 *Hoffman v. The Supervisor of the Western Wall,* 48(2) P.D. 265 (1994); H.C.J 3358/95 *Hoffman v. Director General of the Prime Minister Office,* 54(2) P.D. 345 (2000); H.C.J (further review) 5428/2000 *Director General of the Prime Minister Office v. Hoffman,* 57(3) P.D. 289 (2003).

6. Non-Orthodox Communities Issues in Overseas Jurisprudence

A. Jewish Free School Case in the UK Supreme Court

The Jewish Free School (currently known as "JFS") is a secondary school in London, England, with over 2000 pupils; it regularly has twice the number of applicants for the places that are available. The culture and characteristic nature of the school is Orthodox Judaism as stated in Clause 8 of the school's Instrument of Government from 2005:

> "Recognizing its historic foundation, JFS will preserve and develop its religious character in accordance with the principles of Orthodox Judaism, under the guidance of the Chief Rabbi of the United Hebrew Congregations of the Commonwealth."[21]

The fundamental criterion of JFS in pupil admission was that it would accept only children who were recognized as being Jewish by the Office of the Chief Rabbi (OCR). The OCR is the head of the largest group of Orthodox synagogues in the United Kingdom; however, it does not represent all Jewish Orthodox sects. The OCR, in conformity with Jewish law, identifies as Jewish any person whose matrilineal descent is from a Jewish mother[22] regardless of the form of Judaism practiced by the family or even if the family does not practice Judaism at all.[23]

The proceedings of the *Jewish Free School* case have been brought in relation to an applicant whose father is Jewish and mother is a convert to Judaism undertaken in a manner that is not acknowledged by the OCR. As a result, the child did not meet the school's criterion for admission and was refused a place at the school, even though the child actively practiced Judaism.[24]

Initially the child appealed to the school's adjudicator, who upheld the school's criteria. Subsequently, he appealed to the Administrative Court, mainly on the grounds that the school's admission policy did not reflect its religious character and discriminated on racial basis against pupils who are not from a Jewish matrilineal descent.[25] The court rejected the claims; however, the Court of Appeal unanimously reversed judgement and held that the school discriminated on the ground of ethnic origin. JFS then appealed to the Supreme Court.

---

21 *R (E) v. Governing Body of Jewish Free School* [2009] UKSC 15 [164].
22 The mother herself also must have been descended from a Jewish mother.
23 *Id.*, p 165.
24 *Id.*, p. 166.
25 *E v. Governing Body of JFS & Anor* [2008] EWHC 15/1536 (Admin) (3 53July 2008).

The appeal was dismissed by seven to two.[26] Lord Phillips in his opinion quoted the membership criteria set forth by Lord Fraser in the *Mandla v Dowell Lee* case.[27] The *Mandla* test set forth several different criteria to determine ethnicity, chiefly the historic and cultural tradition associated with religion along with geographical origins or common ancestors, common language and literature, and a common religion that differs from other neighboring groups, or by being a minority or oppressed group within a larger community.[28]

Therefore, it was Lord's Phillip view that one could be identified either by the *Mandla* criteria or by the OCR criteria. Lord Phillip argued that it was the *Mandla* criteria which formed the Jewish ethnic group, principally regarding the long-shared history and common unique cultural traditions of the Jewish people. Even though there is great overlap between the two, as many would satisfy the matrilineal test, there would be some who do not.[29] Thus, in his eyes, it was clear that the matrilineal test was a test of ethnic origin; consequently, Lord Phillips concluded that the school racially discriminates:

> "JFS discriminates in its admission requirements on the sole basis of genetic descent by the maternal line from a woman who is Jewish, in the *Mandla* as well as the religious sense. I can see no escape from the conclusion that this is direct racial discrimination."[30]

The case has helped confirm that, regardless of positive or negative intent, reason or cause cannot be justified in terms of direct discrimination. Accordingly, the law of discrimination and the laws relating to employment and admission policies have been significantly impacted. The impact on Jewish faith schools is extensive in scope because the judgement means that the admission criteria cannot require a matrilineal test, but rather an emphasis will be given on aptitude and Judaic practice.

---

26 Lords Phillips, Mance, Kerr and Clarke, and Lady Hale held that there had been direct discrimination against M on grounds of his ethnic origins; Lord Hope and Lord Walker held that there had been no direct discrimination, but that there had been unjustifiable and disproportionate indirect discrimination. Lords Rodger and Brown would have allowed the school's appeal; Frank Cranmer, *Who Is a Jew? Jewish Faith Schools and the Race Relations Act 1976* (2010).
27 *Mandla (Sewa Singh) and Another v. Dowell Lee and Others* [1983] 2 AC 548.
28 *R (E) v. Governing Body of Jewish Free School* [2009] UKSC 15 [41–46].
29 *Id.*, p.30.
30 *Id.*, p.46.

B. Ran-Dav's Case NJ Invalidating Exclusively Orthodox Kosher Regulation

The case of *Ran-Dav's County Kosher, Inc. v. State of New Jersey*[31] is one of the most noteworthy challenges to the kosher food laws in the United States. In this case, the Ran-Dav County Kosher food business in New Jersey was subject, like many other food businesses, to regulatory supervision both privately through a rabbi, and publicly through the State's Bureau of Kosher Enforcement. The Bureau of Kosher Enforcement was created as part of the Attorney General's Consumer Affairs Division to enforce kosher food regulations. The NJ Attorney General, through an executive directive, created a committee consisting of ten members responsible for advising him on kosher issues relating to the kosher regulations. The term "kosher" was defined as food "prepared and maintained in strict compliance with the laws and customs of the Orthodox Jewish religion."[32]

The Bureau of Kosher Enforcement charged the store for violating the kosher food regulation with regards to possessing meat which was not prepared in a way that meets dietary kosher rules. This action contends that the kosher food regulations violated the Establishment Clause of the federal and state constitutions because the regulations imposed by the state "directly and substantially entangle[ed] government in religious matters."[33] According to the store, as long as they complied with the standards set by their rabbi, the state had no grounds for setting different standards (*Id Est* orthodox Hebrew requirements).[34]

The New Jersey State Supreme Court held, in a 4-to-3 decision that the regulations set forth by state regarding the preparation, maintenance, and sale of kosher products violated the federal and state establishment clauses by applying the *Lemon* test to the regulations; the Court found unconstitutional by excessively entangling the government with religion.[35]

The court also examined the composition of the Bureau of Enforcement along with the Advisory Committee to the New Jersey Attorney General. It found that the Chief of the Bureau is an orthodox rabbi, and the committee is predominantly composed of orthodox rabbis as well. Therefore, it found that "it underscores the theological or religious nature of the State's regulatory en-

---

31 *Ran-Dav's County Kosher, Inc. v. State*, 129 N.J. 141 1992, 608 A.2d 1353.
32 *Id.*, at 145.
33 *Id.*
34 *Id.*
35 *Id.*, at 152; Catherine Beth Sullivan, *Are Kosher Food Laws Constitutionally Kosher?*, 21 B.C. ENVTL. AFF. L. REV. 201, 233 (1993).

deavors."[36] Finally, the court concluded that the appointment of persons with religious qualifications as enforcement officials confirms that the kosher regulations relate mainly to a religious meaning. For these reasons, the court concluded that the state can impose and regulate the labeling of products, but it cannot impose religious standards on those products.[37]

---

36 *Id.*, at 157.
37 *Id.*, at 167.

Part VI: **Law and Religion:**
International Perspectives

Chapter 13:
Selected Jewish and Other Religious Issues in International Jurisprudence

1. Religious Holidays and Days of Rest

The state of affairs existing between issues of religion and issues of state is, in most countries, a subject of prolonged dispute. Every government conciliates the wishes and demands of different religions with the beliefs of others, and the communal welfare at whole. Two sets of difficulties arise most often. First is the extent to which the majority community can express their beliefs publicly. Second is the extent to which a community can regulate and restrict religious practices and beliefs.[1]

The scope of freedom that legislatures and courts have granted individuals and institutions to pursue their religious activities varies. In the United States, the nature of these exemptions falls into two main categories. The first category, *direct conflict*, deals with specific laws and religious beliefs that directly contradict each other, and cannot both simultaneously coexist. The second category, *indirect conflict*, deals with laws that indirectly affect those who follow certain religious principles.[2]

The case of *Sherbert v. Verner*[3] demonstrates a direct conflict between a regulation that required Sherbert to work on Saturday and her Jewish beliefs. Adell Sherbert, a member of the Seventh-Day Adventist Church, was fired from her job because she refused to work on Saturday. Furthermore, Sherbert refused to work at other jobs for the same reason. Therefore, the South Carolina Employment Security Commission rejected her application for employment benefits. The Supreme Court ruled that the South Carolina state law, despite the fact that is it secular by nature, creates a direct and severe hardship on many people who hold religious beliefs regarding the day of Shabbat. The court deduced that the secular statute "substantially burdens" a religious practice,[4] as the observance of the Shabbat is a "cardinal principle"[5] of the faith.

---

1 2 Donald P. Kommers et al., *American Constitutional Law*, 485–486 (3rd ed. 2009).
2 Shimon Shetreet, *Exemptions and Privileges on Grounds of Religion and Conscience*, 62 Ky. L.J. 377 (1973–1974).
3 *Sherbert v. Verner*, 374 U.S. 398, 83 S. Ct. 1790, 10 L. Ed. 2d 965 (1963).
4 Kommers, *supra* note 1, at 575.
5 *Sherbert*, *supra* note 3, at 406.

DOI 10.1515/9783899497946-014

In the case of *McGowan v. State of Maryland*,[6] seven employees of a department store were convicted under the State of Maryland's "Sunday Closing Laws," also known as "Sunday Blue Laws." The laws prohibited petitioners from selling prohibited general goods products to individuals for twenty-four hours on Sunday. The employees challenged their convictions, arguing that the laws were irrational because they provided for exceptions on goods and people who could sell goods on Sunday. They further argued that the laws violated the Equal Protection Clause and the Establishment Clause. The Court affirmed the petitioners' convictions, holding that the laws were secular in nature, since the State's purpose was to give its citizens a common day of rest.[7] In other words, the law forced the petitioners to follow a law of religious principles and, consequently, caused economic loss.[8]

The Canadian Charter of Rights, which was promulgated in 1982, entrenched *inter alia* freedom of religion and included it in the list of rights which are constitutionally protected.[9] Article 2 of the Canadian Constitution reads as follows: "Everyone has the following fundamental freedoms:

a) freedom of conscience and religion;
b) freedom of thought, belief, opinion and expression, including freedom of the press and other media of communication;
c) freedom of peaceful assembly; and
d) Freedom of association."[10]

Although the legislative branch of Canada referred explicitly to the supremacy of God in its Charter of Rights and Freedoms, the judicial branch in Canada is less ready to accept religion as a guiding light. The Supreme Court of Canada struck down the Lord's Day Act for violating Section 2 of the Canadian Charter of Rights and Freedoms because the act was not enacted for any secular reason, but for the purpose of establishing a religious based requirement in the state.[11] In a later case, the Supreme Court of Canada[12] decided that the Ontario provincial Sunday Closing Law was constitutionally valid because the act was not trying to advance any religious agenda, but instead was aiming to provide all work-

---

6 *McGowan v. State of Maryland*, 366 U.S. 420 (1961).
7 *Id.*
8 Shetreet, *supra* note 2, at 383–384.
9 Canadian Charter of Rights and Freedoms, 1982.
10 Article 2 of the Canadian Charter of Rights and Freedoms, 1982.
11 R. v. Big M Drug Mart Ltd., [1985] 1 S.C.R. 295, 1985 CanLII 69 (S.C.C.).
12 *R. v. Edwards Books and Art Ltd.*, [1986] 2 S.C.R. 713.

ers with a day of rest – a purpose of a secular nature. The Canadian Judiciary recognized the primary secular purpose when adjudicating.[13]

The degree and extent of protection of freedom of religion shown in the United States is very high. Unlike the US Constitution, the Canadian Charter does not contain a non-establishment clause, reflecting a different approach to the protection of freedom of religion.[14] Therefore, the Canadian government is not compelled to act neutrally towards religion. As such, governmental actions that are to the advantage of a certain religion over another are not viewed as transgressive in comparison to the US government. However, laws that heavily burden the exercise of belief may be found in violation of Article 2 of the Canadian Constitution.[15]

In situations such as the *Sherbert* case, where the court holds that the law is directly conflicting with the religious beliefs of an individual and thus contradict the free exercise clause, the Canadian Supreme Court may hold that the law is, similarly, religiously burdening and conflicts with the guarantee of freedom of religion.[16]

Nevertheless, in *R. v. Big M Drug Mart Ltd,*[17] the Supreme Court of Canada held that the Lord's Day Act violated freedom of religion as it forced the act of keeping the Christian Sabbath; therefore, it promoted the Christian faith over other religions. It should be noted, however, that the Lord's Day Act is different than the "Sunday Closing Laws" of the state of Maryland. It is not a secular law by nature, but rather was enacted by the Canadian Parliament solely for its religious purpose.[18]

At a later time, the Province of Ontario enacted the *Retail Business Holiday Act,*[19] which makes it an offense to conduct retail business on a holiday.[20] However,

---

13 Meanwhile, in the United States, its Declaration of Independence references the "firm reliance on the protection of divine Providence," similarly to the "Rock of Israel" in the Israeli Declaration of Independence. In the US Constitution, however, no such reference to any divine protection is made.

14 Robert A. Sedler, *The Constitutional Protection of Freedom of Religion, Expression, and Association in Canada and the United States: A Comparative Analysis,* 20 Case W. Res. J. Int'l L. 577, 582 (1998).

15 *Id.,* 584.

16 *Id.,* 580.

17 *R. v. Big M Drug Mart Ltd.,* [1985] 1 S.C.R. 295, 1985 CanLII 69 (S.C.C.).

18 Sadler, *supra* note 11, at X.

19 *Retail Business Holidays Act,* R.S.O. 1980, c. 453.

20 In this act, "holiday" means Sunday, New Year's Day, Good Friday, Victoria Day, Dominion Day, Labour Day, Thanksgiving Day, Christmas Day, and Boxing Day; see section 1, *Id.* of the *Retail Business Holidays Act.*

the act contains numerous exceptions, mostly towards "corner store" operations such as gas stations, pharmacies, and other businesses permitted by the local municipality.[21] Of particular note is the exemption contained in Section 3(4), which applies to businesses on Sunday that have seven or less employees, and less than five thousand square feet used for the service, allowing business to operate on Sunday if they had been closed on Saturday. In 1983, four Ontario retailers were charged with failing to follow the Act, and the legislation was challenged in *R. v. Edwards Books and Art Ltd.*[22] The Supreme Court dismissed the challenge, this time supporting the constitutional legitimacy of the Act. The Court found that even though the Act does abridge the freedom of religion of some Saturday observers, it is a justifiable limit. Furthermore, in the opinion of the court, the act was not enacted to encourage religious worship, but rather for the secular purpose of providing a uniform holiday for retail workers.[23]

Similarly, the Sunday Trading Act of 1994[24] enacted by the Parliament of the United Kingdom allows businesses to be open on Sunday with certain restrictions. Most notably, businesses larger than 280 square meters ("large shop") may be open up to a maximum of six hours. However, Part II of the Act, termed *Shops Occupied by Persons of the Jewish Religion*, allows Jewish occupiers of large shops to give a notice to the local authority stating that they are following the Jewish religion and that the shop will be closed on the day of Shabbat.[25] By doing so, they will be exempt from the restrictions set upon large shops on Sunday.[26]

However, not all jurisdictions are favorable when accommodating for religious beliefs. For example, in *Prais v. Council of the European Communities*,[27] the European Court of Justice refused to accommodate for the claimant's beliefs. The case concerned the request of a Jewish woman to reschedule an exam since it took place on the day of the Jewish holiday of *Shavout*, during that time she was unable to travel or write. The European Court of Justice failed to accommodate her request for two reasons. First, the date had allready been notified to the other examinees, nor was it possible to allow others to take the exam on a different day. Second, human rights in the European Union have not been promulgated.[28]

---

21 Sections 3 and 4 of the *Retail Business Holidays Act, supra* note 16.
22 *R. v. Edwards Books and Art Ltd.*, [1986] 2 S.C.R. 713.
23 *Id.*, at paragraph 62.
24 Sunday Trading Act 1994, c. 20 (Eng.).
25 *Id.*, article 8(1).
26 *Id.*, article 2.
27 130/75 *Prais v Council*, [1976] ECR 1589.
28 *Id.*

Elsewhere[29] I have written on the development in the European Union from its original form, transforming itself from an economy-based coalition into a joint body emphasizing human rights, freedom, and democracy. Only by completing this process has the European Union been given the ability to create a culture of peace (political, economic, cultural, and religious peace). This integration originated from the Lisbon Treaty. Later on, human rights and democratic values were provided through the European Convention on Human Rights, to which all member states were party.[30]

More recently, and after the integration of human rights provisions in the treaties of the European Union, a case similar to prais case was rejected. In *Sessa v. Italy*,[31] a Jewish attorney faced with a hearing set on the Jewish holiday of *Yom Kippur* raised the issue before the initial hearing four month in advance; however, the Italian courts repeatedly refused his requests for adjournment. The European Court of Human Rights held, by a majority, that there was no violation of the right to freedom of religion of the European Convention on Human Right on the basis that he could pass the case on to another lawyer, thus allowing him to observe his religious rituals. The majority further claimed that had there been an interference, this should be considered against the public's right to proper administration of justice.[32] The dissenting opinions stressed how the accommodation of Mr. Sessa's religion would not have burdened the Italian judiciary while at the same time there was a clear interference with his right to freedom of religion.[33] The approach which emerges from this jurisprudence is a restrictive one, and that is to be lamented.

For a contrasting judgement, one could point towards the recent judgement of the Court of Appeals of Maryland in the case of *Neustadter et al. v. Holy Cross Hos-*

---

29 Shimon Shetreet, *The Culture of Peace and Human Rights: The Development of Human Rights Protection in the European Union*, in The Culture of Judicial Independence—Rule of Law and World Peace at 102 (ed. Shimon Shetreet, 2014).

30 For a detailed report of the development of the European Union from a solely economy-based community it once was to that of the current human rights and economy based union, see *Id.*

31 *Prais v. Council of the European Communities*, 75–130, Eur. Ct. H.R. 1589 (1976); *Sessa v. Italy*, App. No. 28790/08 2012 Eur. Ct. H.R.

32 *Id.*; Katayoun Alidadi, "Reasonable Accommodations for Religion and Belief: Adding Value to Article 9 ECHR and the European Union's Anti-Discrimination Approach to Employment," 6 European Law Review 693, 705 (2012).

33 Sessa, *supra* note 28; see also Wolfgang Wieshaider, *Sessa czyli przestrzeń dla mniejszości religijnych*, Studia z Prawa

Wyznaniowego 18:113–121 (in Polish), available at https://www.ceeol.com/search/article-detail?id=342561 (accessed February 9, 2017).

pital of Silver Spring, Inc.[34] The petitioner appealed the judgement of the Circuit Court, asserting that his right to free exercise of his religion was infringed by rulings that denied four motions for postponement of his case so that he could observe the Jewish holiday of *Shavuot.* The Court of Appeals held that: "the judges abused their discretion in denying the requests for a continuance of the trial where the movant's religious beliefs prohibited any appearance or advocacy on his behalf in the pending civil court proceeding".[35]

2. Circumcision

Male circumcision is the surgical process of removal of some, or all, of the foreskin from the penis. It is one of the most commonplace procedures in the world. In 2007, the American Academy of Pediatrics evaluated the medical evidence regarding male circumcision and concluded that the health benefits of newborn circumcision outweigh the risks. The benefits include "prevention of urinary tract infections, acquisition of HIV, transmission of some sexually transmitted infections, and penile cancer."[36]

The religious practice of male circumcision by the Jewish people dates back to the Mosaic times; it was first mentioned as being performed by Abraham on his son Isaac as part of his original covenant with God.

> "Every male among you shall be circumcised. And ye shall be circumcised in the flesh of your foreskin, and it shall be a token of a covenant betwixt Me and you. And he that is eight days old shall be circumcised among you, every male throughout your generations."[37]

At that time, other ancient societies practiced male circumcision; however, it was performed around the age of puberty as a function of an initiation right before marriage. The Israelites separated from this religious tradition as the ceremonial tradition of circumcision on the 8th day after birth was created and enshrined.[38] Today circumcision is seen as an essential act for the Jewish male to enter the covenant (brit) with God (and the community).[39]

---

34 *Alexander H. Neustadter, et al. v. Holy Cross Hospital of Silver Spring, Inc.*, No. 12, September Term 2010.

35 *Id.*

36 American Academy of Pediatrics, "Technical Report: Male Circumcision," Pediatrics 130 issue 3 (2012).

37 Genesis 17:11–12.

38 Paul Johnson, *A History of the Jews* 37 (First Perennial Library Ed. 1988).

39 Encyclopedia Judaica, Circumcision 730, 732 (2d ed. 2007).

A. An Oral Suction (Metzitzah B'peh)

The circumcision consists of three different stages. Firstly, the cutting of the foreskin (*milah*), then, revealing the mucous membrane (*peri'ah*), and lastly, the performance of oral suction (*Metzitzah*). Traditionally the blood is sucked by the circumciser (*mohel*); however, due to medical and political criticism, it has been replaced by either sucking through a glass tube or by use of a swab.[40] Today, *Metzitzah* is not widely practiced; however, some groups such as the ultraorthodox Jewish communities—still do so.

Between 2004 and 2011 New York City learned of eleven herpes infections which were most likely caused by the *Metzitzah* act; two of the babies died and two others suffered brain damage.[41] On September 2012, the New York City Board of Health amended the NYC Health Code (§ 181.21) by prohibiting any person from performing direct oral suction as part of a circumcision without obtaining, prior to the circumcision, a written and signed consent of the parent:[42]

> "A person may not perform a circumcision that involves direct oral suction on an infant under one year of age, without obtaining, prior to the circumcision, the written signed and dated consent of a parent or legal guardian of the infant being circumcised using a form provided by the Department or a form which shall be labeled "Consent to perform oral suction during circumcision," and which at a minimum shall include the infant's date of birth, the full printed name of the infant's parent(s), the name of the individual performing the circumcision and the following statement: "I understand that direct oral suction will be performed on my child and that the New York City Department of Health and Mental Hygiene advises parents that direct oral suction should not be performed because it exposes an infant to the risk of transmission of herpes simplex virus infection, which may result in brain damage or death.""[43]

The amended health code caused outrage in the Orthodox Jewish community, which viewed the regulation as an initial measure to completely stop the tradition of *Metzitzah*.[44] Furthermore, three circumcisers who perform *Metzitzah*, along with three organizations, filed suit in the United States District Court for the Southern District of New York seeking declaratory and injunctive relief.[45]

---

40 *Id.*, at 733734.
41 Sharon Otterman, "Board Votes to Regulate Circumcision, Citing Risks," The New York Times (September 14, 2012).
42 *Cent. Rabbinical Cong. of the USA and Canada, v. N.Y.C. Dep't of Health & Mental Hygiene,* No. 12-cv-7590, 2013 U.S. Dist. LEXIS 4293 (S.D.N.Y. Jan. 10, 2013).
43 § 181.21 (b) Consent for direct oral suction as part of a circumcision.
44 Seth Berkman, *N.Y. Board Orders Forms for Circumcision Rite,* Forward (September 13, 2012).
45 Cent. Rabbinical Cong. of the USA and Canada, *Supra* note 42.

They sought a declaratory and injunctive relief arguing that the amendment violates the rights to free speech and free exercise under the First Amendment. The plaintiffs also sought a preliminary injunction pending adjudication.[46]

The court denied the preliminary injunction, holding that the likelihood of success on the merits of the free exercise claim was not proven by the plaintiffs. The court found that the regulation is neutral and, therefore, subject only to rational basis review, emphasizing the legitimate interests of the government in taking precautionary measures of protecting infant's health, with no discriminatory objective against Judaism. Thus, it concluded that the legislation was likely to be upheld under the rational basis review.[47] As a result, the plaintiffs appealed to the US Court of Appeals for the Second Circuit.

The court of appeals held that the regulation is not neutral and specifically targets a religious practice:[48]

"The Regulation is neither neutral nor, on this record, generally applicable and therefore must satisfy strict scrutiny. The Regulation is not neutral because it purposefully and exclusively targets a religious practice for special burdens. And at least at this preliminary stage, the Regulation is not generally applicable either, because it is underinclusive in relation to its asserted secular goals: The Regulation pertains to religious conduct associated with a small percentage of HSV infection cases among infants, while leaving secular conduct associated with a larger percentage of such infection unaddressed."[49]

The court of appeals vacated the district court's order of denying the plaintiff's motion for a preliminary injunction. Furthermore, the court remanded the judgement of the court for further proceedings while applying the strict scrutiny review when assessing the regulation.[50] Consequently, Mayor Bill de Blasio's administration announced, as part of an agreement with the plaintiffs, that it will be repealing the regulation; stating that they had received only one consent

---

46 *Id.*, at 18.

47 There are two potential degrees in which the constitutionality of a law can be assessed on free exercise grounds. Under "rational basis," the law is presumed to be valid and will be justified if there is a legitimate state interest; however, under "strict scrutiny," it is required that the law be justified by a compelling governmental interest and narrowly tailored to advance that interest.

48 *Cent. Rabbinical Cong. of the USA and Canada v. N.Y.C. Dep't of Health & Mental Hygiene*, 763 F.3d 183; 2014 U.S. App. Lexis 15726 (2014).

49 *Id.*, at 185.

50 *Id.*

since the regulation's inception, and fear that further regulation would drive the *Metzizah* practice into secrecy.[51]

3. Ritual Slaughter of Animals (Shechitah)

The assortment of Jewish laws regarding the types of foods which can be eaten, and in what way they can be prepared, is called *Kashrut*. Among the different dietary regulations, laid out in both the *Torah* and H*alacha*, is the special ritual slaughter process—*Shechita*—of animals. This is to comply with the prohibition of eating any blood and ill animals. Thus, an animal will be restrained and killed by a quick knife stroke to the throat, this is to ensure that the greatest amount of blood will be removed as the principal blood vessels are severed. After, the animal must be steeped in water and salted so that any blood that remains is removed.[52]

Today, many countries across the world require that an animal must be stunned, i. e., placed in a state of unconsciousness, prior to the slaughter. This conflicts with the ritual of *Shechita* (and Muslim ritual slaughter). However, a great number of countries specifically authorize ritual slaughter and regulate the act.[53] For example, French law decrees:

> "It is forbidden to perform ritual slaughter save in a slaughterhouse. Subject to the provisions of the fourth paragraph of this Article, ritual slaughter may be performed only by slaughterers authorized for the purpose by religious bodies which have been approved by the Minister of Agriculture, on a proposal from the Minister of the Interior. Slaughterers must be able to show documentary proof of such authorization.
>
> The approved bodies mentioned in the previous paragraph must inform the Minister of Agriculture of the names of authorized persons and those from whom authorization has been withdrawn. If no religious body has been approved, the prefect of the department in which the slaughterhouse used for ritual slaughter is situated may grant individual authorizations."[54]

---

51 Aaron Short, *NYC Repealing Jewish Circumcision Law Requiring Consent*, New York Post, (February 24, 2015). The issue and certain aspects and circumcision has been adjudicate in israeli courts as well. See HCJ 578/98 *Against Cutting Reprodactive Organs of Babies v. Minister of Health* (published on Nevo, 30.5.1999); C.A. 2055/99 *Ploni v. Zeev* 55(5) P.D. 241 (2001); HCJ 2618/00 Peerot Ltd. v. Minister of Health, 55(5) P.D 49 (2001); Eliav Shochetman "Circumcision with Ratification of the High Court of Justice" 3 Shaarei Mishpat 203 (2003).
52 *Cha'are Shalom Ve Tsedek v. France*, Merits, App NO. 27417/95 ECHR 2000-VII, IHRL.
53 *Id.*, at paragraph 20.
54 Decree No. 80 – 791 of 1 October 1980, promulgated to implement Article 276 of the Countryside Code, as amended by Decree No. 81– 606 of 18 May 1981.

The guidelines for Jewish ritual slaughter in France were approved on 1982, and authority was granted solely to the Joint Rabbinical Committee, which is part of the Jewish Consistorial Association of Paris. Almost all of the Jewish denominations are represented in the Consistory, outside of the liberal sect who believe's in a lax interpretation of the Torah in accordance with modern times, and the ultra-orthodox who are in favor, and follow, a strict interpretation.

Many of the ultra-orthodox Jews wish to comply with strict *Shechita* rules, requiring that the slaughtered animal must not have any traces of ailments or illness, most particularly in the lungs. This type of meat is referred to as *glatt*. However, the Joint Rabbinical Committee does not adhere to these *Shechita* guidelines in France. Therefore, in order to consume *glatt* meat, the ultra-orthodox were required to import meat from other countries, or illegally slaughter animals.

Thus, in a series of proceedings from 1984 to 1994, the ultra-orthodox association "Cha'are Shalom ve Tsedek" attempted to approve the strict rules of ritual slaughter in France with no success. Thus, the association brought the case before the European Court of Human Rights in the *Cha'are Shalom ve Tsedek v. France* case. In its decision, the majority of the court found that the difference of treatment given by the French government between the applicant and the Joint Rabbinical Committee—approving the latter association to perform ritual slaughter while denying the former—was legitimate. This is because, in the opinion of the court, there was no interference with freedom of religion:

> "In the Court's opinion, there would be interference with the freedom to manifest one's religion only if the illegality of performing ritual slaughter made it impossible for ultra-orthodox Jews to eat meat from animals slaughtered in accordance with the religious prescriptions they considered applicable."[55]

Furthermore, the majority judges found that the different treatment by the French government between the applicants and the Joint Rabbinical Committee was reasonable, and also proportional between the means which were employed by the government and the goal of regulating ritual slaughter:

> "The Court further considers that the fact that the exceptional rules designed to regulate the practice of ritual slaughter permit only ritual slaughterers authorized by approved religious bodies to engage in it does not in itself lead to the conclusion that there has been an interference with the freedom to manifest one's religion. The Court considers, like the Government, that it is in the general interest to avoid unregulated slaughter, carried out in conditions of doubtful hygiene, and that it is therefore preferable, if there is to be ritual slaughter,

---

55 Cha'are Shalom Ve Tsedek v. France, *supra* note 52, at pargraph 80.

for it to be performed in slaughterhouses supervised by the public authorities. Accordingly, when in 1982 the State granted approval to the *ACIP*, an offshoot of the Central Consistory, which is the body most representative of the Jewish communities of France, it did not in any way infringe the freedom to manifest one's religion."[56]

The minority opinion, however, elected a broader approach. In their view, the state is obliged to give careful consideration to all applications made by other religious groups, even at times when there is an alternative approved body. Furthermore, it is the state's role to facilitate the plural diversity within divided communities, and not dismiss other alternatives in the sake of homogeneity.[57]

The issue of preceding slaughter by electrical, mechanical, or gaseous stun prior to slaughter has risen and been promulgated in many civil legislative efforts. The reasoning behind this movement is for the welfare of the animal, as slaughter without stunning is seen as cruel. As stated, because pre-slaughter stunning is considered *non-kosher,* such laws are in conflict with the religious ritual.

In many different countries, especially European ones, the subject has been debated at length, and there have been numerous attempts – both successful and unsuccessful – to make it more difficult, or even banning, non-stunning ritual slaughter.[58]

The Polish Animal Protection Act of 1997 requires that all slaughter of animals must be performed by humanitarian techniques which reduce the pain caused by the process. Therefore, stunning prior to the slaughter was mandatory. Then in 2002 the Polish Parliament repealed an exception to the law which allowed ritual slaughter without stunning. Because Poland does not have large Jewish and Muslim religious communities, the change did not bring about large public resistance. Nevertheless, two years later the Polish Minister of Agriculture reintroduced an exception by way of a statutory dictate. The provision contradicted by amended Animal Protection Law; thus, in 2012, the provision was challenged before the Polish Constitutional Tribunal. The Tribunal ruled that in case of conflict between the statute and the minister's exception, the stat-

---

56 *Id.,* at 77.

57 *Id.,* Joint Dissenting Opinion of Judges Sir Nicolas Bratza, Fischbach, Thomassen, Tsatsa-Nikolovska, Panţîru, Levits, and Traja.

58 R. J. Delahunty, *Does Animal Welfare Trump Religious Liberty? The Danish Ban on Kosher and Halal Butchering,* 16 San Diego Int'l L.J. 341, 342 (2015).

ute prevails. As a result, the prohibition of ritual slaughter without prior stunning was formally reinstated.[59]

On the 10th of December, 2014, the Polish Constitutional Tribunal gave a judgement regarding the legality of the prohibition of ritual slaughter without prior stunning set forth in the Animal Protection Act. The motion was triggered by the Union of Jewish Religious Communes in Poland, which claimed that the act contradicted the Polish Constitution's provision on free exercise of religion. That provision states, *inter alia*, that the freedom can be limited only "where this is necessary for the defense of State security, public order, health, morals or the freedoms and rights of others".[60] The applicants further claimed that the Act contradicted Article 9 of the European Convention on Human Rights, which similarly provides, *inter alia*, for freedom of religion. Therefore, the Union of Jewish Religious Communes claimed that, due to the prohibition, the members of the religious groups are treated less favorably, and the act of importing meat is both costly and burdensome.[61]

The Constitutional Tribunal accepted the Union of Jewish Religious Communes claims. By referring to the *Cha'are Shalom Ve Tsedek v France* case, the Tribunal stated that ritual slaughter is protected by Article 53 of the Polish Constitution and Article 9 of the European Convention. The judgment further stated that the prohibition, set forth in the Animal Protection Act, was not a proportionate measure in order to achieve a constitutionally listed goal (as mentioned in Article 56(5) of the Constitution). Therefore, in sum, the prohibition did not correctly balance the values of animal protection and freedom of religion.[62]

Similarly, during early 2011, the lower house of Parliament in the Netherlands passed a bill, by a wide majority, which was introduced by the Animal Rights Party; the bill would have banned all ritual slaughter in the Netherlands outright. However, the Senate rejected the bill, on the grounds that it would have infringed too severely on religious freedom.[63]

Many countries (chiefly Western European) including Norway, Sweden, Iceland, and Switzerland, prohibit ritual slaughter. in February 2014, the Danish

---

59 Aleksandra Lis and Tomasz Pietrzykowski, *Animals as Objects of Ritual Slaughter: Polish Law After the Battle over Exceptionless Mandatory Stunning*, 2 Global Journal of Animal Law 1 (2015).
60 Article 53(5) of the Polish Constitution.
61 Aleksandra Gliszczyńska-Grabias and Wojciech Sadurski, *Freedom of Religion versus Humane Treatment of Animals: Polish Constitutional Tribunal's Judgment on Permissibility of Religious Slaughter*, 11:03 European Constitutional Law Review, 596, 600 (2015).
62 *Id.*, at 603.
63 *Dutch Compromise on Ritual Slaughter*, Radio Netherlands Worldwide Radio, https://www.rnw.org/archive/dutch-compromise-ritual-slaughter (accessed February 9, 2017).

government joined the group of countries which prohibit the slaughter of animals without prior stunning.[64] The Danish government defended its decision on the basis of animal welfare, and argued that ritual slaughter without prior stunning diminishes it.[65]

4. Exhuming the Dead

The general rule of *Halacha* forbids any action regarding the exhumation of a deceased body. Therefore, there is a general prohibition of the removal of remains from their burial place. For instance, the Jerusalem Talmud, in *Moed Katan*, states:

> "Corpses or skeletons may not be removed from an honorable grave to an honorable grave, from one unworthy grave to another, from an unworthy grave to one that is honorable and no need to state, from an honorable grave to one that is unworthy."[66]

There are several reasons for the prohibition of disinterment of human bodies. Chiefly, in general, Jewish Halacha forbids the disrespecting or the defiling or the breach of the dignity of the dead. For instance, Rabbi Akiva declined the exhumation of a body in order to verify if the man was a minor or not, as he thought of the action as humiliation of the dead. This is referred to as the rule against *Nivul Hamet* or *Hilul Hamet*. Another reason is the fear that, by exhuming a body, the remains will be disturbed, which will cause the dead to be disturbed and confused. The prophet Samuel scorned King Saul who went to a woman in *Ein Dor* and asked to communicate with the Prophet Samuel after his death. After doing so, Samuel said to Saul "Why hast thou disquieted me, to bring me up?"[67] This reasoning against disrespecting the dead is referred to as the rule against *Bilbul Hamet*, i.e., the rule against the disarrangement of the bones of the dead. Lastly, the concern is that the process is egregious and disrespectful, especially when the flesh has not completely decomposed.[68]

In spite of the general prohibition of exhumation, there are numerous sources supporting disinterment or the operating of a deceased performed on a

---

64 Article 9 of the "Order on the Slaughter and Killing of Animals" states "[...] Slaughter must take place with prior stunning in accordance with this notice [...]", https://www.retsinformation.dk/Forms/R0710.aspx?id=161815 (in Danish; accessed February 9, 2017).

65 Delahunty, *supra* note 58, at 346.

66 Mo'ed Katan, 2:4.

67 1 Samuel 28:15.

68 Mo'ed Katan 1:13.

human body. On the issue of the autopsy on human bodies there are conflicting views.[69] It has been ruled by rabbis that it is permissible to order disinterment of a body for the purpose of releasing an *aguna* from her marriage bond.[70] Also, it was ruled by The chief Rabbi of Israel, Bakshi Doron, that disinterment is permissible in the case of a mass grave of the victims of the Hadassah hospital convoy of 49 doctors nurses and staff killed in a terror attack In 1948.[71] Exhumation was necessary in order to move the remains to a permanent grave from the discovered mass grave.[72]

Israeli courts have ruled on a number of cases regarding exhumation for the purpose of DNA tests at the request of the plaintiffs. For example, one case involved a minor who requested the exhumation in order to ascertain that he is the son of the person who claimed to be his father, all the while his grandparents refused to provide samples of the father's tissue. The court allowed for the disinterment as it analyzed the Jewish Halacha and concluded that the process was allowed because the interest of the child prevails over the interest of maintaining the dignity of the deceased. However, in another case, the Tel Aviv Family Court ruled that, in the absence of express statutory power to give an order for a DNA test of a dead person, the court should not give such an order.[73]

More recently, the Federal Constitutional Court (*Bundesverfassungsgericht*) refused to intervene to prevent in advance a judicial determination regarding an exhumation of a body for the purpose of determining parenthood based on DNA tests of a deceased. The court decided that there was no constitutional right infringed in the circumstances because the determination of parenthood could be resolved without exhumation; it was not clear if the court would or would not order exhumation. Furthermore, even if the court did order the examination of DNA tissue, it was considered not necessarily a violation of a constitutional right. This ruling was in line with the general rule of Jewish *Halacha*, which, in certain circumstances, allows exhumation and is not considered a violation of religious faith.[74]

---

69 See http://www.medethics.org.il/articles/bib/R0061303.asp (accessed February 9, 2017).

70 See, for example, Rabbi Shaul Nathanson and Rabbi Eliezer Fleckles. "Aguna" is a wife that could not get divorced due to disappearance or refusal of her husband.

71 *Id.*

72 Rabbi Rishon Lezzion Bakshi Doron responsa ,Binyan Av, page 408

73 See Family Court Case (TA) 8090/96 *Plonit v. Wolfson Hospital*, Dinim Mishpahay Vol. 1, pp. 74.

74 Constitutional Court, decision of the 2nd Chamber of the First Senate of 03 July 2015–1 BvR 2405/11–Rn. (1–7), http://www.bverfg.de/e/rk20150703_1bvr240511.html

5. The Enforcement in Civil Court of the Duty to Deliver Get (Divorce Certificate)

In a Court of Appeals in New York, a decision was made involving a Jewish couple married under Jewish law and divorced by civil law. In the decision, the husband was required by the state court of New York to appear before a religious tribunal and grant his wife a religious divorce. This reversed the appellate court's decision that the *ketubah*, the religious marriage certificate stating that wife and husband recognized the Jewish law of marriage and the authority of the Rabbinical tribunal, was a religious agreement, and the State had no interest in their marital status after it had granted a civil divorce. The court stated that the wife was not requesting the enforcement of a solely religious practice, but of an agreement to perform a certain civil obligation to appear before and accept the decision of a designated tribunal. Even though the agreement was part of a religious ceremony, the wife was requesting the court to compel the husband to carry out a secular obligation that he bound himself to when he signed the *ketubah*.[75] The Supreme Court of Canada also supported the right of the wife to receive a Jewish get after a civil divorce.[76] As a result of these cases, a practice has developed for Jewish couples to sign a pre-marriage contract expressly providing for the duty to give a *get*, a Jewish divorce certificate.

6. Jurisprudence Relating to Islamic Sharia and Religious Practice

A. Workplace Accommodation

In 1981, the European Court of Human Rights (ECtHR) heard the case of *X v. The United Kingdom*.[77] The applicant was a school teacher in a London public school; he that the school authorities refused to accommodate his work hours so to allow him to take a forty-five-minute break on Friday afternoons to pray at a mosque. The Court rejected the applicant's claims; it held that the applicant on his own free will accepted the terms of the teaching obligations under his employ-

---

75 *Avitzur v. Avitzur*, 58 N.Y.2d 108; 445 N.E 2d 136; 459 N.Y.S.2d 572 (1983), Court of Appeals of New York.
76 *Bruker v. Marcovitz*, [2007] 3 S.C.R. 607, 2007 SCC 54.
77 *X v. The United Kingdom*, App. No. 7215/75 ECHR (1981).

ment contract and that, as a result, he was unable to attend Friday Prayers. Therefore, the authorities did not infringe on his freedom of religion.[78]

B. Clothes Regulations

The issue of wearing of religious clothing and symbols in public areas, such as schools and universities, has in recent years been a prevailing issue before the European Court of Human Rights. However, all of the holdings upheld the standpoints of the states in perusing their aims. For example, on November 10, 2005, the ECtHR ruled in the case of *Şahin v Turkey*,[79] in which the applicant was refused access to an examination and registration to a course in the University of Israel for wearing an Islamic headscarf. The court found that there was no violation of the European Convention (specifically Articles 8, 9, 10, and 14), as the banning of wearing Islamic headscarves in the university was proportionate in the balance between the applicant's freedom of religion and the state's aims to preserve secularism, public order, and protection of gender equality.[80]

C. Circumcision and the Right to Bodily Integrity

On May 7, 2012, the District Court of Cologne,[81] Germany, ruled that ritual circumcision of young males constitutes an unlawful offense as it is a form of bodily harm. The court's judgement concerns the prosecution of a physician who performed a circumcision on a four-year-old child, whose family adheres to the Islamic faith; the procedure resulted in bodily harm which required medical attention shortly after. As a result, the physician was charged with causing bodily harm by using a dangerous instrument under Sections 223–224 of the German Criminal Code.[82]

The court declared that circumcision for religious reasons is illegal by defending the child's right to bodily integrity and self-determination: "the right of the parents to raise their child in their religious faith does not take precedence

---

78 *Id.*
79 *Sahin v Turkey*, (2007) 44 EHRR 5 (Grand Chamber).
80 European Parliament's Committee on Civil Liberties, Justice and Home Affairs, *Religious Practice and Observance in the EU Member States*, 65 (2013).
81 Cologne District Court [Landgericht Köln] 7 May 2012—Docket No. 151 Ns 169/11 available at: http://www.dur.ac.uk/resources/ilm/CircumcisionJudgmentLGCologne7May20121.pdf
82 *Id.*

over the right of the child to bodily integrity and self-determination."[83] This, in the eyes of the court, is especially true, as the procedure was found to have no medical benefits or essential elements for the child's well-being. Furthermore, by performing the act of circumcision, the child's body has been "permanently and irreparably" changed.[84] Put differently, the Cologne Court ruling addresses two questions: firstly, whether non-medical circumcisions performed on male children infringes upon basic constitutional rights and, secondly, whether circumcision is part of a parent's right to raise a child up in a particular way.[85]

However, the Cologne judgment pertains only to the unique case mentioned above. As with all German Court decisions, and in accordance with the German legal system, court decisions are non-binding beyond the specific case. In other words, German court decisions are only binding between the parties involved. They do not count as precedent, particularly not for the purpose of *stare decisis*. With that being said, to a certain extent, decisions of the supreme courts do impact the interpretation of statutes.[86]

The ruling brought about heated debates from critics who regarded it as an offense to freedom of religious expression and a fundamental human right, while supporters welcomed the ruling. In December 2012, the German parliament passed a new section into the German Civil Code which secures the legality of religious circumcision by allowing parents to give their consent to non-medical circumcisions.[87]

D. Forced Divorce

There are three main forms of traditional divorce in Islam: *ṭalāq*, *tafrīq*, and *khul'*. The first, *ṭalāq*, is a unilateral rejection of a wife by the husband. In other words, a husband can end his marriage by following a fixed formula with no intervention of a court, or ability to contest by the wife. There are three types of *ṭalāq* which are discussed by the modern Islamic jurists: The first, *ahsan*, is characterized by a slow and gradual divorce in which the husband must refrain from sexual relations for three menstrual cycles, after which they

---

83 *Id.*
84 *Id.*
85 Diana Aurenque & Urban Wiesing, *German Law on Circumcision and Its Debate: How an Ethical and Legal Issue Turned Political*, 29 J. of Bioethics 203, 204 (2015).
86 Jan F. Orth, *Explaining the Cologne Circumcision Decision*, 77 The J. of Crim. L. 497, 505 (2013).
87 Diana Aurenque & Urban Wiesing, *German Law on Circumcision and Its Debate: How an Ethical and Legal Issue Turned Political*, 29 J. OF BIOETHICS 203, 207 (2015).

would be divorced. The couple can remarry if they wish. In the second, *Hasan*, the husband audibly emits three pronunciations of divorce in three sequential menstrual cycles. The couple, however, cannot remarry unless the woman has married another man between the initial divorce and the time they wish to remarry. Lastly, is the *ṭalāq al-bid ʿa (*also known as the triple *ṭalāq*) in which the husband simply audibly pronounces three times the word divorce. The divorce according to this type of *ṭalāq* is irrevocable.[88]

In the United States, the law recognizes divorces which are non-judicial of persons who legally reside in the United States and which were obtained within countries that legally recognize the dissolving of marriage. However, the United States does not recognize non-judicial divorces that US residents obtain within its borders.[89] Accordingly, in the case of *Shikoh v. Murrif,*[90] the Second Circuit Court of Appeals ruled that a *ṭalāq* divorce is invalid. A Pakistani male who was studying in New York wished to divorce his wife, living in Pakistan, by writing her a declaration of divorce. As stated by the declaration, the marriage had ended in accordance with Islamic law. However, the court ruled that the declaration was invalid, and it was not a "judicial proceeding" according to the provisions in New York's constitution, which recognizes divorce only by means of judicial proceeding.[91] That is to say, the court held that the divorce proceeding must follow the law of the state where the proceedings took place, even in situations where the procedure is in compliance with the law of the nationality or the domicile of the couple.[92] Similarly, in Israel, forced divorce is forbidden; it is a crime set by Article 181 of the Israeli Criminal Code, with a maximum punishment of 5 years' imprisonment.

7. The Debate in India on Implementing Uniform Civil Code in Personal Matters

Another interesting example of the relationship between religion and state can be found in India. The Constitution of India declares India to be a secular state.[93]

---

88 Judith E. Tucker, *Women, Family, and Gender in Islamic Law,* 86 (2008).
89 Alan Reed, *Transnational Non-Judicial Divorces: A Comparative Analysis of Recognition under English and U.S. Jurisprudence,* 18 Loy, L.A. Int'l & Comp, L.J. 311 (1996).
90 Shikoh v. Murff, 257 F.2d 306 (2d Cir. 1958).
91 Reed, *supra* note 84, at 314.
92 Edward Kaufman, *Conflicts of Law—Non-Judicial Divorces,* 13 U. Miami L. Rev., 240 (1958)
93 See Shimon Shetreet, *Academic Blueprint for the Implementation of Uniform Civil Code for India,* Utah Law Review, pp. 97–120 (2011).

Secularism is not an obvious choice for India due to the plethora of religions and cultures, as well as the deep integration of religion in societal life in India. Interpersonal relationships are governed by personal laws determined by religion. India's constitution is somewhat unique in that instead of reflecting India's society, one of its main aims was, and still is, to shape Indian society and to bring around social reform. Indeed, freedom of religion has been limited in certain cases, when it was deemed to be against the good of the people, such as the outlawing of polygamy for Hindus.[94]

Article 44 of the Constitution states that the "State shall endeavour to secure for the citizens a uniform civil code throughout the territory of India."[95] Many minorities fear that the entire population will be forced to adopt a Hindu character. In addition, another obstacle to creating a uniform civil code is the seemingly necessary impact it will have on the freedom of religion. A uniform civil code will apply, by definition, to all areas of civil life, including those currently covered by personal law. It is feared that it will create law pertaining to marriage and divorce, inheritance, personal status, and so on. Muslims who wish to carry out a Muslim way of life would no longer be able to do so because the personal laws regarding them would be those dictated by the secular state, and not the Shari'a. This is evident from the response to the *Shah Bano* case, which held that a divorced Muslim wife is entitled to apply for maintenance under Section 125 of the Code of Criminal Procedure.[96] Many Muslims were outraged by the court's ruling and saw it as an attempt to force upon them a uniform code. This is understandable, as the court elaborated much upon Article 44, even though it seemingly did not call for any good reason or need to refer to this Article. Very soon after, the Muslim Women (Protection of Rights on Divorce) Act, 1986 was passed,[97] which overturned the *Shah Bano* ruling, thus reinstating Muslim personal law as previously understood.

---

94 See The Hindu Marriage Act, No. 25 of 1955, India Code (1993), *available at* http://indiacode.nic.in.

95 See Shimon Shetreet, *Academic Blueprint for the Implementation of Uniform Civil Code for India*, Utah Law Review, pp. 97–120 (2011).

96 *Mohd. Ahmed Khan v. Shah Bano Begum & Ors*, (1985) 3 S.C.R. (India) 844.

97 The Muslim Women (Protection of Rights on Divorce) Act, No. 25 of 1986, India Code (1993), available at http://indiacode.nic.in (accessed February 9, 2017). For a detailed analysis of the debate in India, see Shimon Shetreet and Hiram Chodosh, Uniform Civil Code in India: Proposed Blueprint for Scholarly Discourse, pp. xxii, 303 (Oxford University Press, 2015).

Part VII: **Equality in Israeli Law**

Chapter 14:
Promoting Equality for Women, Minorities, and Jews from Different Countries

1. The Social Gap among Jews in Israel and Positive Preference

In Israel, there exists a social gap, creating tensions between the Ashkenazim and the so-called Sephardim.[1] Ashkenazim are Jews born in Europe and their descendants, while Sephardim are generally Jews born in Asia and Africa and their descendants. It should be noted, however, that Sephardim may also be descendants of Jews from such European countries as Bulgaria, Greece, and Spain. Israel employs a form of affirmative action, referred to as positive preference, in order to help disadvantaged individuals or groups to improve their position in society. Positive preference should be understood as corrective action that includes positive preference for disadvantaged groups and individuals.[2]

Firstly, positive preference is directed towards promoting the interests of the numerical majority of the population, rather than the numerical minority. While the Sephardim constitute more than 50% of the population, they are in fact a substantive minority because they endure many of the problems that characterize the experience of a minority population.[3]

Secondly, Israel has always maintained an official policy of Jewish solidarity and a commitment to the attainment of a united Jewish people. There has never been an officially sanctioned policy of discrimination. Instead, there has been a

---

1 The problems of inequality between the Ashkenazim and the Sephardim are conceptually similar to inequality based on sex and in some aspects to inequality between the Jewish and Arab populations in Israel. For a discussion of sex inequality, see Prime Minister's Office, Proposal of the Committee on the Status of Women (1981); Shapira-Libai, *The Concept of Sex Equality: The UN Decade for Women*, 11 Israel Yearbook on Human Rights132 (1981); Raday, *Equality of Women Under Israeli Law*, Jerusalem Q. (No. 21) 81 (1983). For a discussion of the status of Arabs in Israel and the preference for Jews (particularly the automatic citizenship granted to Jews under the Law of Return), see Klein, *Le Caractere Juif de l'Etat d'Israel*; Gouldman, *Israel Nationality Law*; Rubinstein, *Israel Nationality*, 2 Tel Aviv University Studies in Law 159; *Every Sixth Israeli* (Hareven ed. 1983)

2 Shimon Shetreet, *Affirmative Action for Promoting Social Equality: The Israeli Experience in Positive Preference*, 17 Israel Yearbook on Human Rights 242–269, 242 (1987) (hereinafter: Shimon Shetreet, *Affirmative Action*). The article is based on a paper presented at a Conference on Affirmative Action held at Tel Aviv University, 30–31 December 1984.

3 Shimon Shetreet, *Affirmative Action, supra* note 2, at 243.

DOI 10.1515/9783899497946-015

negative, or discriminatory, impact on the Sephardim resulting from certain policies in such matters as placement of immigrants in development towns, their transfer from such towns to the center of the country, and the criteria for providing uniform free housing (i.e., all families, regardless of size, received one-and-a-half room apartments of approximately 50 square meters).[4] There has also been personal-informal bias by Ashkenazi officials favoring Ashkenazi individuals to the disadvantage of Sephardim.[5]

Thirdly, Israel has been and remains a highly centralized society. The central government touches almost every aspect of the life of its citizens, while the role of local government is quite limited. This centralization was even greater in the early years of the State. Informal contacts in a highly centralized society are much more important for attaining success than in other systems.[6] In Israel, this is referred to as *protektsia*, similar to the English "old boy network. *Protektsia* has been defined[7] as the assistance that bureaucrats may give to members of the public, not necessarily because they deserve it, but because they may be friends, come from the same town, be members of the same community, or have served with them in the Army. *Protektsia* may be found in the everyday relations between the public and the bureaucracy, and in the web of relationships that form the country's power elite. The result is that a lack of informal access to places of power may curtail one's ability to succeed in government or business.[8]

Lastly, in Israel some of the affirmative action programs with goals to narrow the social gap would be successful even if they were not based on criteria such as country of origin, specifically targeting the Sephardim. They could be successful with more generally applied criteria. For example, preference to students with

---

4 The size of the typical Sephardi family is significantly larger than its Ashkenazi counterpart; thus, policies that seemed fair in actuality resulted in indirect discrimination against Sephardim. For a discussion of these policies and their impact on the Sephardi immigrants, particularly the Moroccan Jews, *see* Inbar and Adler, *Ethnic Integration in Israel: A Comparative Case Study of Moroccan Brothers Who Settled in France and* in *Israel* esp. Ch. 10, at 125–136 (1977).

5 Shimon Shetreet, *Affirmative Action, supra* note 2, at 243.

6 On friendship networks in Israel, *see* Goravitz and Vinograd, "Who Knows Whom? Networks of Contacts in the Israeli Elite," *Megamot* 357 (Hebrew, 1976). Research has shown that the brothers of Moroccan-born Israelis who settled in France were more successful than their Israeli brothers who migrated to *Israel*. See Inbar and Adler, *supra* note 4, esp. Ch. 6, at 73–85. For a detailed discussion of family ties within the political, social and business elites, see Elizur and Salpeter, *Who Rules Israel?* (1973).

7 Elizur and Salpeter, *supra* note 6, at 21–22.

8 Shimon Shetreet, *Affirmative Action, supra* note 2, at 243–244.

low socio-economic status would still largely favor Sephardim and would favor Ashkenazim only marginally.[9]

2. Distribution of Wealth and Power

The inequality among Jews in Israel is manifested by wide gaps in all areas, including public services, housing, per capita income, education at all levels, social status, and the allocation of employment opportunities in centers of power, such as in public administration and public and government institutions, government enterprises, the political system, the Histadrut (the Federation of Labor in Israel) and Histadrut-related companies, and the Zionist bodies and their branches. In all of these areas, the distribution is pyramid-shaped, with the Sephardim at the bottom constituting a clear majority, and their numbers decreasing as they go up the hierarchy. The top echelons contain few or no Sephardim.[10]

The following examples are given in order to highlight the discrepancies in political representation: The Sephardi community, which constitutes about 55% of the population,[11] is barely represented in the centers of power.[12] Of the twenty-four government ministers, usually only four or five are Sephardim, two or three of the twenty-three-member Board of Directors of the Jewish Agency are Sephardim, 25% of the members of the Executive Committee of the Histadrut are Sephardim, as are two of the twenty-four Director General positions in the various departments of the Jewish Agencies.[13] Despite these discrepancies, it must be noted that several Sephardim have obtained high positions, such as the Presi-

---

9 *Id.*, at 244.

10 For further details, see Menahem, *Tensions and Ethnic Discrimination in Israel (Socio-Historical Observations)*, 20 – 24 (Hebrew, 1983); Swirski, *Orientals and Ashkenazim in Israel: The Ethnic Division of Labour*, esp. 12 – 72 (Hebrew, 1981); Peres, *Ethnic Relations in Israel*, esp. 101 – 134 (Hebrew, 1977); Inbar and Adler, *supra* note 4.

11 According to the *1983 Census of Population and Homing* (Vol. 7) (Israel Central Bureau of Statistics, 1985), the Jewish population of Israel included 1,476,400 persons born either in Africa, Asia, or the children of such persons; 1,339,700 persons either born in Europe or America, or the children of such persons, and 533,900 persons classified as of Israeli origin, meaning that they were born in Israel to persons who were also born in Israel.

12 See Adler, "Desegregation in Schools and Developments in the Israeli Educational System," *School Desegregation* 38 – 40 (Amir and Sharan eds., Hebrew, 1985).

13 For a more detailed look at the data, see Smooha, *Israel: Pluralism and Conflict (1918)*; Peres, *supra* note 10, at 123 – 132; Inbar and Adler, *supra* note 4; Swirski, *supra* note 10, at 46 – 48.

dent of the State, Chief of Staff of the Israel Defense Forces, General Secretary of the Histadrut, and Deputy Prime Minister.[14]

For the most part, the socioeconomic division of Israeli society parallels the division according to country of origin.[15] The lowest socioeconomic class, which is around the poverty line, is composed mostly of Sephardim. Most of the working class is also Sephardim, the middle class is mixed and balanced, while the upper middle class is predominantly Ashkenazi. The upper class, including the professional, political, and administrative elites, is 90% Ashkenazi, while 90% of the prison population is Sephardim.[16]

The pyramid repeats itself in education. At the elementary school level, Sephardim constitute 65% of the students, while the rate declines to about 24% in the universities. Professor Ozer Shield has observed that the probability of an Ashkenazi student gaining admission to university is four times greater than that of a Sephardim student.[17]

3. Negative Attitudes towards the Sephardim

The initial attitudes of the dominant Ashkenazi group regarding the mass immigration of Sephardim after the establishment of the State of Israel was benevolent and paternalistic. It viewed its Jewish brethren from Egypt, Morocco, Iraq or Yemen as objects of cultural transformation, disregarding their rich Jewish heritage and deep Jewish values. The view among the Ashkenazi founders of the state was that Israel was a "Melting Pot" and the Jews from the Middle Eastern countries had to be transformed into "Israelis," westernized and modernized. Any failure to be absorbed was interpreted either as a deficiency in the Middle-Eastern family structure, an individual personality problem, or traditional (i.e., cultural) deficiency showing reluctance for change. Thus, "cultural gaps" and "cultural inferiority" became much-used slogans, and for several generations such slogans became part of both formal and informal socialization efforts.[18]

---

14 Shimon Shetreet, *Affirmative Action, supra* note 2, at 244–45.

15 See, e.g., Eisenstadt, *Change and Continuity in Israeli Society (1919)*; Smooha, *supra* note 13; Peres, *supra* note 10; *Studies in Israeli Society* (Krausz ed. 1980); Menahem, *supra* note 10.

16 Shimon Shetreet, *Affirmative Action, supra* note 2, at 245.

17 *Ha'aretz* (Israeli daily newspaper, Hebrew), 26 June 1986, at 2. Professor Shield of the School of Education, the University of Haifa, made a number of observations on the inequality between Ashkenazi and Sephardi students in the educational system at a seminar at the Van Leer Institute, Jerusalem, May 1986.

18 Shimon Shetreet, *Affirmative Action, supra* note 2, at 246.

The assimilation of the Sephardim was at the expense of their cultural pride and identity. Another result was a loss of the collective pride of the Sephardim Jews. This loss of pride was reinforced by the "desert generation" concept, which viewed the generation of the Sephardim parents as "lost," like the "desert generation" in the days of Moses that was doomed to die in the desert and never to enter the Promise Land.[19]

4. The Role of Non-Ashkenazi Jews in Lessening Social Inequality

Non-Ashkenazi Jews played an important role in lessening the social inequality in Israel, most notably during the last century. It is the view of this author that the non-Ashkenazi social protests contributed significantly to the democratization of the Israeli society by a series of social and political protests conducted by the Mizrachi leadership, and predominantly North African Jews.

Elsewhere, I wrote about the North African Jewry,[20] stating that the North African Jewish communities, and especially the Moroccan one, constituted the nucleus of social and political protests in Israel. The beginning of the social protests in Israel's political history can be pointed towards the Wadi Salib protest of 1959, which later resulted in the Public Commission Inquiry led by Judge Dr. Moshe Etzyoni. Later on, in the early 1970s, the North African Jewry were at the center of the Black Panthers organization; at the end of the 1970s, they also played an important role in the Tents movement. The North African Jews during the 1980s were the central figures in the Tami[21] and Shas[22] political parties; later on, the North African Jews also played a crucial role in the larger political parties, such as Ha'Likud and Ha'Avoda.[23]

One could point towards the Wadi Salib protest as a decisive time establishing the importance of the non-Ashkenazi Jews as leaders of social protest. During the first years after Israel was established, many Jewish immigrants arrived, among them approximately 300,000 Mizrachi and 300,000 Ashkenazi. Many of the Mizrachi Jews were sent to live in borderland towns or peripheral neighborhoods of holder cities, such as the Wadi Salib neighborhood in the city of

---

19 *Id.*
20 See Shimon Shetreet, *Pioneers in Tears: Studies of North African Jewry* (Am Oved Publishing, 1991) (Hebrew).
21 Movement for the Heritage of Israel (Tnu'at Masoret Yisrael).
22 *Religious Guardians of the Sephardim* (*Shomrei Sfarad*).
23 Shimon Shetreet, *Pioneers in Tears*, supra note 20, at 265.

Haifa.[24] At that time, there was a strong economical, intellectual, and artistic exercise of authority over the Mizrachi Jews. As the gaps of disparity and unfairness grew year by year, so too did the tensions and unrest grow between the Mizrachi and Ashkenazim.[25]

The Wadi Salib protest, therefore, represents an apex of Mizrachi frustration caused by over a decade of aggressive cultural and economic policies, which later on spread across many other cities in Israel. Wadi Salib was an Arab neighborhood in the city of Haifa; after 1948, many of the Arab residents left, and, in turn, Mizrachi Jews later inhabited the neighborhood. The living conditions were low, characterized by high density, poverty, and poor levels of infrastructure.[26]

On the 8th of July, 1959, an officer decided to open fire upon a drunk man in a local café, located in the Wadi Salib neighborhood, after he failed to arrest him. This caused hundreds of residents to arrive at the scene and started hurling stones at the officer. Later on the next morning, a commerce strike was called for, and many activists visited the injured man at the local hospital. While on their way back from the hospital towards Wadi Salib, the crowd began to destroy all property that came in their way. As a result, the police arrived and began to prevent any further damages by way of, *inter alia*, beating up women and children, resulting in many injuries.[27] The news of the protest spread throughout Israel to other highly populated Mizrachi towns and settlements, such as in Acre and the neighborhood of Musrara in Jerusalem. The violent clashes between protestors and police forces continued, despite a visit by Israel's Prime Minister David Ben-Gurion at Wadi Salib, and the protest continued to spread. All the while, many of the protest leaders, such as David Ben-Harouche, were under arrest and contact with the outside world was withheld. The protest was at the center of public attention.[28]

Afterwards the Israeli government ordered a Public Inquiry Commission into the event. The results of the commission, which were filed a month later, docu-

---

24 Sami Shalom Chetrit, *Intra-Jewish Conflict in Israel: White Jews, Black Jews*, 53–54 (2010); I consider highly objectionable the use of the terminology of "riots," "rebellion," or "events" which have been used by official authorities and by writers in relation to the Wadi Salib Protest. It was the first social protest of major significance in the history of Israel and the use of the other terms is misleading and should not be accepted.
25 *Id.*, at 58.
26 Public Inquiry Report, "The 9/7/59 Wadi Salib Events" (1959) available at: http://www.ar chives.gov.il/archives/#/Archive/0b0717068001c167/File/0b07170684e6e689 (accessed February 9, 2017). See also Shetreet, supra note 20, at 265.
27 *Id.*
28 *Id.*

mented the different issues of the lack of ethnic integration and social gap; however, it denied ethnic discrimination.[29]

Later on, in 1971, the Black Panthers (*Panterim Schchorim*) movement emerged. The Black Panthers was a group of Mizrachi Jews from the neighborhood of Musrara in Jerusalem. They put forward a series of demands, chiefly the end of discriminatory practices against non-Ashkenazi Jews by the government. This was to be done by improving the educational opportunities, housing, and more for the Mizrachi Jews. The movement quickly gained attention soon after a violent demonstration that took place in May 1971.[30] This large-scale ideological wave that many identified with alarmed the Israeli government, and the Panthers' leaders were arrested under administrative detention. Consequently, in response to the police repression, thousands went to the streets in violent protest, resulting in the arrest of 170 activists. All the time the government denied the claims of oppression, claimed that the acts were a result of the violence-prone Moroccan Jews.[31] However, the protests did lead to the Public Inquiry Commission regarding "Children and Teenagers in Need." The commission published its report in 1973, recommending further financial support of poverty-stricken areas and developing the informal education in Israel.[32] In 1973, the Yom Kippur War took place, which steered the public attention from issues of social inequality to those of national security.

However, the influence of the Black Panthers movement did not subside, nor did the issue of dilapidated housing, poor infrastructure, and high unemployment rates resolve. The non-Ashkenazi Jews held the government responsible for the neglect, and wished to transform the nature of their neighborhoods.[33] In 1980, the Ohalim (tents) Movement arose; it aimed to resolve the housing issues in the poor neighborhoods of Jerusalem. The movement constructed the *Ohel Moreh* settlement (as a play on words to the Elon Moreh settlement) in which young couples resided in tents to protest the allocation of government monies towards the settlement movement instead of the poor neighborhoods. This author represented the movement in the case of *Cohen v. Minister of Interior and Police*[34] regarding the question of the power of the state to remove the pro-

---

29 *Id.*, at 67; see also Sammy Smooha, *Israel: Pluralism and Conflict*, 209 (1978).

30 Erik Cohen, *The Black Panthers and Israeli Society*, 147 in Studies of Israeli Society: Migration, Ethnicity and Community (1980, ed. Ernest Krausz).

31 Ella Shohat, *Sephardim in Israel: Zionism from the Standpoint of Its Jewish Victims*, 19 Social Text 1, 29 (1988).

32 Prime Minister Public Inquiry Commission for Children and Teenagers in Need (1973).

33 Shlomo Hasson, "Territories and Identities in Jerusalem," 53 GeoJournal 311, 314 (2001).

34 H.C.J 407/80 *Azar Cohen v. Minister of Interior and Police* (published on Nevo, 10.07.1980).

testers from the premises they occupied—and whether a court order was needed or, rather, could the state do so unilaterally without a court order. After an interim injunction was granted, the court ordered that the state may request the protestors to leave the place.[35]

Lastly, it is important to note the case of *Viki Shiran v. Broadcasting Authority*[36] revolving around the documentary TV series *Pillar of Fire (Amud Ha'Esh)*. The series was created by the Israel Broadcasting Authority and presented the history of Zionism from the 19th century until the establishment of the state of Israel. It first aired in 1981. This author represented a group of non-Ashkenazi petitioners against the Israel Broadcasting Authority for disregarding the contribution of the non-Ashkenazi communities in the Zionist enterprise of building and developing towns and settlements (*moshavim)* in the 1950s and prior to that. The Supreme Court refused to intervene on the grounds that the content review of TV programs and series is an authority solely entrusted to the public council of the Israeli Broadcast Authority.[37]

The recognition of the history and the role of non-Ashkenazi Jewish communities continue to be a controversial issue in Israeli society. In 2016, a commission appointed by the Minister of Education, Naftali Bennet, reviewed the question of the role of non-Ashkenazi studies and rabbinical works in the educational school programs. The commission, termed the Biton Commission (chaired by Erez Biton), recommended rectifying the deficiencies in the present programs and including in the programs adequate discussion and analysis of the non-Ashkenazi history, culture, and artistic works.[38]

From the above report on Wadi Salib demonstrations, the Black panthers movement, the Tents movement events, and Tami and Shass political parties, it is clear that the North African Jewish communities, and especially the Moroccan community, played a significant role in the social and political protests in Israel; those protests helped democratize the country.

---

35 *Id.*

36 H.C.J 1/81 *Viki Shiran v. Broadcasting Authority*, 35(3) P.D. 365 (1981).

37 *Id.*

38 See the Biton Report for the Enhancement of the Sephardic and Orient Jewry in the Educational System (2016) available at (Hebrew) http://edu.gov.il/owlHeb/Tichon/RefurmotHinoch/Documents/bitonreport.pdf (accessed February 9, 2017).

5. Equality in Education

The response to the challenge of social inequality has been focused mainly on education. Some of the measures taken were expressly based on the notion of affirmative action, or "a policy of positive discrimination," as it was phrased by the then Minister of Education.[39] For example, in the early 1970s, high school education until age 15 became free in Israel. Additionally, schools became integrated in 1975.[40]

Under the school integration plan, school districts were reorganized in order to merge affluent areas with more disadvantaged neighborhoods. The redistricting was coupled with a prohibition against registration in schools located beyond a pupil's own school registration area.[41] This program was challenged, but was upheld by the Supreme Court.[42] However, the program is still frustrated or impeded by external and internal avoidance. External avoidance of integration is accomplished through the establishment of private schools that are not subject to public regulation. The religious school system, whether in the form of private religious schools, boarding schools for girls, or Talmudic academies (*yeshivas*) for boys, characterizes this technique. The result is that disadvantaged students tend to remain in the public school system while students (mostly Ashkenazi) from better backgrounds enroll in private schools beyond the reach of the official school integration program.[43]

Internal avoidance of integration is accomplished by classifying the students in an integrated school according to level of academic achievement. The natural and foreseeable consequence is that less able students, who are mostly from disadvantaged backgrounds, are placed in separate classes, and do not benefit from integrating with better students. The end result is integration at the school level, but segregation within classes, in effect maintaining "separate but unequal" classes within schools.[44]

---

39 Minkovich, "An Evaluation Study of Elementary Education in Israel," in *Law and Equality in Education* 22 (Goldstein ed. 1980).

40 Shimon Shetreet, *Affirmative Action, supra* note 2, at 250.

41 This system was implemented through regulations and not legislation. See further, Minkovich, *Id.*, Lewis, in Goldstein, ed., *supra* note 22, at 108; Amir and Bluss, "The Development of Ministry of Education Policies in the Area of Social Integration in the Israeli Educational System," in Amir and Sharan, *supra* note 12, at 75 – 78; Reshef, "National Aims and Educational Policy," *Jerusalem* Q. (No. 20) 96 (1981).

42 H.C.J 152/71 *Kremer v. Jerusalem Municipality et al*, 25(1) P.D. 767, 771 (1971).

43 Shimon Shetreet, *Affirmative Action, supra* note 2, at 251.

44 See Schwarzwald, "Inter-Ethnic Encounter on Separate Conditions: Public Education as Opposed to Religious Public Education," in Amir and Sharan, *supra* note 12, at 100 – 120; Sharan,

The universities in Israel have pre-academic programs that offer a second opportunity for disadvantaged students who have not satisfactorily passed all their high school matriculation examinations, yet who wish to improve their chances of acceptance to university. The admissions policy to the pre-academic programs is largely based on socioeconomic criteria, and predominantly benefits Sephardim students. In recent years, the admissions policy has been expanded to include additional groups, such as students from the kibbutzim.[45] Additionally, at the Faculty of Law of Tel Aviv University, there is a one-year, pre-law program, whose graduates are accorded preference in admission to the Law Faculty.[46]

Social considerations are used in the admissions procedures at many Israeli universities, but most notably at Tel Aviv University. Sephardim with poor socioeconomic backgrounds are given preferential treatment. Such practices occur in both the Faculty of Law and the Faculty of Medicine. In the Faculty of Law, preferential treatment is granted in admission to the Pre-Law Program. This program is part of the Faculty of Humanities, and its graduates are admitted to the Faculty of Law on the basis of their grades in the Pre-Law Program, rather than on university admission tests and the results of the official state-administered high school matriculation examinations.[47]

6. Other Programs

Affirmative action is also utilized for the military draft. In the past, many young men and women were rejected from military service. In Israel, failure to serve in the army can seriously affect one's future, particularly in connection with employment and career opportunities. Now, these young men can be inducted, trained, and educated during their army service.[48]

Since 1976, measures have been taken to rectify the disregard of Sephardim cultural heritage. Research programs and curricula have been introduced to ensure the study of the history, literature, and culture of Sephardim Jews in an at-

---

Amir and Ben-Ari, "Grouping *(hakbaza)* methods and placement according to ability and achievement that still prevail in the middle school as the typical way for resolving the great heterogeneity in student abilities result in resegregation of classes."

45 In some departments at Tel Aviv University, preference in admission is given to Arab students.

46 Shimon Shetreet, *Affirmative Action, supra* note 2, at 251.

47 See *State Comptroller's Report on the Institutions of Higher Education* 14–15 (Jerusalem 1985).

48 Shimon Shetreet, *Affirmative Action, supra* note 2, at 252.

tempt to compensate for the many years that these subjects have been totally ignored. Special radio and TV programs have also been developed to reflect Sephardim aspects. However, this measure sometimes brings about "separate but equal" programming, which seems objectionable. It would be preferable, when appropriate, to integrate Sephardim aspects within the regular programming.[49]

In the year 2000, the Knesset amended the Employment Service Act (Nominations) which, *inter alia*, regulates the nomination of candidates for governmental positions, by adding an "Adequate Representation." The provision requires that among the workers employed by the states, there will be an adequate number of representations from both sexes, people with disabilities, peoples native to the Arab sector including Druze, and Circassians.[50] In March 2011, the provision was amended by expanding the representation to people of Ethiopian heritage.[51] Over the years, other amendments to the provisions were proposed. Among them was the "Positive Preference"[52] provision which stated that, if two candidates are of equal skill and characteristics, then preference should be given to the one who completed military or alternative national civil service. The proposed amendment, however, was not legislated. Some, including the Attorney General of Israel, Yehuda Weinstein, expressed their concerns because the amendment provided affirmative action to those who completed military service; thus, certain parts of the Israeli populous wouldn't be included—mainly Arabs and the ultra-Orthodox. It is the opinion of this author, however, that the amendment was not intended to shun or reject certain groups, but rather grant positive preference on the credit of a person's characteristics, in similar fashion to the way "credit points" are given to people from certain backgrounds or gender. I supported this amendment on the ground that it is perfectly legitimate and widely practiced; it has been traditional both in state and federal jurisdictions in the United States to give preference to veterans seeking employment in public service.

I have supported positive preference not only in my academic writing, but also I implemented this policy when I held public positions in the Israeli cabinet. In this framework, I initiated a cabinet resolution during the Rabin government providing for hundreds of positions in public service exclusively designed for non-Jewish candidates for public service, allocating these positions to various

---

49 *Id.*
50 See the notes on amendment (at the time) here (Hebrew): https://www.nevo.co.il/law_word/law17/prop-2901.pdf (accessed February 9, 2017).
51 The Adequate Representation of Ethiopian Descendants in Public Service (Legislation Amendments), 5771–2011.
52 Employment Service Act (Nominations) (Amendment—Positive Preference), 5768–2009.

ministries. Also, I initiated a program in the ministry of Religious Affairs to allocate additional funds and services provided by the ministry to promote equality of services. The resolution was implemented and resulted in the appointments of hundreds of non-Jewish employees in the public service.[53] The program was called "One Law."[54] The program I initiated and implemented during my term of office as Minister of Religious Affairs was discussed in the judgement of the Supreme Court in a case that was filed by an Arab NGO seeking additional funding for religious services for non-Jewish citizens.[55]

The Labour Party Constitution provides for minimum numerical standards in the representation of Sephardim, women, and young people in the various party bodies. The allocation is 33% for Sephardim, 20% for women, and 15% for young people.[56] However, these quotas are not strictly enforced, as the young people of party institutions and candidate lists are always brought for ultimate approval before the body that is constitutionally empowered by the party to authorize deviations from these numerical standards.[57]

7. Justifications for Positive Preference in Israel

There are several justifications for introducing positive preference programs in Israel. They are based on the need to counterbalance the disadvantages of preferred groups, to compensate for past injury, and to serve as a visible symbol of the social commitment to equality.[58]

Positive preference as a method for promoting equality of results is needed to compensate for disadvantages under which the weaker socioeconomic groups labor. It is also required to counterbalance the indirect discrimination directed at Sephardim.[59]

Studies have demonstrated bias against Sephardim. Research shows that there is a clear preference for Ashkenazim by both Ashkenazim and Sephardim.

---

53 For the program to encourage non Jewish candidates see Shimon Shetreet *The Good Land: Between Power and Religion*, at 339–341 (Yediot Hemed Books 1998 Herew):for the one law program in the ministry of religious affairs see *Id*. At 341–349.

54 Leviticus 24:22 King James Bible: "Ye shall have one manner of law, as well for the stranger, as for one of your own country", Thou shall have one law to the citizen and to the alien [S.Shetreet translation];

55 H.C.J 1113/99 *Adala v. Minister of Religious Affairs* (18.4.2000).

56 Labour Party Constitution, Sec. 161.

57 Shimon Shetreet, *Affirmative Action, supra* note 2, at 252.

58 *Id*., at 261.

59 See *supra* note 10.

This naturally has a negative impact on people's attitudes towards Sephardim when they apply for a job, when they compete for admission to an educational institution,[60] or when they sit for examinations.[61] Positive preference has the potential to compensate for this negative impact.[62]

Likewise, because Israel has such a small population and is a highly centralized society, the importance of personal networks and contacts is crucial. As previously stated, in such a society, the weaker groups are at a disadvantage compared to the more privileged groups with greater access to the ruling elite and to the centers of power.[63] Positive preference is aimed to help the disadvantaged groups counterbalance these advantages.

Positive preference is also necessary to compensate for past injuries suffered following grave mistakes in the absorption of the immigrants from the Islamic countries in the 1950s. These include the discriminatory impact of official policies, the loss of collective pride, and serious injury to their own and the public image.[64]

---

60 The findings of the Israel State Comptroller regarding admission procedures in the Department of Architecture in the Technician. *See supra* note 30.

61 See, e. g., Staal, *Inter-Ethnic Tensions Amongst the People of Israel* (Hebrew, 1979), who reports that students with Sephardi-sounding names received one grade lower than students with Ashkenazi-sounding names on the same examination.

62 Shimon Shetreet, *Affirmative Action, supra* note 2, at 261.

63 It is clear that members of the dominant Ashkenazi group enjoy advantages over the weaker group, such as higher prestige, informal bias in their favor, and increased access to the personal contact networks and the centers of power. If one examines the findings of the State Comptroller on admission procedures at Tel Aviv University and the Technion (see *supra* note 30 text at Sec. III (H)), one may safely conclude that members of the dominant group benefit much more than other groups from the current admission standards and procedures. In this regard, the picture is probably not any different at the other universities in Israel. In addition to the general informal bias in their favor and higher prestige, members of the dominant group in society enjoy numerous other advantages. Studies have shown a positive correlation between level of income and rate of success in admission tests to higher education institutions. See Bell, "Awakening after Bakke," 14 *Harv. C.R—C.L.L. Rev.* 1, at 2 and n. 3 (1979). There are also instances of positive preference towards members of the dominant group, such as preference to sons of doctors in admission to medical schools (which until recently meant the Hebrew University Medical School), or the preferential treatment accorded relatives of contributors, as recorded by the State Comptroller with regard to Tel Aviv University. See *supra* note 30 text at Sec. III (E). There is also a strong claim that the admission tests to universities are culturally and socially biased in favor of the dominant group and indirectly discriminate against socially and economically disadvantaged groups, or groups which are culturally different from the dominant culture. *See* Bell, *Id.*, at 3.

64 Shimon Shetreet, *Affirmative Action, supra* note 2, at 262.

Advancement of the position of members of weaker groups in society will improve their public and self-image and will increase their access to the centers of power. This not only will help the individual members of those weaker groups who will also actually be preferred under the programs, but also will assist disadvantaged groups as a whole. After all, members of the Ashkenazi group, which dominates a society that has shown bias towards the weaker groups, enjoy the benefits of being a part of the stronger group. The effort to tip the scales of social justice in favor of weaker groups cannot be totally unrelated to one's position as a member of a stronger group.[65]

Many opponents of positive preference argue that such programs stigmatize the members of the preferred groups.[66] However, if the programs are administered in good faith, and qualified members are selected, any such stigma will be limited or even eliminated. Moreover, any stigma that may attach ("token Sephardim") is worth the price of promoting equality on an expedited basis. In light of the fact that the gap between Sephardim and Ashkenazim is wide, it is not possible to promote social balance between the groups within a reasonable period of time without formalized, direct measures. Even with the institution of such measures, the time needed to promote equality will be quite substantial and measured in decades. The alternative to positive preference—sitting back to see if the passage of time itself can heal the social evils emanating from the sharp social imbalance in wealth and the distribution of power—will make the inequalities almost permanent.[67]

Additionally, there are legal justifications for maintaining positive preference programs in Israel. The law in Israel does not follow a result-oriented approach to affirmative action, but focuses on an analysis of the rules themselves: if a rule provides for differential treatment of similarly situated persons, the courts will set it aside as discriminatory. If, however, the rule is not facially discriminatory, but its application may still result in indirect discrimination, it will be difficult to challenge its legal validity under present law. Nevertheless, the present case law could be extended to make indirect discrimination unlawful, by interpreting it to hold that a rule or criterion that results in indirect discrimination is illegitimate or unreasonable. However, judicial development takes a long time and depends on what kinds of cases are brought before the courts.[68] Given this, it may be preferable to adopt a result-oriented definition of discrimination by legislation, as

---

65 *Id.*

66 See e.g., Goldstein, "Reverse Discrimination—Reflections of a Jurist," 15 *Israel Yearbook on Human Rights* 28, at 33 (1985).

67 Shimon Shetreet, *Affirmative Action, supra* note 2, at 262–263.

68 *Id.*, at 264.

was done in the United Kingdom by a 1976 legislative amendment to the Race Relations Act.[69]

Two main questions arise in connection with the application of the law of discrimination to the topic of positive preference. First, to what extent will the court compel State agencies to introduce affirmative action programs to attain or promote equality in result? Second, will the court uphold the validity of preferential treatment if it is voluntarily introduced by the administrative authorities?[70]

As to the first question, the courts will be unlikely to issue an order to the agencies to introduce positive preference. This is due to the approach to discrimination articulated in case law, which is based on a process-oriented definition of discrimination.[71] True, a different trend has emerged in recent cases dealing with financing and allocating television time to election campaigns,[72] but this tendency relates to an area in which a Basic Law applies. It is likely that the court takes a special approach to constitutional adjudication,[73] as distinguished from judicial review of administrative actions based on its general supervisory jurisdiction of administrative authority.[74]

It is important to point out that the courts have been generally reluctant to grant affirmative action remedies. A petition seeking an order directing a government agency to introduce an affirmative action program requires the court to issue an order to allocate certain resources and to establish an enforcement mechanism. The courts have been reluctant to grant such affirmative remedies; they are much more inclined to grant relief ordering state agencies to refrain from an act that interferes with individual rights.[75] As Professor Stephen Gold-

---

69 Race Relations Act 1976 (c. 74).
70 Shimon Shetreet, *Affirmative Action, supra* note 2, at 265.
71 In H.C.J 555/77 *Babcock v. Securities Exchange*, 32(2) P.D. 377, at 384, Asher J. stated: "In order for the petitioner to succeed in this Court on a claim of discrimination, he must show that the discrimination was intentional and malicious." Asher J. delivered a dissenting judgment in this case, but the majority judges did not expressly disagree with him. Moreover, Bechor J. agreed with him on the question of discrimination; *Id.*, 387. The Court cited H.C.J. 30/55, *Admot Nazrat v. Minister of Finance*, 9 (2) P.D. 1261, the holding of which was later revised on this point in H.C.J 118/62 *Landau v. Minister of Agriculture*, 16 P.D. 2540, at 2544: "I do not attribute to the respondent's intentional discrimination against the producers, which are not closed farms; but discrimination that exists in fact, even if not intentional when justified, will also be invalidated."
72 H.C.J 141/82 *Rubinstein v. Speaker of the Knesset*, 37(3) P.D. 141 (1983) (Hebrew); H.C.J 246, 260/81 *Derekh Erect v. Broadcasting Authority*, 35(4) P.D. 1.
73 *Id.*
74 Shimon Shetreet, *Affirmative Action, supra* note 2, at 265–266.
75 *Id.*, at 266.

stein has written: "The Israeli courts have not shown the same enthusiasm for promoting equality as they have for liberty."[76] While the courts are reluctant to grant an order compelling preferential programs to compensate for policies that result only in indirect discrimination, the courts have upheld certain preferential policies as legitimate.[77] Thus, the government, for economic reasons, may decide to grant subsidies to one industry and not to another, or may grant larger subsidies to one branch of an industry than to another.[78] Likewise, it has been held that location may serve as basis for preferential treatment. Thus, residents of a town may be charged less than non-residents to rent municipal property,[79] and may be accorded preference in the award of public contracts by the municipality.[80]

When the nature of the treatment calls for encouraging one group even at the exclusion of others, courts have supported preferential treatment.[81] Thus, a policy encouraging Jews to settle in the reconstructed Jewish Quarter in the Old City of Jerusalem and, to that end, to exclude others (e. g., Moslems), was upheld by the Israel Supreme Court.[82] Likewise, the Court approved an arrangement encouraging immigration to Israel by young doctors from Western countries by paying their full salary during compulsory army service, while not granting this privilege to immigrant doctors from other countries.[83] The case law has also supported programs to promote equality even when it conflicts with other rights. Thus, the school integration program was upheld by the Supreme Court, even though it interfered with the right of parents to choose the kind of education their children will receive (e. g., private, religious, non-religious).[84]

In the area of equality in elections, such as the allocation of television time and election campaign financing, the Court has employed broader standards of

---

76 Goldstein, "Judicial Intervention in Education Decision Making," in *Law and Equality* in *Education*, 100 (Goldstein ed., 1980).
77 Shimon Shetreet, *Affirmative Action, supra* note 2, at 266.
78 See H.C.J 332/78, *Scitex Corporation Ltd. v. Minister of Finance*, 33(2) P.D. 594.
79 H.C.J 482/78, *Elkaam v. Mayor of Beer Sheva*, 33(1) P.D. 133.
80 H.C.J 148/64 *Katzof v. Mayor of Eilat*, 18(3) P.D. 423 (1964); H.C.J 119/65, *Sharbiv v. Mayor of Ashkelon*, 19(2) P.D. 220.
81 Shimon Shetreet, *Affirmative Action, supra* note 2, at 266.
82 H.C.J 114/78, 451/78, 510/78, *Borkan v. Company for Development of the Jewish Quarter*, 32(2) P.D. 804, at 805; see also H.C.J 200/83 *Watad v. Minister of Finance*, 38(3) P.D. 113.
83 H.C.J 78/68 *Kraus v. Minister of Defence*, 22(2) P.D. 464, at 467–468. See also Judicial statements supporting preferential policies in allocation of grants to needy groups, H.C.J 175/71, *Abu Gosh v. Minister of Education*, 25(2) P.D. 821, at 839 (per mister J.).
84 *Kramer, supra* note 42.

equality. Using this approach, an ordinary statute violating the entrenched provision in the Basic Law: the Knesset, which guarantees "equal" elections was set aside.[85] This approach is explained by the broader concept employed by the Supreme Court in constitutional adjudication.[86]

Even when there is legislation prohibiting discrimination, the Court has been prepared to permit preferential policies. Thus, the policy of Bar Ilan University Law School preferring graduates of Yeshiva (Talmudic academy) high schools was upheld even in the face of a regulation prohibiting discrimination, and even though it tends to exclude access by preferred groups such as immigrants.[87] Further, if the impact of a policy is to create separate, but not necessarily equal employment groups, the labor court will invalidate such a policy.[88]

In the *Hazin* case,[89] the National Labour Court rejected the contention that employment structures for men and women could be separate, but nevertheless immune from a claim of discrimination if, on the whole, men and women are equally remunerated under each structure. The Court justified its authority to declare void the discriminatory provision in the collective agreement on the basis of the power of the Court to void any contractual condition contrary to public policy. Similarly, in *Elite v. Lederman*,[90] the National Labour Court held that where a woman's job is prima facie similar to a man's, the burden of proof to show that a substantive difference exists lies with the employer.

8. Women's Rights

Women in Israel enjoy formal equality before the law. The Declaration of Independence, which acts as fundamental legal and political document, reads that the State of Israel shall ensure complete social and political equality to all of its inhabitants without regard to religion, race, or sex.[91] However, like many other countries, there are different impediments hindering full equality

---

85 See for example H.C.J 142/89 *Laor Movement v. The Speaker of the Knesset*, 44(3) P.D. 529, at 539 (1990).
86 Shimon Shetreet, *Affirmative Action, supra* note 2, at 267.
87 H.C.J 131/81 *Dover v. Logier Education Council*, 35(4) P.D. 263.
88 For example, *see* 9–88/71 *Edna Hazin v. El Al* (Tel Aviv Regional Labour Court, File No. LA/9/88, not published) and 3–25/73, *Air Stewards Work Committee El Al v. Edna Hazin*, 4 P.D. 365, with regard to the employment of airline stewardesses.
89 *Id.*
90 3–71/77, 9 *P.D.A.* 255.
91 The Declaration of the Establishment of the State of Israel (1948).

of women in the Israeli society, such as widespread gender concepts, and the gendered nature of different institutions and bodies. Furthermore, Israel is also characterized by idiosyncratic obstacles, mainly the influence of religion in the public sphere, and its militarization of society.[92]

With that being said, the Israeli legislature and courts have taken many positive steps towards minimizing gender inequality both in the private and public sphere.

In 1951, the first Knesset enacted the Equal Rights for Women[93] law, making Israel one of the first countries in the world to pass an equality law. The purpose of the law was to "cement full equality between women and men, according to the principles set forth in the establishment of Israel,"[94] by asserting that any discriminatory regulations against women are invalid. However, the law never had any real constitutional strength, and in the year 2000 the law was amended. The revision attempted to increase the law's relevance and expand the principle of equality by transforming its meaning into a proactive one. Thus, the amendments integrated affirmative action into the law.[95]

Similarly, in 1959 the Employment Service Law incorporated a provision forbidding the discrimination on the basis of gender. In 1964, the Equal Pay Law was enacted, providing that an employer had to pay female employees equally to that of male employees for similar work.[96]

The principle of affirmative action developed throughout the years, chiefly through the judiciary. In the case of the Israel Women's Network from 1994,[97] a petition was brought forth against the non-appointment of a female director.[98] The Supreme Court declared that affirmative action, and appropriate representation, is an integral part of equality in Israeli law, and that the burden of proof to show that all efforts were done to achieve equality is imposed upon the appointing body.[99]

---

92 Galia Golan, *Militarization and Gender: The Israeli Experience*, 20 Women's Studies International Forum 581 (1997).

93 Equal Rights for Women law, 5711–1951.

94 *Id.*, Article 1.

95 *Id.*, see Article 1(b)(2).

96 Yael Yishai, *Between the Flag and the Banner—Women in Israeli Politics*, 159 (1997).

97 H.C.J 453/94 *Israel Women's Network v. The State of Israel* (1994).

98 Section 18a of the Governmental Corporations Act states that a government-owned company must provide for adequate representation of both sexes in the board of directors. When adequate representation is lacking, the minster will employ a director from the unrepresented sex.

99 *Israel Women's Network v. The State of Israel, supra* note 93, pp.19–23.

In 1998, the Israel Women's Network petitioned against the Minister of Labor and Welfare[100] regarding the appointment of a man to the role of assistant director general to the National Insurance Institute of Israel. The petitioners argued that the court ruling given in 1994 should be broadened in such a way that appropriate representation is required without a specific law, as it is part of the general requirement of equality. The Supreme Court ruled that another consideration when appointing high ranking positions in the public sector should also take into account the affirmative action of discriminated groups within the public.[101]

Another example of appropriate representation in the Israeli jurisprudence of the Supreme Court can be seen in the case of *Yael Aran*. A search committee for the Israeli Anti-Drug Authority recommended the appointment of Yael Aran, a female candidate, for the position of CEO over a male candidate with a military background. However, the CEO of the Prime Minister's Office decided in favor of the male candidate instead. Aran petitioned to the court, claiming that rejecting the committee's recommendations without any explanation implies favoritism. The state argued that is it important to allow the government to appoint whoever it thinks is most suitable. The court granted the petition on the ground that the CEO of the Prime Minister's Office did not sufficiently address in his decision process the different considerations set forth in the law.[102]

After the court's petition was granted, the male candidate was chosen over Aran once again. Therefore, Aran petitioned to the court claiming that the decision to choose a male was unreasonable. However, the court ruled that women should be favored over men only when their abilities are equal; in this case, the CEO of the Prime Minister's Office followed the court's procedural directive and was aware of the appropriate representation norms, thus dismissing Aran's claims.[103]

---

100 H.C.J 2671/98 *Israel Women's Network v. The Minister of Labor and Welfare*, 52(3) P.D. 630 (1998).
101 *Id.*
102 H.C.J 5755/08 *Aran v. The Government of Israel* (published on Nevo, 21.04.2009).
103 *Id.*, Moshe Cohen-Eliya, *Negligence and Appropriate Representation—The Israeli Case, 133* in Affirmative Action—A View from the Global South (ed. Ockert Dupper and Kamala Sankaran, 2014).

A. Women in the Army

The state of Israel has been in a constant state of war since its establishment. Therefore, the military in Israel is a central institution within the Israeli society and lives of its citizens. This is enhanced by the compulsory service prescribed by law.

Article 16a of the Israeli Defense Service Law anchors the equality of service between females and males in the military. However, according to some, the military is "the quintessence of a patriarchal institution, reinforcing and perpetuating the stereotypical role of women as subordinate, subservient and superfluous."[104]

Throughout the years, different breakthroughs took place with regards to equality of women in the military, most noticeably the 1995 Supreme Court case of Alice Miller.[105] In this case, Alice Miller held a civil pilot's license and degree in aeronautics; when she enlisted, she requested to take the qualifying tests for the pilot's course. Miller petitioned to the Supreme Court, and the court in turn compelled the Israeli Air Force to enroll women in its pilot training courses, dismissing the military's claims that doing so would be too costly. The court held that a society that respected human rights must be prepared to bear financial burdens.[106]

B. Women on the Bench

In 1977, Miriam Ben-Porath became the first woman to be appointed to the Israeli Supreme Court. She was later joined by Justice Shoshanah Netanyahu. In the years after both of these Justices' retirements, three more female justices were appointed. Appointing female justices ensures that the Court will be more reflective of society. In particular, the principle of a reflective judiciary is related to the principle of substantive independence and to the need to maintain actual impartiality, as well as in appearance, in order to ensure that justice should not only be done, but should be seen to be done. Appointment of women also helps maintain judicial independence and public confidence in the courts.[107]

---

104 Golan, *supra* note 86, at 115.
105 H.C.J 4541/94 *Miller v. Minister of Defense*, 49(4) P.D. 94 (1995).
106 Id; Cohen-Eliya, *supra* note 97 at 130.
107 Shimon Shetreet, *Equality of Women on the Bench: The Theoretical Reasoning: The Principle of Fair Reflection*, in S. Shetreet (ed.) Women in Law 183–194, 183 (Kluwer Law International, London—The Hague, Boston 1998).

The authorities charged with appointing must carry out their duty to ensure a balanced composition of the judiciary—ideologically, socially, and culturally. On the same doctrinal basis, a society should legitimately expect the judiciary to include women among its ranks in a fair, reflective manner. This expectation applies both to the judiciary as a whole and to the various judicial levels. This is based on the doctrinal principle of fair reflection. The judiciary is a branch of government, and not merely a dispute-resolution institution. As such, it cannot be composed in total disregard of the makeup of a society. Hence, due regard must be given to the consideration of fair reflection.[108]

There are other arguments for maintaining a well-balanced composition of the judiciary: first, the need to preserve public confidence in courts; second, the need to ensure balanced panels in appellate courts, particularly in cases with public or political overtones. A reflective judiciary is an imperative factor for maintaining the important valued of public confidence in the courts. Because adjudication involves a certain degree of imposition of the judges' own values, there is great need for a reflective judiciary. The process and standards of judicial selection must ensure fair reflection of social classes, ethnic and religious groups, ideological inclination, women as well as men, and, where appropriate, geographical areas. The reflection should be fair and not numerical or strictly proportional. Likewise, compliance with this principle of a reflective judiciary is subject to the requirements of maintaining the professional quality and the moral integrity of the judiciary.[109]

9. Equality on the Basis of Sexual Orientation

The legislation and jurisprudence in Israel regarding the status of lesbians and gays reflects the changes which took place in the Israeli society regarding sexual inclination. It is widely accepted that the rights of gays and lesbians should not be constrained, nor should they be discriminated against.[110] During the late 1980s, extensive legislation and jurisprudence took place regarding the status of gays and lesbians in Israel.

In 1988, the Knesset amended the Criminal Code by abolishing the criminal prohibition against homosexual intercourse.[111] In 1992, the Knesset amended the

---

108 *Id.*, at 190.
109 *Id.*
110 See the opinion of Justice Amit in Administrative Petition Appeal 343/09 *The Open House in Jerusalem for Pride and Tolerance v. City of Jerusalem*, p. 54 (14.09.2010).
111 Amendment No. 22 to the Penal Law (1988).

Equal Employment Opportunity Act by prohibiting discrimination on the basis of sexual inclination,[112] and in 1993 the IDF regulations were also amended so discrimination based on sexual inclination was prohibited.[113]

In 1994, a landmark Supreme Court judgement was given in *El Al v. Danilowitz*.[114] El Al, Israel's national airline, used to give out once a year airline tickets to the spouses of married employees (or those in common law marriages). Danilowitz argued that he and his partner should also be recognized as a couple, as they also share a household together. However, El Al rejected his request, claiming that it is not part of the collective agreement which has been made. The Supreme Court held that equality is a basic right, and denying the ticket perk was discriminatory and unjust.[115]

The Knesset further amended legislation in 1997: The Defamation Act (*Lashon Ha'Ra*) was amended such that individuals may not be humiliated by their sex or sexual inclination.[116] At the same year the Supreme Court held that the decision of the Minister of Education to withhold the broadcast of a TV program concerning homosexual teenagers was annulled.[117]

Later on, in 2006, five same-sex couples married outside of Israel, in countries which recognize same-sex marriage. The couples then returned to Israel and requested from the Ministry of Interior (Population and Immigration Authority) to change their status from single to married. However, they were refused on the remark that same-sex marriage is not recognized in Israel. The Supreme Court held that the Population and Immigration Authority is a statistical-official record body; it must record the information which is presented before it. Therefore, the question is not whether such a record constitutes recognition of marriage, but rather whether same-sex couples can be registered in the Population and Immigration Authority.[118]

Most recently, in 2012, one of the couples who married abroad in the case of *Ben-Ari* (above) asked to divorce each other; they drafted a separation agreement which was recognized by the family court. Afterwards, the plaintiffs requested from the Population Authority that their divorce be recognized, however,

---

112 Equal Opportunities Law (amendment) 1992.

113 See also Alon Harel, *Gay Rights in Israel—A New Era?*, 1 Int'l J. Discriminatin & L. 261 (1996).

114 H.C.J 721/94 *El Al Airlines v. Danilovich and others*, 48(5) P.D. 749 (1994).

115 *Id.*

116 Amendment No.5 Defamation Act (28.2.1997).

117 H.C.J 273/97 *The Association for the Protection of the Individual's Rights—For Homosexuals, Lesbians, and Bisexuals in Israel v. The Minister of Education Culture and Sport*, 51(5) P.D. 822 (1997); The Association is more commonly known as "The Israeli National LGBT Task Force."

118 H.C.J 3045/05 *Ben-Ari v. The Population and Immigration Authority* (21.11.2006).

they were refused because in the authority's opinion the couple should divorce through the rabbinical courts. (Divorce is, according to Israeli law, under religious law, and therefore the jurisdiction of the rabbinical courts.) The rabbinical courts, nevertheless, denied their request to start a case. As a result, the plaintiffs petitioned to the family court. The legal question which stood before the court was to determine the authorized jurisdiction to untie a same-sex marriage: the rabbinical or family courts? The court held that the family court is the correct jurisdiction because the rabbinical courts lack authority. The law states that the rabbinical courts have authority over marriages and divorces of Jews according to the Halacha, and because the Halacha does not recognize same sex marriage, then the court lacks authority. Secondly, it is the opinion of the court that the family courts are the *forum conveniens* as they recognize the validity of same-sex marriages, unlike their rabbinical counterparts.[119]

10. Miscellaneous Topics

A. The Court's Correction of Inequalities

Due to Israel's constant state of emergency, many restrictive laws are passed in the name of security. These laws impact civil rights. The courts in Israel are charged with protecting civil rights, as well as fixing inequalities. The Supreme Court uses a high standard, "due strictness," when reviewing decisions of security decisions.[120] Examples of the Court's exercise of this standard are found in the following cases:

In the *Inash El Usra Association* case,[121] the court considered the validity of an order to close the offices of a women's association in Judea and Samaria. The authorities claimed that the association's offices were being used for political activity hostile to Israel. The court held that the closing period in the order was unreasonably long, and that the period should be reduced. The reduced period had meanwhile elapsed, and the court ordered the authorities to reconsider the intention to prolong the closing order. Another example is the *Nafsu* case.[122] In that case, the Supreme Court overturned a conviction for treason after it became

---

119 F.C 11264 – 09 – 12 *Plonim v. Ministry of Interior* (published on Nevo, 21.11.2012).
120 Shimon Shetreet, *Law and Social Pluralism* (The Nambyar Trust Lecture Series, New Delhi, Lexis Nexis Butterworths 2003), 1– 10, 1– 2 (hereinafter: *Law and Social Pluralism*).
121 H.C.J 660/88, *Inash El Usra Association v. The Commander of the I.D.F. Forces in Judea and Samaria*, 43(3) P.D. 673.
122 Cr.A 124/87 *Nafsu v. Chief Military Prosecutor*, 41(2) P.D. 631.

clear that General Security Service investigators had misled the prosecution and had falsely testified in court. Several of the Court's decisions reveal a tendency to limit governmental authorities in other aspects related to the employment of security considerations. For example, the Court has ruled that if an authority is permitted by law to not disclose the reasoning of its decision, yet chooses to do so, then those stated reasons are subject to High Court review.[123]

The trend of the Supreme Court is that it has extended its scope of judicial review of security decisions in order to safeguard civil rights. It has done so in the face of legislation granting wide or absolute discretion and extensive powers to the authorities, and despite the continued force of emergency powers under the Defense (Emergency) Regulations, absent a constitution or charter of basic rights.[124]

While the Courts do as much as they can to protect civil rights, reform is necessary. The existence of the state of emergency has wide legal implications. It makes possible the enactment of laws that grant wide powers of search and detention, and the establishment of economic arrangements through administrative orders issued under general-framework statutes.[125] Likewise, the state of emergency enables the enactment of emergency regulations which are valid for up to 90 days, unless extended by the Knesset; those regulations may amend or repeal almost any existing Knesset laws.[126] In addition, most of the Defence Regulations, left over from the time of the Mandate over Palestine, are still in force. They provide wide powers for restricting civil liberties (such as provisions regarding censorship), restrictions on the formation of political associations, and restriction on freedom of movement. These regulations apply regardless of the formal declaration of a state of emergency. In these circumstances, the judges of Israel, as the protectors of the rule of law and of personal liberties, have had to confront the problems of security and deal with legal challenges regarding the validity of acts based on security considerations.[127]

---

123 H.C.J 2/79, *Al-Asad v. Minister of Interior*, 34(1) P.D. 505; H.C.J. 541/83, *Asli v. Jerusalem District Commissioner*, 37(4) P.D. 837.
124 *Law and Social Pluralism*, supra note 114, at 4.
125 See S. Shetreet, *A Contemporary Model of Emergency Detention Law: An Assessment of the Israeli Law*, 14 Israel Yearbook on Human Rights (1984) 182, at p. 192–193.
126 Sec. 9 of the Law and Administration Ordinance, 1948 (1 L.S.I. 7). In this connection, see H. Klinghoffer, *Emergency Regulations in Israel*, in Pinhas Rosen Anniversary Book (Jerusalem, 1962) 86 (Hebrew); B. Bracha, *Emergency Legislation According to the Basic Law: Legislation Bill*, 31 HaPraklit (1977) 491; B. Bracha, *Restriction of Personal Freedom without Due Process of Law According to the Defense (Emergency) Regulations, 1945*, 8 Israel Yearbook on Human Rights (1978) 296; H.C.J 7/48 *Al Karbuteli v. Minister of Defense*, 2 P.D. 5.
127 *Law and Social Pluralism*, supra note 114, at 5.

B. Extremism and Freedom of Speech

Because of extremism, Israel has a unique challenge in balancing religious free-speech interests with national security interests. Political speech is considered by many as deserving wider protection than commercial speech. In this respect, Israeli jurisprudence is similar to that of the United States.[128] It is also generally accepted that academic speech is accorded wide protection, as well as artistic speech. The issue of incitement against democracy in the Israeli context is very much associated with religious speech, that is, expression of opinion about the halachic law by religious leaders such as Rabbis, and *dayanim*—judges of state religious courts. In recent years, they have often expressed halachic opinions on issues such as killing of a gentile,[129] the validity of withdrawal from territory in peace agreements, and the expression of opinion whether the late PM Rabin was a "rodef," that is, someone who is pursuing another in order to harm him (and, therefore, by halacha, it is permissible to use force, even causing his death, in order to prevent him from causing danger to others).[130]

At first glance, it seems that religious speech should be accorded similar protection to that given to academic speech. However, there is one difference in terms of content, which distinguishes religious speech and academic speech. Academic speech is an expression of opinion by academic persons who have no binding power in the eyes of their audience or readers. They enjoy personal prestige and professional status, but their speech has merely convincing power—morally or academically. Religious speech, on the other hand, has binding power in the eyes of the followers of the religious leader. Examining the probability that the religious expression of incitement against democracy will cause action is legally and conceptually relevant according to the established principles of the unprotected speech.[131] In regards to religious speech, the courts employ a "clear and present danger" standard of review.[132]

A private individual is less restrained in expression than an appointed public civil servant or office holder in regards to criticizing or attacking the government. Elected officials, such as Parliament members, enjoy substantive immunity on

---

128 See H.C.J 606/93 *Kidum Entrepreneurship and Publishing Inc. v. The Broadcasting Authority*, 48(2) P.D. 1 (1981); H.C.J 5118/95 *Maio Simun Marketing Advertisement and Public Relations Inc. v. The Second Authority for Radio and Television*.
129 *See* C.A 2831/95 *Eido Elba v. State of Israel*, 50 (5) P.D. 221.
130 *Law and Social Pluralism*, supra note 114, at 8.
131 *Id.*
132 H.C.J 73/53 *Kol Ha'am v. Minister of Interior*, 7(2) P.D. 165, 871 (1953).

things said within the scope of their duties.[133] As for academics, they are not considered civil servants because the universities are defined as private. In contrast, Rabbis who were chosen under statutory law or who serve in publicly financed local bodies are restrained by law. Nevertheless, one must distinguish between the Rabbis' capacity as office holders and their capacity as spiritual leaders, in which they express his views separately from their office. This can become problematic.[134] In *Bilet v. Rabbi Goren*,[135] Justice Cohen asserted that the only way to restrict political activity of a statutory official was by legislative means. In *Tzaban v. Minister of Religious Affairs*,[136] Justice Barak equated *Dayanim* to judges and held that, in order to preserve the public's confidence in the judicial system, no adjudicators could involve themselves in political activity. He said that although a *Dayan* must be a Rabbi, it does not follow that every action permissible to a Rabbi is permissible to a Dayan. Rabbis who ascend to the chair of the Dayan accept even more responsibilities, and are further limited in what they might do; political activity may be within acceptable behavior for a Rabbi, but never for a Dayan, who must uphold the public's confidence and the appearance of impartiality.[137]

There is quite a supportable argument advocated by a number of academics, that an incitement cannot be punishable unless it is an incitement of unlawful acts. Therefore, an incitement of an act that does not involve criminal behavior should not be punishable. Beyond the question of criminal punishment, there is also the issue of sanctions *vis-à-vis* incitement against democracy in the administrative and disciplinary spheres. This includes withdrawing state benefits, revocation of a license and closure of a newspaper,[138] and demand for resignation or removal from office.[139] It is obvious that if protection is accorded, it would provide both an administrative and criminal shield. This could potentially be very dangerous for democracy in Israel. In any case, the statute and the offenses provided by the law do not stand on their own, for they are enforced according to a policy the norms applicable in that particular society. For example, Israel had a statute forbidding homosexual intercourse, but it was tacitly not enforced. The

---

133 Art. 1 of The Knesset Member's Duties and Immunities Act.

134 *Law and Social Pluralism, supra* note 114, at 9.

135 H.C.J 291/74 *Bilet v. Rabbi Goren*, 29 (1) P.D. 98.

136 H.C.J 732/84 *Tzaban v. Minister of Religious Affairs*, 40(4) P.D. 141 (1986).

137 *Law and Social Pluralism, supra* note 114, at 9.

138 H.C.J 87/53 *Kol Ha'am v. Minister of Interior*, 7(1) P.D. 871 (1953).

139 On Rabbi Ariel Affair and other cases of conduct that may call for removal, see Shimon Shetreet, *The Good Land,* "Between Power and Religion," pp. 450–462 (1998 Yedioth Ahronot, Hemed Books).

Legal Advisor to the Government at the time, Haim Cohen, issued guidelines which effectively rendered the statute unenforceable—his direction was to refuse prosecution on this statute in the case of homosexual intercourse between consenting adults. The norms that are applicable in a particular society affect the enforcement policy; they are part of the legitimate system of considerations taken when deciding whether to enforce a law.[140]

C. Citizenship and Aliens

Israel is a Jewish state. It is the state of Jewish people. Here it is important again to emphasize that "Jewish" refers both to faith and also to people. As a Jewish state, its official language is Hebrew, its holidays are of Jewish tradition, and every Jew has the right to immigrate to Israel.[141] The right of jews to immigrate to Israel is one of the principal reasons for establishing the state. This "right to return" provides an almost automatic citizenship for Jews;[142] citizenship by virtue of being born to a Jewish mother gives clear preference to Jews in immigration policy.[143] The policy reasons for this are to maintain the Jewish character of the state and protect the Jewish people's right to self-determination through maintaining a majority of the country as Jewish.[144] An immigration policy heavily favoring Jews is justified in three ways: (1) it derives from the rights of Jews to become citizens of a state where they can exercise their right of self-determination. (2) The state of Israel has a right to promulgate laws that help it fulfill that right of self-determination. (3) There is a collective right of the Jewish people to prefer those belonging to their own national community.[145]

The right of return gives every Jew—as a basic, innate right—citizenship immediately upon treading on Israeli soil and with the expressed desire to settle in Israel.[146] Therefore, every Jew has a right to return and every Jew that does return is granted citizenship when expressing the desire to settle in Israel.[147] Under the

---

140 *Law and Social Pluralism, supra* note 114, at 9–10.
141 Law of Return, 5710–1951; Article 18 of King's Order in Council 1922–1947.
142 See Israeli Declaration of Independence.
143 Law of Return, *supra* note 141, Article 1.
144 See explanatory notes for the Law of Return (27.06.1950) available at (Hebrew): https://www.nevo.co.il/law_html/Law17/prop-0048.pdf (accessed February 9, 2017).
145 Law of Return, *supra* note 141, Article 1.
146 *Id.*, Article 3; Section 2 of the Citizenship Law 1952.
147 *Id.*

law of Return, the applicant must be a Jew or a family member of a Jew.[148] A Jew is defined as a person born of a Jewish mother or who has converted to Judaism and is not a member of another religion.[149] This definition was added in 1970 by the Knesset to include the religious aspect of maternal lineage as well as the cultural aspect of being a Jew or belonging to the faith through conversion.[150] It is unclear whether conversion must be orthodox or if it may be a non-orthodox conversion in order to qualify for citizenship.[151]

Citizenship is also given to the child and grandchild of a Jew, the spouse of a Jew, the spouse of the child of a Jew and the spouse of a grandchild of a Jew, even if the person has not immigrated to Israel.[152] In this way, those who are born to a non-Jewish mother will not have their rights curtailed and may still have citizenship.

There is a clear preference in immigration policy towards Jews. The state actively encourages Jewish immigration and even offers financial benefits to new Jewish immigrants.[153] Citizenship is not conferred on the basis of residence or birth in Israel.[154] Citizenship is based on both Jewish bloodline and physically returning to Israel.[155] Citizenship is granted to those with a Jewish parent and if the person returns to Israel with the intent to settle there.[156] A person can also achieve citizenship by adoption by Israeli citizens.

Achieving citizenship as a non-Jew is much more difficult.[157] Citizenship can be achieved by naturalization, which requires residence in Israel for three out of the last five years, entitlement to permanent residence in Israel, having settled in Israel, having some knowledge of Hebrew, and having renounced prior nationality. Spouses of Israeli citizens are usually able to achieve citizenship, but it is

---

148 *Id., Article 4b.*

149 *Id.*

150 See the Law of Return (Amendment-1970).

151 See, for example, H.C.J 1031/93 *Pesaro v The Minister of Interior,* 49(4) P.D. 661 (1993).

152 Law of Return, *supra* note 141, Article 4a.

153 These include different tax exemptions, "Absorption Basket" (Sal Klita), which provides financial assistance, income insurance, and more. See Israeli Ministry of Aliyah and Immigrant Absorption website: http://www.moia.gov.il/English/Subjects/FinancialAssistance/Pages/default.aspx (accessed February 9, 2017).

154 Birth can confer citizenship if the father or mother was an Israeli citizen at the time of the person's birth. See Section 4(a)(1) of Citizenship Law.

155 Law of Return, *supra* note 141.

156 *Id.*

157 See H.C.J 7052/03 *Adalla v. Minister of Interior* 14/05/2006 wherein the court upheld a temporary law banning Palestinian citizens from receiving licenses for family reunions in Israel due to the fact that Israel was in a state of war.

subject to several restrictions. Citizenship for the spouse occurs through the process of naturalization, which requires eligibility for permanent residence in Israel and through approval of the Minister of the Interior.[158]

Citizenship can be lost either voluntarily or by force of law.[159] Individuals cannot waive their citizenship unless they cease or intend to cease to be a resident of Israel.[160] Nor can they waive citizenship in an effort to avoid legal obligation like military service.[161] In order to waive citizenship, a person must be an adult, who is a citizen by force of return, and where the waiver is intended for retaining other citizenship.[162] People who convert to a different religion from Judaism forfeit their rights of citizenship.[163] They may lose citizenship by force if they unlawfully exit Israel to one of several prohibited state or becomes a citizen of one of those states.[164]

The Minister of Interior has wide discretion when determining qualifications for citizenship. For Jews that come under the Law of Return, the Minister must decide whether the applicants are engaged in an activity directed against the Jewish people, or are likely to endanger public health or the security of the State, or had a criminal past and are likely to endanger the public peace.[165] For those that are non-Jews, the Minister has more flexibility in determining whether to confer citizenship. Section 5 of the Citizenship Law for naturalization gives discretion to the Minister of the Interior to grant citizenship if deemed appropriate[166] as well as to set further requirements than those imposed by the naturalization process.[167] The Minister has a wide discretion when determining if applicants pose any security or health concerns.[168]

Israel has a large number of foreign workers, many of whom work in nursing or caregiving, construction and agricultural industries. At its peak, foreign workers constituted about 8% of the employees in the country.[169] Due to security clo-

---

158 The process for naturalization requires qualifying as a temporary resident who has lived at least four years in the country and has a life centered in Israel for three of those four years
159 Citizenship Law, *supra* note 146, Article 10.
160 *Id.*, Article 12.
161 See H.C.J 296/80 *Bokovza v. State of Israel*, 35(I) P.D. 492.
162 Citizenship Law, *supra* note 146, Article 10.
163 Law of Return, *supra* note 141, Article 4a.
164 Citizenship Law, *supra* note 146, Article 11
165 Law of Return, *supra* note 141, Article 2.
166 *Id.*
167 *Id.*
168 *Id.*
169 Population and Immigration Authority, *Forgein Workers in Israel*, 8 (2016): http://www.justice.gov.il/Units/Trafficking/MainDocs/ovdim_zarim%202016.pdf (accessed February 9, 2017);

sures, Palestinian workers were restricted from entering Israel, resulting in damage to economic sectors.[170] In order to meet the demand for workers, Israel started giving work permits to non-Palestinian laborers.[171] This program resulted in a labor migration; by 2003, the number of legal and illegal foreign workers were 240,000.[172] In 2003, the government began to restrict the number of foreign workers that were allowed to enter and expelled 23,000 workers.[173] The government does not seem to have a consistent comprehensive policy to handle foreign workers. Israeli law requires that health services be provided to all those present in the territory of the state and employers must arrange for private medical insurance for workers.[174] However, foreign workers are covered only for emergency medical needs, not long-term chronic illness.[175]

Children of foreign workers pose a particular problem to the country. Since citizenship is based on bloodlines and not place of birth, the children of foreign workers do not have citizenship in Israel.[176] According to Israeli law, children born in Israel to whom Section 4 of the Law of Return applies will have the same status in Israel as their parents. This statute was meant to protect the integrity of the family unit[177] The Ministry of Interior has the power to expel illegal resident children, but, in practice, the Minister does not expel children and refrains from pursuing expulsion of families that include children.[178] Children who are in Israel illegally may apply for naturalization upon becoming adults. However, as adults, they are also subject to expulsion, whereas as children were not likely to be expelled.[179] In order to remedy the difficulties for children of foreign workers, the government has granted Israeli citizenship to children of foreign born workers born in Israel whose parents entered Israel

---

See LABOR MIGRATION TO ISRAEL (2016) by E.U: https://www.gov.il/BlobFolder/reports/foreign_workers_in_israel_2016_report/he/foreign_workers_israel_review_0916.pdf (accessed February 9, 2017).

170 *Id.*, at 6.
171 *Id.*
172 *Id.*, at 9.
173 *Id.*
174 *Id.*, at 10.
175 *Id.*
176 Knesset Research and Information Center, Etti Wiessblay, *The Authorities Treatment of the Children of Labor Immigrants and Aslyum Seekers*, 3 (Knesset Research and Information Center, 2009).
177 See Regulation 12 of the Entry into Israel Regulations 1974; Section 4 of the Law of Return, 1950.
178 Wiessblay, *supra* note 179, at 4.
179 *Id.*

legally.[180] Further, the government passed a graduated naturalization process for naturalization, where children of foreign laborers may have a path to citizenship.[181]

---

180 *Id.*
181 *Id.*

Part VIII: **Israel Meets the Challenges of Holocaust Dilemmas**

Chapter 15:
Holocaust Dilemmas in Israel

The Shoah, or Holocaust, is a subject that preoccupies the Jewish society in Israel and the Diaspora. Holocaust study and research are viewed as very significant educational subjects in Israeli society. The Holocaust is researched from interdisciplinary perspectives: history, psychology, education, sociology, medicine, and more. In the world of law, as well, there are aspects of the Holocaust that have attracted extensive writing in the professional literature—for example, the Nuremberg Tribunals,[1] in which 22 major figures in the Nazi leadership were put on trial by the Allies, and the Eichmann trial in Jerusalem. At the same time, from the perspective of the legal world, it seems the Holocaust, with its myriad facets, has not attracted the broad attention it deserves from a research and study perspective.

There is no question, however, that the Holocaust and subsequent events have left their mark on Israeli society. This chapter will survey legal aspects of the Holocaust that are important components in the consciousness of Israeli society: grappling with the memory of the Holocaust, the Reparations Agreement between Israel and Germany, the Kastner trial, the Eichmann trial, the Demjanjuk trial, and the failure to bomb Auschwitz. In addition, the chapter will address legal issues that arose and took form in later decades following the establishment of the State: the rights of survivors and their treatment, various aspects of the return of victims' property in the hands of various institutions in the State of Israel, and the compromise reached with Swiss banks for the return of hidden assets belonging to Holocaust victims. Lastly, the chapter will discuss the impact of the Holocaust on decisions of Israel's Supreme Court.

The topics addressed in this chapter are important because of their impact on Israeli society. The establishment of Yad Vashem—Israel's living memorial to the Holocaust—is emblematic of the way society has coped with the memory of the Holocaust. Yad Vashem constitutes a cornerstone of the educational perspective adopted by the Jewish state to instill the memory and lessons of the Holocaust to future generations. Particularly outstanding in terms of impact is the Reparations Agreement, which at the time threatened to split society asunder due to controversy over such a step. A host of demonstrations took place protesting the agreement taking shape, some considerably violent, charging that the

---

1 See: Keven Jon Heller, *The Nuremberg Military Tribunals and the Origins of International Criminal Law* (2011)

DOI 10.1515/9783899497946-016

agreement constituted "blood money" for the actions of the German people during the Holocaust, and an immoral step that cast disgrace on Israel and the memory of the victims. In the course of the demonstration on 6 January 1952, the protesters even pelted the Knesset building with stones and clashed with police. The leaders of opposition to the agreement and any negotiations with Germany altogether was Menachem Begin, at the time leader of the Herut party. In his speech before the protesters Begin declared: "I gave the order: 'No!' Today I give you the order: 'Yes!'" The word 'No' referring to Begin's actions during the Altalena Affair, defusing the situation to avoid the violent confrontation deteriorating into a civil war.[2]

The Kastner trial also caused a storm in Israeli society, both the perceptions and its implications on a political level. Kastner was a senior civil servant and closely associated with the ruling *Mapai* party[3]—a storm that did not abate even after Kastner's acquittal, and ultimately led to his murder.

Several years after these episodes, the Eichmann trial took the fore, considered to this day one of the most important and influential trials in the history of Israeli jurisprudence. The Eichmann trial, which deeply engaged the Israeli public, contributed greatly towards inculcating knowledge of the horrors of the Holocaust within Israeli society, and even brought with it a certain sense of "justice being done," even if only on a small scale, while emphasizing the importance of the State of Israel as the defender of the Jewish people. It was not the trial of one mass murderer, rather a journey to unmask the face and the iniquities of the Nazi extermination machine. It was particularly the opening address of chief prosecutor Gideon Hausner, and author and Auschwitz survivor Ka-Tzetnik (Yehiel DeNur), who collapsed in the witness box after giving his testimony, that remained etched in the public's memory. The trial left such an indelible impression on the Israeli public that Hausner cited this as the reason he saw no need to compose his memoir *Justice in Jerusalem* in Hebrew.

The 1987–1988 Demjanjuk trial also generated broad public interest. Here again, the trial made the horrors of the Holocaust part of public discourse, and nurtured the desire to bring Nazi criminals to justice. Even the uniqueness of the trial—which concluded in an acquittal of Demjanjuk in 1993 for lack of suf-

---

2 Avi Shilon, Begin 1913–1992, p. 176–177 (2007) Altalena was a ship of "Etzel" (The Irgun) full with that was on the way to Israel without permission from the Israeli Provisional government and was sunk at the order of PM David Ben-Gurion.
3 Yechiam Weiz "B'heksher ha-Politi – ha-Me'mad ha-Politii shel Zikaron ha-Shoah b-Shnot ha-Chamishim (Regarding the political linkage-political dimension of Holocaust memory in the Fifties), Iyunim b'Hakamat Yisrael (Scrutiny of the Establishment of Israel), (1995–1996).

ficient evidence [that he was indeed 'Ivan the Terrible' the Treblinka guard]—raised moral issues among the public.

The controversy over the failure of the Allies to bomb Auschwitz, and the loaded association of Auschwitz in the collective memory in general, remains cogent to this day.[4] Senior politicians, such as Prime Minister Benyamin Natanyahu and others, have expressed their belief that as a lesson from the Holocaust and from the Allies' refraining from stopping the extermination of the Jews, the State of Israel should not place its destiny in the hands of other nations. The term "Auschwitz" became an icon paraphrased in Israeli discourse. For example, the term "Auschwitz borders" is often employed in the Israeli political arena, particularly among right-wing politicians who oppose return to the June 4, 1967 borders. The source of the phrase is a comment made by the late Minister of Foreign Affairs Abba Eban in a 1969 interview with the German paper *Der Spiegel* in which Eban said, "the June 4 map reminds Israeli Jews of Auschwitz."[5].

The other issues, as already noted, relate primarily to the treatment of survivors and heirs of Holocaust victims, from the end of the war to date—both care for survivors and return of assets overseas and in Israel. This issue has also been raised from time to time in the social discourse, arguing that the status of Holocaust survivors still among us and the level of care they receive constitute a yardstick of Israel's society's morality. Public discourse of this issue was a decisive factor in the promotion of legal developments in this area.

The last topic addressed in the chapter is the impact of the Holocaust on Supreme Court decisions in Israel. This section examines the impact of the memory of the Holocaust on outlooks of what it means to be a "Jewish and democratic state"[6]—reflected in comments by justices on the Supreme Court, some of whom, over the years, have been Holocaust survivors themselves.

---

4 For deliberation of the impact of the Holocaust on Israeli identity and politics, see: Yair Oren "ha-Shoah b-Zehut oob-Zikaron ha-Yehudi" (the Holocaust Jewish Identity and Memory) in Zikaron ha-Shoah Sugiyot ve-Etgarim (Memory of the Holocaust Issues and Challenges), 17 (2011).
5 Mr. Eban said to *Der Spiegel:* "We have openly said that the map will never again be the same as on June 4, 1967. For us, this is a matter of security and of principles. The June map is for us equivalent to insecurity and danger. I do not exaggerate when I say that it has for us something of a memory of Auschwitz."
6 As stated in the Basic Laws (discussed extensively in earlier chapters in this book).See also Minister Landau ynet 26.5.13 using the term "Auschwitz borders."

1. Grappling with the Memory of the Holocaust

The Holocaust and its horrific events have presented the Jewish people in the world and Jews in Israel with the quandary of how the Holocaust should be dealt with as a collective memory. As a collective, the Jewish people has chosen to perpetuate the memory of the Holocaust—to commemorate and nurture public awareness, Jewish and Israeli.

The establishment of Yad Vashem by Israel, as the core institution for documentation of the Holocaust and perpetuation of its memory, which is discussed below, reflects this trend.[7]

A. Establishment of Yad Vashem[8]

The idea of establishing an institution devoted to commemorating the memory of events during the Holocaust and their victims was raised already in the course of the Second World War.[9] The idea was formulated by Mordechai Shenhavi, a member of a kibbutz Mishmar HaEmek at the time who, in the course of August 1942, after the first reports about mass exterminations were received, wrote a piece calling for "the idea of commemorating all the losses from the calamity of the Jewish people due to the oppression of Nazism and the war."

Indeed, already in September 1942, at a time when the mass extermination of Jews had already become widespread, and industrialization of the Final Solution was in process, Shenhavi placed a plan before the board of the Jewish National Fund (JNF) in London entitled "the People's Memorial to the Memory to the Fallen of the Diaspora and a Monument to the Jewish Soldier." Shenhavi believed that it was imperative to erect such a monument forthwith, and not wait until the end of the war, but his call was not adopted.

---

7 While Diaspora communities have followed suit with their own institutions designed to document and teach the Holocaust, the messages are not necessarily identical to those adopted by Israel.

8 Bella Gutterman, "Ve-Natati l-hem Yad Vashem—60 Shnot Hantzacha, Te'ud, Mechkar ve-Chinuch" ("And I gave them Yad Vashem—60 years of commemoration, documentation, research and education"), 16–48 (2013).

9 Regarding other avenues of documentation and commemorating the Holocaust in the State of Israel, see: Nili Koren "k-tzad miyatzvim zikaron" (How is memory shaped), Ee'im shel Zikaron—ha-Shoah b-Moze'onim b-me'ah ha-21—Kovetz Mesu'ah Lamed-Heh (Islands of Memory—the Holocaust in Museums in the 21st Century—Beacon Digest 35 (Kovetz Me'ssua 35), 9 (2007).

In mid-1944, Shenhavi renewed his attempts to convince the Yishuv's institutions and leadership to put into action his vision of such a national project, submitting a proposal entitled "The Idea of Commemorating All Victims of the Jewish Catastrophe Caused by the Nazi Horrors and the War." In accordance with a proposal raised by the head of the JNF's Religious Department Moshe Borstein, the name "Yad Vashem—A Memorial to the Murdered" was chosen. The name was drawn from a verse in the book of Isaiah: "And to them will I give in my house and within my walls a memorial and a name (a *yad vashem*)... that shall not be cut off."[10] In August 1945, Shenhavi's proposal was adopted by the Zionist Executive Committee in London. It was stipulated that the commemoration site would be Jerusalem, as Shenhavi suggested. In his papers, Shenhavi wrote: "Only in the place where the 'pulse' of the [Jewish] people is found can and should this memorial be established. Only the Land of Israel will know how to carry and safeguard this national asset."

Only in May 1946 did preparations and work on establishment of Yad Vashem begin, and the gathering of documentary material and books sent from Europe and brought by survivors commence.

On 1 June 1947, the founding convention of the Yad Vashem convened, appointing Professor Chaim Weizmann to stand at its head. Operations were disrupted by the War of Independence and work suspended from time-to-time. Approximately a year after the signing of the Armistice that ended the War of Independence, construction resumed under Shenhavi's direction.

At different junctures, various individuals voiced their opposition to the form of commemoration Shenhavi envisioned, that is, construction of buildings, gardens, and memorial stones. Architect Rozov sent a letter to Shenhavi saying: "I am not only opposed to the project's form and the way it is being carried out, but also to the principle of commemorating the devastation of European Jewry by creating 'a horror garden with halls'." Zerach Warhaftig, a leading figure in the Mizrachi party, who was a member of the project's board, was opposed to the existing plan due to its engagement in "stone memorials" while disregarding traditional Jewish modes of commemoration such as memorial books (*sefrei zikaron*).

At the same time, there was general agreement about the importance of Shenhavi's work. In February 1953, Minister of Education Professor Ben-Zion Dinur announced that the establishment of Yad Vashem would be built on the Mount of Remembrance (*Har HaZikaron*) on a site adjacent to Mount Herzl.

---

10 Isaiah, Chapter 56, Verse 5._

Thus, the road was paved for the establishment of Yad Vashem as a site of core importance within the national culture.

B. Legislation of the Law of Remembrance of Shoah and Heroism— Yad Vashem

At the outset of January 1952, Shenhavi submitted to Ben-Gurion a draft of a bill for a "Yad Vashem Law." Towards the end of June of the same year, a special ministerial committee was established to discuss the wording of the law. Members of the committee were Ben-Gurion, the Minister of Education Professor Ben-Zion Dinur, and Minister of the Interior and Religions Haim-Moshe Shapira.

In May 1953 the bill was passed in its First Reading (first stage of proposing a bill in the Knesset, one of three readings) unanimously. After the vote, members of the Knesset stood for a minute of silence in commemoration of the victims. The bill was passed into law with the Third Reading on 19 August 1953, entitled the "Law of Remembrance of Shoah and Heroism—Yad Vashem 1953."

The law declared:

> "There is hereby established in Jerusalem a Memorial Authority, Yad Vashem to commemorate "the six million members of the Jewish people who died a martyrs' death at the hands of the Nazis and their collaborators."

In presenting the law before the Knesset, Professor Dinur said the following:

> "It is a unique law that has no precedents within any nation and state because the matter referred to in this law is also one of a kind unprecedented in the annals of man on earth. In the name of the 'Shoah' we mark the devastation of European Jewry, the extermination of more than six million Jews [...] the devastation of thousands of Jewish communities [...] Yad Vashem also signifies a space [...] a site and a name, a place and a name [...] and this name also says that Israel, our country, and Jerusalem, our city, is the rightful place for them and the only fitting place for such a memorial."[11]

The Law's first clause stipulates and defines the Authority to constitute a memorial—a memorial and a name (*yad vashem*) for those murdered and lost in the Holocaust, for their families, for their communities, and for their Jewish culture made extinct in the Holocaust, and at the same time to constitute a memorial to heroism, the war against Nazism and attempts to revolt, and unauthorized immigration (*ha'pala* or Aliyah Bet) to reach safe haven in Israel. The foundations that

---

11 Gutterman, *supra* note 8, at 52–54.

linked the Holocaust and heroism were already raised in the title given to the law, and was already part of the original draft submitted by Shenhavi during the war. There are those who believe that the "marriage" between *shoah* (Holocaust) and *gvurah* (heroism) reflect the inability of Israeli society—at least in the first years of statehood—to cope with the memory of the Holocaust on its own, necessitating that the Holocaust be raised entwined with heroism or revival (*tkuma*).[12] Another principle underlying the Law is appreciation and recognition of Righteous among the Nations, gentiles who saved Jews, whose immortalization constitutes a part of the definition and role of the Authority.

In the second clause of the Law, the role or missions and authority of Yad Vashem is defined. Its task is "to gather into the homeland" the memory of those who perished, and perpetuate the memory of Righteous among the Nations.

The authorities invested in Yad Vashem under the Law express Yad Vashem's status as an educational and commemorative center of the Holocaust and heroism, and as a research center. As such, clause 2(3) states that Yad Vashem shall "firmly to establish in Israel and among the whole [Jewish] people the day appointed by the Knesset as the memorial day for [the] disaster and its heroism and to promote a custom of joint remembrance of the heroes and victims."

The Law clearly views the Memorial Authority as a core institution for commemorating the Holocaust and its memory.[13] For example, clause 6(2) states that Yad Vashem is authorized "to represent Israel on international projects aimed at perpetuating the memory of the victims of the Nazis and of those who fell in the war against them."

In a unique legal arrangement, clause 2(3) provides that Yad Vashem has the authority "to confer "commemorative citizenship" on Jews exterminated during the Holocaust. Professor Dinur explained this step as follows,

"Commemorative citizenship will be a legal expression of the concept 'to gather into the homeland.' What, in essence, was the vile intention of the murderers? To erase the

---

12 Yehiam Weitz "Eetzuv Zikaron ha-Shoah b-Chevrah ha-Yisraelit b-Shnot ha-Chamishim" (Shaping the Memory of the Holocaust in Israeli Society in the Fifties) in T'murot Yesod b-Am ha-Yehudi b-Ekvot ha-Shoah (Fundamental Changes in the Jewish People in the Wake of the Holocaust) 473, pp. 478–479 (1993).

13 Despite the core role it is asigned, over the years, there have been periods when the economic straits of Yad Vashem has been difficult. For example, in December 1990, MK Shevach Weiss registered a parliamentary question to the Minister of Education Zvuloon Hammer titled "The Danger of the Closure of Yad Vashem." Weiss asked Knesset members from the rostrum "whether the institution is destined to constantly go from door to door [to support itself]." See: Gutterman, *supra* note 8, at 174.

> Name of Israel forever, to scatter their ashes, to erase their name and their memory, but we —the [Jewish] people as a whole, the Land [of Israel], the [Jewish] state—receive them as its citizens, gathering them as its citizens, gathering them to her. This commemorative citizenship symbolizes the repatriation, the memorial (*yad*), their place."[14]

In 1985, an amendment to clause 2(4) was added stating that the Righteous among the Nations would receive "honorary citizenship and if they had passed away—commemorative citizenship." On 29 July 1954, the cornerstone was laid for Yad Vashem. The same year, the endeavor to collect the names of the victims commenced. This project (of witness pages for each Holocaust victim, filled out by surviving kin) was viewed as very important, both as another form of immortalization and as a document for generations to come, providing proof for the nations of the world of the sheer enormity of the calamity that the Jewish people underwent during the Holocaust. Yad Vashem's National Committee was headed by Supreme Court Justice Moshe Zilberg.[15]

In 1956, the first memorial ceremony was held on Holocaust and Heroism Remembrance Day (*Yom HaShoah veha-Gvurah*) on the Mount of Remembrance (*Har HaZikaron*), the site of Yad Vashem. This practice has become a permanent custom of state.[16]

C. Legislation of the "Holocaust and Heroism Remembrance Day"

Establishing the Holocaust and its memory as part of the collective memory was sealed in the passage of the Holocaust and Heroism Remembrance Day Law, 5719–1959. (on the "Martyrs and Heroes" Remembrance Day Law 5719–1959.) A 1961 amendment of the Law stipulated that commemoration of this day would be held on 27 Nisan, according to the Jewish calendar.[17]

In the title of the Law as adopted, the Holocaust and heroism are again coupled together *Yom ha-Zikaron l'Shoah ool'Mered ha-Gheta'ot* (although the name proposed in the original bill was "Holocaust and Ghetto Revolts Day").[18] The Law provided that the day would be devoted to "communion with the memory of the Holocaust," and would be marked in a host of ways designed to carry out this

---

14 Gutterman, *supra* note 8, at 54.
15 *Id.*, at 66.
16 *Id.*, at 77.
17 This date is a few days after Passover and a few days before Israel's Memorial Day (for the I.D.F soldiers) and Independence Day.
18 Weitz, *supra* note 12, at 478.

objective: First of all, the directive that there should be a "two-minute silence, during which all work and all road traffic shall be suspended."

In addition, the Law shapes the manner of commemoration by determining that "memorial gatherings and ceremonies would be conducted throughout the country on this day." Third, the law prohibits opening places of entertainment on this day, and requires cultural institutions, radio networks, and places of entertainment "to present only features consonant with its spirit."

The memorial programs and projects now exist in other countries. Noteworthy are the Montreal Holocaust Memorial Centre, the Holocaust Memorial in Washington, DC, and both the Jewish Museum in Berlin and Holocaust monument there. On 1 November 2005, thanks to the vigorous actions of the Minister of Foreign Affairs at the time, Silvan Shalom, a resolution was brought forth before the United Nations General Assembly setting 27 January—the day Auschwitz-Birkenau was liberated—as International Holocaust Remembrance Day. The resolution was passed unanimously. The resolution "urges Member States to develop educational programmes that will inculcate future generations with the lessons of the Holocaust in order to help to prevent future acts of genocide."[19]

2. The Reparations Agreement

The roots of the Reparations Agreement signed between Israel and the Federal Republic of Germany on 10 September 1952 date back to the middle of the 1940s, the end of WWII. Zionist organizations began to prepare the groundwork for a collective reparations claims against Germany once the war ended. The Paris Peace Conference convened at the end of 1945 and beginning of 1946; the objective, among other things, was to discuss compensation quotas the attending nations would receive from German assets. Representatives of Jewish organizations, including the Jewish Agency, lobbied the gathering to allocate a specific sum as collective compensation for the Jewish people for everything Germany had inflicted upon the Jewish people. At the same time, the representatives refrained from discussing compensation to individuals in the framework of collective compensation, and the issue was pushed to the sidelines. The handling of personal claims was left to the lawyers and specialized claims agents and immigrant organizations. The Jewish organizations, and later the heads of the State of Israel, earmarked the monies received as reparations for building the Jewish

---

19 The web of the "Montreal Holocaust Memorial Centre.": http://www.mhmc.ca/en (accessed February 9, 2017); Gutterman, *supra* note 8, at 292.

state and underwriting absorption of refugees from Europe who had survived the Holocaust and sought to rebuild their lives in Israel.[20]

Passage of the German Property Law, 5710–1950, constituted the "opening shot" for a restitution law. The crux of the law was collection of all assets in Israel belonging to German subjects and placing them in the hands of a special Custodian (i. e., the British Custodian of Enemy Property), excluding the property of German churches and German Jews. Most of the property belonged to Templers, a Christian German sect whose members began to buy land in the Land of Israel at the beginning of the 1860s. There is no connection between the Templers and the Knights Templar, members of the Temple Society (or *Tempelgesellschaft*, in German). The Templers were a German Protestant sect that believed their settlement of the Holy Land would lead to the Second Coming. At the beginning, they established a German colony in Haifa, and then founded a Templer settlement in Jaffa; in 1871, German Templers established an agricultural village on a site north of Jaffa, on the road from Jaffa to Nablus which they named Sarona (today the heart of Tel Aviv). In a second wave of settlement that began only at the outset of the 20th century, Templers established three more agricultural villages: Weilhelma (today, Bnei Atarot near Ben-Gurion Airport), Bethlehem of the Galileee (near Nazareth), and Waldhelm (today, Alonei Abba in the Lower Galilee). The Templers who bought land in the Holy Land kept their German citizenship. After the rise of the Nazis to power, many expressed anti-Jewish sentiments; most supported and many joined the local branch of the Nazi party.

At the outbreak of the Second World War, the Templers held some 46,000 dunam (11,500 acres) of land in the Land of Israel. With Great Britain at war with Germany, a "Trade with the Enemy Ordinance 1939" was adopted in Mandate Palestine, designed to prevent Germany and its Axis allies from making use of property in Mandate Palestine belonging to German nationals and alien subjects whose native countries had been conquered by Germany. The Ordinance commanded that all assets in Mandate Palestine belonging to German citizens who had already returned to Germany be transferred to the British Custodian of Enemy Property. Such assets would serve as compensation to the Allies at the end of the war. The Templers who remained in Mandate Palestine were considered "alien enemy subjects" and imprisoned in local internment camps or exiled to Australia. At the beginning, their assets remained in their hands, but in late 1947 it was also expropriated and turned over to the British Custodian of Enemy Property. This step reflected the desire of the British to transfer to England

---

20 Yossi Katz, al Cheshbon ha-Korbanot (At the Victims' Expense) pp. 12–14 (2009).

as many monetary assets as possible before their withdrawal from Mandate Palestine.

Following the establishment of the Jewish state, Israel demanded Britain return to Israel the assets (funds and securities) that were in the hands of the British Custodian of Enemy Property; in March 1950, an agreement was signed between Great Britain and the State of Israel for the partial return of such assets that had been removed from the country. Nevertheless, in the course of negotiations that began in mid-1949, it became evident to Israeli representatives that England was liable to claim German real estate assets in Israel as part of the compensation Germany owed the British under the terms for reparations, restitution, and indemnification that the attending nations drew up in the 1946 Paris Peace Conference. Israeli representatives were increasingly skeptical as to the readiness of the British to return German monetary assets.[21]

Parallel to this, many claims of rights to German property in the Land of Israel from the Australian Government became to emerge (since most of the Templer community that had left Palestine were in Australia). The Australians argued that the Templers were no longer German subjects, but rather Australians.

The pressures applied by German property owners and signs that Great Britain had no intention to return to Israel the monies in the hands of their Custodian, (at first the British Custodian, afterwards the Israeli Custodian) fueled apprehensions in the halls of government in Israel. The State of Israel felt it was out of place to even consider releasing German property—neither to England, nor, all the more so, to German subjects who had supported the Nazis. Therefore, Israel came to the conclusion that it must legislate a law that would block such moves by addressing German assets in Israel and establishing the State of Israel's standing vis-à-vis such assets to ensure that no other entity—except the State of Israel—would have rights to such property. The issue led to legislation of the German Property Law, 5710–1950. In essence, the law presented the claim to reparations, although not directly or explicitly, as a formal legal demand even before the State of Israel approached the major powers on the reparation issue. Likewise, in passing the law, Israel sought to declare that it had monetary claims against Germany of a magnitude at least equal to that of German property located within its territory. Thus, Israel deserves these assets on account of the huge reparations that Germany owed Israel—as the sovereign representative of the Jewish people—due to the Holocaust.[22]

---

21 *Id.*, at 21–26.
22 *Id.*, at 33–35.

In March 1952, the Knesset confirmed the Government's decision to embark on negotiations with Germany on the reparation issue, after German Chancellor Konrad Adenauer declared in September 1951 his Government's readiness to enter negotiations with the Israeli Government over the reparation issue. The declaration came after the United States applied pressure on Germany on this issue, but was also fueled by the desire of Germany to normalize its relations in the Family of Nations.[23]

On the eve of the signing of the Reparations Agreement, Israeli Foreign Minister Moshe Sharett, who had participated in drafting the German Property Law, defined the principle underlying the Agreement and its wording:

> "Regarding civilian German property, on the basis of what assumption did we take it? On the basis of what justification did we take it? We took it because we said to ourselves: the German people stole massive property of immeasurable magnitude, destroyed, obliterated and stole property, the German people has something here in the Land of Israel, we're taking this. We're taking this on account of that larger demand."[24]

A. Formulation of the Agreement and Its Signing

Signing the Agreement depended on agreeing the original Israeli demand of $1.5 Billion in reparations, the burden of which was supposed to be shared by both East and West Germany. The Agreement was designed to pay Israel for absorbing hundreds of thousands of Holocaust refugees and resettling them in Israel. In the end, in practice, the Agreement was signed with West Germany only, and stood on half the original sum: $0.75 billion. The sum was supposed to be spread out over a period of twelve to fourteen years, and to be paid in goods and services from Germany, as well as Germany paying for all the crude oil Israel was supposed to purchases from Great Britain. An additional sum of $113 million was transferred to Israel towards compensation for Jewish Holocaust survivors not living in Israel.

In the framework of the Agreement, it was stated that Israel would preclude demanding restitution for loss of property in the wake of Nazi persecution. At the same time, this did not preclude Israeli citizens *as individuals* from demanding the return of their property in Germany in the framework of compensation or "correction after the fact of injustices of National Socialism." In addition, as negotiations progressed between the German and the Israeli delegations, demands

---

23 *Id.*, at 14.
24 *Id.*, at 35.

on the part of the German delegation regarding German property in Israel grew in intensity. The demand became a condition for the successful conclusion of negotiations.[25]

The German delegation used the German Property Law to leverage return of German property in Israel. The Germans argued that the property held by Israel had served as a guarantee for Israeli citizens demanding compensation from Germany beyond the framework of the State of Israel's global recompense claim (in the name of the Jewish people). Since Germany had removed "collective" demands in the framework of the Agreement with world Jewry and had expanded its domestic laws to accommodate individual compensation claims, there was no longer any need for the State of Israel to continue to hold German property as "collateral."[26]

The Agreement hammered out constituted a concession on the part of Israel, exemplified by the conciliatory gesture to agree to enter negotiations regarding Templer property in Israel, despite an entrenched state policy that rejected such negotiations on principle. Likewise, it was agreed that the Reparations Agreement would not be open to change, even if circumstances changed or new facts emerged (as occurred with the influx of mass Russian immigration in recent decades, including Holocaust survivors). Another Israeli concession concerned Israeli citizens filing personal claims against the German government. Despite the wording of the Agreement that it did not preclude Israeli citizens from demanding their property or other rights from Germany, a letter was appended to the Agreement which limited the rights of Holocaust survivors to demand personal compensation from Germany for disabilities they incurred at the hands of the Nazi regime.

After the Agreement was signed, Germany legislated laws designed to apply compensation laws in force in the American Zone with those in the rest of the German Federal Republic. In the framework of these laws, laws were passed that mandated compensation for revocation of liberty and for damage to health and bodily harm, excluding countries that have a compensation agreement with Germany. Israel fell into this category. Invalidation of the rights of Israeli citizens to receive compensation who had immigrated before 1 October 1953, led to legislation in Israel of the Disabled Victims of Nazi Persecution Law, 5717–1957, which

---

25 *Id.*, at 14–16; Eldad Beck, *Germany, at Odds* (2014), according to the writer the reperations agreed upon were only a fraction of the properties that the German-Nazi regime robbed from the jews.

26 *Id.*, at 48–49._

was designed to provide compensation from the State of Israel's treasury to those ineligible for compensation from Germany.

Some writers argue[27] that the Reparations Agreement contained a concession of sorts on the part of the State of Israel. It had an indirect impact on the way aspirations to bring Nazi criminals to justice in the Nazis and Nazi Collaborators (Punishment) Law, 5710–1950 was expressed. Thus, in 1951, at the height of negotiations over the Reparations Agreement, Hjalmar Schach who had been a high-placed economist and a member of the cabinet in the Nazi regime, entered and left the jurisdiction of Israel without being arrested or questioned.[28]

There are a host of explanations that can elucidate the reason Israel agreed to concessions in the framework of the Agreement with Germany. Among them, Israel's economic situation at the time was dire, so much so that it constituted an existential threat. At the time, Israel was absorbing mass immigrants at unprecedented rates, parallel to financing the cost of the War of Independence. Reparations were the primary source of financing since the country had very small foreign currency reserves, imports exceeded exports, and grants loans from the United States and donations from Diaspora Jewry were unable to stem deterioration of the economy. The Director-General of the Ministry of Finance at the time, David Horowitz, characterized the situation looming should Israel not receive reparations from Germany "an economic Holocaust."[29]

In addition, policymakers in Israel feared that if Israel would not compromise with Germany—with emphasis on the issue of frozen German assets—Germany would retreat from its agreement in principle to grant Israel restitution, against the backdrop of public opinion and strong opposition in Germany to granting reparations. Apprehensions were substantiated when the German delegation made it clear to the Israeli delegation (and even to the Minister of Foreign Affairs Moshe Sharett *directly*) that without a solution for the return of German property, Germany would refuse to sign the Agreement. Moshe Sharett described things as follows:

"We understand that there is no escape from satisfying the demands [of the German delegation] but we are totally opposed to the formula of paying compensation on our part for this property."

---

27 Yoram Sheftel, Parashat Demjanjuk (The Demjanjuk Affair) p. 13 (1993).
28 For an overview of the affair and the public storm in its wake, see Yehiam Weitz "Nose'a avar b-sdeh ha-te'ufa Lod: Parashat Schach b-Lod' ve-mashma'uta" (A traveler passes through Lod Airport: the 'Schach in Lod' Affair and its significance), Yisrael (Israel) 9, 87 (2006).
29 Katz, *supra* note 20, at 16–17.

A compromise was finally reached between the German and Israeli delegations—an agreement that the German property issue would be resolved in a separate agreement from the Reparations Agreement. On the one hand, Israel could credit itself with having blocked compensation to Germans for their property being bound together with the Reparations Agreement itself. On the other hand, Israel could not deny that it was paying compensation to Germany for property, setting a precedent for payment of compensation for German assets elsewhere in the world.[30]

B. Compensation Agreement for Templer Property

On 10 September 1952, at the signing of the Reparation Agreement, an agreement was signed to open within four months' negotiations over German property. The agreement was based on four principles: Firstly, it was stipulated that negotiations would deal solely with Templer assets. Secondly, it was clarified that the German Government would be the one representing German individuals with claims. The objective of this principle was to take the Australian government out of deliberations. Thirdly, the German Government would not support claims against the Israeli Government not conducted through its own auspices. Fourthly, it was agreed that any payment the State of Israel would give would be according to the value of the property within its borders at the time of negotiations. Lastly, it was agreed between the sides that if negotiations would not be concluded within nine months, the matter would be decided by the King of Denmark, the King of Norway, or the King of Sweden.

In the end, the agreement between Israel and Germany was signed in 1955: Israel committed to transfer regular payments to Germany based on an estimation of the value of Templer property, set at 3.2 million pounds sterling. The final agreement was signed on 1 June 1962, after ten years of exhausting and arduous negotiation.

The area agreed upon for which Israel was to compensate Germany was 33,193.090 dunam (approximately 8.3 million acres); the final sum agreed upon was 4.82 million pounds sterling, which constituted 1.5 percent of the reparations Israel and the Claims Conference [the Conference on Jewish Material Claims Against Germany] of Claims] had received from Germany together.

---

30 *Id.*, at 48–54._

In order to ensure that the Templers would not demand compensation as individuals or as an organization, the head of the German delegation Bernhard Wolf wrote his Israeli counterpart on the day of the signing, saying:

> "Therefore I have been ordered by the German Government to reiterate and confirm to the Government of Israel that with the removal of the claims that are the subject of the agreement from 10 September 1952 by the Government of Israel to the order of the German Government according to the agreement from that day, the claims of all previous owners regarding the above as already stated above, will be removed and paid in full."[31]

3. The Kastner Trial

Israel (Rudolf) Kastner was born into a Zionist family in Cluj, the capital of Transylvania, a region that had changed hands numerous time. At one time or another, it was controlled by Austria-Hungary, Romania, and Hungary, then in 1944 belonged to Romania. Kastner was a jurist with a PhD, a Zionist activist and journalist, and served as the secretary of the Jewish faction in the Romanian parliament. He was reputed to be a seasoned politician who won both ardent admirers and rivals, adept at forging ties with people of wealth and power, who had played a key role in achieving impressive gains for the Jewish community.

In 1939, on the eve of the outbreak of the Second World War, there were some 450,000 Jews in Hungary. Thirty percent were non-Zionist *haredi* Jews—the "Orthodox community" led by Rabbi Pinchas Fülöp von Freudiger. Sixty percent belonged to the Neolog community led by Shmuel ('Samu') Stern, a wealthy and educated community that had only a partial tie to Judaism, including some members who belonged to the Hungarian ruling class. Approximately five to seven percent of the community were members of the Zionist movement who, from a sociological standpoint, were affiliated with one of the two abovementioned camps. The Zionists, led by Natan (Otto) Komoly, were roundly criticized by both the religious- and the cosmopolitan-oriented camps of the Jewish community; the former accused them of "rushing the Messiah," the other of fueling anti-semitism by their "dual loyalties."[32]

---

31 *Id.*, at 57–62.
32 Arieh Barnea, "Kastner: Matzil oh Boged—Mechkar Chadash al ha Masa oo-Matan le-hatzalat Yehudei Hungaria ba-Shoah" (Kastner: Savior or Traitor—New Research on the Negotiations to Save Hungarian Jewry during the Holocaust), *Kivunim Chadashim* 19 109, pp. 110–111 (2009).

A. Hungary and Hungarian Jews in the Second World War[33]

Germany considered Hungary of great strategic value, and expressed this in territorial concessions that led to the expansion of the Jewish community to some 825,000 people. This growth in the Hungarian Jewish community was viewed by Hungarian admiral Miklós Horthy as an achievement. Horthy protected the Jews for a long time, but when he saw that it was in his personal and the national interest, he did not hesitate to collaborate with the Germans and send the Jews to their deaths. Nevertheless, in the years 1941–1944, two significant processes were afoot in the Jewish community: antisemitism increased and worsened, among them the law that mobilized 55,000 Jews into the Hungarian army to serve as work details, forced labor units in which 42,000 Jews lost their lives in various ways. At the same time, since these decrees were mild compared to what was taking place in neighboring countries where 90 percent of the Jewish population were being exterminated, by comparison, Hungary was considered a "Garden of Eden for Jews." Tens of thousands of Jews from Poland, Germany, and Slovakia tried to flee to Hungary and some 15,000 succeeded in doing so.

Furthermore, beginning at the close of 1942, Hungary faced a turbulent change of fortune. Beginning with the close of 1942, a series of Nazi defeats in North Africa and Russia led Horthy to the conclusion that his ally was nothing but a weak reed; he sent amorous signals to the Soviet Union and curbed the Hungarian army's involvement in the war, while presenting the image of a loyal ally to Germany. Nazi intelligence warned Hitler of the change. By the outset of 1944, he considered Hungary as, in essence, an enemy state and ordered the German army to take control of it. The order led to pro-Nazi Hungarian forces from the fascist pro-Axis Arrow Cross to take control of Budapest with minor German assistance. In March 1944, local pro-Nazis seized power. With SS officer Edmund Veesenmayer in charge of occupied Hungary, Döme Sztójay (who had been the Hungarian ambassador to Germany since 1935) was appointed prime minister. A special contingent of SS headed by Adolf Eichmann arrived in Hungary with the mission to liquidate the greater part of Hungarian Jewry, without German manpower, trains, budgets, or a timetable.

Under the erroneous assumption that local Jews knew what was in store for them, to trick Jews into thinking they could influence their fate, Eichmann invented two non-existent labor camps at two geographical points along the rail line to Auschwitz which were purported to be the destination of the transport. At first, young men were deported and then given postcards to be sent to Buda-

---

33 *Id.*, at 112–118.

pest and distributed by Jewish community institutions to their families, with pre-written messages to calm recipients. From 15 May 1944, over a period of seven weeks, more than 430,000 Jews were sent to Auschwitz at an unprecedented pace that presented "logistic problems" at Auschwitz in dealing with the masses arriving at the camp. The commander of Auschwitz at the time, Richard Baer, requested that Eichmann slow down the pace. Eichmann was enraged, and requested that his superior, Oswald Pohl, replace Baer, who indeed was replaced by Rudolf Hess, the founder of the camp. Hess began to increase the processing capacity by sending only half the corpses to the crematorium, incinerating the other half in piles within the camp compound—a solution that raised apprehensions that the pillars of smoke could be seen from afar. Hess argued that this was a calculated risk. In retrospect, it became evident that he was right: The Americans spotted the smoke, understood what was happening, but decided not to intervene.

In a speech in the spring of 1944, President Franklin D. Roosevelt warned Horthy not to continue to collaborate with the Nazis. Horthy, indeed, halted collaboration and deportations ceased; Eichmann left Hungary and returned to Berlin. On 17 October 1944, Eichmann returned to Budapest, to organize the "death march" of 76,000 Jews who were to be marched on foot from Budapest to Austria under the command of SS officer Hans Jüttner. The march dispersed before reaching its destination; 11,000 Jews were murdered in the course of the "death march;" however, a group among the marchers was saved after they received orders from Jüttner to remain where they were and not go on with the others.

B. Kastner's Efforts to Save Hungarian Jewry

Parallel to his position as deputy chair of the Zionist movement in Hungary, Kastner was also the driving force and deputy to the chair of the Aid and Rescue Committee in Budapest, Otto Komoly, who tried through the framework of the Committee to work via various avenues to save Jews—efforts that began prior to the mass transports to Auschwitz. Already on the eve of the Nazi invasion, Kastner and other Zionist activists realized that the Nazis would take over their country; the fate Jews would face would be the same as that of their brethren in neighboring countries. They gave representatives of the Zionist youth movement a mission: to travel throughout Hungary and speak with the heads of Jewish communities, to warn them, and to offer the assistance of the Zionist movement to help them flee. The campaign was codenamed *tiyul* (a hike in Hebrew); unfortunately, all the Jewish communities rejected the offer.

In the wake of similar rescue efforts that took place in Slovakia to bribe the Nazi officer Dieter Wisliceny with money to halt deportations to the extermination camps, a letter was circulated among the leaders of Hungary Jewry from Slovakian Rabbi Chaim Michael (Dov) Weissmandl—written at the request of Wisliceny himself in the hopes the recommendation would prompt them to pay more than their brethren in Slovakia. Despite Weissmandl's hints in the letter's content, Hungarian Jews viewed the letter seriously, and representatives of the leadership met with Wisliceny for negotiations. Kastner got wind of this, and met with Wisliceny himself, together with Joel Brand, a Jewish activist, in rescue endeavors. On the way to their meeting with Wisliceny, Kasner met with Moshe Kraus, a member of the inner circle of Mizrachi (the religious Zionist stream) and head of the Palestine Office in Budapest. Kraus gave him a telegram from Jerusalem indicating that British Mandatory authorities had agreed to allow 600 Hungarian Jews to immigrate to Palestine, in exchange for payment. In the course of the meeting, Wisliceny responded in the affirmative to Kastner's request to refrain from deporting Jews to Poland, establishing ghettos in Hungary, or executing Jews on Hungarian soil, and even allowing Jews holding visas to leave Hungary. In practice, however, Wisliceny did none of these things.

On 23 March 1944, Kastner met with Hermann Krumey, an officer in Eichmann's unit. Krumey told Kastner that they were willing to allow 600 Jews to immigrate to Mandate Palestine, in accordance with the British telegram. Komoly, the head of the Zionist movement, took upon himself to organize the group of visa holders; meanwhile, Kastner served as liaison with the Nazis, and took responsibility for mobilizing the required "blood money." As a result of Kastner's negotiation skills, the group was expanded to 1,350 persons and Kastner hoped to raise the number even further by giving bribes to lower-echelon authorities.

In addition to the difficulties mobilizing the required amounts demanded by the Nazis, Kastner encountered distrust among many Jews who questioned the sincerity of the Nazi offer and, at times, even harbored distrust of Kastner himself. A portion of the designated passengers made efforts to transfer from the "Kastner train" to a more "secure" train—the one whose destination was purported to be the non-existent Waldsee labor camp designed to camouflage the real destination, which was Auschwitz.

On 30 June 1944, the train departed with 1,684 persons, including Kastner's wife Erzsébet, who boarded the train as the last passenger—a step perhaps taken to cope with the distrust towards him and his plan. A few days later, it became evident that the train had gone to the Bergen-Belsen concentration camp in northwest Germany, where the passengers were housed in a separate sub-unit in the camp, where they were held under conditions similar to those of Allied POWs. Kastner accosted Eichmann in his office, angrily accusing Eichmann of having misled the Jews. Eichmann, in response, swore on his honor as a German officer that the train passengers would not be harmed—one of the few promises Eichmann made to the Jews that he indeed kept. At Kastner's request, in order to reestablish the trust of those who had financed the journey, Eichmann ordered the release of 318 of the passengers, including Erzsébet Kastner, who were dispatched for Zurich on 21 August 1944. It appears that the willingness of the Nazis to allow such a release created the erroneous belief that the Jews could influence their own fate. This belief by the Jews led the Nazis to the idea of engaging Jewish leaders in actions that had little value, but lured them away from trying to sabotage the overall extermination process. Kastner for his part, and against Eichmann intentions in the matter, viewed the train affair as only a starting point in future efforts to save Jews.[34]

Parallel to this, in June 1944, Kastner conducted negotiations with SS officers who allowed him to be involved in the organization of groups that were sent to Austria for slave labor, so they would not be sent to Auschwitz. In the Austrian camp, 13,500 inmates survived the war. In addition to the episodes described above, Kastner promised Krumey that he would testify on his behalf after the war, in exchange for the latter refraining from deporting some 150,000 ghettoized Jews to Auschwitz. In retrospect, it seems that Krumey misled him. At the time, Eichmann's office was incapable of carrying out such a massive deportation, but Krumey wasn't certain about this and was "paid" with Kastner's promise to testify.

The most important tie Kastner had was with SS officer Kurt Becher, who was an economist who had established a friendly relationship with Heinrich Himmler during his service in the police force. In the war, he had served on the Eastern front and later was posted in Budapest as, among other things, Himmler's personal representative. Kastner understood that Becher was a very influential officer, and wasted no effort gaining his trust. In the spring of 1945, Becher was appointed by Himmler to the special post of Emergency Commander of the Concentration Camps. At the same time, Himmler issued an order personally to all the commanders of the concentration camps to burn them to the ground along with the inmates, before retreating in the face of approaching Allied forces. Becher bought his main alibi by touring the camps with Kastner, He made efforts to convince commanders to ignore the order, and leave the inmates alive when they departed. In some of the camps where they visited, indeed, the commanders ignored Himmler's command, and tens of thousands of Jews survived due to this. It is hard to assess to what degree the decision to ignore the

---

34 *Id.*, at 118–123.

order stemmed from Becher's appeal, but it is clear that Kastner's intervention (his promise to Becher) paved the way for Becher's efforts and, at least in some cases, the commanders followed suit.

In an interview that Becher gave to Israel's Second Channel in 2002, shortly before his death, he said that Kastner recommended to him that Becher take action to stop the mass killings in a prominent location. The reason was to convince the United States of the sincerity of Himmler and his associates, who aspired to establish contact with the Allies and stop the war, while Himmler took the helm. Becher indeed passed on the recommendation to Himmler. In his autobiography, the commander of Auschwitz, Rudolf Hess, wrote that he received an order in October 1944 to halt extermination with gas (without giving the reason); on 3 November 1944, Hess indeed did so, two-and-a-half months before evacuation of the camp.

Assuming at least a thousand persons were murdered in the course of a day at Auschwitz, at least 60,000 Jews were saved by the order that Hess received—an order that may have been the product of Kastner's and Becher's recommendation.

After the war, Kastner arrived in Israel after a lengthy period in Switzerland, where he had joined his wife after the war. Kastner was determined to uphold his commitment to the four Nazis who sought to save their skins: Wisliceny, Krumey, Jüttner, and Becher. The rationale behind such determination was Kastner's desire to demonstrate to the four and the world as a whole that Jews keep their promises, out of hope that in the future, down the road, there would be readiness on the part of the Jews' worst enemies for a rescue deal with Jewish leaders. Kastner indeed testified on their behalf, with the prior approval of the Jewish Agency, which also covered his trip. In 1951, Kastner was appointed spokesperson of the Ministry of Commerce and Industry under the Minister at the time, Dr. Dov Yosef. Already, rumors could be heard accusing Kastner of having betrayed the Jews, primarily from those whose families had not been saved, and others who claimed that had Kastner revealed the horrors he knew about in time, others would have succeeded in avoiding deportation to the camps, and perhaps saved the lives of their families.[35]

---

35 *Id.*, at 129–133; For another view see Eli Reichental 'Was He Murdered Twice? Kastner Affair in a Renewed Review (2010).

C. The Unfolding of the Kastner Affair as It Occurred [36]

The Kastner Trial was the product of the actions of Malchiel Gruenwald, a reli-giously-observant Hungarian Jew who ran a small hotel, the Zion Hotel on Zion Square in Jerusalem. Gruenwald had immigrated to Israel in 1938. After the Holocaust, he discovered his entire family had been murdered and he re-mained alone in the world. The hotel owner was a member of the Mizrachi Zion-ist stream; he habitually attended meetings of the party's institutions, voicing his opinion although he was not a member of the bodies. In September 1953, while sitting in the Vienna Cafe in Zion Square, Gruenwald overheard a conversation in Hungarian between two Jews whom he did not know, discussing rumors about "Kastner's crimes." Gruenwald rushed to disseminate a flier titled "Letters to Mizrachi Members" in which he detailed all the rumors—which became the talk of the town in the newly-established Jewish state.

Kastner's superior, Minister Dov Yosef, asked Kasner to make his stand pub-lic by lodging a slander complaint with the police. Following an investigation, Gruenwald's trial commenced. He engaged the services of attorney Shmuel Tamir (who years later served as a Minister of Justice). Tamir was convinced that the rumors about Kastner were true, and the trial indeed succeeded in pre-senting Kastner as morally guilty and publically flawed. In the public mind, the trial was rapidly transformed from a trial of Gruenwald into a trial of Kastner himself.

The plaintiff assumed from the start that the trial would be simple and swift since it pitted the word of Gruenwald—a self-styled journalist and individual of dubious reputation—against the word of Kastner, who was a well-placed public servant with good ties with the ruling Mapai. Thus, Kastner put the libel case in the hands of a young and inexperienced attorney, Amnon Tel. Further on in the court battle, Tel was replaced by more skilled legal counsel, Haim Cohen (the then Attorney General and Chief Legal Advisor to the Government, although this was a criminal suit), but for Kastner, it seems, the change came too late.

The turning point in the trial occurred when defense attorney Tamir cross-ex-amined Kastner regarding his ties with Kurt Becher. In response to Tamir's ques-tion, Kastner replied that he didn't know the nature of the considerations that led the American military court in Becher's case, and the extent to which his af-fidavit impacted on their decision to release Becher. In the wake of this declara-tion, Tamir waved a letter in the air, a letter Kastner had written to the Minister of Finance Eliezer Kaplan, requesting the Minister's permission to undertake nego-

---

36 *Id.*, at 133–139.

tiations with Becher to uncover large sums that the Nazis had stolen from their victims, closing his statement saying that it appeared to him that Becher would cooperate because "he had been released thanks to my personal intervention." The clear contradiction between Kastner's testimony and his letter were a turning point in the trial.

On 22 June 1956, Gruenwald was acquitted, except for libel in saying Kastner had gotten rich at the expense of those who perished. The judgement included harsh criticism of Kastner. Judge Halevi said that there was a moral prohibition against such close contact with the Nazis, to engage in choosing who would live and who would die (*livchor bein dam l'dam*). He noted that Kastner's obligation as a Jewish leader was to spread the word, inform, and update the community with what he knew about Nazi crimes, to enable Jews to seek ways to save themselves, and to initiate armed resistance; and that Kastner had added insult to injury by volunteering to testify on the four Nazi criminals behalf. In regard to the "rescue train," Halevi branded Kastner someone who had "sold his soul to the devil." Later, Halevi said he regretted using that particular expression but not its underlying premises.

In the wake of the trial, Kastner was forced to resign from his government post, ending up working as a night editor at the Hungarian-language newspaper where he had been one of the founders. Few remained on his side. The incitement against him was so massive that the personal security branch of the General Security Service (GSS, Israel's internal security service) had to assign him a bodyguard for many months.

The state appealed the judgement to the Supreme Court; on 17 January 1958, a decision was handed down with five justices on the bench (including Deputy President Yitzhak Olshan together with Justices Dr. Shimon Agranat, Dr. Moshe Silberg and David Goitein). The Government's appeal to overturn the acquittal of Gruenwald was admitted by the Supreme Court, except for the acquittal on the charge of libeling Kastner for testifying on behalf of the Nazis. Kastner's name had been cleared, and he was labeled in the decision a "rescuer of [Jewish] lives" (*matzil nefashot*).

D. The Murder of Kastner[37]

Just after midnight between 3 and 4 March 1957, Kastner was shot near his home as he returned from work, and died on 15 March. His assassin, Zeev Ekstein, was

---

37 *Id.*, at 140 – 142. For the judgements of the Courts in the Kastner Cases regarding Kastner, see

a member of a tiny extremist right-wing group called "Kingdom of Israel" (*Malchut Yisrael*). In the wake of the first meeting of the group that Ekstein attended, astounded by the extremist line of the speakers, he informed the police that he feared that an insurrection would emerge from the group. The GSS (General Security Service, also known as the Shin Bet) asked him to serve as a paid informer, and Ekstein agreed. Arieh Elieshvili from the counterintelligence and political subversion branch (a veteran informer in the same group) quickly discovered that Ekstein had become enchanted with their nationalistic passion. Elieshvili's report to his superiors led to Ekstein's dismissal as a GSS informer. In the group's meetings, Ekstein, Yosef Menkes (a former member of the pre-state right-wing LEHI movement), and Dan Shemer (a solider) stood out in their extremist view of individuals they viewed as traitors, including Kastner. At the outset of 1957, Menkes convinced the other two to assassinate Kastner. Menkes provided the murder weapon and Shemer served as driver in the jeep "getaway car" as Ekstein turned to Kastner and asked him "Are you Dr. Kastner?" When Kastner affirmed that he was, Ekstein fired three shots at Kastner.

Today one can hear various opinions about Kastner's personality, but it is hard to find any scholar or professional in Holocaust Studies well-informed on the Holocaust who does not view Rudolf Kastner as a saver of Jewish lives under extraordinary difficult circumstances. Nevertheless, in the 1990s, when the mayors of Tel Aviv (Shlomo Lahat) and Haifa (Amram Mitzna) proposed to name a street to commemorate Kastner, in both cases, the majority on their city councils rejected the proposal. Later, Yad Vashem included the Kastner Affair in the annals of its wing that records efforts to save Jews during the Holocaust, which can be viewed as a fitting and courageous rejoinder to vestiges of public opposition that still remain.[38]

4. The Eichmann Trial

In May 1960, Israeli security forces succeeded in capturing Adolf Eichmann and bringing him to Israel from his hiding place in Argentina. On 14 July, 1960, six weeks after the Israeli Police began to interrogate Eichmann, he was allowed to choose a lawyer to represent him from among three attorneys: Dr. Robert Ser-

---

Crim, Case 124/53 *Attorney General v. Gruenwald* 44 P.D. 3 (1955), Crim. App. 232/55, *Attorney General v. Gruenwald* 12 P.D. 2017 (1958).

38 For recent literature that criticizes Kastner's actions, see Eli Reichental, Ha-omnam Nirtzach Pa'amiyim—Parashat Kastner b-Re'iya Mechudeshet (Really Killed Twice?—The Kastner Affair from a Fresh Perspective), 5770/2010.

vatius, who in the past had represented Nazis arraigned at the Nuremberg Trials; another German lawyer who lived in Chile; and an American lawyer from a New York law firm. Eichmann immediately chose Dr. Servatius. Nevertheless, with the passage of time, Eichmann came to realize that the trial could become a problematic procedure from his perspective because the prosecution was represented by a battery of lawyers, while he was represented by Dr. Servatius alone (although his counsel claimed to stand at the head of a group of attorneys). Therefore, in the course of the trial, in addition to writing books for future generations, Eichmann also took a significant part in the trial and worked very hard along side Dr. Servatius.[39]

The Eichmann Trial opened in April 1961 in the Jerusalem District Court. Eichmann was convicted under the Nazis and Nazi Collaborators (Punishment) Law, 5710–1950 (henceforth: the Law), for committing crimes in four categories:[40]first, "crimes against the Jewish people"; second, "crimes against humanity"; third "war crimes"; and fourth, "membership in an enemy organization."

Eichmann was convicted for an array of deeds: causing, together with others, the killing of millions of Jews in order to execute the plan known as "the Final Solution of the Jewish Question," along with the intention of exterminating the Jewish people; placing millions of Jews under living conditions which would bring about their physical destruction; causing grave damage to millions of Jews, physically and spiritually; preventing any further births; causing the murder, enslavement, starvation, and deportation of the civilian population. Eichmann deported, persecuted, and stole the property of millions of Polish Jews, Gypsies, and Slovenians, and was a member of three organizations of the Nazi regime declared by the International Military Tribunal at Nuremberg as criminal organizations. As a member in the organizations, he participated in execution of actions that have been declared criminal.[41] Nevertheless, it should be noted that Eichmann himself claimed that he should only be charged with "aiding and abetting" the actions attributed to him, not their execution itself.[42]

On 15 December, 1961, Eichmann was found guilty and sentenced to death. Three months later, on 11 March, 1962, Eichmann's appeal was heard before the Israel Supreme Court. This time as well, Eichmann was represented by Dr. Servatius alone.

The course of the legal deliberations in the appeal lasted a week only, closing the trial, while the judgement was handed down only two months later, on

---

39 Hannah Arendt. *Eichmann in Jerusalem*, pp. 243–244, 1963.
40 According to Cr.A 336/61 *Eichmann v. Attorney General*, 16(3) P.D. 2033, 2037 (1962).
41 *Id.*, at 2037–2038 of the Judgement.
42 Arendt, *supra* note 39, at 22.

29 May, 1962. The judgement constituted an additional version of the judgement of the District Court, and ran 51 pages long. Nevertheless, in contrast with the District Court, the Supreme Court found that Eichmann had not received orders from above; rather, he was the one giving all the orders regarding the "Jewish Question."

The appeal was based on claims that the court in Israel lacked authority to try him for said crimes; there were also factual arguments such as the claim that Eichmann was merely a "small cog" in the system.[43] His appeal was dismissed.

On the day the final judgement was handed down, the President of the State of Israel, Yitzhak Ben Zvi, received Eichmann's request for clemency. The request was dismissed in a four-page reply written in longhand, to which the President appended letters to Eichmann's wife and family Likewise, the President received hundreds of letters and telegrams from around the world asking him to pardon Eichmann. Among them were a telegram cable from the two heads of the Reform Movement's Central Conference of American Rabbis (who supported "Israel's right to try Eichmann and applauded the scrupulous fairness of the trial but which in principle is opposed to the death penalty"),[44] and a letter from a group of Hebrew University professors led by Martin Buber (who opposed the trial from the beginning, not only the sentence).[45]On 31 March, two days after the final judgement was given, the President turned down the request for clemency on the same day, shortly before midnight, Eichmann was hung, his body cremated, and his ashes scattered in the Mediterranean beyond Israeli territorial waters.

The sentence was carried out swiftly, in an extraordinary fashion. Two hours after Eichmann was informed that his appeal for clemency had been turned down, he was executed. There are two possible reasons. The first, Dr. Servatius, Eichmann's lawyer, requested to appeal to the court in West Germany, to force Israel to extradite Eichmann to Germany. The second reason, Dr. Servatius threat-

---

43 *Judgement in Eichmann Case* (henceforth, The Eichmann Case), *supra* note 40, at 2038–2039 (Hebrew).

44 *Telegram from Rabbi Albert G. Menda, President and Rabbi Leon I. Feuer, Vice-President of the CCAR to Yitzhak Ben-Zvi, President of the State of Israel*, May 31, 1962, The Jacob Rader Marcus Center of the American Jewish Archives, Central Conference of American Rabbis Manuscript Collection Number 34, Box 19, Folder 5, http://www.americanjewisharchives.org/ (accessed February 9, 2017), scanned copy March 23, 2016 from Dr. Gary P. Zola, American Jewish Archives Executive Director.

45 For this letter and others sent to the President of the State regarding Eichmann's death sentence, see the State Archives: www.archives.gov.il/ArchiveGov/pirsumyginzach/HistoricalPublications/EichmanTrial/EichmanTrial11.htm, http://www.haaretz.com/israel-news/we-have-to-carry-out-the-sentence-1.226299.

ened to appeal to the Human Rights Commission, under the authority of the European Convention on Human Rights. Israel, it seems, wanted to carry out the sentence before Dr. Servatius could turn to these entities. Furthermore, Dr. Servatius and his assistant (a German attorney named Dieter Wechtenbruch) were not in Israel at the time the sentence was carried out.

Eichmann's execution led to protests which were short in duration and did not involve prominent or influential elements. They argued that it would have been possible to sentence Eichmann to a "more humane punishment" and that executing criminals of such a magnitude was useless. It was also argued that execution was not very creative, and other options were even raised by the critics.

Hannah Arendt said that Eichmann had "gone to the gallows with great dignity." He requested a bottle of red wine and drank half of it. He asked the guards who had tied his ankles and knees to loosen the bonds so that he could stand straight. They agreed. Just prior to being executed, Eichmann said the following last words:

> "After a short while gentlemen, we shall all meet again. Such is the fate of all men. Long live Germany, long live Argentina, long live Austria. I shall not forget them."

According to Arendt, Eichmann's last words "banally" reflected the essence of evil.[46]

A. The Course of the Trial and Its Aftermath

The trial opened with the chief prosecutor Gideon Hausner's opening statement:

> When I stand before you here, Judges of Israel, to lead the Prosecution of Adolf Eichmann, I am not standing alone. With me are six million accusers. But they cannot rise to their feet and point an accusing finger towards him who sits in the dock and cry: "I accuse." For their ashes are piled up on the hills of Auschwitz and the fields of Treblinka, and are strewn in the forests of Poland. Their graves are scattered throughout the length and breadth of Europe. Their blood cries out, but their voice is not heard. Therefore I will be their spokesman and in their name I will unfold the awesome indictment.
>
> There was only one man who had been concerned almost entirely with the Jews, whose business had been their destruction, whose place in the establishment of the iniquitous regime had been limited to them. That was Adolf Eichmann. If we shall charge him also with crimes against non-Jews, committed as it were by the way, this is because we make no ethnic distinctions. But we should remember that the mission of the Accused,

---

46 Arendt, *supra* note 39, at 250–252.

in which for years he saw his destiny and calling, and to which he devoted himself with enthusiasm and endless zeal, was the extermination of the Jews.[47]

The first argument raised by the Counsel for the Defence was that the court lacked competence[48] "to consider and to decide on the present indictment [because] the law for punishing Nazis and their collaborators of 10 August 1950 sought to provide punishment in regard to persons and acts before the existence of the State of Israel, outside the present boundaries of the State, which wronged persons who were not residents of the State of Israel."[49] The court dismissed the claim. Firstly, in terms of jurisdiction, the Supreme Court accepted the decision in the judgement of the District Court that stated:[50]

> The court must validate the laws of the Knesset, and we cannot resort to the argument that this Law is contrary to the principles of international law—the issue of contradiction between domestic law with international law, application of international law in domestic law is merely a matter of custom, and when it contradicts domestic law that has not been settled by interpretation to bring it into accord [with international law], domestic law takes precedence.

Secondly, it was stated that there was, in fact, no clash with international law. From a legal standpoint, there isn't at all any international law against criminal legislation that is retroactive—there is no such universal phenomenon. Also, from an ethical standpoint, the ethnical quandary inherent in retroactive punishment pales compared to the ethical quandary of *lack* of punishment for actions such as the crimes at hand. One cannot claim at the time they were committed, the perpetrator did not sense that universal ethical values were being violated.

The defense's second claim was that the law created "extraterritorial crimes", that occurred outside the state's domain by a person who is not a citizen of the state towards someone who is not a citizen of the state, in contradiction with the principle of territorial sovereignty. This argument as well was dismissed, while establishing an important and central legal principle of great importance: universal jurisdiction. The court dismissed the argument by a process of elimination when it stated that there was no contradiction between the law and interna-

---

47 See   http://www.nizkor.org/hweb/people/e/eichmann-adolf/transcripts/Sessions/Session-006-007-008-01.html (accessed February 11, 2017).
48 Eichmann Case, *supra* note 40, at 2040–2043.
49 See   http://www.nizkor.org/hweb/people/e/eichmann-adolf/transcripts/Sessions/Session-001-02.html (accessed February 9, 2017).
50 Criminal case 40/61, *The Attorney General of the Government of Israel v. Adolf Eichmann*, p. 14 (released in book form by the GPO, 1962)._

tional law. It reasoned that the principle of territorial sovereignty demands only that a state applies its criminal jurisdiction within its borders and not beyond them. Only when there is a specific rule grounded in a convention that prohibits punishment is a state permitted to deviate from this principle. It is precisely the concept of sovereignty that behooves one not to assume in advance that there are limits on the judicial independence of the state. In practice, almost every country has expanded its authority to impose penalty in a manner that encompasses crimes committed beyond its domain. Even if there had been a contradiction of the territorial sovereignty principle, there is nothing here of benefit to the appellant, since this would, at most, create a breach of rights of the *state* to which the defendant belongs—in that international law only recognizes such states, and them alone. On the other hand, Germany did not accept Eichmann's appeal requesting Germany claim the right to put him on trial and thus relinquished its rights.[51]

In addition, this argument was dismissed from the positive perspective when the court stated that the Law was oriented and in keeping with the principles of international law. This was justified on two grounds. The first ground was that the actions perpetrated by Eichmann had been declared international crimes for which there was individual criminal responsibility. The second, in light of the universal character of these crimes, was that universal jurisdiction applied to them and all states could try them.

The first of these grounds holds that the said actions constituted crimes that were prohibited by international law in the past as well and carried individual criminal liability.[52] The rules of international custom are created issue-by-issue. A principle that constitutes a common denominator in the legal systems that operates in many countries should be viewed as a rule of international law. This is particularly true in the criminal branch of international law in the first stages of its development. The identifying mark that characterizes crimes recognized in customary international law—crimes that interfere with crucial international interests, strike at the foundation of the international community and its security, or violate universal moral values and humanitarian principles—are present in the crimes in the case at hand. The categories of "war crimes" and "crimes against humanity" were defined by the bench of the International Military Tribunal at Nuremberg as international crimes, creating a precedent which was ratified by the United Nations General Assembly. The Convention on the Prevention and Punishment of the Crime of Genocide adopted the following lan-

---

51 The Eichmann Case, *supra* note 40, at 2043–2047.
52 *Id.*, at 2047–2064.

guage: that "the Contracting Parties confirm that genocide... is a crime under international law." In a 28 May 1951, legal opinion by the International Court of Justice upon which the District Court relied,[53] it was ruled that the language employed signified that the principles set forth in the Convention, apart from the contractual obligations within, were part of international law already at the time the crimes were committed.

The second of the grounds notes it was ruled that the universal nature of these crimes grant every state the jurisdiction to judge anyone who participated in their perpetration and to punish the perpetrator. The principle of universal jurisdiction is customary in the crime of piracy. A survey of schools of thought as to the scope of the principle's application leads to this conclusion: that the fundamental rationale for recognizing universal jurisdiction vis-à-vis the crime of piracy—which stands on the interest in preventing harm to the persons and properties of those on the high seas and the joint interest in unfettered commerce of all nations—applies all the more forcefully vis-à-vis the crimes at hand in the Eichmann case. In addition, the inclination is to expand application of the principle beyond the scope of the international crime of piracy and to apply it to conventional war crimes as well.

It should also be noted that the accused, in fact, appealed to the German government to request extradition to the state of Germany, and the German government declined to do so. The refusal rested on practical grounds. Generally speaking, the country that requests extradition is one where most of the evidence is concentrated and where most of the witnesses are situated, and, therefore, constitutes the *forum conveniens* for conducting the trial. (In other words, in any particular case, the doctrine of international law directs competing jurisdictions to defer to the court in the jurisdiction most suitable to the ends of justice.) In the case at hand, the *forum conviens* was clearly the State of Israel. Moreover, while other states had a linkage to the crime, the criminals, or their victims, in these cases as well, practicality (*forum conviens*) took precedence. Furthermore, there were no protests of the venue from these countries. The fact that the crimes and their outcomes were spread over so many countries drained the territorial principle of content because it is impossible to decide which state among these countries is worthiest of extraditing the appellant.

In its decision, the District Court also justified the existence of the court's judicial authority under the "privileged protection" and the "passive personality" principles, which allow states, in limited cases, to claim jurisdiction to try a foreign national for offenses committed abroad that affect its own citizens. In this

---

53 The Eichmann Case in the District [Court], *supra* note 50, at 24.

case this justification was based on the linkage between the Jewish national homeland and the Jewish victims.[54] The Supreme Court accepted the justification and chose to add to the grounds of its decision the above-mentioned rationale that focus on the *international* character of the crimes, since some of the crimes under deliberation were committed against non-Jewish groups.[55]

Another core point raised by the defense was that the appellant had been brought to the State of Israel against his free will by agents of the State of Israel, without the consent of the country in which Eichmann resided (Argentina), and such actions deprive Israel of the right to put Eichmann on trial. The argument was dismissed at the District Court level because, in the absence of an extradition treaty, the Court would not investigate the circumstances of his arrest and his being brought to the judicial jurisdiction where he now stood in the docket, even if the defense claimed that the act of abduction of the defendant was carried out by envoys of the prosecuting state. After all, if a right had been violated, then it was the right to sovereignty of the injured state (Argentina) that had been abrogated, and not Eichmann's rights.[56]

As for the question at hand, on 3 August, 1960, prior to submission of the indictment, Israel and Argentina issued a joint declaration that said the two countries: "view as settled the incident which was caused through the action of citizens of Israel that has violated the basic rights of the State of Argentina." Thus, Argentina waived its claims, including any demand for the return of the accused; thus, any violation of international law which might have been linked with the incident in question was considered remedied. Therefore, according to the principles of international law, no doubt can be cast on the jurisdiction of Israel to bring the Accused to trial after 3 August 1960. After that date, no cause remains on the score of a violation of international law which could have been adduced by him in support of any contention against his trial in Israel."[57] Considering that Eichmann had concealed his identity from the outset, Argentina had not granted him asylum. Argentina's final decline to grant Eichmann asylum is validated in the above declaration.

In his appeal, Eichmann's defense lawyer argued that the District Court relied on rulings dealing with fugitives from justice from the jurisdiction of an authorized court at the time of the offense, whereas, in this instance, the State of Israel didn't exist. This argument was also dismissed since Eichmann was a

---

54 *Id.*, at 42–46.
55 The Eichmann Case, *supra* note 40, at 2060–2067._
56 The Eichmann Case in the District [Court], *supra* note 50, at 46–65.
57 See   http://www.nizkor.org/ftp.cgi/people/k/ftp.cgi?people/e/eichmann.adolf/transcripts/Judgment/Judgment-009 (accessed February 11, 2017).

fugitive from justice from the standpoint of the Law of Nations. Consequently, every nation had the right to judge him under the universal authority. The State of Israel operated as an organ of the Law of Nations. From the moment the right to put him on trial was recognized, there was no need to investigate how the fugitive was arrested and its legality.[58]

Another argument raised in the appeal was that one could not infer from the joint declaration that the Argentinean government had waived its rights, as the District Court had deduced. This argument was dismissed since the declaration was clear and unequivocal. In addition, the defense claimed that the defendant's rights to liberty and personal security under international law had been violated, based on Article 5 of the European Convention for the Protection of Human Rights and Fundamental Freedoms (i. e. "Everyone has the right to liberty and security of person."). The Court ruled that Israel is not a party to the Convention. Furthermore, from the standpoint of customary international law, it was clarified that abduction does not constitute grounds to revoke the authority to try a person when the accused is already within the judicial domain of the Court.

The fourth argument of Eichmann's defense lawyer was that the crimes he was accused of fell, at the time of their perpetration, within the realm of "an act of State"; therefore, the defendant was exempt from criminal liability for his actions.[59] The concept "an act of State" related to actions carried out by a person as an organ of the State and, therefore, the action should be viewed solely as the action of the State. Thus, only the State bears responsibility for such acts. Another state cannot punish the perpetrators, save with the consent of the country that bears responsibility. If not, the state standing in judgment would be intervening in the internal affairs of the state whose bidding that person carried out. This is contrary to the concept of equality among nations, a concept founded on the principle of sovereignty of nations.

The concept of sovereignty from which the doctrine of "acts of State" derives is, however, not an absolute, nor is the doctrine itself. The country in whose domain the act was committed agreed explicitly or seems to have waived its territorial right to punish. Nevertheless, the foundations of the doctrine give way as long as the case at hand concerns prohibitions in international law, and particularly Crimes against Humanity which, by their very essence, supersede the domain of sovereign authority of the State that ordered their perpetration or approved their perpetration *post factum*. That is to say, the State cannot give authorization for actions that constitute grave prohibitions under international

---

58 The Eichmann Case, *supra* note 40, at 2067–2070.
59 *Id.*, at 2070–2075; The Eichmann Case in the District [Court], *supra* note 50, at 33.

law. It is important to note that, even prior to the Second World War, defending charges of perpetration of offenses against the rules of warfare (conventional war crimes) claiming they were "acts of State" was not recognized.

Therefore, on several grounds, the court dismissed the above claim, as well as the claim that actions carried out "under orders" were legal. From a technical standpoint, there was never any law according to which Eichmann operated. The Nazis concealed their actions, were ashamed of them, and did not legislate them into law, evidence that they knew their actions were a crime. West Germany itself viewed as illegitimate the Nazi regime's laws, and denounced their validity from the day of their issue and enforcement. Furthermore, international law does not view these laws as lawful.

In its fifth argument, Eichmann's defense claimed his actions were only "obedience to superior orders." In contrast with "acts of State," this argument held that Eichmann had no choice but to fulfill the orders he received; the fact that he acted under orders of an authorized body served as justification. At the same time, it is clearly apparent that this claim does not apply to the case at hand since Eichmann operated independently—and even exceeded the roles imposed on him in the official chain of command. Furthermore, Section 8 of the Nazis and Nazi Collaborators Law stated that their reduction in culpability under "obedience to superior orders" would not apply, although in Section 11 the Law does state that it is permissible under certain conditions to take into account mitigating circumstances in setting the sentence. Last, the Supreme Court accepted the District Court's ruling that under the general [criminal] law (that is, "basic ideas of law and justice" in the Supreme Court judgment), such a defense should be dismissed because it is a case of a "blatantly illegal order"[60] that Eichmann himself admitted, saying: "Your Honour, President of the Court, since you call upon me to tell and give a clear answer, I must declare that I see in this murder, in the extermination of the Jews, one of the gravest crimes in the history of mankind [And in answer to Judge Halevi] ... I already at that time realized that this solution by the use of force was something illegal, something terrible, but to my regret, I was obliged to deal with it in matters of transportation, because of my oath of loyalty from which I was not released."[61]

---

60 "a blatantly illegal order" is an Israeli legal concept set in 1957 that holds some orders are manifestly illegal, and these must be disobeyed, defined in the judgment by Judge Benjamin Halevy in the 1957 Kfar Kasim trial: "The distinguishing mark of a manifestly illegal order is that above such an order should fly like a black flag."

61 The Eichmann Case in the District [Court], *supra* note 50, at 240 (Session 95, Vol. IV) http://www.asser.nl/upload/documents/DomCLIC/Docs/NLP/Israel/Eichmann_Appeals_Judgement_29-5-1962.pdf (accessed February 9, 2017).

From the perspective of international law, it was found that up until the Second World War there was not one leader who recognized this defense. Indeed, the charter of the Military Tribunal in Nuremberg states that the defense would not use this argument since the very perpetration of such crimes necessitates awareness of the criminal nature of the act by the perpetrator. Therefore, one can conclude that the section that dismisses protection under the Nazis and Nazi Collaborators (Punishment) Law is not a departure from international law and is even in keeping with the basic rules of international law. The prosecution quoted the charter of the Military Tribunal in Nuremberg which stated: "The principle of International Law, which under certain circumstances, protects the representatives of a state, cannot be applied to acts which are condemned as criminal by international law. The authors of these acts cannot shelter themselves behind their official position in order to be freed from punishment in appropriate proceedings."[62]

Lastly, the defense claimed that the judges in the District Court and the Supreme Court, as Jews, were unable psychologically to judge the matter objectively. The argument was dismissed when the Supreme Court accepted the ruling of the District Court regarding the validity and objectivity of the court: "While on the bench a judge does not cease to be flesh and blood, possessed of emotions and impulses. However, he is required by law to subdue these emotions and impulses, for otherwise a judge will never be fit to consider a criminal charge which arouses feelings of revulsion, such as treason, murder or any other grave crime. It is true that the memory of the Holocaust shocks every Jew to the depth of his being, but when this case is brought before us we are obliged to overcome these emotions while sitting in judgment. This duty we shall fulfill."[63]

---

62 The provisions of Article 228 of the Treaty of Versailles already referred to illustrate and enforce this view of individual responsibility. The principle of international law, which, under certain circumstances, protects the representatives of a state, cannot be applied to acts which are condemned as criminal by international law. The authors of these facts cannot shelter themselves behind their official position in order to be freed from punishment in appropriate proceeding. Article 7 of the Charter expressly declares:

"The official position of defendants, whether as Heads of State, or responsible officials in government departments, shall not be considered as freeing them from responsibility, or mitigating punishment." See http://avalon.law.yale.edu/imt/judlawch.asp (accessed February 9, 2017).
63 The Eichmann Case, *supra* note 40, at 2075–2081; http://www.nizkor.org/hweb/people/e/eichmann-adolf/transcripts/Sessions/Session-006-01.html (accessed February 9, 2017).

B. The Knesset's Intervention in Setting the Composition of the Court

According to the laws at the time, the plan was to try Eichmann before a district court. Expectations were that the trial would be conducted in the district court in Jerusalem. The president of the district court in Jerusalem at the time—Judge Benyamin Halevi, had expressed his intention to head the panel of judges; he announced that if the defense requested that he disqualify himself, Halevi would decline to do so. The basis for possibly disqualifying himself rested on concern of prejudice and bias on Judge Halevi's part regarding Eichmann. This concern was raised by the judge's remarks in his June 1955 judgment in the criminal libel case against Gruenwald (which subsequently became known as "the Kastner trial") regarding the accusations Gruenwald had leveled at Dr. Kastner—that Kastner had collaborated with Eichmann. In his judgment, Halevi ruled that Dr. Kastner "sold his soul to the devil" and it was clear that the devil in this context was Eichmann.

Due to such apprehensions, a bill was put before the Knesset supported by Justice Yitzhak Ulshan, the President of the Israeli Supreme Court at the time. The bill states that, in criminal cases carrying the death penalty, a Supreme Court judge would sit in judgment. The president of the Supreme Court would determine the judge and that judge would preside over the panel.

The first debate on the Courts Law (Crimes and Capital Punishment)—1961 bill in the Knesset plenum focused on the personality and authority of Judge Halevi. The bill was presented by Pinchas Rosen, the Minister of Justice. Rosen argued that it would be fitting to establish a special judicial panel for cases where capital punishment was expected. In addition, he argued that appointing the president of the Supreme Court judge to head the bench would ensure a higher level of adjudication. He added that appointment of the other two judges on the bench should be left to the discretion of the president of the district court in which the trial would be conducted, and the chief justice could even appoint himself. As for Judge Halevi, Rosen dismissed the argument that the Government intended to deny him sitting in judgment in the case, but remarked "I assume he [Halevi] will want to weigh whether he should appoint himself to sit in judgment [of Eichmann] in light of factual evidence he set forth regarding Adolf Eichmann while adjudicating another case." The Minister of Justice's comments were intended in the subtext to "recommend" Judge Halevi to reach such conclusions in advance and refrain from sitting in judgment.[64]

---

64 Knesset Debates 30, pp. 754–755 (1960–1961).

By contrast, the opposition supported Judge Halevi. Some members of the House opposed the bill on various grounds. Among the critics was MK Eliyahu Meridor from the leading opposition party *Herut*, who argued that the real reason behind the proposed law was the desire to prevent Halevi specifically from sitting at the head of the panel of three judges. He added that a law against a specific person was unjustified when it expressed lack of confidence in that individual's ability to judge fairly and exercise discretion. Meridor also stressed that such legislation would enable the Government to reject, with the assistance of the Knesset, judges they considered undesirable. He suggested the bill undermined the independence of the courts and upset the separation of powers. In addition, he rejected the arguments against Halevi sitting in judgment in the case: No one, he said, could say they didn't know anything about Eichmann; even among the judges at the Nuremberg Trials, there was not one person on the tribunal who could say honestly that he was unfamiliar with the accused and his deeds. Yosef Serlin from the centralist opposition party (the General Zionists) joined Meridor's criticism. He called for returning the bill to the Government for redrafting since in its current form it undermined the court system and established a dangerous precedent. Instead, a special tribunal for judging Nazis and Nazi Collaborators should be established, rather than legislators intervening in the composition of the bench, said Serlin.[65]

At the same time, there were Members of the Knesset who argued in favor of the proposed law. Among them was MK Baruch Osnia from the ruling Mapai party, who agreed with Rosen that capital crimes should require a special panel of judges on the bench, and took issue with Meridor, arguing that Halevi's involvement was greater than others.

Among the range of arguments, MK Nahum Nir-Rafalkes from the leftist member of governing coalition (the Achdut HaAvodah party) suggested that, since the Eichmann trial represented a trial of the Nazis and antisemitism, one should create special conditions and conduct the proceedings in the Supreme Court. Another suggestion was raised by MK Moshe Sneh from the left-wing Mapam party (also part of the governing coalition), who declared that a Sanhedrin of 71 jurors comprised of Israeli citizens should be established.[66] In addition, Sneh sharply rebutted the notion that Halevi was unfit to serve on the bench in the Eichmann case, arguing that every judge was linked to this matter. He noted that, in the Kastner affair, Halevi had produced a stellar judgment that

---

65 Statement by MK Meridor, *Id.*, at 756; statement by MK Serlin, *Id.*, at 760–761.
66 Sanhedrin is the name of the Jewish court system in antiquity that was comprised of an assembly of twenty-three to seventy-one men appointed in every city in the Land of Israel, with a Great Sanhedrin in Jerusalem serving as a court of appeals among its other national functions.

was a source of pride for the Israeli judicial system; furthermore, Halevi did not deserve such a blow to his stature due to apprehensions that the defense attorney of the "arch-butcher" would call for his disqualification.[67]

Pinchas Rosen closed the debate. He expressed his regret that the discussion had digressed to a personal level. Furthermore, he claimed that the objective of the law emanated from the desire that jurists around the world would be impressed by the manner in which the trial was conducted and that, even if proceedings had been conducted in Haifa or Tel Aviv, he would have chosen this path. He revealed that the possibility of conducting the trial in the Supreme Court had been weighted and rejected. Rosen closed his comments with a broad hint to Judge Halevi, saying "he knew what he would do in his place."[68]

The issue of Halevi being part of the composition of the court did not cease after the First Reading of the bill; rather, it continued throughout the Second and Third. The reactions of parliamentarians were varied. General Zionist MK Shneor Zalman Abramov was in favor of putting the president of the Supreme Court at the head of the court only in proceedings dealing with crimes under the Nazis and Nazi Collaborators (Punishment) Law. The proposed legislation was special since it dealt with punishment for acts that, at the time of their perpetration, were not crimes under the law of the land where they were committed. Jurisdiction was warranted, he argued, considering the crimes were exceptional in their gravity and cruelty. It was justified not only as an exception from common norms in international law, but also because they constituted a departure from the instructions of Israeli law about how the composition of the court should be set.[69]

MK Yosef Shufman from Herut argued that the law was directed specifically against Judge Halevi and was unjust. In the Kastner Affair, the facts regarding Eichmann were not subject to controversy between the sides in the trial, and there was no need to examine them; thus, Halevi had not formed an opinion against Eichmann. He argued that the proposed legislation was discriminatory since, in military crimes that carried the death penalty, three officers sit in judgment—only one a jurist. In addition, he expressed his apprehensions that passage of such a law would be a dangerous precedent in Rule of Law. He reasons there could be other trials where concern for the fate of the accused could be raised, with the law at hand serving as a precedent for changing the basic rights of the accused, with a simple majority in the Knesset.[70]

---

67 Statement of MK Osnia: *Id.*, at 758–759; statement by MK Nir-Rafalkes and MK Sneh, *Id.*, at 761–762.
68 *Id.*, at 762–763.
69 *Id.*, at 854–855.
70 *Id.*, at 855–856.

In his speech, MK Sneh declared that taking judicial authority out of the hands of the district court constituted gross intervention of the executive and legislative branches in judicial authority. This intervention includes not only writing judgments, but also conducting proceedings and composing the bench. In addition, Sneh argued that the Kastner Affair constituted a historical trial. As such, Judge Halevi had exhibited an historical approach—a broad view and historical pathos towards the vision of the Shoah and its causes.[71]

MK Zerach Warhaftig from the National Religious Party supported the bill and replied to the arguments raised by its critics. He argued that the law was general—not tailored to one individual, but addressing all capital crimes, not just Eichmann's. In that the composition of the district court had yet to be set, there was no personal dimension against Halevi, whose influence on the decision would not, in any case, be changed by the law if Halevi did not head the court, but occupied one of the three seats on the bench. Warhaftig argued that there was no detriment to the authority of the district court; the matter remained its authority and only a third of the composition would be changed by the law. There was no flaw in legislation that, in effect, benefits the accused, who is awarded with a judge with greater judicial experience.[72] The bill was passed into law by a majority of 39 votes in favor and 16 against and, in the end, Halevi sat on the panel of judges hearing the case, but did not head the court.

In preparation for the trial and choosing the composition of the bench, a central issue raised in deliberations was that legislation on composition of the court carried the risk that the legislative branch and the executive branch were intervening in the judicial branch's domain. The setting of the composition of the bench by the other two branches of government could be detrimental to judicial independence and the nature of democratic judicial proceedings in general, generating the need to strengthen legal protection for an independent judiciary. While such an action was never repeated, this was not due to any legal obstacle or other obstacle to doing so. Rather, it was due to the self-restraint legislators exhibited, and fear of negative public sentiment. Nevertheless, it seems there has been a pattern over the years, a number of cases where the legislative branch and the executive branch intervened in matters that are the prerogatives of the judicial branch.

Thus, shortly before the president of the Supreme Court Yitzhak Ulshan was scheduled to retire, the Knesset intervened in the procedure for appointing judges by proposing a reform, raising the chief justice's retirement age from age 70 to

---

71 *Id.*
72 *Id.*, at 757–758.

age 75. The official justification was that it would be fitting to bring the terms of office of the president of the Supreme Court into line with the terms of office of the head of the Rabbinical Court of Appeals, which set retirement age at 75. How- ever the general feeling was that the real objective was to extend Ulshan's term of office, a reprehensible maneuver that in the end was unsuccessful.[73]

Another case of "personal legislation" of convenience that comes to mind took place following the appointment of Rabbi Simcha Asaf to serve on the Su- preme Court in 1948. He was an expert in Jewish Law, but he did not meet the criteria set by law (i.e., education and training in secular law).[74] The Minister of Justice sought to pass into law a bill that would retroactively validate the ap- pointment, against fierce opposition to retroactive legislation and legislation fit to serve a specific circumstance. In the end, the law (dubbed "the Asaf Law") was adopted, perhaps because a Judges Law that would set in place a new meth- od of appointing judges was about to be legislated, and there was no logic in standing on principle on the issue.[75]

A more recent case is the 2012 amendment to The Courts Law—1984. Up until this time, the Supreme Court judge with the most seniority was appointed pres- ident of the Court when a chief justice resigned (the seniority system). Clause 8(c) stipulated that a Supreme Court judge who had less than three years to retire- ment could not be appointed to head the court. Justice Asher Grunis was the most senior Supreme Court judge on the bench when the president of the Court Dorit Beinisch retired. (Actually, Justice Eliezer Rivlin had more seniority, but waived the appointment since he had only three months to retirement.) Grunis, however, stood to retire in another three year—minus 41 days; thus, he fell under the limitations of Clause 8(c). Therefore, the Knesset passed an amend- ment sponsored by MK Yaakov Katz that abolished the minimum time left to serve before retirement, to allow Grunis to be appointed president of the Su- preme Court. The amendment, dubbed by the media the "Grunis Law," was met with broad-spread criticism. The critics argued that the law constituted gross intervention of the legislature in the independence of the justice system

---

73 Shimon Shetreet, *On Adjudication: Justice on Trial*, Hemmed Books—Yedioth Aharonoth Publishing, pp. 423–424, (2004) (in Hebrew).
74 Recognizing the ethnic, religious, and political diversity of Israeli society, Israeli governance is on-the-whole based on consensus building—seeking to widen the base of "stake holders" in the political system, which is reflected not only in a multi-party electorate and coalition govern- ments, but also in balance (diversity) in the composition of the Supreme Court, with unwritten "slots" (which are a matter of custom, not law) "reserved" on the bench for representatives of the religious community, the Mizrachi community, the Arab sector, etc.
75 Shetreet, *Justice on Trial*, *supra* note 73, at 422.

and constituted "personal legislation," adopted with the objective of advancing a specific individual.[76] A petition against the legality of the Grunis Law was submitted to the High Court of Justice, but the petition was rejected.[77]

5. Demjanjuk Trial

On 28 February 1986, John Ivan Demjanjuk was extradited from the United States to Israel. Demjanjuk, who lived in Cleveland, Ohio, and worked as a mechanic in a Ford auto plant, was suspected of being "Ivan the Terrible," the monstrous criminal from the Treblinka extermination camp. Surveillance and investigation in regard to Demjanjuk had begun in 1976. Already at the time, the Nazi Criminals Investigation Unit of the Israeli Police Force had conducted a line-up based on photos of Demjanjuk, in which he had been identified by former inmates as "Ivan the Terrible."[78]

Ivan the Terrible ("Ivan Grozni" in Polish and Russian—the moniker alluded to the infamous Czar Ivan IV, renowned for his cruelty) was a Ukrainian *Wachmann* (guard)[79] in the Treblinka death camp. Together with another Ukrainian *Wachmann*, he was responsible for operating the engine that discharges the poisonous pellets into the gas chambers. He was known for his extraordinary cruelty, tormenting the Jews who had arrived at the camps on the transports, as he shoved them into the gas chambers. Survivors of the Treblinka camp spoke of hair-raising exploits and the countless atrocities he committed. For example, Ivan the Terrible was in the habit of hacking at the living flesh of Jews on the way to the gas chamber, cutting off extremities before sending them to their deaths. Consequently, due to his extreme cruelty, the Jews working in the camp had nicknamed him Ivan the Terrible.

---

76 Yonatan Liss "The Knesset Confirmed the Grunis Law," *HaAretz*, January 2, 2012, at www.haaretz.co.il/news/law/1.1607453 (accessed February 9, 2017).

77 H.C.J 85/10, *The Movement for Quality Government in Israel v. the Knesset* (published on Nevo)

78 Yoram Sheftel, *Parashat Eichmann* (The Eichmann Case) pp. 7–14 (1993); At the same time, it is important to note that, at the beginning, Demjanjuk was suspected to being only a *Wachmann* (guard) in the Sobibór camp, not at Treblinka.

79 *Wachmänner* in German means "member of the guard or guards," a name given to the German's auxiliary forces comprised of Red Army POWs who volunteered to serve in these capacities. The *Wachmänner* carried out the lion's share of extermination work, particularly in Operation Reinhard—the code name for the German plan to mass-murder Polish Jewry. See details in Criminal Appeal 347/88 *Demjanjuk v. the State of Israel*, 15–17 (published as a book in Hebrew by the Government Press Office, 1993), henceforth, *The Demjanjuk Affair*.

In February 1987, a year after Demjanjuk arrived in Israel, the Demjanjuk trial opened. Demjanjuk was charged for crimes under Sections 1 and 2 of the Nazis and Nazi Collaborators (Punishment) Law, 5710 – 1950. Section 1 covered crimes against the Jewish people, crimes against humanity, and war crimes. Section 2 covered crimes against persecuted persons. The prosecution claimed that Demjanjuk had operated the gas chambers in Treblinka in October 1942. Extermination at Treblinka was ceased in the fall of 1943, whereas from March 1943, he was transferred part of the time to the Sobibór camp.[80]

The trial took place in the International Convention Center in Jerusalem (*Binyanei HaUmah* or "Buildings of the Nation") in Jerusalem. Supreme Court Judge Dov Levin headed the court, together with members of the Jerusalem District Court Judge Dalia Dorner and Tzvi Tal on the bench. The prosecution team for the State was presided over by the Attorney General Yona Blatman and attorney-at-law Michael Shaked. Demjanjuk's defense were American attorney Mark O'Connor, who resigned in the midst of the trial in the District Court, and Israeli attorney Yoram Sheftel who, after O'Conner's resignation, became the chief defense attorney and, in the course of the appeal process to the Supreme Court, served as Demjanjuk's sole legal representative.

In the Eichmann trial, deliberations focused primarily on the legal authority of an Israeli court to try the defendant, and the question whether criminal responsibility applied to Eichmann's actions as a "small cog" in the system; there was no disagreement that the defendant was the person accused of the actions at hand. By contrast, the line of defense in the Demjanjuk affair was different. The defense pleaded guilty to all the facts in the bill of indictment, including the atrocities carried out by Ivan the Terrible himself in the Treblinka extermination camp. They pleaded "not guilty" to only one fact: the identity of John Demjanjuk as Ivan the Terrible.[81]

The trial was widely covered in the media, attracting attention and public interest in Israel and abroad. The judges, of course, had to overcome the emotional difficulty in trying the individual accused of being the self-same monster from Treblinka. The District Court expressed this as follows:[82]

---

80 Criminal case (District Court–Jerusalem) 373/86 The *State of Israel v. Demjanjuk*, District Court Judgment, 5748(c) P.D. 1, 318 (1988), henceforth *The Demjanjuk Affair in the District Court*.
81 Sheftel, *supra* note 27, at 32, 50.
82 *The Demjanjuk Affair in the District Court*, *supra* note 80, at 2.

"This sense of responsibility behooves us to examine and to weight the facts that prove with equanimity, with prudence and with precision, removing emotional considerations and ignoring all that has been said and written and discussed outside the walls of the court, whether in the media and whether among the public at large."

The Supreme Court reiterated this sentiment in a more general sense, writing in its decision on appeal process in regard to this matter:[83]

"It is hard, very hard, our work [sitting] in judgment in the matter of the Holocaust; we shall stand up to our duty, shall judge truly, without bias, and our passing of judgment shall be right and fitting."

The evidence regarding Demjanjuk's identity was based primarily on two elements. The first was a line-up employing photographs, carried out before Treblinka survivors who were requested to identify Ukrainian *Wachmänner* (guards) they knew from the death camp. The line-up was conducted by the Israel Police Force, initially at the request of the US Government, where legal proceedings were in progress to revoke Demjanjuk's American citizenship (on suspicion it had been granted under false pretences) and, after the investigation, to lay the foundations for putting Demjanjuk on trial in Israel had progressed.

The need for a line-up through photographs, and not direct scrutiny of the person in a line-up, was raised. The reasons given included the time lapse since the events had occurred—35 years—and the assumption that a person's facial features would have changed over time. The photos used in the line-up were from photos taken soon after the Second World War, primarily the photo from 1951 when Demjanjuk requested to immigrate to the United States.

The second primary evidence of Demjanjuk's identity was a document called the "Trawniki Certificate." Trawniki was an SS training camp where volunteers to serve in the SS from among Red Army POWs were inducted, trained, and prepared to serve as *Wachmänner* for the Nazis. For the most part Ukrainians, the *Wachmänner* were sent from Trawniki to serve in various death camps, including Treblinka.[84]

This document, which was transferred to Israel by the KGB, was said to be the service record of Demjanjuk as a soldier in the SS. The certificate carried a photograph which was claimed to be of Demjanjuk during the war, signed by the commander of the camp (SS officer Karl Streibel) and by the camp quar-

---

83 *The Demjanjuk Affair in the District Court*, supra note 80, at 12.
84 *Id.*, at 59; Sheftel, *supra* note 27, at 81.

termaster (Toifel); it bore the signature of the card-bearer, which was claimed to be the signature of Demjanjuk himself.

In addition, the service record card contains biographical details that match Demjanjuk's particulars: his name, the names of his parents, his place of birth, and so forth, and even cites an identifying scar on his back that matches one Demjanjuk sustained while serving in the Red Army. The document also notes the places where Demjanjuk was first stationed (in Okshov on 22 September, 1942) and his second posting (Sobibór on 27 March, 1943).

Another important piece of evidence worth mentioning is the defendant's retort during his interrogation, when asked by his Israeli interrogator whether he had ever been in certain villages in Poland (which the interrogator knew were on the route between Treblinka and Sobibór): "You are pushing me to Treblinka."[85]

Most of the court's deliberations focused on a variety of evidence that identified Demjanjuk as Ivan the Terrible, including various aspects of "rules of evidence." The main issues examined in the trial were as follows:

A. Competence to Try Matters of Genocide

As already noted, Demjanjuk was tried for crimes under Sections 1 and 2 of the Nazis and Nazi Collaborators (Punishment) Law, 5710 – 1950.

The problem is, Demjanjuk was extradited from the United States to Israel in order to stand trial for the crime of murder. The defense argued that there is a significant difference between the crime of murder and the crime of genocide. Therefore, Demjanjuk should not be put on trial for the crime of genocide in Israel. First of all, this crime does not appear in the extradition request, and the crime of genocide does not exist in the framework of criminal law in the United States. The defense counsel's claim was based on two legal precepts: The first is the requirement of "dual criminality," which requires the act for which extradition is requested constitute a punishable crime in both the requesting and the requested states. The second principle is "the principle of speciality," by which a person who is extradited to a country to stand trial for certain criminal offenses may be tried only for those spe-

---

85 *The Demjanjuk Affair in the District Court, supra* note 80, at 360 – 361.

cific offenses cited in the extradition request, not for any other pre-extradition offenses.[86]

In this respect, the District Court ruled that:

> "Murder is murder, whether it takes place vis-à-vis elements of the regular crime of murder or whether it takes place vis-à-vis additional elements of murder as a crime according to another law."[87]

In judging this question, the Supreme Court ruled that total congruence is not required between the crimes, but rather:[88]

> "It suffices that one of the alternatives of the crime in the requesting state arises from the factual legal foundation of the basis of the extradition request—is included in the alternatives of the crime in the requested state, in order for the speciality proviso to be met."

In the case at hand, the Supreme Court ruled that the crime of murder in the United States is based on two foundations: one, causing the death of a person; and two, the killing is premeditated. Thus, Section 1 of the Nazis and Nazi Collaborators (Punishment) Law, which covers the crime of "crimes against the Jewish People" defined as "intent to destroy the Jewish people in whole or in part," encompasses within it the criminal foundations of the stated murder. Section 2 of the Law, as well, specifies that "crimes against persecuted persons" encompasses explicitly the crimes of murder. Therefore, one can put Demjanjuk on trial under these sections, reasoned the court. At the same time, the Court ruled that in the framework of these sections, which include many forms of criminality, the defendant can be tried only on the alternatives that encompass within them the crime of murder, as stated. For example, one cannot charge Demjanjuk with "starvation, deportation, preventing births" and so forth cited in other sections of the Law.[89]

B. The Trawniki Certificate

As already noted, one of the most important pieces of evidence for the prosecution was the Trawniki Certificate. Its importance was tied to the fact that it proved Demjanjuk was a *Wachmann* in the service of the SS, refuting Demjan-

---

86 *The Demjanjuk Affair in the District Court*, *supra* note 80, at 41–42.
87 *Id.*, at 40.
88 *Id.*, at 50–51.
89 *Id.*, at 51–56.

juk's alibi, which claimed he was never a *Wachmann*, but rather had remained a Russian Army POW in the hands of the Nazis at various camps. Demjanjuk further claimed that during the relevant period, when the prosecution claimed he was in Treblinka, he was actually in a POW camp near Chelm. At the same time, there is no documentation that proves Demjanjuk was in Treblinka, since this camp does not appear in the list of places where the bearer was posted. This fact required the prosecution to claim that the posting at Treblinka took place approximately in October 1942, but was not recorded on the document, and that, at a later stage (March 1943), Demjanjuk was transferred to Sobibór to contribute his "experience" at Treblinka.

The Supreme Court ruled that the document should be judged on three levels: the admissibility of the article as evidence, its authenticity, and its admissibility from a substantive standpoint (its content).[90]

On the authenticity issue, the defense argued that the Trawniki Certificate was a forgery; it even brought a string of witnesses to prove that the high level of forgery the KGB possessed as evidence was not authentic.

For example, the defense pointed out that the photo of Demjanjuk attached to the document had staple holes—evidence that it had been removed from another document. The defense also brought various forensic experts who claimed that the signature on the document was not Demjanjuk's signature. The defense said that Soviet authorities had a vested interest in incriminating Demjanjuk as someone who "went over to the enemy side." (Note that, parallel to the extradition request for Demjanjuk submitted by Israel, an extradition request was also submitted to the United States by authorities in the Soviet Union.)

Countless experts were brought to the court by both sides to clarify the question of the document's authenticity, Demjanjuk's signature, and the photo attached to it. The court did not accept the defence's argument; it ruled that the document was authentic[91] and that the signature was indeed Demjanjuk's. Also, it was established that the photo attached to the document was Demjanjuk.

As for the document's admissibility on substantive grounds (the truth of its content) that Demjanjuk was a *Wachmann* who served in Sobibór, the District Court ruled that the Trawniki Certificate was a "vintage document" according to Section 43 of the Evidence, adding to the strength of its authenticity. This was based on the fact that the document's expected and logical

---

90 *Id.*, at 63.
91 *Id.*, at 82.

location was indeed the place from which it was brought to the court—the offices of the Soviet Union's KGB.[92] In this context, the Supreme Court overturned the ruling of the District Court; the law stipulates that, in order for a document to be considered a "vintage document," it has to be "suitably preserved." This proviso did not exist in light of ongoing suspicion towards the KGB and its reputation as a forger of documents.[93] At the same time, the court ruled that truthful content of a public document stood on four conditions. First, the document was created under the force of statutory demands, that is, SS orders. Second, the document was of a public nature. Third, the document was designed to preserve its content for the future. Fourth, the document was open to public scrutiny—this conditional existed since the objective of the document was to present the identity of a *Wachmann* in the various camps.[94]

An additional important aspect that should be mentioned in the matter of the Trawniki Certificate—a point that was recognized as a weighty point by the Supreme Court—was the testimony of a *Wachmann* named Danilchenko; his statement was given in a judicial investigation carried out in the Soviet Union in 1949. Danilchenko said that he remembered Demjanjuk from the Sobibór camp. He testified that he had served with a *Wachmann* named Ivan Demjanjuk in Sobibór approximately at the time noted on Demjanjuk's service card. In addition, Danilchenko identified Demjanjuk in a photographic line-up; he gave many biographical details that matched those of Demjanjuk.[95] Additional documents that showed Demjanjuk was a *Wachmann* in the service of the SS was presented by the prosecution during the appeal process, including weapons logs and military orders in which Demjanjuk's name appears.[96]

C. Identification Line-ups

As already noted, the principal evidence in the trial was identification of Demjanjuk as "Ivan the Terrible" by survivors of the Treblinka death camp. The identification process was carried out by presenting a sheet of paper or an album of

---

92 *Demjanjuk Affair in the District Court, supra* note 80, at 262.
93 Criminal Appeal 347/88, *supra* note 79, at 68.
94 *Id.*, at 69–74.
95 *Id.*, at 137.
96 *Id.*, at 327.

photographs to survivors, who in most cases were requested to say whether they identified a Ukrainian person they were familiar with from Treblinka.

One of the problems that arose is that some of the prosecution's witnesses who identified the photo of Demjanjuk as Ivan the Terrible had died in the interim and could not testify at the trial. Nevertheless, the District Court and, after that, the Supreme Court ruled to accept the statements of the deceased as evidence, based on Section 15 of Nazis and Nazi Collaborators (Punishment) Law, 5710 – 1950:

> "In an action for an offence under this Law, the court may deviate from the rules of evidence if it is satisfied that this will promote the ascertainment of the truth and the just handling of the case."

In this context, lengthy deliberations took place analyzing the value of various identifications. A central argument of the defense was that in the majority of the line-ups, the size of the photos varied, and Demjanjuk's photo was larger than others. Thus, the identification line-up was flawed by a "prohibited hint."[97] Another argument was that the other photos were of other Nazi criminals, for the most part *Wachmänner,* whose features were not similar enough to Demjanjuk's, thus adding value in the eyes of the beholder to identifying Demjanjuk among others.

In regard to the first point, the court ruled that the difference in size between Demjanjuk's photo and the other photos did not diminish the weight of the identification. The court gave several reasons to justify this—both in light of the fact that there were other larger photos, and the fact that the survivors were not instructed to find Ivan the Terrible specifically, but rather *Wachmänner* from Treblinka in general.[98]

As for the second argument, the court ruled that when the line-ups were conducted, the objective was "general pinpointing" (i. e., "identification and extraction") of *Wachmänner* that the survivors recognize; the Demjanjuk picture had no objective of its own. Under such conditions, it is possible to conduct a line-up of pictures among photos of various suspects, not necessarily among similar photos.

---

97 For the photos in the line-up, see: Sheftel, *supra* note 27, at 39.
98 *Demjanjuk Affair, supra* note 79, at 168 – 169.

D. The Decision of the District Court

On 18 April, 1988, the Court handed down its decision. The District Court found that Demjanjuk was Ivan the Terrible from Treblinka. The court thus ruled, based on the testimony of the survivors identifying him. In the testimonies, the court ruled that there was sufficient evidence to find Demjanjuk guilty. At the same time, identifying testimony was strengthened by additional evidence: the Trawniki Certificate that showed Demjanjuk had served as a *Wachmann* in the SS and in Sobibór; Demjanjuk's fraudulent alibi (which according to the court was not found to be in line with various historical facts, and was nothing but a fabrication); and Demjanjuk's own incriminating statements, such as "You are pushing me to Treblinka." Accordingly, the court convicted Demjanjuk for the following crimes: a crime against the Jewish people, a crime against humanity, a war crime. and crimes against persecuted persons.

The court ruled that even a small cog wheel such as a *Wachmann* in an extermination camp was not protected as an instance of coercion, justification, or necessity; furthermore, rejection of such a defense applied not only to key figures in the extermination such as Adolf Eichmann:

> "Even a small cog wheel, even a low-grade driver, is liable [i.e., accountable] to be accomplices to a criminal offense ... and their standing is the same as the standing of the actual exterminator or murderer; orders from above do not liberate the transgressor when the illegality is obvious and prominent before the eyes of the perpetrator."

On 25 April, 1988, the District Court sentenced Demjanjuk to death.

E. New Evidence during the Appeal Stage

Just prior to the appeal to the Supreme Court, new evidence was received—evidence requested both by the prosecution and the defense in the Demjanjuk case. The new evidence was brought to light and submitted to the court due to warming of relations with the Soviet Union and, afterwards, the sudden collapse of the USSR. These events opened the door for exposure of many documents of Soviet investigation authorities. Thus, at various junctures, powers-of-attorney in Eastern Europe representing both the prosecution and the defense could embark on searches for new information.

One form of new evidence was German SS documents, some of which were received from Soviet authorities and some from German archives in

East Germany, where the name Ivan Demjanjuk appears as an SS *Wachmann*, as well as further evidence of Demjanjuk's posting in Sobibór in March 1943. Another form of new evidence that emerged at this point was various confessions made over the years by Ukrainian *Wachmänner* and forced laborers in Treblinka, taken by Soviet investigative authorities. The confession files revealed over 40 confessions by various persons who noted the fact there was a *Wachmann* named Ivan Marchenko in Treblinka. Many of the confessions cited that he was the one operating the gas chambers together with Nicholai Shelayev. A number of confession-givers mentioned the marked cruelty of Ivan Marchenko, and even mentioned the nickname given him by the Jews working in the camp—Ivan the Terrible. However, the biographical details they gave regarding the self-same Ivan Marchenko did not match those of Demjanjuk. A portion of the confession-givers, including Nicholai Shelayev, who operated the gas chambers along-side Ivan the Terrible, identified the photo of Ivan Marchenko as the photo of someone different from Demjanjuk.[99] The defense argued that these confessions proved the innocence of Demjanjuk, and Ivan the Terrible was another man known by the name Ivan Marchenko.

Furthermore, a Polish peasant named Kazimetz Dudek, who lived in a village near the Treblinka camp and operated a small grocery during the war, spoke of Ivan the Terrible, whose name was Ivan Marchenko, but at the same time, Dudek identified Demjanjuk's picture as this man Marchenko.

Defense attorney Yoram Sheftel argued that the farmer's wife, Maria Dudek, worked as a prostitute during the war and Treblinka *Wachmänner* habitually availed themselves of her services. Sheftel said that she also said that Ivan the Terrible's last name was Marchenko, and even claimed that he was *not* the person who appears in Demjanjuk's photo. The situation became all the more complicated since when Demjanjuk signed his immigration request in the early 1950s, he listed his mother's maiden name as Marchenko.[100]

F. Decision of the Court on Appeal

On 29 July 1993, the Supreme Court's decision on Demjanjuk's appeal was handed down, with five judges sitting on the bench.

---

99 *Id.*, at 354–361.
100 *Id.*, at 343–346.

The Supreme Court decision found that Ivan Demjanjuk was without doubt a *Wachmann* who had served in Trawniki and, after that, in the Sobibór extermination camp—both according to the Trawniki Certificate, and according to the testimony of *Wachmann* Danilchenko, noted above. At the same time, despite the identifying witnesses (the survivors who identified Demjanjuk as Ivan the Terrible from Treblinka), in the wake of new evidence brought at the appeal stage of the trial—that is, the confessions of *Wachmänner* regarding the identify of Ivan the Terrible as Ivan Marchenko—reasonable doubt now existed as to the question whether Demjanjuk was Ivan the Terrible, the appalling operator of the gas changers at Treblinka.[101]

In an important passage of the acquittal, the Supreme Court dealt with the question of what constitutes "reasonable doubt" and ruled that not every possibility, distant as it may be, is sufficient to create the doubt necessary for an acquittal:[102]

"Doubt alone is not sufficient, only doubt that is reasonably supported by the evidence[...] [that passes] the test of reasonable intelligence, that is to say, the test of common sense and life experience."

As noted already, the Supreme Court found that there was new evidence to raise reasonable doubt as to the identity of Demjanjuk as Ivan the Terrible. Another important question addressed by the Supreme Court in its decision was whether one can find Demjanjuk guilty for an alternative-parallel offense—for being a *Wachmann* in the Sobibór death camp, a fact that was proven beyond reasonable doubt. The court ruled that this was impossible. Firstly, Demjanjuk had not been extradited for being an accessory to murder (there was no testimony that he himself committed murder there, although the *Wachmänner* surely spilled a lot of blood), and no request had been submitted to the US government by the prosecution in Israel for arraignment on an alternative charge. Secondly, Demjanjuk had not been given the opportunity to defend himself against this charge.

Opening a new judicial procedure due to Demjanjuk's service in Sobibór was not possible, ruled the court, since, after all, Demjanjuk had already been incarcerated in an Israeli prison for more than seven years.[103] The court closed its decision with the following words:

---

101 *Id.*, at 383 – 392.
102 *Id.*, at 383.
103 *Id.*, at 400 – 405.

"The *Wachmann* Ivan Demjanjuk has been acquitted by us, because of doubt, of the terrible charges attributed to Ivan the Terrible of Treblinka. This was the proper course for judges who cannot examine the heart and mind, but have only what their eyes see and read. The facts proved the appellant's participation in the extermination process. The matter is closed —but not complete, the complete truth is not the prerogative of the human judge."[104]

In 2011 (after Demjanjuk's return to the United States and his extradition to Germany), Demjanjuk was convicted in Germany and sentenced to five years in prison for his service in the Sobibór extermination camp. He was found guilty of being an accessory to murder of more than 28,000 people.[105] In March 2012, Demjanjuk died at age 91 while still waiting to serve his sentence.[106]

There are those who believe the outcome of the Demjanjuk trial reached by the Israeli Supreme Court in overturning the District Court's judgement constitutes the victory of jurisprudence (the letter of the law) over justice (bringing Nazi criminals to justice).[107] Others argue that it was a victory for justice. After all, justice behooves one to exercise caution in matters of human life and in the punishment of persons with utmost caution, in the presence of reasonable doubt, the public interest notwithstanding.[108]

G. The Objective of the Trial and Public Opinion in Its Course

As already noted, the Demjanjuk trial attracted wide media coverage. The judges viewed the trial as an educational tool vis-à-vis the Holocaust and Nazi criminals. Both the ruling of the District Court [109] and the Supreme Court[110] were overflowing with descriptions of the horrors of the Holocaust and its course. Numer-

---

104 See http://www.nytimes.com/1993/07/30/world/acquittal-jerusalem-israel-court-sets-dem janjuk-free-but-he-now-without-country.html (accessed February 9, 2017).

105 News agency report "Germania: Damjanjuk horsha b'siyua l'retzach Yehudim" (Germany: Damjanjuk found guilty of accessory to murder of Jews), *nrg–Maariv news* (in Hebrew), 12 May, 2011, at www.nrg.co.il/online/1/ART2/240/105.html (accessed November 6, 2015).

106 "Sochnuyot HaYediot, "Poshe'a ha-Natzi John Demjanjuk met b'gil 91" (News Agencies, Nazi criminal John Demjanjuk dies at age 91), *nrg–Maariv news* (in Hebrew), 17 March, 2013, at www.nrg.co.il/online/1/ART2/347/248.html (accessed November 6, 2015).

107 Itamar Warhaftig, "Al Mishpat Demjanjuk—D'guva l-Ma'amaro shel Arieh Barnea" (On the Demjanjuk trial—Response to Arieh Barnea's Article). *Mechkarei Mishpat*, 11/207 (1993) (in Hebrew).

108 Arieh Barnea "Demjanjuk – ha-Chok veha-Tzedek" (Demjanjuk—Law and Justice), *Mechkarei Mishpat*, 11/201 (1994) (in Hebrew).

109 *The Demjanjuk Affair in the District Court, supra* note 80, at 14–.15

110 *The Demjanjuk Affair, supra* note 79, at 14–24.

ous testimonies were heard in the District Court that dealt with descriptions of the atrocities of extermination. Thus, the Supreme Court wrote:[111]

> "The judgement of the District Court constitutes not only a legal document. It serves as a historical and educational document of great significance. From this perspective, special importance was placed—in addition to certificates, documents, protocols and books—to description and documentation of the Holocaust in the judicial process, from the mouths of those numbered among the survivors who experienced its terrors, of a terrible inferno to their bodies and souls in proximity to the act of extermination, during its perpetration, and in its aftermath and thus they spoke, testified, and were cross-examined in the court ..."

As already noted, the venue chosen for holding the trial in the District Court was the International Convention Center in Jerusalem (*Binyanei HaUmah* or Buildings of the Nation, in Hebrew).

It appears that the judicial system sought to follow in the footsteps of the seminal Eichmann trial and to forge another historic trial. It is hard to say this attempt on the part of the judicial system did not come at a price:

The trial was accompanied by a storm of emotions that at times spelled over into violent channels. Attorney Sheftel described how, in many of the court sessions, curses and profanities were hurled at him and the defendant, in the course of the trial in the District Court.[112]

In the interim between the trial in the District Court and the appeal to the Supreme Court, former district judge Dov Eitan joined the defense team. On 28 November 1988, prior to the opening of deliberations in the Supreme Court sitting as an appellate court, Eitan committed suicide.[113] At the close of Eitan's funeral, an individual named Israel Yechezkeli accosted Yoram Sheftel and threw hydrochloric acid in his face, almost blinding Sheftel.[114]

---

111 *Id.*, at 12.
112 See, for example, Sheftel, *supra* note 27, at 49.
113 *Id.*, at 273–274. The retired judge did not leave any suicide note explaining his motivations, but it is surmised that Eitan felt "trapped"—between his commitment to join the defense and angry public sentiment and pressure to back out. In a 1994 interview, Sheftel said: "...maybe he was threatened in a way that on one hand he was afraid of pursuing his role as a defense attorney, and on the other hand he said to himself that this is impossible to retreat from as well, from the moral point of view. And, maybe, the solution to it was committing suicide." See Roma Hadzewycz, "Interview: Yoram Sheftel, Israeli Defender of John Demjanjuk," *Ukrainian Weekly*, July 21, 1996, at:
http://www.ukrweekly.com/old/archive/1996/299607.shtml (accessed February 9, 2017).
114 *Id.*, at 279.

During the course of the trial, there was great difficulty in handling breaches of the principle of *sub judice* (under judicial consideration) and, therefore, prohibited from public discussion elsewhere. This was expressed, among other things, in the High Court of Justice ruling[115] that the decision of the attorney general not to open an investigation against *Yediot Aharonot* journalist Noach Klieger (a survivor of Auschwitz), who breached *sub judice* in his writings concerning Demjanjuk, was flawed by lack of reasonableness.

It is difficult to criticize the decision of the justice system to mold the trial as an historic-educational act, beyond it being a criminal judicial proceeding. At the same time, it seems that the Demjanjuk affair—certainly after his acquittal—raises questions regarding the boundaries of judicial proceedings, and the boundary between a purely criminal proceeding and a trial serving as a social-educational tool. This question arises in particular in trials involving war crimes and crimes against humanity, which, it should be kept in mind, are not limited to Israel.

6. Failure to Bomb Auschwitz

In April 1944, the possibility of bombing Auschwitz was raised by Rabbi Michael Dov Weissmandl. He raised this possibility after an anti-Nazi Slovakian operative from the railway authority in his country leaked information that the heads of the Slovakian, German, and Hungarian train authorities had signed an agreement to carry 120 transports to Auschwitz. His proposal came as a reaction to the Verba-Wetzler Report, a report that detailed testimony, based on eye-witness accounts of two inmates of the Auschwitz concentration camp who had escaped the camp in April 1944.

In a letter that the Slovakian Weissmandl sent to Jewish organizations in Switzerland, he advised bombing the Košice-Prešov train tunnel in Czechoslovakia on the route to the gas chambers at Auschwitz, and other bridges and tunnels used to transport passengers to Auschwitz. In June of the same year, a letter was received by officers in the US government and the Jewish Agency; on 18 June, the BBC broadcasted a short summary of the content.

The initial position of the Jewish Agency was to give preference to taking the "goods for blood" plan forward in order to save Hungarian Jewry, rather than the plan to bomb Auschwitz. At the outset of June, in order to take the plans forward, Malchiel Gruenbaum, the head of the Rescue Committee (the body established

---

115 H.C.J 223/88 *Sheftel v. the Government Legal Counsel*, 43(4) P.D. 356 (1986).

by the Jewish Agency during the war to take action to save Jews in Europe), met with Lowell C. Pinkerton, the American consul in Jerusalem, to transmit the same request. In doing so, Gruenbaum went beyond the mandate he had received from the Committee in occupied Europe, driven by Gruenbaum's own distrust of other members of the Committee. In the meeting, he raised a number of courses of action. One suggestion was to renew American warnings to Hungary not to assist Germany, and to add Bulgaria to the warning. Another suggestion was to bomb the death camps in Poland.

In the exchange, Pinkerton raised various apprehensions in regard to the suggestion that Auschwitz be bombed, but Pinkerton agreed to pass the proposal on to Washington, provided Gruenbaum put it in writing. However, since this was a significant deviation from Gruenbaum's authority to take such a decision in the name of the Jewish Agency, he agreed to compromise and put in writing only the proposal that the railroad lines between Hungary and Poland be bombed. Indeed, when, at the 11 June meeting of the Jewish Agency, Gruenbaum raised the proposal to bomb Auschwitz, opposition was voiced to such an idea. The organization did not want to take responsibility for bombing the slave labor camp at the site, since such a bombing mission would entail killing Jews in the process.[116]

In the period between 23 and 27 June, the Jewish Agency began to receive confirmed information proving the sheer scope of Hungarian Jews being sent to the Auschwitz death camp. This realization led to a change in thinking among members of the Jewish Agency and strengthened Gruenbaum's position regarding the necessity of bombing the camp. Members of the Rescue Committee sought by various other channels to convince the powers-that-be to bomb Auschwitz, but to no avail.

The appeal to Washington via Pinkerton "enjoyed" a laconic and disappointing reply:

"The Department of State asks me (Pinkerton) to advise you that efforts to protect the status of the Jews of Hungary are conducted in a variety of channels and via the Red Cross. Warnings relating to the treatment of Jews are frequently conveyed to Hungary in radio short waves and others."

Concurrently, Haim Weizmann (at the time, president of the World Zionist Organization) and Moshe Sharett (called Moshe Shertok at the time, head of the Political Department of the Jewish Agency) sought to save the remnant of Hungarian Jewry by taking forward the "goods for blood" plan (negotiations with Adolf

---

116 Shabtai Tebeth, *Ben-Gurion and the Holocaust*, (1996), pp. 186–189.

Eichmann to exchange one million Jews for trucks and other goods, a deal the Nazis proposed and called "Blut gegen Waren" or "blood for goods"). In this regard, they sent heart-rending letters to British entities requesting to meet with British Foreign Minister Anthony Eden. Nevertheless, their efforts came to naught since the Foreign Minister had already decided on 31 May not to approve the "goods for blood" plan.[117]

Parallel to this, the idea of bombing Auschwitz was raised by additional parties. In the wake of appeals from Jewish leaders, on 24 June, 1944, the executive director of the War Refugee Board John W. Pehle contacted John J. McCloy, Assistant Secretary of War and requested, cautiously, that McCloy examine the possibility of bombing Auschwitz.[118]

McCloy viewed the proposal to bomb the railway line used to deport Jews as a clear breach of his own and Secretary of War Henry Lewis Stimson's view that military resources should solely and exclusively be employed to win the war. McCloy responded on 4 July 1944 to Pehle's June 29 memorandum, in which Pehle had raised the proposal, but took issue with it at the same time, questioning the wisdom and utility of bombing the railway lines. McCloy wrote:

> "The War Department is of the opinion that the suggested air operation is impracticable. It could be executed only by the diversion of considerable air support essential to the success of our forces now engaged in decisive operations and would in any case be of such very doubtful efficacy that it would not amount to a practical project."[119][120]

Today, it is clear that the United States military indeed used military resources for targets other than purely war targets. An example is the establishment of the unit called the "the Monuments Men," whose objective was to save art treas-

---

117 *Id.*, at 193–196.

118 Some argue that Pehle did not seriously promote the proposal or pass it on in good faith, rather he was only "going through the motions" and, in fact, Pehle told McCloy that he had "several doubts" about the proposal, including (1) the propriety of using military airplanes for this purpose; (2) "whether it would be difficult to put the railroad line out of commission for a long enough period to do any good"; and (3) "even assuming that this railroad line were put out of commission for the same period of time, whether it would help the Jews in Hungary." Pehle made it clear to McCloy that he was not "at this point at least, requesting the War Department to take any action on this proposal other than to appropriately explore it. See quotes from primary sources here:

http://savingthejews.com/html/auschwitzexcerpt.htm#_edn8 (accessed February 9, 2017).

119 Michael Beschloss, *ha-Minatzchim* (The Conquerors: Roosevelt, Truman and the Destruction of Hitler's Germany 1941–1945) (in Hebrew), Yediot Aharonot publishers, 2003, pp. 77–78.

120 http://savingthejews.com/html/auschwitzexcerpt.htm (accessed February 9, 2017).

ures plundered by the Nazis across Europe.[121] Another example is the deployment of battle units to rescue a group of Lipizzaner horses in Czech territory (fearing advancing Red Army units might turn the prized breeding stallions into horse meat). The horses were put "under the special protection of the US Army" and spirited to safety by a special task force, on orders from General George S. Patton himself.[122]

For many years, conventional wisdom held that John McCloy had decided himself not to bomb Auschwitz, without consulting President Roosevelt. But three years before his death, he gave a taped interview to the son of Henry Morgenthau, who was Secretary of the Treasury during World War II. (Henry Morgenthau III was writing a family history.) In his interview, McCloy admitted that the individual who objected to the idea of bombing Auschwitz and squashed the idea was President Roosevelt himself, who responded angrily to the proposal and expressed his objection in the following words:

"Why, the idea! They'll only move it down the road a little way." One can take FDR's meaning that the Nazis would have built other death camps and continue the killing. McCloy recollected that FDR "made it very clear" to him that bombing Auschwitz "wouldn't have done any good." Moreover, Roosevelt said that bombing Auschwitz would be "provocative" to the Nazis and he wouldn't "have anything to do" with the idea. FDR warned Morgenthau that Americans would be accused of "bombing these innocent people" at Auschwitz, adding, "We'll be accused of participating in this horrible business!"[123]

The lack of willingness to bomb Auschwitz was part of the Roosevelt's policy of pushing the "Jewish Problem" aside. By 1943–1944, the American government had become aware of the slaughter of Jews by Germany. Nevertheless, Roosevelt chose not to bring the matter to the attention of the American public. There are a number of reasons, including apprehension that it would only spur Hitler to persecution of the Jews more, and the fear that such a move would provide fuel for anti-Semites and isolationists in America who charged American was "fighting a

---

121 Rafael Medoff, "'The Monument Men' Shows America Saved Paintings While Letting Jews Die," *Tablet*, January 29, 2014, http://www.tabletmag.com/jewish-arts-and-culture/160918/ monuments-men (accessed November 6, 2015).

122 Karen Jensen, "How General Patton and Some Unlikely Allies Saved the Prized Lipizzaner Stallions," Historynet.com (quoting Patton's diary and other sources) at http://www.historynet. com/patton-rescues-the-lipizzaner-stallions.htm (accessed February 9, 2017).

    Also described in detail in Michael Keane, *George S. Patton: Blood, Guts, and Prayer*, Chapter: "Saving the Lipizzaners," Regnery Publishing, 2012 pp. 133–148.

123 Beschloss, *supra* note 119, at 80; in regard to Roosevelt's attitude to Jews, see Richard Breitman and Allan J. Lichman, *FDR and the Jews*, 2013 SOURCE of quote in English http://www. newenglishreview.org/blog_direct_link.cfm/blog_id/40186/ (accessed February 9, 2017).

war for the Jews." This blunder on the part of the President's attitudes and priorities along with his lack of action reflected ongoing indifference to the Jews' fate (exhibited from Hitler's rise to power). This predisposition led senior government officials to view post-war Germany as solely a reconstruction problem; after solving this issue, the Americans could leave Germany and leave it to chart its own fate.[124] In terms of war priorities, research reveals that the United States bombed the Monowitz industrial sites (a huge industrial complex quite close to Auschwitz) and bombers flew directly over Auschwitz on their way to other missions.[125] Therefore, arguments that Auschwitz was out of the range of operation of the Allied force, and that such a mission would entail "diverting" planes to the area, were untrue.[126]

After publication of the Verba-Wetzler Report, British Foreign Secretary Anthony Eden was asked on 5 July, 1944, if he knew about the mass deportation of Hungarian Jews to Poland in order to kill them, and whether Britain could take steps to prevent the murder of European Jews by Hitler. Eden replied that he had no definitive knowledge, but there were rumors to the effect that authorities in Germany and Hungary had begun deportation; the best way to assist the Jews, he added, was to win the war.

On 7 July, 1944, Churchill requested that Eden examine whether the Royal Air Force could bomb Auschwitz. The Secretary of the Air Ministry stipulated that only American bombers were suitable for carrying out such a mission, but this would be "expensive and dangerous."[127]

At the same time, it should be noted that, already in January 1944, the American War Refugee Board (WRB) had been established by Roosevelt (at the urging

---

124 There is ample evidence tshat he could turn "empathy" on and off, but the "Question" was hardly at the top of his priorities. See *Roosevelt and the Jews* published by the United States Holocaust Museum in 2013. http://www.amazon.com/dp/0674050266/ref=rdr_ext_tmb (accessed February 9, 2017).

125 In this regard, see the documentary film by Haim Hecht, *Tisa Achat Bishbeilenu—ha-Matas me'al Auschwitz* (One Flight for Us—The Flyover over Auschwitz), at www.youtube.com/watch? v=MEtnXiE5MsY (accessed February 9, 2017), (Part IV in Hebrew with Hebrew subtitles), downloaded 6 November, 2015. For full version in Hebrew with English subtitles, see https://vimeo.com/47767264 (accessed February 9, 2017). The documentary presents aerial photography and interviews about the capabilities of the American Air Force and whether it had the potential to bomb the extermination camp; this against the backdrop of the symbolic "flyover" conducted by the Israeli Air Force over Auschwitz in 2003, marking 60 years to the liberation of the camp.

126 Refael Medoff, *In Dialogue: Bush on Auschwitz—Refael Medoff Speaks with Shimon Shetreet*, Jerusalem Post, January 16, 2008, at http://www.wymaninstitute.org/articles/2008-1-dialogue.php (accessed February 9, 2017).

127 Beschloss, *supra* note 119, at 77.

of his Secretary of the Treasury Morgenthau). However, despite its operations—based on working with Jewish organizations, diplomats from neutral countries, and resistance groups in Europe to rescue Jews from occupied territories and provide them with safe havens (i. e., elsewhere, not in the United States)—the WRB's ability to gain the support of the other Allies was low. The British were opposed to collaborating with the War Refugee Board on which the American Secretary of War sat, apprehensive that his attempts to save Jews and resettle them elsewhere would undermine the 1939 White Paper that had cut Jewish immigration to British-controlled Mandate Palestine (to appease the Arabs). Furthermore, support remained low for the idea of saving Jews by bombing Auschwitz and the railroad tracks leading to the camp.

Although there is was no express principle that *required* the Allies to intervene to save Jews, including by bombing Auschwitz, a *special* legal duty existed in light of the Allies' knowledge that heinous crimes of genocide were being committed. By virtue of the right of States to protect themselves and their nationals as a humanitarian objective, this right becomes a legal duty.[128]

President Roosevelt's decision not to bomb Auschwitz was one of the most disturbing decisions in the course of the Second World War. Those who justify the decision, then and today, argue that the best way to save Jews was to win the war in Europe as swiftly as possible. A number of scholars argue that bombing would have stopped the slaughter only for a short time until the Nazis fixed damage to the gas chambers, roads, and rail lines, or until they took other measures—swifter and crueler methods of killing Jews. They hold that bombing would only have spurred the Nazis to speed up the killing.

Those who criticize the decision not to bomb argue that, considering the tempo and scope of extermination (particularly during the period when bombing was raised), disruption of the operation of the death camps and transports to them could have saved tens of thousands.[129]

Nobel Laureate Eli Wiesel (the most famous inmate of the Auschwitz III slave labor camp) challenged apprehensions of jeopardy to inmates of the camps. He recalled the bombing of the nearby IG Farben plant in August 1944, saying that

---

128 Medoff, *supra* note 126.
129 "During the deportation of Hungarian Jews in the spring of 1944, Auschwitz-Birkenau reached a peak killing capacity: the SS gassed as many as 6,000 Jews each day." Source: see US Holocaust Museum, here https://www.ushmm.org/wlc/en/article.php?ModuleId=10007327 (accessed February 9, 2017). Other source: "The highest daily number of people gassed and cremated actually achieved in 1944 during the extermination of the Hungarian Jews was 24,000," at http://www.holocaustresearchproject.org/othercamps/auschwitzgaschambers.html (accessed February 9, 2017).

even if the bombing would have killed Jewish inmates "we no longer feared death."

> "To see the whole works go up in fire—what revenge! ...We were not afraid. And yet, if a bomb had fallen on the blocks, it alone would have claimed hundreds of lives on the spot. We were no longer afraid of death; at any rate, not of that death. Every bomb filled us with joy and gave us new confidence in life."[130]

Today it is clear that bombing Auschwitz would have been perceived as a moral statement by the Allies, signaling that they understood the historical gravity of the Holocaust. Historian Gerhard Weinberg wrote that the bombing of Auschwitz might not have saved many Jews, but "the record of the Allies would have been brighter, and each person saved could have lived out a decent life."[131] This outlook does not, however, take into account that the bombing of the rail lines and extermination facilities might have saved Jews as a result of the damage inflicted. Moreover, it ignores the possibility that damage to facilities and rail lines might have led the Nazis to refrain from further transports.[132]

A. The Public Trial (Moot Court) Conducted by the Lapid Movement over the Question of Allied Guilt for Not Bombing Auschwitz

In 1990, the Lapid movement (a movement dedicated to instilling the lessons of the Holocaust) conducted a moot court in Israel dedicated to the question of whether the Allies were guilty for not bombing the Auschwitz extermination camp and the rail lines leading to it. The author of this part of this book served as judge in this moot court.

---

130 https://books.google.co.il/books?id=3MDOAgAAQBAJ&pg=PA493&lpg=PA493&dq=see+the +whole+works+go+up+in+fire%E2%80%94what+revenge&source=bl&ots=O6rGb0UFKu&sig= FWfhyQDFaaUrw-99oGqddTkDfPI&hl=en&sa=X&ved=0ahUKEwjIqdqVuoTNAhUEiRoKHaYLDq YQ6AEIGjAA#v=onepage&q=see%20the%20whole%20works%20go%20up%20in%20fire%E2% 80%94what%20revenge&f=false (accessed February 9, 2017).
131 Beschloss, *supra* note 119, at 79. Michael R. Beschloss, *The Conquerors: Roosevelt, Truman and the Destruction of Hitler's Germany*, p. 65 at https://books.google.co.il/books?id= gKbNF1BnCRgC&pg=PA65&lpg=PA65&dq=Gerhard+Weinberg++Auschwitz&source=bl&ots= 08Y3Ygdj4X&sig=xmCGS0iortzokw8Ra5BjHebkTiI&hl=en&sa=X&ved=0ahUKEwjBv_G4i__MA hUH2hoKHV4rBZgQ6AEIIzAB#v=onepage&q=Gerhard%20Weinberg%20%20Auschwitz&f=false (accessed February 9, 2017).
132 In this regard, see the documentary film by Haim Hecht, *supra* note 125.

The primary argument raised in the trial was that the Allies had a legal responsibility under international law to bomb Auschwitz, an argument that rested on two points. The first was the right of a state to intervene to defend the lives of its civilians beyond its own borders. There were 2,000 American citizens and an unknown number of British nationals imprisoned at Auschwitz. In addition, domestic and international law uphold the duty to protect citizens of the state.

At the same time, this begs the questions whether the state can exercise discretion as to when this duty should be applied. Does this also exist in regard to a small number of civilians? There are apprehensions that this approach could encourage avoidable use of force and disrupt the international order.

The answer rests on the principle of proportionality, a key conditional in the doctrine of intervention to save civilians abroad, which holds that the use of force is justified only of a magnitude proportional to the level of danger. Thus, in wartime, when the world order is already disrupted, and when one is dealing with the crime of genocide or mass murder, the principle of proportionality is clearly manifested.

The second argument rests on the right of any state to exercise humanitarian intervention to save people from death, even if they are not nationals of the intervening state. International law upholds the right to intervene, even on behalf of those who are not citizens. Moreover, when, as in the case at hand, one is dealing with genocide or mass murder, this right becomes a duty.

In addition, the case at hand involves exceptional crimes that justify exceptional treatment. The exceptionality of such crimes is recognized in the exceptions that apply. There is no statute of limitations, the defense based on necessity or justification ("higher orders" or coercion) is inapplicable, and criminal punishment may be applied retroactively to such crimes. Thus, one should recognize that states are duty bound from a legal standpoint to intervene, even in cases where there is no clear express principle of the existence of such a legal duty. Its criminality is self-evident.

Furthermore, there are those who declare that the Allies had a moral duty to prevent genocide. In wartime, prevention of genocide is perceived as a secondary objective to the primary objective of winning the war. But the second duty exists, subject to the above order of priorities—that is, as long its realization does not unreasonably undermine the objective of bringing victory that would end the war.

In the course of the moot court, the defense (Katriel Ben Arie) raised various arguments, but they were all rejected. Its first argument was that, from a military standpoint, it would have been difficult and too dangerous to get to Auschwitz. In the trial, proof was presented that three times the Allies bombed targets very close to Auschwitz—in Monowitz. Moreover, this argument was rejected in light of the fact that "dangers and limitations" did not prevent approval of other military missions, including rescue missions whose purposes were similar to those of preventing genocide. Auschwitz was not even defined as a secondary target when the opportunity arose to attack it.

The defense's second argument suggested that such a mission to bomb Auschwitz would have come at the expense of other essential military operations. This argument was rejected as well, on the premise that the free world should have sent a clear message of condemnation of the extermination, as well as a clear message to the perpetrators that the world knew about their deeds. As part of the war effort, there is great importance to preventing genocide, parallel to the primary objective of victory. Furthermore, just as the Germans invested enormous resources in extermination, the Allies should have invested efforts of equal magnitude to prevent this crime against humanity.

The defense's third argument was that such bombing would have killed a portion of the camp inmates. The court rejected the argument, ruling that this was irrelevant to failure to bomb the railroad lines leading to the camp. As for the camp itself, such an argument did not justify refraining to bomb, considering the distinct possibility that thousands Jews could have been saved had Auschwitz been bombed.

The defense's fourth argument was that bombing Auschwitz could have been exploited by the Nazi propaganda machine. Such an argument pales by comparison and does not stand the test of logic, when the value of saving human lives is taken into account.

In addition, the defense voiced criticism of the role of Jewish leadership, which didn't sound the alarm in time or protest loud enough against the Allies refraining from bombing. The bench in the public trial ruled that there was substance to this argument, and perhaps a clearer and more vigorous stand would have helped. At the same time, the legal and moral duty of the Allies to take action existed, irrespective of the actions or inactions of the Jewish community.

In January 2008, during a state visit to Israel, President George W. Bush, Jr., declared that the United States should have bombed Auschwitz.[133] Even in retrospect, recognition of the duty of those in power to act militarily during wartime to prevent genocide parallel to the main objective of war—recognition declared by a sitting President of the United States—contributes towards setting norms of behavior for all leaders and nations in this respect for the future: that they are duty bound to act should the situation demand it.

---

133 "Associated Press, "Bush at Yad Vashem: US Should Have Bombed Auschwitz," *ynet news*, Nov. 1, 2008, at http://www.ynetnews.com/articles/0,7340,L-3492988,00.html, (accessed November 6, 2015).

7. The Efforts for the Holocaust Survivors

A. The Dorner Commission Conclusions

In 2008, a commission was formed, headed by retired Justice Dalia Dorner. The commission intended to examine the assistance given to Holocaust survivors and the implementation of their rights by the Israeli government. The commission was formed after the State Control Commission exercised the powers granted to it under the law. The commission was later called the *Dorner Commission*. The commission arrived at several conclusions and recommendations.

Among other things, the commission recommended reducing the bureaucratic procedures the survivors encounter in order to maintain the principle of immediacy, which is necessary for the survivors because to their advanced age. To this end, the commission recommended "reducing proof tests as much as possible and giving automatic eligibility according to criteria known in advance and deductible by the ability of the survivor." The commission also recommended "vouchers system" that will give the Holocaust survivors the freedom to choose a service from a service package.[134]

In addition, the commission noted that only one-third of the Holocaust survivors receive reparations from Israel and that they are members of Clalit who have exhausted their rights (Clalit is Israel's largest health service organization). The Dorner Commission also added that receiving their right to reparations is conditional on the survivors' awareness of those rights when requesting Clalit to recognize their rights, and when they file a claim to the relevant officers to review their claim. The commission stated that it is "a cumbersome bureaucratic procedure and the state has an obligation to change it and set an organized transformation of the lists of Nazi persecution victims to the HMOs in order for them to address to the Holocaust survivors and inform them directly about their rights."[135]

In terms of professional decisions (e. g., medical eligibility, placement in institutions), it was determined that survivors cannot be accepted at the discretion of an individual and that such decisions should be made by multi-professional and inter-professional panels. The Dorner Commission noted that only 1,049 of the Holocaust survivors who are Clalit members and who receive payments from Germany (which are only 11% of all the Holocaust survivors who are mem-

---

134 The State Commission of Inquiry into the Governments' Treatment of Holocaust Survivors (Hereinafter: *The Dorner Commission*) 240–242 (2008).
135 *Id.*, at 192–193.

bers of Clalit) were identified in Clalit's computer systems as automatically eligible for exemption from payment for various medications and fees, although the compensation authorities in Germany transferred funds for 9,815 survivors to Clalit. Since Clalit does not have information on the identity of those who receive payments from Germany, it cannot trace them in order to help them realize their rights.[136]

As the Dorner report shows, through the National Health Insurance Act, Israel citizens cover the medical expenses of many Holocaust survivors who are entitled for payments from Germany. Therefore, the state was asked to promote the subject of transferring the information of the identities of the survivors insured in Clalit who are eligible for funding from Germany to the German authorities.[137]

The Dorner Commission proposed that, as part of the array of services to Holocaust survivors, mobile professional inter-regional teams will be set up. The role of these teams will be to coordinate the daily care routine of the survivors in order to avoid duplication in treatment and in order to coordinate existing services, with an emphasis on treatment on a professional level and shortened timetable. The main job of the teams will be to identify the survivors' needs and take care of them. It was also recommended that every mobile team include a team leader who is a social worker or a gerontologist, a public health nurse, a geriatrician or psych geriatrician physician, and a social worker accompanied by volunteers who will exercise and extract the rights. The teams will be trained and specialize in locating survivors, identifying their needs, and developing and adapting unique treatment plans for them.[138]

Only some of the recommendations were implemented:[139]

At first an amendment was made about harm to the property of disabled Holocaust survivors whose right to submit a claim under the German Federal Compensation Act (BEG) was denied as a result of the Reparations Agreement.[140] The amendment was that the payments for these survivors were updated in relation to the amount paid under German law. In addition, an information center

---

136 *Id.*, at 242.
137 *Id.*, at 191–192.
138 *Id.*, at 239–240.
139 The Knesset's Research and Information Center, *The Implementation of the Dorner Commission Report (The State Commission of Inquiry into the Governments' Treatment of Holocaust Survivors)* 2 (2009).
140 *The Dorner Commission , supra* note 134, at 115–116; on blocking the possibility of the disabled to make a claim under the German Compensation Act, see The Reparations Agreement, *supra* chapter 13.2 at pp. 54–59.

for clarifying rights for Holocaust survivors was set up. The center is operated by the Ministry of Social Services.

By the time the report was published in 2008, 54,610 Holocaust survivors had applied to the information center. Applicants are asked a few guiding questions and, depending on their answers, receive a questionnaire for special treatment that is forwarded to a "fast lane" of the body taking care of the matter: the Ministry of Finance, the Department of Rehabilitation, the Section 2 Foundation of the Claims Conference, the Foundation for the Benefit of Holocaust Victims in Israel, and the Department for Personal Compensation from Germany. Each body has a contact person who knows the rules by which the body works. Six months after the operations started in the information center, in which data on the Holocaust survivors was gathered, the work on segmenting the data began. This work was intended to assist the Services Basket Committee in making decisions for 2010.

Israeli governments have acted to implement other recommendations. For example, social workers have been trained on behalf of the Ministry of Health to assist Holocaust survivors living in retirement homes and hospitals supervised by the Ministry of Health to complete a questionnaire. They signed an agreement with the Jewish Agency regarding the volunteers going to homes of survivors in order to help them fill their questionnaire and operation of this system, and they also trained volunteers for these purposes by the student union, and more.[141] In addition to the above, in recent years, we have witnessed a trend of willingness from the government to increase the amount rationed for assistance to Holocaust survivors and, thus, to expand the circle of survivors who are entitled to it, as well as the amount of benefits.[142]

The culmination of this trend was in the plan that was presented in April 2014 by the Minister of Finance, Yair Lapid, and the Minister of Welfare and Social Services, Meir Cohen. According to the plan, an extra billion NIS a year will be allocated to assist Holocaust survivors. The program is supposed to improve the assistance to survivors on several levels. First, it expands the circle of those entitled to benefits and various conditions. The most important change in this context is comparing the conditions of Holocaust survivors who immigrated to Israel after 1953 to the terms of the survivors who immigrated before 1953. In ad-

---

141 The Implementation of the Dorner Commission Report, *supra* note 139, at 16–18.

142 See, for example, "The Government Will Increase the Budget of Holocaust Survivors in 225 Million NIS," nrg-business www.nrg.co.il/online/16/ART2/358/565.html (accessed February 9, 2017); Roni Singer "The Ministry of Finance Offers: Holocaust Survivors Who Immigrated to Israel after October 1953 Will Receive Assistance," Calcalist http://www.calcalist.co.il/local/ar ticles/0,7340,L-3626143,00.html (accessed February 9, 2017).

dition, the eligibility for assistance to spouses of Holocaust survivors who have died will be expanded. Another significant change which is planned is that, for the purpose of examining the entitlement to a nursing benefit from Social Security, the income of the survivors from benefits paid to them because they are Holocaust survivors will not be considered. Second, the program intends to increase the amount of money the survivors will receive by raising the minimum pension for a Holocaust survivor from 1825 to 2,200 ₪; furthermore the program will fully fund drugs. The plan also includes an annual grant for needy Holocaust survivors. Third, the program intends to reduce bureaucratic procedures that the survivors are forced to pass in order to exercise their entitlement. In order to receive various grants, the survivors will not need to show receipts, but instead will receive the grants directly to their bank accounts.

Finally, the program seeks to expand the therapeutic and human assistance to survivors; assistance in the form of home visitations, social services, and psychological treatments.[143]

B. The Restitution of Holocaust Victims' Assets

In 1997, an article was published by Yossi Katz saying that the Administrator General had a lot of property in real estate and funds coming from investments of European Jews in Israel during the 1920s and 1930s. These Jews died during the Holocaust and, according to the British command from 1939, their property was transferred to the British Custodian of Enemy Property. When the state was established, this property was transferred to the Israeli heirs.

Unfortunately, the news did not cause the government to make a comprehensive examination and return the property to their heirs. Moreover, the Administrator General justified his indifference on the matter through the Administrator General Act of 1978.

The property of the Jews who died in the Holocaust was held not only by the Administrator General, but also the Jewish National Fund (JNF) and its subsidiary, Himnuta. In addition, it was held in the form of cash and securities in banks and in the hands of the Jewish Colonial Trust (JCT). At that time, Israel acted vigorously to restore the property of victims and survivors from Europe.

---

143 Moti Bassok "The Finance and Social Affairs Ministers Decided to Increase Aid for Holocaust Survivors in Billion NIS," The Marker—Health, 13.4.2014 http://www.themarker.com/news/1.2295709 (accessed February 9, 2017).

Prof. Katz believes that, in general, it was not malice that led the bodies that held most of the properties, e.g., the JNF and the Administrator General, to act with indifference to Jewish assets that were in the hands of the State of Israel. They justified their indifference in that Israeli law does not require them to locate missing property owners and return their property. The property that was seized by the Administrator General was not nationalized, so that anyone who proved affinity to the property and demanded its return was entitled to it. However, it is important to note that the Administrator General records held no separate registration of property of people missing in the Holocaust. Similarly, the plaintiffs retained the right to the property when it was held by the Jewish National Fund, or sold to its subsidiary, Himnuta (with the approval of the Administrator General).

However, according to Katz, in some cases the question arises whether the missing property was mistakenly or deliberately forgotten. He brings a number of examples; one involves an American Jewish organization.

In 1914, the American Zionist Commonwealth was established; its job was to buy land in Israel for private Jewish capital. Many land purchases were made for European Jews who later died in the Holocaust. In light of the tragic events before and during World War II, a situation was created whereby many of the sales did not materialize, although the buyers paid the company. The company also suffered numerous economic difficulties; in order to resolve them, it borrowed money from the United Israel Appeal. In 1950, before the process of liquidation began, it was suggested that the company announce publicly it was heading towards liquidation so that people who had interest in the company or investments could come and demand their money. However, in the end, the heads of the company decided not to announce the company's situation in the hope that survivors who invested in the company or their heirs would forget about the property and settle for warnings that were already issued in 1934.[144]

In view of the challenges regarding Holocaust survivors' property, the Knesset decided unanimously on 15 February, 2000, to establish a parliamentary commission of inquiry on the subject of "locating and restituting assets of Holocaust victims that are located in Israel"; this commission was headed by MK Colette Avital.[145] It operated for several years and was dissolved in the second half of 2004.[146]

---

144 Katz, *supra* note 20, at 147–155.
145 Concerning the Commission see *supra* chapter 15.5.C.
146 Katz, *supra* note 20, at 157.

The commission investigated only the issue of the Holocaust victims' bank accounts. The main attention was directed towards Bank Leumi, which on the eve of the establishment of the state was the largest Zionist bank in the Land of Israel.

The commission dealt with valuating the funds to which the victims were entitled. It even included those cases in which money was returned to in the past, but not in its real value.

The commission established a sub-commission to investigate the issue of real estate property and securities property belonging to the Holocaust victims. But in light of the dismantling of the commission, the sub-commission also dismantled and therefore its activity was not completed.

As part of the commission's work, the Minister of Justice at the time, Yosef Tommy Lapid, ordered drafting a bill for the establishment of a quasi-government agency, that would have three functions: the documentation and registration of Holocaust victims' property which is located in the country and is held by governmental and private bodies, and transferring it the agency; publishing the names of the owners and the types of properties registered in their names with the intent that their heirs will turn to the company to get their property (this is also included actively searching the property); and transferring the property to the Holocaust survivors and to Holocaust memorial and education bodies if the owner was not found.

On December 21, 2005, the law was approved in second and third readings under the name *Assets of Holocaust Victims Law (Restitution to Heirs and Dedication to Aid and Commemoration) 5766 – 2006*.

The basis which guided the formulation of the law was that the chances were not big that many heirs of victims who could demand the property would be found, as happened with the private property remaining in Europe. The reason was that most of the investors and property owners in Israel and Europe were hurt, and sometimes their families as well, by the Nazi extermination machine. This basis is presented in the explanation of the law:

"This is partly due to the fact that during the Holocaust entire families and even communities were cut down, and many documents and knowledge relating to Holocaust victims and their assets were lost. Many of the survivors still living today were minors at the time of the Holocaust, and some did not even get to know their relatives who were perished".

During the preparation of the bill for second and third reading, representatives of Holocaust survivors' organizations and the Forum of Holocaust Survivors Organizations were invited to the meetings of the parliamentary commission of inquiry. The intention was that, according to the law, property which could not be traced to the owners would be used primarily for the aid of Holocaust survivors who live in Israel.

Following the law, in the summer of 2006, the Company for Location and Restitution of Holocaust Victims' Assets, Ltd., began to operate under the provisions of the law, i. e. locating and collecting the assets of those who perished, publishing the names of the owners and the types of property, receiving requests for restitution and locating of property, restitution treatment, and preparation for assistance to survivors. However, in early December 2007, an HCJ petition was brought against the company by the Chairman of the Foundation for the Benefit of Holocaust Victims in Israel, Ze'ev Factor. The essence of the petition was to instruct the company to publish, urgently and immediately, the standards by which it would use the assets that were transferred to it for the purposes of assistance to needy survivors. The petitioner also asked the court to instruct the company to begin providing assistance to needy Holocaust survivors immediately.

At the beginning of 2008, one of the most important decisions of the company's board was made. It involved the transfer of 100 million Israeli shekels until April 2008 for the benefit of about 12,000 needy Holocaust survivors. In addition, until that year, two years since it began its operations, the company published on its website the names of about 66,000 property owners, of whom approximately 55,000 were shareholders at JCT, 2,300 were real estate property owners whose property was held by the JNF, and the remainder had bank deposits.[147]

C. The Commission for Location and Restitution of Holocaust Victims' Assets that Are in Israel[148]

At the beginning of 2000, a proposal was submitted by then-Knesset member Colette Avital to set up a parliamentary commission of inquiry for location and restitution of Holocaust Victims' Assets that are in Israel. On 15 February 2000, the Knesset unanimously approved the establishment of the commission. MK Colette Avital headed the commission. As consultants for the commission, attorney Zvi Barak, who gained experience in the agency's struggle against the Swiss banks, and Prof. Yossi Katz, mentioned above, were appointed. The commission acted within the framework of two Knesset assemblies: the 15th and the 16th; there-

---

147 Katz, *supra* note 20, at 157–164.
148 A Report of the Commission of Inquiry on the Subject of Checking Holocaust Victims' Assets in Banks in Israel 7–15 (2000).

fore, the assemblies changed in composition over time. In early 2005, the commissions were disassembled by then Speaker of the Knesset Reuven Rivlin as part of his policy to cancel commissions of inquiry and merge them into the permanent commissions of the Knesset. The commission was active for four years.

The commission heard testimonies from many people, including the Administrator General, the heads of the JNF, the heads of the banks, the Supervisor of Banks, the Minister of Justice, the Accountant General, the heads of the Israel Lands Authority, and more. During its work the commission published two interim reports and a summary report regarding deposits in banks located in Israel, which was published in December 2004. Publishing this report was, in fact, the final note of the commission's work.

The commission of inquiry was assisted by two advisory sub-commissions: one which focused on assets located at the Leumi, Hapoalim, Mizrahi, Mercantile Discount, and Israel Discount banks; and another which focused on assets held by real estate bodies and non-banking bodies, including the Administrator General. The work of the first sub-commission was made possible after the banks mentioned signed a special agreement which expressed their readiness to be examined by external auditors on behalf of the Knesset and to fund the cost of this examination. Zvi Barak headed the advisory sub-commission on banks. Among the conclusions of this sub-commission, it was determined that:[149]

"Under an order issued by the British Custodian of Enemy Property upon the outbreak of WWII, the banks handed over most of the deposits that were defined as 'enemy property' to the British Custodian, and from there, with the establishment of the State of Israel, to the Government of Israel, through the Israeli Custodian of Enemy Property and the Administrator General; the examination also found, in various documents and findings, that after WWII funds and accounts belonging to Holocaust victims or their heirs were left in the banks; the deposits were not transferred to the state in their real value at the date of transfer; deposits that were transferred to their owners by law, whether by the state or by the banks, were not returned at their full real value; after the establishment of the state the banks did not act vigorously to return the funds to their owners, and even after Holocaust survivors and/or heirs of victims contacted the banks they did not act with determination to locate the accounts; Holocaust survivors or their heirs, who acted to receive their money and were answered positively received their money at an unreal value; the Administrator General published the list of property owners (of all kinds) [in its possession] for the first time only in 1998. There was no separate category in this list for property owners who are likely to be Holocaust victims ...; the commission of inquiry established two methods for the revaluation of said funds: a maximum revaluation and a minimum revaluation. The first method is based on linking the amount of the deposit to the index from the date of the outbreak of the war (1939) + 4% interest per annum until September 2004. The second

---

149 *Id.*, at 8.

method is based on linking the amount of the deposit from 1948 + 3% interest per annum until September 2004. The first revaluation method will be used in cases where Holocaust victims and/or their heirs will prove their eligibility; the second method in cases where the owners or their heirs will not be found ...."

According to the sub-commission findings and calculations, the state's liability in accordance with the second revaluation method amounted to approximately 101 million ₪, and the banks' liability to approximately 37 million ₪. According to the first revaluation method, the state's liability amounted to approximately 587 million ₪, and the banks' liability to approximately 323 million ₪. It should be noted that the sub-commission did not at all investigate the issue of banks shares and the chances of Holocaust victims owning them. As an appendix for the sub-commission work, a list of approximately 9,000 names of bank accounts owners who could be suspected as Holocaust victims was published on the Knesset website.

The second sub-commission was formed only a year after the first sub-commission and was headed by Prof. Yossi Katz. Five bodies expressed their consent to be examined as part of the commission of inquiry, and signed an examining agreement with the Knesset: the Administrator General, the Israel Lands Authority, the Jewish National Fund, the Jewish Agency, and Keren Hayesod. Other bodies might have potential assets of Holocaust victims and made it difficult for the sub-commission and did not sign an agreement. Except for the Jewish National Fund, the other bodies that agreed to be examined—and not like what happened with the banks—found it difficult to finance the work of the sub-commission. Because of all these reasons as well as the pressure put on the Knesset speaker to prevent investigations in the areas that the sub-commission was supposed to examine, the sub-commission held only a small number of work sessions. These sessions included, among others, meetings with the Administrator General and the Jewish National fund. Finally, with the disbandment of the commission of inquiry at the beginning of 2005, this sub-commission was also disbanded.

During the commission of inquiry's discussions, the following main issues arose. First was the amount transferred to England by the government of the Land of Israel from the British Custodian of Enemy Property fund, as well as the amount that was returned to the Israeli Custodian fund in 1950. Another issue that arose was the question of the sale of assets by the custodian—whether he was permitted to do so and what was done with the proceeds. A third issue was the degree of compliance to the Trading with the Enemy Ordinance, 1939, by Jewish banks and real estate bodies in the Land of Israel. This was a key issue because the banks' representatives who appeared before the commission maintained there was full compliance (i.e., nothing was left in the hands of the banks) whereas the commission's auditors, on the basis of the research they carried out, disagreed. A fourth issue was that the commission sought to learn the history of releasing assets that were seized at the time based on command: Did the custodian (followed by the Administrator General) collect commissions before discharging the funds? What evidence did they require as a condition of release? In particular, in what value were the deposits released—in nominal values or real values? This issue was critical because it turned out that the custodian released deposits at nominal values whereas the commission had decided in principle that the state would return the deposits in real values.

Another issue the commission discussed was what to do with the property if lawful owners could not be found. The issue was raised in light of precedents in Europe and Switzerland, where it turned out that only a few property owners were found. In this matter, the commission received the opinion of Prof. Katz, on which he expanded in his book *Forgotten Property* from 2000,[150] that the remaining assets should be divided among Holocaust survivors, as well as allocating funds in favor of Holocaust commemorations.

As part of the work of the commission of inquiry, the Administrator General carried out a thorough examination of all the asset portfolios in its hands, then edited and published a separate list of asset portfolios which were probably owned by Holocaust victims. The Administrator General made such an examination in 2001. According to its findings, approximately 15% (2,500) of the asset portfolios in its hands (approximately 17,000) were owned by Holocaust victims. In addition, at the request of the commission, a small unit was opened at the Administrator General; its purpose was to locate the relatives of the victims and their heirs in order to return their property to them. The chairman of the commission also promoted an amendment in the Administrator General Law, 5738–1978, according to which the Administrator General was required to look for the properties of the Holocaust victims as well as the legal owners of the properties. Initial ideas for the establishment of a body whose purpose would be to implement the findings of the commission on the location and restitution of property belonging to Holocaust victims were also raised during the commission's discussion.

---

150 Yossi Katz *Forgotten Property: the Fate of the Property of Those Who Perished in the Holocaust in Israel* (2000).

D. A Class Action against the Swiss Banks over Hiding Assets of Holocaust Victims

From 1996 to 1997, several class actions were filed in the US District Court against three Swiss banks. Two of them were the largest banks in Switzerland: Credit Suisse and Union Bank of Switzerland (UBS). The third bank, Swiss Bank Corporation, merged with UBS later.

The suits claimed that the banks helped the Nazi authorities in receiving and laundering illegally obtained property, as well as laundering funds received as a result of slave labor. Another claim was that the banks hid accounts of Holocaust victims which were deposited before the war.[151]

The legal proceedings were conducted before Justice Edward Korman of the US District Court for the Eastern District of New York. During the years 1998–1999, the various parties reached a settlement compensation in the current value of $1.25 billion. On March 30, 1999, the compensation agreement, which was signed by 17 international Jewish organizations, was approved by Justice Korman. As part of the agreement, the organizations waived any future claim on the matter to Swiss government bodies, banks, or business.[152]

It was agreed that the amount of compensation would be divided to five categories:

The first category included forced laborers who worked for the Nazis and whose financial profits were deposited in Swiss banks; the second category included forced laborers of Swiss corporations. Refugees who were deported, expelled, or not allowed to enter Switzerland during the relevant period made up the third category. The fourth category included looted property—property that was stolen during the war and deposited by the Nazis in Switzerland. The last cateogry included assets that were deposited in accounts owned by Swiss banks, and which were not delivered to its owners after the war.

In four of these categories, all except forced laborers of the second type, the victims had to be included in one of the following groups: Jews, Romanians (Gypsies), Jehovah's Witnesses, homosexuals, or handicapped (physically or

---

151 For additional information on the theft of the property of Holocaust victims by Swiss banks, see Itamar Levin, *The Last Deposit: Swiss Banks and Holocaust Victims' Accounts* (1999).
152 For a chronological overview of the procedure, see Holocaust Victim Assets Litigation (Swiss Banks Settlement): Chronology: In re Holocaust Victim Assets Litigation: http://www.swissbankclaims.com/Chronology.aspx (accessed February 9, 2017). *Weisshaus v. Union Bank of Switz* (In re: Holocaust Victim Assets Litigation.), .No. 96–4849, 2000 U.S. Dist. LEXIS 20817 (E.D.N.Y. Nov. 22, 2000).

mentally). According to the agreement, these groups were defined as "victims or targets of Nazi persecution."

In order to determine how to distribute the compensation, Justice Korman appointed an expert (Moshe Gribetz) in March 1999 to develop a proposal for allocating and distributing the settlement funds in an honest, just, and fair way. The expert had the authority to conduct an independent investigation regarding the facts and the law. In September 2000, Gribetz filed a proposal for the distribution of the money; in November the same year, the final plan was approved by Justice Korman.[153; 154]

As of March 2013, most of the amounts had been allocated or distributed by the banks as follows: approximately $727 million in favor of deposited assets; over $205 million in favour of assets looted during the Holocaust; nearly $288 million in favor of compensation for slave labor of different kinds; over $11 million in favor of compensation for Holocaust survivors; and $10 million in favor of the victims' names project.[155]

Thus, various German bodies, as well as German, Austrian, and French banks, were sued for the theft and hiding of deposits of Jews after the Holocaust.[156]

8. The Impact of the Holocaust on Court Decisions

The Holocaust and its events were mentioned from time to time by Supreme Court judges in their rulings. Some of these are important milestones in the rul-

---

153 Swiss Bank Sattlement, Claims Conference (Mars. 26, 2014) http://www.claimscon.org/about/history/closed-programs/swiss-banks-settlement (accessed February 9, 2017).

154 Edward R. Korman *Rewriting the Holocaust History of the Swiss Banks: A Growing Scandal,* in Holocaust Restitution: Perspectives on the Litigation and its Legacy 115 (Michal J. Bazyler and Roger P. Alford editors NYC Press, 2006).

155 Holocaust Victim Assets Litigation CV 96–4849—Swiss banks settlements fund distribution statistics as of March 31, 2013, available at http://www.swissbankclaims.com/Documents/2013/Distribution%20Statistics%20as%20of%20March%2031%202013.pdf (accessed February 9, 2017).

156 See Micahel J. Bazyler, *Holocaust Justice: The Battle for Restitution in America's Courts* (2003). See also Bazyler's work which claims that this method of compensation for injustices and conflicts between groups was studied and copied from compensation for Holocaust victims and in other conflicts around the world; Michael J. Bazyler, *The Post-Holocaust Restitution Era: Holocaust Restitution as a Model for Addressing Other Historical Injustices,* Working Paper No. 2–03 Bar Ilan University—Faculty of Law (2003), available at: http://www.biu.ac.il/law/unger/working_papers/2-03.pdf (accessed February 9, 2017).

ing of the Israeli Supreme Court. It seems that, in general, the Supreme Court has been affected by the Holocaust in two ways. First is understanding to the importance of the State of Israel and ensuring its existence. The second lesson is the importance of the protection of human dignity and the equality between human beings, whatever their religion, race, or nationality.

In the *Jeris* case, a citizen who was a founding member of an association called Al-Ard petitioned the High Court of Justice. In the associations' regulations, there were, among other things, sections that arose suspicions that the movement was not peaceful toward the Jewish state. For example, there was a section defining the Palestinian problem as an "indivisible unit," the Palestinian people's aspiration for liberation and unification with the Arab nation, and resistance to imperialism. Based on its regulations, the association was disqualified by the authorities. The petitioner asked to revoke the disqualification. The HCJ rejected the appeal unanimously. In the decision, Justice Witkon (who also sat in the appeal panel in Eichmann's Trial) referred to the limits of the freedom of speech and of democracy in this context. He mentioned the rise of the Nazi regime under the approval of democracy as proof that democracy and its values have limits—when they are used to undermine the democratic regime itself:[157]

> "No free regime would accept nor recognize a movement which acts to destroy the very same regime... Not once during the history of sound democratic regimes did various fascist and totalitarian movements rise against them using democratic rights such as freedom of speech, free journalism and free association, in order to lead their destructive activity by democratic consent. Those who witnessed what has happened to the Weimar republic would never forget the lesson". [158]

A similar principle also rose in the Yardor decision,[159] a principle which was named: "defensive democracy." The Yardor decision is, in fact, a continuation of the Jeris decision. Not long after Al-Ard was disqualified, a new Knesset list called the Socialist List was created. The list was based on members of Al-Ard. The Central Elections Committee for the sixth Knesset refused to approve the list for the reason that it was directed against the existence of the state. The main legal problem which arose was that, at the time, there was no explicit legal basis for the committee to disqualify a list that complied with the law.

---

157 H.C.J 253/64 *Jeris v. The Haifa District Supervisor* 18(4) P.D. 679, 683 (1964).
158 Judge Alfred Witkon, H.C.J 253/64 *Jeris v. The Haifa District Supervisor* 18(4) P.D. 679, 683 (1964), see p. 679.
159 E.A 1/65 *Yardor v. Central Elections Committee*, 19(3) P.D. 365 (1965).

Justice Haim Cohn, in a minority opinion, reasoned that since there was no legal authority for disqualifying a list by the committee, the decision should be disqualified and the list should be approved.

In the majority opinion, Justice Zussman and Justice Agranat (who also sat in the appeal panel in Eichmann's Trial) thought that the list should be disqualified although there was no explicit provision authorizing it. President Agranat declared not only that Israel is a sovereign independent state which seeks peace and is characterized by a goverment of the people, but that it is also "the Jewish State in the Land of Israel":

> "The acts of its foundation were firstly authorized by 'the natural and historical right of the Jewish people to live as any other nation, independent and in a sovereign state, and that act fulfilled the inspiration over generations for Israel salvation.'[160]
>
> "It is redundant to mention at this point that the comments mentioned above express the people's vision and credo; the meaning of this credo is that the continuity of the State of Israel is a basic constitutional fact[161] which cannot be denied by any authority of the state when it exercises an authority. If this is not said, it would be shear contempt of the two wars Israel had fought since its foundation, and an absolute contradiction of the history of the Jewish people and its longing, including the contradiction of the fact that the Holocaust that occurred to the Jewish people before the establishment of the State, during which millions of Jews were massacred in Europe, and which proved again—as the Declaration of Independence put it—'the need for a solution to the Jewish people without homeland and independence, by reviving the Jewish State in the Land of Israel.'"[162]

Justice Zussman also mentions the Holocaust and the rise of the Nazi regime in Germany in order to justify the existence of unwritten norms whose status is higher than that of a constitution, while mentioning Witkon's words above:

> "In his decision [...] my esteemed colleague, Justice Witkon, mentioned the need to learn from the Weimar Republic. Perhaps it is no coincidence that the Supreme Court of the German Federal Republic, which was established after WWII, is, as far as I know, the first court which established the principle that a judge must also rule according to unwritten laws, and that they not only stand above a normal law, but also above the constitution."

In *The Public Committee Against Torture in Israel v. the Government of Israel* decision, Justice Aharon Barak spoke about physical means during investigations of security forces:

---

160 Justice President Shimon Agranat, Adolf Eichmann, *supra* note 40.
161 *Id.*, p. 385–386.
162 *Id.*, p. 389.

"We began our ruling by describing the difficult military situation of Israel, and we will end it with this tough situation. We are aware that our judgement does not easily deal with this situation. This is the lot of democracy, that not all means are legal and appropriate and it cannot take measures such as those used by its enemy. Democracies fight with one of their hands bound. Nevertheless, democracy has the upper hand, because protecting the authority of law and recognizing the rights of individuals are part of its security strategy. At the end of the day they strengthen democracy and enable it to overcome hardships. However, it is possible to have an opinion that the military hardships are too many, and that there should be an authority that endorses physical means during investigations. If this is decided upon, naturally the court does not express any opinion at this stage. "The decision of whether or not it is appropriate for Israel, with its unique security problems, to use physical means during investigation, and the extent of such use which exceeds any rule of regular investigatory means. This decision is up to the legislating authority which represents the people, and various considerations should be made there.

"The discussion on the topic should be serious, and the proper legislation could be obtained here, with the restriction that laws which violate individual rights would match the values of the State of Israel, and it would be exercised only for a proper cause, and would not exceed what is necessary according to circumstances. (Section 8 of Basic Law: Human Dignity and Liberty.)

"The decision on these appeals is very difficult for us. Indeed, from a legal standpoint the matter is clear. However, as we are part of the Israeli society we are aware of the hardships, and we experience life here. We do not live in an ivory tower and we are part of life in this country. We are aware of the terror attacks that take place at times. We are concerned by the fact that our judgement might jeopardize appropriate dealings with terrorists. However, we serve as judges. We require that others abide the law, and we require also from ourselves to behave accordingly. When we judge a trial we also stand on trial. We must judge to the best of our conscience."[163]

In the *Bet Surik v. The IDF commander in Gaza* decision, Barak spoke about the alignment of the Israeli West Bank barrier:

"Our task is difficult. We are part of the Israeli society. Although we sometimes live in an ivory tower, this tower is located in Jerusalem which was hit many times by ruthless terror. We are aware of the killing and destruction which the terror inflicts upon the state and its citizens. As any other Israeli citizen, we acknowledge the need of the state to protect its citizens from terror attacks. We are aware that our judgement does not ease the battle of the state against its enemies in the short term. This knowledge torments us. However, we serve as judges, and when we judge trials we are on trial as well. We act to the best of our conscience. As for the battle of the state against terror, we are convinced that in the long run abiding by the law strengthen its spirits. There is no security without justice. Abiding by the law is an important constituent of national security. I made this comment in a previous case ... the same applies in this case. A separation wall which is built only accord-

---

163 Justice Aharon Barak, H.C.J 769/02 *The Public Committee Against Torture in Israel vs. The Government of Israel.*

ing to legal principles could give security to the state and to its citizens. Alignment which is based only on justice could lead the state to the desired security."[164]

In the *Berger* case, Justice Berenson stressed the obligation of the court to ensure equality on the basis of the experience and suffering of the Jewish people in the Diaspora:[165]

> "We were exiled from our homeland and we became victims of prosecutions and discrimination from our host nations, and in every generation we tasted the bitter taste of persecution, malicious suits and discrimination just because we are Jews and our religion is 'different from other people.' This bitter experience penetrated deep into our human and national conscience, and, therefore, it is expected that we do not exercise the improper behavior of the gentiles, and since our renewed independence we should be aware of any act of discrimination and improper conduct towards non-Jewish, law abiding citizens who live among us according to their religion and faith. Xenophobia is a double curse: it spoils the image of God of the hater and it is disastrous to the hated who did not commit any wrong. We have to exhibit human and tolerant attitude towards all human beings and live by the rule that all human beings are equal with regard to their rights and duties".[166]

President Barak quotes Berger in the *Kaadan* case[167], which dealt with the issue of establishing a settlement for only military veterans. In this case, it was held that this practice is discriminatory on the basis of religion and nationality, and violates the state's duty to provide equal treatment, in light of the above.[168]

In a speech he gave at the 34th Zionist Congress in Jerusalem on June 18, 2002, President Aharon Barak described the impact of the Holocaust (which he experienced firsthand as a child) on his perception of both the importance of the State of Israel and of Zionism on the one hand, and of equality and human dignity on the other hand:

> "The declaration of Independence called for 'the Arab citizens of the State of Israel to preserve the peace and take part in building the country on the basis of full and equal citizenship.' Zionism is not based on discrimination toward non-Jews but on the integration of Jews in the national Jewish homeland. Zionism was established as a response to discrim-

---

164 Justice Aharon Barak, H.C.J 2056/04 *Bet Surik v. The IDF Commander in Gaza*, 58(5) P.D. 807 (2004) (Hebrew).
165 H.C.J 392/72 *Berger v. The Haifa District Land Planning Committee* 27(2) P.D 764, 771 (1973).
166 Justice Aharon Barak, H.C.J 6698/95 *Kaadan v. Katzir*, 54(1) P.D. 258.
167 *Id.*, at 275; for discussion and criticism on their decision and its conclusions, see Shimon Shetreet "The Kaadan H.C.J Was Not Related to Reality," *Land* 56, 27 (2003): Ruth Gavison "Zionism in Israel? Following H.C.J Kaadan," Mishpat Umimshal (Hebrew) 6 25 (5761).
168 Yoav Yitzhak Israel's Values as a Jewish and Democratic State *News1*, 18/6/2002 http://www.news1.co.il/archive/003-d-1202-00.html?tag=21-53-48 (accessed February 9, 2017).

ination and persecution. It is obvious that the values of the State of Israel as a democratic state oppose any form of discrimination and require equality. The Declaration of Independence says that 'the State of Israel...would maintain social and political equal rights to all its citizens regardless of religion, race or gender.' Indeed, a democratic country must respect the basic right of all individuals in the country for equality, and to protect it. Equality is the basis of social existence, and is the cornerstone of the democratic regime. It is vital to the social agreement which is the basis of the social structure.

"Accordingly, our ruling that the assignment of state lands to Arabs and Jews should be performed on the basis of equality and is not anti-Zionist, nor post-Zionist. It is a Zionist ruling; it is the fulfillment of Zionism, which desires to see Israel as the Jewish homeland, in which all the citizens are equal. Indeed, only a homeland which is based on equality could exist for a long time; only a state which treats all its citizens equally could be in the company of the freedom seeking nations; only a society which is based on foundations of equality could live in peace with itself.

"Therefore, I stand before you today to tell you my words and to present my opinions. Let me conclude my words with a personal note. I was born in 1936 in Kovna, Lithuania. My grandfather—Avraham Meirovitch—served as a rabbi in one of the towns there. My father— Zvi (Hershel) Brick—was the director of the Israeli Agency Office in Lithuania. My father remained in his office in Kovna even when the Nazis came. That was what his commitment to the Zionist vision required him to do. My father took place in the Zionist Congress in Basel after World War II. In 1941, we were forced into the ghetto. Only a few were left out of thousands. Most of the children were murdered. Life in the ghetto were a living hell. Human life had no value; however, we preserved our identity as human beings. My life was saved thanks to a Lithuanian gentile, who later was declared as a Righteous among the Nations. What lesson did I learn from all of this? My lesson is twofold: first, the central role of the State of Israel and its Jewish character in the Jewish life, the importance of the Zionist state and the need to secure its future, its security and its Jewish character. I fully consider myself as a Zionist. Second, the central importance of human beings, the respect of whom was trampled by the Nazis and their collaborators, but who managed to survive under the worst conditions. I consider the State of Israel as the Jewish homeland which must be strong and secure. Jewish immigration to Israel should be encouraged, and Zionism should be strengthened. Nevertheless, the state should protect the dignity and freedom of all its inhabitants, whether they are Jewish or not. With that feeling I enter the court every day, because I know that when I am judging, I myself am on trial."[169]

In one of his last decisions, President Barak disqualified a section of the law which ruled that Palestinians will not be able to claim compensation from Israel.[170] Two weeks later, in a conference at Bar-Ilan University, he described the impact of the Holocaust and its lesson on his perception of human dignity and the rights of minorities:

---

169 Justice Aharon Barak, The 34th Zionist Congress, Jerusalem (18.06.2002).
170 H.C.J 826/05 *Adalah—The Legal Centre for Arab Minority Rights in Israel v. Minister of Defense* (published on Nevo, on 12.12.2006) (Hebrew).

"I have a story and it is not a post Zionist story. My story is a Zionist story and a story of human dignity and human rights. I have learned a double lesson: one, Zionism—the existence of the State of Israel. If we had a state then, the Holocaust would not have happened. Therefore, this state is very dear and important to me. The security of this state is important to me as much as it is important to the most right winged people in the State of Israel. The existence of this state is a key factor for the existence of the Jewish people. Therefore, I am not a post-Zionist. However, I have learned another lesson: the Germans tried to grind us into human dust. The right of every human being and the right of every minority are my top priorities. The dignity of every man who was created under God is very dear to me.

"The law is part of our national security. This is not post-Zionism. These two foundations—state security on the one hand and human rights on the other—do not conflict, as far as I am concerned. They agree with each other. It is possible to maintain security and to ensure human rights; beyond that, securing human rights is part of the security. A state that does not uphold human rights puts its security in jeopardy, and a state that protects human rights enhances its security. This is real Zionism. We came here to live in decency and integrity and in peace with our neighbors and with our other brothers, but first and foremost with ourselves, and as long as we do not act that way—in equality, decency and integrity while taking risks—we will not have peace within ourselves."[171]

9. Concluding Remarks

The Holocaust and subsequent events have left their mark on Israeli society. This chapter analyzed the legal aspects of the Holocaust that are important components in the consciousness of Israeli society: grappling with the memory of the Holocaust, the Reparations Agreement between Israel and Germany, the Kastner trial, the Eichmann trial, the Demjanjuk trial, and the failure to bomb Auschwitz. The chapter also discussed the impact of the Holocaust on decisions of Israel's Supreme Court.

The chapter addressed the important issue of the rights of survivors and their treatment, and the return of victims' property in the hands of various institutions in the State of Israel, and the compromise reached with Swiss banks for the return of hidden assets belonging to Holocaust victims. As we finalize the last touches of this book further developments take place on holocaust survivors and victim assets.In November 2016 the Company for the Restitution of Holocaust Victims'Assets reached another important achievement. It reached a settlement on its lega suit against the *Ozar Hityashvut Hayehudim* -Jewish Colonial Trust (JCT), for the sale of the company's holdings of JCT's shares according to

---

171 Abraham Zeno "Aharon Barak: I am Not Post-Zionist; Defence Is Important to Me," Law and Criminal Proceedings-ynet, 29.12.06 http://www.ynet.co.il/articles/0,7340,L-3345936,00.html (Hebrew, accessed February 9, 2017).

their real value as of the Leumi bank shares.[172] According to the settlement, the shareholders of the JCT received 12.5% extra value over the value of the JCT shares, resulting from the difference in value between the JCT shares and the Leumi bank shares, which amounted to 20%. Additionally, the Company for the Restitution of Holocaust Victims' Assets received contribution of 9.5 million shekels in addition to the value according to the percentage in the JCT shares.[173]

The law originally provided that the company would operate for fifteen years, dismantling in 2021. This period was changed, setting the date to the 31st of December 2017, unless the company decides to terminate its operation at an earlier date.[174]

---

172 Michael Rochwerger "The fate of Leumi shares worth more than a billion shekels would be decided today" *The Marker* (20.08.2016).
173 CM (TA) 19308 – 05 – 15 *The Company for the Restitution of Assets of Holocaust Victims v. the Jewish Colonial Trust* (28.11.2016).
174 Sec. 60 to the *Assets of Holocaust Victims Law (Restitution to Heirs and Dedication to Aid and Commemoration), 5766 – 2006*; Book of Laws 2449 (2014), 467; Diana Bechor Nir, "Turning a Holocaust Survivor to a Millionaire" *Calcalist* (25.01.2017).

Part IX: **Israeli Private and Commercial Law**

Chapter 16:
Commercial and Business Law

In this chapter, we will begin with a brief analysis of the Israeli legal system, which is a mixed jurisdiction combining two legal traditions: civil law and common law. In the following three chapters, we will briefly review the private and business law in Israel. The review includes corporate law, labor law, and economic law in Israel. In addition, the review includes contract law, property law, and torts law. Finally, we will analyze environmental law and laws regarding dispute resolution.

1. Mixed Jurisdiction

The Israeli legal system is influenced by a number of legal traditions. Historically, Ottoman legal codes were a major part of the overall legal system. Through the progress of time, much of the Ottoman legislation was repealed or replaced, but remnants of that are still present in Israeli law. Today, Israeli law is influenced by both civil and common law traditions. Therefore, Israel is among the states that are classified as a mixed jurisdiction.

Common law influence manifests itself largely in the court system. From the British occupation in Eretz-Israel in 1917 until the declaration of independence of the state of Israel in 1948, and even afterwards—until 1980, when Article 46 of the Privy Council was abolished—there was a warm and brave connection between the common law and Israeli law. Therefore, many institutions that characterize the Israeli legal system are the result of common law, among them: law of admissability (evidence law), trust, the adversarial system of criminal law[1] and estoppel (a legal doctrine whereaby a person is prevented from making assertions that are contradictory to his or her prior position on certain matters before the court).

In addition, judicial decisions are considered a source of law and form Israeli common law. Therefore, precedent, judicial procedure, and court's decision making are very important to Israeli courts (legal system). The Supreme Court gives great importance to its previous decisions, but is not bound by its own precedent. Supreme Court decisions are legally binding on lower courts. Ameri-

---

1 Aharon Barak, "The Israeli Legal System: Culture and Tradition" in *Selected Writings*, p. 41 (1999) (Hebrew).

DOI 10.1515/9783899497946-017

can common law traditions and the wisdom of American judges have heavily influenced the emerging Israeli Constitutional jurisprudence.[2]

The civil law tradition is largely reflected in the codification of public and private laws. Civil law manifests itself through the major role that academics play in shaping the law and through private law principles, such as good faith (both in negotiation and in the execution of any charge), a contract in favor of a third party, and the principle of codification itself.[3]

In addition to the common law and civil law traditions, Israel has had almost seven decades to develop its own additions to the inherited legal systems. All of these influences have created a mixed jurisdiction system which strongly resembles the common law, but with obvious civil law influences.[4]

2. Corporate Law

Corporate law in Israel is part of civil and private law; it deals with the legal status of the different corporations including the rights and duties of the corporation, the officers, the corporation itself, and the shareholders. Unlike other branches of civil law—such as contract or property law, which regulate the relations between the person and his fellow man[5]—the aim of corporate law is to regulate the various organs of the corporation, such as general meetings, the chief executive officer, and the board of directors. The purpose of the regulation is to achieve the common goal and to allow the corporation to act properly. Corporate laws apply throughout the entire course of the life of the corporation, from its establishment, to its current conduct, and until its liquidation.

---

2 Gad Tedeschi, "The Law's Shortcomings" in *Legal Research in Our Country* (2nd Edition, 1959) (Hebrew).
3 Aharon Barak, "The Israeli Legal System: Culture and Tradition," (1992) Hapraklit 40 (Hebrew).
4 *Id.*
5 For further information about Property Law and Contract Law in Israel, see Chapter 17 in this book ("Private Law"); for general analysis of Israeli business law, see Alon Kaplan and Paul ogden, editors, *Israeli Business Law: An Essential Guide* (1999 Kluwer) (hereinafter: *Israeli Business Law: An Essential Guide*).

A. The Corporation

The corporation is a separate legal entity—a somewhat fictitious legal entity eligible for actions, obligations, and rights. The corporation contains a number of individuals incorporated together for a common goal, depending on the category of the corporation.

There are several forms of incorporation recognized by law. A limited company, which is the most widespread corporation, is a form of incorporation which serves business people; its aim is to accumulate gains and divide them between shareholders. On the contrary, a cooperative society (company/organsation) is a form of cooperation based on solidarity and joint activity. It reflects a way of business conduct which is based on cooperative business activity and social commitment of its members. A registered society (company) is a form of incorporation which is not for pecuniary gain; instead, it is categorized by ideological activity, both social and cultural.

Roughly speaking, one may divide corporations into groups according to their characteristics. Some corporations forbid the distributions of dividends or gains to their members, as stemmed from the Associations Act of 1980. [6]Contrary to this, the Companies Act of 2000 regulates the distribution of dividends by corporations. [7]Some characteristics exist in all corporations: they are all separate legal entities, and they are all managed by organs such as general meetings, boards of directors, CEOs, and they are all subject to the duties imposed on the officers of the corporation.[8]

B. The Agent Issue

An additional characteristic which exists in all corporations is the issue of the agent, which is addressed by the companies act. Three characteristics are noted: the relations between shareholders and creditors, the relations between creditors and the management, and the relations between the majority shareholders and the minority shareholders.

Tension naturally exists between the shareholders and the creditors of the company. The shareholders want to distribute the dividends, which mean that

---

6 Association Act, 5740–1980; for general analysis of corporations, see Braude Bavly, "Business Entities" in *Israeli Business Law: An Essential Guide, supra* note 5, at 39–46.

7 Companies Act, 5759–1999.

8 Hadara Bar-Mor, *Corporate Law*, Volume B, p. 5 (2007) (Hebrew); for further information on the corporation, see *The Economic Approach to Law*, Ch. 14 (Uriel Procaccia ed., 2012) (Hebrew).

money is taken out of the company for their benefit. On the other hand, creditors want to leave the gains in the company so that they can get paid for the debt on fixed dates. The corporation act in Israel regulates the rules regarding dividend distribution in a very clear matter. The company's board of directors is the body in charge of making decision of dividend distribution, subject to criteria provided by law.

There is also a tension between the shareholders and the management of the company. The shareholders would like to take dividends from the company, whereas the management would wish to reinvest the gains in business development of the company. In addition, the company managerial officers runs the affairs of the company according to its expertise. The shareholders would like to pay less to the managers of the company to allow them to distribute dividends, whereas the interest of the management is to have as high salary as they can.

In addition, there is a tention between the majority and minority shareholders. As an example, this tension can emerge when the company sells assets to or buys assets from the controlling shareholder. In such a case, the minority shareholders are concerned about the validity of the consideration regarding the transaction. Therefore, the Corporations Act provides for special duties imposed on the controlling shareholder, such as reporting, good faith, fairness, and preventing the deprivation of rights from minority shareholders.[9]

C. The Enactment of the Companies Act of 2000

Until 1999, the central enactment dealing with corporate law was the Companies Ordinance, which was based on an English act from 1929. The act was enforced during the mandatory British rule in Eretz-Israel.[10] The Companies Ordinance was replaced by the Companies Act of 2000, although part of the Companies Ordinance provisions are still enforced, such as the provision dealing with liquidation of companies. Therefore, the ordinance continues to apply parallel to the Companies Act of 2000.[11]

---

9 For further information on the subject, see Irit Haviv-Segal, *Corporate Law*, Volume A, Ch. 7 (2007) (Hebrew).

10 Companies Ordinance (New Version), 5743–1983.

11 Irit Haviv-Segal, *supra* note 9, p. 1–3; for further information on the background of the Companies Act enactment, see Josef Gross, "The New Companies Act," Ch. 1 (4th ed, 2007) (Hebrew).

With the enactment of the Companies Act on 1.2.2000, a significant change occurred both in Israeli corporate law and in the business environment in which Israeli companies operate. The various changes included four key aspects:[12]

First was the proliferation of judgments and judicial decisions which were issued following the enactment of the Companies Act;

Second was the enactment of Amendment No. 3 to the Companies Law. This amendment brought enormous changes in the field of indemnification of directors and officers, in the area of special professional competence requirements for external directors, often reffeerd as outside director, and in the field of applicability of Israeli law to foreign companies;

Third was the Goshen Committee report regarding "Corporate Governance," which imports significant parts of US regulations enacted following to the Enron affair. The regulations deals with understanding the essence of the corporation for society and the intervention of the law in the internal activities of the corporation;[13]

Fourth was the enactment of the Class Action Act in 2006,[14] which governs the different types of class actions; claims under cooperate law are only a part of them.

Alongside changes in the law, the Israeli business environment experienced an unprecedented transformation which significantly affected Israeli companies. Among the changes were privatization processes;[15] transformation in the field of pension funds and mutual funds; fundamental change in the Kibbutz and the Cooperative Societies; various changes in the designation of agricultural land; the process of globalization and its impact on the israeli economy; the economic crises of early years of the new millennium; and the development of private capital and hedge funds.[16]

It should be noted that after the enactment of the Companies Law of 2000, the Supreme Court of Israel has looked predominantly to US cases as models for corporate law, and less to English law. The main model in American law in this field comes from the state of Delaware, whichwas the first jurisdiction to enact company law can be seen as friendly to corporations and entrepreneurs. Moreover, Delaware has a commercial court; the identity of the judges in Delaware

---

12 Irit Haviv-Segal, *supra* note 9, at 1–3.
13 The Code Review Committee Report Corporate Governance in Israel (Hebrew) (2006), available at: http://www.isa.gov.il/Download/IsaFile_45.pdf (accessed February 9, 2017).
14 Class Action Law, 5766–2006.
15 The privatizations carried out in recent years includes the port of Eilat, Bezeq (telecommunications), El Al (aviation), and so forth.
16 *Id.*

is pluralistic, including practitioners, academics, and judges who are experienced in corporation practice. In fact, Israel has established an economic department in the district court of Tel-Aviv, based on Delaware practice features. The department is a court that specializes in corporate law which includes three judges. These judges deal with all disputes pertaining to the Companies Law as well as securities and exchange issues.

3. Labor and Employment Law

A. Statutory Frame

Israeli employees enjoy a constantly evolving level of protection through a web of labor laws and regulations created by the Israeli legislature, working together with an active labor judiciary.[17] Among the various laws and regulation that apply to both employers and employees includes the following:

Minimum Wage: The Minimum Wage Law (1987)[18] provides a minimum hourly rate, which is updated from time to time. Currently, the hourly rate is NIS 25; however, it is due to gradually rise (NIS 26.88 on January 1st 2017).[19]

Mandatory Pension Fund: The Mandatory Pension Insurance Expansion Order (2008) provides that all employees, with few exceptions, are entitled to pension insurance. The pension funds require employers to contribute, for the "remuneration" of the employee, an amount equal to 5–6% of the employee's monthly salary, up to a maximum amount determined based on the average monthly salary in Israel. These contributions will constitute the employee's pension fund at retirement, along with additional statutory contributions for severance payments (6–8.33% of the employee's salary). Israeli pension funds also include a disability insurance component, part of the aforementioned contribution, which can also be paid separately. In addition, the employer is obligated to deduct 5.5–6% from the employee's monthly salary and transfer such amount to the employee's pension fund.

Severance Payment: The Severance Payment Law (1963)[20] provides that, upon dismissal, and under certain circumstances of resignation, employees

---

17 Tal Enat-Ben Arieh, "Labor Law," in *Doing Business in Israel: Legal and Business Guide* 2015, p. 92, available at: https://www.pwc.com/il/en/home/assets/-doing-business-in-israel-2015.pdf (accessed February 9, 2017).
18 Minimum Wage Law, 5747–1987, LB 68.
19 To this date, December 2016, NIS is aproxematly 0.25$ U.S Dollars.
20 Severance Pay Law, 5723–1963, LB 136.

are entitled to receive severance payment equal to the amount of their latest monthly salary multiplied by the number of years of continuous employment (with the same employer or at the same place of employment).

Each month, employers may set aside 8.33 % of the employee's salary to ensure compliance with the law. Since the severance payment is calculated based on the employee's latest monthly salary, shortfalls could occur. In order to avoid this scenario, the law allows the parties to agree that employees shall only be entitled to receive, upon termination of their employment, all severance payment amounts actually set aside during the course of their employment. This arrangement also provides that employees will be entitled to severance pay upon resignation, as opposed to dismissal, something they would not otherwise be entitled to.[21]

Termination—Prior Notice: The Notice for Dismissal and Resignation Law (2001)[22] provides that employees who have been employed by the same employer for more than one year are entitled to receive, at minimum, a 30-day prior notice. Employees who are employed on an hourly basis or have been employed for less than a year are entitled to a shorter prior notice period. Further more, same obligation for prior notice is placed on the employees' shoulders. Lack of notice from their side will couse a fee of up to a month salary.

Work Week and Overtime: The Hours of Work and Rest Law (1951)[23] sets forth a 5 – 6 day working week consisting of 43 hours (8 or 9 hours of work per day). In addition, the law limits the maximum number of overtime hours an employee is premitted to perform and regulates the payment for such working hours. Generally, each of the first two hours of overtime is paid on a 125 % basis, and any additional hour is paid on a 150 % basis. The law provides for several exceptions, including for employees holding management positions that require a special measure of "personal trust," who are not entitled to special remuneration for overtime.

Weekly Rest Day: The Hours of Work and Rest Law (1951)[24] provides that the weekly rest day for a Jewish employee is Saturday and, for employees who are not Jewish, a day that is acceptable to their religion. Generally, employment of Israeli employees on a Saturday is subject to receipt of regulatory permits from the Ministry of Economy.

---

21 Tal Enat-Ben Arieh, *supra* note 17, at 92–93.
22 Early Notice of Dismissal and Resignation Law, 5761–2001, LB378.
23 Work Hours and Rest Law, 5711–1951, LB 204.
24 *Id.*

Vacation Leave: The Annual Vacation Law (1951)[25] sets forth the minimal number of annual vacation days to which employees are entitled. Furthermore, the laws establish certain legal holidays during which the employees are entitled to a day off, in addition to their annual vacation days.

Sick Leave: The Sick Leave Payment Law (1976)[26] provides employees the entitlement of one and a half days of paid sick leave per each full month of employment, up to a maximum of 90 days. Sick days may be accumulated and carried over, but not redeemed. Employees are entitled to sick leave payment, as of the second day of absence, in an amount equal to 50% of their daily salary and, as of the fourth day of absence, for full pay.

In addition, there are several laws aimed at protecting the employee's nonfinancial rights:

Employment Agreement: The Law of Notice to an Employee (Terms of Employment) (2002)[27] provides that, within 30 days from beginning of employment, the employer is required to provide each new employee with a written notice outlining certain terms of the employment.[28]

Non-Discrimination: The Law of Equal Opportunities at Workplaces (1988)[29] prohibits a differential treatment of employees based on gender, race, sexual orientation, religion, etc. (with exceptions of specific nature or characteristics required for thejob or position). Furthermore, the mandatory retirement age for both female and male employees in Israel is 67. Moreover, in recent years, labor courts have held that the mere fact of reaching mandatory retirement age by an employee does not necessarily constitute a reason to terminate employment.

Female Employees: The Employment of Women Law (1954)[30] prohibits the termination of an employee (women or men who are willing to take on the role of primary child caregivers) undergoing fertility treatments or who is pregnant (the only exception is if the employer obtained the approval of the Commissioner of Women Employment in the Ministry of Economy). In the same matter, the law prohibits termination of the term of employment of employees on maternity leave until 60 days after their maternity leave ends.

---

25 Annual Vacation Law, 5711–1951, LB 234.
26 Sick Pay Law, 5736–1976, LB 206.
27 Notice to Employee and Candidate (working conditions and procedures for screening and hiring), 5762–2002, LB 210.
28 Tal Enat-Ben Arieh, *supra* note 17, at 94.
29 Equal Opportunity at Work Law, 5748–1988, LB 38.
30 Women's Work Law, 5714–1954, LB 154.

Disabled Employees: A recent expansion order, obligates employers with over 100 employees to integrate people with disabilities (whether physical or mental) in their organization.

B. Key Non-Statutory Elements

Collective Agreements and Arrangements: this area of the organiazed labor law, typically address issues such as wages, social rights, working hours, payment for overtime and dismissal-related matters. Employers are subject to all agreements and arrangements to which their organization is a party on.[31]

Expansion Orders: These orders expand the provisions and arrangements of collective agreements so that their provisions shall apply to employers and employees that were not initially represented by a party thereto. The orders are administrative orders issued by the Minister of Economy, and some of them apply to all Israeli employers and employees.

Hearing Proceedings for Termination of Employment: This is a prerequisite for termination porecedure of employment of any employee, regardless of their position or seniority. The employer must present a written hearing notice, which contains valid reasons for termination of the employment, and give the employee a reasonable response time. At the hearing, the employer must give the employee the opportunity to reply to the issues mentioned in the hearing notice. Failure to hold any of these demands might lead to a wrongful termination suit against the employer.[32]

C. Recent Trends

Unionization Attempts: The Israeli labor courts have upheld a number of initial attempts by employees to organize collective employment relationships at their respective companies by joining labor unions, several of which are in the advanced technology industry. In light of these precedents, the applicable rules in this area are evolving at a rapid pace.

Security, Catering, and Cleaning Service Providers: The Israeli legislature has imposed increasing obligation on contractors engaging workers in these certain sectors to ensure that these workers are being compensated in accordance with

---

31 Tal Enat-Ben Arieh, *supra* note 17, at 93.
32 *Id.,* at 94.

applicable laws. Moreover, administrative, civil, and criminal liability was put on any contrators or companies benefiting from such services, and who fail to meet their statutory oversight obligations.

4. Economic Law

A. Custom System and Law

a. Import Policy

The Department for Import Policy, located in the Foreign Trade Administration in the Ministry of Economy, is responsible for the Israeli Government policy relating to imports of goods into the country. One of the department's main objectives is to enhance transparency of government activities in all aspects connected with the import process.[33]

In addition, the department deals with the following issues: examining foreign countries' import policies towards Israel in the framework of the World Trade Organization (WTO) agreements;[34] enhancing quality and efficiency of service to businesses dealing with international trade. in order to do so, the department carries out reforms in the import process and increasing its transparency; and gradually exposing the Israeli market to foreign imports while enabling Israel's local industries to adjust and protecting the Israeli public.[35]

Since the 1990s, the Government has actively implemented a liberalization process in international trade in order to expose domestic industry to foreign competition and to simplify the import process for all. The liberalization program has been duly implemented over the years: import restrictions and non-tariff barriers have been eliminated and most-favored-nation (MFN) tariff rates for manufactured products have been reduced drastically to rates of 12% or lower. The policy fully complies with Israel's commitments taken in the framework of the WTO.[36]

---

33 Ministry of Economy—Foreign Trade Administration, available at: http://www.moital.gov.il/ NR/exeres/ADE1812D-CF28-4109-A90A-0E11E88F0D32.htm (accessed February 9, 2017).

34 Ministry of Industry, Trade and Labour—Foreign Trade Administration—Import Policy, available at: http://www.moital.gov.il/NR/exeres/1B363981-F3D1-4374-8923-533E56DEC171.htm (accessed February 9, 2017); For more information about the WTO, see: https://www.wto.org/ (accessed February 9, 2017).

35 *Id.*

36 *Id.*

Over the years, Israel continues to actively implement policies directed at creating an efficient and outward looking economy. Including among others: trade and foreign exchange liberalization, as mentioned above; reduction of state subsidies; and the budget deficit, deregulation, and privatization.[37]

In addition, while enhancing the process of trade liberalization at the multilateral level, Israeli trade policy is aimed at continuing the expansion of its network of bilateral trade agreements. After completing free trade agreements with its two major trading partners, the European Union and the United States during the 1980s and with the EFTA countries (Iceland, Norway, Liechtenstein and Switzerland) in 1992, Israel has extended its free trade agreements to Canada, Turkey, Mexico, Romania, and Bulgaria.

b. Export Policy

The Ministry of Economy and Industry is the body that exercises supervision over exported products, knowledge, and dual-use (civilian and military use) services. Supervision is done by using an Import and Export order (control over exported products, services, and dual-use technologies), which was issued under the Import and Export Ordinance.[38] The purposes of the order are two-fold. The one hand supervises the export of products and dual-use technologies (i.e., material and equipment inherently meant for civilian use and also for military use); the other hand maintains a free flow of products to overseas.

The Import and Export Order is based on a list from the Wassenaar Arrangement (the WA),[39] which was established in July 1996 as the first international authority to supervise the export of conventional weapons and dual-use equipment. Today, the authority has 41 member states, thus focuses as well on global objectives such as: contributing to regional and international security and stability by promoting transparency and accountability in the transfer of conventional weapons and goods and dual-use services; preventing the sale of weapons and dual-use equipment to problematic countries; preventing the transfer of weapons to terrorist organizations; and preventing the transfer of such weapons to areas of concern. It should be noted that the authority would not prevent a legitimate civilian deal or the purchase of weapons for self-defense.[40]

---

37 *Id.*
38 The Import Export Order [New Version], 5739–1979.
39 The full name being The Wassenaar Arrangement on Export Controls for Conventional Arms and Dual-Use Goods and Technologies.
40 For further details see: http://www.wassenaar.org/about-us/ (accessed February 9, 2017).

Export items are divided into several categories, depending on the classification of the Wassenaar Arrangement: dual-use equipment,[41] sensitive products, very sensitive products, and munitions. According to the Wassenaar authority, the supervision over export is implemented by every member state individually. Despite the fact that the scope of the supervision is determined by the Wassenaar lists. It should be noted that the practical implementation changes from state to state, depending on the national procedures of each state.

The export and import order requires an export licence. The decision to issue licenses is made in collaboration between the Ministries of Foreign Affairs and Defence, based on accumulated experience, and the desire to maintain balance. Among the considerations before issuing an export license are state considerations (including the relationship between Israel and the destination state, as well as the relationship with the destination states neighbors) and technical considerations (about the equipment and its operation, checking the final user, and examining the destination and the entities operating within the state).

B. Foreign Trade System and Law

a. The Multi-Lateral Channel

The multi-lateral agreement department in the Ministry of Economy leads the discussions with organizations that design the policies and laws of trade global scale—such as the WTO, which is the framework for the rules of global trade.[42] The active involvement of Israel in such processes dictates the rate of progress and inclusion of Israel in global procedures, which eventually allow Israel to improve and expand its trade options.[43]

The WTO was established in 1995 on the foundation of the GATT Agreement (General Agreement on Tariffs and Trade)[44] to serve as a platform for multi-national trade negotiations between the representatives of the member states. In essence, WTO is the most important organization in the world today in terms

---

41 For instance, advanced materials, materials processing, electronics, computers, telecommunications, sensors and lasers, navigation, marine equipment, and propulsion.

42 The rules of the organization are decided via negotiation between the member states, in the framework of the "rounds" that occur every few years and on an ongoing basis in the organization headquarters in Geneva.

43 Foreign Trade Administration—Ministry of Economy, available at: http://www.moital.gov.il/NR/exeres/F983A359-253C-4442-AA06-BC80AD1B9F0A.htm (accessed February 9, 2017).

44 In contrast to the rules of the WTO, which cover wide areas of the economy, the GATT agreement deals primarily with removing barriers from trade in products and goods.

of supervising and enhancing the liberalization of international trade. As such, it is of the greatest importance to the State of Israel with regards to foreign trade, due to the large number of countries who are members of the WTO and who are bound by its various agreements.[45]

Generally, the WTO works on three main levels: managing and maintaining the existing agreements; being a forum for innovation and for multi-national negotiation in international trade; being a dispute resolution forum between the member states.

WTO activity is founded on several fundamental ideals that are intricately woven into the different trade agreements. The first is preventing discrimination in two ways. One, a state that offers a benefit to a foreign government must make the same benefit available to all the member states that are a part of the WTO. Two, the agreement prevents discrimination between imported and homemade product. The second ideal is transparency. During negotiations, the states submit a table which depicts the various products and the maximum rate that a state may charge in customs for these products, as well as other trade limitations; the table can be viewed by the public and constitutes an international legal norm that may not be derogated from. The third ideal provides favorable treatment for developing countries—relaxation and concessions during negotiations, with regards to the period of time in which the agreements must be implemented as well as the depth of the commitment that the countries must take upon themselves towards negotiations framework.[46] The fourth ideal addresses consensus in decision making—the organization makes decisions following the acceptance of all sides; there is veto power to the "lone state," whoever they may be. The fifth ideal provides exclusion of exceptions. Similar to all legal arrangements, there are exceptions to the fundamental ideals mentioned above which are an inseparable part of the agreements.[47]

The WTO covers a wide range of economic areas, including: tax reductions and, in certain instances, tax exemptions on trade in industrial products; significant reductions in customs on food and agriculture, removing support fors export and lowering local subsidization; plans to remove customs on trade in textiles around the globe; liberalization of trade in services (communications, transportation, finances, etc.); strengthening trade and treatment in the field

---

45 As of February 2016, the organization numbers 162 states with the status of Member States and 25 states with the status of observers.

46 It should be noted, there is no official definition of the WTO regarding what constitutes a developing country.

47 Foreign Trade Administration—Ministry of Economy, available at: http://www.moital.gov.il/NR/exeres/A5E90C0B-C1F0-475C-BC35-436C87A9E0DF.htm (accessed February 9, 2017).

of intellectual property; setting rules for regional trade agreements to ensure that they comply with the multi-lateral WTO agreements; and recognition of the connection between trade and the environment.

Due to fact that Israel joined the WTO at its inception, Israel is referred to as a founding member. Due to its membership in the organization, Israel must abide by the disciplinary rules stemming from the multi-lateral agreements. These rules are mandatory for all members of the organization and are the framework foundation for all international negotiations in order to improve international trade conditions.

The WTO agreements deal with a wide variety of aspects pertaining international trade. They include agreements on trade of goods (GATT), intellectual property, agricultural products (TRIPS), sanitary and phytosanitary products (SPS), technical barriers for proper trade (TBT), levies on dumping and underwriting, subsidization agreements, dispute resolution mechanisms, and more. Among other things, the agreements encourage governments to continue to reduce customs fees and to remove trade restrictions; limit conduct regards subsidizing agriculture; prohibit granting subsidies to exporters; and require the governments to publish information on their public acquisitions while allowing foreign manufacturers to compete with local manufacturers on equal ground for tenders.

In addition to the multi-national agreements, it should be noted that Israel has chosen to partake in several plurilateral initiatives as well. As these are voluntary initiatives, not all WTO members partake in them. Among these initiatives are the Government Procurement Agreement (GPA) and the Information Technology Agreement (ITA).

Despite the fact that bilateral agreements grant Israel greater trade benefits than those received as a member of WTO, the multi-national channel is of greater importance to Israel for several reasons. Whereas the regional trade agreements deal primarily with trade benefits for goods, the WTO agreements deal with services, IP (Intellectual Property), subsidization, trade levies, and more. The effect of international trade on the GDP is high and therforegreat importance is granted to the agreements set by the organization. In concert with the goal of preventing discrimination, Israel is granted benefits on trade as a member of the WTO, even when Israel does not directly negotiate for these benefits. It is a tool, used successfully in the past, to remove trade boycotts on Israel under the demand that countries not discriminate against a founder of the organization. Membership allows Israel to integrate, keep current, and fit itself to the current international economic procedures. In recent years, Israel's representatives have been chosen to chair negotiating committees of the organization and have been chosen as panelists in international dispute resolutions.

b. The Bi-Lateral Channel

The Bi-Lateral Agreement department in the Ministry of Economy is entrusted with Israel's trade agreements as well as its commercial and economic relationship with the European Union (EU). The department works to prevent discrimination of the local market and ensure the rights and proper place of Israeli industry in the various markets. Among the multitude of the department's functions are: examining the profitability of regional free trade agreements and assisting in setting policy for maintaining existing trade agreements and updating them when necessary; initiating and managing negotiations of trade agreements in various areas (free trade zones, services, standardization, governmental appropriation, and more); taking care of trade issues such as diffefernt barriers; and taking care of trade relationships in various areas of industrial cooperation with bodies of the EU.[48]

Today, Israel has several Free Trade Areas Agreements with other countries and unions: The United States,[49] the EFTA states (Switzerland, Norway, Iceland, and Lichtenstein),[50] Canada,[51] Turkey,[52] the EU,[53] Mexico,[54] Colombia,[55] Jordan,[56] Egypt,[57] and the Mercosur states (Uruguay, Argentina, Brazil, Venezuela, and Paraguay).[58]

---

48 Foreign Trade Administration – Ministry of Economy, available at: http://economy.gov.il/English/InternationalAffairs/ForeignTradeAdministration/TradePolicyAgreements/Pages/TradeEconomicAgreements.aspx (accessed February 9, 2017).

49 http://economy.gov.il/English/InternationalAffairs/ForeignTradeAdministration/TradePolicyAgreements/BilateralAgreements/Pages/USA.aspx (accessed February 9, 2017).

50 http://economy.gov.il/English/InternationalAffairs/ForeignTradeAdministration/TradePolicyAgreements/BilateralAgreements/Pages/EFTA.aspx (accessed February 9, 2017).

51 http://economy.gov.il/English/InternationalAffairs/ForeignTradeAdministration/TradePolicyAgreements/BilateralAgreements/Pages/Canada.aspx (accessed February 9, 2017).

52 http://economy.gov.il/English/InternationalAffairs/ForeignTradeAdministration/TradePolicyAgreements/BilateralAgreements/Pages/Turkey.aspx (accessed February 9, 2017).

53 http://economy.gov.il/English/InternationalAffairs/ForeignTradeAdministration/TradePolicyAgreements/BilateralAgreements/Pages/EU.aspx (accessed February 9, 2017).

54 http://economy.gov.il/English/InternationalAffairs/ForeignTradeAdministration/TradePolicyAgreements/BilateralAgreements/Pages/Mexico.aspx (accessed February 9, 2017).

55 http://economy.gov.il/English/InternationalAffairs/ForeignTradeAdministration/TradePolicyAgreements/BilateralAgreements/Pages/Colombia.aspx (accessed February 9, 2017).

56 http://economy.gov.il/English/InternationalAffairs/ForeignTradeAdministration/TradePolicyAgreements/BilateralAgreements/Pages/Jordan.aspx (accessed February 9, 2017).

57 http://economy.gov.il/InternationalAffairs/TradePolicyAndAgreements/BilateralAgreementsDivision/Pages/Egypt.aspx (Hebrew, accessed February 9, 2017).

58 http://economy.gov.il/English/InternationalAffairs/ForeignTradeAdministration/TradePolicyAgreements/BilateralAgreements/Pages/Mercosur.aspx (accessed February 9, 2017).

c. Economic Relations with Middle Eastern Neighbors

Considering the progress of building a culture of peace in the Middle East, record of relations is not goot enough. Israel and Egypt signed a peace treaty in 1979. Jordan and Israel signed a peace treaty in 1994. Israel withdrew from the Southern Lebanon safety zone in May 2000—unfortunately, without any accord being signed. As oppose to above, Israel and Syria have not been able to arrive at any peace accord so far.

The Palestinians and the Israelis are in the midst of a conflict after signing the Oslo Accords. They will have to continue their road to peace as charted by Prime Minister Rabin in the Oslo Agreement, signed in September 1993 on the White House lawn. it was later followed up by the Cairo Agreement in May 1994, and the signing of the Interim Agreements in Washington in September of 1995. Two years later, a supplementary agreement was reached at Wye Plantation, Maryland, between Israel and Palestine during the Netanyahu's first term as prime minister. The Camp David II summit in July 2000 failed, as Arafat rejected Prime Minister Barak's proposals. Later, the Aqaba summit was held in 2004, led by President Bush and leaders of the Palestinian Authority, Egypt, Jordan, and Israel. In November 2007, President Bush hosted the Annapolis Peace Conference, aimed at invigorating the peace process between the Palestinian Authority and Israel; negotiations are taking place between the leaders of Israel and the leadership of the Palestinian Authority. Secretary Kerry, of President Obama administration, tried in 2013–2014 to promote the peace process with no success. We now have to wait and see developments during President Trump addministration.

The importance of building strong foundations of peace in the Middle East is evident. Peace should be built on four foundations: political and security peace, economic peace, cultural peace, and religious peace. Serious attempts have been made towards the creation of a culture of peace in the Middle East.

The first peace agreement with Egypt focused mainly on political and security peace. It regulated the relationship between Israel and Egypt and determined the legal status of the land and settelemet, and provided for security arrangements, and diplomatic relations.

Furthermore, the agreement included another agreement on oil trading between the two countries in the amount of $400M a year. However, the trade and economic relations remained at a very modest and disappointing level, long after the peace treaty of 1979. The two countries, Egypt and Israel, whose joint Gross National Product at the time amounted to over $200B (Israel $150B and Egypt $60B), produced annual trade of no more than $100M. The flow of tourists from Israel to Egypt was predominantly one-way; in recent years, it has declined mainly because of terrorist attacks by radical Islamic groups and the resultant insecurity. Certain professional unions and associations in Egypt remain hostile towards peace with Israel. Members of professional associations who visit Israel or have contacts with Israeli organizations expose themselves to sanctions, even expulsion, from their associations. Even though we have witnessed a very favorable development with the establishment of a peace movement in Egypt led by Ambassador Salah Bassiuni in the past, without economic peace and social support for greater peace, there is great difficulty in moving towards a culture of peace in the Middle East. The Israel Egypt peace treaty remains stable and has survived all the internal changes in Egypt which shows its viability.

The peace treaty with Jordan and other agreements with the Palestinian Authority have been formulated with a greater focus on the desire to achieve economic peace. The agreements with the Palestinian Authority created a custom union, making Israel and the Palestinian Authority areas one custom region. The Casablanca Economic Summit convened in November of 1993, two months after the Declarations of Principles of Peace between Israel and the Palestinians was signed in Washington. It was a clear indication of the recognition that the foundation of true peace must include economic cooperation and economic relations.

It is clear that peace must bring practical projects that will improve the daily life of the residents of both nations. Peace treaties are signed between governments. They are no more than bridges or roads. It is for the people to cross these bridges and to walk these roads in order to translate the provisions of the treaties into reality. Economic peace gives the opportunity for citizens to participate in the realities of peace.

The economic relations between Israel and the Palestinian Authority (PA) were agreed upon in the 1994 Paris Protocol. According the Protocol, a custom union was established between Israel and the Palestinian Authority. The agreement stipulated that the unified customs union will be managed by Israel, and that PA will use the Shekel, the Israeli currency (NIS), as its official currency.

According to the agreed conditions, Israel collects the customs taxes on the goods that are shipped in to the Palestinian areas and then transfers it to the PA. On the same matter, VAT and revenues are collected for goods and services sold in Israel and intended for consumption in the Palestinian Territories. These indirect taxes account for 70% of the Palestinian government's income. The amount is estimated at 120 million NIS per month.

The PA calculates its earned VAT against invoices collected from Palestinians trading with Israeli firms or individuals. Many traders seek to avoid adding VAT, significantly reducing the PA's revenues. The collection of invoices is especially difficult in Gaza, where Hamas has maintained control since 2006 and the PA's ability to operate is limited.

A new agreement was reached between Israel and PA in 2012. According to the new model, a greater access to Israeli data will be given to PA officials. This will increase joint oversight of trade, as well as internal Palestinian trade figures. One of the challenges that the PA is faced is the black market, which is assessed at about 30% of trade between Israel and PA.

C. Foreign Direct Investment System and Law

a. The Development of the System

International investing is one of the main instruments of states' economies.[59] In a globalized world, characterized by increased interstate movement of people, technology, and equity, this subject is identified as one of the key leverages of economic growth in general and specifically of small countries. This follows the substantial socio-economic influences of industry and trade developments —movement of technology knowledge, which occurs in four ways (transferring the knowledge to suppliers and customers of the multi-national company, transfer of the knowledge to competing companies or companies which manufacture complementary products in the same field, transfer due to the migration of competent and highly qualified employees, and finally the framework of multi-national cooperation). In order to remain competitive, countries introduce reforms to improve education and to adopt proper regulations and standards in the workforce with regards to Human Rights and preventing discrimination. These reforms make a country more attractive as a marketplace for doing business on an international level. Foreign investment in developing countries leads to adoption of international standards in various areas: worker's rights, transparency, preserving the environment, assisting struggling sectors of the population (there is a negative correlation between the incoming foreign investment stock

---

59 International Centre for Trade and Sustainable Development, "The Evolving International Investment Law and Policy Regime: Ways Forward" 11 (2016), available at: http://www3.wefo rum.org/docs/E15/WEF_Investment_Law_Policy_regime_report_2015_1401.pdf (accessed February 9, 2017).

See Alberto Aharonowitz, "The Development of the Issue of Investments in International Law and Their Protection: The Case of the Paper Plant on Uruguay River and Remarks on Oil and Gas Industry in Israel", 8 Moznei Mishpat 355 (2013) (Hebrew).

and the size of the population surviving on less than one dollar a day),[60] and the strengthening of international relationships. [61] Aside from these influences, it should be noted that within the practice of international investments lies the potential for stabilizing international relations between the states.[62]

The EU, which was developed after the Second World War due to cooperation in coal, steel, and atomic energy industries, is an excellent example for this. The contribution of an organized economic framework to eradicate conflict and hatred between countries following the war was invaluable, and today is one of the pillars of modern Europe.

b. Culture of Peace and Economic Growth

In contrast with political and economic peace, the recognition of cultural peace came into being rather late. For example, in the first years of the European community, the culture of peace in the European Union was based predominantly on economic and political foundations. The European Union countries have similar political interests. The European Union's economic foundation is embodied in the Euro currency and in the other aspects of the economic union.

Until 2000, the cultural peace in the EU was reflected in the European Convention on Human Rights. It did not derive from the EU constitutional documents.

In the EU, human rights were recognized and integrated into the constitutional documents only in the year 2000, by the adoption of the Charter of Fundamental Rights, which was amended in 2007. Later, it was embodied and recognized in the Treaty on the Functioning of the EU Institutions and the recent adoption of the Reform Treaty of Lisbon—the Constitution of the EU.

For a long time, the European Union countries shed away from addressing culturel plain. Only now, the Treaty of the European Union—which has yet to be finally ratified—is in its Preamble addressing itself to its cultural identity. One of the opening paragraphs of the Preamble reads as follows: "Drawing inspiration from the cultural, religious and humanist inheritance of Europe,

---

60 See: World Development Indicators—OECD, "Foreign Direct Investment for Development— Maximizing Benefits, Minimizing Costs," 2002.
61 See p. 54 in: http://www.mifellows.org/Research/HEB_F/74-HB-F.pdf (accessed February 9, 2017).
62 Alberto Aharonovitz, *supra* note 60, 356. For an elaboration of this analysis, see Shimon Shetreet, "The Culture of Peace and Human Rights: The Development of Human Rights Protection in the European Union," in Shimon Shetreet, *The Culture of Judicial Independence: Rule of Law and World Peace*, 99 (Brill Nijhoff 2014).

from which have developed the universal values of the inviolable and inalienable rights of the human person, freedom, democracy, equality and the rule of law". There was a controversy in the drafting in the EU Constitution in its previous draft, as well as in the later drafting of the Lisbon Treaty, whether or not to use the terminology "Christian Culture." In the end, as a compromise, they decided to adopt the terminology of "cultural, religious and humanist inheritance of Europe."

The human rights in the EU are expressly provided for in the Charter of the Fundamental Rights of the EU, passed in December 2000 and adapted again in 2007. The EU Treaty also considers the European Convention for establshing the Protection of Human Rights and Fundamental Freedoms as the result from the constitutional traditions common to the member states as "General Principles of the Union's Law" (Article 6 of the Treaty of the European Union).

The previous proposed European Constitution was rejected in the referendum by Holland and France. Later on, the Reform Treaty of Lisbon was adopted and, of the 27 member states, Ireland failed to ratify the Treaty of the European Union, again by referendum. The Union is awaiting a remedy to this failure for the completion of the ratification of the European Union's Lisbon Treaty.

These developments are to be commended. If the economic foundation is shaken, it is better that the European Union be dependent not only on political-security aspects and the economic foundations, but also on the cultural and religious foundations. It is, therefore, very important that the Union was able, after so many years, to forge the foundations of culture, religion, and human rights to enhance the EU.

There exists a number of frameworks in which a company can invest in a foreign country and create a multi-national cooperation. First, it can create a subsidiary company in the target country, either as a headquarters or a factory, which is under the sole control of the parent company. Second, it can turn a local company into a multi-national one by either acquiring the foreign-based company or merging with it. Third, in concert with a company based in the foreign country, it can use supply chains and local infrastructure, or joint ventures for developing new products, but without creating a new business entity.[63]

Building the global value chain of multi-national companies, and placing the different links around the world, is done in order to fit the relative advantages of the foreign states. From the accumulated data, we see that Israel's relative advantage lies in Research and Development (R&D), and stems from its unique

---

63 See p. 4 of http://www.mifellows.org/Research/HEB_F/74-HB-F.pdf (accessed February 9, 2017).

characteristics: government development of technology hubs in the defense systems; advanced human equity; an elaborate financing foundation for quick establishment of young and innovative companies; and a system of relationships and knowledge cooperation with the United States. In light of this, a large amount of the foreign investments are directed toward R&D in Israel.[64] Other criteria that make countries appealing to foreign investment include: proximity to large markets, raw materials and cheap labor, tax benefits, and additional incentives that the governments offer.[65]

With its establishment, Israel has been very much concerned with creating a foundation for the state's economy and the promise of economic growth. This idea can be expressed in its body of legislation: the Income Tax Ordinance,[66] the Foreign Investment Encouragement Law,[67] the Industry Encouragement Law (Taxes),[68] the Agriculture Investment Encouragement Law,[69] and the Industry Research and Development Law.[70] These laws, for years, have created a wide statutory pattern intended to encourage foreign investment in Israel.[71]

Despite the above, the majority of the foreign investment policy in Israel is based on Capital Investment Encouragement Law (here in after: the Law), which has gone through many stages over the years.[72] The Law has several main goals. The first is to develop the production capabilities of the state's economy. The second is to improve the ability of the business sector to deal with the competition on an international scale. The third is creating infrastructure for existing and future employment places.[73] The law's main goal is to draw foreign investors to Israel, new and innovative methods and technologies to create efficiency, allowing

---

64 As of August 2013, see p. 11 of http://www.mifellows.org/Research/HEB_F/74-HB-F.pdf (accessed February 9, 2017).

65 "Why Israel?" Ministry of Economy, at: http://www.investinisrael.gov.il/why_israel.html (accessed February 11, 2017); see D Senor, S Singer, *Start-Up Nation: The Story of Israel's Economic Miracle*, McClelland & Stewart (2009).

66 Income Tax Ordinance [New Version], 5721–1961, NV 120.

67 Encouragement of Capital Investments Law, 5719–1959, LB 234.

68 Encouragement of Industry (Taxes) Law, 5729–1969, LB 232.

69 Encouragement of Capital Investments in Agriculture Law, 5741–1980, LB 56.

70 Encouragement of Industrial Research and Development Law, 5744–1984, LB 100.

71 Ministry of Finance—International Affairs Department, Opportunity Israel: Enhanced Legislation, R&D Incentives, Grants and Support Programs 13 (2012), available at: http://www.finan ceisrael.mof.gov.il/financeisrael/Docs/En/publications/InvestorsBooklet.pdf (accessed February 9, 2017).

72 See p. 3 of: http://www.mifellows.org/Research/HEB_F/74-HB-F.pdf (accessed February 9, 2017).

73 Article 1 of the Encouragement of Capital Investments Law.

the state to improve its economic growth and to bring its products and services to international level.[74]

During the years 2011–2012, the Law was amended in drastic fashion, revolutionizing the way gains were treated in the market.[75] According to the older version, companies received extensive benefits on their profits while simultaneously they were taxed more for dividend distribution or for continued investment in their operations abroad. Because of this, many companies chose to avoid dividend distribution in order not to pay taxes. They just deposited the money in the bank. Because of this, the Law was coined the "Jailed Profits" Law, due to the unrecognized profits of the company used to avoid the additional tax.

Following the amendments, the "Jailed Profits" problem was resolved, even retroactively, in order to encourage market growth (the new amendments applied also to profits accrued during the tenure of the previous law). The resolution was that companies would pay a lower tax on Jailed Profits, at a rate of 6.5%–17.5%, on the time and amount of the distribution of the profits. This reduction would be allowed under the condition that the companies must invest half the profits in Israel (i.e., a 40%–70% discount from the original tax due).[76]

Along with legislative development, a significant contribution to investments development was made by a project called the "Yozma Initiative," a government project to encourage venture capital investments in Israel, implemented in the years 1993–1998. The project encouraged and accelerated growth of the high-tech industry. The Israeli government directly invested approximately 100 million dollars in ten venture capital funds, while the funds could choose whether or not to make the government a partner in the fund. Decling the partnership will require the fund to return the amount given by the govermentwith interest. At first, the government held 40% in every fund, but allowed the private partners to acquire its shares in good conditions after five years. The government's investment, albeit a small investment, was a welcoming signal for the funds to raise more equity from overseas. The investment pushed, *de facto*, the venture capital industry in Israel; it brought together local and foreign investors and created a climate that encourages investments in the Israeli high-tech sector.

Evaluation of the investments, took place twelve years after the project began, showed that the project invested in 168 start-ups (13 foreign and 155 Israeli). Additionally, the survival rate of companies was raised to two-thirds, while

---

74 See p. 8 of: http://www.mifellows.org/Research/HEB_F/74-HB-F.pdf (accessed February 9, 2017).
75 Encouragement of Capital Investments Law (Amendment No. 68 and 69), 5719–1959, LB 234.
76 Lior Farber and Michael Goral, *Favour for the Rich or Good Solution for the Deficit: The Tied Profits Act*, Commercial 2, at 15–16 (2013).

the accepted percentage around the world ranges from one-third to a half. The project was dubbed the "Israeli Model," and inspired many national projects in other countries such as Ireland and Hungary.[77]

c. Law for Encouragement of Capital Investments

The Law for Encouragement of Capital Investments 5719–1959 (LECI) was originally drafted in 1959 in order to incentivize the local economy by appealing to non-resident investors. By means of different incentives prescribed by the law, it sets out to promote not only attractiveness of the Israeli market within the global competition, but also to a socio-geographically balanced distribution of commerce and industry, and in turn strengthening peripheral regions. The Law does so by two chief governmental incentives: governmental grants and tax incentives.

At the end of 2010, the Israeli parliament amended LECI, taking into account different studies showing inefficiencies in the allocation of the law's incentives—chiefly emphasizing encouragement of investments and increasing competition. LECI now grants the Israel Investments Centre further leeway in determining suitable investment schemes. It has simplified the tax scheme and established flat tax rates on all incomes of select "preferred companies"; it gives tax preference to companies operating in peripheral regions. Moreover, it solves inherent distortions in the allocation of tax benefits by preventing the use of tax benefits to certain foreign investors, companies which exploit natural resources, and state owned companies.

LECI now applies to companies which qualify as an "International Competitive Enterprise," in other words, companies which have export capabilities (except biotechnology and nanotechnology companies). The high-tech industry, being an integral part of Israel's economy, has also been promoted to the LECI.[78]

(1) Tax Benefits

The LECI uses a flat tax scheme: enterprises located in "Area A" are eligible for a reduced corporate tax of 9 percent on all preferred income, while the corporate tax in other regions is 16 percent.[79]

---

77 See respectively: http://www.finfacts.ie/irishfinancenews/article_1020127.shtml; http://nkfih.gov.hu/english/archive/israeli-hungarian (both accessed February 9, 2017).
78 Crowe Horwath, *Doing Business in Israel 2015*, Paragraph 4.2.
79 EY, *Doing Business in Israel 2015*, p. 13.

As stated above, in order to receive the tax benefits, an enterprise has to be classified as a "preferred corporation": a company which was incorporated under Israeli law, the business of which is controlled and managed within the state, and the corporation owns an International Competitive Enterprise (ICE).

An ICE is classified as a competitive enterprise within international market and contributes to the gross domestic product of Israel. To do so, the enterprise must fulfill one of the following conditions: engage mainly in biotechnology or nanotechnology, and obtain approval of the Head of Industrial R&D Administration; produce at least 25 percent of its Preferred Income[80] from direct exporting to international markets; or engage mainly in the field of renewable energy.[81]

(2) Grants

An enterprise located in "Area A" (the Jordan Valley, the Negev, Jerusalem, and the Galilee) may be eligible for grants as a percentage of the approved investment, up to 20 percent of the actual investments of the enterprise on the following assets: land development, building renovations, buildings, machinery, and other equipment.[82]

d. Investments in Israel by Non-Residents

During 2014, most of the investments in Israel by non-residents were in government bonds, *makam* (short-term Bank of Israel bills), and shares traded in Israel and abroad. During 2013, non-residents invested 12,412 million USD, and while 2014 the amount decreased to 9,499 million USD. In 2015 the net transactions totaled 9,529 million USD[83] of which direct investments were 11,566, portfolio investments were 3,238, and other investments were 5,275 (million USD).[84] Non-residents increased the rate of redeeming their deposits in Israel.[85]

---

80 Preferred Income will be determined as the gross income of the enterprise.

81 Ministry of Economy, Invest in Israel, Tax benefits: http://www.investinisrael.gov.il/what_can_we_do.html; See also http://www.financeisrael.mof.gov.il/FinanceIsrael/Docs/En/publica tions/InvestorsBooklet.pdf (both accessed February 11, 2017).

82 Ministry of Economy, Invest in Israel, The Support: http://economy.gov.il/English/Inter nationalAffairs/InvestInIsrael/WhyIsrael/Pages/WhyIsraelLong.aspx; See also http://www.fi nanceisrael.mof.gov.il/FinanceIsrael/Docs/En/publications/InvestorsBooklet.pdf (both accessed February 11, 2017).

83 Bank of Israel, "Non-Residents' Investments in Israel, and Israelis' Investments Abroad in January 2016," (March 2016). http://www.boi.org.il/en/NewsAndPublications/PressReleases/Pages/10-03-2016-Investments.aspx (accessed February 9, 2017).

84 *Id.*

e. Limits on Government's Undertaking to Investors

Arrangements and agreements between the government and investors may be subject to legal scrutiny and judicial review by the courts. A recent and illustrative example is the major litigation before the Supreme Court of Israel on the gas deal between American and Israeli energy companies to develop Israel's largest offshore deposits in the Mediterranean Sea.[86]

The agreement between Noble Energy (a US-based corporation) and Israeli partner Delek was signed with Israel in December 2015. The deal purpose aimed at allowing the companies to start extracting gas from the massive Leviathan field off Israel's Mediterranean coast. The offshore deposits are estimated to contain nearly 623 billion cubic meters of gas. Noble Energy and Delek own the Leviathan gas field as well as a number of other recently discovered gas fields and supply factories.

Five NGOs and a number of political parties and members of Parliament challenged the legality of the agreement on a number of grounds. The Supreme Court held the agreement to be unconstitutional on the ground that a stability clause, set in the agreement, restricted the government's ability to use its discretion. The court suspended the project for a year to enable the executive to amend the agreement or pass legislation.

By a majority of 4 to 1, the court held that a stability clause in the agreement restricting the government from introducing major regulatory changes for ten years was unacceptable. The condition was aimed at giving the energy companies pricing and regulatory stability for ten years despite future changes in government. The companies needed to spend major amounts of investments in the development of the underwater gas deposits and so wished to get protection from regulatory changes in taxation, antitrust limitations, and export quotas. Per Deputy Supreme Court president Elyakim Rubinstein, the Court ruled that "The stability clause in this chapter of the plan, in which the government undertakes for a decade to not only avoid legislate but rather fight any legislation against the plan's provisions, was determined without authority—and as such is rejected." He further ruled that this was especially the case when the government seeks to limit the discretion of future governments, who may have different composition and may hold different ideology. The Court ruled that government cannot bind itself or future governments by virtue of the stability clause to refrain from initiating new regulatory provisions.

---

85 Bank of Israel, Annual Report of 2014, p. 108 (2015), available at: http://www.bankisrael. gov.il/en/NewsAndPublications/RegularPublications/Pages/DochBankIsrael2014.aspx (accessed February 9, 2017).
86 H.C.J 4374/15 *The Movement for the Quality of Government v. The Prime Minister of Israel.*

The stability clause was the most controversial section of the agreement. By virtue of this clause, the state agreed to refrain from substantial regulatory changes in the gas industry during the next decade, in particular in taxation, exports, and ownership of the fields.

Following the judgement of the Supreme Court, political leaders and representatives of Noble Energy expressed their disappointment. Prime Minister Benjamin Netanyahu called the ruling "mystifying" and said the court's decision seriously threatened the development of gas reserves of the State of Israel.

The prime minister said in a statement that was later criticized: "Israel is seen as a state in which excessive judicial intervention makes it difficult to do business with. We will search for other ways to overcome the severe damage caused to the Israeli economy following this surprising ruling." David L. Stover, Noble Energy's CEO, stated that developing such a project with a huge investment made over a number of years requires Israel to provide a stable investment climate. He stated that "The court's ruling, while recognizing that timely natural gas development is a matter of strategic national interest for Israel, is disappointing and represents another risk to Leviathan timing."[87]

In response to the criticism of statement mentioned above, Prime Minister Netanyahu said that no institution in Israel is above criticism, and political leaders as well as citizens have the right to voice their disagreement with the Supreme Court rulings. Further criticism was expressed by Justice Minister Ayelet Shaked: She told the Israeli Bar Association that the Court had exceeded its authority with the ruling, turning itself again into a place for determining political policy and refined macroeconomic questions whose resolution is in the power of elected members of Knesset.[88]

According to Professor Norman A. Bailey, of the University of Haifa and The Institute of World Politics, Washington, DC, the recent decision of the Supreme Court on the gas plan[89] has had two consequences. First, it is likely that an alternative method of ensuring stability will be found in the coming months; second, judicial activism is a problem for many countries. In Israel, the court's controversial decision may cause the legislature to legislate rules that will reduce the Court's powers to strike down executive and legislative decisions and laws. At a later development a solution was found by mutual agreement between all parties concernd.

---

87 https://www.rt.com/business/337449-israel-court-us-deal/ (accessed February 9, 2017).

88 http://www.timesofisrael.com/justice-minister-takes-fresh-aim-at-supreme-court-over-gas-deal/ (accessed February 9, 2017).

89 http://www.globes.co.il/en/article-can-the-israeli-gas-phoenix-rise-again-1001115575 (accessed February 9, 2017).

D. Monetary and Banking System and Law

The Israel's central bank, the Bank of Israel, acts as advisor and banker to the Government and is in charge of the monetary policy. It is responsible, *inter alia*, for setting base interest rates through its Monetary Policy Committee. Overdrafts with fluctuating interest rates are the most commonly used facility for financing working capital or for funding seasonally affected business. Technically, overdrafts are repayable on demand.

Commercial Banks also offer short, medium, or long-term loans. The repayment terms are negotiable and the rate of interest may be fixed or variable. To obtain bank financing, business will normally be required to provide adequate security. Security will typically be in the form of a fixed or floating charge over the business assets, as well as, in certain circumstances, personal guarantees of its owners.

In addition to these traditional services, banks offer various financing arrangements through subsidiaries or affiliates. These include installment credit, leasing, factoring and invoice discounting, and "mezzanines" finance.

a. Monetary Policy

The Bank of Israel (the "Bank") is the body responsible for fiscal policies of Israel. Its primary purpose is to maintain the value of money, meaning to maintain stable prices and to prevent inflation, in order to achieve a stable economy and to create conditions for continued growth of the economy. Along with that, the Bank has other roles: support for achieving other financial goals of the government, especially growth, industry, and closing social gaps', supporting stability of the financial system in its daily actions while maintaining the prices stability over time.[90]

To reach its primary goal of maintaining stable prices, the government, in consultation with the Bank Chancellor, sets a target for stable prices. The annual rise in the price index for the consumer is defined, as of this writing, as a range of 1–3% inflation rate. The Bank makes use of policies at its disposal, mainly short-term monetary interest. The Bank sets the interest rate to maintain the inflation in the target range or for a return to the target range in no more than two years. It should be noted that the Bank acts independently in setting the short-term interest rate and its use of monetary tools. The Bank interest rate is set by

---

90 Bank of Israel website, available at http://www.boi.org.il/he/MonetaryPolicy/MonetaryPolicyFramework/Pages/Default.aspx (accessed February 9, 2017).

the monetary committee.[91] which is headed by the Chancellor. That rate is the touchstone by which other interest rates, in the economy, are set, such as: the interest rate that the public (households and businesses) pay the bank on loans and the interest rate the public receives for depositing their money there.[92]

The interest rates in the economy affects the scope of expenses and savings, and consequently the prices. Low interest rates can create an increase in spending of business and household, and subsequently pressure to raise prices, whereas high interest rates restrict spending and saving too much, bringing a slowes economic activity and eventually leads to unemployment. Based on that premise, during times of inflation, the Bank raises interest rates and, during periods of recession and stagnation, when there is no inflation risk, the Bank lowers the interest rates.[93]

b. Supervision of Banks

The banking system plays a central role in every modern economy. The public deposits most of its monetary savings and funds in banks. These funds are then used by the banks for, among other uses, providing credit to businesses and home owners. The currency accounts that are used in banks are used for a large amount of the transactions in the economy, as well as for foreign currency transactions. The vital roles of the banking system in the economy, and the serious implications of a failure in this system would cause, led to the establishment of a system to oversee the banks and the way they function.[94] The main roles of the supervising body are: overseeing the stability of the banking corporations from the perspective of protecting the public's deposited money; preserv-

---

91 According to Article 55 of the Bank of Israel Law, 5770 – 2010, the monetary committee submits to the government and to the finance committee, at least twice a year, a periodical report on the monetary policy. The report includes an overview of the developments in pricing and the industry in the period concerning the report, as well as the necessary policy, according to the committee to maintain the prices in the range previously set by the government and to achieve other goals. For previous monetary reports see http://www.boi.org.il/he/MonetaryPolicy/Monetar yPolicyReports/Pages/Default.aspx (accessed February 9, 2017).

92 Bank of Israel website, available at: http://www.boi.org.il/he/MonetaryPolicy/MonetaryPolicy Framework/Pages/Default.aspx (accessed February 9, 2017).

93 For other terminology and exact definitions of the Bank of Israel, see http://www.boi.org.il/ he/Markets/Pages/dictionary.aspx (accessed February 9, 2017).

94 Article 4(7) of the Bank of Israel Law defines that the Bank must "supervise and regulate the banking system."

ing the proper management of the banking corporations; and preserving the fair treatment in the relationships between the banks and their customers.[95]

The Chancellor of the Bank appoints the supervisor. In addition, there are two active committees. One, the licensing committee, advises the Chancellor and the supervisor on issues dealing with licensing permits for banking corporations; these permits are used for acquiring control in corporations, and bank branches. Furthermore, the committee can take certain measures, listed in the Bank of Israel Law, to stabilize problematic banks. The other committee is the advisory committee on banking issues, with whom the supervisor consults on new banking regulations.[96]

Supervision over the banks is achieved through a variety of tools:

Licensing: Licensing procedures and, in particular, licenses from the chancellor are required for a corporation to become a banking corporation and for those who wish to hold 5% or more shares of a banking corporation. The licenses are given following a thorough examination made by the banks supervisor, in consultation with the licensing committees. The procedures are meant to ensure the proper functioning of the bank. Moreover, they are intended to prevent unsuitable developments, both in terms of their economic strength and their integrity; as well as to prevent people whom are not fit from working, owning or becoming dominant players, office holders or shareholders in a banking corporation.

Setting Norms and Restrictions: With the norms and restrictions that were set for the banking operations in the fields of proper management and in risk control, there are rules that deal with banking corporation board of directors structure and conduct, a minimum equity requirement commensurate to the value of the bank's at risk assets, and limiting the maximum amount that may be given as a loan to an individual (and to factors related to the bank), the owners, concerned parties, management, and others.

Review and Evaluation: Reviewing and evaluating banking activities, based on the vast amount of information that is brought to the supervisor, is meant to estimate the strength and economic status of a bank, to prevent it from taking non-calculated risks, and to ensure the existence of proper managing practices as directed by the supervisor. Based on the review findings, the supervisor may

---

95 The roles and authorities of the supervision of banks in the normative framework is as follows: The Banking Ordinance, 1941, Addition 1, 69; Banking (Licensing) Law, 5741–1981, LB 232; Banking (Customer Service) Law, 5741–1981, LB 258; Checks Without Cover Law, 5741–1981, LB 136.

96 Bank of Israel website, available at: http://www.boi.org.il/he/BankingSupervision/Pages/about.aspx (accessed February 9, 2017).

require a bank to set right the deficiencies. in extreme cases, the supervisor can impose sanctions on the bank and its management;

Encouraging Market Supervision: Inspection of customers as well as different parts of the equity market is an important component of the supervision system. The Bank of Israel attempts to strengthen this supervision, primarily by expanding the duties of the bank to provide adequate information regarding their business status, their customer service, and their prices. Directives of the supervisor regarding the composition of the financial reports that banks must publish include the information necessary to analyze a bank's development, profitability, and the risks that characterize its balance sheet. This formula for information requirements is one of the most advanced in the world. Supervision over the banks has greatly expanded the directives detailing the information that banks must pass on to their customers regarding the interests the bank charges, the fees for services, and directives in the field of contractual relationships between the bank and customers.

Investigations into Public Complaints: A customer who believes that the bank acted in an inappropriate way can lodge a complaint with the public inquiry unit. The unit investigates the complaint, and then notifies the inquirer and the bank of its findings. If the complaint is found to be just, the unit has the authorization to order banks to fix the wrongs found;

Economic Analysis: Publishing periodical surveys that reflects and analyse the developments in the banking system.

Information and Reporting: Banks regularly submit data to the Bank of Israel, which is stored and analyzed in a special unit and used to assist different units on their work.[97]

c. Money Laundering

Israel has joined the fight against money laundering by enacting the Money Laundering Law.[98] In addition, in October 2014, Israeli government confirmed the conclusions of the "Loker Committee" that was established in order to minimize the use of cash in the Israeli economy. The main purpose of the committee was to fight undeclared capital ("Black Capital"), and money laundering in order to enable "real tax" collection.[99]

---

97 Bank of Israel Website is available at http://www.boi.org.il/he/BankingSupervision/Pages/about.aspx (accessed February 9, 2017).
98 Money Laundering Law, 5760 – 2000, LB 293.
99 Crown Horwath (Israel), Doing Business in Israel 2016, p. 14. available at: https://www.google.co.il/url?sa=t&rct=j&q=&esrc=s&source=web&cd=1&cad=rja&uact=8&ved=0ahU

The committee recommendations are as follows: limiting cash transactions between individuals carrying on a business to 10,000 NIS (instead of 20,000 NIS as set); limiting cash transactions between individuals to 15,000 NIS (instead of unlimited amount); limiting the possibility of paying off checks that were transferable more than once (up to 10,000 NIS); prohibiting transferring checks without a beneficiary's name; and starting using debit cards that are credited immediately and debit cards that can be loaded.[100]

As a result, the government imposed certain identification and reporting obligations on financial institutions, including banks, stock exchange members, and money changers. These institutions are required to positively identify anyone, either a person or a corporation, requesting services such as opening of an account, change of ownership of an account, or execution of certain transactions. In addition, the aforementioned institutions are required to report two kinds of transactions to the authorities: transactions which exceed defined amounts, and transactions which appear to be unusual in light of the information the institution possesses.[101]

KEwjUwr_Lq4jSAhWEXhQKHfqlANoQFggdMAA&url=https%3A%2F%2Fwww.crowehorwath.net %2Fuploadedfiles%2Fil%2Fadditional-content%2Fhome%2Fdoing%2520business%2520in% 2520israel%25202014%2520.pdf&usg=AFQjCNELJcVuW_gkfrorAuiSDNj6KmuRXw&sig2=rJ5- 2RPmOISEtT74Ivwolg (accessed February 11, 2017).
100 The committee's full conclusions available at *Id.*, at p. 15.
101 *Id.*

Chapter 17:
Private Law

1. Contract Law

A. Contract Principles

Freedom of Contract: The first of the two fundamental principles of contract law in Israel that recognize as a constitutional principle. Freedom of contract applies to both freedom to enter a contract (or refrain from entering) and freedom to shape the contract content and its terms by the engaging parties. However, there are some limitations to this fundamental principle, including: good faith duties, protection of weaker parties, specific requirements of form, and invalidity on grounds of public policy.

As for the last constraint, contract law states that a contract (execution, content, or purpose) which is illegal, immoral, or contrary to public policy is void. Despite the nullity of such a contract, the court may order either party to make restitution or—if unilateral performance (in whole or in part) has already taken place—order a party to perform its obligation in part or in full under the contract provisions. Courts are allowed, and often tend to, sever the void element from the rest of the contract and uphold the non-objectionable portions (the "blue pencil rule"). Additionally, courts may take into account the legitimate interests of third parties who relied on the void contract in good faith and issue orders accordingly.[1]

Good Faith: The second fundamental principle of Israeli contract law. The courts apply the duty to act in good faith extensively; they tend to relate it as a guardian of the principle of freedom of contract, discussed above, than as a substantive limitation on it. Good faith obligations apply in three contexts: first, in contractual negotiations, whether a contract was eventually formed or not (a personal as well as vicarious duty); second, in performance of the contract, including in exercising a right arising from it; and third, the duty of con-

---

1 Jonathan Yovel & Ido Shacham, "Israeli Contract Law: An Overview," p. 5 (2014), available at: https://www.researchgate.net/publication/46417901_An_Overview_of_Israeli_Contract_Law (accessed February 9, 2017).;

For further information on the freedom of contract principle, see: Gabriela Shalev, *Contract Law—General Part*, Ch. 4 (2005); see also Gabriela Shalev, "Law of Contract" in Alon Kaplan & Paul Ogden, Eds., *Israeli Business Law: An Essential Guide*, pp. 25–38 (1999 Kluwer) (hereinafter: *Israeli Business Law: An Essential Guide*).

DOI 10.1515/9783899497946-018

duct in good faith may be extended *mutatis mutandis* to legal acts or obligations in non-contractual contexts.

Since there is no statutory definition regarding the nature or scope of good faith duty, the courts developed and interpreted the principle over the years. Examples include: misleading or failing to disclose required information, retiring from advanced negotiations without justifiable cause (Opportunistic retairment), negotiating with no intention to enter into a contract, raising new demands at advanced negotiation stages, and insistence on strict performance of the contract where cost to the debtor far outweighs any benefit to the creditor.[2]

B. Contract Formation

Contract formation is governed by the Contract Law (General Part)[3] as well as by some peripheral statutes and a wealth of precedents. In addition, courts apply a fairly liberal approach to contract formation, focusing of the parties' mutual intent to enter a bonding relationship as manifested by their language and/ or conduct, rather than insisting on discrete acts discernible as "offer" or "acceptance."

A contract under Israeli law typically entails the fulfillment of four basic elements, broadly construed: offer, acceptance, definiteness, and intention (in order to create a legal relationship). There are no general formal requirements for contract formation, such as a written document or consideration for the completion of a contract, except for certain types of contracts or areas.[4]

a. Offer

A person's proposal to another constitutes an offer if it attests to the offeror's intention to enter into a contract with the offeree and is sufficiently definite to enable the contract to be concluded by acceptance of the offer. The offeror's intention to enter into contract is adduced from the objective communicative facts: statements (contextually interpreted), conduct, etc. (as a general rule, language is not more significant than one's conduct).

An offer may be made to the public, although tenders addressing the public are normally classified as an invitation to make offers rather than as actual of-

---

2 Jonathan Yovel & Ido Shacham, *supra* note 1, at 6; for further information on the good faith principle, see: Gabriela Shalev, *supra* note 1, Ch. 5.
3 Contract Law (General Part), 5733 – 1973.
4 Jonathan Yovel & Ido Shacham, *supra* note 1, at 7.

fers. Like other principles of contract law, it is a question of interpretation; therefore, prudent offerors make this matter clear in the language of the tender.

An offer expires when rejected by the offeree, when a reasonable time has elapsed since its tender, or when the offeror or offeree either passes away or becomes incompetent (in the case of corporations, entering receivership or liquidation). Firm offers that set a time for acceptance or indicate their time of expiration may not be withdrawn, and the offeree may accept or reject them until that time, whereupon they automatically expire.[5]

b. Acceptance

A contract may be tendered either by notice delivered by the offeree to the offeror or by conduct, as long as it attests to the offeree's intention to form a legal contractual relationship, or otherwise indicating the offeree's assent. The offeror may restrict the methods of acceptance available to the offeree, but cannot determine a stipulation that the absence of any response on the part of the offeree would count as acceptance. Such a stipulation is generally invalid, unless the parties made a prior agreement to the contrary. An exception to this rule is a purely beneficial offer, where the contract in question would require no performance from the offerees and puts them to no disadvantage, cost, or inconvenience at all.

Israeli law does not apply a "mailbox rule" for acceptance; thus, acceptance is binding once it reaches the offerors or their place of business. However, once a notice of acceptance has been discharged, even before it reached the offerors, a revocation of the offer by the offerors is no longer effective.[6]

c. Definiteness

An offer should be sufficiently definite to enable acceptance. While this requirement applies to all the essential components of the offer, courts would normally not consider an offer to have failed for lack of definiteness where it may be supplemented or completed by an internal or external mechanism or source. Courts normally tend to uphold offers rather than disqualify them for lack of definiteness as long as the matter of mutual assent has been settled.

---

5 Jonathan Yovel & Ido Shacham, *supra* note 1, at 8; for further information on the subject, see: Gabriela Shalev, *supra* note 1, Ch. 9.

6 Jonathan Yovel & Ido Shacham, *supra* note 1, at 8; for further information on the subject, see: Gabriela Shalev, *supra* note 1, Ch. 10.

Specifically, sources for supplementing a wanting offer may be: the offer itself and the presumed intention of the parties; the circumstances in which the offer was made; existing practices between parties or, in the absence of such practices, practices customary in contracts of that kind; or statutory supplementation, namely the importation of default provisions into the deficient offer.[7] Such supplementary details may include matters of place for performance, time, quality, terms of payment, price, conformity, documents of title, etc.[8]

d. Intention

According to Israeli law, the essence of contract is mutual assent. The law follows the so-called "objective" doctrine of contract formation whereby intent is inferred from conduct as well as entailed by appropriate language. The issue is not whether certain parties had or did not have a subjective intention to contract, but whether by their language and conduct communicated such an intention to a reasonable party under specific circumstances.

Courts follow a pragmatic approach and would seek to infer the parties' intention from both language and conduct—before, during, and after the preliminary agreement—in cases of disputes regarding intention to contract. The performance of obligations pursuant to a memorandum of agreement is strong evidence of intention to enter into the contract.[9]

e. Form

The Israeli law places no general requirements regarding the form of a contract, such as writing, seal, or registration, except for certain types of contracts. The most important of these are: an undertaking to make a transaction in land; arbitration agreements; consumer banking agreements; and an undertaking to make a gratuitous transfer (gift). The requirement of writing in these cases is substantive and is a material condition for the making of a binding contract.

A written document may be required as evidence of common contracts, as well when contesting another written document in court. This requirement is not substantive but merely evidential and the courts apply it pragmatically. Electronic transmissions may generally satisfy the evidentiary requirement, although

---

7 Two main sources for such provisions are: The Sales Law, 5728–1968 and The Contract (General Part) Law, 1973.
8 Jonathan Yovel & Ido Shacham, *supra* note 1, at 9; for further information on the subject, see: Daniel Friedman & Nili Cohen, *Contracts*, Volume 1, Ch. 8 (1991).
9 Jonathan Yovel & Ido Shacham, *supra* note 1, at 9.

both courts and the legislature still require a "tangible form" for the fulfillment of the requirement (such as a computer printout or retrievable, stored digital data).[10]

C. Interpretation of Contract

Israeli courts customarily apply a model of "purposive interpretation" to all legal interactions and texts. Regarding the interpretation of a contract, the aim is to reconstruct the agreement in light of the manifested common purpose made by parties at the time of formation. Thus, Israeli courts allow interpretative evidence regarding context, circumstances, and the parties' behavior before, during, and sometimes even after formation. Customs, courses of conduct, prior agreements, and even *lex mercatoria*, the "merchant law", may be brought as an evidence for the parties' purported agreement and sometimes form interpretative presumptions.

Good faith is applied as an interpretative principle as well. Thus, when reconstructing the parties' purposes, a party may not benefit from having failed to disclose information that should have been disclosed under the good faith requirement. In addition, Israeli law enforces third-party beneficiary contracts. Whether a contract empowers a third party to enforce an obligation or not, is determined by analysis according to the standard rules of contract interpretation.[11]

2. Property Law

In general, Israeli property laws are tailored to our modern time. However, there are still parts that were inherited from regimes that ruled the state of Israel before its establishment (May 14, 1948). These parts are divided into two groups. The first group includes the remaining laws from the period when the country was part of the Ottoman Empire; the second group includes the laws that have survived from the period of the British Mandate.[12]

---

10 Jonathan Yovel & Ido Shacham, *supra* note 1, at10.
11 For further information on the subject, see Eyal Zamir, *More about the Interpretation and Completion of Contracts*, 43 Mishpatim p. 5 (2012).
12 Joshua Weisman, *Property Law—General Part*, Volume 1, p. 27 **(1993)**; for for general analysis of property law see Arie Wiernik, "Law of Real Property," in *Israeli Business Law: An Essential Guide, supra* note 1, at 93–102.

A. The Remains of the Ottoman Period

According to the Ottoman Land Law of 1858, which was the main real estate law in the Ottoman period, land in Israel was classified into five categories, and each category had different laws. These types were: "Mulk"—land that could be purchased, including full ownership, as chattels; "Miri"—land that was owned by the State, while a private holder could receive, at most, a right to hold and use; "Matruka"—land intended to serve the public needs, such as roads and markets; "Mawat"—rocky lands distant from inhabited areas that were not under private ownership; and "Mawkufha"—land devoted to religious endowment.

Antiquated Ottoman Land Law was abolished long ago in Turkey and in other countries that were part of the Ottoman Empire. However, it can be noticed that in Israel some Ottoman real estate categories continue to apply even to this date, despite the legislature's statement made in the land law of 1969. Thus, there was no change in the law regarding the statute of limitations occurred previously on unregulated land and about the "Mawkufha" land. These are the two main remains of the Ottoman period, waiting until today to removal from the Israeli legal system.[13]

B. The Remains of the British Mandate

The remains of English law from British Mandate period are fairly few in the field of property law, but they are not insignificant. These remains come from two sources: the first, directly applying English law on certain matters; the second, mandatory orders that are still implemented today and reflect, in most cases, the tradition of English law.

Examples of the first source: Article 46 of the Privy Council in 1922, which have previously used to fill lacunae domestic law with English law; Section 44 of the Land Rights Settlement Ordinance [New Version] 1969, which states that in a land settlement the court must take into account the beneficial rights to land. Examples of the second source: Companies Ordinance [New Version] 1983, that regards floating charge; Bankruptcy Ordinance [New Version] 1980, that regards the status of a secured creditor in bankruptcy.[14]

---

13 Joshua Weisman, *supra* note 12, at 27–29; For further information on the Ottoman empire, see: Haim Zandberg, Land Rights Settlement in Land of Israel and in the State of Israel, ch. 10 – 11 (2001).

14 Joshua Weisman, *supra* note 12, at30; For further information on the British mandate, see: Haim Zandberg, *supra* note 13, at ch. 12.

C. Laws

In general, property law in Israel is mainly governed by the following statutess; *The Land Law*, 1969:[15] This law sets out rights, rules, and regulations concerning "immovable property," or "land, everything built or planted on land and every other thing permanently fixed to land, except severable fixtures." The law determines, particulars for ownership and possession of land; land registration; joint ownership; building and planting; rules for common property such as boundary fixtures (e. g., fences) and cooperative houses; and lease, mortgage and easement rights. The law further establishes a Land Registry, sets fees for land registration and other transactions, and cancels or repeals certain legal categories concerning land, and Ottoman period land laws.

Ownership of land includes ownership of buildings and plants on land, as well as "the whole depth below the surface of the land subject to any law relating to water, petroleum, mines, minerals... and to the airspace above the surface of the land; however, subject to any law, this provision shall not prevent passage through such airspace." Land owners may demand that a person unlawfully possessing that land will surrender it to the rightfull owners. They may also use "reasonable force" to reclaim their land, provided that they act within thirty days. When a person has illegally built a structure on another person's land, the owner may decide throughout the strcturs life, to have the builder remove it or whether to retain it. If owners keep the structure, they must compensate the builder.

Land owned by the Israeli govermment, a local authority, or any authority established by any enactment is considered a public land. Reserved land is public land intended for public use; it includes the seashore, ports, rivers and streams, roads and railways, airports, and other lands defined by regulations as such. Land under Israel's territorial waters and lakes are public property and belong to the State.[16]

Basic Law: Israel Lands: This law applies to lands owned by the State of Israel, the Jewish National Fund (JNF or KKL) and the development authority ("state lands"). These lands constitute approximately 90% of Israel's terrain; the law determines that they shall not be transferred either by sale or in any other manner.[17]

---

15 Israel Ministry of Foreign Affairs, Land Law – 5729 – 1969 (summary), available at: http://mfa.gov.il/MFA/PressRoom/1998/Pages/Land%20Law-%201969.aspx_(accessed February 9, 2017).
16 *Id.*, at 1969
17 Basic Law: Israel Lands, 5720(1960); see also Haim Sandberg, *Basic Law: Lands of Israel* (Yitzhak Zamir, editor, 2016); H.C.J 729/10 *Dror Israel v. The Government of Israel* (published

Land (Settlement of Title) Ordinance [New Version], 5729 – 1969:[18] This ordia-nance regulates the registration of rights in land that have not yet undergone certain verification procedures, such as rights to title and the boundaries of the property.

Sale Law (Apartments), 1973[19] and Sale Law (Apartments) (Assurance of Investments of Persons Acquiring Apartments), 1974:[20] These laws impose special obligations on sellers of newly-built premises, aimed at giving increased protections to purchasers of apartments from contractors. These include the following obligations. A technical specifications detail must be attached to the sale contract, in the detailed format set out by the Law. The Law provides that in situations when contractors have not fulfilled their obligations to the purchaser in a number of defined circumstances. The purchasers have one year to inform the contractor of any non-conformity in the apartment, commencing from when they receive possession of the apartment. Compensation is to be paid to the purchaser resulting from late handover. There is a cap on the interest that a contractor can charge a purchaser for late payments.

In addition, there are other laws: Protected Tenancy Law (Combined Version), 1972 (affords protection to certain types of tenants in business and residential premises);[21] Lease and Lending Law, 1971 (relates to the lease of immovable and movable property); Land Taxation Law (Appreciation, Sale and Purchase), 1963; Chattels Law, 1971;[22] and Sales Law, 5728 – 1968.[23] The constitutional protection of general property rights is set forth in the Basic Law: Human Dignity and Liberty.

The accepted interpretive rule regarding property law means to maintain restraint and avoidance of innovative interpretive initiatives; therefore, the tendency is to attribute special weight to the stability of the mentioned laws.

---

on Nevo, 24.05.2012). The court rejected a claim that a decision to transfer land owned by the state to private ownership was unconstitutional based on the interpretation of Basic Law: Israel Lands, allowing such transfer.

18 The Land (Settlement of Title) Ordinance [New Version], 5729 – 1969.
19 Sale Law (Apartments), 5733 – 1973.
20 Sale Law (Apartments) (Assurance of Investments of Persons Acquiring Apartments), 5735 – 1974.
21 Protected Tenancy Law [Combined Version], 5732 – 1972.
22 Chattels Law, 5731 – 1971.
23 Sales Law, 5728 – 1968.

3. Law of Torts

The law of tort in Israel belongs to the sphere of private civil law, alongside with contract law and property law; all deals with the relation between private individuals. The main distinction among private branches of law lies in the element of consent. For example, the law of contract exists only on basis of parties consent to the contract, whereas the law of torts deal with involuntary obligations imposed upon a person as a result of bodily or property damage sustained by the injured person—for the damage, the injured person seeks compensation from the person who caused the damage.

The situations where the law of tort applies include: accidents (whether traffic accidents or accidents in the work place), negligence including medical malpractice, assault, libel, various forms of nuisance (such as smell, noise, and air pollution), and other of forms of torts.

In Israeli tort law provisions, one cannot find negotiations between two parties. The way to prevent damages and injuries is by providing efficient law of tort that will prevent people from committing acts of damage. Tort legislative goals can be summarized in three main purposes: first, mitigating the initial damages to the utmost by investing in effective preemptive measures; second, distributive Justice, divding tort damage in a just manner, so that the cost of the damage shall not be imposed on one party only; and third, compensation for the damage in preventing secondary damages.[24]

A. History

Before the Mandatory period of British rule, the law of tort during the rule Ottoman Empire in Palestine–Eretz Israel was based on Ottoman Law. This was the state of law until 1944. According to the provision of the *Mejelle* (the Ottoman legal code) in force to that period, the law of tort provided protection only against property damage, but not against bodily injuries. In spite of the British rule in Eretz Israel, it was not until 1944 that the Mandatory British legislature decided to apply the English tort law in Eretz Israel. The British decided to integrate the English law of tort and the tort ordinance of Cyprus, which was legislated in 1933, and apply it to Eretz Israel.

---

24 For further information on the aims of the law of torts, see: Israel Gilad, *Tort Law—The Limits of Liability*, Ch. 2 (2012) (Hebrew).

In 1968, twenty years after the establishment of the state of Israel, a new version of the tort ordinance originally legislated by the British mandatory government, was legislated by the Israeli legislature.[25] Section 1 of the tort ordinance (new version) refers to the English legal system for the purpose of interpreting the tort ordinance in its new version. Therefore, the link between the tort ordinance new version and English law has not been disconnected. However, eventually after the enactment of the Foundations of Law Act, 1980, the duty to recourse to English law for interpretation of Israeli legislation was disconnected. Thus, the legislature, in the Foundations of Law Act, opened the way for the development of an Israeli original creation tort law. Indeed, in early 1980s, Israeli tort law was developed by original interpretations of the courts. However, the influence of British tort body of laws continues to prevail. One can see these influences in the recourse of the Israeli courts to English laws when they have to adjudicate issues of principal.

B. Tort Ordinance

Tort ordinance in its new version, legislated in 1968, is the bedrock legislation of Israeli tort law. The ordinance is composed of a number of main parts. The first part contains a list of torts, the second deals with a list of defenses, and the third deals with a list of remedies.

The first part contains a list of torts, actions which constitute torts giving rise to tort liability. This is a closed list of torts; therefore, the court cannot create new torts, even if it convinced that there is an absence of a certain regulation relative to torts. The tort ordinance deals with two framework torts: tort of negligence, and tort of breach of statutory duty. Their application extends to endless factual situations without prior definition. The tort ordinance also deals with a number of torts which relate to specific conduct: the tort of assault, false imprisonment, trespass, private and public nuisance, and causing breach of contract.

The second part lists a number of defenses from alleged liabilty. Contrary to the list of torts, this list of defenses is an open list; therefore, it is accepted that the courts have the authority to extend it beyond the ones listed in the ordinances. For example, in situations where the plaintiff has been injured as a result of criminal conduct, and the defendant argues that the plaintiff is a criminal himself, and therefore should not be entitled to a remedy. This defense claims referred to "the culprit should not be rewarded" or "unlawful cause should not give

---

25 Civil Wrongs Ordinance (new version), 5728–1968.

rise to a claim of action" (in Latin: "ex turpi causa non oritur actio"). This defense is not listed expressly in the tort ordinance and was created by the courts. Another example is the defense of contributory negligence. According to this defense, the plaintiff should assume part of the liability for the damage; therefore, the defendant has to be liable for a partial liability and not to the full liability of the injury sustained by the plaintiff. Another example is *volenti non fit iniuria*. According to this principle, an injured person who willfully assumes the risk and is aware of the possibility of being injured cannot claim liability of others when such an injury takes place.

The third part deals with tort remedies, the main remedy provided by law to injuries, is pecuniary compensation. The aim of the compensation to return injured persons to their original situation if the tort had not been occurred (restitute damages). The list of remedies is not closed, and can be extended by the courts. Therefore, sometimes the court orders punitive damages, which reflect not only compensation for the injury rather a penalty for the its conduct. The main rule of thumb on the issue of remedies for torts is that an injured person should never receive double compensation for the same injury. Remedies are determined according to the following principles: pecuniary damages aimed at covering expense in the past and expenses in the future such as medical expenses and assistance to the injured by other parties, loss of income in the past and in the future. In addition to the pecuniary damages, there are also non-pecuniary damages aimed at compensating pain and suffering, and shortening of longevity of the injured.

a. The Structure of the Cause of Action in Tort
There are three basic elements which constitute cause of action in tort: injury, fault, and causal link.

The requirement of injury distinguishes criminal law from tort law. Whereas criminal law the requirement is of risk for the creation of an offense, the requirement in tort law is of injury or harm to occur.

Fault is a breach of standard by action or omission.

The requirement of causal link is divided into two parts: factual link, according to the test of *sine qua non*, and legal causal link. This issue is more ambiguous; it is determined according to the circumstances that caused the harm—the category of the injury and the category of the injured.

b. Levels of Tort Liability

Laws of tort are based on a number of categories of liability which apply to the parties. The categories are based on on stricter and less strict defendant liability. These categories of liability include absolute liability, strict liability, increased liability, negligence, malice, and immunity.

Absolute liability focuses on the result regardless of the fault of the malefeasant and, therefore, the malefeasant will be held liable, regardless of whether or not fault has been proved. This is the conceptual model of the law regarding no-fault traffic accidents, which provides for compensation to the injured without having to prove fault of whichever caused the accident.

The next category of liability is strict liability, which is not conditioned on negligence and focuses on result. Contrary to absolute liability, the defendant can present a number of defense claims, such as contributory negligence. An example for strict liability is the rule regarding deficient products.

Another category of liability is increased liability. This model imposes liability on defendants who cause the damage. However, they can reverse the onus of liability by proving that they did not commit negligence.

The other category of liability is negligence. This is the central form of liability in the law of tort. Unlike criminal law, which is dominated by the requirement of intention or *mens rea* (intention or knowledge of wrongdoing), the law of tort deals with unreasonable conduct which reasonable persons would not have conducted themselves. Reasobale person in tort is in most cases one that takes preventive measures that are cheaper than the damage. Whereas intention in criminal law is a subjective element, negligence in tort law is an objective element; it can be proven in a much easier way than intention, knowledge, or malice. At the foundation of negligence lies social fault.

Another category of liability in tort law is intention, knowledge, and malice. In principle, the distinction between these concepts does not have significant meaning in the law tort as distinguished in criminal law. Nevertheless, it may be noted that in case of intention vis-à-vis knowledge, one cannot receive punitive damages and it is not possible to argue a defense claim of contributory negligence. At the foundation of this model of liability lies moral fault.

The final relative tort liability concept is immunity. Under this concept, public officers and judicial officers enjoy immunity because of their office for tort claim.[26]

---

[26] For further information in the Israeli torts law, see Ariel Porat, *Torts* (2013) (Hebrew).

C. Specific Acts Dealing with Tort Law outside the Tort Ordinance

Tort ordinance is not the only statute dealing with tort actions. There are a number of acts dealing with specific areas of damages:

The first is the Road Accident Victims' Compensation Law of 1975 (RAVC), which provides for principles of compensation for persons who were injured in traffic accidents suffering bodily injuries.[27] This law is based on compulsory insurance that incorporates no-fault absolute liability. This conceptual arrangement is very different from the tort ordinance methodology; as a result, different procedural rules applied to this rule. It should be noted that the plaintiff in traffic accidents under RAVC cannot not sue under the tort ordinance, except for unusual circumstances. Most of the tort claims that are filed in the courts deal with traffic accidents.

Another specific act dealing with damages is the Prohibition of Defamation Law of 1965, which provides for specific causes of action that define injury of defamation.[28] In view of the fact that free speech is a protected constitutional right, the Prohibition of Defamation Law provides a balance between the law of torts and constitutional law.

Another law is the Liability for Defective Products Law of 1980, which provides for the liability of an importer or producers for bodily injury resulting from a product that was produced or imported by the defendant.[29] The law imposed strict liability.

Other specific acts deal with environmental torts; these include the law for the prevention of nuisance of 1961,[30] and environmental nuisances of 1992.[31] These laws deal with legal remedies given to persons injured as a result of different environmental torts.

The other legislative regulations deal with restitution for bodily injuries (the law for civil torts—restitution for bodily injuries of 1964),[32] the law deals with state liability in tort (the law of civil tort state liability of 1952),[33] and regulate causes of tort action in commercial matters such as violation of commercial secrets, unfair trade practice, and the like (commercial torts act of 1999).[34]

---

27 Road Accident Victims Compensation Law, 5753–1975.
28 Prohibition of Defamation Law, 5725–1965.
29 Liability for Defective Products Law, 5740–1980.
30 Abatement of Environmental Nuisances Law, 5721–1961.
31 Prevention of Environmental Nuisances (Civil Action), 5752–1992.
32 Torts Amendments (Repair of Bodily Harm) Law, 5724–1964.
33 Civil Wrongs (Liability of the State) Law, 5712–1952.
34 Commercial Torts Law, 5759–1999.

Chapter 18:
Environmental Law

1. Laws

Israel's wide-ranging environmental legislation uses all forms of legislative in-struments: laws, regulations, administrative orders, and bylaws. These encom-pass laws for the protection of nature (air, water, and soil), the abatement and prevention of environmental nuisances (air, noise, water, and marine pollution), and the safe treatment of contaminants and pollutants (hazardous materials, ra-diation, and solid and liquid waste). Aside from laws and regulations dealing with specific environmental issues, Israel's legislation also includes comprehen-sive laws, such as the Planning and Building Law and the Licensing of Business-es Law, which provides a framework for controlling the use of resources and pro-moting sustainable development.[1]

The Licensing of Businesses Law[2] empowers the Minister of the Interior to designate and define businesses requiring licenses in order, *inter alia*, to ensure proper environmental conditions including: appropriate sanitary conditions; pre-vention of nuisances; compliance with the Planning and Building Law; the safe-ty of those on or near the premises of the business; and the prevention of pollu-tion of water resources by pesticides, fertilizers, or medical substance. Business licenses are granted by the Ministry of the Interior, by means of local authorities, in consultation with the relevant ministries: Environment, Public Security, La-bour and Social Affairs, Agriculture, and Health.[3] The law also provides admin-istrative and judicial powers for the closure of a non-complying business.

The Freedom of Information Law[4] assures open access to public information. The law enables individuals and public organizations to apply to a public au-

---

1 For more information regarding specific categories (health and safety; marine and coastal en-vironment; nature, biodiversity, and open spaces; planning and building; pollution and nuisan-ces; waste and recycling; water and wastewater), see http://www.sviva.gov.il/English/Legis lation/Pages/Legislation.aspx (accessed February 9, 2017); for general analysis of environment law, see Alon Tal, "Law of the Environment," in Alon Kaplan & Paul Ogden, editors, *Israeli Busi-ness Law: An Essential Guide*, 165–176 (1999, Kluwer).
2 Business Licensing Law, 5728–1968, LB 204.
3 Special environmental provisions, stipulated by the Minister of the Environment, which relate to both infrastructure and operation, may be imposed within the framework of the license with regard to air quality, solid waste, hazardous substances, and water and sewage (including indus-trial effluents).
4 Freedom of Information Law, 5758–1988, LB 226.

DOI 10.1515/9783899497946-019

thority in the request to recive information. The 2005 amendment to the Freedom of Information Law specifically relates the publication of environmental information with "relevance to public health, including data on substances that are emitted, spilled, discharged or released to the environment and the results of measurements of noise, odours and radiation, not on private property." The objective is to make environmental information which exists in government agencies more accessible, through its publication on websites and by other means, and to reduce the need for applications and fees.

The Public Health Ordinance[5] defines the powers to control public health and to prevent and eliminate environmental nuisances of various kinds and insect-carried diseases.[6] The ministry's inspection system is empowered to undertake the necessary action in cases of failure to comply with Nuisance Removal Orders.

The Abatement of Environmental Nuisances Law[7] is the main legislative instrument for the control of air quality, odor, and noise. The law makes it illegal to cause "any considerable or unreasonable noise or air pollution (include odors), from any source whatsoever, if it disturbs or is likely to disturb a person in the vicinity or a passer-by." The Minister is authorized, under this law, to issue Nuisance Removal Orders and, in case of non-compliance, to remove the nuisance and to charge the person responsible with double the expenses. All payments and fines under the law are paid to a designated fund providing for public health, established under the Maintenance of Cleanliness Law.[8]

The Plant Protection Law[9] grants the Minister of Agriculture authority, following consultation with an advisory interdisciplinary committee, to regulate the import, sale, distribution, and packaging of pesticides, fertilizers, and other materials. The law authorizes the Minister of Agriculture to regulate the use of pesticides, to require a permit for their use, to promulgate regulations on the safe use of pesticides, and to prohibit or limit the use of pesticides deemed hazardous to human health and the environment.

The Planning and Building Law[10] is a comprehensive statute that monitors and regulates all building and land use designations in Israel. The law establishes a hierarchy of planning bodies (national, regional, and local) responsible for land-use planning, taking into consideration all potential impacts, including

---

5 People's Health Law, 1940, Addition 1, 191.
6 Nuisances may include air pollution, odors, or unsanitary conditions.
7 Environmental Hazards Prevention Law, 5721–1961, LB 58.
8 Cleanliness Law, 5744–1984, LB 142.
9 Plant Protection Law, 5716–1956, LB 79.
10 Planning and Building Law, 5725–1965, LB 307.

environmental ones. The law provides for a public notification and participation process. Public bodies and individuals are free to inspect plans submitted to regional and local planning authorities and to file opposition during the deposition period of any given plan. The law also provides for an appeal process in case an objection is rejected.

2. Environmental Protection and the Kyoto Protocol

The Kyoto Protocol is a mechanism of the international community to devise responses to the danger of climate change. The Kyoto Protocol is the international protocol aimed at reducing greenhouse gas emissions through a series of credits and sanctions manifested in the United Nations Framework Convention on Climate Change (UNFCCC). The main objective of the Kyoto Protocol is to delay global warming and clean the environment through domestic policies and measures. It is a legally binding amendment to the United Nations' international treaty on global warming.

Industrialized countries as a whole are required to reduce certain types of greenhouse emissions by 5.2% for the 2008–2012 commitment period whereas non-industrialized countries are not legally bound to any kind of reductions. This division between industrialized and non-industrialized countries was made as it was felt that, because non-industrialized countries generally produce lower levels of emissions than industrialized counties, they should not be bound to the same reductions.

Pursuant to the Kyoto Protocol, each country has its own reduction target levels based on a percentage of base year emissions. As a result, some countries do not have to reduce levels at all, while others have to reduce emissions by a tremendous amount. Generally, the base year for setting reduction goals is 1990, and Countries must show "demonstrable progress" prior to the 2012 deadline.

Bali, the United States and other countries which refuse to take part in the Kyoto Process, agreed to negotiate the formula for the reduction of the emissions outside of the agreed protocol.

The latest meeting on global warming and air quality standards, the 2015 United Nations Climate Change Conference (COP 21 and CMP 11), was held in Paris in late 2015. It was the 21st yearly session of the Conference of the Parties (COP) to the 1992 UNFCCC and the 11th session of the Meeting of the Parties to the 1997 Kyoto Protocol. The conference negotiated the Paris Agreement, a global agreement on reduction of change. The expected key result was an agreement to set a goal of limiting global warming to less than 2° Celsius (°C) compared to pre-industrial levels.

Israel signed the Kyoto Protocol in 1998 after ratifying the Convention on Climate Change in 1996. The protocol was ratified in 2004. Israel is defined as a developing country.

Maintaining environmental quality and sustainability, including water resources and water quality, is an important part of a culture of peace. The Middle East had witnessed long periods of tensions due to claims over water.

Water is vital for life. The oceans are abundant, and yet there is very little fresh water. Of the 1.39 billion cubic kilometers of water in the world, 97.5% (1.34 billion cubic kilometers) is salt, brackish, or mineralized water; only 2.52% (35,029,000 cubic kilometers) is fresh water. Rivers and streams account for 0.006%, fresh-water lakes for 0.26%, and water contained in the atmosphere for 0.001% of the total quantity of fresh water. The rest of the fresh-water component occurs as soil moisture, permanent snow cover, marshes, and active groundwater. Potential groundwater reserves are estimated to be as high as 30 percent of total freshwater reserves.

However, due to scant rainfall, ground-waters in the Middle East either do not replenish or replenish only minimally. In most areas of the Middle East, rainfall is negligible, being between only 250 and 400 millimeters annually; is the precipitation that does fall concentrated in a rainy season lasting between six and eight months per year. This amount of rainfall is less than the minimum required for basic agriculture, which is at least 400 millimeters annually of regular rainfall. Furthermore, due to the minimal renewing of the Middle East groundwater, the groundwater tends to be brackish.

The Middle East is a good case study of water rights in the world. There is a severe shortage of water and a fast-increasing population. As the difference between the amount of available water and the amount of water required enlarges, water is becoming an ever-increasing political flashpoint in the Middle East. It is, therefore, a key for maintaining peace and sustainability in the Middle East.

3. Proposal for a Kyoto Protocol Model for Water resource

In order to protect the world's water resources and to introduce aqua sustainability, protocol similar to the Kyoto Protocol could be developed for water—a "Kyoto Protocol for Water" (KPW). In a Kyoto Protocol for Water, signatory countries could be assigned water conservation goals, equivalent to a baseline measure of water resources. Water resources could be measured in terms of quantity and quality—the amount of a country's non-renewable water resources including aquifers and ground water, fresh-water sources, and ice caps; water from renewable sources including rainwater; preservation of rivers and other water bodies; level of cleanliness of a country's water resources, measured by salinity and pollution levels; and the cleaning of sewage waters. A Kyoto Protocol for Water's goals could be sustainability, the maintenance of water resources including non-renewable water sources, increasing renewable water sources, and improvement of water quality. Water quantity and pollution baselines could be adopted, with countries needing to reach baseline levels either through domestic improvements, or else by receiving credits for enhancing water sustainability in other countries.

A Kyoto Protocol for Water could be more complicated than the Kyoto Protocol for environmental change due to the existence of riparian owners, those who possess land along water path. Controls would need to be instated to ensure that riparian owners do not gain credits at the expense of downstream owners. Problems could be reduced or eliminated by awarding credits for increasing benefits to other riparian owners, and through imposing sanctions when flows were decreased to an unreasonable degree to other riparian owners. In Credits and sanctions mechanism, some amount of diversion is normal, realistic, and necessary and would taken into account. Sanctions could be associated with dams that diverted large amounts of water flows from downstream neighbors. A county's baseline could be tied to its naturally occurring water resources, creating different water requirements for water rich and water poor countries.

As with the Kyoto Protocol for environmental change, credits in a potential Kyoto Protocol for Water could be traded by creating water programs in other nations. Thus, a sponsored irrigation program could provide credits for a sponsoring country that is investing resources into increasing water sustainability in a second country. The idea on which the Kyoto Protocol is premised on, is that the sustainability, preservation, and cleanliness of water anywhere on earth benefits all of its dwellers.

A further impetus for a Kyoto Protocol for Water is that the pattern of population demographics and water resources demands a flexible system of credits and sanctions in order to be effective. The relationship between areas of large population growth and regions of water shortages leads to those countries with the smallest amounts of available water, often being most in need of increasing their scant resources.

A Kyoto Protocol for Water might not distinguish between the obligations of developed and non-developed countries, as the Kyoto Protocol does. Unlike situation of air pollution, water shortages are not focused in industrialized countries. This variation might increase global acceptance of and enthusiasm for a Kyoto Protocol for Water.

When in its urgent national interest, a contracting party deletes or restricts the boundaries of a wetland included in the list, it should compensate as far as possible for any loss of wetland resources. In particular, it should create additional nature reserves for waterfowl and for the protection of an adequate portion of the original habitat, either in the same area or elsewhere.

A Kyoto Protocol for Water could thus be a strong harborer to peace. By binding signatories to sustainable water conservation and cleanliness globally, water sustainability could be dealt universally, allowing water sustainability to act as a platform to peace.

Chapter 19:
Dispute Resolution

1. The General Law Courts

Israel is a unitary state with a single system of general law courts. The law courts in Israel constitute a separate, independent unit within the Ministry of Justice. The Basic Law: The Judiciary[1] established three Hierarchical levels of courts: The Supreme Court, district courts and magistrates' courts. The latter two are trial courts, while the Supreme Court is essentially an appellate court, which also operates as the High Court of Justice. The Israeli judicial system does not include the use of juries.[2]

Magistrates' Courts: The basic trial courts of the Israeli system. They have jurisdiction in criminal matters where the accused is charged with an offense that carries with it a potential punishment of up to seven years of imprisonment. In civil matters, these courts have jurisdiction in matters up to a million shekels (approximately US $300,000). These courts also have jurisdiction over the use and possession of real property. Magistrates' courts also act as traffic courts, municipal courts, family courts, and small claims courts.

District Courts: The middle level courts of the Israeli judiciary. They have jurisdiction in any matter that is not within the sole jurisdiction of another court. In criminal matters, district courts hear cases where the accused faces more than seven years imprisonment. In civil cases, district courts' jurisdiction extends to matters in which more than 2.5 million shekels (approximately U.S. $600,000) are in dispute. District courts also hear cases dealing with companies and partnership, arbitration, prisoners' petitions, and appeals on tax matters. These courts hear appeals of judgments of the magistrates' courts.

Supreme Court: The Supreme Court has jurisdiction to hear criminal and civil appeals from judgments of the district courts. Cases that begin in the district courts are appealable, as a right, to the Supreme Court. Other matters may be appealed only with the Supreme Court's permission. The Supreme Court has special jurisdiction to hear appeals in matters of Knesset elections, rulings of the Civil Service Commission, disciplinary rulings of the Israel Bar Association, ad-

---

1 Basic Law: Adjudication S.H. (1984) 5744, 78.
2 Israel Ministry of Foreign Affairs, available at: http://www.mfa.gov.il/mfa/aboutisrael/state/democracy/pages/the%20judiciary-%20the%20court%20system.aspx (accessed February 9, 2017).

DOI 10.1515/9783899497946-020

ministrative detentions, and prisoners' petitions appealed from the District Court.

The number of justices on the Court is fixed by Knesset resolution. By convention, the most senior justice is the President (Chief Justice) of the Court and the next senior justice is the Deputy President. The President of the Court is the head of the entire judicial system in Israel.

High Court of Justice: The Supreme Court also sits as the High Court of Justice. This function is unique to the Israeli system because, as the High Court of Justice, the Supreme Court acts as a court of first and last instance. The High Court exercises judicial review over the other branches of government, and has powers "in matters in which it considers it necessary to grant relief in the interests of justice and which are not within the jurisdiction of any other court or tribunal."

In addition, the Israeli legal system recognizes various types of tribunals with limited jurisdiction, the most important of which are the military courts, the labor courts, and the religious courts. These tribunals are distinguished from most other tribunals in terms of both their personal and material jurisdiction. Each tribunal is comprised of a judicial system with independent administration and its own appellate system which includes legally-trained judges.

The success of the judicial system in Israel, with the Supreme Court at its head, in the enforcement of the rule of law and defense of civil rights is, to a great extent, a result of the independence given to judges. Judges enjoy both substantive and personal independence. Substantive independence is set out in Basic Law: The Judiciary: "[a] person in whom judicial power is vested shall, in judicial matters, be subject to no authority but that of the law." It should be emphasized that the general language of this section applies to any person vested with judicial power, and not only to judges within the regular law courts. In addition to substantive independence, judges have wide personal independence that begins with the procedure for their selection and continues during their term of office.[3]

---

3 http://www.mfa.gov.il/mfa/aboutisrael/state/democracy/pages/the%20judiciary-%20the%20court%20system.aspx (accessed February 11, 2017). Shimon Shetreet, Justice in Israel: A Study of the Israeli Judiciary, 497–522 (Martinus Nijhoff: London, 1994).

2. Arbitration and Mediation

Normally commercial entities favor arbitration over court proceedings. This is due to the expeditious process of arbitration, private proceedings, professionalism of the arbitrators, as well as other advantages such as low costs. In many jurisdictions, there are arbitration institutions which provide arbitration forums for commercial disputes. In Israel, the Israeli Institute of Commercial Arbitration serves as a leading arbitral institution, which is appropriate and convenient for commercial entities.

The Israeli Institute of Commercial Arbitration (IICA) was founded in 1991 by the Federation of Israeli Chambers of Commerce. The IICA provides two kinds of alternative dispute resolution—arbitration and mediation—in a professional, speedy, and high quality manner at a relatively low cost. During its years of existence, the IICA has acquired substantial experience. It has administered thousands of arbitration cases in all areas of business and in all fields of law, including real estate, corporate disputes, media, construction, business transactions, and more. The list of arbitrators and mediators includes those from different backgrounds: retired judges, lawyers, accountants, engineers, appraisers, economists, and more.[4]

A. Arbitration

Arbitration is the resolution of disputes through adjudication by an arbitrator instead of in court. In order for a matter to be brought before an arbitrator, both parties must give their consent in writing. Such consent may be expressed prior to a dispute arising, such as through an arbitration clause in a contract, or it can be expressed in a subsequent agreement after a dispute has arisen. The arbitration process ends with an arbitral award, which may be submitted to court for confirmation. A court-approved arbitral award has the same legal standing as a court judgment, and it can be enforced through the Execution Office.

There are a number of ways to initiate an arbitration process before the IICA: through an arbitration agreement; through the parties' written agreement; or pursuant to a court order. The arbitrator is appointed by the President of the

---

4 The Israeli Institution of Commercial Arbitration, available at: http://eng.borerut.com/about/ (accessed February 9, 2017); for general analysis of law of arbitration, see: Gideon Koren, "Law of Arbitration," in Alon Kaplan & Paul Ogden, editors, *Israeli Business Law: An Essential Guide*, pp. 219–238 (1999 Kluwer) (hereinafter: *Israeli Business Law: An Essential Guide*).

IICA in one of two manners. First, after receipt of the pleadings (or description of the dispute) from the parties, the arbitrator can be selected from the roster of IICA arbitrators. The parties select the most suitable arbitrator, on the bases of his or her skills, experience, and fields of expertise. Second, based on the parties' joint request, the arbitrator may be appointed from a roster of recommended arbitrators which is compiled specifically for those parties based upon the facts of their dispute. The advantage of both of the aforementioned methods of appointment is that the arbitrator selected is experienced and knowledgeable in the issues in dispute.

Parties to an International Arbitration Agreement[5] agree that the dispute will be adjudicated by or under the auspices of the IICA. Thus, the arbitration will be conducted according to International Rules of the IICA:

When parties to an applicable arbitration agreement wish to commence an arbitration, they are required to submit to the IICA a typed application describing the nature of and the amount in dispute. The claimant will also serve a copy of this application to each defendant.[6] Within thirty days of receiving the claimant's application (along with exhibits and annexures), the defendant is required to file its statement of defense.[7] During said timeframe, the defense may also file a counterclaim. The claimant can file a defense to the counterclaim within fifteen days of receiving the counterclaim.[8]

The parties may jointly request an appointment of a specific arbitrator (or arbitrators) from the IICA's list of international arbitrators.[9] The list includes a general description of each arbitrator, including that person's credentials and experience.[10] However, if the parties do not request to appoint an arbitrator, the IICA president shall propose a sole arbitrator.[11] If the arbitration agreement stipulates more than one arbitrator, then the president shall appoint the appropriate number of arbitrators.[12] Any party may file an objection regarding the proposed appointment of an arbitrator on the grounds of prejudice, bias, and interest in

---

5 A document which includes the parties' consent for future disputes to be resolved by arbitration.
6 Article 1 of the International Rules of the Israeli Institute of Commercial Arbitration (Tel Aviv), available at: http://eng.borerut.com/wp-content/uploads/2014/06/Rules-institute-of-arbitration-English.pdf (accessed February 9, 2017).
7 *Id.*, Article 2.1 (a).
8 *Id.*, Article 2.2–2.3.
9 *Id.*, Article 4.1.
10 *Id.*, Definitions and Interpretation.
11 *Id.*, Article 4.2 (a).
12 *Id.*, Article 4.2 (b).

the outcome or involvement in the dispute. The IICA president , rule on each objection in writing.[13]

The arbitrator and arbitration proceedings shall not be bound by the rules of evidence unless the parties agree otherwise. The arbitrator shall determine the rules of the procedure subject to the stipulation by the parties and the IICA International Rules.[14] The language of the arbitration shall be in English when the language of the arbitration is in English. If the agreement is in more than one language, and does not address the issue of language in which the arbitration will take place, then the arbitrator will have the discretion to determine the language of the arbitration. Nevertheless, if the arbitrator concludes that significantly all of the possible witnesses are Hebrew speakers, the arbitrator will have discretion to order that oral examinations {of said witnesses} will be conducted in Hebrew.[15]

The arbitrator has the prerogative to suggest that the parties conduct negotiations in order to reach a settlement. If the parties reach a settlement agreement, the arbitrator may accord the agreement the status of an arbitral award.[16] The possible relief granted by the arbitration award can be in any form available under the Israeli law, including declarative and injunctive relief.[17]

B. Mediation

Mediation means bringing about a resolution through consent. The mediation process does not result in any adjudication. The purpose of the mediation process is to reach a resolution acceptable to both parties. A successful mediation process ends in parties' agreement, which may also be submitted to court in order for it to be given the force of a judgment.

3. International Agreements and International Litigation

The state of Israel is a signatory of a multitude of international agreements; in recent years, there has been a significant increase in the amount of international contractual obligations that Israel performs. It is estimated that the state enters

---

13 *Id.*, Article 4.3.
14 *Id.*, Article 6.1.
15 *Id.*, Article 6.2.
16 *Id.*, Article 7.
17 *Id.*, Article 8.

into hundreds of new contracts each year. Many of these agreements give rise to significant obligations, including policy, legislation changes, and, in many cases, convergence with existing judicial bodies or other conflict resolution mechanisms. In recent years, many states, including Israel, have started to accept provisions pertaining to the ways of resolving disputes and, more specifically, conflict resolution dispute mechanisms. These mechanisms vary between mediation and arbitration of different kinds, and also quasi-judicial international mechanisms which directly bind the country as part of its state law.

These developments in international law, and their local ramifications, have compelled many states to deal with this subject. The state of Israel has established the Department for International Agreements and International Litigation (DIAIL) in order to enable the state to cope with the changes that have occurred in the last decade in the international sphere, to advise the state on these subjects, and to represent the state in disputes involving a foreign element.

The DIAIL is entrusted with the responsibility, *inter alia*, to advise in negotiations of international agreements and contracts; examine compatibility of the proposed agreements or contracts with the Israeli and international law; examine possible ramifications of agreement in terms of Israeli and international law; represent the state in all the stages of a dispute; and monitor breaches of agreements.[18]

4. Recognition and Enforcement of Foreign Judgements

The judgments of one State's courts have no force by themselves in another State. In many countries, the recognition and enforcement of foreign judgments is governed by local domestic law and the principles of comity, reciprocity, and res judicata.

The Israeli legal system, like many countries, does not operate in a legal void. The Israeli courts and legislature have drawn inspiration from many foreign legal systems, especially in cross-border trade and disputes. For instance, Israel is a part of many multinational treaties concerning arbitration, and their interpretation will be subject to the interpretation of treaty and international law.[19]

---

18 Office of the Deputy Attorney General (International Law)—International Agreements and International Litigation, available at: http://www.justice.gov.il/En/Units/HumanRightsAndForeignRelations/Pages/default.aspx (accessed February 9, 2017).

19 Haggai Carmon, *Foreign Judgments in Israel—Recognition and Enforcement* 5 (2013); for general analysis of enforcement of judgments, see Louis Garb, *Enforcement of Foreign Judgements*, in *supra* note 4, at 239–244.

In Israel, a judgment in a civil matter rendered in a foreign country is not automatically recognized. Before a judgment is recognized or enforced, it first must go through an integration process. In other words, a foreign judgment must meet certain conditions specified by the Foreign Judgments Enforcement Law, 5718–1958[20] (Enforcement Law) in order for it to be enforceable in Israel. Only after the conditions are met can a foreign judgment be given validity.[21]

The criteria in which a court in Israel may declare a foreign judgment are as follows: the judgment was given according to the laws of the foreign state; the judgment is no longer appealable; the judgment is enforceable in Israel and does not contradict public policy in Israel; and, finally, the judgment is executory in the State in which it was given.[22]

In addition, Article 4 of the Enforcement Law provides that a foreign judgment will not be declared enforceable if it was issued in a State the laws of which do not provide for the enforcement of judgments of Israeli Courts.[23] However, the court may enforce a foreign judgment, even where the reciprocity element is non-existent. It is understood that the reciprocity principles expresses the intention of the state to encourage foreign countries to enforce Israeli judgments.[24]

Recently the Supreme Court of Israel upheld the Tel Aviv District Court[25] that a judgment of the Moscow Commercial Court is enforceable in Israel on the basis of reciprocity. The Court, per Justice Daphne Barak-Erez, held that there is adequate evidence for finding that the Russian courts enforce judgments of foreign courts, even without bilateral treaties between their country of origin and Russia. This is the first time the Supreme Court ruled on the enforceability of Russian court rulings on the reciprocity requirement.[26]

In the context of the enforcement of foreign judgements in domestic courts, it is important to refer to a number of cases dealing with enforcement of foreign judgements by domestic courts in a number of countries. The first two cases that are cases in point are the *Yukos* case and the *Merchant International* case.

---

20 Foreign Judgments Enforcement Law—1958, available at: http://www.goslaw.co.il/uploads/_20_%20Foreign%20Judgments%20Enforcement%20Law%205718-1958.pdf (accessed February 9, 2017).

21 Haggai Carmon, *supra* note 19, at 1.

22 Foreign Judgments Enforcement Law, *supra* note 20, §3.

23 *Id.*, at 68.

24 Amos Shapira, *Recognition and Enforcement of Foreign Judgments* 38, Iyunei Mishpat 4 (1974); *Id.*, at 69.

25 D.C.C 30752–05–11 *Gazprom Transgaz Ochta Ltd. v Double K Oil Products*, 1996 Ltd.

26 *Id.*, at 71.

Per Lord Justic Rix, the English Court of Appeal, in the *Yukos* case,[27] held that "It must ultimately be for the English court to decide whether the recognition of a foreign judgment should be withheld on the grounds that that foreign judgment is a partial and dependent judgment in favour of the state where it was pronounced. That is a question so central to the respect and comity normally due from one court to another that to accept the decision of a court of a third country on the matter would be an abdication of responsibility on the part of the English court. On matters of this kind, we should accept our own responsibilities just as we would expect courts of other countries to accept theirs."

The *Yukos* case raised this issue: Should a state follow the decision made by a second state recognizing the judicial independence, or lack thereof, of a third state?

The English Court held that the question regarding the validity of the Russian process, which according to Dutch public policy was invalid, is not enough, and thefore must be reviewed according to English public policy. The Mount Scopus International standards for judicial independence may serve as a global standard for judging judicial independence.

The ability of courts to enforce foreign decisions plays a vital role in transnational economies. Nationals and non-nationals alike may have a holding in the national territory and still be subjected to foreign decisions. Parties must trust that the decision they have received may be enforced in the national court, thus not requiring further adjudication recognized and enforced internationally.

The second decision of the English Court of Appeal, *Merchant International Co. Ltd. v. Natsionalna Aktsionerna Kompaniia Naftogaz Ukrainy* (2012),[28] concerns the finality of a foreign civil judgment, Here the English court declared a decision to be a violation of "the rule of law." The result was that the English court elected not to disturb the English decision, which had been entered in recognition of the, then, valid foreign judgment, even though that judgment was later set aside by the court in the foreign jurisdiction and has ceased to have validity within the relevant foreign jurisdiction. The English court, in its second decision, employing a transnational criterion of finality (so-called "legal certainty"), chose not to give recognition to a later decision of a foreign jurisdiction setting aside its previous decision

---

27 [2012] 2C.L.C. 549, 159.

28 [2012] EWCA Civ 196, [2012] 1 W.L.R. 3036; [2012] 2 All E.R. (Comm) 1; [2012] C.P. Rep. 25; [2012] 1 C.L.C. 396; noted M. Ahmed, "Setting aside judgment in default, Article 6 of the European Convention on Human Rights and the Principle of *Res Judicata*" (2012) C.J.Q. 417 (the Supreme Court of the United Kingdom has refused permission for a further appeal).

There has recently been a number of decisions dealing with the enforcement of Russian judgments in different countries:

On 30 January 2013, the French Cour de Cassation confirmed that a judgment of a district court in Moscow rendered against a French national should be recognized and enforced in France.

According to a recently published decision of the Munich Court of Appeal (OberLandsgericht OLG), enforcement of a Russian judgment was refused since enforcement had been sought on the basis of the New York Convention. However, it has been argued that enforcement of Russian judgments in Germany would be problematic as there is no evidence of German judgments being enforced in Russia save for decisions made in the course of insolvency proceedings.

5. The Exercise of Jurisdiction

Service of process outside of a state's jurisdiction is an expression of judicial exercise of the state on a defendant outside of the natural jurisdictional boundaries. Such use of judicial exercise may be in conflict with local jurisdictions, and international good manners.[29]

Israeli courts usually acquire jurisdiction over foreign defendants upon service on that defendant. Generally, service abroad is done by the plaintiff obtaining a leave of court to serve the process outside of Israel. The regulation for doing so is set forth in Rule 500 of the Civil Procedure rules.[30] The rule grants an Israeli court permit to service abroad any of the following cases: Relief is sought against a person whose regular residence is in Israel; The action concerns an obligation regarding real estate in Israel; The action is to enforce, nullify, or invalidate a contract, or to receive damages or other relief for the violation of a contract, provided that the contract was incepted in Israel, made by or through an agent in Israel; Israeli law applied to the contract; The suit seeks to prohibit activity in Israel; The suit is based on any action or omission which took place in Israel; The action seeks the enforcement of a foreign judgement of arbitral award; The person outside of Israel is a necessary or proper party to an action which was lawfully brought against another defendant duly served in Israel.[31]

Therefore, a service of process via Rule 500 requires the plaintiff to prove that the Israeli court is the *forum conveniens* to hear the case, rather than in

---

29 Uri Goren, Topics in the Civil Procedure Rules 445 (2013).
30 Civil Procedure Rules, 5744–1984.
31 *Id.*, at sec. 500; Eric S. Sherby, "A Primer on Commercial Litigation in Israel" 4 (2013), available at: http://www.sherby.co.il/pdf/Primer.pdf (accessed February 9, 2017).

the country of residence of the defendant. Hence, in instances of international business cooperation, it is plausible that the Israeli courts will refrain from granting the permit to service abroad, as the forum might not be in Israel, even if the foreign partner has an authorized representative in Israel.

Index

www.ingramcontent.com/pod-product-compliance
Lightning Source LLC
Chambersburg PA
CBHW020812100426

42814CB00001B/32